THE EPISTLE
TO THE
ROMANS

THE EPISTLE
TO THE
ROMANS

By KARL BARTH

TRANSLATED FROM THE
SIXTH EDITION

BY

EDWYN C. HOSKYNS

BART., M.A.

SOMETIME FELLOW OF CORPUS CHRISTI COLLEGE
IN THE UNIVERSITY OF CAMBRIDGE

LONDON
OXFORD UNIVERSITY PRESS
NEW YORK   TORONTO

Oxford University Press, Amen House, London E.C.4
GLASGOW NEW YORK TORONTO MELBOURNE WELLINGTON
BOMBAY CALCUTTA MADRAS KARACHI KUALA LUMPUR
CAPE TOWN IBADAN NAIROBI ACCRA

First edition 1933
Fifth impression 1960

PRINTED IN GREAT BRITAIN

THE AUTHOR'S PREFACE
TO THE ENGLISH EDITION

THE unselfish and laborious task of translating this book into English has been undertaken by Sir Edwyn Hoskyns. Partly owing to my insufficient familiarity with the English language, and partly because my time has been so fully occupied with other work, I have unfortunately not been able to go through the whole of the translation in detail. Sir Edwyn has, however, laid before me a fairly long section of his work, and, after comparing it with the original German, I am persuaded that he has performed his task with great skill. He has combined fidelity to the text with a considerable freedom of presentation; and that is, surely, the mark of a good translator. Though a translation, however skilfully made, must be in some degree a transformation of the original, yet I feel certain that those who think and speak in English will have before them what I wished to say. I should like therefore to take this opportunity of thanking him publicly.

In its English dress my book is now set in a new context; and I cannot refrain from asking those who propose to read it to bear with me whilst I make of them certain demands which seem to me to be important.

1. I beg my English readers to remember that this book was written eleven, or, to be precise, fourteen years ago. When I first wrote it—of the First Edition only the Preface now remains[1]—it required only a little imagination for me to hear the sound of the guns booming away in the north. The man who sat writing his commentary was then just a young country pastor, only vaguely aware of what responsibility in ecclesiastical and scientific matters really means. Altogether ignorant both of the forces which were ranged against him and of those upon which he might call for help, he tumbled himself into a conflict, the inward and outward significance of which he could not foresee. Nor was the situation

[1] See p. 2.

materially different when in 1921 he rewrote the whole book, and let it go out in its second and present form. When, however, I look back at the book, it seems to have been written by another man to meet a situation belonging to a past epoch.[1] Those who now read it—and this applies, perhaps, even more to English than to German readers—ought therefore to remember that they have in their hands what is, in fact, the *beginning* of a development. They ought not to bind the Professor at Bonn too tightly to the Pastor of Safenwil, nor to assume that the present state of theological controversy in Germany can be directly gauged from this book. When they come across opinions expressed in it which seem to them to be open to very grave criticism and to raise very delicate problems, they must not assume too readily that the author is unaware of them. Indeed, it is most improbable that criticisms suggested by a first reading of the book will not already have been made by the author or by his friends or by his opponents, and will not already have been reconsidered and rediscussed in his later publications. For English readers the book is therefore an introduction. It invites them to take a part, according as they are best qualified, in the further work which has opened up as a consequence of the publication of this commentary.

2. It is both an honour and a pleasure to me to know that already many English theologians are not wholly unacquainted with my work. This translation has been preceded by the publication in English of a collection of addresses and of some of my more occasional writings. I have had in my hands a number of books and articles —some good, some less good—which have been written about me both in England and in America. I have also been kept in touch with the endeavours of Adolf Keller to make use of my theological work in order to further the cause of 'Oecumenical' Christianity.[2] Lastly, I know

---

[1] See the Preface to the Sixth Edition.

[2] Dr. Adolf Keller is one of the Pastors of the Reformed Church in the Canton of Zürich. He was for some time secretary of the Life and Work Movement. In 1924 he contributed two articles to the *Expositor* under the title 'A Theology of Crisis', and in 1931 his book *Der Weg der dialektischen*

something of the influence exercised in the English-speaking theological world by Emil Brunner's exposition in English of his theological work, work which is closely allied to mine. Am I wrong, therefore, in assuming that those who read this book will already have some notion or other of what is often called 'Dialectical Theology', or the 'Theology of Krisis', or 'Barthianism', or the like? Perhaps they will also already have some prejudices with regard to such things. If this be so, is it asking too much if I now beg them, while they read this book, to lay aside, so far as is possible, such 'notions' and such 'prejudices', and to read it as though they knew nothing of those well-known glosses and catch-phrases? Is it too much to ask them to read it as though they were for the first time confronted by what is the especial theme of the book? May I also ask my English readers—and I do this because of what has occurred in Germany and in Holland and in Switzerland—not to look at me simply through the spectacles of Emil Brunner, not to conform me to his pattern, and, above all, not to think of me as the representative of a particular 'Theological School'? I ask my readers to judge my work, at any rate to begin with, on its own merits. Only if this be done will it be possible to read the book as it was meant to be read in 1921, and as it evoked the discussions which have arisen as a result of it. If it be not thus approached, it will be impossible for those who read it to take their part independently in the task which has been opened up by it. Let me speak quite openly and honestly: I am sure that it will be to their interest, and in the interest of the theme of the book, if my English readers will be generous enough not to disregard the advice I have just given.

3. Sir Edwyn has asked me to say that the book should not be treated as a collection of fragments, but that it should be read as a whole. It may perhaps sound rather strange for an author to ask his readers to read the whole of his book. Obviously I cannot request my readers to be so delighted with my book, and to gain so

Theologie durch die kirchliche Welt was published by the Kaiser Verlag in Berlin. An English translation of the latter work is now being prepared by the Lutterworth Press. [Tr.]

great a benefit from it, that they will be compelled to go on reading it to the very end. But I know what Sir Edwyn means; and he is quite right. There have been in Germany those who have read and reviewed the book after skimming through, I am quite certain, no more than the First Preface and a few other pages selected at random. They have then for years afterwards behaved as though they had read the book and knew what was in it. Some of them have approved of it, others have subjected it to severe criticism, but all of them have acted like bulls in a china shop. There are also those who have loudly asserted that there are very significant omissions in the book. They would, however, have discovered, had they taken the trouble to look for them in the right place, that these significant things were not in fact omitted. A great deal of tilting at windmills would have been avoided if reviewers in Germany had followed Sir Edwyn's acute and quite simple advice. The truth is that it is the Epistle itself which cannot be split up into fragments. Chs. I and II must not be read apart from Ch. III; nor Ch. V apart from Ch. VI; nor Ch. VIII apart from Ch. VII; nor Ch. IX apart from Ch. XI: and above all, Chs. I–XI must not be separated from Chs. XII–XV. If this be so, is it really defensible for an interpreter of the Epistle to do otherwise than preserve with great care this interlocking of the whole? Since the Epistle can be understood only as a whole, it must clearly follow that any proper interpretation of it must also form one whole. I cannot, of course, communicate to my readers the incentive to busy themselves with discovering this unity; but I am bound to remind them that, if they are possessed of any sense of responsibility, they ought not to busy themselves with speaking *about* this book, unless it has first spoken *to* them as one whole. Indeed, the book would not be an interpretation of the Epistle of Paul to the Romans if it did not follow in detail the various stages through which Paul moves so impressively. There can therefore be no possible understanding of this book if the reader has not himself also followed through these stages.

4. Lastly: it may not be irrelevant if I now make it quite clear both to my future friends and to my future opponents in England that, in writing this book, I set out neither to compose a free fantasia upon the theme of religion, nor to evolve a philosophy of it. My sole aim was to interpret Scripture. I beg my readers not to assume from the outset—as many in Germany have assumed—that I am not interpreting Scripture at all, or rather, that I am interpreting it 'spiritually'. In this context the word 'spiritually' is used, of course, to convey a rebuke. It may be, however, that the rebuke turns back most heavily upon those who launch it so easily against me. The publication of this book in English may perhaps lead to a fresh formulation of the problem, 'What is exegesis?' No one can, of course, bring out the meaning of a text (*auslegen*) without at the same time adding something to it (*einlegen*). Moreover, no interpreter is rid of the danger of in fact adding more than he extracts. I neither was nor am free from this danger. And yet I should be altogether misunderstood if my readers refused to credit me with the honesty of, at any rate, *intending* to *ex*-plain the text. I must assure them that, in writing this book, I felt myself bound to the actual words of the text, and did not in any way propose to engage myself in free theologizing. It goes without saying that my interpretation is open to criticism; and I hope to hear as soon as possible of important and proper criticism of it at the hands of my English-speaking theological colleagues. But I do not want to hear of criticisms which proceed from some religious or philosophical or ethical 'point of view'. Proper criticism of my book can be concerned only with the interpretation of the text of the Epistle. In other words, criticism or approval should move strictly within the realm of Theology. I shall not be impressed in the least by general propositions concerning the value or lack of value of my 'spiritual outlook', or of my 'religious position', or of my 'general view of life'. My book deals with one issue, and with one issue only. Did Paul think and speak in general and in detail in the manner in which I have interpreted

him as thinking and speaking? Or did he think and speak altogether differently? The fourth and last request I have to make of my English readers is therefore quite direct. Of my friendly readers I ask that they should take nothing and believe nothing from me which they are not of themselves persuaded stands within the meaning of what Paul wrote. Of my unfriendly readers I ask that they should not reject as an unreasonable opinion of my own what, in fact, Paul himself propounded. The purpose of this book neither was nor is to delight or to annoy its readers by setting out a New Theology. The purpose was and is to direct them to Holy Scripture, to the Epistle of Paul to the Romans, in order that, whether they be delighted or annoyed, whether they are 'accepted' or 'rejected', they may at least be brought face to face with the subject-matter of the Scriptures. I wished, and still continue to wish, this book to be of definite service. But whom or what ought it to serve? No doubt it should be of service to those who read it. But, primarily and above all else, it must serve that *other* Book where Jesus Christ is present in His Church. Theology is *ministerium verbi divini*. It is nothing more nor less. The conflict in which we have been engaged in Germany during the past ten years revolves round the apprehension of this truth. My purpose in permitting this commentary upon the Epistle of Paul to the Romans to appear in English is to summon an ever increasing number of men to engage themselves in this conflict.

BONN
October, 1932.

THE TRANSLATOR'S PREFACE

WHEN, in 1921, the author of this commentary on the Epistle to the Romans completely rewrote the earlier commentary which he had published in 1918, he stated in his preface that the First Edition, whatever its merits or failings, could now 'disappear from the scene'. It was therefore impossible for the translator to summon back the vanished volume even had he wished to do so. In consequence, it is not the original, but the revised edition of this modern attack upon the vigour of idolatry and upon the arrogance of that scepticism which holds itself aloof that is here presented in an English dress. Whether the translation will be adequate to explain the hubbub and commotion created by this commentary upon its first appearance is for its English readers to decide. Whether it reproduces the original with sufficient accuracy must be left to the judgement of those familiar with the author's works. But of one thing the translator is quite persuaded: to produce a translation worthy of the dignified language of English divinity has been beyond his power. The vehement and explosive character of the German lies intractably behind the English, and for his inability to be rid of it, or to transform it into properly explosive English, he offers his apologies to the readers, both patient and impatient, of this book. As Professor Maitland once said, an English translation is always a 'distorting medium'.

What Karl Barth had to say lies embedded in a wealth of allusions which must be largely unfamiliar to the English reader. Indeed, the disturbing effect of his book among German-speaking people was due in no small degree to his extremely critical sensitiveness to movements of thought of which we in England may perhaps have heard, but which do not hang heavily in the air we breathe. This sometimes delicate, sometimes rough, allusiveness has presented an almost insoluble problem to the translator. What was he to make of such a sentence as this?—'Warum nicht mit Marcion fortschreiten

zur Proklamierung eines neuen Gottes im Gegensatz zu
dem alten des Gesetzes, oder mit Lhotzky zu einer recht
handgreiflichen Anspielung von "Reich Gottes" gegen
"Religion", oder mit Johannes Müller zur Aufweisung
eines Weges aus der Mittelbarkeit zurück in das Land
der zwar verlorenen, oder immerhin hier und jetzt
auffindbaren Unmittelbarkeit, oder mit Ragaz zur
Aufforderung, aus der hoffnungslos gewordenen Kirche
und Theologie in die bessere Welt der Laien überzu-
siedeln, oder mit manchen Seiten der 1. Auflage dieses
Buches im Anschluss an Beck und altwürttembergischen
Naturalismus zur Behauptung eines organisch wachsen-
den göttlichen Seins und Habens im Menschen im Gegensatz zu der Leerheit der idealistischen Forderung. . . .?'
Or of this?—'Er ist—nicht ich, mein existentielles Ich,
ich, der ich in Gott, in der Freiheit Gottes bin'. Or
even of this?—'Die Philosophen nennen diese Krisis des
menschlichen Erkennens den Ursprung'. The introduction of a long series of footnotes would merely have
disturbed the reader and distracted his attention from
the movement of the book itself. And indeed they are
for the most part unnecessary, for we are not so far
detached from European civilization as to be untouched
by its problems, unmoved by its hopes and fears. We
may be ignorant of the theories which German theologians and philosophers have so laboriously constructed,
but we are not ignorant of the ideas or notions which
underlie their theories. We or our neighbours hold the
same opinions, and the same notions buzz in our English
heads. An allusion to some particular theory is more
readily intelligible to us than the theory itself would be.
Many of the unknown persons whose names are scattered
about in the book can, therefore, be taken by the reader
in his stride without bothering to find out precisely who
or what they were or are, or how they worked out their
systems. Those who desire more detailed information
will usually be able to find it in the second edition of
Die Religion in Geschichte und Gegenwart.[1] There are, of

[1] *Die Religion in Geschichte und Gegenwart—Handwörterbuch für Theologie
und Religionswissenschaft;* 2nd edition edited by Hermann Gunkel and Leopold
Zscharnack (J. C. B. Mohr, Tübingen), completed 1931.

course, passages which are wholly unintelligible without further explanation. In such cases a note has been added in order to avoid too great obscurity. There are also passages where the rich allusiveness of the author's language must escape the English reader, and yet not altogether escape him, for the Biblical background is common to the author and to all his readers. When, for example, he plays round the word 'High', we are not ignorant of the words, *Set not your mind on high things*, nor are we unfamiliar with the *High Places* of the Old Testament narrative or with their significance. It is, therefore, not difficult for us to catch a modern application of this Biblical language, even though we may not know that *Das Hochland* is the title of the most cultured Roman Catholic monthly journal in Germany, or even though we may not associate a wedding with the adjective 'high' (Hochzeit).

Quite apart, however, from this peculiar allusiveness, the task of translating a German theological work is never quite straightforward. Words pregnant with meaning often have no precise English equivalent. The words *Sachlichkeit* and *Dinglichkeit*, for example, are quite proper German words, but, though attempts have often been made to do so, we have never been able to build upon the foundation of the word 'Thing'. 'Thinginess', 'Thinghood', 'Thingal', 'Thingish', 'Thingness', 'Thingship', 'Thingsomeness' are, as the *New English Dictionary* shows, intolerable words. A German, moreover, is free, as we are not, to build up comprehensive phrases by the generous use of hyphens. 'Seelisch-geschichtlich' and 'Das Da-Sein und das Wie-Sein der Welt' are, no doubt, congruous with the genius of the German language, but, when turned into literal English, they make nonsense. With these and other such-like troublesome words and phrases the translator has done his best, being guided in each case by the context. English readers will undoubtedly find difficulty in attaching a precise meaning to important words round which the whole commentary tends to revolve. Such words as 'Dialectical', 'Krisis', 'Existential', are stumbling-blocks upon the very threshold. They were, however, as difficult in German as they are in English, and only a steady concentration upon the actual commentary itself will enable the reader to grasp their meaning. The awkward words *Aufheben* and *Aufhebung* of which, because of their double meaning, Hegel was so proud, have been rendered by 'dissolve' and 'dissolution'. If their use to describe a chemical process be borne in mind, they have in English also a positive as well as a negative meaning.

The author intended his book to be read not only with the eyes but also with the ears. He therefore frequently printed particular words in a different type in order to lay emphasis upon them. The meaning of a difficult sentence often becomes clear when it is read aloud. This method of underlining words by the use of a different type is hardly legitimate in an English book, at least not to the extent to which it is allowable in German. The translator has endeavoured, wherever possible, to secure the appropriate emphasis by care in translation; but sometimes he has been compelled to fall back upon the use of a different type, and sometimes he has dared to introduce a hyphen into a word in order to ensure the proper stress (e.g. 'Purpose-full,' 'Pre-supposition').

Something needs to be said also about the translation of the Text of the Epistle. The author made his own translation. Luther's version formed, of course, the basis, but the modern translations of Weizsäcker, Stage, and Jülicher were also consulted and, at times, preferred. Sometimes the author paraphrased rather than translated the original Greek, and distinguished paraphrase from translation by using a different fount. It did not seem necessary or advisable to attempt to make an independent translation into English of the author's resultant Text. The translator has found it possible to reproduce his meaning by selecting the rendering sometimes of one, sometimes of another, of the authorized English Versions. Taken together, the A.V., R.V., A.V.mg., R.V.mg., offer a wide choice of translations. Where, however, the author has no support from the

English versions or where he has paraphrased the Greek, a different fount has been used, in order that the divergence may be at once apparent to the English reader.

A word as to the use of various types throughout the book. The Author bases his commentary upon shorter or longer sub-sections of the Epistle, which are first printed in full. Then, as he builds up his interpretation, he fastens upon sentences or phrases or even upon single words from the sub-section, for special discussion. In order to make this 'lay-out' of the commentary clear to the English reader, the sub-sections of the Epistle are printed in **bold** type. Sentences or phrases or single words are then, on their first appearance for special comment, picked out in **a less bold** type. All other Biblical quotations, including quotations from the Epistle to the Romans and even from the passage under comment, are printed in *italics*. Further, it has been thought advisable, for the sake of clarity, to use SMALL CAPITALS for certain transliterated Greek words, as well as for emphasis, and to space out quotations in other languages.

In conclusion, the translator cannot allow this book to be published without bearing witness to the unfailing kindness of Mr. Humphrey Milford and to the skill of the ·Printer to the University of Oxford, or without expressing his thanks to those who have helped him in tracking down allusions or in translating unfamiliar words. To Professor A. B. Cook, Dr. W. H. S. Jones, the Rev. C. J. Shebbeare, Canon J. K. Mozley, Professor G. Kraft of the University of Freiburg, and Professor Gerhard Kittel of the University of Tübingen, Frau Dr. E. Sommer, the Dean of York, Brig.-General W. Evans, C.M.G., D.S.O., and to the Rev. Charles Smyth, he is more particularly indebted. To the nice mathematical knowledge of his wife he owes the unravelling of the mathematical analogies which occur so frequently in the commentary. But it is to the author himself that his thanks are most especially due. Many questions have been asked, and these have been

b

answered, always by return of post, always graciously,
and always strictly to the point. The Rev. Noel Davey
and the Rev. Charles Smyth have not only given
generously of their time to the correction of the proofs
but have also helped to rid the translation of some of its
more glaring literary absurdities. There are, no doubt,
many mistakes in the translation, but for these the
translator is himself wholly responsible.

NOTE TO SECOND IMPRESSION

THROUGH the kindness of the Rev. Noel Davey a few
minor corrections which the translator had noted during
his lifetime have been incorporated in this impression.

BIOGRAPHICAL NOTE

A BIOGRAPHY of the author would be inappropriate, but the place-names at the conclusion of the various prefaces need some explanation. Karl Barth was:

Pfarrer in Safenwil (Canton Aargau, Switzerland), 1911–21.

Honorary Professor of Reformed Theology in Göttingen, 1921–5.

Professor of Dogmatics and New Testament Exegesis in Münster (Westphalia), 1925–30.

Professor of Systematic Theology in Bonn (1930–35).

OTHER WORKS BY KARL BARTH

IN addition to the Commentary on the Epistle to the Romans, Karl Barth is the author of the following works:

1. *Die Auferstehung der Toten*, 1924. Pp. v+129.
2. *Das Wort Gottes und die Theologie*, 1925. Pp. 212.
3. *Vom christlichen Leben*, 1926. Pp. 39.
4. *Die christliche Dogmatik:* Band I, *Die Lehre vom Worte Gottes*, 1927. Pp. xv+473.
5. *Erklärung des Philipperbriefes*, 1928. Pp. iii+126.
6. *Die Theologie und die Kirche*, 1928. Pp. iii+391.
7. *Fides Quaerens Intellectum: Anselms Beweis der Existenz Gottes*, 1931. Pp. x+199.
8. *Die kirchliche Dogmatik:* Band I, *Die Lehre vom Worte Gottes*, 1932. Pp. xiv+528.

With Heinrich Barth:

9. *Zur Lehre vom Heiligen Geist*, 1930. Pp. iii+105.

With Eduard Thurneysen:

10. *Zur inneren Lage des Christentums*, 1920. Pp. 39 (reprinted in No. 6 under the title: *Unerledigte Anfragen an die heutige Theologie*).
11. *Komm Schöpfer Geist!* 1924. Pp. 266.
12. *Suchet Gott, so werdet ihr Leben!* 1928. Pp. 191.

All these works were published by the Chr. Kaiser Verlag, Munich. In addition, the same firm publishes every two months the journal *Zwischen den Zeiten*, edited by Georg Merz, to which Karl Barth, Friedrich Gogarten, and Eduard Thurneysen are regular contributors.

Of the above-mentioned books, No. 1 has been translated into English by H. J. Stenning under the title: *The Resurrection of the Dead*, published by Hodder & Stoughton, 1933; No. 2 has been translated by Douglas Horton under the title: *The Word of God and the word of man*, published in 1928 by Hodder & Stoughton in England and by the Pilgrim Press in America; No. 3 has been translated by I. Strathearn McNab and published by the Student Christian Movement Press, 1930, under the title: *The Christian Life*. One of the addresses contained in No. 6 has been published by the Lutterworth Press, 1932, under the title, *Questions to Christendom*. A few isolated sermons have also been translated and published in America.

MODERN GERMAN COMMENTARIES ON THE EPISTLE TO THE ROMANS

In the course of his exposition of the Epistle, Karl Barth refers more particularly to the following modern commentaries in German:

JOHANN CHRISTIAN KONRAD VON HOFMANN: *Die heilige Schrift des neuen Testamentes zusammenhängend untersucht,* dritter Teil (Römerbrief), 1868.

JOHANN TOBIAS BECK: *Erklärung des Briefes Pauli an die Römer,* 1884.

HANS LIETZMANN: in vol. iii of the *Handbuch zum Neuen Testament,* 1906, 3rd ed. 1928.

ADOLF JÜLICHER: in *Die Schriften des Neuen Testaments,* vol. ii, 1908, 3rd ed. 1917.

THEODOR ZAHN: *Der Brief des Paulus an die Römer,* 1910.

ERNST KÜHL: *Der Brief des Paulus an die Römer,* 1913.

CONTENTS

CONTENTS xxi

CONTENTS

THE PREFACE TO THE FIRST EDITION

PAUL, as a child of his age, addressed his contemporaries. It is, however, far more important that, as Prophet and Apostle of the Kingdom of God, he veritably speaks to all men of every age. The differences between then and now, there and here, no doubt require careful investigation and consideration. But the purpose of such investigation can only be to demonstrate that these differences are, in fact, purely trivial. The historical-critical method of Biblical investigation has its rightful place: it is concerned with the preparation of the intelligence—and this can never be superfluous. But, were I driven to choose between it and the venerable doctrine of Inspiration, I should without hesitation adopt the latter, which has a broader, deeper, more important justification. The doctrine of Inspiration is concerned with the labour of apprehending, without which no technical equipment, however complete, is of any use whatever. Fortunately, I am not compelled to choose between the two. Nevertheless, my whole energy of interpreting has been expended in an endeavour to see through and beyond history into the spirit of the Bible, which is the Eternal Spirit. What was once of grave importance, is so still. What is to-day of grave importance—and not merely crotchety and incidental—stands in direct connexion with that ancient gravity. If we rightly understand ourselves, our problems are the problems of Paul; and if we be enlightened by the brightness of his answers, those answers must be ours.

> Long, long ago the Truth was found,
> A company of men it bound.
> Grasp firmly then—that ancient Truth!

The understanding of history is an uninterrupted conversation between the wisdom of yesterday and the wisdom of to-morrow. And it is a conversation always conducted honestly and with discernment. In this connexion I cannot fail to think with gratitude and respect of my father, Professor Fritz Barth. For such discernment he signally displayed throughout his whole active life.

It is certain that in the past men who hungered and thirsted after righteousness naturally recognized that they were bound to labour with Paul. They could not remain unmoved spectators in his presence. Perhaps we too are entering upon such a time. Should this be so, this book may even now be of some definite, though limited, service. The reader will detect for himself that it has been written with a joyful sense of discovery. The mighty voice of Paul was new to me: and if to me, no doubt to many others also. And yet, now that my work is finished, I perceive that much remains which I have not yet heard and into which I have not as yet penetrated. My book is therefore no more than a preliminary undertaking. Further co-operation is necessary. If only many, better equipped than I, would appear on the scene and set to work to bore for water at the same source! However, should I be mistaken in this hope of a new, questioning investigation of the Biblical Message, well, this book must—wait. The Epistle to the Romans waits also.

SAFENWIL,
August, 1918.

THE PREFACE TO THE SECOND EDITION

οὐδὲ ἀνῆλθον εἰς Ἱεροσόλυμα
. . . ἀλλὰ ἀπῆλθον εἰς Ἀραβίαν.—Gal. i. 17.

THIS book was described in the preface to the first edition as a 'preliminary investigation'. If as great attention had been paid to this description as to the much-abused final sentence— 'this book must wait . . .'—, no justification would be necessary for presenting a new edition in which the original has been so completely rewritten that it may be claimed that no stone remains in its old place. What I hardly dared to hope has been fulfilled. The book brought Paul and the Bible to the notice of some who had thought little about them. That was indeed the 'definite, though limited', purpose for which it was written. Whatever its merits and failings, the first edition can now disappear from the scene. The work has been continued, and the reader is now offered further tentative results. New advance positions have been occupied, and, as a result, the original position has been completely reformed and consolidated. Consequently the position as a whole has an entirely different aspect. And yet identity of historical subject-matter as well as of the theme of which both editions treat, guarantees a definite continuity between the old and the new. In this second 'preliminary investigation' the co-operation of the serious reader is once again required, for the new edition also is concerned only with PROLEGOMENA. This does not mean that a third revision is promised, still less that the work may some day be completed. There can be no completed work. All human achievements are no more than PROLEGOMENA ; and this is especially the case in the field of theology. I emphasize this, in order that those who saw in my previous commentary the appearance of the horrible spectre of a new orthodoxy may not so misunderstand the situation as to be led to blame me now for too great flexibility of opinion. Such contradictions of criticism are not impossible in certain quarters!

Of the relation between the two editions it is unnecessary for me to speak. The book provides its own evidence of the nature of the revision. Strangely enough, the chief weakness of the original edition seems to have passed altogether unnoticed by those who criticized it, at least in public. And it is surely not for me to provide my readers, and certainly not my reviewers, with the formula for the damaging criticism which might have, and indeed ought to have, been made upon it.[1] Some reference must, however, be made here to the circumstances which have led to an advance and to a change of front. First, and most important: the continued study of Paul himself. My manner of working has enabled me to deal only with portions of the rest of the Pauline literature, but each fresh piece of work has brought with it new light upon the Epistle to the Romans. Secondly: the man Overbeck. Elsewhere, Edward Thurneysen and I have drawn attention, at some length, to the warning addressed by Overbeck to all theologians.[2] This warning I have first applied to myself, and then directed upon the enemy. Whether I have dealt at all adequately with the questions raised by this eminent and pious man I must leave to the judgement of those who are able to perceive the nature of the riddle he has formulated so precisely, and are willing at least to attempt its

[1] On the eve of publication there has come into my hands an essay by Ph. Bachmann which appeared in the *Neue Kirchl. Zeitschrift* (Oct. 1921). The essay contains some friendly criticisms which I recognize to be justified and far-reaching. The author will notice that I too have recently been concerned with the same points.

[2] Franz Overbeck (1837–1905) was from 1872 to 1897 Professor of Critical Theology in the University of Basel. The reference is to two polemical pamphlets in which he launched an attack upon his theological contemporaries, conservative and liberal alike. The first pamphlet appeared in 1873 under the title *Über die Christlichkeit unserer heutigen Theologie*; the second—*Christentum und Kultur*—was published in 1919 from Overbeck's literary remains. According to Overbeck all Christian theology, from the Patristic Age onward, is unchristian and satanic, for it draws Christianity into the sphere of civilization and culture, and thereby denies the essentially eschatological character of the Christian religion. In their brochure, *Zur inneren Lage des Christentums*, 1920, Barth and Thurneysen drew attention to Overbeck and especially to his pamphlet *Christentum und Kultur*, and asserted that the questions he had addressed to all theologians still remained unanswered. See *Religion in Geschichte und Gegenwart*, 2nd ed., vol. iv, pp. 183/4. [Tr.]

solution. To the judgement of men like Eberhart Vischer I cannot submit myself! He sees in the riddle no more than a biographical and psychological problem. Thirdly: closer acquaintance with Plato and Kant. The writings of my brother Heinrich Barth have led me to recognize the importance of these philosophers. I have also paid more attention to what may be culled from the writings of Kierkegaard and Dostoevsky that is of importance for the interpretation of the New Testament. The latter I owe more particularly to hints given me by Edward Thurneysen. Fourthly: a careful consideration of the manner in which the first edition of this book has been received. I am bound to say that the more favourable reviews have been most valuable in compelling me to criticize myself. Their praise has caused me such dismay that I have had sometimes to express the matter otherwise, sometimes even to adopt an entirely different position.—These four circumstances I have set out in order that those who are unhappy until they have exposed the immediate cause of this or that occurrence may at least be put upon the right road. Everything in this world has its immediate cause. How indeed could it be otherwise?

More important, however, are those fundamental matters which are common to both editions.

The book does not claim to be more than fragments of a conversation between theologians. It is quite irrelevant when Jülicher and Eberhard Vischer announce triumphantly that I am—a theologian! I have never pretended to be anything else. The point at issue is the kind of theology which is required. Those who urge us to shake ourselves free from theology and to think—and more particularly to speak and write—only what is immediately intelligible to the general public seem to me to be suffering from a kind of hysteria and to be entirely without discernment. Is it not preferable that those who venture to speak in public, or to write for the public, should first seek a better understanding of the theme they wish to propound? Ragaz and his friends reply hurriedly that this proceeds from callous theological pride. But this cannot be granted for one moment. Those who are genuinely convinced that the question is at present trivial must be permitted to go their way. Some of us, however, are persuaded that the question, What are we to say? is an important one, particularly when the majority are prepared at any moment to lift up their voices in the street. I do not want readers of this book to be under any illusions. They must expect nothing but theology. If, in spite of this warning, it should stray into the hands of some who are not

theologians, I shall be especially pleased. For I am altogether
persuaded that the matters of which it treats and the questions
which it raises do in fact concern every one. I could not make
the book more easily intelligible than the subject itself allows.
And I must beg my untheological readers to be indulgent when
they are confronted with citations in a foreign language, which
defy translation without loss of meaning; or when I have from
time to time made use of philosophical or theological abra-
cadabra. If I be not mistaken—and here I must contradict
Arthur Bonus—we theologians serve the layman best when we
refuse to have him especially in mind, and when we simply live
of our own, as every honest labourer must do.

A friend of Ragaz has thought fit to dismiss me with one of
the elder Blumhardt's aphorisms: 'Simplicity is the mark of
divinity'. My answer is, that it has never entered my head to
suppose that what I say or write is 'divine'. So far as I am
aware, divinity is set out in no book. Not being the elder
Blumhardt, we have undertaken rather to ask the question,
'What is divinity?' The simplicity which proceeds from the
apprehension of God in the Bible and elsewhere, the simplicity
with which God Himself speaks, stands not at the beginning
of our journey but at its end. Thirty years hence we may perhaps
speak of simplicity, but now let us speak the truth. For us
neither the Epistle to the Romans, nor the present theological
position, nor the present state of the world, nor the relation
between God and the world, is simple. And he who is now
concerned with truth must boldly acknowledge that he cannot
be simple. In every direction human life is difficult and complicated. And, if gratitude be a consideration that is at all
relevant, men will not be grateful to us if we provide them
with short-lived pseudo-simplifications. Does the general demand for simplicity mean more than a desire—intelligible
enough, and shared by most theologians—that truth should be
expressed directly, without paradox, and in such a way that it
can be received otherwise than by faith alone? I am thinking
here of an experience in relation to that earnest and upright
man, Wernle. As a modern man he is deeply hurt when I say,
for example, plainly and simply—Christ is risen! He complains
that I have made use of an eschatological phrase, and have
ridden rough-shod over very, very difficult problems of thought.
However, when I endeavour to say the same thing in the
language of thought, that is, in dialectical fashion, he protests
in the name of the simple believer that the doctrine of the
Resurrection is wonderful, spiritual, and hard to understand.

How can I answer him? He would be satisfied only if I were to surrender the broken threads of faith, and to speak directly, concretely, and without paradox. This means that the wholly childlike and the wholly unchildlike belong within the realm of truth, but that everything between must be excluded. I earnestly desire to speak simply of those matters with which the Epistle to the Romans is concerned; and, were some one competent to do this to appear, my work would at once be superseded. I am in no way bound to my book and to my theology. As yet, however, those who claim to speak simply seem to me to be—simply speaking about something else. By such simplicity I remain unconvinced.

Turning now to another matter. I have been accused of being an 'enemy of historical criticism'. Such language seems to me nervous and high-strung. Would it not be better to discuss the point at issue quite calmly? I have, it is true, protested against recent commentaries upon the Epistle to the Romans. The protest was directed not only against those originating in the so-called 'critical' school but also, for example, against the commentaries of Zahn and Kühl. I have nothing whatever to say against historical criticism. I recognize it, and once more state quite definitely that it is both necessary and justified. My complaint is that recent commentators confine themselves to an interpretation of the text which seems to me to be no commentary at all, but merely the first step towards a commentary. Recent commentaries contain no more than a reconstruction of the text, a rendering of the Greek words and phrases by their precise equivalents, a number of additional notes in which archaeological and philological material is gathered together, and a more or less plausible arrangement of the subject-matter in such a manner that it may be made historically and psychologically intelligible from the standpoint of pure pragmatism. Jülicher and Lietzmann know far better than I do how insecure all this historical reconstruction is, and upon what doubtful assumptions it often rests. Even such an elementary attempt at interpretation is not an exact science. Exact scientific knowledge, so far as the Epistle to the Romans is concerned, is limited to the deciphering of the manuscripts and the making of a concordance. Historians do not wish, and rightly do not wish, to be confined within such narrow limits. Jülicher and Lietzmann, not to mention conservative scholars, intend quite clearly to press beyond this preliminary work to an understanding of Paul. Now, this involves more than a mere repetition in Greek or in German of what Paul says: it involves the recon-

sideration of what is set out in the Epistle, until the actual
meaning of it is disclosed. It is at this point that the difference
between us appears. There is no difference of opinion with
regard to the need of applying historical criticism as a prolego-
menon to the understanding of the Epistle. So long as the critic
is occupied in this preliminary work I follow him carefully and
gratefully. So long as it is simply a question of establishing
what stands in the text, I have never dreamed of doing anything
else than sit attentively at the feet of such learned men as
Jülicher, Lietzmann, Zahn, and Kühl, and also at the feet
of their predecessors, Tholuck, Meyer, B. Weiss, and Lipsius.
When, however, I examine their attempts at genuine understanding and interpretation, I am again and again surprised how
little they even claim for their work. By genuine understanding
and interpretation I mean that creative energy which Luther
exercised with intuitive certainty in his exegesis; which underlies the systematic interpretation of Calvin; and which is at least
attempted by such modern writers as Hofmann, J. T. Beck,
Godet, and Schlatter. For example, place the work of Jülicher
side by side with that of Calvin: how energetically Calvin, having
first established what stands in the text, sets himself to re-think
the whole material and to wrestle with it, till the walls which
separate the sixteenth century from the first become transparent! Paul speaks, and the man of the sixteenth century hears.
The conversation between the original record and the reader
moves round the subject-matter, until a distinction between
yesterday and to-day becomes impossible. If a man persuades
himself that Calvin's method can be dismissed with the old-
fashioned motto, 'The Compulsion of Inspiration', he betrays
himself as one who has never worked upon the interpretation
of Scripture. Taking Jülicher's work as typical of much modern
exegesis, we observe how closely he keeps to the mere deciphering
of words as though they were runes. But, when all is done, they
still remain largely unintelligible. How quick he is, without any
real struggling with the raw material of the Epistle, to dismiss
this or that difficult passage as simply a peculiar doctrine or
opinion of Paul! How quick he is to treat a matter as explained,
when it is said to belong to the religious thought, feeling, experience, conscience, or conviction,—of Paul! And, when this does
not at once fit, or is manifestly impossible, how easily he leaps,
like some bold William Tell, right out of the Pauline boat,
and rescues himself by attributing what Paul has said, to his
'personality', to the experience on the road to Damascus (an
episode which seems capable of providing at any moment an

explanation of every impossibility), to later Judaism, to Hellenism, or, in fact, to any exegetical semi-divinity of the ancient world! Orthodox commentators are, it is true, better placed than their more liberal colleagues. For orthodoxy, or any other form of Christianity which retains a sense for the importance of history, does at least offer a safer shore on which to alight after they have left the Pauline boat than does the cultured conscience of modern Protestantism. But, in the end, they have no greater advantage than this—that they are the better able to conceal their lack of any tenacious determination to understand and to interpret. The whole procedure assuredly achieves no more than the first draft of a paraphrase of the text and provides no more than a point of departure for genuine exegesis. The matter contained in the text cannot be released save by a creative straining of the sinews, by a relentless, elastic application of the 'dialectical' method. The critical historian needs to be more critical. The interpretation of what is written requires more than a disjointed series of notes on words and phrases. The commentator must be possessed of a wider intelligence than that which moves within the boundaries of his own natural appreciation. True apprehension can be achieved only by a strict determination to face, as far as possible without rigidity of mind, the tension displayed more or less clearly in the ideas written in the text. Criticism (κρίνειν) applied to historical documents means for me the measuring of words and phrases by the standard of that about which the documents are speaking—unless indeed the whole be nonsense. When documents contain answers to questions, the answers must be brought into relation with the questions which are presupposed, and not with some other questions. And moreover, proper concentration of exegesis presses behind the many questions to the one cardinal question by which all are embraced. Everything in the text ought to be interpreted only in the light of what can be said, and therefore only in the light of what is said. When an investigation is rightly conducted, boulders composed of fortuitous or incidental or merely historical conceptions ought to disappear almost entirely. The Word ought to be exposed in the words. Intelligent comment means that I am driven on till I stand with nothing before me but the enigma of the matter; till the document seems hardly to exist as a document; till I have almost forgotten that I am not its author; till I know the author so well that I allow him to speak in my name and am even able to speak in his name myself. What I have just said will, I know, be severely handled. But I cannot prevent myself asking what comment and interpretation really mean. Have men like Lietzmann ever seriously put this question to themselves? Can scientific investigation ever really triumph so long as men refuse to busy themselves with this question, or so long as they are content to engage themselves with amazing energy upon the work of interpretation with the most superficial understanding of what interpretation really is? For me, at any rate, the question of the true nature of interpretation is the supreme question.—Or is it that these learned men, for whose learning and erudition I have such genuine respect, fail to recognize the existence of any real substance at all, of any underlying problem, of any Word in the words? Do they not perceive that there are documents, such as the books of the New Testament, which compel men to speak at whatever cost, because they find in them that which urgently and finally concerns the very marrow of human civilization? —let the last word stand for the moment. Do they not see that their students' future in the Church presents a problem which lies at the heart of the whole matter, and which cannot be dismissed as though it were merely a matter for 'Pastoral Theology'? I myself know what it means year in year out to mount the steps of the pulpit, conscious of the responsibility to understand and to interpret, and longing to fulfil it; and yet, utterly incapable, because at the University I had never been brought beyond that well-known 'Awe in the presence of History' which means in the end no more than that all hope of engaging in the dignity of understanding and interpretation has been surrendered. Do the historians really suppose that they have exhausted their responsibility towards their readers, when, re bene gesta, they permit Niebergall to speak—in the fifth volume?[1] It was this miserable situation that compelled me as a pastor to undertake a more precise understanding and interpretation of the Bible. Is the whole learned society of New Testament scholars really satisfied that this work can be left to what is called 'Practical Theology', as Jülicher in attacking me has reasserted with intolerable and old-fashioned assurance? Jülicher calls me an 'esoteric personage', but I am not that, nor am I a 'bitter enemy of historical criticism'. I am quite

[1] The reference is to the critical commentary on the Books of the New Testament published in four volumes under the title, *Handbuch zum Neuen Testament*, and edited by Prof. Hans Leitzmann. Finally, a fifth volume with the title 'A Practical Commentary', was entrusted to Pastor Niebergall. Niebergall was killed in the War, and in the second edition of the commentary his work has been replaced by a volume containing an exegesis of the Lutheran Epistles and Gospels for the liturgical year, planned as an aid to preachers: *Die alten Pericopen für die Theologische Praxis, erläutert von Dr. L. Fendt*, 1931. [Tr.]

aware of the difficulty of the problem. But no agreement with
regard to the difficulties and dangers inherent in what I understand by 'critical' theology is possible, nor can there be any
discussion as to how they may be avoided, unless my opponents
acknowledge that there is a problem, and show some signs of
penitence. Otherwise, nothing can be done.

What, then, do I mean when I say that a perception of the
'inner dialectic of the matter' in the actual words of the text
is a necessary and prime requirement for their understanding
and interpretation? It has been asserted—a Swiss reviewer
has said it peculiarly roughly—that I mean, of course, my own
'system'. I know that I have laid myself open to the charge of
imposing a meaning upon the text rather than extracting its
meaning from it, and that my method implies this. My reply
is that, if I have a system, it is limited to a recognition of what
Kierkegaard called the 'infinite qualitative distinction' between
time and eternity, and to my regarding this as possessing negative
as well as positive significance: 'God is in heaven, and thou art
on earth.' The relation between such a God and such a man,
and the relation between such a man and such a God, is for me
the theme of the Bible and the essence of philosophy. Philosophers name this KRISIS of human perception—the Prime
Cause: the Bible beholds at the same cross-roads—the figure
of Jesus Christ. When I am faced by such a document as the
Epistle of Paul to the Romans, I embark on its interpretation
on the assumption that he is confronted with the same unmistakable and unmeasurable significance of that relation as I
myself am confronted with, and that it is this situation which
moulds his thought and its expression. Nor am I unique in
making an assumption at the outset. Other commentators do
the same, though their assumptions are more pragmatic: as, for
example, when they assume that the Epistle was written by
Paul in the first century A.D. Whether these assumptions are
justified or not becomes clear in the course of the investigation,
when each verse comes to be examined and interpreted. That
the assumptions are certainly justified is at the end only a
relative certainty. They cannot be proven. In this uncertainty
my fundamental assumption is, of course, included. For the
present, however, I assume that in the Epistle to the Romans
Paul did speak of Jesus Christ, and not of some one else. And
this is as reputable an assumption as other assumptions that
historians are wont to make. The actual exegesis will alone
decide whether this assumption can be maintained. If Paul
was not primarily concerned with the permanent KRISIS of the

relation between time and eternity, but was dealing with some
other theme, the absurdity of a false assumption will become
clear in the course of a detailed examination of the text.
Questioned as to the ground of my assumption that this was,
in fact, Paul's theme, I answer by asking quite simply whether,
if the Epistle is to be treated seriously at all, it is reasonable
to approach it with any other assumption than that God is God.
If the complaint is made that I have done violence to the author,
I shall maintain the counter-complaint that the real violence
is done to him by those who suppose that, in speaking of Jesus
Christ, he is referring to some anthroposophical chaos—to some
relative-absolute, or to some absolute-relative. Surely it is
precisely of this kind of chaos that Paul stands in such evident
horror in all his Epistles. I do not, of course, for one moment
claim to have provided an adequate interpretation of the Epistle.
But, even so, I am persuaded that there is no reason whatever
for me to abandon my prime assumption. Paul knows of God
what most of us do not know; and his Epistles enable us to
know what he knew. It is this conviction that Paul 'knows'
that my critics choose to name my 'system', or my 'dogmatic
presupposition', or my 'Alexandrianism', and so on and so forth.
I have, however, found this assumption to be the best presupposition, even from the point of view of historical criticism.
Modern pictures of Paul seem to me—and not to me only—
simply incredible. It is true that their creators do frequently
refer to modern problems in order to fill in the picture. But
they do so only by way of illustration. I, however, wish to
understand and to explain the Epistle to the Romans, not to
provide it with a series of illustrations. Moreover, judged by
what seems to me to be the fundamental principle of true
exegesis, I entirely fail to see why parallels drawn from the
ancient world—and with such parallels modern commentators
are chiefly concerned—should be of more value for an understanding of the Epistle than the situation in which we ourselves
actually are, and to which we can therefore bear witness.

The attitude that I have adopted towards the text has been
called 'Biblicist'. For this some have blamed and some have
praised me. The word is not mine, but I accept it, provided
I am allowed to explain what I mean by 'Biblicism'. Wernle
wrote of me with some bitterness: 'No single aspect of Paul's
teaching seems to cause Barth discomfort. . . . There remain for
him no survivals of the age in which Paul lived—not even
trivial survivals.' Wernle then proceeds to enumerate what he
finds to be 'uncomfortable points' or 'survivals' which should

be permitted to 'remain' relics of the past. They are: the Pauline 'depreciation' of the earthly life of Jesus—Christ the Son of God—Redemption by the blood of Christ—Adam and Christ—Paul's use of the Old Testament—his so-called 'Baptismal-Sacramentalism'—the Double Predestination—his attitude to secular authority. Now, imagine a commentary on the Epistle to the Romans which left these eight points unexplained; which allowed them to 'remain uncomfortable points'; and in which a maze of contemporary parallels did duty for an explanation of them. Could such a commentary really be called an interpretation? In contrast with this comfortable dismissal of uncomfortable points it has been my 'Biblicism' which has compelled me to wrestle with these 'scandals to modern thought' until I have found myself able to undertake the interpretation of them, because I have discovered precisely in these points the characteristic and veritable discernment of Paul. Whether I have interpreted them correctly is, of course, another matter. There are passages in the Epistle which I still find very hard to understand. But I concede much more to Wernle than this. Strictly speaking, no single verse seems to me capable of a smooth interpretation. There 'remains' everywhere, more or less in the background, that which subtly escapes both understanding and interpretation, or which, at least, awaits further investigation. But this cannot be thought of as a 'residuum' simply to be put on one side or disregarded. It is my so-called 'Biblicism' and 'Alexandrianism' which forbid me to allow the mark of competent scholarship to be that the critic discloses fragments of past history and then leaves them—unexplained. I have, moreover, no desire to conceal the fact that my 'Biblicist' method—which means in the end no more than 'consider well' —is applicable also to the study of Lao-Tse and of Goethe. Nor can I deny that I should find considerable difficulty in applying the method to certain of the books contained in the Bible itself. When I am named 'Biblicist', all that can rightly be proved against me is that I am prejudiced in supposing the Bible to be a good book, and that I hold it to be profitable for men to take its conceptions at least as seriously as they take their own.

Turning now to what is contained in my commentary on the Epistle to the Romans: I must confess that after all these years I am still concerned with the veritable rather than with the whole Gospel. This is because only by laying hold of the veritable Gospel does it seem to me to be possible to reach out towards the whole Gospel. No one has yet comprehended the whole in a single perspective. The normal practice of speaking or writing fluently and comprehensively of the whole—of faith, hope, and love, of earth, heaven, and hell, each playing its noble and proper part in the balance of the whole—seems to me an unedifying procedure. I do not complain, however, if others, speaking in the name of Christianity, think differently. I only beg them not to pass by what is said here, as though it were totally irrelevant. Paulinism has stood always on the brink of heresy. This being so, it is strange how utterly harmless and unexceptionable most commentaries on the Epistle to the Romans and most books about Paul are. Why should this be so? Perhaps because the uncomfortable points are treated according to Wernle's recipe. May I be permitted, out of deference to Wernle, a word of warning to those who are babes in the study of theology, that is, to any undergraduates who may chance to read this book? Read it, please, carefully and not too quickly. Check it by referring to the Greek text and to other commentaries. Above all, do not be 'enthusiastic'. This is a critical work in the full and most serious meaning of the word 'critical'. K. Müller of Erlangen has rightly pointed out that the book may exercise a fatal influence upon immature minds. And yet, the man who makes this criticism ought seriously to reflect whether the persistent covering up of the dangerous element in Christianity is not to hide its light under a bushel. Perhaps Spengler was right when he told us that we were entering upon an 'iron age'. If this be so, theology and the theologians are bound to bear the marks of it.

Harnack's book on Marcion appeared whilst I was immersed in the writing of my commentary. Those who are familiar with both books will understand why I am bound to refer to it. I was puzzled, on reading the earlier reviews of Harnack's book, by the remarkable parallels between what Marcion had said and what I was actually writing. I wish to plead for a careful examination of these agreements before I be praised or blamed hastily as though I were a Marcionite. At the crucial points these agreements break down. Even before the appearance of Harnack's book, Jülicher had already bracketed my name with Marcion's. Harnack joined me to—Thomas Münzer; Walter Koepler, I think, to Kaspar Schwenckfeld. Before these learned theologians made up their minds to throw me to some ancient and venerable heresiarch they would have done better if they had agreed in their choice. As it is, I remain unscathed, and can only wonder at the varied selection the three theologians have made.

And now, a word concerning a matter of detail. A quite unforeseen importance has been attached to the translation of πίστις by—*the faithfulness of God*. Jülicher selects this as an illustration of that 'joyful sense of discovery' of which I spoke —rather romantically it is true—in the preface to the first edition. As a matter of fact, Rudolf Liechtenhan was the spiritual father of this innovation. He had first drawn my attention in a private letter to the possibility of translating it thus. He has now put it into print. The protest has been so general that I have cut down the number of passages in which the rendering occurs. My critics will note, however, that I have retained it with uncomfortable frequency in Ch. III. My purpose in retaining the translation at certain points is to direct attention to a particular nuance of the word, which would be missed were it rendered monotonously by *faith*, just as it would were I sufficiently pedantic to translate it always by *faithfulness*. That the latter meaning is suggested can hardly be denied in view of Rom. iii. 3, of the well known variant in the LXX Version of Hab. ii. 4, and of similar nuances attached to such words as ἀγάπη, γνῶσις, ἐλπίς, χάρις, δικαιοσύνη, εἰρήνη.

For various reasons I have omitted to provide a bibliography. I should like, however, to call attention to the verbal agreement, from Ch. III onwards, between the commentary on the Epistle by C. H. Rieger (1726–91) published in 1828 amongst his *Considerations upon the New Testament*, and the commentary by Fr. Chr. Steinhofer (1706–61), edited for publication in 1851. The plagiarism cannot be charged to the worthy Rieger. Perhaps some Tübingen specialist can throw light upon this puzzling affair.—Jülicher has endeavoured to exclude me from the scholarly world and to set me firmly in the harmless world of practical theology by pointing out my aberrations in the field of textual criticism. It is true that I have sometimes ventured to disagree with Nestle's text, which is the text used by most theological students. I had, however, no intention of claiming any authority in a field in which I am obviously incompetent. And yet, in spite of my incompetence, I could not avoid attempting to justify my adoption of certain variant readings in important passages. I only did this—pending further instruction.

May I, in conclusion, utter a warning to some of my reviewers? I wish to impress upon them that, in reviewing the second edition, it is even more dangerous than before to write about this book either with enthusiasm or with peevishness. I beg them to consider what is implied if the book be wholly accepted or wholly rejected. I beg them to consider what it means to mingle in friendly fashion praise and blame. Nevertheless, I know that it is beyond my power to put this so that they will understand what I mean.

Nothing more remains except for me to thank my friends Eduard Thurneysen of St. Gall, Rudolf Pestalozzi of Zürich, and Georg Merz of Munich, for their loyal assistance in correcting the proofs. The first of these friends has read the whole manuscript with approval, and has suggested many additions. Some of these additions penetrated deeper than my original comment, others were explanatory and added greater precision of expression. I have adopted these additions for the most part without alteration, and they remain a silent testimony to his self-effacement. So close has been our co-operation that I doubt whether even the specialist could detect where the one leaves off and the other begins. The completion of the second edition coincides with the moment when I have to bid farewell to the people of Safenwil. During the past years they have had to put up with a pastor who lived in his study. They have also had to put up with much from his disturbing preoccupation with the Epistle to the Romans. On the whole they have borne this with real patience and sympathy, and I cannot forbear to put on record my gratitude to them. No pastor to whom this book is welcome will find it a light task to make it simple either for himself or for his parishioners.—And now, when I am compelled to leave one field of work behind me and to enter upon a new task, it is a peculiar privilege and pleasure to send a word of greeting to all those friends known and unknown, German and Swiss, who in different ways share the same tribulation.

SAFENWIL,
September, 1921.

THE PREFACE TO THE THIRD EDITION

DETAILS apart, the third edition is a reprint of the second. A time may come when it will be necessary for me once again to rewrite the whole. I hardly know whether I ought to fear or to desire this. Our modern life is subject to strange and rapid changes. Whether this is a symptom of decay, or whether it is a sign that we are moving towards momentous spiritual decisions, who can say? At all events, the situation alters from day to day, conference succeeds conference, men instruct and are instructed, a man says something, and then, finding it echoed in the mouths of others, fears to say it again lest its meaning be altogether lost in the noise of its echo, and yet, side by side with all this dangerous applause, fresh, valuable criticism makes itself heard, and requires most careful consideration. 'We can never plunge a second time into the same river, for now it narrows, now it broadens out, but always it flows on and on.' How then can such a living and responsible undertaking as a commentary on the Epistle to the Romans ever remain stationary? Nevertheless I do not at present feel myself obliged to rewrite the book. This being so, I have no alternative but to sanction the reprinting of what I wrote a year ago. I have caused the preface to the second edition to be reprinted, because otherwise this book would be incomplete. I do not, however, regard its repetition as of very great importance, certainly not the repetition of the polemic contained in it.

The strangest episode in the history of the book since the appearance of the second edition has been its friendly reception by Bultmann and its equally friendly rejection by Schlatter. From the one I conclude to my very great satisfaction that the original outcry against the book as being an incitement to a Diocletian persecution of historical, critical theology was not demanded; from the other that the course I have taken is independent of that positive theology to which I feel myself most nearly related. For the present I have simply noted carefully and gratefully the criticisms and questions put to me by Bultmann and Schlatter, and also by Kolfhaus. Some of their criticisms are new to me; of others I have been long aware.

I should like, however, to take this opportunity of adding something to what was said in the preface to the second edition about 'Historical Criticism', about the 'Dialectic of the Matter', and about 'Biblicism', because they affect the general method of approach. Bultmann complains that I am too conservative. He agrees with me that criticism must begin with the subject-matter, but thinks that this must lead on to the criticism of some of Paul's opinions, because even he fails at times to retain his grip upon what is, in fact, his subject. Bultmann writes: 'Other spirits make themselves heard, as well as the Spirit of Christ.' I do not wish to engage in a controversy with Bultmann as to which of us is the more radical. But I must go farther than he does and say that there are in the Epistle no words at all which are not words of those 'other spirits' which he calls Jewish or Popular Christian or Hellenistic or whatever else they may be. Is it really legitimate to extract a certain number of passages and claim that there the veritable Spirit of Christ has spoken? Or, to put it another way, can the Spirit of Christ be thought of as standing in the Epistle side by side with 'other' spirits and in competition with them ? It seems to me impossible to set the Spirit of Christ—the veritable subject-matter of the Epistle—over against other spirits, in such a manner as to deal out praise to some passages, and to depreciate others where Paul is not controlled by his true subject-matter. Rather, it is for us to perceive and to make clear that the whole is placed under the KRISIS of the Spirit of Christ. The whole is litera, that is, voices of those other spirits. The problem is whether the whole must not be understood in relation to the true subject-matter which is—The Spirit of Christ. This is the problem which provides aim and purpose to our study of the litera.

The commentator is thus presented with a clear 'Either—Or' The question is whether or no he is to place himself in a relation to his author of utter loyalty. Is he to read him, determined to follow him to the very last word, wholly aware of what he is doing, and assuming that the author also knew what he was doing? Loyalty surely cannot end at a particular point, and certainly cannot be exhausted by an exposure of the author's literary affinities. Anything short of utter loyalty means a commentary ON Paul's Epistle to the Romans, not a commentary so far as is possible WITH him—even to his last word. True exegesis involves, of course, much sweat and many groans. Even so, the extent to which the commentator will be able to disclose the Spirit of Christ in his reading of Paul will not be everywhere the same. But he will know that the responsibility rests on his shoulders; and he will not let himself be bewildered by the voices of those other spirits, which so often render inaudible the dominant tones of the Spirit of Christ. He will, moreover, always be willing to assume that, when he fails to understand, the blame is his and not Paul's. Nor will he rest content until paradoxically he has seen the whole in the fragments, and has displayed the fragments in the context of the veritable subject-matter, so that all the other spirits are seen in some way or other to serve the Spirit of Christ.

It may be, on the other hand, that the commentator is unable to accept the presupposition which such fidelity requires. This may be because he does not perceive, or at least does not perceive sufficiently clearly, what is the veritable subject-matter of such a document as the Epistle to the Romans. Or it may be because, so noisy are those other spirits which shriek at him from every verse, he despairs of ever being able to detect the dominant tones. If this be so, for whatever reason, he must content himself with writing a commentary ON Paul. He cannot speak WITH him, except perchance when Paul says something

c

which even he can understand. Such a commentator will only
discover the Spirit of Christ 'here and there'; and he may not
attribute to the Spirit of Christ even those fragments which he
finds illuminating. He stands irresponsibly before the text,
confronted, as a spectator, with a mixture of Spirit and spirits.
Though he may here and there follow his author, he does not
feel bound to wrestle with the understanding of him, for the
simple reason that he has never made up his mind to stand or
fall with him. I cannot, for my part, think it possible for an
interpreter honestly to reproduce the meaning of any author
unless he dares to accept the condition of utter loyalty. To
make an oration over a man means to speak over his body,
and that is to bury him finally, deeper and without hope, in his
grave. No doubt despair leaves no other course open. Indeed,
there are many historical personages whom it is possible only
to speak ABOUT. Even so, it is still open to question whether the
riddle they propound is really due to their obscurity or to our
lack of apprehension. In any case, I am completely unable to
understand Bultmann's demand that I should mingle fire and
water. He asks me to think and write WITH Paul, to follow him
into the vast unfamiliarity of his Jewish, Popular-Christian,
Hellenistic conceptions; and then suddenly, when the whole
becomes too hopelessly bizarre, I am to turn round and write
'critically' ABOUT him and against him—as though, when all
is strange, this or that is to be regarded as especially outrageous.
Is Bultmann incapable of understanding that, even were we
concerned with an author's literary style, such a method
of procedure would be illegitimate? His demands seem to me,
therefore, to involve not merely a return to the older theory
of 'relics of a bygone age' and 'uncomfortable points', but also
an error in literary taste. Bultmann further goes on to hint that
there lurks behind my whole method of exegesis a 'modern form
of the dogma of Inspiration'. Schlatter also noticed the same
tendency with disapproval. But, from the preface to the first
edition onwards, I have never attempted to conceal the fact
that my manner of interpretation has certain affinities with the
old doctrine of Verbal Inspiration. As expounded by Calvin,
the doctrine seems to me at least worthy of careful consideration
as capable of leading to spiritual apprehension, and I have
already made it clear how I have, in fact, made use of it. Is
there any way of penetrating the heart of a document—of any
document!—except on the assumption that its spirit will speak
to our spirit through the actual written words? This does not
exclude a criticism of the letter by the spirit, which is, indeed,

unavoidable. It is precisely a strict faithfulness which compels
us to expand or to abbreviate the text, lest a too rigid attitude
to the words should obscure that which is struggling to expression in them and which demands expression. This critical freedom of exegesis was used by Calvin in masterly fashion, without
the slightest disregard for the discipline by which alone liberty
is justified. The attentive reader will perceive that I have
employed this method, believing it to be demanded by the text.
I can only hope that I have not fallen into the snare of indis-
cipline which inevitably threatens those who employ it. I have
resolutely determined not to make use of the method in order
to criticize Paul; and it is my serious intention always to avoid
this temptation. The Spirit of Christ is not a vantage-point
from which a ceaseless correction of Paul—or of any one else—
may be exercised schoolmaster-wise. We must be content if,
despite other spirits, we are not wholly bereft of the Spirit;
content if, standing by Paul's side, we are able to learn and to
teach; content with a readiness to discern in spiritual fashion
what is spiritually intended; and satisfied also to recognize that
the voice with which we proclaim what we have received is
primarily nothing but the voice of those other spirits. No
human word, no word of Paul, is absolute truth. In this I agree
with Bultmann—and surely with all intelligent people. But
what does the relativity of all human speech mean? Does
relativity mean ambiguity? Assuredly it does. But how can
I demonstrate it better than by employing the whole of my
energy to disclose the nature of this ambiguity? More than one
reader of my book has learned from it to understand the
uncertainty of Paulinism. I do not object to the book being so
used. But nevertheless, we must learn to see beyond Paul.
This can only be done, however, if, with utter loyalty and with
a desperate earnestness, we endeavour to penetrate his meaning.

It may help those who find much that is contained in the
second edition of my commentary strangely unfamiliar, if I
quote, in passing, the opening sentences of Calvin's interpretation of the eleventh chapter of the Epistle to the Hebrews.—
'Grace', he writes, 'has always the appearance of contradiction.
The foundation is faith. For faith is the pillar and possession
upon which we are able to plant our feet. But what, in fact,
do we possess? Not things that are present, but what is set
far distant under our feet—nay more, what is beyond the
comprehension of our spirit. Faith is therefore named the
evidence of things not seen. But *evidence* means that things
emerge into appearance, and is applicable only to what concerns

our senses. In the realm of faith the two apparent opposites—evidence and things not seen—struggle with one another and are united. It is precisely the hidden things, inaccessible to sensible perception, that are displayed by the Spirit of God. He promises eternal life—to those who are dead. He speaks of the blessedness of resurrection—to those who are compassed about with corruption. He pronounces those in whom sin dwells —to be righteous. He calls those oppressed with ceaseless tribulation—blessed. He promises abundance of riches—to those abounding only in hunger and thirst. God cries out to us that He is coming quickly to our aid—and yet He seems deaf to every human cry for help. What, then, would be our fate, were we not powerful in hope, were we not hurrying through the darkness of the world along the road which is enlightened by the Spirit and by the Word of God?'

I must again thank those who have assisted me so loyally. Georg Merz corrected the proofs and compiled the index. Lukas Christ of Pratteln has smoothed out the roughness of my style in many passages—a very necessary piece of work.

GÖTTINGEN,
July, 1922.

THE PREFACE TO THE FOURTH EDITION

SINCE the appearance of the last edition, further work and further reflection have made it obvious that the book needs to be rewritten. It requires clarification; and other improvements are necessary also. But it is no use patching it up, and for a long time to come I shall have no opportunity of recasting the whole. Further, I do not, as yet, see my way through those difficult passages which ought to be the starting-point of a new revision. Could I see my way clearly, I should have to find time to rewrite the whole book. I must therefore send the book out once more unaltered. This, however, need not inconvenience those familiar with current theological discussions. They tend, in one form or another, to revolve round the Epistle to the Romans. The reader will therefore be in a position to make for himself the necessary reservations and amplifications.

As regards the external history of the book: it should be noted that Jülicher has reviewed it for a second time. He pronounces it to have proceeded from the 'arrogance of a spiritual enthusiast'; and this, he says, is his 'final word'. On the other hand, the literary organ of the Dutch Reformed Church is outraged by the 'negative' character of the book, and its readers are warned to 'exercise great care in using it', since it is 'foreign to their piety'. Of greater interest to me personally are the appreciations which have reached me from the Catholic side. Catholic reviewers have, for the most part, displayed a genuine understanding of the point at issue. They have, moreover, conducted the discussion in a proper atmosphere of theological controversy —an atmosphere seemingly foreign to most of my reviewers on the other side of the great gulf. Now, what is the meaning of this fundamental, and to me quite unexpected, understanding? Erich Przywara, S.J., contrasts our 'school'! with that of Otto and Heiler, judging it to be a 'genuine rebirth of Protestantism', a reappearance of the 'passionate fervour of the old Reformers'. Joseph Engert, on the other hand, brings forward evidence to show that, apart from the doctrine of the Church elaborated in Chs. IX–XI, my commentary does not differ from the teaching of Thomas Aquinas, of the Council of Trent, and of the Roman Catechism; only my formulation of it is far more obscure and complicated. The two reviewers are clearly not saying quite the same thing. Should they agree together as to what it is precisely they wish to say to us, we should be bound to answer them. Meanwhile, I cannot help saying that I regard it as a most hopeful sign for both sides that an opportunity should now be provided of entering into genuine theological, as opposed to merely historical, discussion with theologians of the Old Church. Those, like ourselves, who are moving in the world of the theology of the Reformation, for this very reason, ought not —and indeed do not—cast in the teeth of others that they are moving with conviction in the world of medieval theology. When that is said, we must, however, own to a horror of mystical, High-Church, Evangelical-Catholic, dilettantism.

GÖTTINGEN,
February, 1924.

THE PREFACE TO THE FIFTH EDITION

THIS book continues to be read and to exert influence, but its very 'success' is such as to compel its author to pause and consider. In his thoughts about his 'success' it is right that his readers should share. Two reflections jostle one another in my mind. When I wrote the book, did I simply put into words what was everywhere in the air—especially in Germany after the War? Did I say what was readily acceptable to the 'rulers of the world' in our generation, and what men's ears itched to hear? And, in becoming fashionable and in the appearance of 'proper Barthians', like the 'Ritschlians' of the Bismarck era!—am I suffering an inevitable punishment? Every word I wrote against human—too human—vapourings, everything I wrote especially against religious vapourings, everything I said about their various causes and effects, seems now to be turned back upon myself. I had set out to please none but the very few, to swim against the current, to beat upon doors which I thought were firmly bolted. Was I altogether deceived? Perhaps I was. For who is able to know even himself accurately, or to gauge his contemporaries? Who knows whether we are not being moved, just when we imagine that we are moving others? My readers can well understand how startling it was for me to note the kind of theological books which at the present time have made a like impression. Was I deceived about the world and about myself? Am I after all merely one of those bad theologians who are no more than servants of public opinion? And are my readers also deceived in supposing a thing to be relevant to-day which was, in fact, relevant only for Paul and for Luther and Calvin? Have they been presented with what is really no more than a rehash, resurrected out of Nietzsche and Kierkegaard and Cohen? If this be what has actually occurred I must accept judgement and recognize that I am just the author of—a best-seller. But why should not this be the truth? And even if it were not true, no credit would be due to me or to my book. When I wrote in the Preface to the first edition that this book could 'wait', it was treated as a piece of arrogance. If this were pride on my part, perhaps I have had to be punished for it, since, unlike so many other better books, it did not have to wait. In common with much else that is empty show, it has gained the applause by which it is condemned. *All flesh is as grass*— the truth of these words is exhibited in this world far more surely by precarious success than by a correspondingly pre-carious failure.—This is the first of my reflections; and I beg my friendly readers to perceive that it is directed against them as well as against myself. They must bear its weight with me. They will then be no more surprised than I shall be, should it one day become apparent that here too—*the grass withereth, and the flower fadeth.*

The second reflection is more serious. It may be that every criticism implied in the former reflection is justified, and yet that nevertheless, in spite of much arrogance and wrong-headed-ness, aye, even in the midst of it, something has been brought out into the open through what has been observed and said in this book—as it were by forensic justification (justificatio forensis). And this applies to what others have also observed and said who are in no way dependent upon my book. It is to this whole situation that the Church and the theologians of to-day are bound to pay attention. But what then is my personal responsibility in all this? And what is the responsibility of my friendly readers? If, perhaps quite apart from me and even in opposition to me, there has emerged something true and right, what am I to say, when, because at the critical moment I sounded the alarm, I am now supposed—to my horror I must acknowledge it—to be in some special way responsible for continuing and deepening and carrying through what has been begun? I can only say that, when I was working at this book in my peaceful parsonage in the distant valley of the Aar, I was convinced, like any other vigorous and keen author, that I was producing something good and valuable. But it never crossed my mind to think that the apostle Paul, as I seemed to hear him, would awaken such an echo that with the publication of this book I should give many earnest men the right to drive me into a corner by asking me questions concerning further implications, consequences, and applications, or even by asking me to repeat what had been brought to light. As though I were competent for all this! In his 'Reminiscences' Admiral Tirpitz says that, whereas it is easy to hoist your flag, it is difficult to strike it honourably. I would add that it is even more difficult—at any rate when there is no question of hauling it down—to continue to fly it honourably. And this is my situation. As it becomes more and more clear how much there remained to be done after the book was written, I often wish that I had never written it. And I feel this even more acutely now that I have been suddenly appointed, in spite of my light equipment, to the responsible position of professor at a university. It is now demanded of me that I should definitely put my hand to the plough every day; and every day I am reminded how difficult it is to plough the field of Christian doctrine, remembering that each furrow is—of bitter necessity —a new furrow.

Should this more favourable explanation of the 'success' of my book also be justified, then, whatever can be rightly said to the contrary, it does mark the moment when a breach, how-ever small, has been made in the inner and outer afflictions of Protestantism. It is, however, oppressively humiliating both for me and for my readers—at least, for my friendly, understanding, and sympathetic readers—to reflect that, when quick speech and action is necessary to do justice both to the misery and to the hope of the Church, we should remain so incompetent—unless indeed the whole present situation be merely a Fata Morgana. I have just come across the following lines written by a pastor in Hessen, who is personally unknown to me.[1] They fit my position so well, that they might have been addressed to me:

> God needs MEN, not creatures
> Full of noisy, catchy phrases.
> Dogs he asks for, who their noses
> Deeply thrust into—To-day,
> And there scent Eternity.
>
> Should it lie too deeply buried,
> Then go on, and fiercely burrow,
> Excavate until—To-morrow.

Yes, God needs . . . ! I wish I could be such a Hound of God—Domini canis—and could persuade all my readers to enter the Order. Understood thus, these lines make the best review of my book that has yet appeared. And no review could be more critical. No man can add a cubit to his stature, and so the 'success' of the book, even according to the second reflection, is a judgement under which we stand.

It is necessary therefore to keep in mind both reflections upon the uncertainty of our position. For I wish my understanding reader—I am not now speaking of or to the others—to apprehend with me the severity and the goodness which together press upon our memory the fact that we have a Master. We must not expect to escape some equivalent of the concrete threatenings and tribulations which Protestant Christians and theologians were compelled to endure for their faith in the sixteenth century. We of the twentieth century must not shrink from being the Church Militant. I am able to understand something of what this equivalent is, when I think of the paradox or dialectic which is contained in the word 'success'.

That is what I wished to say. And now I can send forth this book once more.

MÜNSTER IN WESTPHALIA,
February, 1926.

[1] Printed in *Kirche und Welt*, January 1926.

THE PREFACE TO THE SIXTH EDITION

THE two years and a half which have passed since the publication of the fifth edition of this book have increased the distance separating me from what I had originally written. Not that, in expounding the Pauline Epistles, or indeed any part of Holy Scripture, I should now wish to say anything materially different from what I then said. I should still retain that which gave so serious and so severe offence; and so long as it still remains unrecognized that such offence had to be given and that the giving of it was justifiable, or until I am myself persuaded that I was wrong in giving it, there seems no reason why I should cease giving offence, and if so, why I should not continue to do so in its original form. However, I do not wish the book to go forth once more without saying that, were I to set to work again upon the exposition of the Epistle, and were I determined to repeat the same thing, I should certainly have to express it quite differently. I have, in the meantime, learnt that in Paul there is on the one hand a far greater variety and on the other hand a far greater monotony than I had then attributed to him. Much would therefore have to be drastically curtailed, and much expanded. Much would have to be expressed more carefully and with greater reserve; much, however, with greater clarity and more emphatically. A great deal of the scaffolding of the book was due to my own particular situation at the time and also to the general situation. This would have to be pulled down. Many threads, on the other hand, which I had not then noticed in the Epistle, would now have to be brought to light. Those who read the book must also bear in mind the quite simple fact that I am now seven years older, and that all our exercise books obviously require correcting. Moreover, since the appearance of the fifth edition, I have embarked upon the publication of my *Prolegomena to Christian Dogmatics*. This means that a certain weight has been lifted from the earlier book, inasmuch as any serious criticism of it has at least to take also into consideration what is said in the second and more comprehensive book, where I have attempted a greater breadth of treatment and also greater precision. Similarly, those who, after reading the earlier book, still retain confidence in me and desire further treatment of the questions which it raises, should also take into account both the later book and other writings of mine, which are, in fact, continuations of the original work. At Neuendettelsau[1]

---

[1] Neuendettelsau is a small village in Bavaria, lying south-west of Nuremburg. It was the scene of the pastorate of Wilhelm Löhe (1808–72. See

the following statement appeared the other day: 'Of Karl Barth
it may now be said that he is already slipping into the position
of a man of yesterday.' (The *Freimund* of 8 Nov. 1928.) Yes,
no doubt! Dead men ride fast, but successful theologians ride
faster (*cf.* the Preface to the fifth edition). How could I have
written this book at all, had I not been both in theory and
in practice pre-pared before I became a 'man of to-day'?
Do I—as I am accused of doing—treat 'time' and 'history'
so lightly as to be hurt when I am told that my day has an
evening and will, indeed, become a past yesterday? Warned
of this, I am, however, glad of the opportunity of still making
some corrections and of adding some explanations; glad to
be able to beg my friendly readers, even if they think (perhaps rightly) that it would be better for me to make no corrections, not to write my obituary notice until what I have said
is proved to have been exhausted and the 'yesterday' which
exists sub specie aeterni has also been manifested in time.

MÜNSTER IN WESTPHALIA,
· *The First Sunday in Advent*, 1928.

Religion in Geschichte und Gegenwart, 2nd ed., vol. iii, p. 1707). Since then it
has become the active centre of the home and foreign missionary work of the
Lutheran Church. The mother-house of the Lutheran Deaconesses is located
there. The Movement has at Neuendettelsau its own press, and from it is
issued a weekly paper entitled *Freimund. Kirchlich-Politisches Wochenblatt
für Stadt und Land*, with the sub-title 'Organ einer öffentlichen Mission
vom Standpunkt ev.-luth. Christentums. [Tr.]

INTRODUCTION

THE AUTHOR TO HIS READERS

I. 1–7

Paul, a servant of Jesus Christ, called to be an apostle, separated unto the gospel of God, which he promised afore by his prophets in the holy scriptures, concerning his Son, who was born of the seed of David according to the flesh, and declared to be the Son of God with power, according to the Holy Spirit, through his **resurrection from the dead—even Jesus Christ our Lord, through whom we received grace and apostleship** to bring into being obedience to the faithfulness of God which is confirmed in the gospel **among all nations, for his name's sake: among whom are ye also the called of Jesus Christ: To all that are in Rome, beloved of God, called to be saints: Grace to you and peace from God our Father and the Lord Jesus Christ.**

Paul, a servant of Jesus Christ, called to be an apostle. Here is no 'genius rejoicing in his own creative ability' (Zündel). The man who is now speaking is an emissary, bound to perform his duty; the minister of his King; a servant, not a master. However great and important a man Paul may have been, the essential theme of his mission is not within him but above him— unapproachably distant and unutterably strange. His call to apostleship is not a familiar episode in his own personal history: 'The call to be an apostle is a paradoxical occurrence, lying always beyond his personal self-identity' (Kierkegaard). Paul, it is true, is always himself, and moves essentially on the same plane as all other men. But, in contradiction to himself and in distinction from all others, he is—called by God and sent forth. Are we then to name him a Pharisee? Yes, a Pharisee— 'separated', isolated, and distinct. But he is a Pharisee of a higher order. Fashioned of the same stuff as all other men, a stone differing in no way from other stones, yet in his relation to God—and in this only—he is unique. As an apostle—and only as an apostle—he stands in no organic relationship with human society as it exists in history: seen from the point of view of human society, he can be regarded only as an exception,

nay, rather, as an impossibility. Paul's position can be justified only as resting in God, and so only can his words be
regarded as at all credible, for they are as incapable of direct
apprehension as is God Himself. For this reason he dares to
approach others and to demand a hearing without fear either
of exalting himself or of approximating too closely to his
audience. He appeals only to the authority of God. This is
the ground of his authority. There is no other.

Paul is authorized to deliver—the Gospel of God. He is commissioned to hand over to men something quite new and unprecedented, joyful and good,—the truth of God. Yes, precisely
—of God! The Gospel is not a religious message to inform mankind of their divinity or to tell them how they may become
divine. The Gospel proclaims a God utterly distinct from men.
Salvation comes to them from Him, because they are, as men,
incapable of knowing Him, and because they have no right to
claim anything from Him. The Gospel is not one thing in the
midst of other things, to be directly apprehended and comprehended. The Gospel is the Word of the Primal Origin of all
things, the Word which, since it is ever new, must ever be
received with renewed fear and trembling. The Gospel is therefore not an event, nor an experience, nor an emotion—however
delicate! Rather, it is the clear and objective perception of
what eye hath not seen nor ear heard. Moreover, what it
demands of men is more than notice, or understanding, or
sympathy. It demands participation, comprehension, co-operation; for it is a communication which presumes faith in the
living God, and which creates that which it presumes.

Being the Gospel of God it was—promised afore. The Gospel
is no intrusion of to-day. As the seed of eternity it is the fruit
of time, the meaning and maturity of history—the fulfilment
of prophecy. The Gospel is the word spoken by the prophets
from time immemorial, the word which can now be received
and has now been accepted. Such is the Gospel with which the
apostle has been entrusted. By it his speech is authorized, but
by it also that which he says is judged. The words of the
prophets, long fastened under lock and key, are now set free.
Now it is possible to hear what Jeremiah and Job and the
preacher Solomon had proclaimed long ago. Now we can see
and understand what is written, for we have an 'entrance into
the Old Testament' (Luther). Therefore the man who now
speaks, stands firmly upon a history which has been expounded
and veritably understood: 'From the outset he disclaims the
honour due to an innovator' (Schlatter).

Jesus Christ our Lord. This is the Gospel and the meaning of history. In this name two worlds meet and go apart, two planes intersect, the one known and the other unknown. The known plane is God's creation, fallen out of its union with Him, and therefore the world of the 'flesh' needing redemption, the world of men, and of time, and of things—our world. This known plane is intersected by another plane that is unknown—the world of the Father, of the Primal Creation, and of the final Redemption. The relation between us and God, between this world and His world, presses for recognition, but the line of intersection is not self-evident. The point on the line of intersection at which the relation becomes observable and observed is Jesus, Jesus of Nazareth, the historical Jesus,—**born of the seed of David according to the flesh.** The name Jesus defines an historical occurrence and marks the point where the unknown world cuts the known world. This does not mean that, at this point, time and things and men are in themselves exalted above other times and other things and other men, but that they are exalted inasmuch as they serve to define the neighbourhood of the point at which the hidden line, intersecting time and eternity, concrete occurrence and primal origin, men and God, becomes visible. The years A.D. 1–30 are the era of revelation and disclosure; the era which, as is shown by the reference to David, sets forth the new and strange and divine definition of all time. The particularity of the years A.D. 1–30 is dissolved by this divine definition, because it makes every epoch a potential field of revelation and disclosure. The point on the line of intersection is no more extended onto the known plane than is the unknown plane of which it proclaims the existence. The effulgence, or, rather, the crater made at the percussion point of an exploding shell, the void by which the point on the line of intersection makes itself known in the concrete world of history, is not—even though it be named the Life of Jesus—that other world which touches our world in Him. In so far as our world is touched in Jesus by the other world, it ceases to be capable of direct observation as history, time, or thing. Jesus has been—**declared to be the Son of God with power, according to the Holy Spirit, through his resurrection from the dead.** In this declaration and appointment—which are beyond historical definition—lies the true significance of Jesus. Jesus as the Christ, as the Messiah, is the End of History; and He can be comprehended only as Paradox (Kierkegaard), as Victor (Blumhardt), as Primal History (Overbeck). As Christ, Jesus is the plane which lies beyond our comprehension. The plane which is known to us, He intersects vertically, from above. Within history, Jesus as the Christ can be understood only as Problem or Myth. As the Christ, He brings the world of the Father. But we who stand in this concrete world know nothing, and are incapable of knowing anything, of that other world. The Resurrection from the dead is, however, the transformation: the establishing or *declaration* of that point from above, and the corresponding discerning of it from below. The Resurrection is the revelation: the disclosing of Jesus as the Christ, the appearing of God, and the apprehending of God in Jesus. The Resurrection is the emergence of the necessity of giving glory to God: the reckoning with what is unknown and unobservable in Jesus, the recognition of Him as Paradox, Victor, and Primal History. In the Resurrection the new world of the Holy Spirit touches the old world of the flesh, but touches it as a tangent touches a circle, that is, without touching it. And, precisely because it does not touch it, it touches it as its frontier—as the new world. The Resurrection is therefore an occurrence in history, which took place outside the gates of Jerusalem in the year A.D. 30, inasmuch as it there 'came to pass', was discovered and recognized. But inasmuch as the occurrence was conditioned by the Resurrection, in so far, that is, as it was not the 'coming to pass', or the discovery, or the recognition, which conditioned its necessity and appearance and revelation, the Resurrection is not an event in history at all. Jesus is *declared to be the Son of God* wherever He reveals Himself and is recognized as the Messiah, before the first Easter Day and, most assuredly, after it. This declaration of the Son of man to be the Son of God is the significance of Jesus, and, apart from this, Jesus has no more significance or insignificance than may be attached to any man or thing or period of history in itself.—*Even though we have known Christ after the flesh, yet now we know him so no longer.* What He was, He is. But what He is underlies what He was. There is here no merging or fusion of God and man, no exaltation of humanity to divinity, no overflowing of God into human nature. What touches us—and yet does not touch us—in Jesus the Christ, is the Kingdom of God who is both Creator and Redeemer. The Kingdom of God has become actual, is nigh at hand (iii. 21, 22). And this Jesus Christ is—our **Lord**. Through His presence in the world and in our life we have been dissolved as men and established in God. By directing our eyes to Him our advance is stopped—and we are set in motion. We tarry and—hurry. Because Jesus is Lord over Paul and over the Roman Christians, the word 'God' is no empty word in the Epistle to the Romans.

From Jesus Christ Paul has received—**grace and apostleship.** Grace is the incomprehensible fact that God is well pleased with a man, and that a man can rejoice in God. Only when grace is recognized to be incomprehensible is it grace. Grace exists, therefore, only where the Resurrection is reflected. Grace is the gift of Christ, who exposes the gulf which separates God and man, and, by exposing it, bridges it. But inasmuch as God knows men from afar and is known by them in His undiscoverable majesty, the man of God must inevitably approach his fellow men as an 'emissary': *Necessity is laid upon me; yea, woe is unto me, if I preach not the gospel* (1 Cor. ix. 16). And yet the distinction between Paul and other Christians can be a matter of degree only. For, where the grace of God is, men participate in proclaiming the transformation of time and of things, the Resurrection—however reservedly and with whatever scepticism they proclaim it. Where the grace of God is, the very existence of the world and the very existence of God become a question and a hope with which and for which men must wrestle. For we are not now concerned with the propaganda of a conviction or with its imposition on others; grace means bearing witness to the faithfulness of God which a man has encountered in Christ, and which, when it is encountered and recognized, requires a corresponding fidelity towards God. The fidelity of a man to the faithfulness of God—the faith, that is, which accepts grace—is itself the demand for obedience and itself demands obedience from others. Hence the demand is a call which enlightens and rouses to action; it carries with it mission, beside which no other mission is possible. For the name of Him in whom the two worlds meet and are separated must be honoured, and for this mission grace provides full authority, since men are shattered by it (v. 2).

The same God who had made Paul the apostle of the Gentiles (i. 1) had also pressed the Roman Christians into the service of His imminent and coming Kingdom. As men called unto holiness, they belong no longer to themselves or to the old world which is passing to corruption. They belong to Him who has called them. Not for Paul only, but for them also, has the Son of man been appointed Son of God through the power of the Resurrection. They too are here and now imprisoned in the knowledge of great tribulation and of great hope. They too after their fashion are separated and isolated for God. They too are constituted anew by the—**grace and peace from God our**

Father and the Lord Jesus Christ. May this presupposition occur ever afresh! May their peace be their disquiet, and their disquiet be their peace! This is beginning, theme, and end, of the Epistle to the Romans.

PERSONAL MATTERS

i. 8–15

v. 8. First, I thank my God through Jesus Christ, because your faith is spoken of throughout the whole world.

The Resurrection has proved its power: there are Christians —even in Rome. And this has come about apart from any personal action of Paul. They have been called, whoever it was that brought the call of Christ (i. 6). This is a sufficient ground for thanksgiving. The stone has been rolled away from the door of the tomb. The Word has free course. Jesus lives; and He is in the metropolis of the world. Everywhere Christians have heard of it (xvi. 19). This may be only a parable, but a parable it is. Paul does not thank God for the piety of the Roman Christians, or for any other observable human advantages they may possess. He simply gives thanks for the fact that there are Christians in Rome. Special gifts or remarkable deeds are less important than the fact that the flag has been planted, that the name of the Lord is announced and received, that the Kingdom of God is being awaited and proclaimed. This then is faith: the fidelity of men encountering the faithfulness of God. Now, when this occurs, the KRISIS introduced by the resurrection of Jesus is set in motion, His appointment as Son of God (i. 4) is made manifest, and the servant of God has reason to give thanks. The doors of Rome have been opened for the Lord, and for His servant also.

vv. 9, 10. More than a casual or merely external relationship has long existed between Paul and the Roman Christians: **For God is my witness whom I serve in my spirit** by proclaiming **the gospel of his Son, how unceasingly I make mention of you always in my prayers, if by any means now at length I may be prospered by the will of God to come unto you.**

The apostle belongs to them—indeed he belongs to many! (i. 14)—as certainly as he belongs to God. The spirit of one who has received and bears witness to the grace of God, and who is consumed with zeal for the honour of his Lord (i. 5), cannot remain estranged from the spirits of those who have been

moved by the same revelation and disclosure. His prayer is
as much a work for them as for himself. When he prays, he
prays for them as they too pray for him—unless indeed they
have grown weary of striving (xv. 30). Those who have never
seen one another and whose paths have never crossed possess
in their attention to the Gospel of salvation a ground of solidarity.
And yet, sharing this solidarity, knowing themselves to be in
God, they not unnaturally desire to see one another, if that be
permitted. But ought there to be such meeting? Is it necessary?
Surely not. The desire has no direct connexion with the Kingdom of God; and the will of God has complete precedence.
He may comply with human desires, but also He may not. In
any case, that alone is right which complies with His will.
Meanwhile, those who have never met must have confidence
in each other, but, beyond that, they must seek only to know the
will of God. And the will of God is perceived when the inner
and outer situation genuinely correspond with the Christian's
perception of what is right (xii. 2). Apart from this moment
of perception the fulfilment of human desires is unthinkable.

**vv. 11, 12. For I long to see you that I may impart unto
you** the grace of the Spirit, **to the end ye may be established;**
or better, **that I may be comforted together with you, by
the mutual faith, both yours and mine.**

There is good reason for Paul's longing. When pilgrims on
the road of God meet one another, they have something to say.
A man may be of value to another man, not because he wishes
to be important, not because he possesses some inner wealth
of soul, not because of something he is, but because of what he
is—not. His importance may consist in his poverty, in his hopes
and fears, in his waiting and hurrying, in the direction of his
whole being towards what lies beyond his horizon and beyond
his power. The importance of an apostle is negative rather than
positive. In him a void becomes visible. And for this reason
he is something to others: he is able to share grace with them,
to focus their attention, and to establish them in waiting and in
adoration. The Spirit gives grace through him. Possessing
nothing, he has nothing of his own to offer, and so, the more he
imparts, the more he receives; and the more he receives, the
more he imparts. There is therefore no question of Christians
saying to one another—'Did you receive from me?' or 'Did I
receive from you?' Since neither is, or possesses, anything,
nothing passes from the one to the other. It is sufficient that what
is, is—above us and behind us and beyond us. Faith it is—the

gospel of faith, the content of faith, the faithfulness of God—
that, in all the human frailty and tribulation with which we
are surrounded, provides comfort alike to the beginner and to
him that hath the pre-eminence. Though fellowship is assuredly
in itself an empty and a trivial thing, we cry out for it, because
we long to join hands in knocking at the doors of the Kingdom
of God and to be moved together by His Spirit.

**v. 13. And I would not have you ignorant, brethren,
that oftentimes I purposed to come unto you—and was
hindered hitherto—that I might** celebrate a harvest **among
you also, even as among the rest of the Gentiles.**

Many times Paul had planned a visit to Rome to satisfy his
own longing and the well-known longing of the Christians who
lived there. But there were still places where no beginning had
been made. And since his life's work was to plant in virgin soil
(xv. 20–2), he had never been allowed to choose the road which
led to Rome. Nevertheless, it remained his desire and intention
to reap where he had not sown, and to cultivate ground which
others had already ploughed. By the will of God (i. 10), however,
this had not yet been possible.

vv. 14, 15. I am debtor—yes, with my whole being—**both
to the Greeks and to the Barbarians, both to the wise and
to the foolish.** It is therefore my great desire **to preach the
gospel to you also that are in Rome.**

Paul was bound under discipline (i. 1), a discipline which
limited his personal wishes, and in so doing provided an opportunity for their fulfilment. Should the proper occasion arise,
he would be able to perform his ministry with as little trepida-
tion in the cultured and religious cosmopolitan society of Rome
as when he had been faced by the crass stupidity of Iconium
and Lystra. He is confined by no cultural or geographical
frontier. And, moreover, his guiding principle of speaking only
where the gospel had not been heard already is not a law of the
Medes and Persians—indeed, no one can claim to have heard
the Gospel already. Even the Christians in Rome are included in
the forces of the Gentiles, to whose service he has admittedly
been consecrated. He proposes to speak to them things old
and new; and what is old and familiar is still unknown, for it
can never sufficiently be brought to remembrance (xv. 15).
Meanwhile, however, only the written word is available. He must
therefore use it as best he can to promote a common knocking at
the doors of the Kingdom and a united movement towards it.

THE THEME OF THE EPISTLE

i. 16, 17

**For I am not ashamed of the gospel: for it is the power
of God unto salvation to every one that believeth; to
the Jew first, and also to the Greek.** For therein is
revealed the righteousness of God from faithfulness **unto
faith: as it is written, But the righteous shall live from**
my faithfulness.

I am not ashamed. The Gospel neither requires men to engage
in the conflict of religions or the conflict of philosophies, nor
does it compel them to hold themselves aloof from these controversies. In announcing the limitation of the known world by
another that is unknown, the Gospel does not enter into competition with the many attempts to disclose within the known
world some more or less unknown and higher form of existence
and to make it accessible to men. The Gospel is not a truth
among other truths. Rather, it sets a question-mark against
all truths. The Gospel is not the door but the hinge. The man
who apprehends its meaning is removed from all strife, because
he is engaged in a strife with the whole, even with existence
itself. Anxiety concerning the victory of the Gospel—that is,
Christian Apologetics—is meaningless, because the Gospel is
the victory by which the world is overcome. By the Gospel
the whole concrete world is dissolved and established. It does
not require representatives with a sense of responsibility, for
it is as responsible for those who proclaim it as it is for those
to whom it is proclaimed. It is the advocate of both. Nor is it
necessary for the Gospel that Paul should take his stand in the
midst of the spiritual cosmopolitanism of Rome; though he can,
of course, enter the city without shame, and will enter it as a
man who has been consoled by the Gospel. God does not need
us. Indeed, if He were not God, He would be ashamed of us.
We, at any rate, cannot be ashamed of Him.

The Gospel of the Resurrection is the—**power of God,** His
virtus (Vulgate), the disclosing and apprehending of His meaning, His effective pre-eminence over all gods. The Gospel of the
Resurrection is the action, the supreme miracle, by which God,
the unknown God dwelling in light unapproachable, the Holy
One, Creator, and Redeemer, makes Himself known: *What therefore ye worship in ignorance, this set I forth unto you* (Acts xvii. 23).
No divinity remaining on this side the line of resurrection; no
divinity which dwells in temples made with hands or which is

served by the hand of man ; no divinity which NEEDS ANYTHING, any human propaganda (Acts xvii. 24, 25),—can be God. God is the unknown God, and, precisely because He is unknown, He bestows life and breath and all things. Therefore the power of God can be detected neither in the world of nature nor in the souls of men. It must not be confounded with any high, exalted force, known or knowable. The power of God is not the most exalted of observable forces, nor is it either their sum or their fount. Being completely different, it is the KRISIS of all power, that by which all power is measured, and by which it is pronounced to be both something and—nothing, nothing and—something. It is that which sets all these powers in motion and fashions their eternal rest. It is the Primal Origin by which they all are dissolved, the consummation by which they all are established. The power of God stands neither at the side of nor above—supernatural!—these limited and limiting powers. It is pure and pre-eminent and—beyond them all. It can neither be substituted for them nor ranged with them, and, save with the greatest caution, it cannot even be compared with them. The assumption that Jesus is the Christ (i. 4) is, in the strictest sense of the word, an assumption, void of any content that can be comprehended by us. The appointment of Jesus to be the Christ takes place in the Spirit and must be apprehended in the Spirit. It is self-sufficient, unlimited, and in itself true. And moreover, it is what is altogether new, the decisive factor and turning-point in man's consideration of God. This it is which is communicated between Paul and his hearers. To the proclamation and receiving of this Gospel the whole activity of the Christian community—its teaching, ethics, and worship—is strictly related. But the activity of the community is related to the Gospel only in so far as it is no more than a crater formed by the explosion of a shell and seeks to be no more than a void in which the Gospel reveals itself. The people of Christ, His community, know that no sacred word or work or thing exists in its own right: they know only those words and works and things which by their negation are sign-posts to the Holy One. If anything Christian(!) be unrelated to the Gospel, it is a human by-product, a dangerous religious survival, a regrettable misunderstanding. For in this case content would be substituted for a void, convex for concave, positive for negative, and the characteristic marks of Christianity would be possession and self-sufficiency rather than deprivation and hope. If this be persisted in, there emerges, instead of the community of Christ, Christendom, an ineffective peace-pact or compromise with that existence which, moving with its own momentum, lies on this side resurrection. Christianity would then have lost all relation to the power of God. Now, whenever this occurs, the Gospel, so far from being removed from all rivalry, stands hard pressed in the midst of other religions and philosophies of this world. Hard pressed, because, if men must have their religious needs satisfied, if they must surround themselves with comfortable illusions about their knowledge of God and particularly about their union with Him,—well, the world penetrates far deeper into such matters than does a Christianity which misunderstands itself, and of such a 'gospel' we have good cause to be ashamed. Paul, however, is speaking of the power of the UNKNOWN God, of—*Things which eye saw not and ear heard not, and which entered not into the heart of man.* Of such a Gospel he has no cause to be ashamed.

The power of God is power—**unto salvation**. In this world men find themselves to be imprisoned. In fact the more profoundly we become aware of the limited character of the possibilities which are open to us here and now, the more clear it is that we are farther from God, that our desertion of Him is more complete (i. 18, v. 12), and the consequences of that desertion more vast (i. 24, v. 12), than we had ever dreamed. Men are their own masters. Their union with God is shattered so completely that they cannot even conceive of its restoration. Their sin is their guilt; their death is their destiny; their world is formless and tumultuous chaos, a chaos of the forces of nature and of the human soul; their life is illusion. This is the situation in which we find ourselves. The question 'Is there then a God?' is therefore entirely relevant and indeed inevitable! But the answer to this question, that is to say, our desire to comprehend the world in its relation to God, must proceed either from the criminal arrogance of religion or from that final apprehension of truth which lies beyond birth and death—the perception, in other words, which proceeds from God outwards. When the problem is formulated thus, it is evident that, just as genuine coins are open to suspicion so long as false coins are in circulation, so the perception which proceeds outwards from God cannot have free course until the arrogance of religion be done away. Now, it is the Gospel that opens up the possibility of this final perception, and, if this possibility is to be realized, all penultimate perceptions must be withdrawn from circulation. The Gospel speaks of God as He is: it is concerned with Him Himself and with Him only. It speaks of the Creator who shall be our Redeemer and of the Redeemer who is our Creator. It is pregnant

with our complete conversion; for it announces the transformation of our creatureliness into freedom. It proclaims the forgiveness of our sins, the victory of life over death, in fact, the
restoration of everything that has been lost. It is the signal,
the fire-alarm of a coming, new world. But what does all this
mean? Bound to the world as it is, we cannot here and now
apprehend. We can only receive the Gospel, for it is the recollection of God which is created by the Gospel that comprehends
its meaning. The world remains the world and men remain
men even whilst the Gospel is being received. The whole
burden of sin and the whole curse of death still press heavily
upon us. We must be under no illusion: the reality of our present
existence continues as it is! The Resurrection, which is the
place of exit, also bars us in, for it is both barrier and exit.
Nevertheless, the 'No' which we encounter is the 'No'—of God.
And therefore our veritable deprivation is our veritable comfort
in distress. The barrier marks the frontier of a new country,
and what dissolves the whole wisdom of the world also establishes it. Precisely because the 'No' of God is all-embracing,
it is also His 'Yes'. We have therefore, in the power of God,
a look-out, a door, a hope; and even in this world we have the
possibility of following the narrow path and of taking each
simple little step with a 'despair which has its own consolation'
(Luther). The prisoner becomes a watchman. Bound to his
post as firmly as a prisoner in his cell, he watches for the dawning
of the day: *I will stand upon my watch, and set me upon the tower,
and will look forth to see what he will speak with me, and what
he will answer concerning my complaint. And the Lord answered
me, and said, Write the vision, and make it plain upon tables,
that he may run that readeth it. For the vision is yet for the
appointed time, and it hasteth toward the end, and shall not lie:
though it tarry, wait for it; because it will surely come, it will not
delay* (Hab. ii. 1–3).

The Gospel requires—*faith*. Only for those who believe is it
the *power of God unto salvation*. It can therefore be neither
directly communicated nor directly apprehended. Christ hath
been appointed to be the Son of God—*according to the Spirit* (i. 4).
'Now, Spirit is the denial of direct immediacy. If Christ be very
God, He must be unknown, for to be known directly is the
characteristic mark of an idol' (Kierkegaard). So new, so unheard of, so unexpected in this world is the power of God unto
salvation, that it can appear among us, be received and understood by us, only as contradiction. The Gospel does not expound
or recommend itself. It does not negotiate or plead, threaten,

or make promises. It withdraws itself always when it is not
listened to for its own sake. 'Faith directs itself towards the
things that are invisible. Indeed, only when that which is
believed on is hidden, can it provide an opportunity for faith.
And moreover, those things are most deeply hidden which most
clearly contradict the obvious experience of the senses. Therefore, when God makes alive, He kills; when He justifies, He
imposes guilt; when He leads us to heaven, He thrusts us down
into hell' (Luther). The Gospel of salvation can only be believed
in; it is a matter for faith only. It demands choice. This is its
seriousness. To him that is not sufficiently mature to accept a
contradiction and to rest in it, it becomes a scandal—to him
that is unable to escape the necessity of contradiction, it becomes
a matter for faith. Faith is awe in the presence of the divine
incognito; it is the love of God that is aware of the qualitative
distinction between God and man and God and the world; it
is the affirmation of resurrection as the turning-point of the
world; and therefore it is the affirmation of the divine 'No' in
Christ, of the shattering halt in the presence of God. He who
knows the world to be bounded by a truth that contradicts it;
he who knows himself to be bounded by a will that contradicts
him; he who, knowing too well that he must be satisfied to live
with this contradiction and not attempt to escape from it, finds
it hard to kick against the pricks (Overbeck); he who finally
makes open confession of the contradiction and determines to
base his life upon it—he it is that believes. The believer is the
man who puts his trust in God, in God Himself, and in God
alone; that is to say, the man who, perceiving the faithfulness
of God in the very fact that He has set us within the realm of
that which contradicts the course of this world, meets the
faithfulness of God with a corresponding fidelity, and with
God says 'Nevertheless' and 'In spite of this'. The believer
discovers in the Gospel the power of God unto salvation, the
rays which mark the coming of eternal blessedness, and the
courage to stand and watch. This discovery is, however, a free
choice between scandal and faith, a choice presented to him
always and everywhere and at every moment. Depth of feeling,
strength of conviction, advance in perception and in moral
behaviour, are no more than things which accompany the birth
of faith. Being of this world, they are in themselves no more
than unimportant signs of the occurrence of faith. And moreover, as signs of the occurrence of faith they are not positive
factors, but negations of other positive factors, stages in the
work of clearance by which room is made in this world for that

which is beyond it. Faith, therefore, is never identical with 'piety', however pure and however delicate. In so far as 'piety' is a sign of the occurrence of faith, it is so as the dissolution of all other concrete things and supremely as the dissolution of itself. Faith lives of its own, because it lives of God. This is the Centrum Paulinum (Bengel).

There is no man who ought not to believe or who cannot believe. Neither **the Jew** nor **the Greek** is disenfranchised from the Gospel. By setting a question-mark against the whole course of this world and its inevitability, the Gospel directly concerns every man. As surely as no one is removed from the universal questionableness of human life, so surely is no one excluded from the divine contradiction that is in Christ, by which this questionableness seeks to make itself known to men. The Jew, the religious and ecclesiastical man, is, it is true, FIRST summoned to make the choice; this is because he stands quite normally on the frontier of this world and at the point where the line of intersection by the new dimensional plane (i. 4) must be veritably seen (ii. 17–20; iii. 1, 2; ix. 4, 5; x. 14, 15). But the advantage of the Jew provides him with no precedence. The problem 'Religion or Irreligion'—not to speak of the problem 'Church or World'—is no longer a fundamental problem. The possibility of hearing the Gospel is as universal as is the responsibility to hear it, and as is the promise vouchsafed to them who do hear it.

In the Gospel is revealed the great, universal secret of the **righteousness of God** which presses upon every man of every rank. In Christ the consistency of God with Himself—so grievously questioned throughout the whole world, among both Jews and Greeks—is brought to light and honoured. What men on this side resurrection name 'God' is most characteristically not God. Their 'God' does not redeem his creation, but allows free course to the unrighteousness of men; does not declare himself to be God, but is the complete affirmation of the course of the world and of men as it is. This is intolerable, for, in spite of the highest honours we offer him for his adornment, he is, in fact, 'No-God'. The cry of revolt against such a god is nearer the truth than is the sophistry with which men attempt to justify him. Only because they have nothing better, only because they lack the courage of despair, do the generality of men on this side resurrection avoid falling into blatant atheism. But in Christ God speaks as He is, and punishes the 'No-God' of all these falsehoods. He affirms Himself by denying us as we are and the world as it is. In Christ God offers Himself to be known as God beyond our trespass, beyond time and things and men; to be known as the Redeemer of the prisoners, and consequently, as the meaning of all that is—in fact, as the Creator. He acknowledges Himself to be our God by creating and maintaining the distance by which we are separated from Him; He displays His mercy by inaugurating His KRISIS and bringing us under judgement. He guarantees our salvation by willing to be God and to be known as God—in Christ; He justifies us by justifying Himself.

From faithfulness the righteousness of God reveals itself, that is to say, from His faithfulness to us. The very God has not forgotten men; the Creator has not abandoned the creation. Though the secret has been *kept in silence through times eternal* and shall be kept in silence (xvi. 25); though men shall continue to prefer their 'No-God' to the divine paradox; though the manifestation of what cannot be made known be the impossibility before which only the thoughtless are not terrified; yet, the faithfulness of God to men still abides; there still abides too that profound agreement between the will of God and that which men, longing to be freed from themselves, also secretly desire; there abides the divine answer which is given to us when the final human question awakes in us.—*We look for new heavens and a new earth, wherein dwelleth righteousness.* And because we have been appointed to this awaiting, we perceive the faithfulness of God.

Unto faith is revealed that which God reveals from His faithfulness. To those who have abandoned direct communication, the communication is made. To those willing to venture with God, He speaks. Those who take upon them the divine 'No' shall themselves be borne by the greater divine 'Yes'. Those who labour and are heavy laden shall be refreshed. Those who do not shun the contradiction have been hidden in God. Those who honestly allow themselves to be set to wait know thereby that they ought, must, and can, await the faithfulness of God. Those who stand in awe in the presence of God and keep themselves from revolt live with God.

In them is fulfilled the prophecy—**The righteous shall live from faithfulness!** (Hab. ii. 4). The righteous man is the prisoner become watchman. He is the guard at the threshold of divine reality. There is no other righteousness save that of the man who sets himself under judgement, of the man who is terrified and hopes. He shall live. He has the expectation of true life, for, recognizing that this life is naught, he is never without the reflection of the true life in this life, never without the prospect of incorruption in that which is passing to corruption.

The GREAT impossibility has announced to him the end and
goal of every trivial impossibility. He shall live of the faithfulness of God. Whether we say *of the faithfulness of God* or 'of
the faith of men', both are the same. The form in which the
prophet's words have been handed down already points in both
directions. It is the faithfulness of God which we encounter
so unescapably in the prophet's 'No': God the Holy One, the
altogether Other. It is the faith of men which we meet in the awe
of those who affirm the 'No' and are ready to accept the void
and to move and tarry in negation. Where the faithfulness of
God encounters the fidelity of men, there is manifested His
righteousness. There shall the righteous man live.

This is the theme of the Epistle to the Romans.

THE NIGHT

ITS CAUSE

I. 18–21

**v. 18. For the wrath of God is revealed from heaven
against all ungodliness and unrighteousness of men, who
hold the truth** imprisoned in the chains of **their unrighteousness.**

In the name of God! We know not what we should say to
this. The believer knows our ignorance. With Job, he loves
the God who in His unsearchable eminence is only to be feared:
with Luther, he loves the deus absconditus. To him is manifested the righteousness of God. He shall be saved, and he
alone. 'Only the prisoner shall be free, only the poor shall
be rich, only the weak strong, only the humble exalted, only the
empty filled, only nothing shall be something' (Luther). But
against the ungodliness and unrighteousness of men there is
revealed the wrath of God.

The wrath of God is the judgement under which we stand in
so far as we do not love the Judge; it is the 'No' which meets us
when we do not affirm it; it is the protest pronounced always
and everywhere against the course of the world in so far as we
do not accept the protest as our own; it is the questionableness
of life in so far as we do not apprehend it; it is our boundedness and corruptibility in so far as we do not acknowledge their
necessity. The judgement under which we stand is a fact, quite
apart from our attitude to it. Indeed, it is the fact most
characteristic of our life. Whether it enters within the light of
salvation and of the coming world depends upon the answer we

give to the problem of faith. But it is a fact, even should we choose the scandal rather than faith (i. 16). That time is nothing when measured by the standard of eternity, that all things are semblance when measured by their origin and by their end, that we are sinners, and that we must die—all these things ARE, even though the barrier be not for us the place of exit. Life moves on its course in its vast uncertainty and we move with it, even though we do not see the great question-mark that is set against us. Men are lost, even though they know nothing of salvation. Then the barrier remains a barrier and does not become a place of exit. The prisoner remains a prisoner and does not become the watchman. Then is waiting not joyful but a bitter-sweet surrender to what is inevitable. Then is the contradiction not hope, but a sorrowful opposition. The fruitful paradox of our existence is then that which consumes it like a worm. And Negation is then—what is normally meant by the word. In the place of the Holy God there then appear Fate, Matter, the Universe, Chance, ANANKE. Indeed, a certain perception is betrayed when we begin to avoid giving the name 'God' to the 'No-God' of unbelief (i. 17). That which we, apart from faith in the resurrection, name 'God', is also a final consequence of the divine wrath. But the God who, contradicting His own name, affirms the course of this world, is God—God in His wrath, God who sorrows on our behalf, God who can only turn Himself from us and say only 'No'. And yet, for this very reason, no upright man can unreservedly name Him 'God'. For the wrath of God cannot be His last word, the true revelation of Him! 'Not-God' cannot seriously be named 'God'. Nevertheless, it is, in fact, always God against whom we are thrust. Even the unbeliever encounters God, but he does not penetrate through to the truth of God that is hidden from him, and so he is broken to pieces on God, as Pharaoh was (ix. 15–18). 'Everything that thwarts and damages the life that has been made by God, all the frailty and bondage of the creaturely life, including the sentence of death under which it lies, is a reaction of the power of God' (Zündel). Yes, but we must add that, if we do not make the apprehension of this divine reaction our own, we must perish at its hands. The whole world is the footprint of God; yes, but, in so far as we choose scandal rather than faith, the footprint in the vast riddle of the world is the footprint of His wrath. The wrath of God is to unbelief the discovery of His righteousness, for God is not mocked. The wrath of God is the righteousness of God—apart from and without Christ.

But what does 'apart from and without Christ' mean? **The wrath of God is revealed against all ungodliness and unrighteousness of men.** These are the characteristic features of our relation to God, as it takes shape on this side resurrection. Our relation to God is *ungodly*. We suppose that we know what we are saying when we say 'God'. We assign to Him the highest place in our world: and in so doing we place Him fundamentally on one line with ourselves and with things. We assume that He *needs something*: and so we assume that we are able to arrange our relation to Him as we arrange our other relationships. We press ourselves into proximity with Him: and so, all unthinking, we make Him nigh unto ourselves. We allow ourselves an ordinary communication with Him, we permit ourselves to reckon with Him as though this were not extraordinary behaviour on our part. We dare to deck ourselves out as His companions, patrons, advisers, and commissioners. We confound time with eternity. This is the *ungodliness* of our relation to God. And our relation to God is *unrighteous*. Secretly we are ourselves the masters in this relationship. We are not concerned with God, but with our own requirements, to which God must adjust Himself. Our arrogance demands that, in addition to everything else, some super-world should also be known and accessible to us. Our conduct calls for some deeper sanction, some approbation and remuneration from another world. Our well-regulated, pleasurable life longs for some hours of devotion, some prolongation into infinity. And so, when we set God upon the throne of the world, we mean by God ourselves. In 'believing' on Him, we justify, enjoy, and adore ourselves. Our devotion consists in a solemn affirmation of ourselves and of the world and in a pious setting aside of the contradiction. Under the banners of humility and emotion we rise in rebellion against God. We confound time with eternity. That is our *unrighteousness.*—Such is our relation to God apart from and without Christ, on this side resurrection, and before we are called to order. God Himself is not acknowledged as God and what is called 'God' is in fact Man. By living to ourselves, we serve the 'No-God'.

Who hold the truth imprisoned in unrighteousness. This second characteristic is in point of time the first. Men fall a prey first to themselves and then to the 'No-God'. First is heard the promise—*ye shall be as God!*—and then men lose the sense for eternity. First mankind is exalted, and then men obscure the distance between God and man. The nodal point in the relation between God and man apart from and without

Christ is the unrighteousness of slaves. Thinking of ourselves
what can be thought only of God, we are unable to think of
Him more highly than we think of ourselves. Being to ourselves
what God ought to be to us, He is no more to us than we are
to ourselves. This secret identification of ourselves with God
carries with it our isolation from Him. The little god must,
quite appropriately, dispossess the great God. Men have *imprisoned* and encased the *truth*—the righteousness of God; they
have trimmed it to their own measure, and thereby robbed it
both of its earnestness and of its significance. They have made
it ordinary, harmless, and useless; and thereby transformed it
into untruth. This has all been brought to light by their ungodliness, and this ungodliness will not fail to thrust them into
ever new forms of unrighteousness. If mankind be itself God,
the appearance of the idol is then inevitable. And whenever
the idol is honoured, it is inevitable that men, feeling themselves
to be the true God, should also feel that they have themselves
fashioned the idol. This is the rebellion which makes it impossible for us to see the new dimensional plane which is the
boundary of our world and the meaning of our salvation.
Against such rebellion there can be revealed only the wrath
of God.

**vv. 19–21. Because that which may be known of God is
manifest to them; for God manifested it unto them. For
the invisible things of him since the creation of the world
are clearly seen, being perceived through the things that
are made, even his everlasting power and divinity; so
that they are without excuse: because that, in spite of
knowing God, they glorified him not as God, neither gave
thanks; but became vain in their reasonings, and their
senseless heart was darkened.**

That which may be known of God is manifest unto them. The
truth concerning the limiting and dissolving of men by the unknown God, which breaks forth in the resurrection, is a known
truth: this is the tragic factor in the story of the passion of
the truth. When our limitation is apprehended, and when
He is perceived who, in bounding us, is also the dissolution
of our limitation, the most primitive as well as the most
highly developed forms of human self-consciousness become
repeatedly involved in a 'despairing humiliation', in the 'irony
of intelligence' (H. Cohen). We know that God is He whom
we do not know, and that our ignorance is precisely the
problem and the source of our knowledge. We know that God

is the Personality which we are not, and that this lack of
Personality is precisely what dissolves and establishes our
personality. The recognition of the absolute heteronomy under
which we stand is itself an autonomous recognition; and this
is precisely *that which may be known of God*. When we rebel,
we are in rebellion not against what is foreign to us but against
that which is most intimately ours, not against what is removed
from us but against that which lies at our hands. Our memory
of God accompanies us always as problem and as warning. He
is the hidden abyss; but He is also the hidden home at the
beginning and end of all our journeyings. Disloyalty to Him
is disloyalty to ourselves.

For the invisible things of God are clearly seen. This we have
forgotten, and we must allow it to be brought once more to our
minds. Our lack of humility, our lack of recollection, our lack
of fear in the presence of God, are not in our present condition
inevitable, however natural they may seem to us. Plato in his
wisdom recognized long ago that behind the visible there lies the
invisible universe which is the Origin of all concrete things. And
moreover, the solid good sense of the men of the world had long
ago perceived that the fear of the Lord is the beginning of wisdom.
The clear, honest eyes of the poet in the book of Job and of the
Preacher Solomon had long ago rediscovered, mirrored in the
world of appearance, the archetypal, unobservable, undiscoverable Majesty of God. The speech of God can always be heard
out of the whirlwind. Always it requires of us that we should
perceive how unwisely we speak of that which is too high for
us, too far beyond our understanding, when, in praising God
or in complaining of Him, we plead with Him as with One who is
like unto us. The insecurity of our whole existence, the vanity
and utter questionableness of all that is and of what we are,
lie as in a text-book open before us. What are all those enigmatic creatures of God—a zoological garden, for example—but
so many problems to which we have no answer? But God only,
God Himself, He is the Answer. And so the boundary which bars
us in and which, nevertheless, points beyond itself, can **since the
creation of the world** be clearly seen **through the things that are
made** by God. By calm, veritable, unprejudiced religious contemplation the divine 'No' can be established and apprehended. If
we do not ourselves hinder it, nothing can prevent our being
translated into a most wholesome KRISIS by that which *may be
known of God*. And indeed, we stand already in this KRISIS if we
would but *see clearly*. And what is clearly seen to be indisputable
reality is the invisibility of God, which is precisely and in strict

agreement with the gospel of the resurrection—**His everlasting power and divinity.** And what does this mean but that we can know nothing of God, that we are not God, that the Lord is to be feared? Herein lies His pre-eminence over all gods; and here is that which marks Him out as God, as Creator, and as Redeemer (i. 16). And so through all history there runs the line of inter-section between time and eternity, between the present and the future world (i. 4). Long ago it was proclaimed (i. 2); always it was visible. The wrath of God needed not to be revealed to those who stood already under His judgement, for they could have known and loved the Judge. **So that,** when they fail to see and fail to hear, **they are without excuse.** Having eyes to see and ears to hear they are doing what they are doing. Inexcusable is their godlessness, for the *clearly seen* works of God speak of His *everlasting power* and they have already risen up in protest against the service of the 'No-God', by which God is ranged in the midst of the natural and 'spiritual' and other forces of this world. Inexcusable also is their unrighteousness, for the *clearly seen* facts bear witness to the *everlasting divinity* of God, and have already risen up in protest against the arrogance of religion, by which men, speaking of God from the welter of their experiences, mean in fact themselves. We have, therefore, encased the truth of God and evoked His wrath. But this was not because no alternative was open to us. God is not far from each one of us: *for in him we live, and move, and have our being* (Acts xvii. 27, 28). The situation might, therefore, have been very different.

But—**in spite of knowing God.** The knowledge of God attain-able through a simple observation of the incomprehensibility, the imperfection, the triviality of human life, was not taken advantage of. The invisibility of God seems to us less tolerable than the questionable visibility of what we like to call 'God'. We make of the eternal and ultimate presupposition of the Creator a 'thing in itself' above and in the midst of other things, of that which is living and abstracted from all concreteness a concrete thing—no doubt the highest—in the midst of other concrete things, of the Spirit a spirit, of what is inaccessible and therefore so nigh at hand an endlessly uncertain object of our experiences. Rather than see in His Light—eternal and which no man can approach unto—the Light, we allow Him to become a light—no doubt the most brilliant and, indeed, immaterial and supernatural—at which we kindle our own lights and then, quite consistently, seek to find in concrete things their own light. If, then, God is to us no longer the

Unknown, what has become of the **glory** we owe Him? If God is to us no longer what we are not, what has become of the **thanks** which are due to Him? The revolt of Prometheus is wholly justified when once Zeus—the 'No-God'—has been exalted to the throne of God.

And so the light has become in us darkness, and the wrath of God is inevitable—**They became vain in their reasonings, and their senseless heart was darkened.** The barrier is now indeed a barrier, and the 'No' of God is now indeed negation. Bereft of understanding and left to themselves, men are at the mercy of the dominion of the meaningless powers of the world; for our life in this world has meaning only in its relation to the true God. But this relation can be re-established only through the—*clearly seen*—memory of eternity breaking in upon our minds and hearts. There is no other relation to God save that which appears upon the road along which Job travelled. If this 'breaking in' does not occur, our thought remains merely empty, formal, critical and unproductive, incapable of mastering the rich world of appearance and of apprehending each particular thing in the context of the whole. Unbroken thought thereby divests itself of any true relation to the concrete world, and, contrariwise, the unbroken heart, that is to say, that sensitiveness to things which is guarded by no final insight, divests itself of the control of thought. Dark, blind, uncritical, capricious, mankind becomes a thing in itself. Heartless, perceiving without observing and therefore empty, is our thought: thoughtless, observing without perceiving and therefore blind, is our heart. Fugitive is the soul in this world and soulless is the world, when men do not find themselves within the sphere of the knowledge of the unknown God, when they avoid the true God in whom they and the world must lose themselves in order that both may find themselves again.

This is the Cause of the Night in which we are wandering: this also is the Cause of the Wrath of God which has been manifested over our heads.

ITS OPERATION

I. 22-32

v. 22. Professing themselves to be wise, they became fools.

The picture of a world without paradox and without eternity, of knowing without the background of not-knowing, of a religion without the unknown God, of a view of life without the memory of the 'No' by which we are encountered, has much to be said in its favour. It evokes confidence, for it is simple and straight-forward and uncramped; it provides considerable security and has few ragged edges; it corresponds, generally speaking, with what is required by the practical experiences of life; its standards and general principles are conveniently vague and flexible; and it possesses, moreover, a liberal prospect of vast future possibilities. Once the possibility that things can be *clearly seen* (i. 20) is abandoned, men are able against this back-ground to profess that they are wise. The Night, too, has its wisdom. But, nevertheless, the vanity of the mind and the darkness of the heart still remain facts to be reckoned with. The brilliance of this unbroken wisdom cannot be maintained in the actual course of events, for they have passed inevitably under the wrath of God. That God is not known as God is due, not merely to some error of thought or to some gap in experience, but to a fundamentally wrong attitude to life. Vanity of mind and blindness of heart inevitably bring into being corrupt conduct. The more the unbroken man marches along his road secure of himself, the more surely does he make a fool of him-self, the more certainly do that morality and that manner of life which are built up upon a forgetting of the abyss, upon a forgetting of men's true home, turn out to be a lie. It is indeed not difficult to show that this is so.

vv. 23, 24. And changed the glory of the incorruptible God for an image made like to corruptible man, and to birds, and fourfooted beasts, and creeping things. Where-fore God gave them up in the lusts of their hearts unto uncleanness, that their bodies should be dishonoured among themselves.

They changed the glory of the incorruptible—for an image of the corruptible. That is to say, the understanding of what is characteristic of God was lost. They had lost their knowledge of the crevasse, the polar zone, the desert barrier, which must be crossed if men are really to advance from corruption to incor-ruption. The distance between God and man had no longer its essential, sharp, acid, and disintegrating ultimate significance. The difference between the incorruption, the pre-eminence and originality of God, and the corruption, the boundedness and relativity of men had been confused. Once the eye, which can perceive this distinction, has been blinded, there arises in the midst, between here and there, between us and the 'Wholly Other', a mist or concoction of religion in which, by a whole

E

series of skilful assimilations and mixings more or less strongly
flavoured with sexuality, sometimes the behaviour of men or
of animals is exalted to be an experience of God, sometimes the
Being and Existence of God is 'enjoyed' as a human or animal
experience. In all this mist the prime factor is provided by the
illusion that it is possible for men to hold communication with
God or, at least, to enter into a covenant relationship with Him
without miracle—vertical from above, without the dissolution
of all concrete things, and apart from THE truth which lies
beyond birth and death. But, on whatever level it occurs, if
the experience of religion is more than a void, or claims to
contain or to possess or to 'enjoy' God, it is a shameless and
abortive anticipation of that which can proceed from the unknown God alone. In all this busy concern with concrete things
there is always a revolt against God. For in it we assist at the
birth of the 'No-God', at the making of idols. Enveloped in
mist, we forget not merely that all that passes to corruption is
a parable, but also that it is ONLY a parable. The glory of the
incorruptible God has been confused with the image (Ps. cvi.
20) of corruptible things. Some one of the relationships of
men to the objects of their fear or of their desire, to some means
of their subsistence, to some product of their own thought or
action, to some impressive occurrence in nature or in history,
is taken to be in itself significant and of supreme importance,
as though even this selected relationship were not broken by
the witness it bears to the unknown Creator whose glory cannot
be confused with the known glory of an image, however pure
and delicate. From such supposed direct communion with God
—genuine only when it is not genuine, when it is not romanti-
cized into an 'experience', when it is at once dissolved and
claims to be merely an open space, a sign-post, an occasion, and
an opportunity—there emerge precisely all those intermediary,
collateral, lawless divinities and powers and authorities and
principalities (viii. 38) that obscure and discolour the light of the
true God. In the realm of romantic direct communion—in India,
for example—these divinities are thrown up in the most extravagant numbers. Wherever the qualitative distinction between
men and the final Omega is overlooked or misunderstood, that
fetishism is bound to appear in which God is experienced in
birds and fourfooted things, and finally, or rather primarily, in
the **likeness of corruptible man**—Personality, the Child, the
Woman—and in the half-spiritual, half-material creations,
exhibitions, and representations of His creative ability—Family,
Nation, State, Church, Fatherland. And so the 'No-God' is

set up, idols are erected, and God, who dwells beyond all this and that, is 'given up'.

Wherefore God gave them up. The confusion avenges itself and becomes its own punishment. The forgetting of the true God is already itself the breaking loose of His wrath against those who forget Him (i. 18). The enterprise of setting up the 'No-God' is avenged by its success. Deified nature and deified spirits of men are, in truth, very gods; like Jupiter and Mars, Isis and Osiris, Cybele and Attis, they come to be the very breath of our life. Our conduct becomes governed precisely by what we desire. By a strict inevitability we reach the goal we have set before us. The images and likenesses, whose meaning we have failed to perceive, become themselves purpose and content and end. And now men have really become slaves and puppets of things, of 'Nature' and of 'Civilization', whose dissolution and establishing by God they have overlooked. And now there is no higher power to protect them from what they have set on high. And, moreover, the uncleanness of their relation to God submerges their lives also in uncleanness. When God has been deprived of His glory, men are also deprived of theirs. Desecrated within in their souls, they are desecrated also without in their bodies, for men are one. The concreteness of the creatureliness of their lives becomes now dishonour; and lust—sexuality both in the narrower and in the wider sense of the word—becomes, as the primary motive-power of their whole desire and striving, altogether questionable and open to suspicion. The whole ignominy of the course of the world they must now bear and bemoan and curse as ignominy; and further, in their separation from God they must continue to give it ever new birth. They have wished to experience the known god of this world: well! they have experienced him.

vv. 25–7. They exchanged the truth of God for a lie, and worshipped and served the creature rather than the Creator, who is blessed for ever. Amen. For this cause God gave them up unto vile passions: for their women changed the natural relation of the sexes **into that which is against nature: and likewise also the men, leaving the natural use of the woman, burned in their lust one toward another, men with men working unseemliness, and receiving in** their own body **that recompense of their error which was due.**

They exchanged the truth for a lie. Complete rebellion from God soon takes to itself more pronounced forms. It would not

be unexpected were direct experience of God to have occasioned
some occasional and rather humorous changes, some superficial
errors, some dissolution of the Truth of God into a number of
worldly-wise maxims. But though this is, no doubt, possible,
it is not long before the Truth is quite seriously exchanged for
a lie. The tiny mist between God and man, by which the far
distance is obscured, soon becomes a veritable sea of clouds.
Some half-conscious resentment at the unknown God very soon
becomes fully conscious. The dazzled eye is soon damaged.
Principalities and powers, formerly but seldom exalted to the
throne, are soon established there, encircled with a halo of
everlasting power and divinity (i. 20). The Creator, the eternal
Archetype, meanwhile grows ever more and more 'abstract',
'theoretical', insignificant, and unloved. The completely concrete 'No-God' has won his victory, even though there may,
perhaps, remain some bleak survival of the Unknown behind
what is thought to be genuinely significant and magnificent,
some occasional reference to a final secret in the midst of so much
busy service of him whom we name 'God'. The only reality,
the unknown, living God, appears nebulous, problematical,
and unreal, whereas the world, separated from Him, and men,
unbroken by any memory of Him, appear in a nimbus of security,
necessity, and reality. The world is **worshipped and served—**
if it be necessary, quite apart from its Creator. In their general
view of the world scientists and historians are in far closer
agreement with philosophers and theologians than is normally
recognized. It is not merely that the world exists side by side
with God: it has taken His place, and has itself become God,
and demands 'the same devotion which the old-fashioned
believer offered to His God' (Dr. F. Strauss). Contradictions
within the deified world—Nature and Civilization, Materialism
and Idealism, Capitalism and Socialism, Secularism and Ecclesiasticism, Imperialism and Democracy—are not so serious as
they give themselves out to be. Such contradictions are contradictions within the world, and there is for them no paradox, no
negation, no eternity.

For this cause God gave them up. Unbroken naturalness is
not pure. Nor are matters improved when 'naturalness' is
penetrated by piety. In 'naturalness' there is always secreted
that which is non-natural, and, indeed, that which actually
contradicts nature. This contradictory factor awaits the hour
when it will break forth. When, by allowing nature to
run its course freely and uncontradicted, God and the world
have become confused with one another, there comes into

prominence a further confusion: what cannot be avoided or escaped from becomes confused with some necessity of nature, and this is in very truth a demonic caricature of the necessity of God. These two confusions stand altogether on one line, they belong together and cohere together. What is at first merely open to suspicion moves inexorably on to what is positively absurd. Everything then becomes Libido: life becomes totally erotic. When the frontier between God and man, the last inexorable barrier and obstacle, is not closed, the barrier between what is normal and what is perverse is opened.

vv. 28–31. A final and even sharper pointing of the whole situation is not only conceivable but actually takes place. In the perversity of this relation to God there still, however, remains a relic of clarity of sight, a last, warning recollection of the secret of God that withstands the arrogance of religion. A reflection of this secret lies even in the deified forces of the world, even in the deified universe itself. From time to time this bare relic of the Unknown reasserts itself in the presentiment of awe. But even this can cease. The damaged eye may become blind. Defective knowledge can become ignorance of God; it may become AGNOSIA (1 Cor. xv. 34). **Even as they refused to have God in their knowledge.**—That is to say, they became no longer capable of serious awe and amazement. They become unable to reckon with anything except feelings and experiences and events. They think only in terms of more or less spiritual sophistry, without light from above or from behind.—**God gave them up to a reprobate mind, to do those things which are not fitting; being filled with all unrighteousness, wickedness, covetousness, maliciousness; full of envy, murder, strife, deceit, malignity; whisperers, backbiters, haters of God, insolent, haughty, boastful, inventors of evil things, disobedient to parents, without understanding, covenant-breakers, without natural affection, unmerciful.** Here is the final vacuity and disintegration. Chaos has found itself, and anything may happen. The atoms whirl, the struggle for existence rages. Even reason itself becomes irrational. Ideas of duty and of fellowship become wholly unstable. The world is full of personal caprice and social unrighteousness—this is not a picture merely of Rome under the Caesars! The true nature of our unbroken existence is here unrolled before us. Our ungodliness and unrighteousness stand under the wrath of God. His judgement now becomes judgement and nothing more;

and we experience the impossibility of men as the real and final impossibility of God.

v. 32. It ought not to be difficult for us to perceive this sequence, but—**Knowing the ordinance of God, that they which practise such things are worthy of death, not only do the same, but also consent with them that practise them.** This is the wisdom of the Night issuing in folly (i. 22): folly, because it holds firmly to a two-dimensional plane, a plane persistently contradicted by actual occurrence. The wisdom of the Night knows whither the unbroken road is leading. It understands quite clearly the meaning of its direction and of its goal. It knows the Cause; it sees the Operation; but it dare not give the command to halt. The road of those who forget their Creator is accompanied always by a strange complaint against the frailty of human existence, and by indictments against human sinfulness. But in spite of all this, with their eyes fixed upon the earth, they affirm the edifice which is erected on it, concentrate their desire upon it, approve it, hope for its continued existence, and, regardless of every protest, constitute themselves its guardians. But why is it so difficult to remember what has been forgotten, though it is quite clear that the operation of this forgetfulness and the end of our wandering in the Night is—Death?

The Second Chapter

THE RIGHTEOUSNESS OF MEN

THE JUDGE

II. 1–13

To whom, then, *is the wrath of God revealed* (i. 18)? And what is the situation which can be seen only in the light of His wrath? Who are these men who have adopted the known God of this world, the No-God, as their God? Who are the ungodly and the unrighteous whom God has given up? Can every single man, all humanity, be meant? Must it be assumed that we all stand before the barrier and that, unless we are aware of our position, we must remain barred up and our lives but vanity and darkness? Or may not some perhaps, even though they be few, be able to avoid this situation? May not the wrath of God be just one possibility, peculiar to a certain type of men and women and characteristic of certain periods of history? Are there in the army of light no heroes who have broken through and escaped from the darkness? Is there not marching side by side with ungodliness and unrighteousness a veritable righteousness of men? Can we not imagine, and does there not actually exist, a humble godliness by which men achieve a higher order of existence and become thereby no longer worthy of death (i. 32)? Is not their faith an obvious psychological and historical fact? Does not this very faith enable them to escape from the ungodliness of this world and free themselves from the bars behind which we all are confined? Have they—*But we*—not scaled a height that is inaccessible to the generality of men, whence, as men apart, they look virtuously down upon those beneath them, incapable, as yet, of the perception to which they have attained? Does not an island of the blest rise from the ocean of the unfortunate: an island of men able to hear the long-promised Gospel of God? If we are able to conceive the possibility of honouring the unknown God of Abraham, Isaac, and Jacob, does not this carry with it the possibility of escape from the burden of His wrath? Has none held himself upright at the bar of the divine judgement of the world as it is, and, after his removal from the darkness, sat down by the side of God as His assessor in judgement? Or must we take it that the circle is closed and that no one has eluded the inevitability of cause and effect, of downfall and apostasy, which is the mark of men as men and of the world as the world?

vv. 1, 2. Wherefore thou art without excuse, O man, whosoever thou art that judgest: for wherein thou judgest another, thou condemnest thyself; for thou that judgest dost practise the same things. But we know that the judgement of God is according to the standard of the **truth against them that practise such things.**

Without excuse. Those who do not know the unknown God (i. 18–21) have neither occasion nor possibility of lifting themselves up. So is it also with those who know Him; for they too are men; they too belong to the world of time. There is no human righteousness by which men can escape the wrath of God! There is no magnificent temporality of this world which can justify men before God. There is no arrangement of affairs or deportment of behaviour, no disposition of mind or depth of feeling, no intuition or understanding, which is, by its own virtue, pleasing to God. Men are men, and they belong to the world of men: *that which is born of the flesh is flesh.* Every concrete and tangible thing belongs within the order of time. Everything which emerges in men and which owes its form and expansion to them is always and everywhere, and as such, ungodly and unclean. The kingdom of men is, without exception, never the Kingdom of God; and since there are no men so fortunate as to be incumbents in the Kingdom of God, no man can exonerate or excuse himself.

Wherein thou judgest another, thou condemnest thyself. Whenever thou dost erect thyself upon a pedestal, thou doest wrong; whensoever thou sayest 'I' or 'we' or 'it is so', thou dost exchange the glory of the incorruptible for the image of the corruptible (i. 23); wherein thou dost undertake to give glory to the unknown God, as though it were a possible undertaking, thou dost imprison and encyst the truth, for thou dost assert godliness and humility to be thine, and thou art thereby marked as ungodly and unrighteous. The removal of thyself from the burden of the world by some pretended insight or vision does but press the burden of the world more heavily upon thee than upon any other. By striding ahead of others, even though it be for their assistance, as though the secret of God were known to thee, thou dost manifest thyself ignorant of His secret; for by thy removal from thy brethren thou dost render thyself incapable of assisting even the most helpless among them. By beholding folly as the folly of others, thine own folly cries out to heaven. Even negation of this world and perception of the paradox of life; even submission to the judgement of God and waiting upon Him; even 'brokenness'; even the behaviour of the 'Biblical Man'—

if these proceed from the adoption of a point of view, of a method, of a system, or of a particular kind of behaviour, by which men distinguish themselves from other men—are no more than the righteousness of men. And even faith, if it proceeds from anything but a void, is unbelief; for it is then once again the appearance of the slavery of unrighteousness seeking to suppress the dawning truth of God, the disturbance of all disturbings. Here again is that contempt and presumption which fails to perceive the distance between God and man, and which inevitably exalts and enthrones the no-God of this world. Here again is that assimilation of God and man, by which God is withdrawn from His isolation. Here again is that 'romance of the infinite' and its venerable shibboleth: *The temple of the Lord are these!* (Jer. vii. 4). Thy present action, then, is human rebellion; and it evokes the wrath of God.

For thou that judgest doest the same things. What is true of the generality of men is true also of the men of God. As men they do not differ from other men (i. 1). There is no fragment or epoch of history which can be pronounced divine. The whole history of the Church and of all religion takes place in this world. What is called the 'history of our salvation' is not an event in the midst of other events, but is nothing less than the KRISIS of all history. There are no saints in the midst of a company of sinners; for where men have claimed to be saints, they are thereby marked as not-saints. Their criticism and invective and indictment of the world inevitably place them—unless they be themselves its object—within the course of this world and betray that they too are of it. Their indictment springs not from their capacity to help but from their own distress; it is of this world; it is a talking about life, not life itself; its illumination is artificial; it marks no rising of the sun nor breaking of the dawn. This is as true of Paul, the prophet and apostle of the Kingdom of God, and of Jeremiah, as it is of Luther, Kierkegaard, and Blumhardt! It applies both to St. Francis, who far surpassed Jesus in 'love', childishness, and austerity, and to the distinctive sanctity of Tolstoy. Everything human swims with the stream either with vehement protest or with easy accommodation, even when it appears to hover above it or to engage in conflict with it. Christ is not one of the righteous. Since power belongs only to God, it is the tragic story of every man of God that he has to contend for the right of God by placing himself in the wrong. This must be so if the men of God are not to usurp the place of God.

We know that the judgement of God is according to the

standard of the truth. The man of God is aware of the true and tragic and paradoxical state of affairs. He knows what he is about when he adopts a point of view which is no point of view, and when he in nowise regards himself as excused by his vocation. The men of God know that belief is faith only when it is the product of no historical or spiritual achievement. They know that faith is the ineffable reality of God, that clarity of sight (i. 20) is no system, no discovery of research, but the eternal ground of perception. They know also that in itself faith can be no more justified than any other human achievement. They do not escape from the paradox by making it another fragment of the concrete world. They do not evacuate the divine negation by too nearly accommodating it to their own human negation. They do not blunt the austerity of judgement by supposing it to be a temporal station through which they have passed in their spiritual pilgrimage (ordo salutis) and which they have left behind. They do not make of the dawning righteousness of the Gospel of salvation a hole into which they can creep or a fortress in which they can resist the attacks of others. They know the judgement of God to be *according to the standard of truth*; and if men are measured by the standard of the truth of God, who can withstand it? Can stability be attained anywhere or at any time?

vv. 3-5. And reckonest thou this, O man, who judgest them that practise such things, and doest the same, that thou in particular **shalt escape the judgement of God? Or despisest thou the riches of his goodness and forbearance and longsuffering,** and dost thou not perceive **that the goodness of God leadeth thee to repentance? but** with **thy hardness and impenitent heart** thou **treasurest up for thyself wrath in the day of wrath and revelation of the righteous judgement of God.**

And reckonest thou that thou in particular shalt escape the judgement of God? The reckoning of the righteousness of men is false; it contains, moreover, a false entry. Thou hast credited to thine own account that which belongs to God. What God has given thee, thou hast accounted a human possibility and achievement. What has been bestowed upon thee in eternity, thou hast counted as possessing temporal validity. Thou dost overlook of what slight importance is the eminence upon which thou art standing. Thou failest to perceive that even now a question is being asked of thee to which thou canst give no answer. Thou dost not understand that the course of history does not in itself constitute the judgement upon history. In laying violent and foolish hands upon the visible and temporal things of this world, thou losest the things that are invisible and eternal. When thou boastest of faith as of some achievement of men, the divine operation in faith is ended, and it is degraded to a worthless and transitory thing of this world. The more thou dost attempt to escape from the judgement of God according to the standard of truth, the more completely is thy way barred.

Dost thou not perceive that the goodness of God leadeth thee to repentance? How does it, then, come about that there are any such stalwarts in the army of light? How is it that there exist any far-seeing and intelligent men—real men, living in the real world—who, like the Jews of the time of Jesus, have caught a glimpse of the Last Things, and to whom waiting upon God, upon God alone, is well known? In such men a miracle has occurred above, behind, and in them. They have encountered the grace of God; have met the incomprehensibility of God, as Job did—*out of the whirlwind*. They were terrified in their ungodliness and unrighteousness and were shaken out of their dreaming. It was as though the veil of the mist of religion was dispersed and the cloud of divine wrath was rent asunder; and they heard the indiscoverable, saw the negation of God! felt the barrier of the judgement, the paradox of existence, and, hopeful in their distress, divined the meaning of life. They came to themselves in fear and awe and trembling and in—'clarity of sight'. In the presence of God they were compelled to stand still. What, then, is all this? Is it mysticism, or intuition, or ecstasy, or a miraculous occurrence granted to peculiarly gifted men or to men who have been especially guided? Can it be described as an experience of certain pure souls, or as a discovery of the intelligence; as an achievement of will, or as a response to peculiarly intense prayer? No, assuredly not. There have been purer souls and wiser heads; there have been men of greater energy of life and of greater spiritual perception; but God has not spoken to them. There are mystics and ecstatics who have never *seen clearly*. The encounter of grace depends upon no human possession: for achievement—even awe and awakening—is of no value and has no independent validity in the Presence of God. When God speaks and is recognized, we are unable to speak of human existence or possessions or enjoyment. He who has been chosen by God cannot say that he has chosen God. When room is found for awe and humility in the presence of God, that is, when there arises the possibility of faith, this is intelligible only as impossibility,—**as the riches of his goodness.** Whereas I was blind, now I see; How have I deserved this?—simply as **for-bearance** of the wrath of God: How is it that I have been chosen out of the great multitude?—simply as the inexplicable **long-suffering** of God towards me. What can He expect of me, that He has granted this unprecedented possibility TO ME? Nothing can be put forward to account for and explain this emphatic 'TO' and 'ME'; absolutely nothing. It all hangs in the air: it is a pure, absolute, vertical miracle. Every phrase descriptive of human experience is here irrelevant; for we cannot claim even to exist. We are once again faced by the undimensional line of intersection. The dialectic of the miracle of God is expressed in the words: *The goodness of God leadeth thee to repentance.* What is demanded of men by God can be demanded only by God, can be only a new call to God, a new call to conversion, awe, humility, a new requirement to abandon every security and to resign every honour, to give glory to God, to the unknown God, as something always new, as something that has never been done before. Every claim to be a proprietor, which might be deduced from such surrender, is a misunderstanding of election, a misunderstanding of the call which has been given, a misunderstanding of God. Every positive claim to be an exception renders the man who has some perception of God like unto him who has no perception whatever: *Dost thou not perceive that the goodness of God leadeth thee to repentance?* Dost thou not know that there is no other possibility of correct perception?

If thou dost not perceive this—**with thy hardness and impenitent heart thou treasurest up for thyself wrath.** Misunderstanding such as this immediately condenses, solidifies, hardens, into a solid mass of misunderstanding. For the initial misunderstanding causes every human thought and word and action, however pure and delicate, to unite as elements in the composition of one hard and solid lump. There comes into being what is known as the 'religious' life, which is regarded as something peculiar, which is contrasted with the life of the generality of men, and which, because it is nothing more than romantic unbelief, has no protection against the enmity of those who despise it. There emerges from the *righteousness of God* of the Prophets the human righteousness of the Pharisees, which is as such ungodliness and unrighteousness. The righteousness of God, when misunderstood, remains hidden. Each concrete and tangible disposition of human affairs so that they may conform to the will of God marks the presence of the prophet turned pharisee: he who engages in dispositions of this sort stands under the authority of him who is No-God, and round him gather the threatening clouds of the wrath of God. He has falsified his accounts by failing to disclose how serious his position is. Though he piles up higher and higher his divine claims, his divine assurance, and his divine delights, he does but build a Tower of Babel. Behind the screen of his daily disposing waits the eternal day of wrath and of the just judgement of God. Standing upon his eminence, he HAS already BEEN cast down; the friend of God, he IS His declared and most bitter enemy; the righteous man, he HAS already BEEN judged. He must not be surprised if what he is be suddenly manifested and made known.

vv. 6–11. The standard by which men are measured is not of this world. It is eternal, as God is; it is itself God. God seeks continually that men should be open to Him and to Him only. By dissolving us, He establishes us; by killing us, He gives us life. We shall be redeemed, because we shall all be changed—at the sound of the last trump. The righteous man, so the passage continues—yes, precisely, the righteous man, the believer—stands upright before this God, **who will render to every man according to his works: to them that by patient** continuing, which is the mark of **well-doing, seek** the **glory and honour and incorruption** of God, with **eternal life: but unto them that** have the minds of slaves **and obey not the truth, but obey unrighteousness,** there waits **wrath and indignation, tribulation and anguish, upon every soul of man that worketh evil, of the Jew first, and also of the Greek; but glory and honour and peace to every man that worketh good, to the Jew first, and also to the Greek: for there is no respect of persons with God.**

Who will render to every man according to his works. Who is it that will thus *render?* He it is in whose presence men are deceitful and of no worth; He, whom men, abounding with ill-gotten riches, ought never to have forgotten; He, whose last word is that to HIM belongeth power and mercy (Ps. lxii. 9–12; LXX); He, before whom men are bound to acknowledge, 'I know Him not', in order that they may perceive that they are known by Him (Prov. xxiv. 12; LXX). He—God—it is who *renders* unto men according to their works and by the valuation which He puts upon them creates their value or their worthlessness; His is the decision between good and evil; in Him we discover our intelligence or our folly, our heaven or our hell. *Works—* our doing and our not-doing, our inner disposition and the outward ordering of our lives—are significant only within the inner and outer course of our temporal existence. Notable our *works*

may be; but we must not over-estimate them, we must not
raise them to the order of infinity. God alone is the merchant
who can pay in the currency of eternity. He alone can make a
valuation which is eternally valid.

The miracle therefore can take place whereby—**to them that
seek his glory and honour and incorruption** He renders **eternal
life.** That is to say, it is possible that to the awe and lowliness
with which men, within the limitations of human experience,
seek after God and after Him only, there corresponds a real
finding of Him. It can be that the earlier vessel of faith,
despite its manifest uncomeliness, does contain eternal life; it
may be that the **patient continuing** of human waiting and
hurrying does mark the presence and operation of a real **well-
doing**; it may be that what a man does is **good**, in spite of the
weakness of the flesh and in spite of all the marks of his inadequacy; it may be that his actions already indicate the **glory
and honour and peace** of the Coming World. But this possibility
can be neither embodied in human conduct nor conceived of by
human thought. When it exists, it exists as the possibility of
God and as His possibility only. Confronted by it, the man
of the world and the man of God, the Greek and the Jew, are assembled together upon one line. They all share in the promise of
God and in His promise only. The possibility of God can never
be embodied in one form of human righteousness which may be
compared and contrasted with other forms of human righteousness or unrighteousness. The believer—who does the *good work*
—can never behave as though this work of his were his possession to be played off against another's lack of possession. The
believer will never say 'I act', but 'God acts'; he will never
say 'God has rendered', but 'God *will render*'! (ii. 13, iii. 30,
v. 17, 19.) Awe and lowliness before God will wish to be nought
but void and deprivation and hope.

There can, however, also take place that other terrible miracle
whereby—**Unto them that obey unrighteousness, there waits
wrath and indignation.** It is possible that to what appears to
human eyes to be undeniably awe and lowliness there corresponds no finding of the true God, but only a finding of him who
is No-God (i. 23, ii. 1, 2). It can be that there awaits it the manifestation of divine displeasure (ii. 5); it may be that God renders
to the work of men wrath and indignation; it may be that
those who plainly conduct themselves as prophets have in His
sight but—**the minds of slaves**; it may be that they are 'work-
men, who, regardless of their employer, labour only for the reward
which is due to them' (Zahn). A brilliant devotion or obedience

to truth may turn out to be utter disobedience, and an all-pervading humility may be nothing but unrighteousness. Those who 'mean well' may be evil and ripe unto judgement. Yet this possibility also cannot be grasped by human intelligence. It too comes from God and from Him only. No man is secure 𝛾 before it. Here again the Jew and the Greek, the men of God and the men of the world, are assembled together on one line under the threat of judgement. There is no form of human righteousness to which the divine Merchant will assign so high a value that He will certainly purchase it for Himself. Godlessness and unrighteousness can never be other than they are, even though they take on the most noble and delicate forms, even 𝑥 though they become that thing of soul and sense which we call faith. The Judge will never deprive Himself of his right to judge even the righteous. He judges; He himself and He only.

For there is no respect of persons with God. The observable superiority which one man has over another is only his *person*, his mask, his form, the part he takes in the play. To their fellow men it is only this mask which distinguishes one man from another. They can see no more than this. It has, of course, its value. But this distinction of character does not reach beyond the KRISIS of everything that passes to corruption: it does not reach into the realm of incorruption. The standard by which God measures is, however, not of this world. God does not regard the mask. Before Him even the righteous man does not play the role of a righteous man, but is what he veritably is: perhaps he is received as one who seeketh after incorruption; perhaps he is condemned as a rebellious servant. In either case, 𝑥 he, the man himself, is searched out and known. Men are men, 𝑥 and God is God. There is now no vestige left of the alluring security of the Pharisees.

vv. 12, 13. For as many as have sinned without the law shall also perish without the law; and as many as have sinned in the presence of the law shall be judged by the law: for not the hearers of the law are righteous before God, but the doers of the law shall be accounted righteous.

Once again the question presses upon us (ii. 4): Whence then, comes the righteousness of men? And the answer is, it comes by the revelation of God; by the setting forth and communication of the divine law; by divine proximity and election through which men now here, now there, are enabled to have faith in God and to obey Him in awe and in humility (ii. 14). But what proceeds from God is in our eyes a miracle, and by it men are entitled to claim neither pre-eminence nor security. Sinners they are, and sinners they remain. Rebellion is rebellion; and who has not rebelled? No doubt we can make a superficial distinction between grades of sin. There are those who have sinned in opposition to the known law; and there are those who have sinned whilst far from the law and in ignorance of it. There is an obvious and important distinction between human unbelief and that faith which is also human. But these are superficial distinctions, which belong within the framework of this world. The veritable distinction between men and men, between the saved and the damned, between those who remain under the judgement of God and those who have been released from it, cannot be made according to a human standard. There is both here and there a passing to perdition. The final distinction is made by the *doing* of the law, that is to say, by the actual realization by men of the demands of God, by the whole content, meaning, direction, and disposition, of a man's behaviour. But when it is said that it is by the whole significance of a man's behaviour and action that he is approved or disapproved, this whole significance is the significance which it has FOR GOD and not for men. It is God's approval or disapproval; and it is indifferent whether a man lives, as he does live, without or with law. For it is not—**the hearers of the law,** that is, those who take notice of it, who have understanding and experience of it, even though they understand and experience the highest revelation of God, who thereby secure His approval. What proceeds from men can neither effect salvation nor itself be—**righteous before God.** It is—**the doers of the law** who truly hear it, the *Jew which is one inwardly* (ii. 29). The righteousness of these just men is defined by the words—**They shall be accounted** (declared) **righteous.** There must be no misunderstanding here! It is not said that they ARE righteous, nor that they HAVE BEEN declared righteous; but that they SHALL BE (ii. 6) accounted (declared) righteous. The future is used in order that the last trace of human righteousness, the last vestige of any concrete form of this righteousness, might disappear. Men have in this world of unrighteousness the prospect of the righteousness of the Coming World; they have received here and now, in time, the impetus to an eternal movement. Their righteousness consists in their surrender of the righteousness of men to God, to whom it rightly belongs, and in their complete renunciation of their own righteousness. Where such doers are disclosed by the law, and where such faith is discovered by revelation, there is Christ— *the end of the law unto righteousness to every one that believeth*

(x. 4, 5) ; and there, too, is the knowledge of Him who has first known us. Nevertheless, the Judge remains the Judge, until there be a new heaven and a new earth.

THE JUDGEMENT

II. 14–29

vv. 14–16. For when it happens that **Gentiles, which have not the law, do by nature the things of the law, these, having no law, are a law unto themselves; in that they show the work of the law written in their hearts (their conscience bearing witness therewith, and their thoughts one with another accusing or else excusing them); in the day when God shall judge the secrets of men (according to my gospel) by Jesus Christ.**

A strangely obscure and provocative piece of information, proceeding, however, from the clear recognition that God is the Judge. Those possessing no revelation stand before God as though they were fully possessed of it ; awake in their sleep, righteous in their unrighteousness, they believe whilst they do not believe! This strange occurrence, this firm fragility, must be carefully considered by those who trust in human righteousness.

Gentiles, which have not the law, do the things of the law. The law is the revelation once given by God, given in its completeness. The law is the impression of divine revelation left behind in time, in history, and in the lives of men ; it is a heap of clinkers marking a fiery miracle which has taken place, a burnt-out crater disclosing the place where God has spoken, a solemn reminder of the humiliation through which some men had been compelled to pass, a dry canal which in a past generation and under different conditions had been filled with the living water of faith and of clear perception, a canal formed out of ideas and conceptions and commandments, all of which call to mind the behaviour of certain other men, and demand that their conduct should be maintained. The men who *have the law* are the men who inhabit this empty canal. They are stamped with the impress of the true and unknown God, because they possess the form of traditional and inherited religion, or even the form of an experience which once had been theirs. Consequently, they have in their midst the sign-post which points them to God, to the KRISIS of human existence, to the new world which is set at the barrier of this world. Thus directed, the stamp of revelation

F

appears to them of such supreme importance that they are busily engaged in preserving its impress. *Gentiles which have not the law* are they who lack this direction altogether. Their individual lives and their experiences of history are not stamped by revelation; and they have no impress of it to guard. They may be named sleepers, for they are disturbed by no memory of some incomprehensible occurrence in their experience or in the experience of others. They may be named unbelievers, for they do not seem to be moved either to awe or to amazement at that which is above them: they are marked by no visible brokenness. They may be named unrighteous, for they accept the course of the world without question and are unconscious of the barrier which hems them in. In no sense can they be described as inhabiting the empty canal of revelation. But it can happen that the *Gentiles, which have not the law, do the things of the law*. Because God is the Judge, the doing of the law is a thing distinct from its possession or its hearing (ii. 13). To *do the law* means that revelation occurs, that God speaks. When a man stands before God, awe and humility are inevitable, and this is the righteousness which is valid with God. But revelation is from God; it cannot be compelled to flow between the banks of an empty canal. It can flow there; but it also fashions for itself a new bed in which to run its course, for it is not bound to the impress which it once had made, but is free. It is therefore a mistake to abide by the description of the Gentiles as asleep in unrighteousness and unbelief. They can become God-fearers; without it being evident to others, they can become His elect, for faith is always in itself hidden and unrecognized. Among the Gentiles there is, moreover, a shattering and disturbing awe which those who inhabit the empty canal neither perceive nor understand; but God beholds it and knows its meaning. Whenever the Gentiles grow sceptical of the righteousness of men, there is exposed to them the righteousness of God. By nature and in the natural order they *do the law*. In their merry and worldly dependence upon the creation, in their simple, unpretentious, matter-of-fact behaviour, they are known of God and esteem Him in return. They are not lacking in perception of the corruptibility of all things human; they do not fail to recognize that the dark cloud which bounds our existence is edged by the silver lining of salvation and redemption; they are not without respect for the negation by which the creation is distinguished from the Creator, or for the affirmation which makes them His creatures. Their lives are assuredly only a parable; but perhaps so perfect a parable that they are thereby

justified. The Gentile world no doubt lies in wickedness; but
it may be a world so disintegrated, so disorganized, and so undermined, that the mercy of God seems closer and more credible
than where the 'Kingdom of God' is displayed in full bloom.
Finally, is it not just where nothing noble can find an entrance;
just where men are incapable of being impressed by anything
at all; just in the midst of the last and deepest scepticism, that
there may perhaps exist that brokenness which is the recollection of God, aye, of God Himself? Disturbance of soul, restless
murmuring, cavil, and protest: such may be sign-posts to the
peace of God which passeth all understanding. What then are
the things of the law? What does it require and call to remembrance in those who possess it? Surely, exactly what is so
strangely presented to us in the children of the world. Can it
be, then, that they veritably *do the law*? Can it be that they stand
at the source of the river? Why should it not be so? Can the
man who has himself known the riches of the goodness of God
(ii. 4), and has himself perceived His revelation to be wholly
undeserved, incomprehensible, and independent of human worth,
dare to limit the sphere of God's operation?

They are a law unto themselves. If there be men who do the
law without possessing it, and who receive it by doing it, they
are then law unto themselves. The living water fashions its
own course, and the visible pre-eminence of the inhabitants of
the canal is destroyed. There has been exposed to view a new
rough river-bed, a very unfamiliar and strange impress of revelation, a disturbing form of faith. But who will deny what God
alone can deny? The religion and the experiences of the
characters in the novels of Dostoevsky have presumably their
counterparts in many other forms of religion and of experience;
but those who *have the law*—even if it be the Gospel!—have no
occasion to regard such men merely as objects of missionary
enterprise, or to speak of them in superior fashion as people
possessed of 'elementary forms of religion'. Such men may long
have been in possession of impressions of God quite different from
those which we ever have had or shall have. And if it were
a matter of religion and of experience, these—which are in any
case trivial—God can, and does, give to the Gentiles.

They show the work of the law, written in their hearts. They
come under the judgement of God; they are even now under
judgement; and that by which men are justified by God is discovered in them. How, we ask, is this so? *The work* which is
displayed before God by the Gentile who has been justified, and
by which he is found pleasing to God, has no positive content or

'extent', for this would be irrelevant. Were he to be judged by the righteousness of men, he would undoubtedly be lost. Even if a righteousness of men were possibly discovered in him, he would not thereby be justified. What is pleasing to God comes into being when all human righteousness is gone, irretrievably gone, when men are uncertain and lost, when they have abandoned all ethical and religious illusions, and when they have renounced every hope in this world and in this heaven. Beyond every concrete visible thing, beyond everything in the law of which those who possess it approve—the 'ethical kernel', the 'idealistic background', the 'religious feeling'—beyond all that is valued in western European culture—'conduct', 'poise', 'race', 'personality', 'delicacy of taste', 'spirituality', 'force of character'—beyond all these things is set that which men have to lay before God, and which He will *render* (ii. 6) with eternal life. There may perhaps be no more than a quite unconscious feeling for religion in no way derived from the Church; perhaps no more than the last stage of human nakedness (Dostoevsky!); perhaps no more than confusion, misery, and destitution; perhaps no more than some last terror before the mystery of death, some final disgusted rejection of the inevitability of the world by a man when he leaves his busy life protesting against its futility. But more than any of these, and better and more beautiful, is that the *rendering* of God—depends upon—nothing at all! There is joy in heaven over one sinner that repenteth, more than over ninety and nine just persons, which need no repentance. But what is Repentance? Not the last and noblest and most refined achievement of the righteousness of men in the service of God, but the first elemental act of the righteousness of God in the service of men; the work that God has written in their hearts, and which, because it is from God and not from men, occasions joy in heaven; that looking forward to God, and to Him only, which is recognized only by God and by God Himself.

Their conscience bearing witness therewith, and their thoughts one with another accusing or else excusing them. Who is there among the lawless and ungodly that hears even the sound of the voice of conscience? Who among them can penetrate the dialectical paradox by which they are enveloped: the paradox of God and destiny, destiny and guilt, guilt and atonement, atonement and—God? God hears and knows. What is muffled and secret and concealed, what is hardly conscious, what Gellert named 'the divine ordering in the context', to Him is eloquent and full of speech. To Him there rises up a testimony on behalf of men which can be uttered before no human judge. God knows what we do not know. Hence emerges the incomprehensible possibility that lawless men are brought to judgement, and yet pass through it into freedom.

For—**in the day when God shall judge the secrets of men by Jesus Christ** the *Gentiles* will show their *work* and shall discover the good pleasure of God. Whence, then, comes this possibility of perceiving that the ungodly are comprehended in God? Whence, then, comes the possibility of the erasure of that transverse section by which men are separated according to the law, the religious from the irreligious, the moral from the immoral? How can there be substituted for it that longitudinal section which reveals to all, even to those most deeply submerged, the possibility of access to God? The new Day which has dawned for men in the resurrection, the Day of Jesus Christ, this—**according to my gospel**—is the Day that ushers in the transformation of all time into eternity. This is the Day when the *secrets of men* are laid bare and it is revealed that men are known by God. *Through Jesus Christ* men are judged by God. This is their KRISIS, but it is both negation and affirmation, both death and life. In Christ there has appeared an end, but also a beginning, a passing to corruption, but also a becoming new; and both are for the whole world and for all men. For the Redeemer who has been manifested in Christ is the Creator of all things. There is no residue. In Christ, high and low, the just and the unjust, after they have received the same command to halt before the unknown God, have the same access to the Father. ALL flesh is as grass; and it is the will of God that ALL should be saved (i. 16, iii. 29, x. 2). For this reason God judgeth the *secrets of men*. The condemnation under which we stand, the mercy, the power of forgiveness by which we are supported and carried, these concern us all and embrace the whole world, but are unobservable, and are directed towards the *secrets of men*. There alone they exist and are true. So long as some stand in the light and others in the shade, visibly confronting one another, they are not true. But at midnight, when there is no light, and at midday when there is no shadow, the distinction between light and shade ceases to have meaning. Christ is both midnight and midday. Then is perceived above all human distinctions the vast comprehensiveness of God. God Himself propounds the problem of God—and answers it. He sets all men of all ranks always under one threat and under one promise. The line of intersection drawn by Him can neither be seen nor approached, and is always unbridgeable and disturbing, but it points us always to the *secret* where God

Himself is the Judge. But it is precisely this sternness of the Gospel of Christ which constitutes its tenderness and gentleness and its power unto liberty. In His utter strangeness God wills to make Himself known and can make Himself known. He, whom none of us is able to comprehend, does not deprive any single human being of witness to Himself. The hidden God is not far from *the secrets of men*; and we recognize this the more clearly when we perceive that in secret He pronounces His judgement upon the secrets of men. Since God takes no cognizance of the impressions which men have about Him, He is the hope of the Gentiles at the judgement, for He is God Himself.

Since God is the Judge, every righteousness of men is thrust into obscurity, every criticism which men exercise upon the ungodly and every busy attempt to convert them become of trivial importance. Beyond human good and evil the arm of God is extended in power; and men are advised to beware of too great daring.

vv. 17–25. But if thou bearest the name of a Jew, and restest upon the law, and gloriest in God, and knowest his will and dost apprehend **the things that are excellent, being instructed out of the law—but art confident that thou thyself art a guide of the blind, a light of them that are in darkness, an instructor of the foolish, a teacher of babes, having** before thee **in the law the** perfect **form of knowledge and of the truth; thou therefore that teachest another, teachest thou not thyself? thou that preachest a man should not steal, dost thou steal? thou that sayest a man should not commit adultery, dost thou commit adultery? thou that abhorrest idols, dost thou rob temples? thou who gloriest in the law, through thy transgression of the law dishonourest thou God? For the name of God is blasphemed among the Gentiles because of you, even as it is written. For circumcision indeed profiteth, if thou be a doer of the law: but if thou be a transgressor of the law, thy circumcision is become uncircumcision.**

A disturbing and surprising piece of information from the invisibility of the OTHER side. God pronounces those who are awake to be asleep, believers to be unbelievers, the righteous to be unrighteous. Men who bear upon them the stamp of the impress of revelation remain still men of the world. Men must note carefully this possibility of the judgement of God upon their righteousness.

Thou bearest the name of a Jew. Yet thou art not therefore the
first and the best. Thou art, it is true, heir to a past history, and
thou awaitest a future history to correspond thereto. Thy life is
set in a context which leads to the supposition that thou art in this
world of the flesh a peculiar person. Thou hast a name; and it is
widely supposed that thou dost live a life different from the
many who possess not the advantage of this name. Thou—
restest upon the law. Thou art stamped with the marks of the
living God; and thou art busily engaged in preserving these
marks. Thou dost take pleasure in the exercise of that authority
which belongs to thee because thou dost live under the authority
of the knowledge of God, which is denied to those outside, who
live in the midst of a chaos of notions and whose judgements
are guided by no fixed standard of truth. **Thou gloriest in God.**
How canst thou do otherwise? for thou hast a veritable impression and memory of Him; and by continuous prayer thy gaze
is directed to the place where He does assuredly stand. How
different are the doubters and the atheists who consider the
place whither thy gaze is directed to be naught but emptiness!
Thou knowest the will of God. Thou knowest that the recollection of God involves obedience, and that from the place whither
thy gaze is continually fixed there comes an active intervention
in thy life, an aggressive incursion into the world; and thou
knowest the direction along which this attack must develop.
Thou art not lacking in the disturbing knowledge that something
must be done, or in the zeal to arise and accomplish it. How
different are those thoughtless ones who are driven onwards by
the rumbling power of fate! **Thou dost apprehend the things
that are excellent.** Thou hast an inherited and developed sense
for things as they really are, a delicate perception of the meaning of history and of the significance of the impulses of the human
heart; and thou art especially sensitive to the things which are
untrustworthy and fraught with peril. Thou art possessed of
spiritual insight and art able to pronounce acute and penetrating
judgements. Thou knowest well how to stake out thy position
so that none can confuse thy property with the land which
belongs to others, and thou hast good reason to mark thy boundaries clearly. Thou seest deep, for thou art deep. How different
are they who live their lives as mere amateurs, immersed in a
thousand superficialities! In short, thou hast much. What dost
thou desire more? What could any man have which is not thine?
Great is the opportunity which has been given thee; great are
the riches of the goodness of God which have been showered
upon thee; great is the forbearance of the wrath of God towards

thee, and great His patience (ii. 4, iii. 2, iv. 11, ix. 4, 5). Great, assuredly, is that which is expected of thee.

And now—**thou art confident that thou thyself art a guide of the blind.** Not without reason dost thou feel thyself entrusted with a mission. The contrast between thyself with all thy marks of revelation and those who can display no such marks provides thee with the sense of vocation. Thy imagination is filled with the picture of a divine plan of God's purpose, in the working out of which the chief role has been assigned to thee. Conscious of this sacred task, and confident of ability to perform it, thou dost undertake the part of mediator of the impress of revelation which thou hast—**having in the law the perfect form of knowledge and of the truth**—and art willing, with passionate earnestness and conviction, to guide the blind who walk in darkness, to instruct the foolish, and to teach babes. Thou hast the intention of spreading the revelation, of extending its influence, of propagating it, of expounding it, in order that many others may possess it; and by the power of what thou art and hast, thou feelest thyself compelled to action and appointed to co-operate with God.

But—**thou therefore that teachest another, teachest thou not thyself?** The missioner must, however, be sent, the instructor must have been taught, and the distributor must have been provided with something to distribute. What comes of the possession of the law, if it be not done, if those who possess it be not authorized by God? What comes of the impress of revelation, if revelation be not continuous? What is the use of fixing attention upon the place where God should be, if He is no longer there? What does it avail at the judgement that thou dost dwell on the banks of the canal, if the canal be empty? Can the possibility that the water has been cut off be ruled out? And if this possibility may not be excluded, who then art thou? What dost thou possess? With what dost thou propose to irrigate the surrounding country? What is the new spirit which thou wouldest pour out over others? No, thy impress of revelation, thy emotion, thy experience and enthusiasm, are of this world, are flesh. With all thy pious worldliness is there any reason to suppose that thou hast less occasion to fear the wrath of God than others have? Hast thou been less occupied than they in imprisoning the truth and in changing the incorruptible into the image of the corruptible? What art thou, if God come not to thy assistance, if He does not discover in the secret of thine heart the *work*, the prayer of the Publican, the appeal of the Prodigal Son, the entreaty of the widow to the Unjust

Judge? Apart from this, thy labour is but THY labour: thy
righteousness is robbery, for who does not steal? thy purity
is adultery, for who is rid of sexuality? thy piety is arrogance,
for where is the piety which does not approach God too nearly?
Is there any advantage in distinguishing before the judgement
seat of God a higher and a lower form of worldliness? If thy
life be without that justification which God alone can give, it is
utterly devoid of any justification at all. If thou hast no more
to boast of than thy impress of revelation, thou hast no ground
of boasting whatsoever. If thou appealest to anything more than
thy faith, and thy faith only, thou canst have no ground of
appeal. If God be not for thee, all is against thee.

But there is more:—**Thou gloriest in the law, and through thy
transgression of the law thou dishonourest God.** If God be not on
thy side, thou canst not be on His side, but only against Him.
The world possesses deep and penetrating insight. It refuses to
admit thy supposed superiority. It recognizes at once that thou
art flesh of its flesh, bone of its bone. Thy corruption renders
thee unfit to work for God and to take the lead in advancing His
cause. Thou dost act in precise contradiction to the profession
which thou hast not unreasonably adopted; for thou dost undertake a mission without being sent. Where law is, the 'world'
expects a doing of the law; where the impress of revelation is, it
expects actual revelation. With inexhaustible patience it believes the exalted claims of the sons of God in their midst to be a
genuine claim. It is not unsusceptible to reality, but it har-
bours no illusions. When, therefore, it finds that it has been
deceived by those who say that they have been called and enlightened, it sees in them no more than another example of
'Potemkin's Villages'.[1] The children of God present nothing
peculiar, nothing new, nothing that exercises a compelling power.
And so, after standing for a moment in amazement before the
comedy of an unreal communion with God, the children of the
world turn away supported and confirmed in their knowledge
that, after all, the world is the world. With proper instinct for the
truth, they do not permit themselves to be imposed upon, and
they are thus protected against any turning towards the 'God' of
the pious man. Whenever men 'adopt the point of view of God';

---

[1] When, in 1787, Catherine II wished to display to the Austrian, English,
and French ambassadors the rapid development of wealth and prosperity in
Southern Russia under her rule, her favourite, Prince Gregori Alexandrovich
Potemkin, organized the famous 'Tauric' journey, and staged the display.
Villages were improvised and inhabited by temporary villagers and other
'property' villages of painted canvas were erected on the horizon. Hence the
phrase 'Potemkin's villages' became proverbial for sham splendour. [Tr.]

whenever He is not everything and they nothing; whenever they desire to be and to do something in co-operation with Him; then, however stimulating their ideas, however noble their actions, God becomes—a notion. When only the empty canals of God are visible, objections and protests against 'God' are wholly justified. How then does it stand with God's fellow-workers?—**For the name of God is blasphemed among the Gentiles because of you** (Isa. lii. 5). Are *these* then the elect children of God by whom the Kingdom of God is sustained? Surely this blasphemous possibility—a possibility realized, alas, everywhere and in all ages—ought to restrain us whenever we are tempted to construct a supreme and final human righteousness out of the prophetic energy of those who wait and hurry!

But if thou be a transgressor of the law, thy circumcision is become uncircumcision. Here bursts upon us the unavoidable relativism. The impress of revelation possessed by the children of God becomes a human worldly factor side by side with other factors. Their claim to absolute superiority over others falls therefore to the ground. The piety of the children of God, their morality and their ideas, ebbs and flows: the history of the Church is a secular history written under the title, 'How the ring was—lost'. For when God does not find the worth which He values and for which He *renders* (ii. 6), mere human advantages have no particular significance. The uncleanness and ungodliness which He discovers in *the secrets of men* necessarily obscure the impress of revelation which men might discover in themselves or which others might find in them. The heroes of God without God may be compared to a traveller who remains standing under the sign-post, instead of moving in the direction to which it directs him. The sign-post has become meaningless; and their faith and prayers and Biblical outlook are meaningless also. The Jewish sacrament of circumcision—and this is true of every other sacrament—is no longer fellowship with God: it remains still—and here, surely, under the wrath of God, Zwingli and the liberals are right—only SIGNIFICANT of fellowship with God. For the crater, by which the holy men sit and wait, is burnt out. The form of holiness is holy only in its form; and no attempt to spiritualize it can protect such holiness from ever-increasing vacuity. Circumcision is, then, equal to uncircumcision, faith to unbelief, and blessedness to godlessness.

Thus the righteousness of men is vulnerable even in its own home. It is mistaken not only in its attitude to those outside, to the Gentiles (ii. 14-16), but also in its attitude to itself. Before the judgement seat of God it is shaken at its roots. There

is no claim which can rest upon what men have achieved in this
world or upon what might emerge in them from this world.

**vv. 26-9. If therefore the uncircumcision keep the
ordinances of the law, shall not his uncircumcision be
reckoned** in fact **for circumcision ? and shall not the uncircumcision which is by nature, if it fulfil the law, judge
thee, who with the letter and circumcision art a transgressor of the law ? For he is not a Jew, which is one out-
wardly; neither is that circumcision, which is outward
in the flesh: but he is a Jew, which is one inwardly; and
circumcision is that of the heart, in the spirit, not in the
letter; whose praise is not of men, but of God.**

A final possibility has now appeared. The ring of cause and
effect, of decline and fall, is completely closed. The ring may,
however, be both closed up and sustained by the incomprehensible
mercy of God. Human righteousness is, as we have seen, in itself
an illusion: there is in this world no observable righteousness.
There may, however, be a righteousness before God, a righteousness that comes from Him. There is no visible company of saints
and exceptional people and heroes and righteous supermen who
are what they are because of their possession of the law, the impress of revelation, or because of some inner spiritual capacity of
theirs, or because of some ethical and sacramental system to which
they have devoted themselves. There may be, however, beyond all
these distinctions—a new man, created by God for God. If that
were so, would not—**his uncircumcision be reckoned for circumcision?** would not then ungodliness before God be *rendered* with
eternal life, as though it were piety? would not then rebellion
and absence of awe be entered in God's ledger as godliness and
humility? might not then the fact that God has not recognized
any human faith as such, but has *shut it up under unbelief*, be—*in
order that he might have mercy upon all* (xi. 32)? Apart from any
merit or visible occasion or human possibility, apart from any
human attempt to bring it about or to prevent its occurrence, there
would then have broken in upon the known context of things the
impossible possibility of the New World, of God Himself, of the
Unknown God! With men this is impossible: with God it is
possible. God reckons according to His standard. In the light of
His fellowship God leads the unbeliever to the *end* (goal) *of the
law*. In a world lying in wickedness, He sets the believer upon
his feet. God passes by all that is concrete, visible, and *outward*,
for He judges in secret according to His justice. God is the Spirit
who dwells, or does not dwell, in the hearts of men, and who is

wholly independent of what is written, or not written, in letters inscribed on human 'Tables'. The rewards of God are presented only according to His will.—Have we anything to say against this? Is God unjust?—But if we think that He is, what superior justice have we to set against His justice? Is not God the eternal truth of our lives? and does not His truth condition His judgement? Of what use are our truths here? The honour of God will enlighten, and the righteousness of God shall be revealed. Consequently, His action must be exercised invisibly and in a manner wholly contrary to our expectation. God does not live by the idea of justice with which we provide Him. He is His own justice. He is not one cause among many; He is not the final solution which we propound to the problem of life. Therefore His appearance is incomprehensible and without known occasion, and His judgement is according to His own justice. And yet, there is a claim to salvation from the wrath of God: the claim IS where every claim is surrendered and broken down by God Himself; where His negation is final and His wrath unavoidable; when God is recognized as God. The claim IS where the history of the relation between God and man begins; where there is no history to record, because it only occurs, and occurs eternally. The claim IS when men dare—but even this is no recipe for blessedness but only the eternal ground of its perception—to go forth into the fresh air and to love the undiscoverable God. And this occurrence IS—in Jesus Christ.

The Third Chapter

THE RIGHTEOUSNESS OF GOD

THE LAW

III. 1–20

HISTORY is the display of the supposed advantages of power and intelligence which some men possess over others, of the struggle for existence hypocritically described by ideologists as a struggle for justice and freedom, of the ebb and flow of old and new forms of human righteousness, each vying with the rest in solemnity and triviality. Yet one drop of eternity is of greater weight than a vast ocean of finite things. Measured by the standard of God the dignitaries of men forfeit their excellence and their serious importance—they become relative; and even the noblest of human moral and spiritual attainments are seen to be what they really are—natural, of this world, profane, and 'materialistic'. The valleys are exalted and the high hills made low. Ended is the conflict of good and evil, for men are ranged upon one line, and their *secrets* (ii. 16) are judged before God and before Him only.

The judgement of God is the end of history, not the beginning of a new, a second, epoch. By it history is not prolonged, but done away with. The difference between that which lies beyond the judgement and that which lies on this side of it is not relative but absolute: the two are separated absolutely. God speaks: and He is recognized as the Judge. By His speech and by His judgement a transformation is effected so radical that time and eternity, here and there, the righteousness of men and the righteousness of God, are indissolubly linked together. The end is also the goal; the Redeemer is also the Creator; He that judgeth is also He that restoreth all things. The disclosure of non-sense is the revelation of sense. What is new is also the deepest truth of what was old. The most radical ending of history, the negation under which all flesh stands, the absolute judgement, which is the meaning of God for the world of men and time and things, is also the crimson thread which runs through the whole course of the world in its inevitability. But when the corruptible is recognized as such, it becomes the parable of incorruption. The final subjection to the wrath of God is faith in His righteousness: and then God is known as the Unknown God. As such, He is precisely no 'thing-in-itself', no metaphysical substance in the

midst of other substances, no second, other Stranger, side by
side with those whose existence is independent of Him. On
the contrary, He is the eternal, pure Origin of all things. As
their non-existence, He is their true being. God is love.

And so it follows that every impress of revelation in history, however little cause there may be in it for boasting of human righteousness, however little peace and security it affords, is not extinguished and destroyed as it passes through the judgement,
but is thereby authorized, established, and confirmed. For in
the radical dissolution of all physical, intellectual, and spiritual
achievements of men, in the all-embracing 'relativization' of all
human distinctions and human dignities, their true and eternal
meaning is made known.

**vv. 1–4. What advantage then hath the Jew ? or what is
the profit of circumcision ? Much in every way: first of all,
that they were intrusted with the oracles of God. For
what if some were without faith ? shall their want of faith
make of none effect the faithfulness of God ? God forbid:
yea, let God be found true, but every man a liar; as it is
written, That thou mightest be justified in thy words,
and mightest prevail when thou comest into judgement.**

What advantage then hath the Jew? If everything be under
the judgement of God, is there, seriously considered, any
advantage? Are not all the advantages of particular salvation or
peace simply obliterated?   Are there in history any high points
which are more than large waves upon the stream of transitoriness, thick shadows where all is shadow? Is there any connexion
between those impressions of revelation which may be discovered
in the events of history or in the spiritual experiences of men, and
the actual revelation of the Unknown God Himself? Is there any
relation between the steadfastness of those who move across the
pages of history as the elect or the illuminated, as the men of
goodwill, as prophets and heroes, and the coming Kingdom of
God where all things will be New? Behind these particular
questions there lies the larger question concerning the general
relation between occurrences and experiences and the eternal
content of all occurrence, between the world as it is and the
veritable existence of the world, between striving and knowing.
May it not be that the perception of God as the Judge involves
the denial of all connexion and relation between here and there?
—What is the profit of circumcision?
We answer:—**Much in every way.** Strangely great and
strangely powerful are the connexion and relation between God

and the world, between there and here. For when we have
clearly perceived that, if divinity be so concreted and humanized
in a particular department of history—the history of religion
or the history of salvation—God has ceased to be God, and
there can be there no relation with him, then we are able to see
that the whole occurrence of the known world derives its content
and significance from the Unknown God; then, too, we are able
to see in every impress of revelation a sign-post to Revelation;
then, too, we are able to recognize that all experience bears within
it an understanding by which it is itself condemned, and that all
time bears within it that eternity by which it is dissolved.
Judgement is not annihilation; by it all things are established.
Cleansing is not a process of emptying; it is an act of fulfilment.
God has not forsaken men; but God is—true (iii. 31).

They were entrusted with the oracles of God. However ambiguous and questionable the position of the righteous man who
searches and waits for God may be as a human position
(ii. 17–25), he, nevertheless, performs a distinct and necessary
function as a symptom of the will and action of God. Set in the
midst of human life, righteous men bear witness to reliance upon
God and to the advent of His Kingdom; and, compelled to be still,
by their own 'experiences' or by the experiences of others they
direct their attention to the possibility that the unknown can as
such become an object of knowledge. By their recollection of the
impossible they are themselves the proof that God stands within
the realm of possibility, not as one possibility among others, but
—and this is precisely what is made clear in their case—as the
impossible possibility. The *oracles of God*, of which they are
the possessors and guardians, are the comprehensible signs of
the incomprehensible truth that, though the world is incapable
of redemption, yet there is a redemption for the world. It is irrelevant whether they possess and are concerned to guard Moses
or John the Baptist, Plato or Socialism, or that moral perception
which dwells in all its simplicity in the midst of the rough and
tumble of human life. In each case there is vocation, promise,
a parabolic possibility, something which is offered to men as
an open road to their deepest perception. If they have been
veritably entrusted with the oracles of God, their claim to peculiarity and to special attention is not necessarily presumptuous.

**For what if some were without faith? shall their want of faith
make of none effect the faithfulness of God?** Submerged and
hidden is the true ground of our existence; unrecognized is the
Unknown God, fruitless the traces of His faithfulness, unused
His promises and gifts. The recognition of this is, however,

irrelevant for the moment. That His confidence is misused is
but a trivial truth, when it is seen from God's side. The action of
some, even if it were the action of all, would neither hinder His
will and action, nor render them of none effect. The faithfulness of
God may be obscured, but we cannot be rid of it; His gifts may
evoke no gratitude, but they will not be withdrawn; His goodness will bring under judgement those who withstand it, but it is
His goodness none the less. The utter godlessness of the course of
history does not alter the fact that it is marked everywhere by
peculiar impressions of revelation, by opportunities and open
doors, which, when seen from God's side, can summon men to recollection and to knowledge. Whenever men wait upon God, they
possess a mission and a character indelebilis, even though God
be shrouded from their eyes and from the eyes of all in utter
incomprehensibility, and even though they themselves be overwhelmed by catastrophes which affect their inner as well as their
outer lives. God never reveals Himself to no purpose. Where
there is *law* (ii. 14), even if it be nought but burnt-out cinders,
there is a word of the faithfulness of God.

Yea, let God be found true, but every man a liar. Of what
importance is the infidelity of those who have received the grace
of God? It preserves and makes known the 'presupposition of
the whole Christian philosophy' (Calvin). GOD is true: HE is the
Answer, the Helper, the Judge, and the Redeemer; not man,
whether from the East or from the West, whether of Nordic
stock or of Biblical outlook; not the pious nor the hero nor the
sage; not the pacifist, nor the man of action; not even the Super-
man—but God alone, and God Himself! If this be forgotten, we
must again and again be reminded of the inadequacy of all who
bear revelation, and of the gulf which separates them from what
they bear, in order that we may be referred once again to the
Beginning and the Origin. The bearer of revelation himself lives of
the recognition that God is declared to be God by his inadequacy.
This is his confession (Ps. cxvi. 10–14): *I believed, and therefore
have I spoken, but I was sore troubled*: and it proceeds—*I said in
my alarm* (*in my ecstasy*, LXX), *all men are liars*. All men! Yes,
precisely. Only when the all-embracing contrast between God
and men is perceived can there emerge the knowledge of God, a
new communion with Him, and a new worship: *What reward
shall I give unto the Lord for all the benefits that he hath done unto
me? I will receive the cup of salvation, and call upon the name of
the Lord. I will pay my vows now in the presence of all his people.*

**That thou mightest be justified in thy words, and mightest
prevail when thou comest into judgement** (Ps. li. 4). We are

wholly unjustified in doubting the vocation of the saints or in criticizing Him who called them, because the theme of despair constantly recurs in the story of their lives. The oracles of God are fraught with a significance wholly independent of the course of human history; indeed, it is the theme of despair and inadequacy which marks the visible operation of the oracles of God in the course of history. This human situation is described in the 51st Psalm, where the Psalmist, illuminated by the light of God, finds himself to be utterly impure, conceives himself competent to offer no sacrifice but his own troubled spirit and his own broken and contrite heart, and recognizes precisely here the triumphant victory of God. Above the rise and fall of the waves of history, in spite of human infidelity—aye, in this very infidelity itself—there remains the faithfulness of God. And there remains also the *advantage* (iii. 1) which the Jew has RECEIVED but does not POSSESS.

vv. 5–8. But if our unrighteousness commendeth the righteousness of God, what shall we say? Is not **God unrighteous who taketh vengeance? (I speak** according to human logic) **God forbid: for then how does[1] God judge the world? But if the truth of God through my lie abounded unto his glory,** what explanation is there of the obvious fact **that I am still judged as a sinner? and why not (as we be slanderously reported, and as some affirm that we say), Let us do evil, that good may come** from it? Those who speak thus confirm their own condemnation.

If our unrighteousness commendeth the righteousness of God, is not God unrighteous who taketh vengeance? A strange light would seem to be thrown upon the nature of God by the insight which has just been provided (iii. 1–4) into the manner in which His pre-eminence is displayed in the despair of His elect. Their despair is occasioned by the *unrighteousness* of the arbitrary and tyrannical egotism of men (i. 18), an egotism by which even they are themselves affected and by which even they imprison truth. If, then, human unrighteousness testifies to the righteousness of God, must not His righteousness also be arbitrary and tyrannical, even a dreadful and terrible and cruel egotism? Does not His wrath at our submission to the dominion of the No-God (i. 22–32) bear witness also against Him? Does not the actual condition of the world and of men declare His nature to be unfathomable,

---

[1] I take it that Bengel was right in reading, in agreement with κρίνομαι in v. 7, κρίνει (cf. ii. 16) in place of κρινεῖ. *Judge the world* occurs in the present tense also in 1 Cor. vi. 2.

capricious, and tyrannical? If the meaninglessness of history be
the revelation of its hidden meaning, must it not follow of
necessity that its meaning is also meaningless?

The words—**according to human logic**—suggest, however, that
a quite different conclusion lies near at hand and must be
substituted for a deduction which, though it appears inevitable,
is nevertheless wholly uncritical, far too straightforward, and,
when applied to God, simply the result of a wild and illegitimate
method of thought. In spite of innumerable warnings, human
logic always tends to arrange its propositions in a series and
to leave out of account what is not pro-posed, which is in fact
the pre-supposition of all pro-positions. In speaking of God,
human logic characteristically ignores both His nature and the
fact that, when the reference is to Him, the argument from
operation to cause is inapplicable, since He is not a known
thing in a series of things.

For then how does God judge the world? If God, as the final
Cause, could, as is implied by the previous indictment, be placed
within the succession of other things in this world, and if conclusions could be drawn about Him from the other things of the
world, what are we then to make of the fact that the whole
concrete world is ambiguous and under KRISIS? There is no
object apart from our thinking of it; nor has an object any clear
characteristics save when we are able to recognize them by some
quick-moving previous knowledge. Therefore if God be an
object in the world, we can make no statement about Him—for
example, that He is capricious and tyrannical—which does not
proceed from some previous superior knowledge. If, therefore,
God were, as the objection in iii. 5 implies, an object among
other objects, if He were Himself subject to the KRISIS, He
would then obviously not be God, and the true God would have
to be sought in the Origin of the KRISIS. And this is clearly the
case: the objection in iii. 5 refers not to God at all, but to the
No-God, who is the god of this world. The true God, Himself
removed from all concretion, is the Origin of the KRISIS of every
concrete thing, the Judge, the negation of this world in which is
included also the god of human logic. It is of this true God we
speak—of the Judge of the world of which He forms no part.
Tempting, therefore, as the argument directly from ourselves to
Him may be, it fails to reach the goal. It is a blind alley. The
true God is not unrighteous, not capricious, not arbitrary. Where
He sits in judgement the all-embracing unrighteousness, caprice,
and arbitrariness of our world meet their contradiction, and in
this contradiction their nature is disclosed.

If the truth of God through my lie abounded unto his glory,
what explanation is there of the obvious fact that I am still
judged as a sinner? This objection is caused evidently by a
shrinking from the irresponsibility which seems to follow from a
recognition by men of the pre-eminence of God—or it springs
also from the desire to be assured of such irresponsibility. If the
faithfulness of God persists, or even triumphs, through the
infidelity of His elect, men can, at any rate, console themselves
with the reflection that the truth of God abounds in their lie.
This conclusion is, however, illegitimate, for it assumes that men
are in a position to further the truth of God by their action.
That assumption is false. God is assuredly not the world,
and it is impossible for men, either by their lies or by their
obedience, to add anything to, or subtract anything from, His
truth and glory. These God Himself assigns. The decision as to
whether our actions are lies or obedience is wholly His; He
renders to every man according to his works (ii. 6) ; He triumphs
whether He receives or rejects us, whether He condemns us or has
mercy upon us. In either case I am in possession of no justification, no excuse, no confirmation either of my being or of my
behaviour. I can only bow to His decision as an object either of
His mercy or of His condemnation. Whatever my fate may be,
I can only give honour to Him. This is uprightness before God,
and it contradicts all our petty, sophistical questionings concerning why God is God. The man who fears lest the divine
sovereignty may remove human responsibility, or desires that it
should do so, must be reminded quite plainly that he stands
before the judgement of God as a sinner. Is this a fact or
not? Human responsibility consists in answering this question
honestly, and in the fear of the Lord which emerges when the
question has been so answered. As surely as he who perceives
God to be the Judge knows that the dishonour of the world does
not bring God into dishonour (iii. 5–7), so surely does the man
who knows himself to be under judgement recognize that the
action of God—whether for him or against him—redounds in no
way to his credit but to God's alone. To shrink from a clear
recognition that the human will is 'enslaved' is profitless; vain
also is the secret desire to profit by this recognition. In it, since
it is the acknowledgement by men of the glory of God precisely
where they have been rejected, lies the free and joyful subjection to God and the rejection of every impure sophistry.

Why not, Let us do evil that good may come from it? Those
who speak thus confirm their own condemnation. Straightforward speaking about God and man, as though they were two

equal parties, is a complete deflection. It would seem clear
enough that, if God permits good to come, even when we do
evil, we must obviously deduce—*Let us do evil that good may
come of it*. This clarity of reasoning is, however, utter darkness.
Those who speak thus do but—*confirm their own condemnation*.
For God and man are not interchangeable terms; and we are
permitted neither to attribute evil to God's account nor to place
to our own account the good which may come out of evil. Our
action is never God's action; nor does the consequence of our
action lie within our competence. Mistakenness here does but
occasion a fresh obscuring of the distance between God and man
as a consequence of our supposed insight into His sovereignty.
But we are not God: the sovereignty is His not ours. Evil
remains evil, in spite of the good which God may bring out of it;
the non-sense of history remains non-sense, in spite of the sense
which is in it from God; infidelity is infidelity, in spite of the
faithfulness of God by which it is not permitted to wander out
of the way. The world is the world, in spite of the mercy of God
by which it is enveloped and established. When we tolerate,
accept, and affirm ourselves, we affirm the existing course of the
world; and in so doing we do not glorify the omnipotent God,
but confirm the condemnation which has already been pronounced over us, and establish the justice of the divine wrath.
The arrogance with which we set ourselves by the side of God,
with the intention of doing something for Him, deprives us of the
only possible ground of salvation, which is to cast ourselves upon
His favour or disfavour. Should we attempt to escape judgement
by appealing to fatalism, we fall under condemnation precisely
because of this appeal, for any plea which we offer to God on the
supposition that He will support our past, present, and future, is
idolatry and godlessness, is in fact simply that *ungodliness and
unrighteousness* (i. 18) which make inevitable the wrath of God.

**vv. 9–18. What then? do we excuse ourselves? No, in
no wise: for we have before charged both Jews and
Greeks, that they are all under sin; as it is written, There
is none righteous, no, not one; There is none that understandeth, There is none that seeketh after God; They have
all turned aside, they are together become unprofitable;
There is none that doeth good, no, not so much as one:
Their throat is an open sepulchre; With their tongues
they have used deceit: The poison of asps is under their
lips: Whose mouth is full of cursing and bitterness: Their
feet are swift to shed blood; Destruction and misery are**

in their ways; And the way of peace have they not known:
There is no fear of God before their eyes.

Do we excuse ourselves when we perceive that the faithfulness
of God persists even in the apostasy of men? The answer, as we
have already seen (iii. 5–8), is—*No, in no wise.* Just as surely as
the recognition of the sovereignty of God overthrows all confidence in human righteousness, it sets erect no other ground
of confidence. Men are not deprived of one security, in order
that they may immediately discover for themselves another.
No man can shelter himself behind the triumphant will of God;
rather, when it is once perceived, he comes under judgement
and enters into a condition of shattering confusion—from which
he can never escape.

We have before charged that . . . all are under sin. The charge
(i. 18—ii. 29) holds. Both Jews and Greeks, the sons of God and
the natural children of the world, are, as men, children of
wrath. They are, without exception, in subjection to the foreign
power of sin (v. 12–14). To us God is, and remains, unknown;
we are, and remain, homeless in this world; sinners we are and
sinners we remain. The word 'humanity' means unredeemed
men and women; the word 'history' implies limitation and
corruption; the pronoun 'I' spells judgement. Neither forwards
nor backwards can we escape from this narrow gorge. There is
therefore no alternative for us but to remain under the indictment; and only he who remains here without making any
attempt to escape, even by spinning sophistries of human
logic (iii. 5–8), is able to praise God in His faithfulness (iii. 1–4).

As it is written. Is there in all this something new and surprising? Is it resignation following upon disillusionment, or
enthusiasm born of pessimism? Is it violence offered to the
riches of human life, a revolt against history, or the arrogance
of some form of Gnostic radicalism? No, the indictment of
which we disapprove so strongly—*is written*; it has been *proclaimed long ago* (i. 2). The whole course of history pronounces
this indictment against itself. How can a man be called 'historically minded', if he persistently overlooks it? If all the great
outstanding figures in history, whose judgements are worthy of
serious consideration, if all the prophets, Psalmists, philosophers,
Fathers of the Church, Reformers, poets, artists, were asked
their opinion, would one of them assert that men were good, or
even capable of good? Is the doctrine of original sin merely one
doctrine among many? Is it not rather, according to its fundamental meaning (see, however, v. 12), THE Doctrine which

emerges from all honest study of history? Is it not the doctrine which, in the last resort, underlies the whole teaching of history? Is it possible for us to adopt a 'different point of view' from that of the Bible, Augustine, and the Reformers? What then does history teach about the things which men do or do not do?

Does it teach that some men, at least, are like God? No, but that—**There is none righteous, no, not one.**

Does it teach that men possess a deep perception of the nature of things? or that they have experienced the essence of life? No, but that—**There is none that understandeth.**

Does it provide a moving picture of quiet piety or of fiery search after God? Do the great witnesses to the truth furnish a splendid picture, for example, of 'Prayer'? No:—**There is none that seeketh after God.**

Can it describe this or that individual and his actions as natural, healthy, genuine, original, right-minded, ideal, full of character, affectionate, attractive, intelligent, forceful, ingenuous, of sterling worth? No:—**They have all turned aside, they are together become unprofitable; There is none that doeth good, no, not so much as one.**

Can it not unearth, perhaps, some secular or spiritual human characteristics more beautiful even than these—whether in the inner realm of intelligence or in the outer realm of conduct—conscious or unconscious—active or passive—theoretical or practical? No:—**Their throat is an open sepulchre; With their tongues they have used deceit: The poison of asps is under their lips: Whose mouth is full of cursing and bitterness.** And in final judgement upon the thoughts and words of men—**Their feet are swift to shed blood; Destruction and misery are in their ways; And the way of peace have they not known.** This is the final judgement upon the deeds and works of men.

There is no fear of God before their eyes. In history we see and are taught that in this world the fear of God is never, in its true character, visible, or comprehended, or directly 'realized'. The fear of God can be perceived neither in the external course of history nor in the hearts of men. What is everywhere visible is precisely not—fear of God. So it is written in Job xiv. 4; Ps. xiv. 1-3, v. 10, cxl. 4, x. 7; Isa. lix. 7, 8; Ps. xxxvi. 2. Are the men who wrote this, and those who agree with them and quote their words, blind to the nobility of human history? Of course they are not, for they deny it nowhere. They could have gratefully acknowledged the greatness of men and sung its praises, had that been their subject. They could have spoken of the value of religion and ethics and civilization and of their significance in

the world. But this was not their theme. Their theme—and it
is the proper theme of history—is not concerned with denying
or affirming what men are IN THEMSELVES; it is concerned with
the perception of the uncertainty of men in relation to what they
are not, that is to say, in their relation to God who is their eternal
Origin. Thence comes their radical attack! It has nothing to do
with that relative criticism which must, of course, be exercised
upon all religion, ethics, and civilization. For the same reason,
it cannot remain satisfied with that relative approval which
must be awarded to every human achievement when placed in
its own context. The disturbance lies far deeper and is infinitely
more than mere unrest, for it reaches out to a peace which is
beyond the experience of normal human life. Its negation is all-
embracing, since it proceeds from an all-embracing affirmation.
Those who lead this attack are moved neither by pessimism, nor
by the desire of tormenting themselves, nor by any pleasure in
mere negation; they are moved by a grim horror of illusion; by
a determination to bow before no empty tabernacle; by a single-
minded and earnest striving after what is real and essential; by
a firm rejection of every attempt to escape from the veritable
relation between God and man; by a genuine refusal to be
deceived by those penultimate and antepenultimate truths
with which human research has to be content both at the
beginning and at the end of its investigation. They allow full
right to the materialistic, secular, 'sceptical' view of the world;
and then, assuming this final scepticism, they set forth upon
the road which leads to the knowledge of God and thereby to
the knowledge of the eternal significance of the world and of
history. No road to the eternal meaning of the created world
has ever existed, save the road of negation. This is the lesson of
history.

**vv. 19, 20. Now we know that what things soever the
law saith, it speaketh to them that are under the law;
that every mouth may be stopped, and all the world may
become guilty before God. Therefore by the deeds of the
law shall no flesh be justified in his sight: for by the law is
the knowledge of sin.**

What the law saith, it speaketh to them that are under the law.
The possessors of the law are the idealists, the especially
favoured, those who have an experience of God or, at least, a
remembrance of such experience (ii. 14, iii. 2). Their impress of
revelation, their religion and their piety, demonstrate and bear
witness to God. Such men are directed to God; but for that very

reason they are not directed by Him. They cannot, however, fail to perceive the true relation between God and man; nor can they be guilty of supposing that some men—they themselves, for example—are, in consequence of their spiritual and historical advantages, in a position of security with regard to God or in possession of any excuse for their actions (ii.1). They cannot by means of *human logic* (iii. 5) proceed to reverse the truth that God is God, or escape from the disturbance and tension, the insecurity and questionableness, of the position in which God has placed them. Genuine faith is a void, an obeisance before that which we can never be, or do, or possess; it is devotion to Him who can never become the world or man, save in the dissolution and redemption and resurrection of everything which we here and now call world and man. We have just (iii. 10–18) heard the voice of the law, of religion and piety. The empty canal speaks of the water which does not flow through it. The sign-post points to a destination which is precisely where the sign-post is not. The impress (*form*, ii. 20) speaks of the genuine signet-ring which is not where the impress is, but which has left upon it its—negative. And so it is history as a chronicle of the nobility of men, not history as a chronique scandaleuse, which contains the accusation of history against history.

That every mouth may be stopped, and all the world may become guilty before God. And yet the Jew has an advantage (iii. 1). He is in a position to know our ignorance of God; he is able to halt before that which no eye hath seen, nor ear heard, which hath not entered into the heart of men. He can fear God. Religion is the possibility of the removal of every ground of confidence except confidence in God alone. Piety is the possibility of the removal of the last traces of a firm foundation upon which we can erect a system of thought. The judgement of history is that those devoted to its investigation are driven to a final deprivation: they become dumb before God. When this possibility is realized; when men who exercise themselves in the law hear the voice of the law pronouncing that God alone is just; when their religion dissolves religion, and their piety dissolves piety; when this historical and spiritual pre-eminence depresses every eminence; when every confident, arrogant mouth, every mouth that thinks that it can give forth even one single truth, is stopped; when men, as men, have scaled the world's highest peaks, and there discover that *all the world* is *guilty before God*—then it is that their peculiar advantage is established, maintained, and confirmed; then it is that there is manifested the eternal meaning of history; then it is that God asserts His faithfulness, and reveals that it has not been deflected by the unfaithfulness of men.

By the deeds of the law shall no flesh be justified in his sight— *Enter not into judgement with thy servant; For in thy sight shall no man living be justified* (Ps. cxliii. 2): *Of a truth I know that it is so: For how can man be just before God? If he should desire to contend with him, he could not answer him one of a thousand* (Job ix. 2, 3, see LXX version). *Long ago* (i. 2) these men uttered the witness of history against history, of which we have been reminded (iii. 10–18). Long ago they assigned to it the same clear significance as we have done. The *living* (Ps. cxliii) may be as truly named the *dead* (Job ix). Caught up in the struggle for existence—eating, drinking, sleeping, yes, above all, sleeping! marrying and giving in marriage—men stand midway between life and death. Immersed in the flux of time and history, fleshly, they are not righteous before God. What, indeed, does *flesh* mean, but the complete inadequacy of the creature when he stands before the Creator? What does it mean, but unqualified and, when measured by human standards, unqualifiable worldliness? What does it mean, but everything that is unrighteous before God? The *works of the law* that are written by God in the hearts of men (ii. 15) do not bear witness for them but against them; they provide them with no security or rest or excuse; they demolish their righteousness, they do not build it up. Seen from within the sphere of human fleshliness—in fact, as we see them—the works of the law negate, they do not affirm. Only God sees them as positive factors, to be treasured up and valued. Men, as we know them, have no resting-place, no peace, no stronghold, not even in the hidden depths or superficialities of their nature. It is God who judgeth the *secrets of men* (ii. 16), and they are, and can be, known only by Him. In all their works men possess nothing which they can put forth on their behalf; but God renders to every man *according to his works* (ii. 6). What men account righteous and valuable is, as such, *flesh*, which, in God's sight, is unrighteous and valueless. That which He pronounces righteous, and for which He *renders*, is not flesh as such, not something we possess nor something which the world accounts weighty and important. God alone is the answer to the question; He alone is our helper in the misery which is the consequence of the separation of the Creator from the creature. Well-grounded, therefore, is the cry—*Therefore is my spirit overwhelmed within me; my heart within me is desolate. I remember the days of old; I meditate on all thy works. I spread forth my hands unto thee: My soul thirsteth after thee, as a weary* *land* (Ps. cxliii. 4–6). Justified also is the complaint: *Lo, he goeth by me and I see him not: He passeth on also, but I perceive him not. Behold, he seizeth the prey, who can hinder him? Who will say unto him, What doest thou? God will not withdraw his anger; the helpers of arrogancy do stoop under him. How much less shall I answer him, and choose out my words to reason with him? Whom, though I were righteous, yet would I not answer; I would make supplication to my judge. If I had called, and he had answered me; yet would I not believe that he harkened unto my voice. For he breaketh me with a tempest, and multiplieth my wounds without cause. He will not suffer me to take my breath, but filleth me with bitterness. If I speak of strength, lo, he is strong: and if of judgement, who shall set me a time to plead? Though I be righteous, mine own mouth shall condemn me: Though I be perfect, he shall prove me perverse. Though I be perfect, I will not regard myself; I despise my life* (Job ix. 11–21; see LXX version). The man of genuine religion and piety, the man who accepts the law, must play his part in the midst of this crying and complaining. He knows that it is precisely the *doing of the law*—in other words, what a man veritably does in God— that is his perpetual coming under judgement.

By the law is the knowledge of sin. The answer is now given to our question (iii. 1), *What advantage then hath the Jew?* He has an advantage. He possesses law—the impress of revelation —experience, religion, piety, perception, vision; in fact, he has a Biblical outlook. The men who possess the law are removed from all romantic sentimentality, for they are moving along the chasm which divides the Creator from the creature, spirit from flesh. By the law they are placed under indictment, and are pronounced to be sinners in God's sight; by it they are deprived of every possession, and handed over to the favour or disfavour of God. When this occurs, men hear the decision of the law, and understand themselves in the peculiarity of their experience and of their piety. Then it is that they hear the final truth, the truth of redemption and of atonement. Once this is heard and understood, it is possible for us to say that there ARE eminences in history. When history points beyond itself and discovers in itself its own inadequacy, when there emerges in history a horror at history, then its high places are made known. When an impress of revelation is nothing but a sign-post to Revelation, the impress is itself eternal reality; when the waiting of the pious is veritably only an expectancy which drives out all memory of piety, this waiting IS a waiting in the Kingdom of God; when a solid sense of possession is known to be itself

wholly questionable, the possession is eternally solid. The whole
course of this world participates in true existence when its non-
existence is recognized. Through the law, therefore, attention
is directed towards God, and by it He is displayed as the Judge.
This is the positive relation between God and men, which is disclosed to men when they perceive the utter separation between
here and there, and become aware of the only possible presence
of God in the world. In the light of ultimate and all-embracing
KRISIS God is known to be God, and His sovereignty is seen.
Here is the peculiarity of the Jew and the meaning of circumcision. God is known as the Unknown God, who *justifieth the
ungodly* (iv. 5), who *quickeneth the dead, and calleth the things
that are not, as though they were* (iv. 17), on whom men can only
in hope believe against hope (iv. 18). When the 'Jew' realizes
this peculiar possibility, when he recognizes that he has been
set at the barrier between two worlds, he is able to rejoice in
his peculiarity. Such realization and perception lie beyond the
possibility of our knowledge, and are the becoming possible of
that which is impossible.

JESUS

III. 21–6

**vv. 21, 22 a. But now apart from the law the righteous-
ness of God hath been manifested, being witnessed by the
law and the prophets; even the righteousness of God
through** his faithfulness **in Jesus Christ unto all them that
believe.**

But now. We stand here before an irresistible and all-
embracing dissolution of the world of time and things and men,
before a penetrating and ultimate KRISIS, before the supremacy
of a negation by which all existence is rolled up. The world is
the world; and we now know what that means (i. 18—iii. 20).
But whence comes this KRISIS? Whence comes our recognition
of it and our ability to comprehend it? Whence comes the
possibility of our perceiving that the world is the world, and of
our thus limiting it as such by contrasting it with another world
which is unknown to us? Whence comes the possibility of our
describing time only as time, and things only as things, and men
only as men? and whence the possibility of our assigning a
value to history and existence by sternly recognizing that they
are concrete, limited, and relative? From what lofty eminence
do all these critical opinions descend? And out of what abyss
arises our knowledge of these last, unknown things, by which

everything is measured, this shattering knowledge of the invisible Judge in whose hands lies our condemnation? All these questions revolve round one point, which is our origin, and sound one presupposition, from which our existence has emerged. From this presupposition we have come, and, regarded from this point, the world and we ourselves are seen to be bounded, dissolved, rolled up, and judged. But this one point is not a point among other points, and this one presupposition is not one among many presuppositions. Our origin evokes in us a memory of our habitation with the Lord of heaven and earth; and at this reminiscence the heavens are rent asunder, the graves are opened, the sun stands still upon Gibeon, and the moon stays in the valley of Ajalon. *But now* directs our attention to time which is beyond time, to space which has no locality, to impossible possibility, to the gospel of transformation, to the imminent Coming of the Kingdom of God, to affirmation in negation, to salvation in the world, to acquittal in condemnation, to eternity in time, to life in death—*I saw a new heaven and a new earth: for the first heaven and the first earth are passed away*. This is the Word of God.

Apart from the law. That God speaks, that we, known by Him, see ourselves and the world in His light, is something strange, peculiar, new; and this 'otherness' runs through all religions, all experience, and every disposition of men, when these are directed towards God. This 'otherness' cuts sharply through all human sense of possession and semi-possession, even through all sense of not-possessing. It is the meaning of all ecclesiastical and religious history, nay, of all history; meaning which, for this reason, cannot be identified with any period or epoch of history or even with any underlying experience in history—for even such experience itself shares in the general ambiguity of all history. It is the confirmation of all these concrete and spiritual factors in the history of religion which we have named the impress of revelation, of all forms of worship, and, in the broadest sense of the word, of all 'beliefs'; confirmation which, for this reason, must not be identified with the things which are confirmed, as though it were a visible thing in the midst of other visible things, and not, on the contrary, visible only in its invisibility. The voice of God which is His *power* (i. 16) is and remains the voice OF GOD; were it not so, and did it not remain beyond all other voices, it would not be the POWER of God. God speaks where there is *law*; but He speaks also where there is no law. He speaks where law is, not because law is there, but because He willeth to speak. God is free.

The righteousness of God. The word of God declares that He
is what He is. By committing Himself to men and to the world
which has been created by Him, and by His unceasingly accepting them and it, He justifies Himself to Himself. Even the
wrath of God is His righteousness (i. 18). To unbelief, His
righteousness is necessarily manifested as divine negation. God
makes Himself known as Creator and Lord of all things through
His anger against unbelief, through the compulsion by which
He drives men helplessly on to the barrier which hems them in,
and hands them over to the god of this world (i. 20, 21). In this
negation God affirms Himself and pronounces His claim upon
men to be decisive, permanent, and final. Beyond the barrier
at which we stand is—God. This is the theme of the Word of
God. The more we become aware of the piercing irresistibility
of this Word, the more powerfully and clearly will God speak
to us of His justice and of His Kingdom; the more everything
human—our good and evil, our belief and unbelief—becomes
transparent as glass, the more pronouncedly do we—as we are
seen and known by God—stand under His sovereignty and
under the operation of His power. The righteousness of God is
that 'nevertheless' by which He associates us with Himself and
declares Himself to be our God. This 'nevertheless' contradicts
every human logical 'consequently', and is itself incomprehensible and without cause or occasion, because it is the 'nevertheless!' of God. The will of God brooks no questioning: because He
is God, He wills. The righteousness of God is His forgiveness,
the radical alteration of the relation between God and man
which explains why, though human unrighteousness and ungodliness have brought the world to its present condition and
are intolerable to Him, He nevertheless continues to name us
His people in order that we may BE His people. The righteousness of God is righteousness from outside—justitia forensis,
justitia aliena; for the Judge pronounces His verdict according to the standard of His righteousness only. Unlike any other
verdict, His verdict is creative: He pronounces us, His enemies,
to be His friends. 'Here therefore is the sermon of sermons
and the wisdom of heaven; in order that we may believe that
our righteousness and salvation and comfort come to us from
outside; in order that we may believe that, though in us dwells
naught but sin and unrighteousness and folly, we are, nevertheless, acceptable before God, righteous and holy and wise'
(Luther). The righteousness of God is the action which sets
free the truth that we have imprisoned (i. 18), and which is
wholly independent of every attempt, or imaginable attempt,

that we could make to achieve liberty. The righteousness of
God is therefore the sovereign and regal display of the power of
God: it is the miracle of resurrection. The righteousness of God
is our standing-place in the air—that is to say, where there is
no human possibility of standing—whose foundations are laid
by God Himself and supported always by Him only; the place
where we are wholly in His hands for favour or disfavour. This
is the righteousness of God; and it is a positive relation between
God and man. 'We can neither doubt nor surrender this article
of faith—though heaven and earth and every corruptible thing
fall in ruins about us' (Luther). In the light of some 150,000
years of human insecurity, can we even consider any other
positive relation? Can we even for one moment conceive of
the emergence of some concrete or direct, historical or spiritual,
relation? European history apart, can Asiatic or African or
American history provide any other answer than God alone,
God Himself, and the mercy of God?

That God is righteous—**hath been manifested**. This is the
answer to our question 'whence?', the meaning of our 'thence',
our *But now*. The mercy of God triumphs! It has been given to
us. The positive relation between God and man, which is the
absolute paradox, veritably exists. This is the theme of the
Gospel (i. 1, 16), proclaimed in fear and trembling, but under
pressure of a necessity from which there is no escape. It proclaims eternity as an event. We declare the knowledge of the
Unknown God, the Lord of heaven and earth, who dwelleth
not in temples made with hands, who needeth not anything,
seeing that He himself giveth to all life and breath and all things.
We set forth everything given by God to men, as given in order
that they may seek Him who is not far from each one of us, in
whom we live and move and have our being, who is beyond all
our life and movement and existence, and whose nature is to
remain faithful, in spite of human depravity. We proclaim that,
because it is His nature to remain faithful, the Godhead cannot
be graven into any likeness by the skill and device of men; that
God has overlooked the times of ignorance, *but* that *now* He
commandeth men everywhere to repent. We announce the
dawning of the day in which He will judge the world of men in
righteousness—in His righteousness! (Acts xvii. 23–31). The
righteousness of God *hath been manifested*. We can no longer
omit to reckon with it; we can no longer see what has been given
otherwise than in the light of this previous giving. We can
come from nowhere except from this pre-supposition. Henceforward the negation in which we stand can be understood only

in the light of the divine affirmation from which it proceeds. This means that the marks of human unrighteousness and ungodliness are crossed by the deeper marks of the divine forgiveness; that the discord of human defiance is penetrated by the undertones of the divine melody 'Nevertheless'. Once the revelation is given, our situation can never be otherwise; if, that is to say, we believe what has been revealed, and if we perceive that men have been dissolved by God, and therefore exalted to be with Him. By faith in the revelation of God we see men bounded, confined, and barred in, but even this is the operation of God. We see men under judgement, yet nevertheless thereby set aright. We see sense in the non-sense of history. We see that truth has burst its bonds. We see in men more than *flesh*. We see salvation breaking through. We see the faithfulness of God remaining firm, even though the noblest human hopes and expectations are dashed to the ground. And so, now that we have beheld what has appeared, been manifested, and displayed, we advance to meet the world, our conversation is of this revelation, and we are occupied in bringing the revelation of God to the notice of those who have eyes to see and ears to hear.

The revelation of the righteousness of God is—**witnessed by the law and the prophets**: it has been *proclaimed long ago* (i. 2). Abraham saw the day when God would judge the world in righteousness; Moses saw it also; the Prophets saw it; Job and the Psalmists saw it. We are encompassed by a cloud of witnesses who stood, all of them, in the light of this day; for the meaning of every epoch in history is directly related to God. In His righteousness every promise is fulfilled. The righteousness of God is the meaning of all religion, the answer to every human hope and desire and striving and waiting, and it is especially the answer to all that human activity which is concentrated upon hope. The righteousness of God is that upon which the whole existence and inevitability of the world is founded, and it is peculiarly visible when the world stands under the negation of judgement. It is the meaning of history, and especially of the complaint of history against its own inadequacy. It is the redemption of all creation, and most particularly when the creature knows itself to be no more than a creature, and so points beyond itself. Wherever there is an impress of revelation —and does anything whatsoever lack this mark?—there is a witness to the Unknown God, even if it be no more than an ignorant and superstitious worship of the most terrible kind (Acts xvii. 22, 23). Where have there not been *certain of your own poets who also* have said it (Acts xvii. 28)? Where there is experience, there is also the possibility of understanding. We proclaim no new thing; we proclaim the essential truth in everything that is old; we proclaim the incorruptible of which all corruptible is a parable. Our theme, therefore, is the theme concerning which the parables speak and to which they bear witness; the theme which eyes have seen and ears heard, and in which men have veritably believed; we proclaim the theme of the Church, which has been believed by all men, everywhere, and at all times.

The righteousness of God is manifested—**through his faith-fulness in Jesus Christ.** The faithfulness of God is the divine patience according to which He provides, at sundry times and at many divers points in human history, occcasions and possi-bilities and witnesses of the knowledge of His righteousness. Jesus of Nazareth is the point at which it can be seen that all the other points form one line of supreme significance. He is the point at which is perceived the crimson thread which runs through all history. Christ—the righteousness of God Himself—is the theme of this perception. The faithfulness of God and Jesus the Christ confirm one another. The faithfulness of God is established when we meet the Christ in Jesus. Consequently, in spite of all our inadequacy, we are able to recognize the veritable possibility of the action of God in all His divers witnesses in history; consequently also, we are able to discover in the traces of the righteousness of God in the world more than mere chance occurrences, and are in a position to see that our own position in time is pregnant with eternal promise, if—nay, because!—we meet truth of another order at one point in time, at one place in that time which is illuminated throughout by reality and by the answer of God. The Day of Jesus Christ is the Day of all days; the brilliant and visible light of this one point is the hidden invisible light of all points; to perceive the righteousness of God once and for all here is the *hope of righteous-ness* (Gal. v. 5) everywhere and at all times. By the knowledge of Jesus Christ all human waiting is guaranteed, authorized, and established; for He makes it known that it is not men who wait, but God—in His faithfulness. Our discovery of the Christ in Jesus of Nazareth is authorized by the fact that every mani-festation of the faithfulness of God points and bears witness to what we have actually encountered in Jesus. The hidden authority of the Law and the Prophets is the Christ who meets us in Jesus. Redemption and resurrection, the invisibility of God and a new order, constitute the meaning of every religion; and it is precisely this that compels us to stand still in the presence of Jesus. All human activity is a cry for forgiveness;

and it is precisely this that is proclaimed by Jesus and that appears concretely in Him. The objection that this hidden power of forgiveness and, in fact, the whole subject-matter of religion, is found elsewhere, is wholly wide of the mark, since it is precisely we who have been enabled to make this claim. In Jesus we have discovered and recognized the truth that God is found everywhere and that, both before and after Jesus, men have been discovered by Him. In Him we have found the standard by which all discovery of God and all being discovered by Him is made known as such; in Him we recognize that this finding and being found is the truth of the order of eternity. Many live their lives in the light of redemption and forgiveness and resurrection; but that we have eyes to see their manner of life we owe to the One. In His light we see light. That it is the Christ whom we have encountered in Jesus is guaranteed by our finding in Him the sharply defined, final interpretation of the Word of the faithfulness of God to which the Law and the Prophets bore witness. His entering within the deepest darkness of human ambiguity and abiding within it is THE faithfulness. The life of Jesus is perfected obedience to the will of the faithful God. Jesus stands among sinners as a sinner; He sets Himself wholly under the judgement under which the world is set; He takes His place where God can be present only in questioning about Him; He takes the form of a slave; He moves to the cross and to death; His greatest achievement is a negative achievement. He is not a genius, endowed with manifest or even with occult powers; He is not a hero or leader of men; He is neither poet nor thinker:—*My God, my God, why hast thou forsaken me?* Nevertheless, precisely in this negation, He is the fulfilment of every possibility of human progress, as the Prophets and the Law conceive of progress and evolution, because He sacrifices to the incomparably Greater and to the invisibly Other every claim to genius and every human heroic or aesthetic or psychic possibility, because there is no conceivable human possibility of which He did not rid Himself. Herein He is recognized as the Christ; for this reason God hath exalted Him; and consequently He is the light of the Last Things by which all men and all things are illuminated. In Him we behold the faithfulness of God in the depths of Hell. The Messiah is the end of mankind, and here also God is found faithful. On the day when mankind is dissolved the new era of the righteousness of God will be inaugurated.

Unto all them that believe. Here is the necessary qualification. The vision of the New Day remains an indirect vision; in Jesus revelation is a paradox, however objective and universal it may be. That the promises of the faithfulness of God have been fulfilled in Jesus the Christ is not, and never will be, a self-evident truth, since in Him it appears in its final hiddenness and its most profound secrecy. The truth, in fact, can never be self-evident, because it is a matter neither of historical nor of psychological experience, and because it is neither a cosmic happening within the natural order, nor even the most supreme event of our imaginings. Therefore it is not accessible to our perception: it can neither be dug out of what is unconsciously within us, nor apprehended by devout contemplation, nor made known by the manipulation of occult psychic powers. These exercises, indeed, render it the more inaccessible. It can neither be taught nor handed down by tradition, nor is it a subject of research. Were it capable of such treatment, it would not be universally significant, it would not be the righteousness of God for the whole world, salvation for all men. Faith is conversion: it is the radically new disposition of the man who stands naked before God and has been wholly impoverished that he may procure the one pearl of great price; it is the attitude of the man who for the sake of Jesus has lost his own soul. Faith is the faithfulness of God, ever secreted in and beyond all human ideas and affirmations about Him, and beyond every positive religious achievement. There is no such thing as mature and assured possession of faith: regarded psychologically, it is always a leap into the darkness of the unknown, a flight into empty air. Faith is not revealed to us by *flesh and blood* (Matt. xvi. 17): no one can communicate it to himself or to any one else. What I heard yesterday I must hear again to-day; and if I am to hear it afresh to-morrow, it must be revealed by the Father of Jesus, who is in heaven, and by Him only. The revelation which is in Jesus, because it is the revelation of the righteousness of God, must be the most complete veiling of His incomprehensibility. In Jesus, God becomes veritably a secret: He is made known as the Unknown, speaking in eternal silence; He protects himself from every intimate companionship and from all the impertinence of religion. He becomes a scandal to the Jews and to the Greeks foolishness. In Jesus the communication of God begins with a rebuff, with the exposure of a vast chasm, with the clear revelation of a great stumbling-block. 'Remove from the Christian Religion, as Christendom has done, its ability to shock, and Christianity, by becoming a direct communication, is altogether destroyed. It then becomes a tiny superficial thing, capable neither of inflicting deep wounds

nor of healing them; by discovering an unreal and merely
human compassion, it forgets the qualitative distinction between
man and God' (Kierkegaard). Faith in Jesus, like its theme,
the righteousness of God, is the radical 'Nevertheless'. Faith
in Jesus is to feel and comprehend the unheard of 'love-less'
love of God, to do the ever scandalous and outrageous will of
God, to call upon God in His incomprehensibility and hiddenness.
To believe in Jesus is the most hazardous of all hazards. This
'Nevertheless', this unheard of action, this hazard, is the road
to which we direct men. We demand faith, no more and no
less; and we make this demand, not in our ôwn name, but in the
name of Jesus, in whom we have encountered it irresistibly. We
do not demand belief in our faith; for we are aware that, in so far
as faith originates in us, it is unbelievable. We do not demand
from others our faith; if others are to believe, they must do so,
as we do, entirely at their own risk and because of the promise.
We demand faith in Jesus; and we make this demand here and
now upon all, whatever may be the condition of life in which they
find themselves. There are, however, no preliminaries necessary
to faith, no required standard of education or intelligence, no
peculiar temper of mind or heart, no special economic status.
There are no human avenues of approach, no 'way of salvation';
to faith there is no ladder which must be first scaled. Faith
is its own initiation, its own presupposition. Upon whatever
rung of the ladder of human life men may happen to be
standing—whether they be Jews or Greeks, old or young, educated or uneducated, complex or simple—in tribulation or in
repose they are capable of faith. The demand of faith passes
diagonally across every type of religious or moral temperament, across every experience of life, through every department
of intellectual activity, and through every social class. For all
faith is both simple and difficult; for all alike it is a scandal, a
hazard, a 'Nevertheless'; to all it presents the same embarrassment and the same promise; for all it is a leap into the void.
And it is possible for all, only because for all it is equally
impossible.

**vv. 22b–24. For there is no distinction: for all have
sinned, and fall short of the glory of God; being justified
freely by his grace through the redemption that is in
Christ Jesus.**

'Note that here is the very centre and kernel of the Epistle
and of all Scripture' (Luther).
There is no distinction. The reality of the righteousness of

God is attested by its universality. It is not irrelevant that it is precisely Paul, who, daring, in Jesus, to put his trust boldly in grace alone, is able, in Jesus, also to perceive the divine breaking down of all human distinctions. Indeed, Paul's courage proceeds from his insight. Because he is the Apostle of the Gentiles, he is the Prophet of the Kingdom of God. Once this interdependence was obscured, there came into being what was afterwards known as 'missionary work'. But this is something quite different from the mission of Paul. His mission did not erect barriers; it tore them down. God can be known only when men of all ranks are grouped together upon one single step; when those of the highest rank regard 'suffering with the whole social order of their age and bearing its heavy burden' (S. Preiswerk) as the noblest achievement of which they are capable; when the rich in spirit think nothing of their wealth—not even in order to share it—but themselves become poor and the brothers of the poor. The Pharisee who prays can indeed become a missionary, but not a missionary of the Kingdom of God. The strange UNION—of men one with another—must assert and expose the strange, and yet saving, SEPARATION—between God and man. In this separation is displayed the righteousness of God. The paradox must be maintained absolutely, in order that the scandal may not be obscured, and in order that Christianity may be disclosed in its true nature as 'a problem which is itself essentially a riddle, and which sets a question-mark against every human achievement in history' (Overbeck). Nothing must be allowed to disturb this paradox; nothing must be retained of that illusion which permits a supposed religious or moral or intellectual experience to remove the only sure ground of salvation, which is the mercy of God. The illusion that some men have an advantage over others must be completely discarded. The words *there is no distinction* need to be repeated and listened to again and again. The demand to believe is laid upon all. All must proceed along the road of faith, and must proceed only along that road; yet it is a road along which no man can go. All flesh must be silent before the inconspicuousness of God, in order that all flesh may see His salvation.

All have sinned, and fall short of the glory of God. Here is exposed the cause of the dissolution of every distinction. The remarkable union is attested by a remarkable separation. There is no positive possession of men which is sufficient to provide a foundation for human solidarity; for every positive possession— religious temperament, moral consciousness, humanitarianism— already contains within itself the seed of the disruption of society.

These positive factors are productive of difference, since they distinguish men from one another. Genuine fellowship is grounded upon a negative: it is grounded upon what men lack. Precisely when we recognize that we are sinners do we perceive that we are brothers. Our solidarity with other men is alone adequately grounded, when with others—or apart from them, since we may not wait for them!—we stretch out beyond everything that we are and have, and behold the wholly problematical character of our present condition. Men *fall short of the glory of God*. The glory of God is his conspicuousness (Gloria divinitas conspicua—Bengel). For us this conspicuousness is lacking; and herein we are united. Consequently, all that is exalted must become abased; and blessed are they who already stand far below. The problem of faith appears where the conspicuousness of God is lacking—*they that have not seen, and yet have believed*; and forgiveness of sins, which is the only relevant salvation, then emerges as a highly significant possibility. The recognition of the need of the forgiveness of sin has nothing in common with pessimism, with contrition and the sense of sin, or with the 'heavy depression' of the 'preachers of death' (Nietzsche); it has no relation to eastern asceticism contrasted with the merriment of the Greeks. The need of the forgiveness of sin might in fact be regarded as a Dionysiac enthusiasm, were it not that it can be placed in no such human category. True negation is directed as much against the denial of this life as it is against the acceptance of it. Both Jew and Greek are set under one condemnation. Our deepest and final deprivation—a deprivation just as real whether we accept or deny the world as it is!— is recognized when we perceive the true and original humanity which lies beyond this world. In his PURITY man is set within the domain of the mercy of God.

Being justified (declared righteous) **freely by his grace.** When we are enabled to hear nothing except the word of the Judge, by which he asserts Himself and by which He upholdeth all things (Heb. i. 3), we know that we stand assuredly and genuinely before God. Our hearing can then be nothing more than faith in God, faith that He is because He is. So long as we are swayed by any other motive except faith, we do not stand before God. Thus all distinctions between men are seen to be trivial. *God declares*: He declares His Righteousness to be the Truth behind and beyond all human righteousness and unrighteousness. He declares that He has espoused our cause, and that we belong to Him. He declares that we, His enemies, are His beloved children. He declares His decision to erect His justice by the complete

renewal of heaven and of earth. This declaration is creatio ex
nihilo, creation out of nothing. Uttered by God from His tribunal,
it is grounded in Him alone, and is without occasion or condition.
Such creation is assuredly genuine creation, the creation of the
divine righteousness in us and in the world. When God speaks,
it is done. But the creation is a new creation; it is not a mere
new eruption, or extension, or unfolding, of that old 'creative
evolution' of which we form a part, and shall remain a part,
till our lives' end. Between the old and the new creation is set
always the end of this man and of this world. The 'Something' which the Word of God creates is of an eternal order,
wholly distinct from every 'something' which we know otherwise. It neither emerges from what we know, nor is it a development of it. Compared with our 'something' it is and remains
always—nothing. However true it is that—THIS mortal must
put on immortality, and THIS corruptible must put on incorruption; nevertheless—*Flesh and blood cannot inherit the Kingdom of
God*—inasmuch as the *putting on* is an act of God, and not a
human action, this mortal remains mortal and subject to corruption: he awaits a radical and qualitative change, a transformation; he awaits, in fact, the Resurrection of the Dead (1 Cor. xv.
50–7). *We await a new heaven and a new earth.* The Righteousness
of God in us and in the world is not a particular form of human
righteousness competing with other forms; rather, *your life is
hid with Christ in God* (Col. iii. 3). If it be not hidden, it is not
Life! The Kingdom of God has not 'broken forth' upon the
earth, not even the tiniest fragment of it; and yet, it has been
proclaimed: it has not come, not even in its most sublime form;
and yet, it is *nigh at hand*. The Kingdom of God remains a matter
of faith, and most of all is the revelation of it in Christ Jesus
a matter of faith. It is heralded and it is nigh at hand as a new
world, not as the continuation of the old. 'Our' righteousness
can be genuine and permanent only as the Righteousness of God.
By *new* must always be understood the eternal world in the
reflection of which we stand here and now. The mercy of God
which is directed towards us can be true, and can remain true,
only as a miracle—'vertical from above'. When the mercy of
God is thought of as an element in history or as a factor in
human spiritual experience, its untruth is emphasized. We
stand really before God, inasmuch as we await in faith the realization of His Word, and inasmuch as we perpetually recognize
that the declaration that we are justified by God in His Presence
takes place *freely by his grace*, and only by His grace. Grace is
the generous and free will of God, His will to accept us; its

necessity proceeds from Him and from Him only. The necessity
of the promise of God that those who in a pure heart lack His
glory shall see Him face to face; the necessity that the imprisoned Truth of God shall break its chains; the necessity that
God shall maintain and show forth His faithfulness, without any
provision by us of an occasion for its display—but simply because He is God; all this necessity is the majestic pre-eminence of
grace. Grace is, then, no spiritual power residing in the man of
this world; no physical energy residing in Nature; no cosmic
power in this earth. Grace is and remains always the Power of
God (i. 16), the promise of a new man, of a new nature, of a new
world: it is the promise of the Kingdom of God. Grace is and
remains always in this world negative, invisible, and hidden;
the mark of its operation is the declaration of the passing of
this world and of the end of all things. Restless, and terribly
shattering, grace completely overthrows the foundations of this
world; and yet, on the Day of days, the creative Word of God
veritably declares the operation of grace to be no mere negation.
Grace is altogether 'Yes'; it is salvation, comfort, and edification. Through the dissolution of the outer man the inner man
is renewed day by day. But all this is true on the Day of all
days through the creating Word; and it must be believed on,
because the creative Word of God has promised it; and we can
believe in it, if our eyes be fixed upon the Day of fulfilment
which has been announced in Jesus.

This creative word is spoken—**through the redemption that is
in Christ Jesus.**

What is there, then, in Christ Jesus? There is that which
horrifies: the dissolution of history in history, the destruction of
the structure of events within their known structure, the end of
time in the order of time. *Hallowed be Thy name! Thy kingdom
come! Thy will be done in earth as it is in heaven!* The Son of man
proclaims the death of the son of man, He proclaims God as
First and Last; and the echo answers: *He taught them as one
that had authority—He is beside himself—He deceiveth the people
—A friend of publicans and sinners.* The answer bears unmistakable witness to the truth of what has been proclaimed. Jesus of
Nazareth, *Christ after the flesh,* is one amongst other possibilities
of history; but He is THE possibility which possesses all the
marks of impossibility. His life is a history within the framework of history, a concrete event in the midst of other concrete
events, an occasion in time and limited by the boundaries of
time; it belongs to the texture of human life. But it is history
pregnant with meaning; it is concreteness which displays the

Beginning and the Ending; it is time awakened to the memory of Eternity; it is humanity filled with the Voice of God. In this fragment of the world there is detached from this world—before the very eyes of men and in their actual hearing!—something which gleams in the darkness and gives to the world a new brilliance; and this 'something' is—Glory to God in the highest, and on earth peace among men in whom he is well pleased!—God Himself, who willeth to draw the whole world unto Himself, and to fashion a new heaven and a new earth. As yet we see but the image of this world and of its dominion. Mighty it is, and lifted up, and very magnificent, terrible to behold, an image of gold and silver, of iron and clay and brass. But in the hidden Life of Jesus we see also the stone fashioned and detached, which smites the image upon its feet and, without any aid from human hands, breaks it in pieces. The whole image is crushed, and the wind carries it away like the chaff of the summer threshing-floors. *But the stone that smote the image became a great mountain, and filled the whole earth* (Dan. ii. 24–35). Satan as lightning is fallen from heaven, his dominion is ended; the Kingdom of God is at hand, and the heralds of His Kingdom are assuredly present: *The blind receive their sight, and the lame walk, the lepers are cleansed, and the deaf hear, the dead are raised up, and the poor have the gospel preached to them; and—blessed is he, whosoever shall not be offended in me.* He that gazes upon this earthly fragment of the world, and perceives in the life of Jesus, and beyond it, the redemption which shall come; he it is that hears the creative Voice of God, and looks henceforward for no other, but awaits all from this redemption and from this Voice of God (Matt. xi. 1–4). Blessed is he who believes what can only be BELIEVED, and what CAN only be believed because of that which is—in Christ Jesus.

vv. 25, 26. Whom God set forth to be a covering of **propitiation, through** his faithfulness, **by his blood, to shew his righteousness, because of the remission of sins done aforetime, in the forbearance of God; for the shewing, I say, of his righteousness at this present time: that he might be just, and the justifier of him that** is grounded upon the faithfulness which abides **in Jesus**.

Whom God set forth to be a covering of propitiation, through his faithfulness, by his blood. In the Old Testament cultus the *covering of propitiation* (EV. *mercy seat*; Hebr. *Kapporeth*; LXX *Hilasterion*) was the sheet of gold, overshadowed by the wings of the two angel-figures (cherubim), which covered and marked the place where the contents of the ark, the oracles of God, were deposited (Exod. xxv. 17–21). In 1 Sam. iv. 4, 2 Sam. vi. 2, Ps. lxxx. 1, it is the place above which God Himself dwells; in Exod. xxv. 22, Num. vii. 89, it is the place from which God speaks to Moses; it is pre-eminently, however, the place where, on the great day of Atonement, the people were reconciled to God by the sprinkling of blood (Lev. xvi. 14, 15). The analogy with Jesus is especially appropriate, because the mercy seat is no more than a particular, though very significant, place. By the express counsel of God, Jesus has been appointed from eternity as the place of propitiation above which God dwells and from which He speaks; now, however, He occupies a position in time, in history, and in the presence of men. The life of Jesus is the place in history fitted by God for propitiation and fraught with eternity—*God was in Christ reconciling the world unto himself* (2 Cor. v. 19). At this place the Kingdom of God is come nigh: so near is it, that here His coming and His redeeming power are recognized; so near, that here God dwells with men and His communing is unmistakable; so near, that here the pressure of faith is a commanding necessity. But, just as in the Old Testament the *Kapporeth* covered the testimonies of God as well as marked their presence among men, so here the Kingdom of God, His atoning activity, and the dawning of the day of redemption (iii. 24), are in Jesus covered as well as displayed. Jesus is presented to us unmistakably as the Christ, but His Messiahship is also presented to us as a sharply defined paradox. It is a matter for faith only. The propitiation occurs at the place of propitiation—only by blood, whereby we are solemnly reminded that God gives life only through death. Consequently, in Jesus also atonement occurs only through the faithfulness of God, *by his blood*: only, that is to say, in the inferno of His complete solidarity with all the sin and weakness and misery of the flesh; in the secret of an occurrence which seems to us wholly negative; in the extinguishing of all the lights—hero, prophet, wonder-worker—which mark the brilliance of human life, a brilliance which shone also in His life, whilst He lived a man amongst men; and finally, in the absolute scandal of His death upon the Cross. By His blood, then, Jesus is proved to be the Christ, the first and last word to men of the faithfulness of God. By His death He declares the impossible possibility of our redemption, and shows Himself as the light from light uncreated, as the Herald of the Kingdom of God. 'In the picture of the Redeemer the dominant colour is blood' (Ph. Fr. Hiller), because, in the way of the Cross, in the offering of His life, and in His death, the radical nature of

the redemption which He brings and the utter novelty of the
world which He proclaims are first brought to light. Brought to
light—nay, rather, put in the shade, when once we recognize
that to comprehend either the radicalism or the novelty of God's
world or the necessary transformation of the hearts of men,
lies beyond our competence—*Behold, this child is set for the
fall and rising up of many in Israel; and for a sign which
shall be spoken against—yea and a sword shall pierce through thine
own soul—that the thoughts of many hearts may be revealed* (Luke
ii. 34, 35). The secret of redemption by the blood of Jesus is, and
remains, the secret of God. Its manifestation also, which is the
invisibility of God becoming visible, is always the action of God,
an act of His faithfulness, or, what is the same thing, an act of
faith. In so far as this occurs and His faithfulness persists, in so
far as the hazard of faith is ventured, the dawn of the new
world, the reality of the mercy of God and of our salvation, of our
future being-clothed-upon with our habitation not made with
hands, eternal, in the heavens (2 Cor. v. 1 ff.), is displayed and
announced, secured and guaranteed to us, in the blood of Jesus.
We stand already, here and now, in the reflection of the things
which are to come; we are perplexed, but not hopeless; smitten
by God, but nevertheless, in this KRISIS, under His healing power.
'Therefore we must nestle under the wings of this mother-hen,
and not rashly fly away trusting in the powers of our own faith,
lest the hawk speedily tear us in pieces and devour us' (Luther).

For the showing of his righteousness. Everywhere there has
been forgiveness of sins, the miraculous outpouring upon men of
the wealth of the divine mercy, signs of the forbearance and
longsuffering of God (ii. 4). Everywhere men are being healed
of the divine wounds. But it is through Jesus that we have been
enabled to see that this is so; through Him the righteousness of
God has been exposed and presented to us; through Him we
have been placed so that we can apprehend history—**sins done
aforetime**—as God sees it, that is to say, in the light of His dissolving mercy; through Him we know the mercy of God to be
the end of all things and the new beginning, and we know what
this means for us—it means that we must be led unto repentance
(ii. 4, vi. 2, 3). Only through Him is the righteousness of God
clearly seen to be the unmistakable governance of men and the
real power in history. By the pre-supposition which has been
given us in Jesus we now see always and everywhere not only
the flesh and the sin, as the law sees (iii. 20), but the Judge who,
in His condemnation, speaks the word of forgiveness wherever
He finds in the *secrets of men* (ii. 16) faithful recognition of His

faithfulness. God is just; and He is the justifier of those who
dare to leap into the void. Believing in Jesus, we believe in the
universal reality of the faithfulness of God. Believing in Jesus,
to us the righteousness and justification of God are manifested
and displayed. This is the pre-supposition by which we can see
ourselves as we are and advance to meet men as they are. In
the light of this presupposition we can dare to do what otherwise
we could never do—to believe in ourselves and in all men. For
this reason and with this pre-supposition we demand coura-
geously of all men (iii. 22) faith—faith in the pre-supposition.
We have peace with God (v. 1), because He is just, and because
He justifies.

BY FAITH ONLY

III. 27–30

**vv. 27, 28. Where then is boasting ? It is excluded. By
what manner of law ? of works ? Nay: but by the law of**
the faithfulness of God! For **we reckon that a man is
justified by** the faithfulness of God **apart from the works
of the law.**

Where then is boasting? It is excluded. To us Jesus has announced the truth which proceeds from beyond the grave. God
is righteous; and He Himself, and He only, declares men to be
righteous. Men are righteous only when their righteousness
proceeds from God, and from Him continuously. From this
pre-supposition it is possible to adopt a critical attitude to the
law, to religion, to human experience, to history, to the inevitability of the world as it is, in fact, to every concrete human
position. In Jesus everything which emerges from men and which
occurs through their agency is subjected to the measurement of
God and by Him pronounced valuable or worthless according to
His pleasure. All existence must be tested, must be disturbed and
weighed in the balance. This critical point of view involves the
apprehension that the world and human history are moving in a
secular and relative context, which is in itself ultimately meaningless; but it involves also the apprehension that they have
meaning as a parable of a wholly other world; that they bear
witness (iii. 21) to a wholly other history; that they are reminis-
cent of a wholly other mankind; that they are, in fact, a parable,
a witness, and a reminiscence, of God. When subjected to this
criticism there is but one aspect of human life which is seen to be
altogether meaningless and incomprehensible. Incomprehensible and meaningless is the view that things—men and their

experiences—are in themselves, apart from their subjection to
the judgement of God and apart from their awaiting His justification, great and important, or are in themselves sufficient to be,
or to desire to be, divine: incomprehensible and meaningless is
all confusing of time and eternity, every intrusion into the
world or appearance in it of the sovereignty of God as a concrete,
tangible thing—and we must include here every 'substratum of
divinity', every 'higher world': unintelligible and meaningless is
all other-worldliness, if other-worldliness is thought of merely
as improved worldliness, all improper notions of immanence,
every non-radical idea of transcendence, every kind of relative
relation between God and man, every divinity which presents
itself as being or having or doing what men are or have or do,
every human figure which calls itself in any way divine. When
all this middle-realm between God and man is clearly recognized,
it must be discarded. Confronted by Jesus, men must die, they
must die daily, save in so far as they stand under the 'No' and
the 'Yes' of God, and are passing from atonement—*by blood* (iii.
25)—to redemption, from the cross to resurrection. That is to
say: so long as men claim to see and know and have and do what is
real, ultimate, and divine, or even conceive of such a possibility;
so long as, failing to recognize that they have nothing which they
have not received and nothing which they must not continue to
receive, they remain unbroken; so long as men have never been
made aware or have ceased to be aware of the paradox of faith;
so long as they have not surrendered or have ceased to surrender
all security and certainty and every concrete ground of comfort,
in order that they may be saved by grace only—they must be
mortified. Men are bereft of every ground of *boasting* except
hope (iv. 18, v. 2, xv. 17). They are bereft of the possibility
of standing upright in the presence of God by appealing to
what, as men, they suppose to be of great importance; just as
they are also bereft of the possibility of standing upright in the
presence of their fellow men by appealing to the one thing which
God regards as of supreme importance. We are deprived of the
possibility either of projecting a temporal thing into infinity or
of confining eternity within the sphere of time. Similarly, it is
impossible for us to detach a fragment of our behaviour from its
human context and to pronounce it to be justified before the
judgement seat of God, just as it is impossible for us to detach
one element from the righteousness of God and to regard it, in
its detachment, as capable of being comfortably inserted within
the structure of human behaviour as it is. Such possibilities are
all *excluded*, and must be cut off. The righteousness of God is a

vast impossibility; and as such it forms an absolute obstacle to the claim of any human righteousness to be either an anticipation of what will finally be or a relic of what once has been. We have nothing of which to boast, nothing past or future, nothing before or after the 'Moment'—which is no moment in time—when the last trumpet shall sound and men stand naked before God, and when, in their nakedness, they shall be clothed upon with the righteousness of God. And so, in the presence of Jesus, all that men are and have and do is perceived to be complete unreality, unless, bowed under the negation of God, they await His divine affirmation. All that men are and have and do is in itself naught but the righteousness of men, and, in the sight of God and men, remains illusion, unless, under the judgement of God, it ceases to be the righteousness of men.

By what manner of law? of works? Nay: but by the law of the faithfulness of God. What is the ground of this pronouncement of impossibility? Why is this pronouncement true, and by what governance is the righteousness of men dethroned? How can we speak of a mortification which neither provides nor desires an opportunity of boasting? And what is the meaning of this dying of men? Is there any law or any religion which can demand this of us? In what piety, or in what experience, or according to what morality, can this death occur? Surely the words 'law', 'religion', 'experience', denote some positive human knowledge or feeling or action or experience—or *work*. Can there, in fact, be any other law except the *law of works*? What can we know of the actions and the works of God? In all this questioning we are threatened by a grave misunderstanding. We may think of knowledge of the Last Things as the supreme achievement of human intelligence; or we may think of silence before God as the final leap of human piety—as, for example, when we read the mystical sayings of Angelus Silesius as so many psychological recipes; or we may suppose that a supreme human experience will be ours, if we take up our position at the eschatological 'Moment' —which is, however, no moment; or we may perhaps imagine the 'wisdom of death' (Overbeck) to be the most up-to-date wisdom of life. But this is the triumph of Pharisaism appearing in a new and far more terrible form; for it is the Pharisaism of humility taking the place of the Pharisaism of self-righteousness. There is no limit to the possibilities of the righteousness of men: it may run not only to self-glorification, but also to self-annihilation, as it does in Buddhism and mysticism and pietism. The latter is a more terrible misunderstanding than the former, because it lies so near to the righteousness of God, and it too is *excluded*—at the last moment. To bow before the negation of God and to await His affirmation is not the last and most courageous achievement of men who are capable of combining perception of God's transcendence with a desire for His immanence. This is still a *boasting* in the *law of works*, which, so long as it is retained, makes even a beginning of the disclosure of the righteousness of God impossible. The man who boasts that he possesses something which justifies him before God and man, even if that something be his own insecurity and brokenness, still retains confidence in human self-justification. No, the solid ground upon which the law of works stands must be completely broken up. No work, be it most delicately spiritual, or be it even a work of self-negation, is worthy of serious attention. In fact, our experience is that which we have not experienced; our religion consists in the dissolution of religion; our law is the complete disestablishment of all human experience and knowledge and action and possession. Nothing human which desires to be more than a void and a deprivation, a possibility and a sign-post, more than the most trivial thing in the midst of the phenomena of this world, survives; nothing which is not, like everything else in this world, dust and ashes—before God. Only faith survives: faith which is not a work, not even a negative work; not an achievement, not even the achievement of humility; not a thing which exists before God and man in its own right. Faith is the ground, the new order, the light, where *boasting* ends and the true righteousness of God begins. Faith is not a foundation upon which men can emplace themselves; not an atmosphere in which they can breathe; not a system under which they can arrange their lives. Regarded from our human point of view, what was once religion and law and a method of life becomes anarchy and a void and an abyss. But the *law of the faithfulness of God*, or, what is the same thing, the *law of faith*, is the place where we are established by God. There there is nothing but God Himself, God only; and there the place is no place; for it is the 'Moment' when men are moved by God, by the true God, the Creator and Redeemer of men and of all human things; the 'Moment' when men surrender themselves and all that they are to God. The 'Moment' of the movement of men by God is beyond men, it cannot be enclosed in a system or a method or a 'way'. It rests in the good pleasure of God, and its occasion is to be sought and found only in Him. *The law of the spirit of life* (viii. 2) is the point of view—which is no point of view!—by which all human boasting is *excluded*.

For we reckon that a man is justified by the faithfulness of God apart from the works of the law. Our transference from the point of view of religion to the point of view of Jesus involves the transference from a well-established attitude towards the relation between God and man to a wholly different method of *reckoning*. All religions either *reckon* that human achievements in this world—some concrete human behaviour or disposition—constitute a claim to the favour of God and must be rewarded by Him (ii. 6); or else they *reckon* that human achievements are themselves the reward of God, since they are the tangible and recognizable products of a transformation of human behaviour that has been wrought by God. So all religions assume either that God will act or that He has acted; making the assumption quite apart from any consideration of the 'Moment' when men stand naked before God and are clothed upon by Him. They do not consider before and after to be before and after the 'Moment' when men are moved by God; or they suppose either that the 'Moment' depends upon some previous behaviour or that it carries with it some subsequent behaviour: that is to say, they conceive of the 'Moment' as in some way comparable and commensurable with human behaviour. Consequently, all religions admit the possibility of boasting of what men are and do and have, as though they were divine. In all religions it is therefore possible to disregard or to escape from the paradox of faith. From the point of view of Jesus, however, we must *reckon* otherwise: fundamentally there are no human *works* sufficiently significant to excite the favour of God; nor are there works so well-pleasing to Him that they become significant in the world. In Jesus everything that occurs in the world is bent under the judgement of God and awaits His affirmation. The words *apart from* cover everything both before and after the 'Moment' when men stand before God and are moved by Him; for no comparison between the 'Moment' and works which are done either before or after it is possible. The Being and Action of God are and remain wholly different from the being and action of men. The line which separates here from there cannot be crossed: it is the line of death, which is, nevertheless, the line of life; it is the end, which is, nevertheless, the beginning; it is the 'No', which is, nevertheless, the 'Yes'. It is God who pronounces and speaks and renders, who selects and values according to His pleasure. And the word which He utters is verily creative, for it brings reality into being. To God belongs what He *renders*: it belongs no longer to men. What God treats as valuable is valuable indeed—but, for this reason, it is not valuable in this world. When the new man arises and the new world appears; when, in the power of the faithfulness of God, the new day dawns; then is His faithfulness glorified by His justification of men. Yet this does not mean that in the light of this new day the man of this world either is glorified or will be glorified, for—*This mortal must put on immortality and this corruptible must put on incorruption.* In so far as the *putting on* occurs by the creative act of God, mortality is taken away from mortality and corruption is removed from corruption. This world is thereby no whit exalted, or established, or transformed. With reference to before and after, the 'Moment' is and remains strange and different; it neither has its roots in the past, nor can it be transmitted to the future. The 'Moment' does not belong in any causal or temporal or logical sequence: it is always and everywhere wholly new: it is what God—who only is immortal—is and has and does. Credo, quia absurdum. Men are forgiven by God only when He condemns them; life rises only from death; the beginning stands at the end, and 'Yes' proceeds from 'No'. Righteousness *by the blood of Jesus* (iii. 25) is always righteousness *apart from the works of law*; apart, that is, from everything human which may, before God and man, be declared righteous. Concerning this righteousness men can boast only in hope—that is, in God. The cross stands, and must always stand, between us and God. The cross is the bridge which creates a chasm and the promise which sounds a warning. We can never escape the paradox of faith, nor can it ever be removed. By faith only—sola fide—does mankind stand before God and is moved by Him. The faithfulness of God can be believed in only, because it is the faithfulness of God. Were it more, it would be less. This is the new *reckoning*.

vv. 29, 30. Or is God the God of the Jews only? is he not the God of the Gentiles also? Yea, of the Gentiles also: seeing that there is one God, and he shall justify the circumcision by faithfulness, **and the uncircumcision through** faithfulness.

Is God the God of the Jews only? is he not the God of the Gentiles also? yea, of the Gentiles also. To have spoken of the truth of the divine word with more assurance would have been less impressive; to have presented in more concrete form what is here perceived would have obscured it; a claim to human certainty would have betrayed ignorance of what is known. God can be apprehended only through Himself and His faithfulness. He is intelligible only by faith. The supposition that He is and has and acts in human fashion robs Him of His divinity; and

any claim to direct relationship with Him depresses Him to the
level of time and things and men, and deprives Him of His true
meaning. The reality of divinity depends upon its universality.
Its universality depends upon every mouth being stopped and
the whole world being guilty before Him (iii. 19); it depends
upon the firm recognition that all men have fallen short of the
glory of God (iii. 23). If relationship with God were to produce
an enhancement of human being and having and doing in this
world, rather than a weakening, or even a deprivation, of these
things, God would become visibly and concretely a spiritual or
historical element in the midst of other elements, differing only
relatively from these other notable spiritual or historical powers
with which men have been endowed. God would then be *the
God of the Jews only*, the God only of certain privileged and well-
disposed people; He would become, like 'religion', a speciality
of certain special circles and epochs and temperaments; He
would be comparatively easy to attain, and to be without Him
would be no very serious deprivation. In that case much use
would be made of the word 'God', but the theme would not be
concerned with righteousness, or redemption, or resurrection, it
would not be concerned with all things, or with the Last Things,
or with Eternity. And therefore what is less—that is, less positively certain and less surely guaranteed—is, in fact, more.
'God' is the eternal, the last word, if we mean 'by faith only',
if we mean the impossible possibility of the faithfulness of
God. In the paradox of faith the faithfulness of God is sufficient,
for through it we stand on firm ground and move forward with
assurance. In this world no union with God is possible. It then
becomes clear that God is the God of all men, the God of the
Gentiles and of the Jews; He is not an element in spiritual
experience or in the course of history; He is, rather, the ground
of all elements, by whom they are measured and in whom they
are contained. He differs absolutely from all our lights and
properties and abilities. This being so, the *everlasting power and
divinity* (i. 20) of God shines forth ever more clearly. When
therefore we use the word 'God', we do not say something but
everything, not the last truth but one, but the last truth of all.
It is the word of judgement, of challenge, of hope; it is directed
to all, and is significant—of supreme significance—for all.

**Seeing that there is one God, and he shall justify the circum-
cision by faithfulness and the uncircumcision through faithfulness.**
In place of the plurality of things which seek to be important
in themselves, in place of all the derived divinities which usurp
authority in this world, there is manifested in Jesus the One-ness

of God. In the righteousness of God, which is known only by faith, is the reality and life and personality of the one Creator and Redeemer. In Jesus is to be found the frame of reference for the co-ordinates of eternal truth, by which, on the one hand, things which normally repel one another (men and men) are held together; and by which, on the other hand, things which normally are mutually attracted (God and men) are distinguished. In the light of this KRISIS God is known and honoured and loved. Here a true understanding of the meaning of the religious phrase 'binding and loosing' is regained. The vast distinction between God and man is their veritable union. Because time and eternity, the righteousness of men and the righteousness of God, here and there, are completely dissociated in Jesus, they are also in Him comprehended and united—in God. All 'law', all human being and having and doing, the whole course of this world and its inevitability, are a sign-post, a parable, a possibility, an expectation. For this reason they are always deprivation and dissatisfaction, a void and a longing. But once this is recognized there appears above them all the faithfulness of God, who forgives by condemning, gives life by killing, and utters His 'Yes' when nothing but His 'No' is audible. In Jesus God is known to be the unknown God. In the light of this KRISIS also the deepest unity of men with men is apprehended, and we regain a true understanding of the individuality, of the historical and personal peculiarity, of the real *advantage* (iii. 1), of each single man. The especial abilities of each individual are not destroyed but realized when he is related to his true purport, which is impossibility. The personality of each man is not destroyed but established by the deep disturbance of this 'Not yet' and this 'No further'. The universal challenge of faith is the creative word which calls men into existence out of the chaos of independent personality. It deprives the circumcised and the uncircumcised of their several boastings: it raises the sinner from his depth and dethrones the righteous from his height. If they stand before God by faith only, they both SHALL—for their present condition is not yet their future rest in God—be justified. The faithfulness of God is where faith is. The *advantage* (iii. 1) begins where *boasting* ceases. This is forgiveness, redemption, and the new creation.

But we know, when we pronounce this, that we are speaking of a possibility of which we are ignorant; a possibility which—and we must repeat it again and again!—can only be believed in.

THE VOICE OF HISTORY

FAITH IS MIRACLE

III 31—IV. 8

v. 31. Do we then make the law of none effect through faith ? God forbid: nay, we establish the law.

Do we make the law of none effect through faith? If we thrust the Resurrection into history, if we set the pre-supposition which is in Jesus within the sequence of events, if we weave the paradox of faith into human spiritual experience, we introduce, as it were, a spectre which devours every living thing. The world would then disappear before God, creation before redemption, experience before apprehension, content before form, and the law would be made of none effect before the sole reality, before the faithfulness of the Lawgiver, which is, however, visible to faith alone. How could we protect such a notion and the criticism which proceeds from it from the dualism of Gnosticism? We could in no way protect it, if the radicalism which here appears be not the extreme radicalism. A negation which remains side by side with the position it negates must itself be negated, and is therefore no truly radical negation. Resurrection ceases to be resurrection, if it be some abnormal event side by side with other events. What, in that case, did rise again? A presupposition which does not apply to every living thing and which is not universally valid, is no absolute, final pre-supposition. The paradox which still retains a relationship with normal spiritual experience, however peculiar or abnormal or even 'ecstatic' it may be, is no real paradox. That Other from which we have come and which is contrasted with all concrete, known, temporal, human existence can be in no manner wholly distinct unless it be in every manner wholly distinct. This complete Otherness is adequately protected only when it is quite strictly the Origin and Fulfilment of human existence, its final affirmation. To *make the law of none effect through faith* is to place faith side by side with the law as another, second, distinct thing, instead of setting it within the law; it is to set Christ side by side with Moses instead of comprehending Moses in Christ. If we do not perceive God's judgement of every human movement and direction to be also that by which they are at once directed; if we do not see in the dissolution by God of all human conduct and desire the doing away of dissolution; if the last question which faith proposes is not—as the last question—at once the answer to all questions—then faith is not faith, and we have concluded wrongly. Such a false conclusion would merely mean that we had been caught up in a reaction and had given expression to a 'resentment'. We should simply have moved in some contrary direction, which itself requires to be dissolved, to be submitted to dialectical criticism, and to be brought back to a final unity.

All this was clearly not intended—**Nay, we establish the law.** Indeed, we rid life and history and spiritual experience of their capriciousness. It is we who proclaim God as Lord of heaven and earth, by naming Him the unknown God; we who recognize the work of the Creator in the creation, by preaching redemption; we who perceive the meaning of all experience, by thrusting it under the light of apprehension; we who retain the eternal truth of the law, by setting forth the paradox of faith as the eternal 'No' of the law. It is precisely we who proclaim the right of the individual, the eternal worth of each single one (Kierkegaard!), by announcing that his soul is lost before God and, in Him, is dissolved—and saved. We demand the subjection of all human being and having and doing under the divine judgement, precisely in order that it may always and everywhere await the divine justification, and because, seen from God and for God, nothing can ever be lost. We remove from the 'Moment' when the last trump sounds all likeness to the past and the future, and thereby proclaim the likeness of all times, of all past and future, for we no longer perceive any past or any future which, in its complete distinction from the 'Moment', does not participate in its dignity and meaning. In the veritable transcendence of the judgement and righteousness of God lies His most genuine immanence. He who is thus in Christ is also he who was and who will be. The revelation in Jesus from which we come is the disclosing of the tireless, necessary reality in the longitude of time. And so it is that history itself bears witness to resurrection, the concrete world to its non-concrete presupposition, and human life to the paradox of faith which is its inalienable foundation. And moreover, the law, rightly understood, bears witness to, justifies, and reveals the faithfulness of God. We do not make the law of none effect, we enable the Law, the Bible, Religion, veritably to speak. We permit them to bear witness (iii. 21) to their proper meaning. We apprehend faith as the meaning of the law, as radical miracle (iv. 1–8), as pure beginning (iv. 9–12), as primal creation (iv. 13–17a),—*we establish the law.*

vv. 1, 2. What shall we say then[1] of Abraham, our fore-father according to the flesh ? If Abraham was justified by works, he hath whereof to glory! but not before God.

What shall we say then of Abraham? We select the venerable and classic figure of Abraham to illustrate the generalization that faith is the meaning of the law. Our task has not been simplified by this selection, for the circumstances of his life were so different from ours that we cannot take our place beside him on the same historical and psychological plane. This selection, however, ought to disclose to us whether the revelation of God in Jesus simply dissolves the law or whether it fulfils it ; whether it is merely some new movement of reform or reaction in the general story of the history of religion, loosely connected perhaps, with the Biblical literature, or whether it is the meaning and substance of the whole history of religion. If the revelation in Jesus be no more than a particular historical happening, an event among other events, a religion among other religions, its relative and incidental and particular character ought to become apparent when contrasted with an occurrence so remote as is the story of the religion of Abraham. If the crimson thread does not run consistently and markedly through history, as in Jesus we suppose it to do ; if it is not the objective link between all, then and now, and here and there; it must snap in our fingers when we say 'Abraham', so great a contrast does he present to what we have seen in Jesus. And also, when it is contrasted with the classical stature, the sterling worth and character, the manifest importance, of that best of men— our forefather according to the flesh—will not all sensible people recognize that negation and deprivation and dissolution of human being and having and doing are merely relative, that resurrection must be understood merely as a shadowy phantom, that radical criticism is pure scepticism, and that the contrast between Abraham and Jesus is no more than a contrast between two characters: in other words, it ought to become evident that the supposed crimson thread is wholly ambiguous and relative. Jesus would not be the Christ if figures like Abraham, Jeremiah, Socrates, Grünewald, Luther, Kierkegaard, Dostoevsky remained, contrasted with Him, merely figures of past history, and did not rather constitute in Him one essential unity; if their positions were merely dissolved by the negation He proclaimed and were not at the same

---

[1] Deleting εὑρηκέναι from the text, since, in spite of strong manuscript support, it would seem to have been interpolated into the text in order to smooth out the grammatical structure of the sentence.

time established. This is the question with which we are concerned. Jesus is established as the Christ, if His light is none other than the light of the Old Testament and of the whole history of religion and of all history; if the miracle of Christmas be the advent of that light, for which the whole world of nature and of men, the whole creation visible and invisible, waits as for its fulfilment. 'The Old Testament did not, in the ordinary sense of the word, "precede" Christ. Rather it lived in Him; or, to put the point in another way, it was the concrete image which accompanied and directly reflected His pre-historical life' (Overbeck). *Before Abraham was, I am.* This is the claim we make for Abraham, but it needs proof.

If Abraham was justified by works, he hath whereof to glory! Abraham's works—his behaviour, disposition, and character, as displayed in his words and actions—are clearly those of a righteous man. He towers above the surrounding paganism; he is possessed of a delicate sense for religion; he is a pure-minded man whose actions declare him possessed of a heroic faith. We expect God to agree with our estimate of the 'righteousness' of Abraham and of men like him. If we were to find that God does in fact declare the visible *works* of Abraham to be righteous, we should be faced by human being and having and doing, which, since they are already justified, clearly require no future justification, and this would be in direct contradiction with what we have already said (iii. 20, 27–31) concerning the divine disturbing and questioning of the whole course of human life. The voice of history proclaims Abraham's fame; it points him out as a remarkable man, a heroic character, and a notable personality. According to this judgement, the righteousness of God, being manifested in the *works* of Abraham, becomes identical with the righteousness of men. And why should not this identity appear elsewhere also? There is, then, here a possible means of escape from the KRISIS of all humanity. And if so, it is no longer necessary for men to proceed along the road which passes through death to life; no longer necessary for them to face the paradox of faith encountered in Jesus. Were there to have existed, even at one point in history, a directly visible divine-humanity or human-divinity, there would indeed be a legitimate ground of boasting, and there would obviously be an easier road to God than the way of death set before us in Jesus. And who would not choose the simpler way? What are we to say to this?

We agree that Abraham has indeed a righteousness of which he can boast—**but not before God.** When a man's behaviour, his mission, his exercise of authority, impress us as being of divine authority, what do we really mean? If we take the word 'divine' seriously, we mean that in this man the invisible has become visible, that what he is calls to mind what he is not, that a secret lies above and behind his behaviour, and is hidden as well as illustrated by his conduct. We do not in any case mean that the secret is to be identified with his actions. When objects are thrown into the shadow by the application of a brilliant light, we do not call the shadow light; nor should we, when the light of the righteousness of God throws the works of men into darkness, call these works righteous. They are neither divinely-human nor humanly-divine; they are, rather, signs of the righteousness of God, and the more clearly they make His righteousness conspicuous, the more certainly are they signs. The *works* which a man does in his concrete and visible life are no more identical with his *work* which is righteous before God than are the fetters with which a prisoner is tightly bound and by which he is led hither and thither against his will, identical with the real limbs of his body. The impression made upon us by a man's works is the memory which they evoke in us of a strange and invisible occurrence. The stronger the impression, the clearer is the recollection. This means that the conspicuous *righteousness* of Abraham and of men like him, their religious genius, the importance of their character and behaviour, may provide a ground of boasting before men and at the bar of history—an ill-advised reading of history may lead to no more than a satisfied boasting in the power of human personality, &c.—*but not before God*. The true ground of boasting before God, however, is repentance (ii.4); this is the work which is valued by God and for which he *renders* (ii. 6). The man whose name is written in the book of God is he that is a *Jew inwardly* and whose *circumcision is that of the heart* (ii. 29). Yet even this is humanly impossible, and is, consequently, invisible to human eyes. Repentance is possible only from God, and is seen only by Him. And moreover, the more obvious it is that conspicuous human achievements point to this further invisible impossibility, the more clearly are they seen and judged to be merely human. The great figures in history are classic figures, not because of their human creative power, but because they are under judgement. Their creative activity is severely limited; a limitation actually displayed by their pre-eminent actions. Moreover, they are themselves aware that their creative genius is so precarious, relative, and arrested, that it provides no ground of boasting. Their positive, absolute, and sure greatness is known only to God, because it rests in Him.

From this it follows that it is not the righteousness of God which is conspicuous in Abraham and in men like him. And if this be so, Abraham, yes, precisely Abraham, stands under the KRISIS of everything human. He proceeds along the road which leads through death to life. His worth, and the possibility of our being able to recognize it, rest in the paradox and miracle of faith. There is no escape from the way of death which is manifested in Jesus.

vv. 3–5. For what saith the scripture? And Abraham believed in God, and it was reckoned unto him for righteousness. Now to Abraham as one **that worketh,** that which is merely his **reward is not reckoned of grace, but of debt. But to** Abraham as one **that worketh not, but** only **believeth on him that justifieth the ungodly, his faith is reckoned for righteousness.**

Abraham believed in God. All that belongs peculiarly to Abraham and his like—their heroism, their mature experience, their conscious or unconscious piety, their notable personalities—is in no way considered righteous before God. Every event in their lives occasioned, as cause and effect, by what precedes it, everything which occurs within the sequence of human life, belongs on this side of the line of death by which men are separated from God, time from eternity. And this remains true, even though such events bear unmistakable witness to that which lies upon the other side. Beyond the line of death is God, the Sustainer Himself unsustained, substantial but without substance, known in His unknowableness, showing mercy in His unapproachable holiness, demanding the obedient recognition of His authority. Merciful in His judgement, He alone is active, for He beareth all things. Because He is not man, He is the true Cause, the House which cannot be dissolved, the first and last Truth, the Creator and Redeemer and Lord of men. To men His ways appear always new, strangely distant, pre-eminent, beyond their horizon and possession. He who says 'God', says 'miracle'. God encounters the soul as 'either–or'; and this involves acceptance or rejection, affirmation or denial, waking or sleeping, apprehension or misapprehension. We, however, are capable only of rejecting, denying, sleeping, and misapprehending. We are incompetent to see what is invisible and to comprehend what is incomprehensible. We have no sensible organ wherewith to perceive the miracle. Human experience and human perception end where God begins. In so far as there is human comprehension and affirmation of God, in so far as spiritual experience is directed towards God, receives its impress from Him, and possesses the form of faith, there has occurred what is impossible, the paradox and the miracle. Abraham's assurance that God is able to perform His word is the impossible assurance (iv. 21); his perception that He would call into being things that are not (iv. 17) is the miracle of perception; his apprehension that Glory (Doxa) belongs to God (iv. 20), moving, as it does, contrary to our opinion (doxa), is the para-dox; and his insight is faith. *Abraham believed.* Here is the action which makes him what he is; here is the hidden source of all his well-known *works* (iv. 2). As a believer Abraham is what he is. In what he is—seer, spiritual and moral hero—his faith—that is to say, what he is not—miracle, the new world, God—is made manifest. If the line of death—his human disestablishment through his establishment by God —be removed from Abraham's faith, its whole significance is removed. For faith would then become no more than a subjective human act, and would be depressed to the level of other relative and precarious human actions. Abraham ceases to be Abraham, if his life be not the consequence of his death. He did not merely believe: he believed—in God (Gen. xv. 6). Thus saith the Scripture.

And it was reckoned unto him for righteousness. The characteristic analogy of *reckoning* or of an entry in an account book (iii. 28) is already in the Genesis narrative used to describe God's favour towards men. In the ledger of life entries are transferred by God from His account to man's account. If men attempt such a manner of reckoning, they are guilty of a fraudulent impossibility (ii. 3). With God, however, such reckoning is both possible and just. The miracle of faith which Abraham encountered was entered in his account as divine righteousness. Contrasted with all human being and having and doing, this transaction is effective and is free, and, because it is free, it is the authentic action of God. Through what they are not, men participate in what God is. By their death they are enlightened by the eternal brilliance of God. His real and powerful action occurs and is encountered only in what men are not, in their death. If faith be an exercise of human competence or disposition or character, it is no more the righteousness of God than is any other human thing. Faith is a vacuum and a limitation encompassed by miracle and by paradoxical impossibility. But because it is void of human content, it is guaranteed by God as His righteousness. The death of Jesus is thus manifested also in the life of Abraham.

To Abraham as one that worketh his reward is not reckoned. The word *reckoned* is used here to mark the distinction between

the notable human righteousness of Abraham and the righteousness of God in which he stands. In so far as his faith was not
miraculous but only the display of remarkable and irrational
heroism, in so far as it was a personal achievement, it would
require for its justification some signal act of grace, of which
there is no mention in the Genesis narrative. As a worker,
Abraham has his reward; if not in the book of life, yet nevertheless in the book of the history of religion, in the record of the
achievements of great men and of delicate souls. Mention must
assuredly be made of the true and good and noble actions of
Abraham and of men like him. He deserves the reward of human
gratitude and respect. This, however, is not a matter of *grace*,
but of clear and obvious *debt*. In the normal course of events he
deserves this reward from men, and he does in fact receive it.
But this direct estimation of a man's historical and psychological
worth has no bearing upon his righteousness before God. It is
the proper estimate of his human righteousness, which is paid
as of debt. If, however, 'God' be involved in this purely human
transaction, it is because He is not thought of as the Creator and
Redeemer and Lord of men whose property is to exercise grace
and to *reckon* righteousness, but as one bound to the notable
works of men as a contractor is pledged to pay the required price
as of debt, if the goods he has ordered be up to sample. Such a
'God' is, however, not God, but the deified spirit of man.

**But to Abraham that worketh not, his faith is reckoned for
righteousness.** There is, however, another method of assessing
human worth: a method employed, for example, both in the
book of Genesis and by Dostoevsky. This method of reckoning
is not concerned to give honour where honour is due. It is not
busied with proving the righteousness of men. It does not overlook or forget the final question, by which the whole procedure
is conditioned. It does not think only of wage-books, but
remembers that there is a Book of Life in which is recorded
the secrets of men which can become known. It is not pre-
occupied with what may be *reckoned* to men *as of debt*, but
with that which is *of grace*. It runs little risk of confusing
the judgements of men with the judgements of God, since
His judgement forms the basis of the whole method of reckoning. It sees the *works* of men upon the background of their
not-working, their lives in the light of their deaths, their
mature nobility by the standard of the sovereignty of God. It
sees their createdness bearing witness to the Creator, and what
is visible in them as void and deprivation, as longing and hope
for that which is invisible. It sees human belief in the light of

faith. It can calmly and with a certain sad humour rejoice in all human greatness, in all confident belief, in all heroism, in all refinement of soul, and in every human achievement in history. It does not, however, finally judge according to these things, but according to the faith which it perceives, contrary to all appearance (para-dox), in all these things. And it supposes that, in thus judging, it is more just than those far too righteous men who are so busy in assigning praise. It can also with the same calm and with a certain smile of forgiveness mourn over all that equally human death in sin, over atheism, heathenism, and degenerate depravity. It does not, however, finally judge according to these things, but according to the faith which it sees, contrary to all appearance (para-dox), in all these things. And it supposes that, in thus judging, it is more just than those far too righteous men who are so busy in assigning blame. It recognizes that in both cases God's reward is rendered according to His pleasure and His valuation (ii. 6), that He does not respect the persons or masks of men (ii. 11), but judges their secrets (ii. 16). It sees faith because it has believing eyes, and because it knows what faith is; the impossibility from which all possibility emerges, the miracle from which proceeds all human experience, the paradox by which all direct and visible human being and having and doing is limited and rendered questionable—and is established and affirmed. And because, itself believing, it sees the faith of men beyond all that they are, because it is able to understand what they are from what they are not, it sees their righteousness as *reckoned*, strictly as the righteousness of God, as the divine 'nevertheless' and not as a divine 'therefore', as forgiveness and not as an imprimatur upon what men are.

He believeth on him that justifieth the ungodly. The meaning of the words *He believeth in God* is here interpreted by a paraphrase, in which Abraham's righteousness is defined. Abraham never 'possessed God': God possessed him. Abraham was God's possession—as one that *worketh not* (iv. 5) and *apart from works* (iii. 28). The occasion of this *possession* does not lie in Abraham, but in God that *justifieth* him. In Abraham it is the wrath of God which is established. Before God, Abraham's human righteousness and unrighteousness is merely *ungodliness* (i. 18). Like all other men, Abraham stands under negation. That he awoke to his position and was aware of the KRISIS, that in this KRISIS he feared God, that he heard the 'No' of God and understood it as His 'Yes'—this is Abraham's faith. In righteousness such as this there can be no *boasting*. Through the classic figure of Abraham we learn the truth that we can boast only in the righteousness which has been manifested *by the blood of Jesus* (iii. 25) and which is *reckoned* unto men. This great, positive affirmation cannot be understood in isolation, but only in the context of the negation of the Last Trump. When it is affirmed in the book of Genesis that Abraham has a righteousness of which he can boast, it must be understood as the model which points to the life of Christ and directs attention to the pre-eminence and purity and earnestness of the 'Moment' with which everything which was before and which shall be hereafter is contrasted—as that which is the sign-post to the Resurrection. The miracle of faith is always the same miracle.

vv. 6–8. Even as David also pronounceth a blessing upon the man, unto whom God reckoneth righteousness apart from works, saying, Blessed are they whose iniquities are forgiven, and whose sins are covered! Blessed is the man to whom the Lord will not reckon sin.

Even as David also pronounceth a blessing upon the man, unto whom God reckoneth righteousness. The Psalter provides a commentary upon the biographies contained elsewhere in the Old Testament. Accordingly we here encounter that manner of outlining human life indirectly which is so characteristic of the Biblical literature. Who is pronounced blessed? Is it the man who possesses heaven and carries it about with him? is it the man who deserves blessedness and displays it in his works? Assuredly not. David is certainly not referring to such blessedness as this. He does not see the blessedness of men, their meritorious pre-eminence and salvation, as a concrete and visible thing. He looks beyond the advantages or disadvantages which belong to men as individuals, and which are capable of psychological analysis. His eyes are fixed upon an invisible relationship between God and men, *apart from works.* His interest is centred upon a divine disposition which, psychologically considered, is merely a vacuum. And in this invisible relationship, which is the righteousness reckoned by God, he beholds the whole fullness and significance of human personality. His blessing is pronounced upon this *reckoned* and invisible life out of death.

Blessed are they whose iniquities are forgiven, and whose sins are covered! Blessed is the man unto whom the Lord will not reckon sin, *and in whose mouth is no guile. When I kept silence, my bones waxed old through my roaring all the day long. For day and night thy hand was heavy upon me. I came into so great misery that my backbone stiffened. I acknowledged my sin unto thee, and mine iniquity have I not hid: I said I will confess my*

*transgressions unto the Lord; and thou forgavest the iniquity of
my sin* (Ps. xxxii. 1–5: LXX). The sequence of thought is
remarkable. What is the righteous life of the pious men of the
Old Testament? Is it not true that their concrete and visible
existence is neither righteousness nor life? The presumption of
righteousness and of life is precisely the *guile* which must be
removed. The Psalmist desires to be silent concerning his *sin*—
that is, concerning the contrast between his piety and that to
which his piety bears witness—and concerning the *iniquity* of his
heart—that is, concerning the unavoidable idolatry of all human
worship; he longs to conceal his wickedness with illusions; he
hopes that, if his transgressions are submerged in the rightness
of his general behaviour, they may be pardoned. He wishes to
live out his own personal life, and not to die in the presence of
God. But over his whole endeavour there hangs the sentence of
death; and, wedged in between the truth of God and the guile
of his own heart, he roars all the day in actual physical pain.
Gripped firmly by God, his own personal arrogance can breathe
no longer, and cries aloud; throttled by lies, the soul, God's
creation, can live no longer, and cries out. Fallen, as into a
crevasse, he groans in pain, like some speechless Zacharias or
blinded Saul, until he gives himself up as a prisoner to God
and crushes every tendency to boast, until he *acknowledges* the
impossibility of acquiring for himself the righteousness of
God and recognizes the inexorable 'No' that is set against all
human righteousness and the judgement to which the whole
illusion of religion is subjected. Thus it is that in fear and
trembling he perceives the line of death running through human
life. Then at last he *acknowledges*, and conceals nothing. He
confesses—*and thou didst forgive me*. Out of the whirlwind God
answers him. But what is the answer? Is it some new, deep,
positive, religious experience? Surely not. His inner life is
radically broken down. This is no psychological occurrence;
rather, it is the advent of the 'Moment' which is beyond all time,
by which everything before and after is set in a new context.
This does not mean that the tribulation and distress of the
righteous man is at an end! It is, however, now made
evident that he suffers for God's sake, that his crying is a
crying unto God. Nor is the iniquity and sinfulness of the
creature at an end! It does, however, now become evident
that there is hope: hope that they have been forgiven, covered,
and not reckoned. Here once more is the miracle of faith
operating beyond the direct, visible reality of men's lives. In
His 'No' God utters His 'Yes'. This new relation between God

and man can occasion no fresh delusion or deceit, for it is based upon a criticism so radical as to exclude all human boasting. The blessing of 'David' is therefore no blessing pronounced upon the life and righteousness of the man of the world or upon what is conspicuous in him; it concerns the inner invisible man, called into being by the creative action of God, which is day by day renewed in the death of the man of the world. This miracle of the reckoning of the divine righteousness, this non-reckoning of human unrighteousness, which is seen only in the visibility of death, is the paradox of faith. By it the pious man is pronounced blessed. What is true of Abraham is therefore true also of the anonymous figure portrayed in the 32nd Psalm. Both are witnesses of the Resurrection, and both live by it. As independent historical figures apart from Christ, they are incomprehensible. They are types of that life of His which is prolonged longitudinally throughout the whole extent of time.

FAITH IS BEGINNING

IV. 9–12

v. 9a. Is this blessing pronounced first **upon the circumcision, or** already **upon the uncircumcision also?**

We have seen in ch. iii. 21, 27–30 that, contrasted with the visible concreteness of religion, the righteousness of faith is peculiar, new, and strange. In its pure other-worldliness we have found it to be the beginning and truth of all religion. We are no longer permitted either to regard it as a thing in history or to subject it, as though it could be identified with religious experience, to psychological analysis. It is neither a constant factor traceable throughout the evolution of human being and having and doing, nor is it a special department of Church History or of the History of Comparative Religion, nor can it be disclosed in the so-called History of Salvation. All these, it is true, bear witness to the faithfulness of God; yet nevertheless, in relation to the concrete things of the law and to all the ramifications of human impressions of revelation, He remains entirely free. Now, can it be shown that the law is not hereby made of none effect, but is established (iii. 31), and that hereby we elucidate the true meaning of historical revelation and do it veritable honour? The problem should be stated as follows: Does the true claim of religion depend upon its being treated as a concrete factor in human life, forming a necessary preliminary to the emergence of a positive relationship between God and man? Does it claim that

God is able to reveal Himself only within the sphere of those
visible impressions of revelation preserved in the piety of the
Church or in that wider field to which we give the name of
'Religion'? Does the blessing pronounced in the law (iv. 6–8)
concern *first* the circumcised Abraham, the Jew, the confessor
and representative of the supreme religion, the father of a
peculiar race and of a particular historical brotherhood? Or, on
the contrary, can the essential meaning of religion be understood
only if its concreteness is conditioned solely by the primal relation
between God and man? Does not religion itself perceive this
relation to be free and unfettered? Does it not itself regard it as
pure Beginning? Does it not look beyond itself and beyond its
own reality to that by which men are established? Does not
it recognize that the place where God wills to reveal Himself
cannot be identified with its own concrete and visible possessions,
but is incomprehensibly more comprehensive? Is not the blessing pronounced upon the pagan and uncircumcised Abraham,
quite apart from his works, apart, that is, from his notable
position in the story of the evolution of religion, theocracy, and
salvation? Is not the blessing pronounced upon him in the non-
particularity of his humanness and createdness? Is it not thus
that we are justified? Is it not necessary for us to perceive that
the line of life which marks the true relation between God and
man is, in its critical significance, the line of death, and that this
applies even to the reality of religion? Are we not compelled
to set the righteousness of faith over against all religious and
ecclesiastical being and having and doing, and to see in it the
true Beginning?

vv. 9b, 10. **For we** read: **To Abraham his faith was
reckoned for righteousness. How then** are we to understand that **it was reckoned? when he was** already **in circumcision, or** whilst he was still **in uncircumcision?**
Clearly, **not** when he was already **in circumcision, but**
whilst he was still **in uncircumcision**.

**For we read : To Abraham his faith was reckoned for righteous-
ness.** The voice of the law and the history of salvation lay
emphasis upon the significant word *reckoned* (iv. 3) ; and we must
follow up the hint which they provide. They are not concerned
with the peculiarity of Abraham's directly visible status. His
righteousness is clearly distinct from his *circumcision*. In any
case, his circumcision is not the divine reckoning, neither is circumcision the divine action which makes him what he is. There is
no miracle either in the act of circumcision or in its significance.

By it he is visibly incorporated into the sphere of visible religion. In so far as the righteousness of Abraham was effected by, and included in, his circumcision, it was a religious righteousness, not that other, *reckoned* righteousness of God, to which reference is made in the book of Genesis.

Clearly, not when he was already in circumcision, but whilst he was still in uncircumcision, was Abraham's faith reckoned for righteousness. According to the law, the reckoning of righteousness unto Abraham can be comprehended only against the background of his uncircumcision, which, it must be remembered, is also a real status in history. When God called him, Abraham was still unrighteous; he was not yet the Patriarch, not yet the representative of theocracy. Even in the temporal sphere the call of God in actual fact precedes the contrasts, circumcised—uncircumcised, religious—irreligious, ecclesiastical—secular. Thus Abraham's faith is not yet circumcision, not yet religion, is not yet accompanied by pious spiritual experiences. Faith is the pre-supposition which underlies these contrasts, which brings them together as contrasts. Faith is neither religion nor irreligion, neither sacred nor profane; it is always both together. In the Genesis narrative the call and the faith of Abraham without doubt constitute the pure Beginning. They are given first and without any occasion. From the standpoint of the history of religion, Abraham is a pagan, and not a Jew; from the standpoint of the history of salvation, he is one of the *ungodly* (iv. 5), a dead man (iv. 12), still impious, and not yet the father of the people of God, which he afterwards became. The world is the world; and Abraham is a man of the world. The word *reckoned* now becomes intelligible. If religious rightness, which is the product of circumcision, is both chronologically and substantially excluded from the picture of Abraham, he has nothing wherewith to clothe his nakedness before God, except that which lies beyond the range of religious phenomena, and is visible only to God, and has value only because it owes its existence to God alone. Since there is nothing left to Abraham except his faith, there is then nothing which can be *reckoned* (iv. 5) except the hearing of that which no ear can hear; except, that is to say, faith. The Genesis narrative emphasizes the invisible righteousness of Abraham, which is his faith. This means that righteousness is there apprehended as the being and having and doing of God, contrasted with the circumscribed series of the world's happenings, in the midst of which religion achieves its victories. To assert that the concrete reality of religion fails to provide the pre-supposition of the relation between God and man, is in complete accord with the

meaning of religion itself. The relation between God and man
precedes, is the Beginning of, and is pre-supposed by, the concrete reality of religion, just as it precedes that which is opposed
to religion! The blessing pronounced upon the pious man (iv.
4–8) is a blessing pronounced upon the man who is not yet pious
(iv. 9). It is a blessing pronounced upon his faith, not upon his
orthodoxy; and righteousness before God is not something
which must be added to the faith either of the pious or of the
impious man.

**vv. 11, 12. And he received the sign of circumcision as
a seal of the righteousness of the faith which he had while
he was in uncircumcision: that he might be the father of
all them that believe, though they be in uncircumcision,
that righteousness might be reckoned unto them also;
and the father of circumcision also, to them who are not
only born of the circumcision, but who also walk in the
steps of that faith of our father Abraham which he had
in uncircumcision.**

He received the sign of circumcision as a seal. The true reality
of all impressions of revelation consists in their being signs,
witnesses, types, recollections, and sign-posts to the Revelation itself, which lies beyond actual reality. Abraham participated also in this typical concrete world: in Circumcision, in the
Church, and in Religion. Circumcision appeared necessarily, as
a physical reminder to Israel of its divinely appointed particularity. Israel was purified and sanctified as the elect people
of God. Religion is the unavoidable reflection in the soul—
in experience—of the miracle of faith which has occurred to
the soul. The Church, from which we can never escape, is the
canalization in history of that divine transaction in men which
can never become a matter of history. The distinction between
the moral and actual content of religion and the divine form by
which it is given character and meaning is absolute and final.
As some noble and spacious flight of vaulted steps springs up
from the ground, and ends, may be, in the fresh open air, so the
rich matter of religion leads out beyond itself. The wealth of
religion has, however, its own peculiar danger, for its proper
function may be misunderstood. Instead of pointing beyond
itself, it may be erected, like some great pyramid, as an immense
sepulchre within which the truth lies mummified in wood and
stone. True religion is a seal, reminding men that they have been
established by God and that they will be established by Him; it
reminds them also of their dissolution and of their redemption,

and of the daily renewed faithfulness of God. As a seal, it points
onwards to the covenant between God and man, which still remains unfulfilled, and which still awaits its inauguration. The
signing of a contract must not be confused with the decision which
preceded it or with the execution which will follow it. Similarly,
the decision of God eternally precedes the *sign*, and the purpose
of God stretches eternally beyond it. The matter of religion
stands midway between the Alpha and Omega of God, between
the Beginning and the End. It has meaning only through its
relation to the Beginning and the End, of which it is a sign and
to which it bears witness. Standing in this retrospective and
prospective relationship, Abraham received the sign of circumcision, and participated in the concrete life of Religion and of
the Church.

**As a seal of the righteousness of the faith which he had while
he was in uncircumcision.** As an uncircumcised believer, Abraham received the sign of circumcision. He was not yet all that
was to be comprehended in the word 'circumcision'; he was
not yet the 'Friend of God', if the phrase denotes one who has
separated himself from the Gentiles; he was not yet a believer,
if the word 'believer' denotes a 'religious personality'. Without
tangible religious experience, he became aware of the judgement
and mercy of God; outside the sphere of the Church and without
participating in its life, he became the human medium of the
covenant between God and man. Nevertheless, he was not as
yet a suitable and selected minister of the covenant, as the
Church understands selection and suitability. His faith *while he
was in uncircumcision* is reckoned unto him for righteousness, and
circumcision is its subsequent and provisional seal and token.

That he might be the father of them that believe. Abraham's
circumcision is therefore significant, not because it conditions or
effects a relationship, but because it makes known the relationship which has come about. It is the token of reality, not reality
itself; and its eternal importance depends upon the line of death
by which Religion is marked as belonging only to the world of
concrete appearance. Circumcision, Religion, the Church, do not
possess positive content: they are tokens and signs which must
be understood negatively, and they are established only in so far
as their independent significance diminishes and finally dies.
The circumcision of Abraham does not require circumcision, his
piety does not require religion; his separation does not require
separation; his theocratical position does not require churchmanship. His pre-eminent moral and historical position does not
impose upon men an ever-developing tradition. All these things,

which are, and can be, no more than signs, ought to point to that which eternally precedes them and extends infinitely beyond them. These temporal things deliver their message precisely as they withdraw and decrease and die in the presence of that eternity in which every finite thing is comprehended. They ought to speak to all as to children of Abraham, as the message was delivered to Abraham himself. The temporal holiness of the saints is the service that they render to the eternal holiness of God; it is, as Grünewald has depicted it,[1] the witness of John the Baptist to that which lies beyond the line of death. The significance of Abraham's circumcision, religion, and churchmanship is indirect. They invite men to faith, not to circumcision; they make men aware of his invisible and *reckoned* righteousness, not of his religion; they summon men to bend before the incomprehensible God, not to embrace Judaism. *In thy seed* (name) *shall all the nations of the earth be blessed; because thou hast obeyed my voice* (Gen. xxii. 18). Abraham's circumcision is, however, not merely a token, for it also effects its purpose, namely, the faith of the uncircumcised. Circumcision is not itself the gate through which Gentiles become Jews or through which men of the world become pious; but it does effectually call to mind the gate through which Jews and Gentiles, in spite of vast differences of temperament and of environment, enter the Kingdom of God. Though not itself the Beginning, it is, nevertheless, its sign. It demands and promises that faith which is *reckoned*, and which veritably is—righteousness before God. In so far as Circumcision, Religion, and the Church, are set in this context and serve this purpose, in so far as they are recognized as factors in this world and are humbled by this recognition, in so far as their activities are directed towards *the faith of the uncircumcised*, they are themselves qualified as righteousness and share in the eternal significance of the Beginning and the End. If, however, they seek to be something more than of this world, something more than the faith of the uncircumcised, if with the arrogance of religion they claim to possess a reality which does not belong to them, they are and must remain disqualified—even in this world.

If Abraham is—**the father of circumcision also,** he is so, in so far as they of the circumcision—**walk in the steps of that faith of our father Abraham which he had in uncircumcision.** The Jews therefore must first become Gentiles, the religious irreligious, churchmen men of the world, rather than vice versa. And yet,

---

[1] The reference is to the crucifixion in the 'Isenheim Altarpiece' painted by Matthias Grünewald (c. 1480–1530), and now in the Museum at Colmar in Alsace. [Tr.]

this is a dangerous manner of expressing the truth; for the deprivation of the Gentiles no more provides the true Beginning than does the advantage of the Jew. Minus has no pre-eminence over plus. It must, however, be clearly stated that faith is always and essentially *faith apart from circumcision*. Whether it be encountered among those who possess religion or among those deprived of it, faith, as pure Beginning, lies beyond the positive content of history and of inner religious experience. The Jewish religion forms but a part of the wider world to which the revelation of God is promised and in which it is encountered. The world is not broken up into fragments; it is one whole, encompassed and sustained by the mercy of God. The circumcised are children of God, not because they stand within Jewish religious and ecclesiastical tradition, but on account of that other conspicuous 'tradition' and continuity of faith, which lies beyond tradition, and in which the living unity of God is perpetually displayed (iii. 29, 30). They are those who *walk in the steps of that faith of our father Abraham which he had in uncircumcision*. They know that, when men, regardless of the extent of their religious or other possessions, are wholly directed towards God and towards Him only, they are found by Him and established by Him. Such men are pilgrims, prepared always for surrender and dissolution, ready always to decrease in honour, ever tireless in descending the ladder of renunciation and death. To be pilgrims means that men must perpetually return to the starting-point of that naked humanity which is absolute poverty and utter insecurity. God must not be sought as though He sat enthroned upon the summit of religious attainment. He is to be found on the plain where men suffer and sin. The veritable pinnacle of religious achievement is attained when men are thrust down into the company of those who lie in the depths (iii. 22, 23). The true faith is the *faith of Abraham which he had in uncircumcision*; the true children of Abraham are they whom God is able to raise up *of these stones*. Where this is overlooked, the first must become the last, for only the last can be first.

FAITH IS CREATION

IV. 13–17a

v. 13. For not through the law was the promise to Abraham or to his seed, that he should be heir of the world, but through the righteousness of faith.

The promise that he should be heir of the world. The command that men should replenish and subdue the earth is here once more laid down. Permission is given to men to rule over all that God has made very good. Putting this in a reverse form: Abraham received the promise by anticipation. The blessedness of every creature is seen in a perspective which stretches beyond Isaac, Abraham's unexpected son, and beyond Jacob (Israel) to the Messiah, who, because He is the true Man from Heaven, is true humanity upon earth. This is the theme and meaning of the life of Abraham. Because he received the promise, he is the classic figure of the law (Gen. xviii. 17–19). He received the clear impression of revelation, and therefore Israel, as his seed, does him honour and claims spiritual kinship with him. Israel's peculiarity consists in readiness and longing to participate in the promise which he received; Israel's history is the story of the varieties of behaviour which this longing has occasioned; Israel's hope is the ceaseless desire to escape from the vicissitudes of history and to receive the promise.

Two questions now become urgent. In the first place, does the promise that, under the blessing of God, Israel should be the heir of the world, also constitute her the mediator of the blessing to the world? And secondly, has not Israel actually received the promise, and will she not always continue to receive it? No doubt a great possibility belongs to Israel. The real question, however, concerns the manner in which she participates in it. Does she participate—**through the law** or—**through the righteousness of faith**? The promise was made to Israel in the law by means of a series of impressions of revelation vouchsafed to Abraham and to others like him. It was, that is to say, made to a particular historical people. The problem is whether their peculiar status and history does or does not confer the promise positively and powerfully. Do the desire and readiness to reproduce Abraham's behaviour, which are the characteristic feature of Israel's history, constitute in themselves the ground of her peculiarity? Do the tradition and behaviour of Israel make her history the history of salvation? Does her fixity of hope create and appoint her children the true children of Abraham? Does Israel rightly understand the law, when she supposes that her status is conferred by her law, and by her history, and by her fixity of hope? Supposing, however, that we deny this altogether, and prefer to find the meaning of the law in its competence to testify and bear witness, rather than in any power conferred by it; do we thereby make the law of none effect (iii. 31)? Surely not; for does not the status conferred by the law point beyond itself to a creative power of a totally different kind? Does not the concrete likeness to Abraham, visible in his children, reflect a light which comes from elsewhere and which in no way belongs to Abraham? Is not the history of Israel the history of salvation, because it forms the boundary at which an unhistorical happening occurs, and because it is the audible answer to the inaudible voice of the divine call? Is not the hope of Israel the product of this peculiar situation? Nevertheless, when it is seen that the real meaning of the law is that, through the righteousness of God which is the righteousness of faith *apart from the law*, the children of Abraham are brought into being and established, the honour of the law is most surely vindicated.

v. 14. For if they which are of the law be heirs, faith is made void, and the promise is made of none effect.

In the book of Genesis it is written that Abraham received the promise *through faith*. This means that, through the creative efficacy of faith, he became the first expectant heir of the Messianic Kingdom (Gen. xv. 6). Faith, it is true, has also its 'legal' aspect, and may then be described as a positive status. But if faith be thought of from this legal and visible point of view, if it be regarded as a condition capable of human attainment, it is manifestly deprived of its dynamic power and remains insecure. If Abraham and his children are what they are *through the law*, faith is evacuated. But faith establishes certainty when it is the advance into what is invisible and eternal, and when it is itself invisible. Every visible status, every temporal road, every pragmatic approach to faith, is, in the end, the negation of faith. Faith is faith, only when it is an 'advance', possible and comprehensible because it comes from God alone, and from God Himself. Faith is creative, only in so far as it is light from light uncreated; living, only when it is life from death; positive, only if by it men are grounded upon the groundlessness of God. Only when it is thus understood is faith *reckoned for righteousness*, and can men through faith become recipients of the divine promise. Apart from this divine authentication of the visible and human impressions of revelation in the law, even the most deep-seated, most sincere, most fiery faith is —unbelief. When faith ceases to be faith, the promise, which can be received only by faith, is suspended also. For the promise which Abraham receives can be neither seen nor described; it is beyond all possibility and beyond all concrete reality. The world which has been blessed and made *good* by God is beyond our comprehending, nor is it possible to transform the dominion of men over this God-created world into an object of human historical endeavour. The Messiah who brings this sovereignty

is, in any case, not man, as we understand humanity. The
grace of redemption, like the grace of creation, is no concrete
thing in the midst of other concrete things. Grace is the invisible
relationship in which all things stand; and the knowledge of it
remains always a dialectical knowledge. The promise has no
point of contact with Abraham's 'Biblical outlook', or with
Israel's disposition of hope, or, in fact, with any positive human
status. The promise agrees with faith, since both involve the
extremity of negation. If the promise be not received through
faith, it is not received at all; it remains no more than an
eschatological myth, which, like other myths, is suspended in
mid-air. If it be not comprehended by faith, it can be comprehended by no substitute for faith: it cannot be experienced or
seen in an 'ecstasy'; it can neither be heard nor seen nor felt.
If we be heirs through the law, we are veritably dispossessed
and excluded from all expectation of the promised heritage. We
are not Abraham or his children.

v. 15. For the law apart from faith **worketh** for men not
the promise but **the wrath** of God; **but where there is no
law, neither is there transgression.**

The law worketh wrath. By this we mean that the law, in
itself and apart from faith, forms an actual obstacle to the
inheritance of the Kingdom of God. This does not mean, of
course, that the law is valueless apart from faith. Indeed, in
assessing the value of the law, no regard need be paid to its
function of testifying and bearing witness to what lies beyond it.
Regarded as a concrete experience from which there emerges a
particular disposition and behaviour, it certainly has significance
in itself, and possesses a brilliance of its own. But we must be
careful to harbour no illusions here, lest we be tempted to define
faith in terms of experience. Any attempt to stretch the relation
between concrete and temporal things to cover their eternal
Origin ends in destructive and incurable scepticism. The claim
that the law *worketh* the promise breaks down on the plain
truth that what is concrete and visible is incompatible with the
promise. The only conspicuous element in the promise is that it
is not coterminous with the actual and moral impressions in the
world of God's revelation. Since the law shares in the corruptibility of the world, it *worketh* not the promise. And indeed, if it
be regarded as possessing reality, rather than as testifying to it,
it *worketh—wrath*. Hence, when the law claims to possess in
itself ultimate reality and to be like God, it becomes *ungodliness*
and *unrighteousness* (i. 18), and attracts to itself the wrath of

God. This inevitability of judgement affects all religions in so far as their reality is merely the reality of temporal and concrete things. It affects religion, even when it is upright and sincere and genuine, even the religion of Abraham and of the Prophets, even the religion of the Epistle to the Romans—and it affects, of course, the religion of any one who undertakes to expound the Epistle. In this context the word 'law' embraces all who set out to experience the infinite, all who venture upon its contemplation or description or representation. This is always transgression. Whenever men suppose themselves conscious of the emotion of nearness to God, whenever they speak and write of divine things, whenever sermon-making and temple-building are thought of as an ultimate human occupation, whenever men are aware of divine appointment and of being entrusted with a divine mission, sin veritably abounds (v. 20)—unless the miracle of forgiveness accompanies such activity; unless, that is to say, the fear of the Lord maintains the distance by which God is separated from men (i. 22, 23). No human demeanour is more open to criticism, more doubtful, or more dangerous, than religious demeanour. No undertaking subjects men to so severe a judgement as the undertaking of religion. The whole rich abundance of the worship of God, from the grossest superstition to the most delicate spirituality, from naked rationalism to the most subtle mysticism of the metaphysician, is under suspicion both from above and from below. God treats it as arrogance, and men as illusion. But we must beware of running to the opposite misunderstanding. If religion is nebulous and lacking in security, so also is everything which is exalted to oppose religion. Antireligious negation has no advantage over the affirmations of religion. To destroy temples is not better than to build them. The silence of devotion is not superior to the words of the preacher. Amaziah AND Amos, Martensen AND Kierkegaard, all the protestations against religion from Nietzsche down to the most degraded and loud-voiced anticlericals, the whole anti-theological romanticism of aestheticism, socialism, and the Youth Movement in its multifarious ramifications, are without exception enveloped in haze, and incompetent to provide security. And the haze solidifies into the cloud of the wrath of God. So long as religious as well as anti-religious activities fail to draw attention to that which lies beyond them, and so long as they attempt their own justification, either as faith, hope, and charity, or as the enthusiastic and dionysiac gestures of the Anti-Christ, they are assuredly mere illusion. Everything which seeks to justify itself, whether by affirmation or by

negation, is under the sentence of judgement. Those who
believe in immanent reality should ponder well the words—*the
law worketh wrath.*

But where there is no law, neither is there transgression. There
is, however, a justification of the Prophet and of the Pharisee,
of the practice of religion in its genuine and penetrating as well
as in its less real and more superficial forms. It is also possible
to justify anti-religious behaviour. But this justification is by
faith only. By faith—in so far as law, the whole concrete visibility of human behaviour, does not condition and control it.
By faith—in so far as faith, as a positive or negative experience
in this world, is rid of all arrogance and aware of its own emptiness before the pure 'No' of God. By faith—in so far as it
stands on the critical line which divides the *religiosus* Luther
from the *religiosus* Erasmus, and which separates the anti-
religiosus Overbeck from the anti-*religiosus* Nietzsche; that
is to say, in so far as faith is the relating of the whole content
of human life to its eternal Origin and the awareness of the life
which proceeds from death. If this invisible aspect of faith be
paramount, *transgression*, affecting, as it does, its visible aspect,
cannot be paramount. When therefore religion, or anti-religion,
is concerned to point beyond itself, it loses its ambiguity,
and absolute scepticism is deprived of all right. And so there
appears, or at least can appear, the justification of sacrifice and
prayer and preaching, of prophecy and mysticism and pharisaism, of theology and piety and churchmanship, of Catholicism
and Protestantism, of books like the Epistle to the Romans
where the paradox is clearly stated, and even of other books
where the paradox is, to a greater or lesser extent, glossed over.
But the justification appears only under the compulsion of the
divine 'Nevertheless', in the recognition of the ever-recurring
necessity of the forgiveness of sins, in a fearful and trembling
consciousness that there is no human or pragmatic road which
may be prolonged so far as to justify itself before God and man.
Justification can be found only in the light of God's sincerity
and of His irony. The use of the words 'in so far as' allows the
possibility of clothing the divine in the garment of the human,
and of the eternal in a temporal parable. But this can be permitted only when the possibility is recognized as the impossible
possibility. We must not conclude from this that we have
achieved a secure standing place. We have done no more than
make room for the 'Moment' which has no before and no after,
and for the decision which lies only in God's hands. We cannot
claim that we have attained this possibility. We can only, in

fear and trembling, assert the possibility of its occurrence. Apart from this fearful faith, the law remains a vast obstacle which renders it impossible for us to await the advent of the Kingdom of God.

vv. 16, 17a. For this cause we say that **it is of faith** that the heirs are what they are, **that it may be according to grace; to the end that the promise may be sure to all the seed; not to that only which is of the law, but to that also which is of the faith of Abraham, who is the father of us all (as it is written, A father of many nations have I made thee).**

For this cause it is of faith. We say this after full consideration, since no other possibility is open to us. The Law, the History, and the Religion of Israel are the context in which men can await the heavenly inheritance; but they are not the effective power through which they enter it. In so far as the law has power, it is an earth-born and worldly and opposite power which actually makes the inheritance of Abraham impossible. The truly creative act by which men become the children of Abraham, by which stones are transformed into sons, does not lie in the possible possibility of the law, but in the impossible possibility of faith.

That it may be according to grace; to the end that the promise may be to all the seed. The consideration of that which makes Abraham to be Abraham (iv. 1) forces us beyond the limit of what is concrete and visible, and directs us to a preceding relationship which, because it lies beyond his soul-and-sense experience, establishes the moral and actual course of his life. Abraham is Abraham according to grace. Law and History and Religion have significance and meaning—*according to grace.* Now, *grace* presupposes the line of death by which all concrete human conspicuousness is bounded absolutely. This line is, however, in God's sight the line of life, since it assumes the final negation which alone contains the affirmation of God. It presupposes the last judgement apart from which there is no justification. In exposing this relationship, the history and experience of 'Abraham' and of 'Israel' have served their purpose, and the law is established (iii. 31). In speaking of Abraham, however, we necessarily speak of Christ; in speaking of Abraham's faith, we inevitably speak of that general KRISIS which we encounter in Him; in speaking of Abraham's sons, we speak with assurance of all those who, having first encountered the KRISIS of Christ, participate also in His Resurrec-

tion. Since the heirs are what they are not through the law but
of faith, not as a consequence of moral and historical status but
according to grace, it follows as a matter of course that participation in their company cannot be confined to those who have been
made the children of Abraham according to the law, cannot be
limited to the historical Israel, or to those who accept a particular and definite historical tradition and doctrine, or to those
who are members of some particular 'movement'. Such limitation in the number of the heirs makes the inheritance itself
more than insecure (iv. 14, 15). As the recipient of the promise,
Abraham stands outside every historical and particular company of men; similarly his true seed, being the race of believers,
likewise stand outside. Of course those who are, through the
doctrine and tradition of the law, his children, can share with
him the expectation of the Kingdom of the Messiah and of the
blessing of God; the decisive and primal relation with God can be
encountered within this particular company of men: but God is
not the God of the Jews only (iii. 29). By the faithfulness of God,
men who move in a different moral and historical environment
can be directed to revelation. Sectarianism, whether crude or
refined, is dissolved, if the children of Abraham are brought into
being by faith only. The word delivered to Abraham *according
to grace*, which he heard by faith, admits of no esoteric confine-
ment; it is valid for all who have the form of a man. It cuts
down vertically, from above, through every particular human
status. Through the emergence of that status which men have
in God, every human status is established by dissolution.

Are we, in saying that in Christ Abraham is the father of us all,
and that this is the meaning by which the law is established, imposing an interpretation upon the Scriptures rather than expounding them? Assuredly not, for what do the Scriptures say? **A
father of many nations have I made thee** (Gen. xvii. 5). Abraham
is, of course, the father of the single nation, Israel; but we have
seen that, because in Christ he is the father of this one nation,
he is also, at the same time and in consequence, the father of
many nations. The historical framework is broken through
when the secret of history is laid bare. We have no occasion to
deny the plain meaning of history, since it is history which
bears witness to the many of the one forgiveness of sins: *And
when they heard these things, they held their peace, and glorified
God, saying, Then to the Gentiles also God hath granted repentance
unto life* (Acts xi. 18).

CONCERNING THE VALUE OF HISTORY
IV. 17b–25

v. **17b.** *Abraham is the father of us all* (iv. 16)—**before him whom he believed, even God, who quickeneth the dead, and calleth the things that are not, as though they were.**

Before him whom he believed, even God, is Abraham the father of us all. Neither the events nor the personalities of history are wholly deprived of this non-historical radiance—*before him whom he believed, even God*. This radiance obliterates the isolation of personality, the remoteness of the past, the aloofness of peculiarity, and all those purely incidental elements of which the individual is made up, and brings out what is common to every happening in history as well as its dignity and importance. Seen in this radiance history makes known its supremacy over human life—Historia vitae magistra—and because of this radiance we pay attention to it. 'The non-historical resembles an all-embracing atmosphere in which human life is conceived and apart from which it shrivels up. For the actions which men propose take shape first in this dim and non-historical vapour. If it were possible for a man to penetrate with his understanding the non-historical in which every great episode in history had its origin, he might, by raising himself beyond the sphere of history, attain to that knowledge which would absolve him from the necessity of taking serious account of the actual facts of history. A single hour chosen from the first, or it might be from the nineteenth, century, or one single individual, whatever his condition, be he Greek or Turk, would suffice to provide an answer to the question how and why men should live' (Nietzsche). To express this sense for the light which is beyond history, or for the 'non-historical atmosphere' of life, those whose thought is bounded horizontally are driven to lapse nervously either into mythology or into mysticism. But we, however, see at the critical 'line which separates what is clearly visible from the impenetrable darkness' (Nietzsche) the light of the LOGOS of all history and of all life; and this is the non-historical, or rather the Primal History, which conditions all history. Abraham is the father of us all—*before him whom he believed, even God*. As absolute Miracle, as pure Beginning, as that Primal Creation, faith brings the known condition and status of human life into relation with the unknown God. The figure of Abraham—and indeed all history, whether we mean by history occurrence itself or its

description,—is the manifestation of the ground of knowledge
and of the power of creation. That Abraham is our father according to the flesh (iv. 1) does not thrust us back into what is concrete and visible, rather it directs us to what is invisible; he is
the father of us all—before God.

**Even God, who quickeneth the dead, and calleth the things
that are not, as though they were.** Faith, as the ground of knowledge and as the creative power in history, is here distinguished
from the whole dim world of mythology and mysticism. There
is here no question of overtopping or deepening or enriching
this world by calling into being another 'inner' or 'higher'
world. There is no question of the 'cosmic-metaphysical' or of
imposing two, or three, or even seven, other worlds upon the
concrete world in which we live. There is nothing but the final
and—because there is no escape from it—the unique contradiction between life and death, between the things that are and the
things that are not. Faith beholds life and existence where
the man of the world sees nothing but death and non-existence;
and contrariwise, it sees death and non-existence where he
beholds full-blooded life. We have seen the figure of Abraham
standing in the bright light of this critical line. There is no
possibility of stretching or elongating or developing or building
up what lies on this side of the line so that it may cross it.
Regarded from the other side, such elongation is equivalent
simply to death and non-existence; regarded from this side, its
collapse is also seen to be death and non-existence. The dilemma
of this double-sided negation is resolved only by the apparent
impossibility that 'minus times minus equals plus'. The relation between the two negations by which both are dissolved is
their true meaning and power. The *living* must die in order
that the *dead* may be made alive. *The things which are* must be
seen *as though they were not* in order that *the things which are
not* may be called *as though they were.* Here is the impossibility
of knowing, the impossibility of resurrection, the impossibility of
God, Creator and Redeemer, in whom 'here' and 'there' are both
one. Abraham is brought within the scope of the impossibility
by faith, itself the non-historical and impossible factor, which
makes possibility possible and by which history is established.
A similar faith appears on the borderland of the philosophy of
Plato, of the art of Grünewald and Dostoevsky, and of the religion of Luther. And yet, it must not be supposed that knowledge is a fortuitous thing, that resurrection is a contingent
happening, and that God is bound to the contradiction between
'here' and 't here'. God is pure negation. He is both 'here' and

'there'. He is the negation of the negation in which the other world contradicts this world and this world the other world. He is the death of our death and the non-existence of our non-existence. He makes *alive* and *calleth all things into being*. This God, and the transformation of all things in Him—*I saw a new heaven and a new earth*—is the faith of Abraham, the radiance from light uncreated, the Genesis narrative, and the LOGOS of all history.

v. 18. Who in hope believed against hope, to the end that he might become a father of many nations, according to that which had been spoken, So shall thy seed be (Gen. xv. 5).

Here we see Abraham manifestly at a loss—and yet making a discovery; manifestly torn asunder—and yet forging a bond of union; manifestly thrown off his balance—and yet standing upright. We are able to hear his 'Yes', whilst the world above and below him cries out to him—'No'. This is Abraham's faith: faith which, **in hope against hope,** steps out beyond human capacity across the chasm which separates God and man, beyond the visibility of the seen and the invisibility of the unseen world, beyond subjective and objective possibility. We watch Abraham as he advances to the place where he is supported only by the Word of God. We do not see him actually take the supreme step; but we see him advancing towards it and moving on from it. The supreme step is invisible to us.

> 'This action is from God alone;
> Apart from Him it is undone.
> But all must praise His power and might;
> And gratefully in Him delight.'

v. 19. And without being weakened in faith he considered his own body now as good as dead (he being about a hundred years old), and the deadness of Sarah's womb.

Abraham was under no delusion concerning the actual situation. He was no optimistic enthusiast; indeed, his honesty leads him to a scornful scepticism: *Then Abraham fell upon his face, and laughed, and said in his heart, Shall a child be born unto him that is an hundred years old? and shall Sarah, that is ninety years old, bear?* (Gen. xvii. 17). Abraham's demeanour is so far wholly intelligible; and such demeanour is also intelligible whenever men are confronted with a similar situation. That God proved Himself too strong for Abraham, and that therefore he could not become weak in faith is, however, beyond our com-

prehension. That he withstood the temptation which the visible
world presented to him, is the incomprehensible which lies beyond our understanding. That he was empowered to see dis-
tinctly and to hear clearly that which is not and cannot be, is
the non-historical which lies beyond history.

v. 20. He did **not** criticize **the promise of God** with unbelieving doubt, **but waxed strong in faith, giving glory
to God.**

'Everything by which we are surrounded conflicts with the
promise of God. He promises us immortality, but we are encompassed with mortality and corruption. He pronounces that we
are righteous in His sight, but we are engulfed in sin. He declares
His favour and goodwill towards us, but we are threatened by
the tokens of His wrath. What can we do? It is His will that
we should shut our eyes to what we are and have, in order that
nothing may impede or even check our faith in Him' (Calvin).
'Reason cannot attain unto it, only faith can achieve it. Faith
is, as it were, creative of divinity. This does not mean that
faith is competent to add to the eternal and divine Being;
nevertheless, it creates It in us. Where there is no faith, God is
deprived of his honour; He ceases to be accounted among us
wise and just and faithful and true and merciful. Where there
is no faith, God retains neither His divinity nor His majesty.
Therefore, everything hangs upon our faith. Our Lord God
requires of us no more than that we should render the honour
due unto Him and that we should take Him for our God; that
is, that we should not take Him for a vain and empty idol, but
for the true and veritable God. . . . The competence to give Him
such honour from the heart is assuredly wisdom beyond all
wisdom, righteousness beyond all righteousness, worship beyond
all worship, sacrifice beyond all sacrifice. He who thus believes
and confides in God's Word, as Abraham did, is righteous before
Him; for he possesses the faith which renders unto God the
honour due to Him; that is, he gives Him what he owes Him
and what he is bound to give Him. . . . True faith thus addresses
God: "God, my God, gladly I believe all thy words." But what
are God's words? Were reason to make answer, it would reply
"God's words are useless and impossible, stupid, petty and
trivial, mendacious and preposterous; yes, even atrociously
heretical and diabolical." And, indeed, what could be more
irrational and laughable, ridiculous and impossible, than God's
words to Abraham? . . . Moreover, all the articles of our Christian belief are, when considered rationally, just as impossible and

mendacious and preposterous. Faith, however, is completely abreast of the situation. It grips reason by the throat and strangles the beast. It effects what the whole world and all that is in it is impotent to do. But how can faith do this? By holding on to God's word and by accounting it right and true, however stupid and impossible it may appear. By this means did Abraham imprison his reason. . . . And in the same fashion do all other believers who have entered the dark recesses of faith, throttle reason, saying: "Listen, Reason, thou blind and stupid fool that understandest nought of the things of God. Cease thy tricks and chattering; hold thy tongue and be still! Venture no more to criticize the Word of God. Sit thee down; listen to His words; and believe in Him." So do the faithful strangle the beast. Thus do they achieve what the whole world is incompetent to achieve. And thereby they do our Lord God supreme and notable service. May such service ever be done Him! In comparison with this worship and sacrifice of the faithful, the whole array of sacrifices and offerings done by the heathen, or by works of monks, or by the deeds of holy men, is but vanity and nothingness' (Luther). He who can hear this, let him hear it; for it is the beginning and the end of history.

v. 21. And being fully assured that, what he had promised, he was able also to perform.

Was he—assured by some religious experience, by intuition, by the consciousness of a divine mission? Perhaps there were these things also; for why should the non-historical assurance not be accompanied by historical assurance? It is more probable, however, that there were no such accompaniments. It is more probable that Abraham was *filled* with deprivation and brokenness and uncertainty. And yet, not even filled with these things, for the assurance of deprivation and hunger and thirst would still be no more than an historical assurance. The riches of grace (Eph. i) lie, like poverty in spirit (Matt. v), beyond historical possession and deprivation. The fullness of Abraham's assurance, however, has no other ground than that he was the recipient of the divine promise. This is beyond history and is indescribable. It is comprehensible only as life from the dead (iv. 13).

v. 22. Wherefore it was reckoned unto him for righteousness.

Wherefore?—Because Abraham's faith is *faith before God* (iv. 17b); because faith is not one element in his character, but forms the absolute limitation which marks his behaviour and dissolves it, the absolute Miracle, the pure Beginning, and the Primal Creation. Because his faith is not comprehended in an historical happening, but is the negation of all occurrence and non-occurrence, it is defined by God as righteousness; and in God, and by God only, Abraham participates in the negation of all negation and in the death of all death. And so his faith, being unimpeded by historical occurrence, shines forth as light from light uncreated.

vv. 23–5. Now it was not written for his sake alone, that it was reckoned unto him; but for our sake also, unto whom it shall be reckoned, who believe on him that raised Jesus our Lord from the dead, who was delivered up for our trespasses, and was raised for our justification.

Not for his sake alone, *but for our sake also.* Particular episodes in history can be of universal importance. The past can speak to the present; for there is between them a simultaneity which heals the past of its dumbness and the present of its deafness, which enables the past to speak and the present to hear. This simultaneity makes possible an intercourse in which time is at once dissolved and fulfilled, for its theme is the non-historical, the invisible, and the incomprehensible. The Genesis narrative opens its mouth and utters the non-historical truth that to Abraham his faith was reckoned as righteousness. In so far as his situation is ours also, our ears too can be open to hear. History reveals its importance, when, through such communing, the present becomes aware of the unity of meaning that is in all history. If, however, the unhistorical be removed, the past remains dumb and the present deaf. However accessible the authorities and sources for the writing of history may be, the keenest historical acumen can discover nothing, if contemporary intercourse be not mingled with it. But Abraham cannot be our contemporary; he can say nothing to us which we are competent to hear, apart from the radiance of the non-historical. Unless, quite apart from the study of documentary sources, there exists a living perception of the one constant significance of all human occurrence, history becomes merely a sequence of epochs and a series of civilizations; it consists of a plurality of different and incommunicable elements, of separate individuals, ages, periods, relationships, and institutions; it teems with phenomena which charge about in all directions. This is non-sense. To say that such non-sense is 'reality' is not necessarily true. To call it 'interesting'

L

is not the equivalent of saying that it is full of meaning. A past, marked by a chaos of faces, is not an eloquent, understood, and apprehended past. If history can present no more than this, it is trivial. Be the material never so carefully and critically brought together; be the devotion in delving into the past never so great, and the accuracy of the scholar never so precise; be the understanding of an ancient culture and manner of life never so sensitive, and the sympathy with different points of view thrown up by the past never so delicate—yet this, for all its competence, is not history: it is photographed and analysed chaos. History is a synthetic work of art. History emerges from what has occurred, and has one single, unified theme. If this work of art, this occurrence, this one theme, be not engraved upon the historian, there can be no writing of history. 'Only the supreme power of the present can interpret the past. Only when human capacity is stretched to its full nobility is it competent to discover past greatness and to recognize what is worthy of being known and preserved. Like through like. Otherwise men depress the past to their own level. . . . It is the mature and pre-eminent man who writes history. He that has not passed through some greater and nobler experience than his contemporaries will be incapable of interpreting the greatness and nobility of the past. The voices of the past speak in oracles; and only the master of the present and the architect of the future can hope to decipher their meaning' (Nietzsche). This means that we perceive the significance of our present existence in the diversity of the unity of past history. When the intercourse between past and present becomes a contemporary intercourse, the meaning of both is discovered in the non-historical factor which is the beginning and end of history, and which lies beyond the scope of our sight and hearing. Consequently, the 'value of history' is displayed in that which precedes its critical investigation; for its value lies in the KRISIS within which all history stands, in the sickness unto death. And so we are confronted by a series of paradoxes. The historian sees when he comprehends, and he comprehends when he has something to proclaim; he sees history when he writes it, and he writes history when he makes it; he draws his knowledge from 'sources', which only, however, become available for his use through a knowledge which he already possesses. After this fashion the Genesis narrative is composed. It is a history which hears and speaks; it is filled with contemporary history, with the history of men whose ears and lips have been unsealed by the KRISIS in which they have been engulfed. It is this which gives them their competence to hear and to speak. They see the radiance and diffuse it, because they have themselves been illuminated by it. Of course, they present non-historical history; but they do so because it is precisely the non-historical factor which forms the veritable substance and quality of all history. Since they themselves start from the non-historical and move towards it, they perceive that all history bears inevitable witness to its non-historical beginning and its non-historical end. For this reason, the description of Abraham was written *not for his sake alone, but for our sake also.*

For our sake also, who believe on him that raised Jesus from the dead, who was delivered up for our trespasses, and was raised for our justification. 'Like through like' and 'like to like'. The past speaks only to those who are now, in the present, capable of hearing. It is possible to blot out the radiance with which the past is illuminated, and to describe the wisdom of the book of Genesis as a wisdom of the past. Abraham can be depicted as a Bedouin sheikh, belonging to a bygone age. If so, epochs have come and gone since his day, and we are able to compare and to contrast him with their rich and fascinating diversity. Abraham thus becomes one in a series of historical figures, strangely different from us and wonderfully apart. Contemporary intercourse has ceased, either because the past is an unworthy partner of the present, or because the present is unworthy of the past. And why should we not admit that this is so? In times of spiritual poverty, historical analysis is a method we are bound to adopt. But one day it will itself reach its limit, and must, to take a single instance, pronounce Abraham's personality to be unhistorical; and then it too will stand before the same commanding necessity of a synthesis which is the starting-point of the Book of Genesis. Thus there is open to us no way of writing history otherwise than as it is written in the Book of Genesis. And rather than claim to be using the method of analysis, we had better openly adopt the other method. Whether we wish it or not, we are involved in a contemporary intercourse between the past and the present. What Genesis tells us about Abraham is what concerns us vitally, though we may find it hard to recognize what it has to say, because our way of thinking is so very different. *We believe on him that raised Jesus from the dead.* Before ever we read the story of Abraham, we are in the same uncertainty as Abraham was. We stand at the barrier between death and life, between deep-seated human corruption, which is the denial of God, and the righteousness of God, which is the denial of men. We are the partners of Abraham; and he is a far more 'unhistorical' figure than critical analysis has ever dreamed of. To us, as to him, knowledge is impossible, resurrection impossible, the union of 'here' and 'there', which is established only by God and can be awaited only from Him, is likewise impossible. We believe: but when we say this, we know that we must go on to say that our belief is compounded of unbelief. Nevertheless, we know also that faith is, as it was with Abraham, what we do not know. This incomprehensible is the transformation of all things, the death of our death, the non-existence of our non-existence (iv. 17). In so far as we, all of us, do *not* believe, there remains for us all, among other possible possibilities, the method of critical analysis which is concerned with the Abraham who does not and cannot concern us. We have no desire to fetter or to cast suspicions upon the critical method. But it also cannot in the end survive the KRISIS, the sickness unto death, under which we stand. Indeed, in its own fashion it hastens the process. For it inevitably shows that the historical Abraham really does not concern us. And just in so far as it comes to this conclusion, it opens the road to the understanding of the non-historical Abraham of the Genesis story, to the necessary synthesis, and finally to the impossible possibility of which we must sooner or later dare to take stock, namely—our faith.

The Fifth Chapter

THE COMING DAY

THE NEW MAN

V. I–II

v. 1. Being therefore justified by faith, we have[1] peace with God through our Lord Jesus Christ.

Being therefore justified by faith : *The night is far spent, and the day is at hand* (xiii. 12). No treatment of faith is adequate which does not take account of the men who believe, the *we* of the Epistle, the new men ; the men of the Day of the Lord which is at hand, but which has not yet come. By faith we attain the status of those who have been declared righteous before God. By faith we are what we are not. Faith is the predicate of which the new man is the subject. Projected into the midst of human life, the new man seems no more than a void, his 'passionate motions of eternity' (Kierkegaard) are invisible. Seen from the human side, he is incomprehensible, a mere negation ; and yet, it is this which marks him out for what he is. He is the zero-point between two branches of a hyperbola stretching to infinity ; and being this, he is, in unimaginable fashion, both end and beginning. The new subject, being that which is radically and absolutely 'other', must therefore be contrasted with what I am ; it is, in fact, what I am not. Nevertheless, I am this new subject ; because, since faith is the predicate, an identity is established between me and it. Under the banner of the death and resurrection of Christ (iv. 25)—by the knowledge of God, who gives life to the dead and calls them that are not as though they were (iv. 17)—the new man comes into being, and I am born—from above (John iii. 3). If there be no gamble of faith, if faith be forgotten or for one moment suspended, or if it be thought of as anything but a hazard, this identity is no more than an entirely trivial enterprise of religious or speculative arrogance. Speaking dialectically: this identification must always be shattered by the recognition that man is not God. In the moment when we dare

---

[1] Reading ἔχομεν (*we have*) not ἔχωμεν (*let us have*). The latter reading is well attested, but not satisfactory: it is peculiarly unsuitable here, and may have been introduced as a means of concentrating the reader's attention upon the passage (cf. Theodoret: προσήκει δὲ ὑμᾶς τὴν πρὸς τὸν θεὸν γεγεννημένην φυλάττειν εἰρήνην). Lietzmann suggests that the misunderstanding goes back to Tertius, to whom the letter was dictated (xvi. 22).

to say we believe, we remain always under suspicion. The necessity of passing through the narrow gate which leads from life to death and from death to life must remain always a sheer impossibility and a sheer necessity. Beyond the gate the path is wholly impassable, the situation incomprehensible, and the power to proceed unattainable. It is dangerous for us to take even one step forward. The comfortable and easy manner in which men advance towards this critical point is the primary curse which lies upon all, or almost all, dogmatic preaching, and is the lie, the poison, which it is so difficult to eradicate from the pastoral work of the Church. The truth that we ARE new men is, however, comprehensible to us only at its starting-point. And this starting-point means for us the end of the old man. This is the only aspect of the truth visible to us; only in the Cross of Christ can we comprehend the truth and meaning of His Resurrection. We can only BELIEVE in what is new, and, moreover, our capacity reaches no further than to believing that we do believe. The point where faith and un-belief part company can be defined neither psychologically nor historically. As far as we can see, our hands are empty: 'We resemble the grass growing on the summit of some steep ravine where no other vegetation can live. Below in the valleys rise the mighty oaks, whose roots are buried in the rich soil. We, however, are weak and tiny plants, hardly visible, unprotected from wind and storm, almost withered away, almost without roots. But yet, whilst the topmost branches of the oak trees lie still wrapt in darkness, the light catches us in the early morning, and we see what none other can see: we see the sun of the coming day, and we cry out our welcome—"Come, Lord!"' (Merejkovski). Therefore we are righteous before God and in our weakness we are strong. We are first, because we are last; we grow, because we wither away; we are great, because we are little. God justifies Himself in our presence, and thereby we are justified in His presence. By making us His prisoners, He sets us free; by rejecting us as we are, He affirms us to be what we are not; He takes our side and uses us for His purpose, and thereby His side becomes our side, His right our right, and His good work is begun in us. He acknowledges us, and is with us. He promises us salvation in His Kingdom. By hope we are His. Thus the new subject emerges in the negation of the old, known, human subject; and by the invisible and personal action of God human personality is fashioned.

We have peace with God. The known man, the man of un-righteousness, enters into the peace of the Unknown God—this is the ineffable light into which we enter by faith. Peace with God is the peace concluded between man and God. It is effected by a God-given transformation of man's whole disposition, through which the proper relation between the Creator and the creature is re-established, and by means of which also the only true and proper love towards God is brought into being —the love which has its beginning in fear (v. 5). Unless we are righteous before God, we must be at enmity with Him; and love which obscures the distance between God and man and which is not grounded upon fear—as for example, the 'intimacy' of mysticism, or of the romantics, or of the disciples of Zinzendorf—is, in the end, directed towards the 'No-God' of this world, (i. 22, 23) and brings men under the wrath of God, as His enemies (v. 10). 'Peace with God is contrasted with every form of intoxicated security of the flesh' (Calvin). Peace is the proper ordering of the relation between man as man with God as God. Consequently it is far more than a 'pleasurable sensation of happiness' (Kühl), a sensation which may or may not accompany the conclusion of peace, but which does not constitute the declaration of it. Peace is declared when imprisoned truth (i. 18) is set at liberty and when the righteousness of God is made manifest (iii. 21). Peace is declared by faith. And yet, peace is something less than 'Life in the reality of God' (Kutter). In it no union of God and man is consummated, no dissolution of the line of death, no appropriation of the Fullness of God, or of His Salvation and final Redemption. The bitter conflict between flesh and spirit remains as intense as before; man remains man, and God is still God. Nor is the necessity of faith removed, for the tension of the paradox remains without even the slightest easement. Men are compelled to wait and only to wait; they are impelled to hope, and not to sight (viii. 24). By faith, however, their waiting is a waiting upon God alone; and this is to be at peace with Him. In the midst, therefore, between human experience and the reality of God, there lies the power and meaning of the peace which is possessed by those who are righteous through faith. But where is this peace? It is found where attention that is focused upon what God is in Christ, encounters the critical separation and union which is manifested in Him.

Through our Lord Jesus Christ. Peace implies its establishment and realization in God. Otherwise it has no existence and cannot be possessed. We encounter the action of God in contemplating the crucified and risen Christ. His action does not depend upon some experience of our souls or upon some stirring of our spirits. Our righteousness before God does not rest there, nor does the proper ordering of our relation with God hang upon such experiences. Faith and its power is invisible and non-historical. Faith is the point at which life becomes death and death becomes life in Christ; and by its operation we are dissolved and reconciled to God.

v. 2. By whom also we have had our access by faith[1] into this grace wherein we stand; and we glory in hope of the glory of God.

By whom also we have had our access by faith into this grace. The peace of the new man is illustrated by the expectant though insecure position of the apostle. He stands within *this grace* (i. 5), but is, nevertheless, in a most remarkable situation. For he has to speak the unspeakable and to bear witness to that of which God is the only witness. He is, moreover, the slave of the Messiah, separated unto the Gospel of God (i. 1). His position is utterly paradoxical, and the paradox is the paradox of grace (1 Cor. xv. 9, 10). Grace makes known to him, and perhaps to his readers also, how inconspicuous is the peace of God and how incomprehensible its significance. There is no doubt as to his own limitations. In fear and trembling he learnt to respect God's justice. As Saul he had been dissolved; he was blinded; the course of his life was broken. Only then did he begin to love God; only then did he know Him as the Creator and Redeemer of men; only then did zeal for God begin to flare up within him. When the destructive holiness of God had become vividly real to him, the mercy of God embraced him in its power. When the relation to God became to him a relation of expectancy, he became one who possessed: he possessed peace and hastened with God. In his weakness and insignificance, God had directed His attention towards him, and had laid upon him the burden of an ever-insistent divine employment. Pressed onwards irrevocably by the power of God, he became what he is—the messenger of Him before whom every man is dust and ashes. He is what he is not; he knows what he does not know; he does what he cannot do— *I live, yet not I.* This is the grace in which Paul stands. Since the message cannot be separated from the man who utters it, and since his exaltation is crossed by humiliation, Paul has nothing to say concerning the peace of God, nothing even concerning his own existence, which is not spoken in a paradox. He is fully aware that, though the words *by faith only* open the door to the

---

[1] τῇ πίστει ought not to be removed from the text. The seemingly unnecessary repetition can be explained, if Paul, according to our interpretation of the passage, intends the words ἐπὶ τὴν χάριν ταύτην to refer not only to the general εἰρήνη of *v.* 1, but also, and particularly, to his own apostolate.

peace of God, the door is also closed with the same words. He has himself entered by the door of faith. Yet he carefully defines his manner of entrance as *by him*, that is, by Jesus Christ our Lord. This means that he has encountered faith, not in the course of a steady growth in experience, but through the action of God upon him, and in the vision of the crucified and risen Christ. Thus, and thus only, he is what he is—not!

And we glory in hope of the glory of God. Paul knows well what he is doing when he says that, in proclaiming the Gospel, he brings men hope, a great hope, full of joy, the hope beyond all other hope, the hope of the glory of God. 'In the Gospel there shines forth upon us the hope that we may share in the divine nature. For when we shall see God face to face, we shall be like Him' (Calvin). The union of men with God is pure sight (iii. 23): it is life in the reality of God, it is salvation and final redemption. The union of 'here' and 'there' and of 'No' and 'Yes' of God in the Resurrection, at the Parousia of Christ when He shall come again, is the heritage promised to Abraham (iv. 13). In this hope the righteous rejoice: 'Although they be now pilgrims upon earth, yet they confidently hasten onwards towards the place which is beyond all heavens, guarding their future heritage peacefully in their hearts' (Calvin). In this hope Paul, the believer, also rejoices; for his present tribulation constitutes the living factor in the paradox of his apostolate. But his Gospel is not more than a Gospel of hope. He possesses no authority to beget the new life; he can but assist at its beginning. He has no greater competence than Socrates had! Faith has no power of anticipation; it travels by no short cut to that future eternity which lies beyond us. We have no secret treasure by which we can avoid the tension of faith or blot out the 'not yet' which confronts us. We cannot transform hope—and deny it—by making of it a present reality. What is, exists, so far as we are now concerned, always in what we are not. We cannot identify the new man with the old, except in so far as there is set between them the predicate of faith, and unless we are advancing in faith through the dreadful valley of death. *And we glory*—yes, no doubt, for we are aware of a final consummation and comfort and pride. But though we shall always know and think upon this final consummation, we shall never count upon it or reckon it as our possession (ii. 17, 22, iii. 27, iv. 2), never appeal to it as an experience or possible possibility of our own. Indeed, we are prevented from so doing, for it depends upon the justification by God, who exalts us by humiliating us, whom we can only receive, but whom we can never spell out for ourselves.

vv. 3–5. And not only so, but we also glory in our tribulations: because we know **that tribulation worketh patience; and patience, probation; and probation, hope: and hope putteth not to shame; because the love of God hath been shed abroad in our hearts through the Holy Spirit which was given unto us.**

We also glory in our tribulations. We do not recognize that final consolation and resting-place only when our inner and outer life runs so smoothly and hopefully that a boast almost rises to our lips. Our hope of the glory of God (v. 2) moves on a higher plane: and to this our lack of the glory of God (iii. 23) is a negative witness. The affirmation of hope and our deprivation of glory do not ebb and flow in accordance with the rise and fall of our human life. The grace in which the Apostle stands and his peace with God are in no way reflected in the inner and outer course of his life, as though he who possesses them must be rewarded with happiness or a 'good time' or, at least, with the ATARAXIA of the Greeks. It is no more necessary for the peace of God to carry these things with it than it is necessary for knowledge of the wrath and judgement of God to be productive of pessimism or to encourage asceticism. Because faith is grounded and centred in God, its affirmation can be maintained in spite of great deprivation; just as the negation which is involved in faith may be retained when the course of human life runs, for the time being at least, entirely smoothly. The peace of God, in which the righteous stand by faith, is contradicted neither by human *tribulations* and calamities, nor by the *dissolution of the outer man* (2 Cor. iv. 16) which affects also his inner being, nor by the *energy of death* which the apostle knows to be at work in him (2 Cor. iv. 12), nor by *fightings without and fears within* (2 Cor. vii. 5), nor by the pressure of enemies on every side. This desperate situation in no way conflicts with the love of God which hath been shed abroad in our hearts (v. 5); nor does it put faith to shame, as though, because of it, God required to be defended, or as though faith would breathe more easily if it were removed. God is justified and the evil is removed—by the word of justification with which He justifies the believer and appoints him the inheritor of His Kingdom. *By faith only* avails here also. Faith which presses onwards and leads to sight does not wait for sight in order that it may believe. It believes in the midst of tribulation and persecution. Yes! in the midst of these things; not when their edge has been blunted, because a means of enduring them has been found, or because happiness has been

once more restored. In the peace of God there is sighing and
murmuring and weakness. 'These words turn and rend those
babblers who desire all Christians to be strong and none weak.
Christians are full of longing; and they cry in their misery:
Abba, Father! To human reason this is a poor meaningless
little word. But Paul says, where that cry is heard, there are
the children of God. We need not always be strong; for did not
God permit His Son to be submerged in the misery of the Cross?
And will He treat the members of Christ otherwise?' (Luther).
There is suffering and sinking, a being lost and a being rent
asunder, in the peace of God. 'Abraham is suspended between
heaven and earth; he combats God, and his heart is torn in
twain. He is told that in Isaac shall be his seed: and then he is
told that Isaac must die. And yet, hope is there all the time;
and no one who is able to stand the blow will ever let it go'
(Luther). In the peace of God there is room also for what the
world calls unbelief: *My God, my God, why hast thou forsaken me?*
This is the onslaught of death and of hell. 'Let no one misunderstand this. If a man does not wish to be thus attacked, he is not
a Christian, but a Turk and an enemy of Christ' (Luther). There
is no calm or merry freedom from hurt in those who hope
for, but who do not possess, redemption. Security is not anticipated. Redemption occurs in the midst of upheaval and amid
the chaos of unredeemed humanity. 'Redemption occurs in
hope. It is in process of becoming. Here we must stand, fence,
and deal out blows. The coward is overtaken by disaster'
(Luther). The merry men of God are merry where there is no
merriment: and this is the boasting of the man who is righteous
by faith.

**Because we know that tribulation worketh patience; and
patience, probation; and probation hope.** We rejoice, not only in
tribulation, but also at it. We are able to say 'Yes' to the negations in our life, just as we are often compelled to say 'No' to its
affirmations. But how is this possible? It is possible *because we
know*. Because, in some way or other, we have penetrated the
reality and meaning of the occasion, because we have seen
through it. Yet, do we know it? No! we do not know it. We
know our ignorance. But God knows it; and we believe, and
dare to know what God knows. We know that for us it is
impossible to know the power and meaning of the tribulation in
which we stand. We know it as the power of death and as having
the significance of death. We think we know its vitality by the
way in which it hinders and destroys and denies our life. We
seem to see in it the terrible riddle of our existence and the

heavy curse of our createdness, and to behold in it the manifestation of the wrath of God. We suppose it to be sent by the
'No-God' of this world (i. 18).—But we believers see the invisible. We see the righteousness of God in His wrath, the
risen Christ in the crucified One, life in death, the 'Yes' in the
'No'. We are able to behold at the barrier the place of exit, and
in the judgement the Coming Day of Salvation. We, as believers,
stand in the negation of the negation of the suffering of
Christ (v. 6). And hereby a new premiss is provided for our
tribulation also. What at first seems nothing but mere human
suffering becomes the action of God, the Creator and Redeemer.
The obstacle to our life becomes a stepping-stone to the victory
of life. Demolition becomes edification. Disappointment and
obstruction become energetic hastening and tarrying for the
coming of the Lord. The prisoner becomes the watchman (i. 16),
and darkness is converted into light (Ps. cxxxix. 12). We understand the questionableness of life as it is; and we become aware
that our limitation and dissolution are inevitable, and no mere
chance occurrence. We affirm the negation which says that we
are creatures, and we *see clearly* (i. 20). We are enabled to take
to ourselves the protest of the creation against the world as it is
(viii. 19, 20); for we recognize that we stand under judgement,
and we love the Judge, because He lets it be known that He
is not to be identified with the god of this world. As Judge,
He manifests Himself as utterly different from us and from
our life. Thus our tribulation, without ceasing to be tribulation
or to be felt to be tribulation, is transformed. We must suffer,
as we suffered before. But our suffering is no longer a passive,
dangerous, poisonous, destructive tribulation and perplexity,
such as invade the souls of those who hate the Judge (ii. 9),
but is transformed into a tribulation and perplexity which
are creative, fruitful, powerful, promising, by which men are
dissolved, cast to the ground, pressed into a corner, and imprisoned, by God. By tribulation we are braced to patience.
Defence is turned into offence. The questionableness of our
situation becomes a source of strength; for we are encouraged
by the knowledge that this is God's way of saving us, and that
it cannot be otherwise (viii. 28). We may doubt, but it is in
God we doubt. We may kick against the pricks, but they are
God's pricks. Blasphemy even, even the blasphemy of Job,
is blasphemy against God. When we know that the attack which
is launched against our position is directed by God, the opportunity is given us of replying with a divine counter-attack. We
possess a divine artillery which silences the enemy and inflicts

upon him the damage he would inflict upon us. Death is deprived of its power. When we recognize that in suffering and brokenness it is God whom we encounter, that we have been cast up against Him and bound to Him, that we have been dissolved by Him and uplifted by Him, then tribulation worketh *probation* of faith, and faith discovers God to be the Originator of all things, and awaits all from Him. Our particular situation proves this general proposition, and the gate at which all hope seems lost is the place at which it is continually renewed. It is more than doubtful whether this *probation* carries with it a 'firm disposition of soul' (Lietzmann). Such mature firmness, at any rate, does not necessarily accompany it. The road, which is impassable, has been made known to us in the crucified and risen Christ; and our thought is the thought to which no man can attain. Therefore we *glory* in tribulations.

Hope putteth not to shame ; because the love of God hath been shed abroad in our hearts through the Holy Spirit which was given unto us. 'Confronted by conflict men always tend to grow restless' (Steinhofer). This is no doubt true, if endurance, and the probation and hope which depend upon endurance, be thought of as lying within human capacity. There is then no security in these virtues; and they may fail. Even those who have endured much and have been much tested and have never lost hope are not able to glory in tribulation. Indeed, if the truth be told, men as men are always restless in tribulation. But our hope is different in kind; for it is the hope of faith. This hope does not rise and fall as ours does. Its nerve-centre lies not in human capacity, but in the capacity and purpose of God. Such hope, then, possesses a real purpose by which its content is shaped and cannot be *confounded* or *put to shame* (Ps. xxii. 5, 6, xxv. 20), even though all hope be removed. It endures, when we have lost all power of endurance. It is approved, when we are not approved. Therefore we *glory* in hope (v. 2), precisely because it is not an achievement of our spirit, but the action of the Holy Spirit, and because the love of God hath been shed abroad in our hearts through the Holy Spirit which was given unto us. The *Holy Spirit* is the operation of God in faith, the creative and redemptive power of the Kingdom of Heaven, which is nigh at hand. As a tumbler sings when it is touched, so we and our world are touched in faith by the Spirit of God, who is the eternal 'Yes'. He provides faith with content which is not a thing in time; if it were a thing, it would be nothing but a void and a negation. He is the miraculous factor in faith, its beginning and its end. He is equal with God, and on His account God reckons righteousness to the believer. He is invisible, outside the continuity of the visible human subject and beyond all psychological analysis. He creates the new subject of the man who stands upright in the presence of God. He is the subject of faith, which 'religious experience' reaches after and longs for, but never finds. He is the subject by whom we are enabled to speak unspeakable things: to say that we have peace with God, that we have entered into grace and that we glory in hope of the glory of God (v. 1, 2). Therefore He is given, given by God. He is the pre-supposition of all human being and having; but to us He is comprehensible and conspicuous only in what is not given. 'The Holy Spirit, who is the effectual cause of holiness of life, was not in us by nature. But now, through Him, the love of God is in our hearts' (Hofmann). And so, there is a human 'I' and 'we', a human *heart*, which God is able to love. In the God-given occurrence, by which men are dissolved in order that they may be established, there takes place also the occurrence in which the *invisible things of God* (i. 20)—so gladly and easily and strangely obscured by men—are made known and offered to us for our observation. Then it is that men are able to encounter finally, as Job did, in the extremity of negation when the inevitability of the world seems unsurmountable—the divine 'Yes'. Following the guiding hand of John the Baptist, and seeing it pointing, as Grünewald depicted it, to the deepest horror of death, they are there met by the promise of ultimate salvation, by supreme blessedness, and by eternal life. This impossibility is the love of God. The creature can love the Creator; the condemned man, his Judge; the vanquished and slain man, his enemy; the victim, the priest who sacrifices it—because He—God—is all in all, and because it would then be still more impossible not to love Him. Men can never wrest love unto themselves, and make it their own possession. They can only continually receive it afresh as something *shed abroad* from above. Such love, which is God's work, is possible only because He first loved us (v. 8). This insight into the invisible, which is ours because it is not 'ours', is the anchor of our hope. Love is that which endures in our endurance, which is proved in our probation; it is the hope in our hope. By its power, hope is not put to shame; by its power, we glory in hope, glory even in tribulation; by its power we have peace with God; and by it we are what we are not—new men. 'After such an occurrence, such an encounter, how can we for one moment imagine that the hope of the glory of God putteth us to shame?' (Hofmann).

v. 6. For while we were yet weak, in due season Christ died for the ungodly.

The peace of the new man with God (v. i) and his love for Him whose ways are past finding out, are beyond all human understanding. So too is his hope which is grounded in love; so too is his glorying in hope. The new man lives by faith, for he lives of the Holy Spirit; and the Holy Spirit is given by faith. All this means that the new man lives by the dying of Christ, whose life is known only through His Resurrection, from which faith springs (v. 10). Now, the life of Christ is His oboedientia passiva, His death on the Cross. It is completely and solely and exclusively His death on the Cross. The doctrine of the munus triplex[1] obscures and weakens the New Testament concentration upon the death of Christ; for there is no second or third or any other aspect of His life which may be treated independently or set side by side with His death. Neither the personality of Jesus, nor the 'Christ idea', nor the Sermon on the Mount, nor His miracles of healing, nor His trust in God, nor His love of His brethren, nor His demand for repentance, nor His message of forgiveness, nor His attack on tradition, nor His call to poverty and discipleship; neither the implications of His Gospel for social life or for the life of the individual, nor the eschatological or the immediate aspects of His teaching concerning the Kingdom of God—none of these things exist in their own right. Everything shines in the light of His death, and is illuminated by it. No single passage in the Synoptic Gospels is intelligible apart from the death. The Kingdom of God has its beginning on the other side of the Cross, beyond all that is called 'religion' and 'life', beyond conservatism and radicalism, physics and metaphysics; on the other side of morals and of that which is beyond morality, of the joy and the sorrow of the world, of the practical and the contemplative life—beyond all human possibilities, whatsoever they may be. The life of Jesus is essentially a passing by all these things; it is essentially a turning-away from every thesis and antithesis, from all human restlessness and repose, from every positive and negative human possibility except the possibility of death. He bids farewell to all those achievements by which men obscure the fact of death; and because He passes by and turns away and bids farewell, His life shines, and human things are enlightened by the light which is reflected from Him. Relative they are seen to be, and yet re-lated to the wealth of God; they are seen to have been created

---

[1] The doctrine of the 'Munus Triplex' is the doctrine of Christ as Prophet, Priest, and King. See the discussion in Ritschl's *Justification and Reconciliation* (Engl. tr. pp. 417–34). [Tr.]

by Him, and yet to await His redeeming work. Their greatness
and their littleness, their importance and their futility, their
'Yes' and their 'No', are clearly perceived, when they are regarded—sub specie mortis (iii. 30). For it is in the perspective of
death that the unseen things of God are made manifest, and the
oneness of God is revealed. By this knowledge the new man lives.
He lives of the life which has been made known to him in the dying
of Christ. Christ *died for us*. *For us*—that is, in so far as by
His death we recognize the law of our own dying; in so far as
in His death the invisible God becomes *for us* visible; in so far
as His death is the place where atonement with God takes place
(iii. 25, v. 9), and where we, who have rejected our Creator,
return to His love; and in so far as in His death the paradox of
the righteousness and the identity of His holy wrath and His
forgiving mercy becomes *for us*—the Truth. The new man is
therefore brought into being by that which is pre-eminent over,
and prior to, all the concrete possibilities of human life. This
paramount factor cannot be identified with human possessions,
because by it they are finally and critically negated, nor must it
be confounded with even the most intimate religious experience
that may be vouchsafed to us as the disciples of Jesus and of
Him crucified, because these 'things of religion' are precisely the
things which Jesus passed by in order to die. What Christ has
done, He has done apart from us, in so far as we are 'we'. It
follows, therefore, that no fundamental deprivation is suffered by
those who, owing to their being separated, either by time or by
locality, from the scene of the Crucifixion, cannot share in the
actual experiences of those who stood by the Cross. If it were not
so, *for us* would be limited to a particular group of men and
women. Those who do not see Christ according to the flesh and
have no direct experience of Him are not less reconciled to
God through Him than others are. In Spirit—*He went and
preached unto the spirits in prison* (1 Pet. iii. 19). The atonement
which occurred in Him is an invisible atonement which is
contrasted with any soul-and-sense relationship between us and
Jesus as impossibility is contrasted with possibility, death with
life, non-existence with existence. Compared with all that we
are and have and do, it is—satisfactio vicaria. He died for us
whilst 'we'—all that we are and have and do—were weak and
godless. How then can this relation between Him and us—
between Him, risen from the dead, and us, still involved in all
questionable possibilities of a life which has not yet been illuminated by the light of His death—be fundamentally altered?
Apart from the faith by which we die with Christ, how can we

who live in this world cease to remain both weak and godless?
For it is precisely dying with Christ—in virtue of which we shall
be what we are not—that establishes the life of the new man.

**vv. 7, 8. For scarcely for a righteous man will one die:
for peradventure for the good man some would even dare
to die. But God commendeth His love towards us, in
that, while we were yet sinners, Christ died for us.**

The new man does not live by direct, personal benefits. He
does not live by sharing in the good things of this life, nor even
by his capacity to procure them for others. He does not owe his
life to what another has procured for him by dying, nor does he
even profit by his own death. Direct benefits can be thus
procured. There are rare, but nevertheless quite possible,
occasions when one man offers his life on behalf of another—as
for example, when a missionary or a doctor dies at his post, when
a soldier dies on the field of battle, or when a mother dies in
giving birth to a child. It is obvious that, as an effective historical
occurrence, the death of Christ, as providing an opportunity for
experience, must be set in the context of martyrdom. It is, moreover, possible that, if the motive of suicide were the receiving of
benefit from a final despair concerning the things of this world,
we might have to respect the man who takes his own life. But we
must beware lest the honour which we are bound to pay to those
who offer up their lives should degenerate into that sentimentality which attributes to a human action, even to the sacrifice of life,
an importance which it cannot in the end bear. For human self-
sacrifice can be no more than a parable of that by which the new
man is brought into being. Its importance stands or falls with the
importance of the things of this life which it mediates, and depends for its effectiveness upon the capacity of the person to benefit by it. In the case of self-destruction, the suicide, by his action,
mediates the benefit to himself. The question remains, however,
whether the good which is mediated by death is, in fact, good;
and also whether the man on whose behalf death is dared is, in
fact, good. There are, no doubt, cases in the world of men and
of things, where good men do benefit by the death of others.
But no atonement is thereby effected. By it we do not escape
from the relativity of this world; there comes into being no
security which stretches beyond the business of this world,
beyond its greatness and its littleness, its competence and its
incompetence; nothing is achieved outside the realm of our lives,
nothing on the other side of our life and death, and if we continue
to think along these lines, even though the 'veritably Good'—

M

which is not a thing which can be experienced in the world—
were to appear in our midst, nothing would come of it, since
men, as men, would not be in a position to appropriate it—
because of their lack of goodness. But the death of Christ is
concerned precisely with this benefit. It is a benefit which,
'rather than providing us with the knowledge of God—where
indeed is such knowledge?—provides us with the assurance that
He knows us' (Overbeck). By the death of Christ—**God commendeth his own love towards us.** By it the things which are of
value in this life are dissolved, and yet it is by it that they are
essentially established. By the death of Christ we are confronted
by the absolute and not merely relative 'otherness' of God, and
therefore by His indissoluble union with us. In manifesting the
utmost limit of the wrath of God, it exposes His unfathomable
mercy. Because in it the problem of God assumes its most bitter
and unavoidable form, it provides His own answer to the
problem. Here is Emmanuel, God with us; and God commendeth His love towards us—**while we were yet sinners.** That is to
say, apart from our capacity to receive it, apart from our
competence to hear the communication and to accept His love.
And indeed, our incompetence is obvious; for we have no eyes
wherewith to see it, and no ears wherewith to hear it. God as-
sures us of that whereof we cannot be assured. He speaks to us in
virtue of that which we do not possess: Amore non provocatus
sponte nos prior dilexit—'God first loved us without being first
provoked thereto by our love' (Calvin). The glory of God (v. 2),
which is presupposed in the death of Christ, is not merely a new
object; it requires a new subject. And this new subject—only
by faith identical with me, a sinner!—is the new man, who with
unquenchable certainty knows himself in Christ to be beloved
of God.

**vv. 9–11. Much more then, being now justified by his
blood, shall we be saved from the wrath of God through
him. For if, while we were enemies, we were reconciled
to God through the death of his Son, much more, being
reconciled, shall we be saved by his life; and not only so,
but we also** glory **in God through our Lord Jesus Christ,
through whom we have now received the reconciliation.**

The peculiar quality of the new man, of his love towards God,
of his hope which is based upon this love, of his glorying in hope,
is that it springs from the pre-eminence of the divine assurance
given in the death of Christ and—**by his blood.** In so far as he
lives of his origin and of the source of his life, in so far as he is

bold unto faith, the new man is what he is not. He is a new subject related to a new object. As the beloved of God, he loves God; endowed with hope, he is confident in hope; the elect of God, he glories in God. Standing in the light of God's 'Nevertheless' (iii. 21), we hurry and tarry under the beetling crag of His KRISIS. To the question, Whence are we?—which is the question of all questions—we receive the answer which is beyond all answers: We are they who have been justified by God. We, before whose blinded eyes God justifies Himself as God; we, who have been brought under His justice and whom He has claimed for His Kingdom; we, who have encountered the divine 'Nevertheless' which is God's decision to come to man's assistance, and the divine forgiveness and freedom which are conferred upon us wholly from outside our competence; we, who have been lifted up into the air, so that we have no standing-place except the protection of God—we are they who have been reconciled to God; we are they who have peace with Him. Our disposition towards Him is simply open-hearted preparedness and willingness to receive. As the beloved of God we have no alternative but to love Him in return. In the dawning splendour of His glory, we have no alternative but hope. 'God takes the initiative, and redresses the world of men which has turned away from Him in fear and enmity' (Weinel). Thence have we come (iii. 21).— And yet: Are we? Do we have? Are we competent? Do we come? Yes! if it be clearly understood that we are not 'we'. This disposition is ours only inasmuch as we believe; only inasmuch as, by the death of Christ, the line of death has passed vertically through our lives; and inasmuch as we, consequently, remain still in fear and trembling, in awe and gratitude. I—and yet not I: Christ in me. The new man has no existence except non-existence; for the pre-eminence of his origin lies in the miracle of God, in His beginning, in His creative act—in the death of Christ. That *we are* does not mean that we have progressed to a higher stage of religion or of life; nor must our new existence be confounded with those eschatological illusions in which the union of 'here' and 'there' is anticipated in our imagination. All such illusion is dammed at its source. In so far as we are anything except that which we are not, in so far as we do not believe and are not enlightened by the death of Christ, we remain within this world, outside the peace of God and outside the reconciliation which He has wrought. For everything which we can know and apprehend and see belongs to this world. No soul-and-sense experience can bridge the gulf by which the old is separated from the new. In so far as 'we' are, we remain at enmity with God, by nature prone to hate both God and our neighbours, in no sense citizens and heirs of the Kingdom of God, but its destroyers. In so far, however, as the new man stands in the light of the death of Christ, all that I am which is not the new man falls beneath its shadow. The light of Christ constitutes a new subject and forms a new predicate: we are— new men! But this new constitution is indirect and dialectical: it comes into being only by faith. *By his blood* we are justified; as **enemies** we are—**reconciled to God through the death of his Son.** We must therefore never allow this dialectical pre-supposition to be hardened or petrified into a concrete and direct occurrence. It is valid only by faith, and it exists only in the fear of the Lord and in the light of the Resurrection. Only so, are we and have we; only so, are we competent and do we come; only so, does redemption draw near; and only so, *shall we be saved from the wrath* under which we still stand here and now. For the life which has been manifested through the death of Christ is salvation to those who are reconciled with God through the death of His Son. How then is it possible for us not to glory in hope through our Lord Jesus Christ? 'We praise God as our God; and the fountain of all possible good things is opened unto us' (Calvin). 'When once again men have God, they have all the fullness of life and its blessedness' (Fr. Barth). Yes! they do veritably have; because through the death of Christ they are now filled with the future of God. Spes erit res —'This hope is possession' (Bengel).

THE NEW WORLD

V. 12–21

v. 12. Therefore—that is to say, in the apprehension of the constitution of the new man through the new life manifested in the death of Christ (v. 1–11) there is involved a further perception—**as through one man sin entered** (as power) **into the world** (of men), **and death through sin** (became the supreme law of the world); **and so death passed unto all men, for that all sinned**—so the one 'coming' man, Christ (v. 14), of whom the former man is a type, inaugurates the precisely reverse context of the world (v.18–19).

Therefore. As new men we stand on the threshold of a new world. But the *old man* also is mankind, humanity, and the world of men. Each particular man is therefore doubly conditioned. He is conditioned, on the one hand, by that which dissolves his particularity, and on the other, by that which affirms it. As the

old man, he is what he 'is', the man 'we' know, who is under the
wrath of God: as the new man, he is what he is not, the man
'we' do not know, who is righteous before God. Accordingly,
in the light of the critical 'Moment', there is opened up a perception which extends backwards to the actual context in which
all men stand by law, and forwards to a radically different, and
indeed opposite, context. Both, however, are universal, orderly,
necessary, and unavoidable. If a man be *in Adam*, he is an old,
fallen, imprisoned, creature: if he be *in Christ*, he is a creature, new, reconciled and redeemed (2 Cor. v. 17). There he
dies, here he enters into life (2 Cor. iv. 12). But these two worlds
do not exist side by side, nor do the old and the new man compose two men. For the possibility of the one involves the impossibility of the other; and the impossibility of the one involves
the possibility of the other. Regarded from the point of view
of the 'first' world, the 'second' ceases to be a second; and from
the point of view of the 'second', the 'first' ceases to be a first.
What is non-existent in the first world forms the very existence
of the second; and what constitutes the existence of the first is
non-existent in the second. Say, *in Adam*: then the old was and
is and shall be, and the new was not and is not and shall not be.
Say, *in Christ*: then the old has passed away, and the new is
come into being (2 Cor. v. 17). But only in the light of the critical
'Moment', when mankind and its world are passing as one
whole, from the old to the new, from 'here' to 'there', from the
present to the coming age, does the distinction between the two
become apparent. The distinction exists therefore only when
this world is dissolved by the dissolution whereby it is established. The two ways meet and go apart where in Adam men
are fallen from God and where in Christ they find Him again.
Here the old and visible world encounters judgement unto
death, and the new and invisible world encounters judgement
unto life. Where the two roads go apart, there they also meet.
There is no discovery of God in Christ, no entering into life,
except men be exposed in Adam as fallen from God and under
the judgement of death. But we cannot stop here: there is no
falling from God in Adam, no judgement of death visible to us,
except at the point where we are reconciled to God in Christ
and assured of life. We might, indeed, comment with Hera-
clitus: 'Immortal—mortal; mortal—immortal. The two alter-
nate. Men live in death, and die in life.' But the matter is not
so simple. The two factors are not of equal weight and
importance; nor is there a strict balance between them. Life in
Adam and life in Christ is not an ever-recurring cycle of sin and

righteousness, death and life. There is unity of movement; but
it is displayed in the advantage that the second has over the first,
in a turning from the first to the second, and in the victory of
the second over the first. If this movement be a genuine movement, the parallelism or polarity of the two contrasted factors,
which appears at first sight permanent and fixed, must break
down. Genuine movement can take place only if the balance
between the two be wholly and finally disturbed. This is the
significance of the critical 'Moment', which we name faith or
resurrection. Christ is contrasted with Adam as the goal and
purpose of the movement. Hence between them there can be
no equipoise. As the goal, Christ does not merely expose a
dis-tinction. He forces a de-cision between the two factors.
By doing this, He is not merely the second, but the *last* Adam
(1 Cor. xv. 45). The new world is therefore more than a variation of the old. There can be no return movement from the
righteousness of Christ to the fall of Adam. The life which
springs from death is wholly pre-eminent over the life which en-
genders death and is enclosed by it. There is a death which is
the death of death: and this is the theme of the Gospel (i. 1, 16).
The Gospel is the power of God, the power of the Resurrection;
it is the 'miraculous warfare' (Luther), the paradox; it is faith,
as the primal and creative factor. The Gospel is our life; and
yet it is not 'our' life. Where faith and the power of God are,
men are what they are not. They stand as new men on the
threshold of the new world, the world of life. When we reflect
that the new world can be none other than the old world dissolved
and overthrown by the victory of Christ, it becomes clear that,
when the invisible operation of the old world becomes visible
in dissolution and overthrow, we are in fact confronted with the
operation of the new world. In the concrete realities of the first
world we perceive the presuppositions which, if they be reversed
and set moving in a contrary direction, form the presuppositions of the second world. Now that we have this dialectical
relationship between 'old' and 'new' in mind, we can concentrate our attention on the 'old'; not, of course, for its own sake
—since it does not exist in itself but only in relation to the pre-
eminence of the 'new'—but in order that we may thereby be
enabled to decipher the law of the new world.

Death is the supreme law of the world in which we live. Of
death we know nothing except that it is denial and corruption,
the destroyer and destruction, creatureliness and naturalness.
Death is engraved inexorably and indelibly upon our life. It is
the supreme tribulation in which we stand. In it the whole

riddle of our existence is summarized and focused; and in its
inevitability we are reminded of the wrath which hangs over
the man of the world and the world of man. So completely is
death the supreme law of this world, that even that which, in this
world, points to the overcoming and renewal of this world, takes
the form of death. Morality appears only as the denial of the
body by the spirit; the dying Socrates is the only fitting emblem
of philosophy; progress is no more than a restless negation of
the existing natural order. No flame—except the flame of the
Lord! (Exod. iii. 2)—can burn without destroying. Even the
Christ according to the flesh must die in order that He may be
appointed the Son of God (i. 3, 4). We too must pass through
death, if we are to render unto God the honour due to Him.
We have to learn that the fear of the Lord is the beginning of
wisdom. We would like to turn our backs on all this, if we could.
We would like to protest against death in the name of life, if it
were not that the protest of death against our life is far more
venerable, far more significant. We try to bury out of sight the
suspicions and reservations which accompany every unbroken
affirmation we make, and to protect our eyes against the grey
light of the final negation which envelops all our healthy,
creative, and positive activities, a final negation which is preceded by a whole host of preliminary negations. But we are
unable to persist long in our attempt; for it is all too evident
that the grey light does not proceed from our caprice, but has
a primary origin. It envelops our whole life (i. 10), for there is no
vital and creative human action which is not born in pain and
revolution and death. We are powerless; we are lost. Death
is the supreme law of our life. We can say no more than that
if there be salvation, it must be salvation from death; if there
be a 'Yes', it must be such a 'Yes' as will dissolve this last and
final 'No'; if there be a way of escape, it must pass through
this terrible barrier by which we are confronted.

Sin. We must now turn our attention to the men who inhabit
this world of death. They are men of sin. Sin is that by which
man as we know him is defined, for we know nothing of sinless
men. Sin is power—sovereign power (v. 21). By it men are controlled. The actual sins of the individual man are the means by
which the general situation is more or less clearly made known.
Particular sins do not alter the status of a man; they merely
show how heavily the general dominion of sin presses upon him.
Sin is the sovereign power in the world as we know it; and it is
wholly irrelevant what particular form it takes in the life of each
individual. Sin is an especial relationship of men to God; and it

derives its sovereign power, and even its existence, from this relationship. Sin is a robbing of God: a robbery which becomes apparent in our arrogant endeavour to cross the line of death by which we are bounded (i. 18, 19); in our drunken blurring of the distance which separates us from God; in our forgetfulness of His invisibility; in our investing of men with the form of God, and of God with the form of man; and in our devotion to some romantic infinity, some 'No-God' of this world, which we have created for ourselves. And all the time we are oblivious that we must die in *ungodliness and unrighteousness*. In its visible and concrete form, then, sin is the disturbing of the relationship with God which is defined by death. However, this concrete, historical aspect of sin points to another aspect which is neither historical nor concrete. Death forms the limit of our life and marks the boundary between us and God. But since God is not death, but the life of the Coming Day, there is a different way of looking at sin. In its non-concrete and non-historical aspect, sin is robbery, in the sense that it is the falling of men out of direct relationship with God, the rending asunder of the spiritual band which unites God with the world and with men, the Creator with His creation. It is an assumption of independence in which God is forgotten. It is the sophisticated, pretentious, unchildlike, wisdom of the serpent: *Hath God said?*— a wisdom to which men attend, and which produces an unreal aloofness from God who is the Life of our life. In its concrete form sin is no more than the ever-widening appearance and expression and *abounding* (v. 20) in time of this Original Fall. It points to the Fall which lies behind time. But there is also another invisible significance attaching to sin. It is *ungodliness and unrighteousness* of men, since it damages the living relationship between God and man, and appropriates to itself the madness of the devil—Eritis sicut Deus (*ye shall be as God*). If, however, we begin with this aspect of sin, we have to take care lest, passing by the Cross, we suppose ourselves capable of undertaking the restoration of our proper position either by some forceful and tumultuous action or by some delicate refinement of thought. For restoration is outside our competence, because, as we know, we are under the law of death. The perception which, originating in the via crucis, sees sin as an inherited status, enables us to make two comments upon the temptation by which we are encouraged to engage upon our own restoration.

First: Sin—**entered into the world**. What is *the world*? The world is our whole existence, as it has been, and is, conditioned by sin. There has come into being a COSMOS which, because we no longer know God, is not Creation. That is to say, there is a world 'without us' which has broken loose from the world 'within us', and what is in us is mirrored again in what is without us:—Eritis sicut Deus! As we see it, the world is the world of time and of things, in which nature and spirit, body and soul, the ideal and the material, interact and oppose one another. It is a world in which things move towards independence, a world of things existing powerfully in their own right, a world of principalities and powers and thrones and dominations. Like men, the world is imprisoned. As their world, it unwillingly participates in the perversity of men and shares their damaged relationship with God. It assumes that relative divinity which is the mark of human greatness and of human fallenness. The disease from which men suffer is transferred to the world, which experiences this suffering (viii. 19, 20). And so, in this world, which is our world, the true life is invisible, unknown, and impossible; and concrete and objective things, our this and that, thus and thus, here and there, become either divinized worldliness or worldly divinity. The only glory of the Creator which remains is that by which this independent validity is limited, for these things do in fact contain their own criticism. They are in fact open to question; for the possibility, even the necessity, of their dissolution is latent in them. That is to say, what they are points to what they are not; and the only possibility of perceiving the glory of God is that perception which operates sub specie mortis. Job's friends marshalled all the arguments for a direct justification of the things of the world—and failed; and in their failure all arguments for a direct justification are also done away. In so far as this world is our world, it is the world into which sin entered. In this world, on this earth, and under this heaven, there is no redemption, no direct life. Redemption can be only through redemption! But redemption can only take place at the coming Day, when there shall be a new heaven and a new earth.

Secondly:—**Through sin death.** Through sin, death entered into the world—as KRISIS. There is here a twofold meaning. Death is the supreme law of the world, but it also points to a Lawgiver who as such is above His law. It is judgement and betterment, barrier and exit, end and beginning, 'No' and 'Yes', the sign of the wrath of God and the signal of His imminent salvation. In any case, death is the divine command—'Stop'—and we cannot disobey it. Through its narrow gate we must pass. It is the point where we must be wise, for there is no other possibility of wisdom. *Through sin death.* Death is the reverse

side of sin. It entered into the world as a result of the original
and invisible sin by which the life, which is the relationship of
men to God, was damaged. Sin is guilt; and the destiny of sin
and guilt is death. Living without sharing in life, men are defined
as mortal; loosed from primary existence, they are non-existent;
in their wild unrelatedness and absoluteness and independence,
they are relative. It is *therefore* inevitable that the relation of
men to God should be made clear by death. It is inevitable that
human existence should break into fragments, and that its
questionableness should be exposed; inevitable that it should
fall apart into a plurality of human temporal and concrete
things, which no optimistic or pessimistic view of life is really
able to combine into one whole; inevitable that human 'life'
should be thwarted, undermined, and finally denied, by insecurity, limitation, suffering, and at the last by death. Where sin
lives, death lives in sin—and we are not alive (vii. 10). Where
sin reigns, it reigns in death (v. 21)—and we are dead. When
sin gives its orders, it pays in the currency of death (vi. 23).
Sin is a bleak, lifeless, unrelated existence. Our life is confronted
with a steep precipice, towering above us, hemming us in on
every side, and on it are hewn the words: *All things come to
an end*. And yet in all the negativity there is no point which
does not bear witness to the summit—'whence Adam fell'
(Luther). There is no relativity which does not reflect a vanished
absolute which can never be wholly obliterated, since it is this
absolute which makes relativity relative. Death never occurs
but it calls attention to our participation in the Life of God and
to that relationship of His with us which is not broken by sin.
The thought of Life and of God is stirred in us by death—by the
reality of death, not by our experience of it. It is unavoidable
that it is for the sake of life that we have to remember that we
must die; unavoidable too that the finger which directs us to
the Cross of Christ should also remind us that we cannot pass
beyond the world of sin except where the barrier has been passed.
Through sin came death, death as judgement, as the breaking of
our life, as the occasion of apprehension, as our misery and our
hope. Death is the reverse side of that sin which is invisible; but
it is also the reverse side of the righteousness which is invisible.

Through one man all this came about! Who then is this one
man? Adam? Yes! Adam is the one through whom death entered
the world. For he committed the invisible sin, and fell from
God. But the Adam who did this is not Adam in his historical
unrelatedness, but Adam in his non-historical relation to Christ.
How could we recognize the invisible sin of the disobedient

Adam, unless we perceived the invisible righteousness of Christ obedient unto death? Whence have we the competence to understand what 'fallen—from God' means? And how could we form any conception of Adam's fall, unless we had in mind the exaltation of Christ from death to Life? Whence could we have known the meaning of a life lived—in order that it may pass to death? Adam has no existence on the plane of history and of psychological analysis. He exists as the first Adam, as the type of the second Adam who is to come, as the shadow cast by His light. He exists as the 'Moment' which forms the background from which Christ advances to victory, the scene where the world and mankind are transformed from fall to righteousness, from death to life, and from old to new. Adam has no separate, positive existence. He does not revolve round his own pole; he is not a second factor. He exists only when he is dissolved, and he is affirmed only when in Christ he is brought to nought. It is evident that neither he nor the Christ risen and appointed to the life of God, the Christ of whom he is the projection, can be 'historical' figures. Leaving out of account what may have occurred to the historical Adam, it is clear that the sin which Adam brought into the world precedes death, just as the righteousness which Christ brought follows it. Our historical knowledge is, however, bounded on the one side by the death of Adam, and on the other side by the death of Christ. What Adam was before he became mortal and what Christ is after He ceased to be mortal—in other words, the operation of the emergence of death from Life and of Life from death—is therefore by definition non-historical. It follows then of necessity that the entrance of sin into the world through Adam is in no strict sense an historical or psychological happening. The doctrine of Original Sin, as it has been generally understood in the West, would not have been to Paul an 'attractive hypothesis' (Lietzmann); it would have been just one of the many historical and psychological falsifications of his meaning. The sin which entered the world through Adam is, like the righteousness manifested to the world in Christ, timeless and transcendental. It is the disposition and relation to God of men who stand facing the old with their backs to the new. Sin is, moreover, meaningless and incomprehensible except as the negation of the righteousness which is in Christ, and apart from its being surmounted by the 'Yes' of that righteousness. In the first man, in his life in the world, and in the world in which he lived, this disposition is seen in actual operation. The non-temporal Fall of all men from their union with God is manifested in that they *imprison the truth in ungod-liness and unrighteousness* (i. 18). This active disposition is explained—and yet not explained—by the divine predestination of men to destruction which follows their divine election in Christ as the shadow follows the light. The Fall is not occasioned by the transgression of Adam; but the transgression was presumably its first manifest operation. In this context the venerable Reformation doctrine of 'Supralapsarianism' becomes intelligible. According to it, predestination unto rejection precedes the 'historical' fall. Only in so far as Adam first did what we all do, is it legitimate for us to call and define by his name the shadow in which we all stand. By the first Adam we mean the natural, earthy, historical man; and it is this man who must be overcome (1 Cor. xv. 45, 46).

And so death passed unto all men, for that all sinned. We now move out from the non-historical background of our 'old' world into the bright light of its observable foreground. And there we see the inevitable working out of the via crucis in the visible world. We see all men doing what Adam did, and then suffering as Adam suffered. We see men sin, and then die. We see men wresting from God what is His, and then being brought to shame. We know that the 'then' is really 'therefore'. We are, however, unable to see the causal relationship; only the concrete facts are visible to us. The sin which broke forth in the visible action of Adam when he pressed forward to the tree of knowledge—a sin in which the woman was also hopelessly compromised—we see recurring repeatedly in varying forms throughout the whole story of human life: *There is none righteous, no, not one* (iii. 10, 23). Moreover, whether it be recognized or no, there runs through the story the line of death, which explains the meaning of the words: *Adam is become as one of us, to know good and evil* (Gen. iii. 22).

And now: as the invisible operation of the old world is illustrated in observable facts, so. . . .—But, before we draw out the analogy, what has been said above requires some further elucidation.

vv. 13, 14. For until the law sin was in the world: but sin is not imputed when there is no law. Nevertheless death reigned from Adam to Moses, even over them that had not sinned after the likeness of Adam's transgression, who is the figure of him that was to come.

What requires to be emphasized is the conception of sin. If it is to provide an explanation of the nature both of the world which is passing to corruption and of the coming world, unobservable sin must be understood in its full significance. We have said that we must not think of sin as an event or as the sum of a series of events or as a particular status, that we must not regard it as sharing in the contingency of moral or of actual happenings. Rather, we must think of it as the pre-supposition which under-lies every human event and conditions every human status. Sin is the characteristic mark of human nature as such; it is not a lapse or a series of lapses in a man's life; it is the Fall which occurred with the emergence of human life. Sin occurs before it has taken concrete form consciously or un-consciously in this or that man, and it is powerful before it takes control of his will or disposition. **Until the law sin was in the world.**

The law with which sin is contrasted is a visible factor in history (ii. 14–16), constantly reawakening in men the recol-lection of that relationship with God which they have—lost. The law is the norm by which divine truth and divine will are made known, and it may be presented to men consciously or unconsciously. The law is the light of the revelation and of the presence of God, broken into beams of different colours in the prism of the sequence and variety of human events. Where law is, there appears also a human righteousness and a divine elec-tion and vocation (ii. 3–5, 12, 13; iii. 2). Happy is the man who knows that the law provides him with no excuse, no comfortable retreat (ii. 1, 2). For where law or religion is, there the unright-eousness of men is evident. Bereft of every covering and naked in their impotent flesh—men are the obstacles of God and the objects of His wrath. And they are so, precisely when they become aware of the demands of the law, when they hear it, and give serious attention to it (iii. 14–20, iv. 15a). Unless we are very much deceived, it is this situation which provokes an arrogant attempt upon the tree of knowledge, and a new forget-fulness of human mortality; in so far, that is to say, as we mis-understand the impossibility of the law, and thereby misjudge its meaning. But, woe to the man of God who is thus deceived, and who forgets that his is a situation of peculiar danger! (ii. 17, 18.) Where law is, there is also transgression (iv. 15b), and sin is *reckoned*. This means that, when we have eyes to see, the darkness in which we stand becomes a torment. The material is inflammable, and a smouldering fire breaks out. Sin becomes burdensome guilt, which has to be borne con-sciously or unconsciously. Sin, having inherited sufficient capital, uses it to work up a flourishing business (vii. 8, 11);

and, as it redoubles its energy, the business soon appears—firmly established. So the man, awakened and devoted to religion, in full possession of the law, becomes a sinner in the most obvious sense of the word (vii. 7, 8; 14, 15).

The disease from which Joseph suffered now breaks out, not in the indifferent masses, but in those who are 'interested in religion'; not in the coarse-minded and disreputable, but in the clergy and their friends; not in the cinema, but in the Church; not in the godless professors of medicine, but in the doctors of the Theological Faculty; not in the capitalists and the materialists, but in those active in Social Reform; not in the wide circulation of frivolous literature, but in the publication of books such as the one I am now writing. The people of Israel are brought to ruin by their law and by their peculiar election and vocation; and they must suffer and decay in a manner unknown to the Philistines and the Moabites. So was it originally with Adam. Only because, having been warned concerning the tree of knowledge, Adam actually possessed the law, could sin enter into the world; and Adam became a sinner, because he was so nearly related to God. Is there any place, any epoch in history, any single human life, in which law plays no part? The period between the law of Adam and the law of Moses is treated as a period without law. Men's eyes were blind, and there was, consequently, no darkness; the world was damp, and there was consequently no burning fire. There was no capital, and, consequently, no business was possible. Human life was in the nursery, and God stood by watching in serious and amused silence. It could not have been otherwise. So we ought not to attempt to defend or to blame this nursery-stage in which there is no trace of those penultimate things which must appear later, when personal sin, conscious or unconscious, breaks out, and when sin is therefore *reckoned*. *Apart from the law sin is dead* (vii. 8). These sleeping sinners require only the final word—forgiveness. Nevertheless, they do await this word; for even such naïve sleepers[1] are not exempted from the sin of the world, as delicate-minded disciples of Rousseau would have us to suppose. This is clear from the words—**Nevertheless death reigned from Adam to Moses.** It has never been known that the law of death was inoperative in the case of these law-less ones, if indeed such men ever existed. They too were natural and created beings, confronted by the same riddle of birth and death as confronts us who

[1] The phrase '*Kanadische Schläfer*' occurs in the German and is a somewhat obscure reference to a poem by R. Seume: 'Ein Kanadier der noch Europens übertüchte Hoflichkeit nicht kannte . . .'. [Tr.]

have been awakened to perceive in these things a punishment
greater even than our sins require. That the universal sovereignty
of death affects them also is an additional indication of invisible
sin, of the Fall, which must not be identified with actual sin or
with those miserable lapses which are so frequent in our lives.
Sleeping sinners they are; and the shrunken Hippocratic[1] look
which appears even on their faces shows that their dreams have
a final non-historical origin. God treats as serious their case
also because they too share in the guilt and responsibility for
the separation of men from the divine life. They too stand under
the wrath of God, although His wrath be hidden. They did not,
it is true, sin—**after the likeness of Adam's transgression,** nor
of Israel's; yet, nevertheless, their dissimilarity provides them
neither with rest nor with excuse. Although, historically speaking, they are wholly uninstructed and innocent, they too stand
within the KRISIS of election and rejection, of justification and
damnation. The distinction between them and those who, under
the law, must die in the full bloom of their sins, is only relative:
*There is no respect of persons with God. For as many as sinned
without law shall also perish without law: and as many as have
sinned under the law shall be judged by the law* (ii. 11, 12). The
sin which entered the world by Adam is—and this must be
emphasized—powerful, supremely powerful, quite apart from
his actual sin and the sin of his followers. The visible sovereignty
of death points backwards to the invisible sovereignty of sin,
even when sin issued in no single concrete and visible action.
A king is not elected by his subjects, and they have no opportunity of deciding whether or no they wish to be his subjects.
He ascends the throne as the heir, and he rules 'by the grace of
God' or without it. Only by revolution and by overthrowing the
dynasty, only by upsetting the transcendental pre-supposition,
can they bring about a change in their general and necessary
dependence.

As a sinner, in the invisible and non-historical meaning of the
word, Adam is—**the figure of him that was to come.** The shadow
in which he stands bears witness to the light of Christ. Were
this not so, the shadow would be invisible to us. The shadow
also provides us with a standard by which we may measure the
light and perceive its nature. The invisible constitution of this
world is, if the minus sign outside the bracket be changed into
plus, the constitution of the new world which is to come. 'The
secret of Adam is the secret of the Messiah' (a Rabbinic saying).

---

[1] The description of the facies Hippocratica (the appearance of the face
before death) occurs in Hippocrates *Prognostic*, II. [Tr.]

The secret is the secret of men immediately fallen from God, and
yet indissolubly bound to Him; the secret which is obscured if
Adam and Christ be treated separately, but which is manifested
when they are brought together. Both figures stand close upon
the barrier between sin and righteousness, death and life; but
the one looks backwards, the other forwards. Utterly separated
by the contrast of what is encountered in them, but indissolubly united in that both the two contrasted things, election
and rejection, originate in one divine predestination; indivisible,
in that the sin and death of the one and the righteousness and
life of the other cover the whole range of human life in all its
dimensions; indivisible also, in that the 'Yes' of the one is the
'No' of the other, and the 'No' of the one is the 'Yes' of the
other. Type, '*figure*', prophecy, questioning, are the notes of
the one; archetype, fulfilment, answer, are the notes of the other.
As surely as (v. 15–17) the movement of the two to separation
is a genuine movement, so surely are the righteousness of God
and His life wholly pre-eminent over sin and death both
initially and finally, so surely is the apparent polarity of the
contrasts dissolved in the light of the critical 'Moment' when
'one death eats up the other' (Luther). From Adam to Christ—
this is God's road to men and among them. Of this we must now
speak further.

vv. 15–17. But there is no equilibrium; and one may **not**
say: **as the trespass, so also is the free gift. For if by the
trespass of the one the many died, much more did the
grace of God, and the gift by the grace of the one man,
Jesus Christ, abound unto the many.**

And, since there is no equilibrium, one may **not** say: **as
through one that sinned** sin entered into the world, **so** through
the one righteous man **the gift** has been given to men. (The
relation is, it is true, similar; **for the judgement came of
one unto condemnation, but the free gift came of the
trespasses** of many men **unto justification.**) But here the
similarity breaks down; **for if, by the trespass of the one,
death reigned through the one; much more shall they
that receive the abundance of grace and of the gift of
righteousness reign in life through the one, even Jesus
Christ.**

The whole passage is diacritical: it is concerned with empha-
sizing a distinction. **Much more!** How completely differently!
How much more certainly (v. 15, 17; cf. 9, 10)! As Jülicher comments: 'All logical argument is discarded.' The dualism of Adam

and Christ, between the old and the new, is not metaphysical but dialectical. The dualism exists only in so far as it dissolves itself. It is a dualism of one movement, of one apprehension, of one road from here to there. The situation is therefore misunderstood, if it be thought of as an equilibrium resulting from two equal forces operating in opposite directions, or if it be compared with the movement of the pendulum of a clock. The two contrasted factors are living and true, because they point in the same direction. This unity of direction is necessitated by an identity of origin and of purpose. Both have their origin and their purpose in God, and to Him they point. They move forward of necessity from guilt and destiny to reconciliation and redemption. The KRISIS of death and resurrection, the KRISIS of faith, is a turning from the divine 'No' to the divine 'Yes'. There is no subsequent reverse movement. Consequently, the invisible constitution of the new world is in form the same as that of the old. It differs, however, in power and significance, because it is altogether superior and utterly opposite. But this requires consideration and formulation.

THE FIRST CONSIDERATION (v. 15). We direct our attention first to the origins, the dominants, which condition on the one hand the old as old and disappearing, and on the other hand the new as new and 'coming'. The two origins are defined as 'Fall' and 'Grace'. Both definitions serve to bring out the relation between God and man. In both cases, whether a man stands 'fallen' in Adam or 'under grace' in Christ, he is what he is in God, in God Himself, and only in God. God is the factor common to both; it is this common factor which makes both appear to exist in equilibrium. But the distinction lies precisely in the common factor—How does the relation between God and man appear in Adam? Clearly—and this lies already in the word 'Fall'— God is here deserted and denied by men; He suffers and is robbed. Sin is, essentially, robbing God of what is His: and because it it is robbing OF GOD, sin is essentially the appearance in the world of a power—like God (v. 12). Sin is an invisible negative occurrence encountered by God and in Him. That—**by the trespass of the one the many died** is wholly congruous with this occurrence; that is to say, it is congruous that the negative relation between God and man should assume concrete form in Adam's world and also among men. In the one man, Adam, what was invisible became visible: in him God utters His 'No', and advances to the attack. He drives us from Paradise, and robs us of life: Sicut homo peccando rapit, quod Dei est, ita Deus puniendo aufert, quod hominis est (Anselm). The sinful

N

and fallen world is as such the world of death. It is a world
enclosed by a final and unresolved question, from which there
is no escape except at the barrier, and in which knowledge is not
attainable except by ignorance, nor hope except out of despair.
In it there is nought except the expectation of final judgement
and final dissolution; and moreover, judgement is already dread-
fully present even in the expectation. Contrasted with this is
the relation of men to God in Christ. Whether this relation be
defined as righteousness (i. 14, iii. 21) or as obedience (v. 19) or
as grace, we are manifestly concerned with the grace of God—
**with the grace of God and the gift by the grace of the one man, Jesus
Christ.** We are concerned with a POSITIVE, invisible relation,
with the operation and action of God, with His activity with
reference to men and their world. He does not simply accept
the robbery of what is His. He makes a claim upon men. Men,
though fallen, are not in His sight lost. He is merciful and
wonderful. He is the God who gives the gift of grace. It is
therefore wholly congruous that *the grace of God* should—
abound unto the many. It is therefore wholly congruous that
the positive relation between God and man should assume
positive form among men in Christ's world. God appears here
as Creator and Redeemer, as the Giver of Life and of all good
gifts. In the one man, Jesus Christ, what was invisible becomes
visible: in Him God utters His 'Yes'. The world to which God
turns actively and positively is as such the world of life,
the world in which nothing that is limited and trivial and
passing to corruption exists as it is, but IS what it signifies.
Related to its final origin and purpose, to its final meaning
and reality, the course of this world becomes, even in its questioning, full of answer; even in its transitoriness, filled with
eternity; even in its penultimate action, filled with final peace.
Thus the divine radiance shines out even over the nature of
men; and the world, too, filled with indescribable hope, is
stretched out before the new men standing on the threshold of
the new world. All this takes place in hope of a final one-ness,
a final clarity and peace, but once again, inasmuch as there is
hope, all is already also blessedly present (v. 11).—Such is the
dialectical balance between Fall and Grace. And what logic
can prevent the opening up of the possibility—the near possibility—of the dissolution of the apparent symmetry of these
contrasts? What logic can prevent our perceiving that the step
forward—the *much more*—is their true meaning? And moreover,
what can prevent our—taking the step?

THE SECOND CONSIDERATION (v. 16, 17). We now turn our

attention to the tendencies characteristic on the one hand of the old world, and, on the other, of the new. We must consider what entered the world—**through the one** sinner, and what entered the world—as the *gift* of God. Again we notice that, in each case human life is disposed in the same fashion, whether by fall or by grace. Both dispositions originate in a decision pronounced by the just and merciful God; both proceed in accordance with a definite though invisible ordering; and both involve further consequences, whether man be represented by Adam or by the *many* who, like him, are fallen sinners, and whether the decision be the sentence of death or of freedom: **The judgement came of one unto condemnation, but the free gift came of the trespasses of many unto justification.** The different characteristics of the old and the new proceed from the same invisible origin. They are old or new according to their relation to God. From Him they flow in different directions, as streams at the watershed of the Alps, or as a river when it passes through separate arches of a bridge. At the point of separation they are united; and it is this that constitutes their similarity (v. 16). When, however, we turn our attention to the nature of God's decision, as it affects men, it is dissimilarity we find. For God elects and rejects (v. 17). —On the one hand, the decision means that—**by the trespass of the one** there came into the world an active causality: **Death reigned through the one.** We see mankind robbed and rejected and suffering. We see men shackled by an iron chain which, starting from the first man, extends to the last. Men are under the control of the visible past and the visible future; the characteristic feature of the whole situation—causality—being the destiny of death. Mind and body lie under the mechanical necessity of destiny (ANANKE), and men are confined in a circle of meaningless growth and decay, of false security and bitter disappointment, of questionable youth and unmistakable old age, of abortive optimism and equally abortive pessimism. Men cannot live, because they have no power of will; they cannot will, because they are not free; they are not free, because they cannot choose their goal; they cannot choose their goal, because they are no more than mortal. Though the sentence of death was not pronounced at any moment in time, yet, like the sword of Damocles, it is suspended over our heads at every moment.— On the other hand, the decision means that through the one righteous man there came into the world the *gift* of God, which is nothing less than—**the abundance of grace and of the gift of righteousness.** This gift men are able to *receive*; and through it they verily *reign in life.* Through the death of Christ (vi. 4, 5)

men are made new and are translated into the realm of life.
The divine constitution under which we live in Christ is revolution against the invisible law of sin which has become visible in
death; it is the rehabilitation of men and their complete freedom
from the authority by which all existence is held in chains.
Nothing more nor less than the world is the heritage that is
promised to Abraham and to his successors (iv. 13). Men shall
not be enslaved to the COSMOS; rather the COSMOS shall lie,
set free, at their feet.

Though mankind has become the slave of all things, yet in
the death of Christ men are lord of all. The historical causality,
which renders them no more than links in a chain, is broken
in fragments, and they stand as individuals under the law of
liberty through the grace of Christ which—*came of the trespasses
of many*. The law of independence and freedom, by which they
are made new, is identical with the law of life (v. 18) which
marks the presence of the Kingdom of God. Established by
God, men are freed from sin and, consequently, from death
which is the consequence of sin. Immortal, they discover the
free purpose of life; and free of purpose, they discover freedom
of will. For those who have discovered this freedom, whether
they employ it victoriously or no, all corruption becomes a
parable of incorruption. Free of will, man has discovered himself. He is regal. His nobility is immeasurable and to his worth
there is no limit; for he possesses the life which is eternal and
true. The fact that those who receive abundance of grace *shall
reign* reminds us, however, that the identification of the old
with the new man has yet to be fulfilled (ii. 13, iii. 20, v. 20);
that we have as yet only been declared free; and that our actual
redemption cannot be identified with any concrete happening in
history. Here, too, men do not pass beyond the threshold of the
Kingdom of God, which is the Kingdom of the free and of the
freed. Yet they do stand hopefully on the threshold; and, because they have hope, they do not wholly lack the anticipatorily
present reality of what is hoped for. Once again the position of
the dialectical balance between judgement and grace may provide
us with the answer to the question as to whether we are right
in inferring—*much more then*—from the operation of the old
world the pre-eminent, victorious, wholly distinct, and infinitely
more significant and more powerful operation of the new world.

**vv. 18, 19. So then as by the offence of one judgement
came unto all men to condemnation; even so by the
righteousness of one the free gift came unto all men to**

**justification of life. For as by one man's disobedience
the many were made sinners, so by the obedience of one
shall many be** appointed **righteous.**

We have seen clearly (v. 13, 14) that the sin by which the old
course of the world is controlled is no less original, invisible,
and objective, than the righteousness with which it is contrasted.
We have also further ascertained (v. 15–17) that the underlying
conflict between the two is presented as movement from fall
to atonement, from imprisonment to redemption, from death to
life, only in order to make evident that the movement finally
disappears. It is now possible for us to complete the setting out
of the contrasts which, at an earlier stage, we were compelled
to break off (v. 12), without fear of being misunderstood.

Adam is the 'old' subject, the EGO of the man of this world.
This EGO is fallen. It has appropriated to itself what is God's, in
order that it may live in its own glory. This fallen state is the
consequence of no single historical act: it is the unavoidable
pre-supposition of all human history, and, in the last analysis,
proceeds from the secret of divine displeasure and divine rejection. Directly related to this 'Fall' is the **condemnation** unto
death, pronounced upon **all men**; whereby the naturalness and
creatureliness, the inadequacy, tribulation, and corruption, of
men, as men of this world, constitute alike their curse and their
destiny (v. 18). For (v. 19)—**by one man's disobedience the many
were made sinners.** The action of Adam does not merely throw
light upon his own individual character; rather, it defines
individuality itself, all individuals,—*the many.* For those who
have eyes to see, the many are discovered and exposed as
sinners. There is no man, who as a man and as he really is, is
not—*in Adam.* As such, therefore, the old and fallen subject
is set under sentence of death, under negation, under the
wrath of God.—Such, then, is the old world by which we are
continually generated.

But Christ is the 'new' subject, the EGO of the coming world.
This EGO receives and bears and reveals the divine *justification*
and election—*This is my beloved Son, in whom I am well pleased.*
This qualification of man, this appointing as the Son of God,
through the power of the Resurrection (i. 3, 4), of Him who was
born of the seed of David, is also non-concrete, unobservable, and
non-historical. Flesh and blood cannot reveal it unto us. Here
also both our knowledge and the object of our knowledge proceed from the secret of divine predestination, by which all
human history is constituted anew and given a pre-eminent and

victorious meaning. As a consequence of the righteousness of
Christ there comes—**justification of life—unto all men.** Here is
the negation of all negation, the death of all death, the breaking
down of all limitations, the rending asunder of all fetters, the
clothing of men with their habitation which is from heaven
(2 Cor. v. 2). For all men death is swallowed up in victory
(1 Cor. xv. 55) and mortality is swallowed up by life (2 Cor. v. 4):
*Christ being raised from the dead dieth no more, death no more
hath dominion over him* (vi. 9). With this declaration of righteousness the new and eternal subject of all men has been directly
created (v. 18). For (v. 19)—**by the obedience of the one shall
many be appointed righteous.** Here again, it is not merely that
A personality, AN individual, has been illuminated by what
is observable and appreciable in the obedience of the life and
death of the one Jesus; rather, it is THE personality, THE individual, which has here been disclosed. In the One the *many*
individuals are, here, for those who have eyes to see, appointed,
illuminated, and disclosed: that is to say, Thou and I are
appointed as righteous before God, as seen and known by God,
as established in God, as taken unto Himself by God. In the
light of this act of obedience there is no man who is not—
in Christ. All are renewed and clothed with righteousness,
all are become a new subject, and are therefore set at liberty
and placed under the affirmation of God. But, as what we are,
Thou and I can think of this positive relation with God only in
terms of hope, as we are reminded by the words: *They shall be
accounted righteous* (ii. 13, iii. 10, v. 17). We stand only at the
threshold. Yes! but we do stand there.—Such, then, is the new
world to which we move.

**vv. 20, 21. Moreover the law has entered between, that
the trespass might abound; but where sin abounded,
grace did abound more exceedingly: that, as sin reigned
in death, even so might grace reign through righteousness unto eternal life through Jesus Christ our Lord.**

Just as what had been said in v. 12 was repeated more
emphatically in v. 13, 14; so here what was said in v. 18, 19
is repeated with greater emphasis. The conception of sin was
deepened and clarified when sin was defined as *trespass* and
disobedience. The definition is now shown to be important
because it enables us to fix our attention finally upon the pre-
eminent significance of the opposing conceptions of *righteousness*
and *obedience*. Once more it is the idea of law which best
serves this purpose. We have already seen that, even where

·there is no law, invisible sin operates as power (in death). We
have now to show that sin becomes visible—precisely where
the law is. This does not mean, of course, that there has
emerged a third factor between the world as 'Fall' and the
world as 'Righteousness', between disobedience and obedience.
The law, as a visible and concrete historical fact, is, rather,
the point at which men become consciously aware of the two
worlds, the place at which the necessity of a change of direction has to be recognized. We have seen the vast, objective,
invisible, new world encounter the old world victoriously. We
have marked how its whole operation is based upon the sovereign
will of God. But has not something been suppressed, or forgotten and overlooked? Has not the relation of men to God,
which we have named *in Adam* and *in Christ*, its subjective side
also? Does there not also exist, side by side with the invisible
possibilities of the *old* and the *new*, the visible possibility that
men may become—religious? Is there not between Adam and
Christ a third figure—Moses! (v. 13, 14) by whose side Aaron
stands? Are there not prophets and priests? Are there not
men who believe and hope and love, devoted and awakened
men, men who wait and hurry, courageous men who venture
the leap into the void, or men who are, at least, faithful in little
things, men of prayer and thought and action? In short, is there
not the vast subject-matter of an 'Encyclopaedia of Religion and
Ethics'? In religion do not men cross the threshold at which we
have seen the new man standing? Is not the dialectical balance
between sin and righteousness replaced in religion by a healthy,
vigorous, divine humanity or human divinity? Is not religion a
tangible and concrete fragment of the new world? We are bound
to face these questions seriously—Yes! the relation with God has
its human, historical, subjective side. We cannot underestimate
the fact that religious men do exist. There is a disposition and
manner of thought and action which is characteristically religious. Religion appears in history in many different forms, but,
where it displays strong and earnest godliness, it is always
attractive. We may venture perhaps upon a relative criticism
of this or of that form which religion assumes, but we are, nevertheless, bound to stand spellbound before it and to give it relative
approval. Nor has religion great difficulty in answering objections to this or to that particular form in which it presents itself,
for it is in religion that human capacity appears most pure,
most strong, most penetrating, most adaptable. Religion is
the ability of men to receive and to retain an impress of God's
revelation; it is the capacity to reproduce and give visible

expression to the transformation of the old into the new man—
so that it becomes a conscious human expression and a conscious
and creative human activity. **The law,** then—precisely as this
human possibility—has **entered between.** The law is an ambiguous matter floating between heaven and earth, at one
moment making extravagant promises, at another knowing
itself helpless to fulfil them. It claims to possess the new
world of righteousness and life, for it avows the possibility
of possessing God and of living in His presence—*Who have
received the law by the disposition of angels* (Acts vii. 53)—*The
law is holy, and the commandment holy, and righteous, and good*
(vii. 12). Manifestly, then, the law has its invisible foundation
and meaning from God; and we are bound to search it out(iii. 31).
This is the relative justification of the whole acceptance and
confession and defence of religion. But, as a human possibility,
it manifestly appears and has its reality in history, it is woven
into the texture of men, it belongs mentally and morally to the
old world, and stands in the shadow of sin and death. The
DIVINE possibility of religion can never be changed into a
human possibility. All criticism of religion can find in this its
relative justification. We see, then, that the relation to God
has necessarily its subjective side, which is under the law of
death. Neither Moses nor Aaron, neither the crudest nor the
most delicate forms of religious experience, can escape from this
twilight of religion. The 'Jesus of History', *born of a woman,
born under the law* (Gal. iv. 4), the paradox of Paul's apostolate,
and our peace with God (v. 1), have no protection against the misunderstanding whereby they are regarded as new forms of this
human possibility—which is, however, not a human possibility!
In this twilight the polemics of one religion against another are
fought out; in the same twilight men engage in anti-religious
propaganda—which is but another form of religion. However
much we may protest that our religion is free of misunderstanding; however delicate may be the scepticism of those
irreligious-religious men who stand outside; yet we and they
still remain within the framework of history, unable to escape
from the twilight of misunderstanding. We must therefore
abandon our superiority and pride of difference. The religion
which we are able to detect in ourselves and in others is that of
human possibility, and, as such, it is a most precarious attempt
to imitate the flight of a bird. And so, if religion be understood
as a concrete, comprehensible, and historical phenomenon in
the world of men and of sin and of death—it must be abandoned.
All our respect and admiration for the part it plays in this world

of ours must not prevent our recognizing that every claim to absolute and transcendent truth, every claim to direct relationship with God, made on its behalf, is utterly worthless. The boldest speculations of religion, its most intimate experiences, its wide-flung plans for taking the Kingdom of Heaven by violence, stick fast in some middle region of materialistic idealism, in some endeavour to stretch nature to super-nature or to metaphysics. They end, that is to say, in the territory of the 'No-God' of this world, where they can be honoured as 'Life' and as the 'Kingdom of God', as 'reality' and as 'other-worldliness'. —No more can be said POSITIVELY about religion than that in its purest and noblest and most tenacious achievements mankind reaches, and indeed must reach, its highest pinnacle of human possibility. But even so religion remains a human achievement. The law has entered between—**that the trespass may abound.** The invisible possibility of religion operates, and must operate, as a visible possibility, in order that the fall of man may become visible, and the necessity of his turning unto *righteousness* may be made manifest—in his visible attainments. In the religious man we are able to perceive most clearly that men are flesh, sinful, hindrances to God, under His wrath, arrogant, restless, incapable of knowledge, and weak of will. Precisely in the religious man we become aware of the inexorable barrier with which we are confronted. The law worketh wrath. Where law is, there is transgression (iv. 15). Where law is, sin is imputed (v. 13). 'Each one of us is utterly guilty in the presence of all; and, more than all others, I am guilty' (Dostoevsky). 'Before, I was free, and walked in the dark without a lantern: now, possessing the law, I have a conscience, and I take a lantern when I walk in the dark. God's law does nothing for me, but to awaken my bad conscience' (Luther). This is the subjective, human side of the relation with God. Esau, who was no dreamer as Jacob was, did not lie as Jacob did. To be Israel, as far as human possibility is concerned, means to be worthless and despicable, full of sorrow and disease: to be Christ, so far as human possibility is concerned, means to die in the midst of evil-doers, to die framing the question, which neither Pilate nor Caiaphas would have allowed to escape from his lips: *My God, my God, why hast thou forsaken me?* So far as human possibility is concerned, prophets and priests, theologians and philosophers, men of faith, hope, and charity, break in pieces on the impossibility of God. They have laboured in vain and spent their strength for nought, although the matter is the Lord's and their work is God's (Isa. xlix. 4). They are boils and

ulcers which enable the disease from which all suffer to be diag-
nosed. If we expect anything else, we are ignorant of the meaning of law and religion and election and vocation; and we had
better leave these things alone. Wherever men pray and preach,
wherever sacrifice is offered, wherever in the presence of God
emotions are stirred and experiences occur—there, yes! precisely
there, the trespass abounds. Precisely there, the invisible truth
that before God no flesh is righteous, which may perhaps have
remained invisible *from Adam to Moses* (v. 14), becomes visible.
Precisely there, men encounter God; and there breaks forth the
KRISIS of God, the sickness unto death.

But where sin abounded, grace did abound more exceedingly.
The final and most significant concrete factor, the possibility
of religion, must be dissolved catastrophically, in order that the
'No' of God may be transformed into His 'Yes', and in order
that grace may be grace. This transformation occurs when the
dissolution and catastrophe are encountered; when the last
human endeavour is found to be useless and ineffective; when
every short cut has failed; when no human movement or
re-volution or e-volution is adequate to provide a positive, or
even a negative, method of proceeding from Adam to Christ;
when the abandoned Servant of God abandons—Himself. Then
it is that the claim of religion is justified. What can be more
healthy than disease unto death? And where should the disease
break out, if it be not where the law has *entered between*; where,
in their utter questionableness, men are not able to contemplate
God; and where, precisely for this reason, human inadequacy
is brought out of obscurity into the clear light of day?—*When
his soul shall make an offering for sin, he shall see his seed, he
shall prolong his days, and the pleasure of the Lord shall prosper
in his hand. He shall see of the travail of his soul, and shall be
satisfied: by his knowledge shall my righteous servant make many
righteous; for he shall bear their sins* (Isa. liii. 10, 11). This is the
dissolution and catastrophe which makes of Saul—Paul; and
which enables and commands Paul to be truly—Saul. For he
is Paul in virtue of what he is not. This is the abounding *more
exceedingly* of grace, which cannot occur in every temporal
moment, unless sin abounds in religion. We must not turn our
backs upon the importance of religion in history; and indeed
care is taken that we should not do so. Grace is grace, where the
possibility of religion in the full bloom of its power is earnestly
accepted—and then offered up as a sacrifice. But does grace
occur only there? We must not dare even to think, still less to
speak, thus,—as though grace were limited. Happy are those

mature and superior humanists who know nothing of the arrogance and tragedy of religion, who seem to be spared the illusions and disillusionments of Israel. We dare not return to the procedure of the Pharisees, and cry out to them: 'If Christ had been born in Athens, we should have no guarantee of so regal a sovereignty of grace' (Zahn).

Sin, then, must *abound* and grace must *abound more exceedingly*—that, as sin reigned in death, even so might grace reign through righteousness unto eternal life. The new world is the Kingdom of God and the sphere of His sovereignty and power. As new men, we stand at its threshold. God Himself, and God alone, wills and elects, creates and redeems. We were concerned with the genuineness of the movement from Adam to Christ, when, associating like to like, we finally brought the whole possibility of religion under the general heading of 'The reign of sin unto death'. This was essential, in order that we might confront everything with its opposite—with grace which *reigns through righteousness unto eternal life*—through Jesus Christ our Lord. Grace is not grace, if he that receives it is not under judgement. Righteousness is not righteousness, if it be not reckoned to the sinner. Life is not life, if it be not life from death. And God is not God, if he be not the End of men. We have seen the old world as a completely closed circle from which we have no means of escape. But, because we have perceived this, we are able to recognize—in the light of the Resurrection of Jesus from the dead—the power and meaning of the Coming Day: the Day of the New World and of the New Man.

The Sixth Chapter

GRACE

THE POWER OF THE RESURRECTION

VI. I–II

v. 1. What shall we say then further? **Shall we continue in sin, that grace may abound ? God forbid.**

What shall we say then further? We have seen Adam and Christ, the old and the new world, the dominion of sin and the dominion of righteousness, linked together in a strict dialectical relationship. We have seen them apparently pointing to one another, determining one another, and authorizing one another. We have been careful, however, to emphasize (v. 15–17) the dialectical character of this relation. The first is dissolved by the second; the reverse process is impossible. It is, in fact, of quite vital importance that we should be competent, not only to emphasize, but also to prove this process to be inevitable, irreversible, and victorious. We boldly claimed that the most important evidence for the eternity of the 'Moment' of perception is provided by the terrifying words: *Where sin abounded, grace did much more abound* (v. 20). That is to say, by an incomprehensible decision of God, the key is turned, the door opened, and men—cross the threshold. We also ventured to find in the relation between Saul and Paul an illustration of the relation between the extremity of sin and the triumph of grace. We were, moreover, compelled to venture upon such an understanding of the relation between sin and grace, since 'We should not silently pass Christ by on the ground that to many He is a rock of offence and a stone of stumbling. For by the same quality He brings both the unbelievers to destruction and the pious to resurrection' (Calvin). And yet, these words are dangerously ambiguous. The 'quality' to which Calvin refers is not an actual or a psychological status or process: it is capable of no physical or metaphysical definition. Misunderstanding is avoided only if the words are taken as referring to the eternal 'Moment' of the knowledge of God. It would, however, be possible to expand Calvin's meaning somewhat as follows: 'Fall and grace stand to one another in an eternal tension, or polarity, or antinomy. The "Yes" and the "No" are alike necessary, important, and divine. "No" must be transformed into "Yes", and "Yes" into "No", for everything is both negative and positive.' Is that, however, what we really mean?

The deduction would then be inevitable—*Let us continue in sin that grace may abound*. The continuity of the relation between sin and grace, Saul and Paul, forms the *actus purus* of an invisible occurrence in God. The unity of the divine will is divided only that it may be revealed in overcoming the division. But it is only too easy to confuse this invisible occurrence in God with that observable series of psychophysical experiences in which it is manifested. Or, to put this another way, the observable flux of human experience which points to the transformation of that experience in God may be projected backwards metaphysically into the will of God. Men will then direct their attention, not towards the Unknown God, but towards their own selves; and the continuity which they perceive existing between their lower and their higher experiences will appear to them invested with transcendent sanction and authority. Once provided in this way with the sanction of eternity, all disquiet is at an end, and the threats and promises involved in the invisible occurrence are totally obscured: in their place we have the sepulchral peace of an immanent tension, a polarity, an allogeneity, an antinomy, between lower and higher conditions of mental or moral behaviour. Since human possibilities are related to one another as cause and effect, the next step is obvious. By analogy the condition of grace is supposed to succeed the condition of sin as one human possibility succeeds another. The reverse may therefore also occur: sin may succeed grace, and grace again follow sin. The causal connexion between the two constitutes a clear invitation to *continue in sin*. So sin, which in God's sight withers as soon as it appears and vanishes in extrusion and destruction, becomes a positive factor, a means, an instrument, a spring-board, by the use of which another human possibility may be achieved. Here we are faced by the same 'human logic' which produced, in an earlier passage (iii. 3–5), the conclusion—*Let us do evil that good may come*. Here again human life is employed to confine the free movement of the will of God within the limits of human experience, and to extend to divinity the contrasts with which men are familiar: as though we were, within the limits imposed by our nature, competent to transform evil into good and sin into grace; and as though a 'God' who vacillates capriciously between evil and good, sin and grace, were the Very God, and not rather the 'No-God' of this world in whom is mirrored the disorderliness of the human soul.

God forbid that such manipulations of human logic should be current among us. *God forbid* that the ineffable and invisible 'Moment' at which the power of sin and the power of grace are equally balanced and both are sanctioned by God, should be translated into terms of psychophysical sensations and experiences which jostle and succeed one another in unabashed visibility. *God forbid* that we should honour and welcome sin as a cause of grace, as though they stood in a mutual relation of cause and effect. *God forbid* that we should piously attribute the sovereignty of God to men, and with equal piety ascribe to Him impotence. *God forbid* that we should play a pseudo-dialectical game with the eternal tension and polarity and antinomy in which we are set, and then imagine that we are acting in accordance with the divine decrees. All this is, however, forbidden by the power of the Resurrection, of which we must now speak.

v. 2. We who died to sin, how shall we any longer be able to live therein ?

As an event, sin is that interchanging of God and man, that exalting of men to divinity or depressing of God to humanity, by which we seek to justify and fortify and establish ourselves. So long as our will and our intelligence continue to press out inevitably into such an event—whether on the lowest or on the highest rung of the ladder of human achievement, is irrelevant—we continue inevitably to be sinners. Continue inevitably, because, in the whole realm of human possibility, our will and intelligence cannot do otherwise. Our limitation, our contingent and fragmentary nature, must inevitably bear witness to the invisible sin of the Fall by which our existence as men—as the men we actually are—is conditioned. *To live in sin* means that by an invisible necessity we cannot do otherwise than wilfully and consciously exalt ourselves to divinity and depress God to our own level.

Grace, however, is the fact of forgiveness. But it can be apprehended only in that continuity which pertains to the will of God, and to His will alone. So far as the eye can see, men reject God; and yet, He accepts them, fallen as they are, as His children, as objects of His mercy, His favour, and His love. This action of God constitutes so deadly an assault upon men *living in sin*, that a radical doubt arises as to whether in fact their status is conditioned by sin visible or invisible.

'Grace is opposed to sin, and devours it' (Luther). The reference here is to the sin of the Fall which becomes concrete in the supreme sin of religion, the sin of anthropomorphism. Grace digs sin up by its roots, for it questions the validity of our present existence and status. It takes away our breath, ignores us as we are, and treats us as what we are not—as new men. To be in grace means that we are no longer treated by God as sinners. For those who have been known by God, sin, instead of determining of necessity our will and intelligence, becomes a withered, defeated, and finished thing. **We died to sin.** We no longer grow up from its roots, breathe its air, and abide under its dominion. **How shall we any longer be able to live therein?** How can we continue to live as we are, as men of whom God knows nothing? What is to become of the visible state of our will and intelligence? How can our existence remain the scene of visible sin? Yes indeed! How? A doubt is here cast upon the pre-supposition of the necessity of sin; for our existence has been thrust under the light of a superior existence by which it is rendered non-existent. The totality of our human will and intelligence, future as well as past, has been superseded by the pre-eminent, ineffable, and invisible power of our eternal future existence —Futurum aeternum—the future of the non-concrete possibility of God. This is grace.

Grace and sin, then, are incommensurable. They cannot be correlated as two stations on a railway, or two links in a chain of causality, or two foci of an ellipse, or two steps in an argument. Mathematically speaking, they are not merely points on different planes, but points in different spaces, of which the second excludes the first. There is no question of a 'relationship' between them, and the possibility of moving from one to the other is excluded. Sin is related to grace as possibility to impossibility. Grace to which sin is a contemporary possibility is not grace. He that has received grace neither knows nor wills sin. He is not a sinner. Between the two is set the dissolution of the old and the emergence of the new man. 'Justification is the act of God by which men are not left as they are but wholly transformed' (Fr. Barth).

vv. 3–5. Or are ye ignorant that all we who were baptized into Christ Jesus were baptized into his death? We were buried therefore with him through baptism into death: that like as Christ was raised from the dead through the glory of the Father, so we also should walk in newness of life. For if we have become united with him in the likeness of his death—that is, by our death—we shall be also in the likeness of his resurrection.

We who were baptized into Christ Jesus. The memory of the sign (iv. 11) of baptism, that concrete event in time which was

the beginning of our knowledge of God, provides us with our
starting-point. Baptism is an occurrence belonging to the concrete world of religion. And why should we not remember it?
For sin, the wilful and conscious dishonouring of God with
which we are concerned, is also a concrete fact: *Redemption in
Christ Jesus* (iii. 24) also is a fact belonging to the concrete world;
its 'historicity', is—*for all who believe* (iii. 22a)—that which
points to the existentiality of its eternal content. Similarly, baptism, especially because of the paradox of its non-repetition, is a
sign. We know, of course, that a sign is no more than a sign;
but why should we for that reason regard it as indifferent?
'Signs are empty and ineffectual only when our wickedness
and ingratitude impede the operation of the truth of God'
(Calvin): when, that is, by identifying truth with some
concrete thing, we deprive a sign of its truth. Mistaking piety
for the content of truth, we take refuge in some ineffectual
ecclesiastical transaction: whether by identifying the truth
of a sign with some religious experience—for example, 'bap-
tismal experience'!—associated with it; or by attributing to
the sign itself a direct mystical and magical communication;
or, more rationally, by treating the sign as a concrete 'symbol'
of the Christian 'myth', and retaining it as an encouragement in
the midst of the chaos of life. But baptism is a sacrament of
truth and holiness; and it is a sacrament, because it is the
sign which directs us to God's revelation of eternal life and
declares, not merely the Christian 'myth', but—the Word of God.
It does not merely signify eternal reality, but is eternal reality,
because it points significantly beyond its own concreteness.
Baptism mediates the new creation: it is not itself grace, but
from first to last a means of grace. As the question which men
put to God is always also His answer to it; as human faith is
enclosed invisibly by the faithfulness of God; so also the human
act of baptism is enclosed by that action of God on behalf of
men which it declares. If, then, baptism is what it signifies, why
should we not choose it as our base of operations in the temporal
and concrete world? What we have been saying throughout
and wish to drive home here also, is supported by the fact that
baptism, as a rite of initiation, is no original creation of Christianity, but was taken over from 'Hellenism'. There is good
reason for this. The Gospel of Christ was not concerned with
the inventing of new rites and dogmas and institutions. Everywhere it can be seen quite naïvely borrowing religious material
already in existence. The Gospel of the Unknown God does
not enter into competition with known divinities, such as

Mithras or Isis or Cybele, to whom the sphere of religious phenomena belongs. Being itself wholly pre-eminent over the middle-
world of magic in which the original and proper meaning of
religious symbolism has been obscured, the Gospel of the Unknown God is competent to understand the mystery religions
better than they do themselves, and, avoiding their dangers,
is free to gather up the sense in their non-sense. The Gospel is
therefore justified in accepting and appropriating the 'witness'
which Judaism and Paganism bear to the revelation of God
(iii. 21). But by grace alone do we become aware of the sense
that is in non-sense (iv. 16); for there is no direct communication
from God, and therefore the appropriation of the sense in the
non-sense of the world of religion can only be by faith. We know
too that we ourselves are subject to a like limitation. Our election, our signs, and our witness, have also their own criticism
latent within them.

Are ye ignorant that we were baptized into his death? To those
who are not ignorant the sign of baptism speaks of death. To
be baptized means to be immersed, to be sunk in a foreign element, to be covered by a tide of purification. The man who
emerges from the water is not the same man who entered it. One
man dies and another is born. The baptized person is no longer
to be identified with the man who died. Baptism bears witness
to us of the death of Christ, where the radical and inexorable
claim of God upon men triumphed. He that is baptized is drawn
into the sphere of this event. Overwhelmed and hidden by the
claim of God, he disappears and is lost in this death. The arrogant illusion of the likeness of men to God is loosened and
stripped from him. In the light of the Cross, what indeed is
left to him? He has forfeited his identity with the man who
sins in will and act; he is free of the power of sin, free also of the
status of sin. The man over whom sin has power and dominion
has died (vi. 2, 7). The death of Christ dissolves the Fall by
bringing into being the void in which the usurped independence
of men can breathe no longer. It digs up the invisible roots of
visible sin, and makes Adam, the man of the 'No-God', a thing
decayed and gone. Beyond this death the man who asks that
he may continue in sin (vi. 2) and be like God lives no longer.
He is dissolved by the claim which God makes upon him. The
perception of this freedom must not be described as 'Heaven-
storming idealism' (H. Holtzmann). It is the end of such
tumult. Nor is it 'pure, harsh doctrinarianism' (Wernle). To
call upon the God who quickeneth the dead (iv. 17b) is not
doctrine; and, moreover, no theorist could for one moment allow

himself so naked and so blatant a contradiction, so glaring a paradox. The conception of divine power in human weakness is neither 'pure' nor 'harsh', and, unlike any 'doctrine', has continually to be thought out afresh as though it had never been thought out at all. Troeltsch names it: 'The theology of the absolute moment.' Yes! that is it; provided that 'absolute' be thought of as 'existential', the knowledge of the most positive and most exclusive existentiality of divine grace. With this the act of baptism is concerned: 'Your baptism is nothing less than grace clutching you by the throat: a grace-full throttling, by which your sin is submerged in order that ye may remain under grace. Come thus to thy baptism. Give thyself up to be drowned in baptism and killed by the mercy of thy dear God, saying: "Drown me and throttle me, dear Lord, for henceforth I will gladly die to sin with Thy Son"' (Luther). This death is grace.

We were buried with him through baptism into death: that like as Christ was raised from the dead through the glory of the Father, so we also should walk in newness of life. But why is this death grace? Because it is the 'death of death, the sin of sin, the poison of poison, and the imprisoning of imprisonment' (Luther). Because the shattering and undermining and disintegration which proceed from it are the action of God; because its negation is positive and its power is the primal authority; because the final word spoken over the man of this world is at once hinge, and threshold, and bridge, and turning-point, to the new man; because the baptized person—who must not be identified with the man who died—is identical with the new man who has been born. Death is not grace so long as it is a merely relative negation; that is, so long as the attack upon the man of this world peters out in mere criticism of, or opposition to, or revolution against, this or that concrete thing. Death is not grace, if human possibilities are multiplied by it through the coming into being of a whole series of negative (?) things, such as, ascetism, 'back to nature', silent worship, mystical death, Buddhist Nirvana, Bolshevism, Dadaism, and so forth: so long, that is, as the attack does not culminate in the final negation of the man of this world and of all his possibilities, and so long as we are not—*buried with him*. But—and this is what gives the attack its real power—the Judgement, the End, the sound of the Last Trump, pass straight through our 'Yes' and our 'No', through life and death, all and nothing, enjoyment and deprivation, speech and silence, tradition and revolution, in fact, through the whole busy activity of the man of this world—

and through his manifest tarrying. And then we encounter the power of the Resurrection: Christ *was raised from the dead through the glory of the Father*; impossibility becomes possibility. In the Resurrection, the full seriousness and energy of the veritable negation, of our being buried, are displayed and ratified. By the creation of the new man, the truth of the redemption which Christ effected is made known (v. 10, 11); by our existence in Him our existence in Adam is manifestly dissolved. By this radical conception of death the autonomy of the power of resurrection is guaranteed as independent of the life which is on this side of the line of death. The void brought into being by the death of Christ is filled with the new life which is the power of the Resurrection. The pre-eminence of the new life does not merely check our *continuance in sin* (vi. 2), it renders it impossible. The sinner in will and act, the man whom alone we can see, know, and conceive of, is thrust against the wall and becomes wholly questionable. How shall we, who have been thus placed in question, live any longer in sin? Dead and buried—*we should walk in newness of life*. As in ii. 13, iii. 30, v. 17, 19, &c., so here (vi. 2, 5, 8, 14), the future of the Resurrection—Futurum resurrectionis—which is our future, is a parable of our eternity. But is it only a parable? We have already seen that the raising of Jesus from the dead is not an event in history elongated so as still to remain an event in the midst of other events. The Resurrection is the non-historical (iv. 17b) relating of the whole historical life of Jesus to its origin in God. It follows therefore that the pressure of the power of the Resurrection into my existence, which of necessity involves a real walking in newness of life, cannot be an event among other events in my present, past, or future life. My new life is the 'ought' and 'can', the 'must' and 'will', of my new EGO which has been created in Christ: it is the assurance of my *citizenship in heaven* (Phil. iii. 20), the vitality of my life which is *hid with Christ in God* (Col. iii. 3): it is the invisible point of observation and of relationship, the judgement exercised by my infinite upon my finite existence; it is the threatening and promising which is set beyond time, beyond all visibility, beyond all the finite and concrete events of my life. Because the world is the world, and time is time, and men are men, and so long as they remain what they are, my new life must exist 'beyond' them; as the deadly and incommensurable power of the Resurrection, my new life presses upon my *continuing in sin*, and, as the criticism of my temporal existence and thought and will, determines also its meaning and significance. In so far as the impossible becomes possible and I am

buried with Christ, in so far as the 'I' which is not I appropriates
both the criticism and the significance of all that strictly contradicts all that I am, I am veritably *dead to sin* (vi. 2). For in
the invisible newness of life whereby the new man walks in the
glory of God, sin has as little light and air and space as in
the glory of God which is manifested in the raising of Jesus
from the dead. It always remains, of course, a burning question
whether we can and do venture (v. 1, vi. 11) to reckon with this
impossible possibility of the new man; but there is no question
at all but that the possible possibility of sin is excluded by it.

**For if we have become united to him in the likeness of his death,
we shall be also in the likeness of his resurrection.** In so far as our
tribulation is not a negation which we have manipulated, it is
a likeness and an analogue of the death of Christ (viii. 17; Gal. vi.
17; 2 Cor. iv. 10; Phil. iii. 10; Col. i. 24) and we are thereby visibly
united to him in time. His death is the means by which men are
able to apprehend themselves in God, that is to say, they apprehend His increase in their decrease, His strength in their weakness, His life in their death (2 Cor. iv. 16, 17). This is the criticism
exerted by the death of Christ; its significance is made known,
because it is the threshold over which we pass from judgement to
the Judge, from tribulation to Him who is free and who sets free,
from sorrow to hope (v. 3, 4). It is the occasion by which we know
ourselves to be in God. This apprehension, however, must not
be identified with some peculiar maturity of human experience.
The sign of baptism reminds us of this invisible fellowship with
God (vi. 3), which rules out any question of being the fellow or
disciple of Christ except in the bearing of His Cross. That is to
say, baptism does not remind us of some attainable and positive
conformity to Jesus, of some moral and actual experience of
likeness to Him, such as trust in God, brotherly love, freedom,
childlike character; it involves, of course, a visible conforming
to Christ of our actual life in the world, but, in the light of His
death, the union with Him upon which everything depends
consists in the wholly irremediable questionableness of human
life from beginning to end. We stand—and who does not stand
with us?—on the threshold of the narrow gate through which
we perceive the graciousness of the Judge and the mercy of the
Holy One. From our union with Christ in dishonour and weakness and corruption we look out—and who does not look with
us?—upon our union with Him in glory and power and incorruption: that is to say, we men, living in time, perceive the Futurum
resurrectionis, which is our true and positive conformity to
Jesus. This is wholly distinct from such moral and actual

experiences or dispositions of character as may accompany the perception. Since the true conformity to Jesus is no human quality or activity, it cannot be either compared or contrasted with these experiences or dispositions. It nowhere swims into the ken either of the historian or of the psychologist, and no man can claim to possess it directly. That life of ours which is positively conformed to Jesus is the life which is hid with Christ in God, and which is only 'ours' here and now as the eternal future. This, however, is sufficient for us, for the grace of God sufficeth (2 Cor. i. 9). Grace is the act of God by which the new man shall be and is, and by which also he is free from sin. Our negative, known, human existence, so little conformed to Jesus, is filled with hope by the positive and secret power of the resurrection.

vv. 6, 7. Knowing this, that our old man was crucified with him, that the body of sin might be done away, that so we should no longer be in bondage to sin; for he that died is justified from sin.

Knowing this. Understanding the sign of baptism, we understand ourselves, and know what God knows about us: *He knoweth whereof we are made; He remembereth that we are but dust* (Ps. ciii. 14). In the frailty and relativity, in the all-pervading KRISIS under which we stand in the likeness of the death of Christ upon the Cross, we know that we are conformed to Him (vi. 3, 5). This inward perception involves, however, an outward perception also, since our conformity to Christ is the starting-point for the psychology of grace, a psychology which is rid of the possibility of direct and non-dialectical analysis, and which is content to contrast grace as a non-concrete factor with the whole concrete behaviour of the soul. Conformed to Christ in the way of death, we perceive our status, as determined by sin, fallen away, withered, and non-existent; and we perceive the pre-eminent power of the new man—we see the mercy of God, and ourselves as His children.

Our old man. That is, as Godet says: 'The fallen Adam, reappearing in every human EGO as it comes under the dominion of self-love occasioned by the first sin.' Our whole concern with the world of time and of things and of men, our continuous business with what the world offers us, is our preoccupation with the fallen Adam. In the world there is no other Adam. All our judgements and analyses of his nature and importance concern the *old man*, since our EGO, unless it be wholly dissolved (*yet not I, but Christ liveth in me*), remains the EGO or subject of the old man; and, consequently, all our judgements concerning human nobility or deprivation, exaltation or humiliation, are judgements on the old man by the old man. Nevertheless, my very recognition of my complete identity with the old man involves the existence of a point outside that identity from which I may know myself, or rather from which I may be known; otherwise I should not recognize myself, or rather be recognized, as nothing but this old man. What, then, is this point of observation? What is this dynamic force which so powerfully and irresistibly drives me to recognize the closed circle in which I live? How is it that I am able to stand aside and see my EGO as an object of knowledge, as something strange and foreign to me? For such knowledge, and in order that the old man may become the object of such knowledge, a new subject, a new x must be presupposed.

Crucified with him. The answer to these questions is provided by our crucifixion with Christ. The invisible point of observation, which lies wholly beyond my identity with myself, and the validity of the observation made from it by the unknown x come into being and are valid through my knowledge of my conformity to Christ in the likeness of His death. In Christ I behold the old man—of whom alone we have knowledge—first raised to the highest pinnacle of human possibility, and then under judgement, handed over to death, finally and manifestly dissolved. In Christ I see the old man exposed in flagrant contradiction to the new man who is righteous before God and lives in Him, and I see the new man invisibly contrasted with the old. With my eyes fixed upon Christ, in this judgement and surrender and dissolution and contradiction I recognize myself. I see the unknown subject or x by whom I am recognized, and I behold the point from which I am perceived as the old man and from which I am denied. This point, then, must be a positive point, and this subject or x must also be positive. This unobservable positive x, contrasted with the death of Christ on my behalf which I die with Him, is the hinge upon which, and by which, the supreme movement from the old to the new turns and is effected. Movement can be described only by a series of contrasted positions—for example, the film of a bird in flight. But even so the movement itself is not thereby described, for it consists neither in a single, isolated position nor in a whole series of positions. And so, although this turning movement is indescribable, nevertheless certain observations may be made from the invisible point x. First: since the 'No' which emerges from the 'Yes' is inexorable, I am, without any consideration for my feelings,

defined as the old man, the man of sin. Secondly: there is no
escape from my identity with this old man. I myself am the
man by whom I am confronted in the mirror of the death of
Christ. Thirdly: I am forced to assent to the sentence of crucifixion pronounced upon the old man, for 'by the advent of Christ
and by His Resurrection on our behalf we, men as we are, have
been outstripped; we have become old and obsolete' (Schlatter).
Fourthly: a gulf is created by which I am distinguished from that
old man, and the mysterious possibility emerges of my regarding
myself as an object not identical with myself. And fifthly: since
my identification with the invisible new man is established, it
becomes the pre-supposition in the light of which the whole
process—which is no process—becomes intelligible.

That the body of sin might be done away. *Body* involves life,
concreteness, personality, individuality, and slavery. Sin has
a body: that is, it has a concrete existence, a sphere of influence,
a basis of operation, a persistent material; it exists, progresses,
acts, with vigorous independence, and possesses substance in
the world of time and of things and of men. Its *body* is always
visible and historical. The question which arises is, whether we
are to continue in sin, that is to say, whether our actions and
wills can any longer remain involved in this observable and
historical process of sin. This body of sin, however, is my body,
my temporal, human, concrete existence, with which I am
wholly and indissolubly united. So long as I live in the body—
so long, that is, as I am what I am,—I am a sinner; and it is
wholly natural and inevitable that I should *continue in sin* and
live therein (vi. 1, 2). The crucifixion of the old man must have
to do, then, with the removal of this 'so long as', with the dissolution of *this body* of my existence determined by time and
things and men. Because and so long as I live in the body,
I remain the old man, and am wholly and indissolubly one with
him. Therefore the death of the old man and the dissolution of
my identity with him also involve the *doing away* of my union
with this body. As the new man, I live no longer in it: as determined by time and things and men, I exist no longer. In the
KRISIS of the death of Christ my whole corporality, my existence
in the course of this world, is, as such, brought into question,
in order that it may be done away by being related to the new
man, with whom I, crucified with Christ, am identical. My
corporality awaits the new body, which is the concrete life, the
personality, the individuality, of the new man, the slave of the
righteousness of God.

So that we should no longer be in bondage to sin. The dissolution

of the body—thought of here as Futurum resurrectionis
—which has come unseen within our horizon and is announced
in the crucifixion of the old man, signifies that the power of sin
has been done away. Since I am not identified with the old
man who is wholly and irrevocably bound to this body, I can
no longer be in bondage to sin. Sin, like a fish out of water, is
out of its element: in the concord of the new harmony it is a
false note. Sin has no power over the new man, because his
body is otherwise constituted. The EGO—which I am not—
is free. Expecting resurrection, and discerning my identity
with the new man beyond the death of Christ, I must, I can,
I ought, and I will, not be a sinner.

For he that died is justified from sin. Grace, then, is not a
human possibility for men by the side of which there is room for
such other possibilities as, for example, sin. Grace is the divine
possibility for men, which robs them, as men, of their own possibilities. Grace is the relating of the visible man to his invisible
personality which is grounded in God. Grace is related to the
visible man as death to life. The Futurum aeternum towers
above our life, casting over it everywhere the shadow of doubt
and shock, of uncertainty and impossibility. What in God we
are, and know, and will, rises like an overhanging precipice over
our past and present and future. The man who shall be (vi. 5)
conformed to Christ at the resurrection, and who appears at the
point from which the attack develops, is another man: his will
and knowledge and being are wholly different from mine. To the
functions of the living man he is dead: he is incapable of changing God into man and man into God, the sin of which I am and
have been and shall be guilty. The forensic justification by
God which is the condemnation of all concrete human behaviour,
the forgiveness of sin, and those possibilities of God Himself
which seem to us impossible, constitute his life. He lives of that
which negates the unobservable sin of Adam, the Fall, and all
human negation. He—and, in so far as I am identified with him,
we—present nothing upon which the existence and knowledge
and will of the man of sin can thrive. We starve him out, under-
mine him, and are wholly sceptical of him; and from us he expects
nothing less. We turn over the page of sin so that no trace of its
writing is visible from the other side. Though I, in my visible
existence and knowledge and will, cannot possibly, as I am,
escape the guilt of sin; yet, in my relation to the new man
which I am not, I cannot even for one moment reckon with the
possibility of guilt. For me, identified by grace with the new man,
this past and present and future possibility—vanished yesterday.

vv. 8–11. But if we died with Christ, we believe that we shall also live with him; knowing, that is, **that Christ being raised from the dead dieth no more; death no more hath dominion over him. For the death that he died, he died unto sin once for all: but the life that he liveth, he liveth unto God. Even so reckon ye also yourselves to be dead unto sin, but alive unto God in Jesus Christ.**

But if we died with Christ, we believe that we shall also live with him. The proof of the impossibility of continuing in sin (vi. 1) rests upon the precise significance for the sinner of the words *died with Christ.* Dying with Christ is the vast negation beyond which by grace we stand. In so far as I am identical with the unknown *x* which lies beyond the dissolution of the known man, I, as a sinner, am crucified, dead, and buried. It is, however, vitally important to show that this negation is consequent upon an affirmation, lest what has been said earlier (vi. 4) be misunderstood. The negation of every human 'Yes' and 'No', here and there, 'not only—but also', is occasioned by an affirmation by which all dualism, tension, polarity, allogeneity, and antinomy, are excluded. The possibility of sin is therefore confronted, not, as may perhaps have been supposed, by a mere negation, but by a POSITIVE impossibility. *If we died with Christ, we believe.* . . . Faith, for the psychology of grace, is the beginning and the end, the decisive and only relevant factor. Faith assumes with implicit confidence, that the invisible existence of men in God has veritable and concrete reality. Faith is the incomparable and irrevocable step over the frontier separating the old from the new man and the old from the new world. Faith presents itself in a series of paradoxes: human vacuum—divine fullness; human speechlessness, ignorance, and expectation—divine words, knowledge, and action; the end of all things human—the beginning of divine possibility. Faith is the divine revolution and upheaval by which the well-known equilibrium between 'Yes' and 'No', grace and sin, good and evil, is disturbed and overthrown. The believer who is dead with Christ sees in His Cross an opportunity for comprehending the insecurity of human existence as a divine necessity pointing beyond insecurity. The believer sees the beginning of God in the end of man, and the light of His mercy in the tempest of His wrath. By faith the primal reality of human existence in God enters our horizon; by faith the incomparable step is taken; by faith the conversion from which there is no return occurs; to faith no looking backwards is permitted: to faith, in the light of the

absolute 'Moment' and of the death of Christ, there is no supposition, but only reality: to faith there is not only vacuum but
also fullness, not only human belief but also divine faithfulness.
What then, we ask, is that in which we believe? We believe
that Christ died in our place, and that therefore we died with
him. We believe in our identity with the invisible new man who
stands on the other side of the Cross. We believe in that eternal
existence of ours which is grounded upon the knowledge of
death, upon the resurrection, upon God. We believe *that we
shall also live with him*. We therefore believe that we are the
invisible subject of the Futurum resurrectionis. Accompanied by many question-marks and marks of exclamation, with
all due reservations and restrictions, we say that this faith is 'our'
faith. But it lies completely beyond the range of psychological
analysis, for faith is the actual and positive impossibility which
is unable to reckon with the possibility of sin having any existence on the plane of grace. 'He that believes is he that also
possesses.' If we believe, sin lies behind us.

**Knowing, that is, that Christ being raised from the dead dieth
no more ; death no more hath dominion over him.** Faith is the
possibility of daring to know what God knows, and of ceasing,
therefore, to know what He no longer knows. Such knowledge,
since it presupposes the questionableness of all human capacity,
lies outside our competence. It is this recognition that constitutes the hazard of faith. Faith is the possibility which belongs
to men in God, in God Himself, and only in God, when all human
possibilities have been exhausted. Faith means motionlessness,
silence, worship—it means not-knowing. Faith renders inevitable
a qualitative distinction between God and man; it renders
necessary and unavoidable a perception of the contradiction
between Him and the world of time and things and men; and
it finds in death the only parable of the Kingdom of God. It is
at this point that we reach the visible significance of the 'Life
of Jesus'. With a growing clarity and precision Jesus, the Healer,
Saviour, Prophet, Messiah, Son of God, is determined by the
fact of the crucifixion, for we are clearly not intended to understand His life as an illustration of human possibility, nor indeed
can we thus interpret Him. Here also we encounter the visible
significance of Christian faith, which consists in the perception
that the line of death which runs through the life of Jesus is
in fact the law and necessity of all human life. We perceive that
we are dead with Christ, that in relation to God we are ignorant,
and that before Him we can only cease to move and speak, we
can only worship. Nevertheless, this strange significance of the

visible life of Jesus, according to which every human possibility is dissolved, requires an invisible centre from which the KRISIS proceeds. It assumes a standard of impossibility by which visible human possibilities are measured. It assumes, in fact, something which directs the life of Jesus, and round which it revolves. If He can be interpreted only in terms of suffering, there must be contrasted with the passive Jesus an active Jesus. Over against Him who announces the end of the Temple and of the world of the Son of man, must be set He that cometh on the clouds of heaven and brings the Kingdom of His Father. Over against the crucified Jesus stands the risen Lord. The visible significance of His life cannot be understood apart from the disclosure and revelation of the invisible glorification of the Father. This is the resurrection of Jesus from the dead. The judgement to which Jesus surrenders Himself is righteousness; the death He suffers is life; the 'No' which He proclaims is 'Yes'; and the contradiction between God and man which is disclosed in Him is reconciliation. In the invisible totality of the new man Jesus, that is, in the concrete, corporeal person of the risen Jesus, the direction in which His visible life had moved is reversed. When this reversal is revealed and perceived, the frontier of all visible human history, including the visible human history of Jesus of Nazareth, is clearly marked. This reversal or transformation is not a 'historical event' which may be placed side by side with other events. Rather it is the 'non-historical' happening, by which all other events are bounded, and to which events before and on and after Easter Day point. If this transformation were a 'historical', that is, a psychical, or superphysical event, it would have taken place on a plane which would render legitimate those many weighty and sophisticated hypotheses which are nowadays held to be more or less compatible with 'belief'. But it would also render legitimate the putting forward and discussion of hypotheses such as apparent but not real death, deception practised by the disciples or by Jesus Himself, objective or subjective visions, and many other spiritualistic or anthroposophistical theories. Common to all these hypotheses is the opinion that it is not God Himself and God alone who here enters upon the scene and utters that Word by which the visible Way of the Cross is reversed, and by which the invisible is set over against the visible Jesus. The Resurrection accordingly becomes merely another of those human possibilities which Jesus in His Crucifixion abandoned. If this were true, the fulfilment of the meaning of His life would require that He should once more die, in order that due honour and obedience

might be paid to the Unknown God who dwelleth in light unapproachable and in whose presence all discernible psychic experience, all concrete physical and super-physical conditions, are
dust and ashes. Over all historical possibilities and probabilities
and necessities and certainties death is supreme, for they all are
mortal and passing to corruption. Were there a direct and
causal connexion between the historical 'facts' of the Resurrection—the empty tomb, for example, or the appearances
detailed in 1 Cor. xv—and the Resurrection itself; were it in
any sense of the word a 'fact' in history, then no profession of
faith or refinement of devotion could prevent it being involved
in the see-saw of 'Yes' and 'No', life and death, God and man,
which is characteristic of all that happens on the historical plane.
There is under this heaven and this earth no existence or occurrence, no transformation, be it never so striking, no experience,
be it never so unique, no miracle, be it never so unheard of,
which is not caught up by a relativity in which great and small
are inextricably woven together. Therefore, if the Resurrection be brought within the context of history, it must share in
its obscurity and error and essential questionableness. Against
the influence which the Resurrection has exerted upon individual
souls must then be set the far more obvious distortions and disfigurements of which it has been the cause; against the social
benefits it has conferred must be set the far more manifest
impotence of Christians and their fraudulent behaviour; with
its purest and most brilliant rays must be compared the rays
which have emanated from other and even greater lights and
powers (Overbeck!). Think of those 150,000 years of human
history and of 'the ebb and flow of great civilizations; consider
the ice-ages which are past and which will presumably return,
and remember that they are caused by the tiniest movement of
the pole' (Troeltsch). Yes, if the Resurrection were an occurrence in history, such thoughts would have weight and importance for the consideration of divine things. But, in fact, they
are irrelevant. Indeed, it is not such considerations that
give us pause. Not only has the world always been able to
threaten 'Christendom'; it has actually threatened it, in so far,
that is, as 'Christendom' formed one factor in history, in time and
in the world, and so long as it has been betrayed by so many
theologians who fail to perceive that its truth must be sought
not merely beyond all negation, beyond death, and beyond
men, but beyond even the possibility of contrasting 'Yes' and
'No', life and death, God and the world, or of ranging them in a
causal sequence, and so playing them off one against the other.

The conception of Resurrection, however, wholly forbids this method of procedure: *Why seek ye the living among the dead?* Why do ye set the truth of God on the plane and in the space where historical factors, such as 'Christendom', rise and fall, ebb and flow, are great and are little? The conception of resurrection emerges with the conception of death, with the conception of the end of all historical things as such. The bodily resurrection of Christ stands over against His bodily crucifixion —and nowhere else can it be encountered. Only in so far as He has been *put to death in the flesh* is He *quickened in the spirit* (1 Pet. iii. 18), revealed and perceived under a new heaven and a new earth as the new man: that is to say, only in so far as He has, in order to die, abandoned and left behind all concrete, human, historical possibilities—even the possibility of some wonderful super-physical existence. He is the Risen—Crucified One. He is the invisible new man in God. He is the end of the old man as such, for He has put behind Him death and the whole relativity of histórical and time-enveloped things. Raised from the dead he dieth no more—because His Resurrection is the non-historical event κατ᾽ ἐξοχήν. *Death no more hath dominion over him.* The new life cannot be extinguished and revoked: it is the life of God, and the life of men known by God. By faith we dare to make God's knowledge of men our own, and to know this life, the risen life of Jesus, to be our life: *we shall live with him* (vi. 8). Obviously, we are not the 'we' who call this life 'our' life, for this knowledge can be visible only as the knowledge of our death. Similarly, the faith by which we know can occur only in our godly and humble and loving, but not-knowing, death with Christ. Only because faith has occurred and we are new men is it a positive impossibility for us to return to that life in which sin is possible. This is our situation in so far as the impossible and invisible object of knowledge which we encountered in the visibility of the Cross is perceived by an equally impossible and invisible subject of knowledge lying beyond the line which both separates and unites death and life. This, however, can occur only if the Futurum resurrectionis—*we shall live*—pre-supposes a new 'we' as the reverse of dying with Christ.

For the death that he died, he died unto sin once for all: but the life that he liveth, he liveth unto God. The doing away of human possibilities as such in the death of Christ is the doing away of the possibility of sin. Since the whole human possibility as such, which lies on this side of death, is in fact the possibility of sin, death must constitute the meaning of the life of Christ. Life in the world of time and things and men is, as such, life in the Fall; it is both the unseen separation of God and man and, in anthropomorphism, His far too visible proximity. There is, in this life, no simplicity or purity or sinlessness or righteousness which is valid before God! Sin is the final meaning and life of this life. But then Christ died. God is the final meaning and death of death—God who stands beyond the death of this life. Hence the new (impossible) possibility which constitutes a real nearness to God can be discerned only in the likeness of death; and sinlessness and righteousness can be observed only in that radical negation of all human possibilities which is the likeness of death. Since, then, sinlessness and righteousness are veritably observed in the death of Christ, the wholly Other has entered within my horizon *once for all*; in so far, that is, as in His death Christ veritably stands in my place, and I by faith (vi. 8) veritably participate in His death in order that I may live with Him. So then, just as I am visibly one with the dying Christ, so I am invisibly one with this 'Other', the risen Christ; and I am therefore the man who lives in God; I am the individual, soul and body, who stands in my place. Because the death of Christ is the end of that life which can and must die, and the final victory of sinlessness over the possibility of sin, it proclaims: *Thy sins have been forgiven thee*; and because, since the order death–resurrection, sin–grace, cannot be reversed, Christ dieth no more,—therefore I, living to God in Christ, am as such dead to sin. I stand only within the sphere of conversion from sin to grace, a conversion which cannot be reversed.

Even so reckon ye also yourselves to be dead unto sin, but alive unto God in Christ Jesus. The question whether the venture of faith has been dared, contains in itself the testing of our conversion and of our perception of the situation in which we stand. Faith means seeing what God sees, knowing what God knows, reckoning as God reckons. God reckons (iii. 28, iv. 3) with the man who has died to sin and liveth unto Himself (vi. 10). The revelation of this new man in whom God is well pleased is discerned in the Resurrection of Jesus from the dead. The power of the Resurrection is, however, the knowledge of the new man, by which we know God, or, rather, are known of Him (Gal. iv. 9; 1 Cor. viii. 2, 3; xiii. 12). Grace is the power of the Resurrection. Not unnaturally, the indicative is here changed to an imperative, meaning that what is said is true, that He who knows and he who is known—and the knowledge of this fact—assuredly exist. In other words, in the nosse is esse. Then the positive impossiblity of being both in sin and under grace actually has existence—well! let it exist.

The forgiveness of sin is valid—well! accept it as valid. 'With Christ thou art dead unto sin, be then now dead! With Christ thou art risen to life for God, then live now for Him! Thou art set at liberty, then be now free!' (Schlatter): 'Be what thou already art in Christ' (Godet). The power of the Resurrection is the key, the opening door, the step over the threshold. Grace is the disturbing and the upsetting of the equilibrium. We actually encounter the impossible possibility of completely exposing the falsity of the reality of 'our' life and of stretching out towards the reality of our life in God. To us, as the subject of the Futurum resurrectionis, as being what we are not, everything which God no longer reckons or knows is—indifferent.

THE POWER OF OBEDIENCE

VI. 12-23.

vv. 12–14. Let not therefore the sin which dwells in your mortal body reign, that ye should obey the lusts thereof: neither present your members unto sin as weapons of unrighteousness; but present yourselves unto God, as alive from the dead, and therefore also your members as weapons of righteousness unto God. For sin shall not have dominion over you: for ye are not under law, but under grace.

Let not therefore the sin which dwells in your mortal body reign, that ye should obey the lusts thereof. Grace is the power of obedience; it is theory and practice, conception and birth; it is the indicative which carries with it a categorical imperative; it is the call, the command, the order, which cannot be disobeyed. Grace has the force of a downright conclusion; it is knowledge which requires no act of will to translate it into action, as though the will were a second factor side by side with knowledge. Grace is knowledge of the will of God, and as such it is the willing of the will of God. Grace is the power of the Resurrection: the knowledge that men are known of God, the consciousness that their existence is begotten of God, that it moves and rests in Him, and that it is beyond all concrete things, beyond the being and course of this world. Inasmuch as men have discovered it, Grace is the existence begotten of God, the new man, created and redeemed by God, the man who is righteous before Him and in whom He is well pleased, the man in whom God again discovers Himself, as a father discovers himself in his child. Of supreme significance, then, is the demand that I, the new man in the power of the

resurrection and within the KRISIS of the transition from death
to life, should by faith and under grace—will the will of God.
As the man under grace, I am in a position to hear and to understand this demand, for existentially and assuredly I live from
God and am what He desires. By this demand, moreover, I
am reminded of that primal Origin by which my existence is
affirmed, and I perceive that I—and yet not I—AM. As the man
under grace, I am created and quickened and awakened. But
I am also disturbed, for the demand bids me take up arms
against the world of men and against the men of the world.
The object which I, as the subject, am bidden to attack is—
myself. To me, who am under grace, sin is completely problematical: it is not merely relative, not just a fatal possibility set
over against other and better possibilities; it is the one possibility, by which all others, whether good or bad, are encompassed; it has dominion over me, a dominion exerted apparently
through my *mortal body*, with which I am indissolubly united.
Nevertheless, under grace, I am unable to recognize any validity
in this dominion; I cannot reckon with it; I can only encounter
with absolute scepticism its claim to be something presupposed
and given. I am, of course, aware of sin; but, although it is the
essential factor in all human possibility, I can only recognize it
as impossibility. Sin dwells in this mortal body, and there it
will continue to dwell so long as death is not swallowed up in
victory and this mortal shall have put on immortality; that is,
so long as time is time and the world is the world and man
is man; so long as I am what I am on this side of the death
of Christ, and am not identical with the new man, not under
grace, not—broken; so long as, with one foot in the grave, I
am just an individual, grotesquely isolated and subject to
chance, bounded by the grim processes of birth and death,
woven into identity with the contingent concreteness of this
'mysterious universe'. This body cannot be a natural and
pure body, a body without sin; if it could, mortality would
be capable of drawing immortality to itself, and corruption
incorruption. Since, however, this body has not yet put on
either incorruption or immortality, it remains the body of sin.
But here we must not allow ourselves to drift into dualism,
as though grace and sin, 'Yes' and 'No', were simply two contrasted factors. The important characteristic of this mortal and
sinful body is that it has been rendered questionable, assaulted,
overwhelmed, and dissolved, by the *crucifixion of the old man*
(vi. 6)—*that so we should no longer serve sin*. The *old man*, the
man of human possibilities, indissolubly and indivisibly united

with the sinful and mortal body, is assuredly an EGO; but
what he is has no validity for me who am under grace and am
dead with Christ: as such, I can no longer recognize the dominion
of sin which dwells in my mortal body, nor can I admit that sin
is the characteristic factor in the sphere in which my mortal body
exercises its functions. There too sin is questioned, assaulted,
and dethroned: for as surely as Christ is my hope by the crucifixion of the flesh, even so does my body share in the hope of the
sinlessness and immortality of the new man. From the relation
of my body to me as I am, must emerge its relation to me as I am
not. I and my body do not form the unchallenged domain
of sin, nor even the unchallenged base from which sin operates:
we are the battle-field in which sin has to fight for its victory.
I am the warrior under grace, the new man, who can neither
admit nor submit to the tyranny which sin exercises over me
and over my mortal body. When I speak of tyranny over my
mortal body, I mean tyranny exercised over the circumstances
in which I live, over history, over all temporal human ends, in
fact, over my whole external life, and indeed precisely there,
because, existentially speaking, there is no 'without' which is
not also 'within'. Of this tyranny I am wholly sceptical, and I
am, consequently, in full revolt against it. I can be no neutral
observer of the conflict between grace and sin. I cannot allow
any alternation between sin and grace, because sin is the
(human!) possibility which the impossibility of grace has
rendered impossible. It is not surprising that sin, as a human
possibility, should extend as far as the eye can see. What is surprising is that I should allow this possibility to be mine. It is
not surprising that sin should dwell in my mortal body. What
is surprising is that I should compromise with it, adjust myself to
it, and permit its reign to provide a modus vivendi. It is not
surprising that the *lusts* of my mortal body should be quite real
things, for in them is exposed the vitality of its sinfulness and
mortality. Yes indeed, the lusts of my body, all of them, effect
this exposure: my hunger and my need of sleep, my sexual desires
and my longing to 'express myself', my temperament and my
originality, my determination to know and to create, the blind
passion of my will—and finally, and presumably supremely,
my 'need of religion', with which is linked a veritable macrocosm
of social lusts. All these various engagements of mine are
grounded essentially in time and insecurity and 'thing-i-ness',
relentlessly bound up with the corruptibility of my body and
with my existence in the world. All these things are the vitality
of my sinfulness and mortality, and make up the life which,

P

because it is sinful, is handed over to death. The reality of this life of lusts is not surprising. What is surprising is that I should authorize a definition, in terms of such lusts, of what I am under grace; that, failing to recognize the relativity of this life, I should obey it and ascribe to it transcendent reality, that—employing a metaphysical term—I should 'hypostatize' it, transmute it, dedicate it, and pronounce it to be holy and religious. This is especially surprising, since all the time my life as the new man encounters the life of my mortal body as existence encounters non-existence. It is, moreover, surely surprising that I should fail to remember that 'everything corruptible is only a parable'; and that, forgetting the holy fear created by the gulf which to the end of days separates what I am from what I am not, I should discover and pursue a road which is unbroken by any radical negation and which claims to stretch from human nature to the divine nature. It is incomprehensible that I, being under grace, should cease to live and move by the vitality of another order strictly contrasted with the lusts of my mortal body. By grace we receive the *gift of righteousness* (v. 17), and it is folly for us not to employ it as a weapon of offence; we shall *reign in life* (v. 17); and it is madness for us to persist in affirming our slavery to death. 'Note that the saints also have evil lusts in the flesh—which they do not follow' (Luther).

Neither present your members unto sin as weapons of unrighteousness; but present yourselves unto God, as alive from the dead. By a man's *members* is meant his psycho-physical organism, his total cosmic existence conditioned by cause and effect. By *weapons of unrighteousness* is meant the arrogant behaviour by which, when men identify themselves with God (i. 18), this organism is employed as an instrument by which the truth is imprisoned; when, surrendering themselves to this organism as prisoners of sin, they vaunt a supposed freedom and rise up in rebellion. Such behaviour is always to us an observable possibility because we are human; but this possibility is denied me, and is existentially precluded for me, by the observable power of obedience which is by grace. Thou art not a prisoner. Thy members are neither intended to erect a Tower of Babel nor competent to do so. Present them not unto sin: present thyself unto God. Thou that art under grace, present thine unredeemed self. Thou that art the new man, present unto God the old man with every member of his body. 'Ought it to be possible for us to engage our whole energies right up to the very end of our days in what is more or less open rebellion against God? Ought we to be able to smite Him in the face with the hand which He has given us—and at the same time to set our hope upon Christ?' (J. Chr. Blumhardt). Though this possibility extends as far as the eye can reach, yet, nevertheless, it is undermined and overthrown by the invisible state of grace in which men stand. This is the cavern or vacuum excavated in the mountain of human possibility, by which the possibility of overthrowing it is opened up. But there is a third alternative— we may 'fight as mercenaries, now on the side of sin against God, and now on the side of God against sin, or we may even serve sin in our material life, and God in our spiritual life' (Zahn). This alternative is, however, ruled out. Ye have passed from death to life. There is no third alternative between death and life. In the war which is waged between them, there are no deserters, no mediators, and no neutrals. Where the mountain is, there is no cavern; and where the cavern is, there is no mountain.

—and therefore also your members as weapons of righteousness unto God. Hic Rhodus, hic salta![1]—This presentation is an existential presentation unto God, which quite positively includes the limbs of our mortal body. The invisible power of obedience transforms the totality of our visible human possibilities, and dissolves them. Where sin now reigns in death, precisely there grace now reigns through righteousness, through the creative word of forgiveness, through that 'And yet' with which God accepts us and reckons us as His. Thus, in its questionableness and dereliction, our mortal body becomes a poem of love, a vessel of honour, and a weapon of the righteousness of God. If a man has not passed from death to life, how can he be capable even of hearing this demand? This is the crux of the matter, for grace, breaking through both mysticism and morality, transforms the indicative into an imperative, and we encounter the absolute demand that the impossible shall become possible (vi. 19).

For sin shall not have dominion over you : for ye are not under law, but under grace. Only in so far as grace is the power of the Resurrection is it power unto obedience. Grace is the power of knowledge by which we recognize that we are the subject of the Futurum resurrectionis, the power of that hazard whereby we dare to reckon our existence as the existence of the new man, the power of the transformation whereby we pass from 'life' to death and from 'death' to life. Under grace we are at God's

---

[1] Hic Rhodus, hic salta!—From the Latin version of Aesop's Fable, *The Boasting Traveller* (fab. 203 Halm). The phrase is frequently used in Germany, and means that what has hitherto been talked of, and boasted of, must now be done. [Tr.]

disposal to do what He wills with our members. We cannot claim
to be and to do all this as 'religious men', but only as men under
the grace of God. We are not what we are because we may be or
probably are *under law* and therefore have some 'experience of
God', or because we may display in our souls, characters, or
dispositions, some visible traces or impressions of contact with
the grace of God, or because we presumably inhabit the canal in
which it is possible for living water to flow. The power of obedience by which sin is overcome depends upon no act of will
or tendency of our nature, it depends upon no enthusiasm or
'movement', however pure. No doubt, all these things are in
some measure possessed by us, and, no doubt, we shall in addition have some 'religion' and be members of some 'church'; we
shall believe this or that, and engage in this or that act of private
devotion. These religious beliefs and practices will, presumably,
moreover affect our moral behaviour, and will direct our dreams
and hopes, our struggles and our sufferings; they will cause
us both gain and loss. In the vast pandemonium of human piety
we shall play our part, the historian and the psychologist will
enter us under one of their well-known 'categories', and we shall
be a 'type' (vi. 17). All this is a sign and a witness, but it is not
the power unto obedience, it will not enable us to say 'No' to
sin because we say 'Yes' to God. These things do not mean that
sin has no dominion over us. The power of obedience is not
'typical' but primary, not derived but original, not religious but
from God, not law but grace. If the power of grace were identical
with what is usually understood by visible piety and observed
experience, the imperative—Present yourselves not to the will
of sin, but present yourselves unto God—would be meaningless.
How can it be that sin will not continue to reign in the vast
realm of human possibility, from which the whole world of
enthusiastic religious exaltation of soul cannot be excluded?
How is it possible for the man of the world to will the will of
God, however pious he may be? How can what is finite, even
though it be mounted upon the highest rung of the ladder of religion, comprehend infinity? Finitum non capax infiniti.
The religious man can, it is true, comprehend the conflict between
his experience of grace and his proneness to sin; but what he
understands is a conflict between one human possibility and
another human possibility. We cannot, if we are honest, describe this conflict as the victory of grace. At best, the truth of
God and the truth of sin are ever balanced against one another
as 'Yes' and 'No'. But this is no radical transformation of human
existence from life to death and from death to life; and in this

experience of conflict we are not existentially at God's disposal;
for the reality of God still remains something which is distinct
from the reality of human *lusts*, and the yearnings of religion are
of the same order as our sexual and intellectual and other
desires. The reality of God is not removed from criticism, it is
not critically proven. Consequently, the will of God operative
in men, when contrasted with the will of L i b i d o, still remains a
very questionable factor. The victory of grace is therefore incomplete: the frontier of human vitality is not crossed, and the divine
territory has not as yet been entered. The power of obedience
which says 'Yes' to God and 'No' to sin does not exist in
any concrete fashion. Indeed, sin abounds rather the more
exceedingly, and, having attained in religion (v. 20) the highest
pinnacle of human achievement, men encounter—the wrath of
God (iv. 15). Ye are, however, *not under law, but under grace.*
That is to say, ye stand beyond the last and noblest human
achievement, where only forgiveness matters (iv. 15, v. 13), and
where forgiveness becomes a matter of fact. Lietzmann has
supposed that the words *under grace* are a 'formula of ideal
moral optimism'. But that is precisely what forgiveness is not.
Grace is the royal and sovereign power of God, the existential
presentation of men to God for His disposal, the real freedom of
the will of God in men. Grace lies beyond all optimism and also
beyond all pessimism. Grace is the power of obedience, because
it is human existence in that plane and space and world in which
obedience is undeniable and unavoidable, because it is the
power of the Resurrection. And grace is the power of the Resurrection because it is the power of death, the power, that is, of the
man who has passed from death to life, who has once again found
himself because he has lost himself in God and in God alone.

vv. 15, 16. **What then** follows from this? **shall we sin,
because we are not under law, but under grace? God
forbid. Know ye not, that to whom ye present yourselves
as servants unto obedience, his servants ye are whom**
also **ye** must **obey; whether** servants **of sin unto death, or**
servants **of obedience** to God **unto righteousness.**

Shall we sin, because we are not under law, but under grace?
Does grace then carry with it in any sense the freedom to sin?
When once we recognize that the life of men in God is invisible,
impossible, and intangible, are we to resign ourselves with a
certain holy humour to the supposition that the conflict of
religion with sin is futile? Are we to allow the visible possibilities of real human life to run their course determined by sin?

Does grace mean that men can survey calmly and without concern the ravages of the lusts of their mortal bodies and the
operations of the powers which control this unredeemed world?
Can we appeal to the fact of creation, and then proceed to treat
the motions of the body and the course of this world as willed
by God, or at least as permitted by Him? Can we, with our eyes
fixed upon a redemption which is not available in this world, proceed to conclude peace, or at any rate to arrange an armistice,
with the world as it is? Are we to understand the contrast of
grace and law in such a manner that, whilst the man under law
must engage in a passionate, wearisome, and sometimes despairing conflict with sin, the man under grace may compromise with
it and continue to live the peaceful bourgeois life of a man of the
world? Can we who are under grace adopt the superior poise
and balance of the sceptic, and come forward as generous
humanists? Or can we select the mingled sorrow and happiness
of mysticism for our devotion, because we suppose that it
occupies a satisfactory position midway between God and the
world, between 'there' and 'here', between the final redemption
and the present fallen creature? If we behave in any such
fashion, does not our all-embracing denial of the sin-controlled
course of this world really amount to an affirmation of it?
Have we not, by consigning that other world, that other possibility, peaceably to the 'other side', rendered it practically unimportant? If grace were simply law in a new guise, if it
were another new and rugged human possibility, if it were some
antinomian mysticism or pietism, if it were the 'waiting' of
quietism and pacifism—we should in very truth have affirmed
the world. If grace were a human possibility, it would be
right and natural to let it run its course adjusting itself to
other human possibilities as best it can. Grace would then
involve a broad freedom to sin. Those who, unlike Paul
and the Reformers, are able to include grace under the
category of law and God under the categories of religion and
human morality; those who cannot contemplate soberly and
clearly that impossibility which with God is possible; those
who are unable to think the thought of eternity: all these men
who perpetually confuse grace with human possibility, are
bound in the end to confound it with the final relative possibility
—the possibility of negative passivity. And then, when this
has occurred and passivity is embraced or rejected, embraced
with enthusiasm or rejected with contumely, there comes into
being a veritable ocean of misunderstandings. If grace means
that, because God does everything, men ought to do nothing,

there are but three alternatives. Either, with the scarcely-veiled approval of the men of the world, we 'do nothing', with the result that the *body of sin* is for the first time firmly set upon its throne. Or, rejecting this 'do nothing' policy, and adopting the grim earnestness of the religious moralist, we 'do' what we can and battle with sin, with the result that it—more exceedingly *abounds* (v. 20). Or—and this is the course more safely and normally selected—without genuine conviction we swing hither and thither between 'quietism' and 'activism', between approval and disapproval, with the result that sin secures a double triumph: it triumphs both in the normal pride of human achievement and in the religious arrogance of human passivity. The utterly human consequences which result from the acceptance or rejection of grace when it is defined as human possibility, make it quite obvious that this is not what we mean by grace. And so we conclude: God forbid that that should be grace!

God forbid. Know ye not, that to whom ye present yourselves as servants unto obedience, his servants ye are whom also ye must obey? Grace, then, means neither that men can or ought to do something, nor that they can or ought to do nothing. Grace means that God does something. Nor does grace mean that God does 'everything'. Grace means that God does some quite definite thing, not a thing here and a thing there, but something quite definite in men. Grace means that God forgives men their sins. Grace is the self-consciousness of the new man, the answer to our question concerning our existence. We are not in a position to say anything which is relevant concerning grace and sin, until our perception has been sharpened and we are protected from pantheism by being reminded of the critical significance of the death of Christ; until we have been liberated from obsession with the problem concerning what we can or ought to do or not to do. Grace is the Kingdom of God, His rule and power and dominion. Grace is radically contrasted with the whole realm of human possibility, the sphere of the sovereignty of sin. Though grace, on account of this contrast, lies beyond all human possibility, yet nevertheless, for the same reason, it judges human life and launches a disturbing attack upon it. In so far as in this contrast God is encountered, human life is refashioned and provided with a new hope and a new promise. Grace, as the power and authority of God over men, can never be identified with the actions or with the passivity of the men of this world. Grace is the unobservable truth of men: it is their impossibility, which constitutes the veritable possibility of their acting or not acting; it is their veritable existence,

which can be defined only as non-existence. The man who is under grace has this contradiction in himself. Grace is not 'something' which a man has in himself, it is that which God has in
him, by which the man of sin is contradicted. Since, however,
we know only the man of sin, this contradiction contradicts all
men, and it contradicts ourselves. We are therefore compelled
to say quite definitely that to possess grace does not mean to be
or not to be this or that, or to do or not to do this or that. The
possession of grace means the existential submission to God's
contradiction of all that we ourselves are or are not, of all that
we do or do not do. 'Grace possessed' means that we are presented *unto obedience* to the contradiction, and that we are
His servants. This possession of grace occurs as the impossible possibility of God which is beyond every possibility of
our own: it is the freedom which God takes to Himself in us. HE
takes it, and He takes it IN US. We are under grace, and we are
ourselves the objective of its attack. Not only is it impossible
for us to escape it, but we cannot even stand aside as spectators
watching the progress of the assault and waiting for it to die
down. We are, moreover, ourselves the attacking party, for, as
objects of the attack, we die, are crucified (vi. 6), in order that
we may pass from death to life, and may discover that we are
ourselves united to God in His active contradiction of our 'life'.
Through this divine contradiction the new individual, created
and redeemed by God, is shown forth as the invisible reality
of our very existence, while our visible reality is declared to
be untruth. The divine contradiction means that we are not
we, and the attack develops from our existence in God—
His servants ye are. There is no other existence running side
by side with our existential existence. We are *servants*, slaves,
existentially appointed *unto obedience*. We are servants *to
God*, existentially appointed unto obedience to the divine 'No',
which is pronounced in us against sin. We are in no position to
say 'Yes' to sin.

We are servants—**whether servants of sin unto death, or
servants of obedience to God unto righteousness.** We see, then,
that both sin and grace are existentially conditions of slavery
Each excludes the other. There is no position midway between
them. Only at the 'incomprehensible moment' when we are
attacked by our existence in God and when we pass from the
authority of the one under the authority of the other, is it
possible to set them side by side. Both sin and grace are defined
as 'slavery' in the strictest sense of the word. Slavery defines the
totality of our individual human existence: it defines it exactly

because it is an existence from which we cannot possibly escape.
Grace and sin are to one another as 'either' is to 'or'. He who
is under grace can no more adjust himself comfortably to sin than
the sinner can toy with grace as with an alternative human
possibility. Both have real existence, yet each excludes the
other. The sinner has no eye for grace, just as he who is under
grace has no eye for sin. Each is a possibility which admits
no other possibility. From both emerges also a *power unto
obedience*. There is, then, no equilibrium between them. Were
we conscious only of obedience unto sin, we should, as servants
of sin, be bound to dismiss out of hand any claim that grace
might conceivably advance against us. Under its authority we
should be already sold and given up to it. *Much more* (v. 15, 17)
obvious would be this incompatibility, if we were *servants unto
obedience to God*. The two slaveries are therefore altogether
mutually exclusive, and a man's existence in Adam cannot be
congruous with his existence in Christ. It should here be noted
that the grim earnestness of the attack which the law and
religion and morality launch against sin is insufficient to create
this disturbance and fissure; they are unable to avoid some
recognition of both God and the world, of both 'there' and
'here'; indeed, they actually effect an adjustment between the
two, by which the antagonism is obscured and composed. It is
therefore precisely because *we are not under law, but under grace*,
and because we await the victory over sin which comes not
from men, but from God, that the condition of human life is
pressed to an ultimate issue and no easement is possible as it is
for the spectator in vi. 15. Because we are under grace and not
under law, we are not free to sin and are confronted with an
either–or, which no bridge can span.

**vv. 17–19. But thanks be to God, that ye were servants
of sin, but ye became obedient from the heart** as a consequence of the impression of **that teaching whereunto ye were
delivered; and being made free from sin, ye became
servants of righteousness. I speak after the manner of
men because of the infirmity of your flesh: for as ye presented your members as servants to uncleanness and to
iniquity** for the creating of **iniquity, even so now present
your members as servants to righteousness** for the creating
of **sanctification.**

**Thanks be to God, that ye were servants of sin, but ye became
obedient from the heart.** The decisive offensive must now be
boldly launched. The advance must now begin. The presentation

of the matter of the Gospel accordingly takes the form of pastoral exhortation. The Gospel is announced and proclaimed: that is, it is addressed to particular men, in this case to the Christians in Rome; and to them as men who stand under grace, and whose power of obedience is presupposed. They receive the crisp command to undertake the conquest of sin. They must now show forth their knowledge in action and this action in knowledge. The appeal, however, has no meaning apart from the reservation contained in the words—*Thanks be to God*. Their obedience is no matter of human possibility, for from this the Roman Christians are wholly free! Nevertheless, with his *Thanks be to God*, Paul dares to inscribe upon them the truth that they are no longer servants to sin. They are servants of God; they are rid of slavery to sin, which is existentially dissolved and excluded. To their past life belongs their visible— far too visible—service to sin. The present and the future exist in their invisible obedience to grace. *Ye were servants to sin, but ye became obedient*—aye, *from the heart*. This direct description is clearly intentional, and is no mere leap of anticipation which leaves the present unaffected. Each man's heart is seen as God sees it (ii. 16). They are summoned to repentance, and the forgiveness of sin is spoken over them as the Word of God. They are bidden think of themselves as existentially under grace, as belonging to God, and as brought within the sphere of resurrection. Looking on Him who has been crucified on their behalf, they are bidden to—believe; yes! to believe in their power of obedience. This is the venture which must be dared. How is it possible to speak of the grace and of the Kingdom of God, if each man be not persuaded that the description concerns him and that he is under grace and within the Kingdom? How is it possible to pronounce the truth that the grace of God concerns all men, if it be not boldly applied to each particular man, if the more than audacious 'Nevertheless' be not exposed existentially in each separate person? How can grace be believed in as the victory of the invisible power of obedience over sin, if grace, anticipating faith and leaping over visible bondage to sin, has not already firmly penetrated each single individual, so that he believes in grace, not without, but within him? Grace is proven, established, and efficacious, in that it boldly *forgives us our debts, as we also forgive our debtors!* Grace pre-supposes that men are *from the heart* under grace; it believes, but it does not see. An apostle is thus distinct from the 'religious man' in that, without being on the watch for experiences of grace, he none the less believes that there are men who do possess it.

As a consequence of the impression of that teaching whereunto ye were delivered. The mention of these particular men does not exclude others. The apostle dares to approach Jew and Gentile alike with the same pre-supposition. The missionary, no less than the writer of the Epistle to the 'already' converted Roman Christians, can appeal with thanksgiving to the— Unknown!—God who finds men before they seek Him and of whom they need but to be reminded. But why should not the visible experiences of grace which belong to the 'Christians' encourage the apostle to single them out with thanksgiving to God as particularly under grace? Is it not indeed inevitable that he should do so, but without thereby depriving others? The—*impression of teaching whereunto they were delivered*—for example, baptism (vi. 3)—is a sign on the plane of 'Christendom'. In the midst of other religions, and not without points of contact with them, 'Christendom' takes human and visible shape, as experience and institution and dogma and cultus. The religious proclamation of 'Christendom' appears in many 'types'. To some such 'type' the Pauline teaching belongs; and, may be, a somewhat different teaching had become 'typical' of Roman 'Christendom'. Difference of form is, however, trivial. Paul accepts their 'type' as a witness of which he can remind them. He does not think it wrong to assume that by an appeal to what is typical, contingent, and visible, they will, in fact, be reminded of what is invisible, primal, and existential: that is, that God has found them; that they have been forgiven; that they are under grace; that they are new men in Christ: to remind them, in fact, of the power of the resurrection, which is the power of obedience. In all this he takes for granted that his reminder is no more than a reminder, for the reality of their state of grace, of which he reminds them, is—of God. Therefore the thanksgiving with which the passage opens does not precede the reminder merely as a matter of form.

Being made free from sin, ye became servants of righteousness. This is the state of grace which the apostle claims on behalf of the Roman Christians. In them the fissure and disturbance have taken place. There is no possibility of readjustment. The attack upon their existence by their existence in God has actually taken place. Their bondage to sin has been broken, and they have become servants of righteousness. The power of the resurrection, the knowledge of God who quickeneth the dead, has con-verted them—yes! has converted THEM, since their conversion was no mechanical process. They have themselves

personally effected it—in the power of the resurrection. What
has taken place, moreover, is unmistakable, irrevocable, and
irreversible. To the man under grace, righteousness is not a
possibility, but a necessity; not a disposition subject to change,
but the inexorable meaning of life; not a condition possessing
varying degrees of healthiness, but the condition by which
existence is itself determined; not that which he possesses, but
that which possesses him. The freedom of the man under grace
is founded upon the good pleasure of God, and has no other
foundation; it is the freedom of the will of God in men, and
freedom of no other kind. Free in God, ye are imprisoned in
Him. This is the categorical imperative of grace and of the
existential belonging-to-God. Knowledge here emerges as the
distinction between the old and the new man; a distinction
which is, however, immediately dissolved in the oneness of the
new man. And ye stand under this imperative.

I speak after the manner of men because of the infirmity of
your flesh. I say 'ye are' and 'ye stand'. I contrast freedom and
slavery. In using such language, however, I speak *after the
manner of men*. We know that all such direct and non-paradoxi-
cal descriptions of the invisible and existential human status are
definitions of the indefinable. We know that, in daring to use
such language, we are entering the twilight of religious romanticism, in which sin and grace, faith and unbelief, take concrete
form and become things which some men 'have' and others
'have not'; which some men 'are' and others 'are not'. But
we know that the passage from death to life by the power of the
resurrection, the freedom from sin and the service to righteousness, may be assigned to no known person. We know that the
names of those who may validly be thus described are written
only in the book of life. We know that the domain of grace has
no existence or non-existence that may be observed; that it is
not the property of this or that man; that it does not belong to
Children or to Socialists or to the Russian Nation or to the
German People, or to Dostoevsky! or to Kutter! And yet we
boldly employ this language, the language of romanticism,
because it is impossible to describe the immediacy of divine
forgiveness except by means of parables drawn from human immediacy. Owing to the *infirmity of the flesh*, since men's ears are
inadequately tuned to the truth, any avoidance of such words
as 'existence' or 'possession' necessarily obscures and weakens
understanding of the reality of forgiveness. Men must not be
permitted to remain spectators, otherwise they will be unable
to apprehend the con-version which God effects. It is vital that

the possibility of an objective knowledge of God should be
wholly eradicated from our minds, because it is only when the
perception breaks upon us that we ourselves—each one of us—
has been forgiven by Him, that it is proved that we can neither
know sin nor commit it. We think we know what we are about
when we dare to use this direct language. It is a necessity for
the preacher, but it lays him open to very severe criticism.
Broken men, we dare to use unbroken language. We must not
forget that we are speaking in parables and *after the manner
of men*. We must remember that what is spoken in faith
must also be heard in faith, and that grace must be both proclaimed and received as grace, that is, as the observed but
invisible establishing of men in God. This warning must be
carefully borne in mind when we come to the words which
follow.

**As ye presented your members as servants to uncleanness and
to iniquity for the creating of iniquity, even so now present your
members as servants to righteousness for the creating of sanctification.** Ye stand under the imperative of grace. Yes! under
the imperative—of grace. And grace is the dissolution of the
sin which dwells in your mortal body. Human limbs are at the
disposal of grace and not at the disposal of sin. Grace, and not
sin, determines mortal men. In grace, and not in sin, God enters
in on their behalf. Grace means that God reckons men's whole
existence to be His and claims it for Himself. Grace is God's
authority over men, over men who are one and indivisible. Grace
is the truth of God about the individual and about the broad
course of his whole life; and because grace is this, it brings him
radically under KRISIS. Grace cannot stand still and rest; it
cannot silently abandon its claim; it cannot hand visible life
over to sin in order that it may be satisfied with the righteousness
of some 'other' invisible and intangible life. That is impossible,
because it would mean a dualism between sin and grace, whereas
grace displays itself as grace precisely in the dissolution of this
dualism. Grace seizes visible life and demands that it be presented to righteousness; the *members* of men are placed at its disposal. The very content and theme of the Futurum resurrectionis is that under grace *this mortal must put on immortality*.
Grace would not be grace, if it were a 'thing' merely contrasted
with our concrete life determined as it is by sin. No promise of
a refuge in another and a better world is sufficient to maintain
the full claim and attack and KRISIS which is, in fact, directed
against the life of our members in this world of time and
things and men. If God be veritably gracious towards us, that

better 'other world' must put in question our life in 'this world',
whether by its absence or by its insistent pressure upon us, by
its invasion and its violent knocking at our doors. Similarly,
if God be gracious towards us, no mere fatalistic discrediting
of our present life can calm us in the presence of the KRISIS.
We must be enabled to discover that we are no more of this
evil world, no more under its power. We must be set in radi-
cál opposition to it, and in such a manner that in the conscious tribulation of discovering its mere this-worldliness and
negativity we discover also the promise, and in apprehending
our deprivation we also apprehend our hope. The mercy of God
towards us means that 'here' and 'there' are related to one
another, and that the barrier between them has been removed.
Grace, as the invisible truth, cannot but press to concretion. It
cannot do otherwise than stretch out with the possibility of impossibility towards that existence, occurrence, desire, achievement, which has the permanent impression of sin. Grace determines to see and hear and touch. It presses to revelation and
to sight. The Resurrection of Christ from the dead (vi. 9) is
this revelation and sight. As history, it lies on the frontier of
that which is not history; as non-history, it lies on the frontier of
history. As the new man, not only am I the man I AM NOT, but
also I AM the man I am not (v. 1, 9–11). Grace means: *thy will be
done in earth as it is in heaven.* Consequently, grace, as the existential relation between God and man, is bound to move from the
indicative of the divine truth concerning men to the imperative
by which the divine reality makes its demand upon them.
They must will what God wills, as hitherto they have not! They
must serve righteousness with the same members, with the same
visible concreteness, with which they have hitherto served
uncleanness and iniquity. They must bring sanctification into
concrete existence by those same instruments which they have
hitherto used to create *iniquity*. They must glorify God with
their bodies, that is, in that same environment and under those
same conditions in which they have hitherto done Him dishonour. There is demanded of them—of each single person—
a different being and having and doing. All this is expressed as
though the answer to the demand were a human possibility!
in fact, as though sin did not dwell in those mortal bodies with
which they are indissolubly united. The demand is uttered as
though neither time were time nor men men nor things things!
It is spoken as though men no longer had one foot in the grave;
as though mortality were already swallowed up in life and death
in victory; as though men were capable of receiving an absolute

demand. The possibility of obedience is not merely not open
to criticism, it is claimed from the standpoint of grace as the
only possibility, and its final advent is awaited with passionate
impatience and zealous longing. This possibility is nothing less
than the fulfilment of the demand, the doing of God's will upon
earth, the emergence of the visible and concrete sanctification
of human life; in fact, it is the comprehension of the temporal
world by eternity. If we are able to endure life apart from this
possibility; if we are content with something less; if we trim
and adjust grace so that it dovetails in with other possibilities;
—grace is not grace. If we are able to escape from that naturally
Christian—Medieval!—disturbance of soul; if all that is in us
does not stretch out towards a sanctified life prepared for and
open to the righteousness of God; if we do not long for a life
running so nigh to the righteousness of God that it would break
visibly through in our members, in our mortal body;—grace is
not grace. And yet, though the Futurum resurrectionis embraces the whole life of the man who is under grace—his heavenly
and his earthly 'part', the new man, 'soul', and the *glorified*
body of the old crucified man,—we must not understand this future life in the ordinary sense of the word 'future', as though men
were to await it as an event in time. Rather, the whole broad
front of human life—past, present, and future—is embraced
and rolled out, so that, without providing a moment's respite
to human waiting, it is defined as life in which *sin shall not have
dominion over you* (vi. 14). All this assumes that this possibility is
the possibility of impossibility. The occurrence is non-historical,
the revelation is the disclosing of the eternal secret, and the
observation is the observing of what is invisible. As such, all
this human being and having and doing is the miracle of the
new creation; it belongs to an order wholly distinct from every
other being and having and doing. So different is it, that it
eludes expression; for when expressed, it appears as though it
were a second or peculiar disposition of human affairs capable of
being compared with other dispositions. It may, for example,
be described as a being *clothed upon with our habitation which is
from heaven* (2 Cor. v. 2), or as the coming into being of a new
order upon a new earth and under a new heaven. The limitations inherent in such language only serve, however, to emphasize as clearly as possible the divine imperative. There are in
fact no limitations. Our human 'but' is none other than the
divine 'therefore'—let him that hath ears to hear, hear. It
would be indeed a notable achievement were human speech
to be rid of such obscurity, and were we competent to speak

otherwise than *after the manner of men*. We must own, however,
that the imperative with its corresponding indicative (vi. 18) is
spoken *after the manner of men*; consequently, the inadequacy of
human language introduces a limitation which does not in fact
exist. The imperative demands from men that which cannot be
demanded of them. In demanding at once the dissolution and
radically new ordering of here and now, it demands that which
it assumes. The event which took place in Christ and on Easter
Day was not directly intelligible; room was left for a choice
between faith and unbelief. And yet there is demanded of us
a clear and directly intelligible occurrence—in our *members!*
Speaking after the manner of men, this means that, under the
parable of direct human address, there is demanded of us what
is intelligible only as the being and having and doing of God. If
we allow our thoughts to move on uncontrolled by the memory
that the imperative assumes an 'as though' and limits our
action so as to compel us to focus our attention on the action
of God, we shall inevitably fall a prey to the anticipations of
religious moralism and to the wildest illusions of romanticism. Becoming sentimental, we shall confuse and intermingle
the righteousness of God with all manner of forms of human
righteousness; we shall mix up Redemption with all manner of re-
demptions, and Eternal Life with the life which we suppose we
can eventually—experience. So long as we endeavour to speak
about grace, our speech must labour under a necessary obscurity.
The real truth is that our whole thought about grace must be
inadequate, since *we must die*, and who has ever been able to
think out to the end what is therein involved? If, then, we must
speak about grace; if we dare to interpret it; our speech and
our interpretation must be undertaken knowing that we are
acting *after the manner of men*. It is inevitable that the last
and final all-embracing word concerning grace, the word which
speaks of the sanctification of our mortal body to be the instrument of righteousness, must run the risk of seeming trivial and
fantastic on our lips. And yet, its impossibility once recognized,
the impossible word, even on our lips, renders sin impossible,
for we speak of God's righteousness as judgement, of His forgiveness as power, and of His Word as Creation.

**vv. 20–3. For when ye were servants of sin, ye were
free from righteousness. What fruit had ye then in those
things whereof ye are now ashamed ? for the end of those
things is death. But now being made free from sin, and
become servants to God, ye have your fruit in what leads**

to sanctification, and the end eternal life. For the wages of sin is death; but the free gift of God is eternal life in Jesus Christ our Lord.

Grace is the KRISIS from death to life. Death is therefore at once the absolute demand and the absolute power of obedience over against sin. No tension or polarity is possible between grace and sin; there can be no adjustment or equilibrium or even temporary compromise between them. As men under grace, we cannot admit or allow grace and sin to be two alternative possibilities or necessities, each with its own rights and properties. For this reason, the Gospel of Christ is a shattering disturbance, an assault which brings everything into question. For this reason, nothing is so meaningless as the attempt to construct a religion out of the Gospel, and to set it as one human possibility in the midst of others. Since Schleiermacher, this attempt has been undertaken more consciously than ever before in Protestant theology—and it is the betrayal of Christ. The man under grace is engaged unconditionally in a conflict. This conflict is a war of life and death, a war in which there can be no armistice, no agreement—and no peace.

Men seem to proceed on their way in a twilight of indifferent neutrality; and this in spite of all their activity and suffering, their influencing and being influenced, their sowing and their reaping. But what fruits do they secure? What is the upshot of their journey? What signifies their behaviour and their prowess? What do they achieve by their words and by their deeds in which they do but discover their own selves? What mean the 'movements', the alliances, and the rules within the framework of which they live their lives? Whither do progress and evolution lead them? What is the goal, the TELOS, the purpose of those innumerable ends for which men strive and to which they may, or may not, attain? Do men know the answer to these questions? Or indeed, can they know? In this harvest of human endeavour wheat and tares grow up in such entangled identity that it is impossible to detect which brings forth iniquity and which *sanctification* (vi. 19). Who is able to judge, and by what objective norm can it be decided, whether the limbs of our mortal body do right or wrong? Who can say whether a thing made by the finite and created spirit of man is evil or good, or whether this or that motion of the soul or historical achievement is iniquitous or holy? May it not be that everything that men do and say and bring into being lies wholly on one side or the other? Is there any visible iniquity which it is

quite impossible to interpret as *santification*? Or is there any
visible *sanctification* which may not be called *iniquity*? We
possess, however, no Rosetta stone by the help of which we can
decipher the unknown language of human life. We are manifestly ignorant of the harvest which the Lord will carry into
His barns; ignorant, too, of the relation between His harvest
and ours. And if the meaning of the things we bring forth is
beyond our comprehension, how can we comprehend the meaning of our existence? If we do not know our end, how can we
know our beginning? Are our affirmations and our negations
anything more than chance or whim? When we judge one man
a criminal and another a saint; when we destine one to hell and
another to heaven; when we believe 'good will grow better and
better, and evil worse and worse' (Harnack), are we not purely
capricious? Moreover, what is good? What is evil? Is it not
right that twilight such as this should mark the realm of tension
and polarity, of dualism and allogeneity? Here 'Yes' and 'No'
confront each other; here both are alike necessary, valuable,
and divine—and yet we can have no very great illusion about the
necessity, value, and divinity of this 'Yes' and this 'No'. Here
wisdom can, no doubt, do its utmost to adjust a balance and
arrange a compromise—so that the play can run on without a
hitch!

The righteousness of God in Jesus Christ is a possession which
breaks through this twilight, bringing the knowledge which sets
even human existence ablaze. The revelation and observation—
of the Unknown God—whereby men know themselves to be
known and begotten by Him whom they are not; by Him with
whom they have no continuity or connexion; to whom there
runs no road or bridge along which they can pass; who is their
Creator and their Primal Origin—this revelation and observation,
in so far as He reveals Himself and allows us to perceive Him
as Father, makes impossibility possible. It is grace. Under
grace mén know that they are—**servants of sin**; guilty victims,
they have fallen from the living God; **free from righteousness,**
men upon whom the light of Forgiveness and Judgement has
never shone. Such—they were. But under grace they are—
free from sin and—**servants of God.** They have been existentially moved, translated, wrenched from 'here' to 'there'. A
great gulf is fixed between what they were and what they are.
Inscribed over the one is **death** and over the other **life.** So the
theme of the revelation and observation of God is nothing less
than the stepping from death to life, nothing less than the life
which comes from death. Under grace we perceive what we

sow; we see the meaning of our existence; we recognize our
beginning; and consequently, we know what we reap, what is
the meaning of our achievements, the purpose and TELOS of our
lives. The lightning which sets our existence ablaze illuminates
at once our being and knowing, our thinking and speaking, our
will and its execution, the motions of our souls and the achievements of our bodies, the aims we yearn after and the purposes
we attain. And then, maybe the lightning leaves these things
untouched; or refines and purifies them; carbonizes them; or
transmutes them into other substances; or perhaps it consumes
and destroys them altogether—and yet, not altogether: Non
omnis moriar! In every case, they are subjected to a radical
testing. What we were is proved by its relation to what we are,
whether it stands on this side or on that side of the gulf which
becomes visible through the revelation and observation of God,
whether its quality be life or death. This, then, is our harvest.
The tares are separated from the wheat; the Purpose in the
purposes is laid bare; the unknown language of human life is
deciphered, for everything is set under the TELOS either of death
or of life, determined by what we were or by what we are, by
our slavery to sin, now existentially vacated, or by our slavery
to God, now existentially restored. Since death and life exclude
one another, nothing can belong to both at once. By this we
are reminded that we can think of death only with reference to
life, and of life only with reference to death. Seen from the standpoint of this TELOS, death or life, which is the theme of the
revelation and observation of God, the meaning of iniquity and
sanctification ceases to be obscure. Iniquity is clearly defined:
there is an evil which no man ought to think or will or do;
there are things—**whereof ye are now ashamed**; there are possibilities, which, in the light of the 'Moment' when all temporal
things are illuminated, are declared to be wholly forbidden and
excluded. Why are they forbidden? Because their end is death;
because they issue from the 'vitality of mortality'; because they
spread death and are dedicated to it; because they cannot exist
in the devouring fire of the life which is perceived through death.
To those who perceive what life is, the criterion by which iniquity
is recognized is sufficiently evident:—**the wages of sin is death.**
Similarly—*sanctification* has but one possible meaning: there
is a—**fruit unto sanctification;** there are possibilities of human
being and having and doing which are defined by the knowledge
of God as altogether necessary and accessible; there is a 'good'
which men ought to be and think and will and do; there is a
'good', because human life, determined by it, is able to survive

the destructive fire; there are purposes and works, alliances and movements, which have their beginning and end in life, which are alive even in their 'middle part', for they are not altogether obscured, even in the world of time and things and men which is under the dominion of death. They survive in the devouring fire of that life which is made known in death. They may be transformed, carbonized, refined; or they may remain untouched—but, in any case, they stand the test. For those who possess it, this criterion points only in one direction; it points to—**the free gift of God,** which is **eternal life in Jesus Christ.**

Sin and grace, then, cannot be placed side by side, or arranged in series, or treated as of like importance, any more than death and life can be so treated. There is no bridge across the gulf which separates them. They have no blurred edges which might be run together. The impassable gulf runs starkly through the fissure between good and evil, between what is valuable and what is valueless, between what is holy and what is unholy. Those who inhabit the dim world of men and are not under grace cannot perceive the gulf which provides them with this clear criterion and enables them to survey the new order. Those, however, who do possess this criterion are again and again compelled to draw up a list of sinners and righteous men and to make a catalogue of what is permitted and what is forbidden. They are bound to attempt a system of ethics. But, when this is said, it must be borne in mind that the criterion by which they are compelled to undertake this systematization also renders it no more than an attempt. The knowledge of God which is the condition of our survey compels us to distinguish clearly between sinners and righteous men; but the human knowledge which emerges is at once dissolved by the very criterion by which it was created. Only because of the power of obedience in which we stand are we able to comprehend and lay hold of the possibility of impossibility. And this power is the power of the Resurrection.

FREEDOM

THE FRONTIER OF RELIGION

VII. 1–6

GRACE is obedience. To understand this, we must understand what is meant by the whole conception of Resurrection. The obedience of grace is that being and having and doing of men which is related to their former being and having and doing, and indeed to every human possibility, as life is related to death. Our present existence is brought within the realm of its final and impossible possibility, and there it is met by an inexorable and predetermined 'either–or'. Grace is the relation of God to men which admits of no compromise. God is not mocked. Already the Victor, He enters the conflict as a consuming fire. In the presence of His 'Yes' and His 'Amen', our stammering 'As If', our muttered 'Yes and No', cannot stand. Upon the threshold of my existence there appears, demanding admittance—the new man of the new world, the new man in Christ Jesus, justified and redeemed, alive and good, endowed with attributes which are not mine, have not been mine, and never will be mine. This new man is no visible figure in history, no metaphysical phantom of my imagination; he is no other, second person, with whom I may be compared; he claims to be me myself, my existential, unobservable, EGO. In God I am what I am; I cannot therefore wait to be what I am. Under grace, and aware of the message of Christ, I am exposed to the full and unavoidable earnestness of His demand, claim, and promise; I am subjected to a vast and vehement pressure. To be a Christian is to be under this pressure. In ch. iv we made use of the 'historical' and illustrative figure of Abraham, in order to explain that grace is the unobservable and incomparable achievement of the freedom of God, and that it can be found and sought, conceived and apprehended, only as Miracle, Beginning, and Creation. We have now to prove this by facing up to the last human possibility—the possibility of Religion. We are not, however, unprepared for this encounter (ii. 1–13, 14–29; iii. 1–20, 27–30, 31; iv. 9–12, 13–17; v. 13, 20; vi. 14, 15). But first we have to show that religion is a human possibility, and, consequently, a limited possibility,

which by its ineffectiveness, establishes and authenticates the
freedom of God to confer grace upon men.

**v. 1. Or are ye ignorant, brethren—I speak to men
that know the law—how that the law hath dominion over
a man as long as he liveth?**

Brethren—I speak to men that know the law. The possibility
of religion is already familiar to the Christians in Rome. To
whom indeed can it be unfamiliar? Paul knows it; men of every
degree and of all classes actually make use of it; for above
all the occurrences of human life there hangs a smoke-screen
of religion, sometimes heavy, sometimes light. The memory of
that lost direct relationship with God is everywhere retained—
the Unknown God is the God both of Jews and of Gentiles!—and
this memory most assuredly evokes actual and moral experience.
Awe and love, and the enthusiasm of men for that which is
above them, are the concrete and negative impressions of that
union with God which is intangible and invisible. Nor must
we divorce grace from the experience of grace which takes form
and shape in religion and in morality, in dogma and in ecclesiasticism. We hear, we believe, we obey, we confess, we express
ourselves with some passion in speech or in print,—with negative
or positive emphasis. We dispose ourselves upon our appropriate
shelf in the emporium of religion and ethics, ticketed and labelled
with this or that philosophy of life; and we are what we are
described to be upon our label. Of course, from time to time we
change our position; but this only suggests to those gifted with
acute powers of observation the triviality of any particular
position: it suggests, in fact, that a particular standpoint is no
standing place. As men living in the world, and being what we
are, we cannot hope to escape the possibility of religion. For
this reason any attempt to occupy a position 'in the air'
denotes—presumably—a lack of prudence and circumspection
on our part. We may move from one department to another,
but we cannot escape from the store to wander away 'into
the blue'. Knowing ourselves to be thus circumscribed, we
are able to see that the last and the most inevitable human
possibility—the possibility of religion—even in its most courageous, most powerful, most clearly defined, most impossible
'variety', is after all no more than a human possibility, and
as such a limited possibility: and, because limited, peculiarly
dangerous, since it bears witness to, and is embraced by, the
promise of a new and higher order by which it is itself severely
limited. Beyond the humanism which reaches its culminating

point in religion we encounter the freedom which is ours by
grace. Grace, however, is not another possibility. Grace is the
impossibility which is possible only in God, and which is unencumbered and untouched by the final possibility, the ambiguity,
of religion: *The wages of sin is death, but the gift of God is eternal
life through Jesus Christ our Lord* (vi. 23).

Do you comprehend this?—**Or are ye ignorant that the law
hath dominion over a man as long as he liveth?** *The dominion
of the law over a man* means that men are wholly entangled in
the uncertainty which exists within the realm of the possibility
of religion. The man of religion changes colour like a film of oil
on the top of the water. Every moment inevitably he changes
his colour. When he reaches the summit, he falls into the abyss.
He is Moses AND Aaron, Paul AND Saul, enthusiast AND obscuran-
tist, prophet AND pharisee, priest AND blatant sacerdotalist.
He is at once positive, in that he bears noble witness to the
relation which exists between God and man; and negative, in that
in him human nature is confronted by the reality of God. He is
always both positive and negative, and he is the first because
he is the second. Neither obedience, nor resurrection, nor God,
can be embraced within the possibility of religion. Religion is
always a thing in the midst of other things; it involves always a
contrast, a positive and a negative pole, a 'Yes' and a 'No'. In
religion the 'Either' never dissolves the 'Or'; and men find in
it neither the 'Yes' which transcends the conflict between 'Yes'
and 'No', nor the life which transcends death. More than any
other human possibility religion is scarred with the dualism of
'There' and 'Here', presupposition and fact, truth and reality;
the religious man above all others is not what he is intended to
be. A dualism controls the whole world of religion, and, consequently, there sin—*abounds* (v. 20). This abounding of sin in
religion proceeds from dualism because, if God be one factor in a
contrast, a positive opposed to a negative pole, a 'Yes' contrasted
with a 'No', rather than the one, pre-eminent, victorious, free
God, He is degraded to the god of this world, who is 'No-God'—
'To be under the Law means to be under sin' (Kühl). But a man
is under law *as long as he liveth*: as long, that is, as his actual
existence in this world is his life, and in so far as his existence is
bounded by the birth and death of his life in this world. The
dominion of law stands and falls with this life. The frontier
of religion, and of the uncertainty into which it plunges men,
is identical with the frontier by which all human possibility is
bounded. Moving within the frontier of human possibility, I
have no alternative but to appear as, and actually to be—a

religious man. At best I might hope to be a St. Francis, but I am certainly a Grand-Inquisitor;[1] I might set out to be a Blumhardt, but I shall assuredly be a Brand.[2] And if I suspect myself of being far nearer to the second than to the first, how can I justify myself? *Are ye ignorant* that the pre-eminent 'Yes' of God refers not to the man *as long as he liveth*, not to me, but to the new man who has passed from death to life? My justification is therefore guaranteed precisely by the strictest limitation of the possibility of religion, moving, as it does, always within the sphere of 'Yes' AND 'No'.

vv. 2–4. For the woman that hath a husband is bound by law to the husband while he liveth; but if the husband die, she is discharged from the law which binds her to her husband. **So then if, while her husband liveth, she be joined to another man, she shall be called an adulteress: but if the husband die, she is free from the law, so that she is no adulteress, though she be joined to another man. Wherefore, my brethren, ye also were made dead to** the life which is under the dominion of **the law through the** slain **body of Christ; that ye should be joined to another, even to him who was raised from the dead, that we might bring forth fruit unto God.**

The distinctive and critical meaning of the words *as long as he liveth* (vii. 1) can be brought out by an analogy. *As long as he liveth*, yes! but no longer! The conception of death, which is both the characteristic feature and the boundary of this life, enables us to reach a decision concerning the existence or non-existence of that which constitutes a man's 'life'.—**While he liveth** a man is authorized to claim that his wife is married to him, for she is bound under a peculiar obligation. He is thereby authorized also to call her faithless, an adulteress, if she give herself to another man. If, however, he should die, his wife has been set free. By virtue of his death she is no longer his wedded wife. If she then gives herself to another man, she is neither faithless nor an adulteress. Thus, in the moral and legal ordering of marriage, men are also bound by a particular possibility, for they are bound by the life of their partner. So also, the particular possibility is ended by death—in this case, the death of one of the partners in the marriage. Within the ordinances of the law

---

[1] 'The Legend of the Grand Inquisitor' is related in the fifth chapter of the fifth book of Dostoevsky's novel *The Brothers Karamazov*. [Tr.]
[2] The reference is to Ibsen's Dramatic Poem, *Brand*. For Johann Christoph Blumhardt see note on p. 312. [Tr.]

neither party is free to select another possibility—apart from death. Should death, however, occur, the living partner, still acting within the law, is free to select another possibility. That is to say, the law also recognizes that death involves alteration, reversal, radical transformation, a metamorphosis of all predicates. So much for the analogy. Now, listen to its application.

Ye also were made dead to the law through the body of Christ. Ye! ye who are under grace! By means of the conception of death ye are both limited and freed. Ye are under law *as long as* ye live, but only *as long as* ye live. So long as ye are under the necessary ordering of the relation between God and man in religion, ye are limited, enclosed, and fettered by its ambiguity; ye are inexorably committed to live under its dominion—as a wife is committed to her husband, apart from his death. Ye are therefore inevitably under law. Nevertheless, in so far as ye are removed from the necessary ordering of the relation between God and man in religion—as a wife is removed from obligation to her husband by his death—ye are loosed, unlocked, freed unto the eternal, essential, existential unity and clarity and fullness of the possibility of God, which lies beyond the entire ambiguity of religion. Ye are therefore not under law. Are ye then to conclude from this that ye occupy a double position? Are ye bounded AND unlimited, fettered AND freed, barred in AND set at liberty? Or, have ye been turned about, changed, transformed, by the conception of death? Surely, in Christ ye are under grace. Comprehending Him, ye are comprehended in His death; with His human body ye are *made dead*. All human possibilities, including the possibility of religion, have been offered and surrendered to God on Golgotha. Christ, who was *born under the law* (Gal. iv. 4); Christ, who submitted, as did all the pious of Israel, to John's baptism of repentance; Christ, the prophet, the wise man, the teacher, the friend of men, the Messiah-King, dies, that the Son of God may live. Golgotha is the end of law and the frontier of religion. In the slain Christ-according-to-the-law, the last and noblest human possibility, the possibility of human piety and belief and enthusiasm and prayer, is fulfilled by being evacuated. And it is evacuated because the man Jesus, in spite of all that He is and has and does, gives honour to God, and to God alone. With this human *body of Christ* we also are dead to the law, for we have been removed from that life under the dominion of law, which is death. Looking outwards from the Cross, we observe religion, as a concrete thing of soul and sense, as a particular aspect of human behaviour, to have been—taken out of the way (Col. ii.

14). Men do not stand upright before God in virtue of their
religion, any more than they stand upright before Him in virtue
of any other human property. They stand upright before Him in
virtue of that divine nature by which also Christ stood when His
'religious consciousness' was the recognition that He was abandoned by God. In the slain body of Christ, we perceive the non-
existence of men and supremely of religious (!) men; and we also
perceive atonement, forgiveness, justification, and redemption.
From death comes life; and what death is, is made known to us
in the death of Christ. So long, therefore, as we live (vii. 1), we
are joined to the 'living', human body of Christ, to the Christ-
according-to-the-flesh: so long, that is, as we are what we are,
born under the law, woven into the vast ambiguity of religious
experience and history, engaged in the game of 'Yes AND No' (a
dangerous game, but one full of promise), we have no right to
expect our situation to be other than it is, any more than the
married woman can expect to belong to another man except her
husband—so long as he liveth. But—through the slain body
of Christ, we are what we are not. Observed from this scene of
death 'we' live no more; we are dead to the law, dead to the
possibility and necessity of religion, dead to every human possibility; we are removed, set free, unfettered. As a widow is set
free by the law to be joined to another husband, so the road to
that other life, where there is no duplicity, no ambiguity, is
thrown open to us.

**That ye should be joined to another, even to him who was
raised from the dead, that we might bring forth fruit unto God.**
We encounter here that Other who stands directly contrasted
with the loftiest pinnacle of human achievement which is the
'living' body of Christ, for we encounter—*him who was raised
from the dead*. For that Other we have been unfettered and set
at liberty. Beyond the evacuation in Christ of the achievement
of religion—evacuation which is fulfilment—we perceive in Him
the power of obedience which is the power of His Resurrection. In this final balance sheet, in which religion and grace
confront one another as death and life, our pardon is assured
and we are enabled to recognize the freedom of God. Not as
religious men do we obey the categorical imperative; not
as religious men do we become *free from sin* and servants to
God; *the fruits unto sanctification*, which God gathers into His
barns, are not our religious thoughts and desires and actions.
Rather, we obey the imperative of God as men under grace; as
men standing within the peace of God which passeth all understanding; as men who have passed from death to life. So it is

that Paul dares to address as *brethren* men who, like himself, *know the law* (vii. 1) only too well. He addresses them thus, because they are not ignorant of their unobservable establishment in God, which lies beyond the frontier of religion and is perceived in the passing of Christ from crucifixion to resurrection.

vv. 5, 6. For when we were in the flesh, the sinful passions, which were through the law, wrought in our members—to bring forth fruit unto death. But now we have been discharged from the law, having died to that wherein we were held prisoners; **so that we serve in newness of spirit, not in oldness of the letter.**

Fruit unto God (vi. 22, vii. 4)—human thought, will, and action—cannot be defined as *sanctified*, apart from that grace which is grounded in the freedom of God. Men, when observed as men, even as religious men, are—**in the flesh.** Their behaviour is turned towards death and away from God, for their thoughts and intentions and actions are of the earth and must be pronounced unholy and sinful,—peculiarly unholy and peculiarly sinful, when, in their fantasies, they imagine that they are like unto God. The mature and well-balanced man, standing firmly with both feet on the earth, who has never been lamed and broken and half-blinded by the scandal of his life, is as such the existentially godless man. His vigour is the vigour of the lusts of his mortal body (vi. 12). If we undertake to catalogue these lusts, we have to own that the higher, as, for example, the excitement of religion, are distinguished from the lower, as, for example, the desire for sleep, only in degree. Apart from the final word of forgiveness, erotic passions are as precarious as the passions of politics, the passions of ethics as suspicious as the passions of aesthetics. It is passion itself which ought not to be allowed to run its course unbroken and entire. Since the passions of sin spring ultimately from the 'vitality of mortality', their vigorous energy can—apart from the final word 'Resurrection'—produce only—**fruit unto death.** Their intentions and achievements are all bounded by time, and can in no sense be stretched into infinity. This whole activity is governed by its inexorable passage from life unto death. And moreover, law hastens rather than checks this inevitable passing to death of the world of the flesh; for law is the highest achievement of 'humanity'—a grim word of double meaning! When we have grasped the significance of the direction in which human passion moves, we are confronted with the possibility of religion. Though religion, it is true, opposes the passion of men, yet it too stands

within the bracket which is defined by the all-embracing word
sin. With acute analysis Feuerbach has penetrated the truth
when he points out that sinful passions are clearly seen, awakened,
and set in motion, with the intrusion of the possibility of religion,
and because of it. In religion the supreme competence of human
possibility attains its consummation and final realization. Under
the scrutiny of law men become sinners (vii. 7–13); for in the
end human passion derives its living energy from that passionate
desire: Eritis sicut Deus! In religion this final passion becomes
conscious and recognizable as experience and event. Can there
be any affirmation of passion that outstrips the passion with
which Prometheus robs Zeus of his fire and uses it for his own
advantage? And yet, is it not perfectly obvious that such stolen
fire is not the all-consuming fire of God, but only a furnace from
which a very peculiar kind of smoke pours forth? Many gases and
different kinds of smoke, many fumes, spread over the broad
plain of human life. Smoke from the fire of Zeus may penetrate
farther than other fumes, it may display greater variety, but
it does not differ in kind. In any case, it is not by the possession
of such fire that we pass from death to life, or put an end to
human passions. Rather, it is the crowning of all other passions
with the passion of eternity, the endowment of what is finite
with infinity, the most exalted consecration of the passions of
men, and their most secure establishment. If, then, by the consciousness of religion we make human thought and will and act to
be the thought and will and act of God, does not human behaviour become supremely impressive, significant, necessary, and
inevitable? Does not human behaviour then cease to be subjective, and become objective? A man may or may not act religiously; but if he does so act, it is widely supposed that he
does well, and is thereby justified and established and secure.
In fact, however, he merely establishes himself, rests upon his
own competence, and treats his own ambitions as adequate
and satisfactory. Religion, then, so far from dissolving men
existentially, so far from rolling them out and pressing them
against the wall, so far from overwhelming them and transforming them, acts upon them like a drug which has been extremely
skilfully administered. Instead of counteracting human illusions,
it does no more than introduce an alternative condition of
pleasurable emotion. Thus it is that the possibility of religion
enables the existentially godless man to attain the full maturity
of his godlessness by bringing forth a rich and most conspicuous
harvest of *fruit unto death*. What human passion is more
obviously temporary than the passion of religion? What

passion, when allowed free course, is more clearly analogous
to death? What region of human activity is so thickly studded
with cemeteries as is the region of Christian apologetics and
dogmatics and ethics and sociology? Consequently, we are
bound to state quite boldly: *the law worketh wrath* (iv. 15).
Having said this, we have laid bare the frontier of religion.

But now we have been discharged from the law. Kühl pronounces this to be a reference to the 'experience of baptism'.
But that is precisely what it is not. We dare once again (as in
vi. 19) to affirm what no man can affirm of himself. We are
bold, knowing that we are compelled to audacity. The limitation, which we have recognized and defined (vii. 1), is broken
through; and we stand on the other side of the last human
possibility, the possibility of religion. But 'our' being under
grace is not an experience, not one type of human behaviour,
not a particular condition of human activity (vi. 14). Not by
virtue of our own freedom are we what we are; but rather we are
what we are not—by the freedom of God. We are unencumbered
by the inner contradictions of religion, and undisturbed by
the questionable ambiguity of its sinful passions, in spite of the
relativity of its experiences and occurrences. The heaven which
bounds this world of ours is rent asunder in the eternal 'Moment'
of apprehension, in the light of resurrection, in the light of God,
in order that our vision may have space to perceive, not what
men think and will and do, but what God thinks and wills and
does. Standing in the shadow of *the law*, we are enabled by the
brilliance of this *But now* (iii. 21)—light from light uncreated!—
to look back upon *the law* and its dialectic as upon that which is
done away. Moved and shaken and tossed hither and thither by
the sudden changes and chances of religious experience, with
which we too are more or less familiar, we are able even now to
reach out towards that calm and peaceful region where the
swinging pendulum is at rest. Woven into the crude texture of
the occurrences of religion, in which everything—yes, everything!
—human is involved, we stand, nevertheless, already in the primal
and ultimate history where all ambiguity, all polarity, every 'not
only—but also', is *done away*, because God is all in all. We stand
already where the temporal order, from which we cannot escape,
stands over against us as one completed whole, bounded by the
Day of Jesus Christ; where we know ourselves to be finally liberated from the coils of our humanity, in which, as religious men,
we are bound and throttled. 'Liberated!' But we have said too
much. We have spoken *after the manner of men* (vi. 19). What
do we mean when we say that we are 'finally liberated'? If we

mean that something observable has taken place in us and in others, we have returned again to law and to religion. Once again we have become irridescent with human possibility. Is there born of woman any Super-man who is not with Christ under law *as long as he liveth*? When we assert that 'we' live no longer under law, that the possibility of religion lies behind us as some finished thing, we know not what we say, and we utter that which it is not lawful for us to utter. Nevertheless, we do make this assertion. As we previously pronounced the ineffable imperative of sanctification (vi. 12–23), so now we proclaim again what is impossible. We pronounce that which should enter no human ear and proceed from no human mouth. The truth has encountered us from beyond a frontier we have never crossed; it is as though we had been transfixed by an arrow launched at us from beyond an impassable river. But woe be to us, if we do not utter what must be uttered, if we do not speak of that of which the un-observability alone is observable. We speak as prisoners at liberty, as blind seeing, as dead and behold we live. It is not we who speak: Christ is the end of law, the frontier of religion.

Having died to that wherein we were held prisoners. The frontier of religion is the line of death which separates flesh from spirit, time from eternity, human possibility from the possibility of God. In so far as this sharp sword has cleft its way through; in so far, that is, as the power and significance of the Cross, which is the token of judgement and of grace, has cast upon us its shadow—we are *discharged from the law*. We supposed that we could escape the all-embracing Memento mori, and we were thereby imprisoned. What seemed to us pure and upright and unbroken was shown to be for that very reason impure and crooked and crippled. Engaged in earnest and vigo-rous acts of piety, we thought ourselves in possession of that which could never be frozen into stark death. And so religion blossomed forth as the supreme possibility; and who can rid himself of this humanity? Is it not demonstrably clear that expectation of life is the most characteristic feature of religious piety; and that men cling to religion with a bourgeois tenacity, supposing it to be that final thing of soul and sense which is deathless and unshattered. But religion must die. In God we are rid of it. We must apprehend this last concrete thing bounded—aye, radically bounded and placed in question. We, like all clear-sighted men from Job to Dostoevsky, are compelled to recognize, whether we acknowledge it or not, that our con-crete status in the world of time and of men and of things lies under the shadow of death. Living under the shadow of the

Cross, we acknowledge our relatedness to Christ (vi. 5); and, when we say that we are discharged from the law, we know what we are doing—as men who do not know! It is permitted to us to say that under law we are more exceedingly under grace; for we are 'devout'—as though we were not so; we live—ignoring our experiences, or rather, transcending them. We are, then, competent to look, it may be but a little way, beyond ourselves, beyond what is in us and through us and of us, to smile and to weep at what we are. Perhaps even our religion retains some vestige of its own insignificance; perhaps it also knows its lack of solemnity and efficacy, and is conscious of its limitations. Perhaps, however, our piety lacks this perception. Whether we perceive it or not, whenever men are *under the law*, there emerges a piety which celebrates no final triumph and boasts no final justification, but which, nevertheless, refuses to regard its failure as the final tragedy, because it is a piety which continually bears witness to a significance lying beyond itself. The road of religion passes through prophecy, through speaking with tongues, through the knowledge of mysteries, through the giving-of-the-body-to-be-burned, through the giving-of-goods-to-feed-the-poor, through all such things—and it passes onwards still. The road is most strangely defined almost entirely in negatives: but it is named the 'incomprehensible way of love' (1 Cor. xii. 31). Can this be rightly named a road? It is no road—which we can observe or investigate or even enter upon. We can only pass along it. It is the road—which is the shadow cast by the Cross upon all 'healthy' human life: which is the place where the tenacity of men is invisibly, yet most effectually, disturbed and shattered and dissolved; the place where the competence of God, of the Spirit, of Eternity, can enter within our horizon. *Having died to that wherein we were held prisoners.* Having died, that is, to the flesh. May this invisible vision be ours! May we perceive that we are without doubt held and moved and directed by the sure and triumphant freedom of God! May we apprehend the command 'Thus far and no further' which bars the flood when it has submerged the loftiest peaks of human achievement.

So that we serve in newness of spirit, not in oldness of the letter. Sanctify yourselves! Be servants of God! This is the imperative of grace (vi. 22). Were this to mean that we were to serve God in some new, more refined, more detailed *oldness of the letter*, we should be confronted merely by a new piety. We have now to show that *newness of spirit* denotes the possibility which has its beginning in God, beyond the frontier of the

old and of every new possibility of religion. Thus far we have
tried to apprehend the limits of religion. We have been concerned with the negative truth. But religion has also a positive
truth; for in religion the Spirit veritably enters in on our behalf
with groanings which cannot be uttered (viii. 26).

THE MEANING OF RELIGION

VII. 7–13

**v. 7a. What shall we say then? That the law itself is
sin? God forbid.**

We have now reached the point where we are bound to discuss
the effective meaning and significance of that last and noblest
human possibility which encounters us at the threshold and
meeting-place of two worlds, but which, nevertheless, remains
itself on this side the abyss dividing sinners from those who
are under grace. Here, at this turning-point, grace and law—
religion—the first invisibility and the last visible thing, confront each other. Grace is the freedom of God by which men are
seized. Within the sphere of psycho-physical experience this
seizure is, however, nothing but vacuum and void and blankness.
The seizure, therefore, lies on the other side of the abyss. Though
religion and law appear to concern that relationship between
men and God with which grace is also concerned, yet in fact they
do not do so. Law and religion embrace a definite and observable
disposition of men in this world. They hold a concrete position
in the world, and are, consequently, things among other things.
They stand, therefore, on this side the abyss, for they are not the
pre-supposition of all things. There is no stepping across the
frontier by gradual advance or by laborious ascent, or by any
human development whatsoever. The step forward involves on
this side collapse and the beginning from the far side of that
which is wholly Other. If, therefore, the experience of grace be
thought of as the prolongation of already existing religious
experience, grace ceases to be grace, and becomes a thing on
this side. But grace is that which lies on the other side, and no
bridge leads to it. Grace confronts law with a sharp, clearly
defined 'No! Anything rather than such confusion!' The first
divine possibility is contrasted with the last human possibility
along the whole frontier of religion. There is no bridge between
service *in newness of spirit* and *service in oldness of the letter*
(vii. 6). What then, we ask, is the meaning of the paradox of
this close proximity and this vast separation, this near parallel-

ism and this unbridgeable gulf, this interlocking relationship and
this harsh opposition? What attitude are we to adopt to that
relationship to God from which no man can escape *as long as he
liveth* (vii. 1)? How are we to think of religion, if it be also the
most radical dividing of men from God?

The law—sin? It seems obvious that we are almost compelled
to the judgement that the law is sin. Whenever we have been
brought to understand the double position which the law
occupies as the loftiest peak of human possibility, we have been
on the brink of subscribing to this judgement (iv. 15; v. 20; vi.
14, 15; vii. 5). And why should we not surrender to the pressure
and say roundly that religion is the supremacy of human arrogance stretching itself even to God? Why should we not say
that rebellion against God, robbery of what is His, forms the
mysterious background of our whole existence? Would not this
bold statement represent the truth? And why, then, should we
not embark on a war against religion? Would not such an
engagement constitute a human possibility far outstripping the
possibility of religion? Why should we not enrol ourselves as
disciples of Marcion, and proclaim a new God, quite distinct
from the old God of the law? Why should we not follow
Lhotzky, and play off the 'Kingdom of God' against 'Religion'?
or Johannes Müller, and, transporting men from the country of
indirect observation, deposit them in the lost, but nevertheless
still discoverable, land of direct apprehension? or Ragaz, and,
waving the flag of revolution against Theology and the Church,
advance from their barrenness into the new world of complete
laicism in religion? Why should we not return to the main
theme of the first edition of this commentary, and, joining
hands with Beck and with the naturalism of the leaders of the
old school of Württemberg, set over against an empty idealism
the picture of humanity as a growing divine organism? Or
finally, why not proclaim ourselves one with the company of
'healthy' mystics of all ages, and set forth the secret of a true
supernatural religion running at all points parallel to natural
religion? Why not? The answer is simply—**God forbid!** The
apparent radicalism of all these simplifications is pseudo-
radicalism: Nondum considerasti, quanti ponderis
sit peccatum (Anselm). The corrupt tree of sin must not
be identified with the possibility of religion, for sin is not one
possibility in the midst of others. We do not escape from sin by
removing ourselves from religion and taking up with some other
and superior thing—if indeed that were possible. Religion is the
supreme possibility of all human possibilities; and consequently

grace, the good tree, can never be a possibility above, or within, or by the side of, the possibility of religion. Grace is man's divine possibility, and, as such, lies beyond all human possibility. When, therefore, on the basis of a true perception that law is the supreme dominion of sin over men, men first deduce that sin and law are identical, and then proceed in crude or in delicate fashion to demand the abrogation of law, in order that they may live in this world without law—that is, presumably, without sin!; when men revolt, as Marcion did, and with equally good cause, against the Old Testament; when they forget, however, that a like resentment must be applied to the totality of that new thing which they erect upon the ruins of the old—this whole procedure makes it plain that they have not yet understood the criticism under which the law veritably stands. The veritable KRISIS under which religion stands consists first in the impossibility of escape from it *as long as* a man *liveth*; and then in the stupidity of any attempt to be rid of it, since it is precisely in religion that men perceive themselves to be bounded as men of the world by that which is divine. Religion compels us to the perception that God is not to be found in religion. Religion makes us to know that we are competent to advance no single step. Religion, as the final human possibility, commands us to halt. Religion brings us to the place where we must wait, in order that God may confront us—on the other side of the frontier of religion. The transformation of the 'No' of religion into the divine 'Yes' occurs in the dissolution of this last observable human thing. It follows, therefore, that there can be no question of our escaping from this final thing, ridding ourselves of it, or putting something else in its place. It follows also that we cannot just identify law and sin, or suppose that we can advance out of the realm of sin into the realm of grace simply by some complete or partial abrogation of law.

v. 7b. Howbeit, I had not known sin, except through the law: for I had not known coveting, except the law had said, Thou shalt not covet.

I had not known sin, except through the law. What then is religion, if it be not the loftiest summit in the land of sin, if it be not identical with sin? The law is quite obviously the point at which sin becomes an observable fact of experience. Law brings all human possibility into the clear light of an all-embracing KRISIS. Men are sinners, only because of their election and vocation, only because of the act of remembering their lost direct dependence upon God, only because of the contrast between their pristine and their present relation to Him. Otherwise they are not sinners. Apart from the possibility of religion, men, as creatures in the midst of other creatures, are sinners only in the secret of God; that is, they sin unobservably and non-historically. God knows good and evil. But not so can men be convinced of sin. Sin does not yet weigh them down as guilt and as destiny. They are incompetent to perceive the sword of judgement hanging above their heads; nor can any man persuade or compel them to this fatal perception. Nor is it otherwise with regard to the new creation, which is the obverse side of the condition of men. Men are righteous, only in the secret of God: that is, they are righteous unobservably and non-historically. They cannot convince themselves of righteousness. Between these two unobservable realities are set observable law and observable religion. In the midst of other things, whether we recognize it or not, is placed the impress of revelation, the knowledge of good and evil, the perception— more or less clear—that we belong to God, the reminiscence of our Primal Origin, by which we are elected either to blessedness or to damnation. Reference is made, it is true, in v. 13, 14, to an exception to this general knowledge; but it is, presumably, only a theoretical exception. We are now concerned with the meaning of this peculiar and final apprehension; and the question as to whether there are exceptions is hardly relevant. We are able to see that, compared with other things of which we are aware, religion is a distinct and quite peculiar thing. A numinous perception of any kind has an alarming and disturbing effect upon all other perceptions; a divinity of any kind tends to bring men into a condition which is more or less ambiguous; a cleavage of some form or other is made between their existence and a contrasted and threatening non-existence; a gulf appears between the concrete world and the real world; there emerges a scepticism as to whether we are competent to elongate possibility into impossibility or to stretch our actual existence into non-existence. Something of this KRISIS underlies all religion; and the more insistent the tension becomes, the more clearly we are in the presence of the phenomenon of religion, whether or no we ourselves are conscious of it. From the point of view of comparative religion, the evolution of religion reaches its highest and purest peak in the Law of Israel, that is, in the assault made upon men by the Prophets. But what is the real significance of this prophetic KRISIS? It is unintelligible unless we first recognize that precisely in the phenomena of religion there occurs visibly a rising of slaves against the authority of

God. Men *hold the truth imprisoned in unrighteousness.* They have lost themselves. Giving pleasurable attention to the words—*Ye shall be as God*—they become to themselves what God ought to be to them. Transforming time into eternity, and therefore eternity into time, they stretch themselves beyond the boundary of death, rob the Unknown God of what is His, push themselves into His domain, and depress Him to their own level. Forgetting the awful gulf by which they are separated from Him, they enter upon a relation with Him which would be possible only if He were not God. They make Him a thing in this world, and set Him in the midst of other things. All this occurs quite manifestly and observably within the possibility of religion. Now the prophetic KRISIS means the bringing of the final observable human possibility of religion within the scope of that KRISIS under which all human endeavour is set. The prophets see what men in fact are: they see them, confronted by the ambiguity of the world, bringing forth the possibility of religion; they see them arrogantly and illegitimately daring the impossible and raising themselves to equality with God. But, if this last achievement of men be the action of a criminal, what are we to say of all their other minor achievements? Clearly, all are under judgement. In the light of the prophetic condemnation of this final achievement we perceive the condemnation also of all previous and lesser achievements. The whole series of human competences becomes to us a series of impossibilities. When the highest competence is seen to be illusion, the lower share inevitably in a general illusoriness. If God encounters and confronts men in religion, He encounters and confronts them everywhere. Remembering their direct relation with Him, its loss becomes an event, and there breaks out a sickness unto death. It is religion, then, which sets a question-mark against every system of human culture; and religion is a genuine experience. But what do men experience in religion? In religion men know themselves to be conditioned invisibly by—sin. In religion the Fall of mankind out of its primal union with God becomes the pre-supposition of all human vitality. *Through the law,* the double and eternal predestination of men to blessedness or to damnation becomes a psycho-physical occurrence; and—*sin abounds* (v. 20).

I had not known coveting, except the law had said, Thou shalt not covet. The sinfulness of my vitality and the necessary dissolution of my desires are not self-evident truths. This qualification of my whole activity is, apart from religion, merely an opinion. Moreover, all my senses object to being disqualified; they protest vigorously against a suspicion and condemnation which is directed against them and against the natural order as such. Surely, if we exclude from our thoughts the primal and final significance of the possibility of religion, this resistance and protest is wholly justified. Why indeed should mere natural vitality be evil? *I had not known coveting—Apart from the law sin is dead* (vii. 8)—unless, that is, with fatal imprudence, I had dared, as a religious man, to leave the region of mere worldliness and press forward into the questionable light of my divine possibility. Religion in some guise or other overwhelms me like an armed man; for, though the ambiguity of my existence in this world may perhaps be hidden from me, yet nevertheless my desires and my vitality press forward into the sphere of religion, and I am defenceless against this pressure. To put the matter another way: I am confronted, as a man of this world, by the clear or hidden problem of the existence of God. It is, then, inevitable that I should do what I ought not to do: that quite inadequately and unworthily, I should formulate the relation between the infinity of God and my finite existence, between my finite existence and the infinity of God—in terms of religion. When I have surrendered to this seeming necessity, law has entered into my life, and my desires and vitality are then subjected, if not to an absolute, at least to a quite devastating negation; if not to a direct, at least to a brilliant indirect lighting; if not to a final, at least to a penetrating and a vigorous ambiguity. Between the experience of religion and all other human experiences there is a relatively quite radical cleavage: in the religion of the prophets, for example, this cleavage is peculiarly terrible. The 'peculiarity' of the Jew is occasioned by his occupation of a position so perilously near the edge of a precipice that its sheer drop may be taken as bearing witness to the sharp edge of that wholly other precipice, by which all human achievements, all concrete occurrences, are bounded; the precipice which separates men from God (iii. 1–20). Though I may with naïve creatureliness *covet*, so long as I know naught but this coveting creatureliness, yet even this is forbidden me whenever, in venturing to know more than my creatureliness, I have pressed so hard on the frontier of divine possibilities that even my created existence is rendered questionable. When this has once occurred, the desires even of my simple createdness are broken desires. They are no longer innocent, and I am no longer justified in their enjoyment. When religion, supreme among all desires, opens its mouth, it proclaims to all coveting—*Thou shalt not!* When eternity confronts human finite existence, it renders that finite existence sinful. When human finite existence is confronted by the

eternity of God, it becomes sin. This applies, however, only
when the action of men who have fallen out of their relationship
with God is not the action of God Himself. We are not concerned here with the precise form or scope or extent of this
KRISIS of human vitality, for such matters belong properly to
the study of history. We are concerned only to bring out the
peculiar significance of the phenomenon of religion and its
relation to other phenomena. We have asked the question:
What is the meaning of religion? We have now discovered its
meaning to be that our whole concrete and observable existence
is sinful. Through religion we perceive that men have rebelled
against God, and that their rebellion is a rebellion of slaves. We
are now driven to the consideration of that freedom which lies
beyond the concrete visibility of sin—the freedom of God which
is our freedom.

**vv. 8–11. But sin, taking occasion by the command-
ment, wrought in me all manner of coveting: for apart
from the law sin is dead. And I was alive apart from the
law once: but when the commandment came, sin burst
into life, and I died; and the commandment, which was
unto life, this I found to be unto death: for sin, taking
occasion by the commandment, deceived me, and through
it slew me.**

**But sin, taking occasion by the commandment, wrought in me
all manner of coveting.** In speaking of the process by which
Word became Myth it is impossible to avoid mythological language! In its primal form, in the secret of God, sin is the
possibility that the union between men and God may be broken.
Sin is the possibility of predestination to blessedness OR to
damnation. This does not mean, of course, that sin originated in
God; but it does mean that He is its final truth. In God men
possess—as slaves do—the possibility of rebellion. They can
separate themselves from Him who is eternally one. They can
lay hold of the shadow which follows the divine glory—but only
as its negation—and make it their eternity. Men have the
opportunity of making themselves God. The knowledge of this
opportunity, and the consequent capacity to make use of it, is
sin. When the sluice-gates are opened, the water, by the force
of its own inertia, pours through to a lower level. So sin, because
its nature is to move downwards and not upwards, because it
belongs properly to what is relative, separated, independent,
and indirect, bursts into the world of time, breaks into concrete
visibility, and stands there in stark contrast with what is un-

observable, non-concrete, and eternal. Sin is sin—in so far as
the world is manifested as an independent thing over against
creation; in so far as the course of the world runs counter to its
existence; in so far as men are opposed to God. And yet, it is
not immediately obvious that the sluice-gates of the lock which
marks the distinction between God and man have been opened.
Originally, there was no separation. Men dwelt in the Garden
of Eden, in which there were no absolute and relative, no
'Higher' and 'Lower', no 'There' and 'Here': such distinctions
marked the Fall. The world was originally one with the Creator,
and men were one with God. The natural order then, as such,
was holy, because holiness is its characteristic mark. Originally,
there was no *coveting*: men were permitted, and indeed commanded, to enjoy all the fruits of the garden. There was, however,
one exception. In the midst of the garden stood *the tree of the
knowledge of good and evil*. The behaviour of men must not be
governed by knowledge of the contrast between the primal state
and its contradiction. That is God's secret. Men ought not to
be independently what they are in dependence upon God; they
ought not, as creatures, to be some second thing by the side of
the Creator. Men ought not to know that they are merely—men.
God knows this, but in His mercy He has concealed it from them.
So long as ignorance prevailed, the Lord walked freely in the
garden in the cool of the day, as though in the equality of friend-
ship. Look how Michelangelo has depicted the 'Creation of
Eve': in the fullness of her charm and beauty she rises slowly,
posing herself in the fatal attitude of—worship. Notice the
Creator's warning arm and careworn, saddened eyes, as He
replies to Eve's gesture of adoration. She is manifestly behaving
as she ought not. Eve—and we must honour her as the first
'religious personality'—was the first to set herself over against
God, the first to worship Him; but, inasmuch as SHE worshipped
HIM, she was separated from Him in a manner at once terrible
and presumptuous. Then the 'well-known serpent' appears upon
the scene. He utters words—the archetype of all sermons—
about God; he—the first shepherd of the souls of men—first
offers advice concerning the commandments of God. Adam's
titanic capacity for wisdom already existed before Eve!;—
now it is turned into tragic reality. Tragic—because, when men,
knowing good and evil, become *like God*, when their direct relation with Him gives birth to independent action, then all direct
relationship is broken off. When men stretch out their hands
and touch the link which binds them to God, when they touch
the tree *in the midst of the garden*, which ought not to be touched,

they are by this presumptuous contact separated from Him. They have handled death—that barbed wire loaded with electricity. Stretching out to reach what they are not, men encounter what they are, and they are thereby fenced in and shut out. With open eyes they see that they are separated from God and—naked. Coveting, lusting after, passionately desiring corruptible things, they become themselves corruptible. Why is the question concerning God as the Creator and us as His creation a question which, in spite of its insistent, compelling, desperate urgency, cannot even be formulated—by us? Yet we know no man who has not done as Adam did. We ourselves have touched the tree; we have formulated the question; and in formulating it we have set ourselves in opposition to God. In opposition to God!—this which God withheld from us for our salvation now governs our lives. Immediately we know good AND evil, the commandment of God transforms Paradise into—Paradise Lost. Our present existence is discredited and rendered questionable, already, perhaps, accused and condemned as actually evil, by the demand which names a thing 'good' which—ought to be so and is not. The covetous desire, which causes men to stretch out their hands towards that one tree, renders also more or less forbidden those many desires to enjoy the fruits of all the other trees. For this one lust sets everything which men think and will and do in direct opposition to the relentless and holy and eternal will of God. This is the triumph of sin. Impetuously sin has sought and found its level in the many-sided vitality of men, and their vitality is now named 'lust'. Opposition to God emerges in the critical distinction between seen and unseen, relative and absolute, independence and primal union. And this opposition comes into being through the divine commandment; through the intrusion of the possibility of religion; through the beguilement of the serpent's sermon on the theme of a direct relation between men and God; through the far too great attention paid to it by men, and especially by women, since they are more acutely disturbed than men are by the riddle of direct relationship. So it is that religion becomes the occasion of sin. Religion is the working capital of sin; its fulcrum; the means by which men are removed from direct union with God and thrust into disunion, that is, into the recognition of their—creatureliness.

For apart from the law sin is dead. And I was alive apart from the law once. The words *I was alive* can no more refer to the historical past than can the words *we shall live* (vi. 2, &c.) to some historical future; the reference is to that life which is primal and

non-historical, just as the previous reference was to that life
which is also final and non-historical. There is no question here of
contrasting a particular epoch in the life of a single individual,
or of a group, or indeed of all mankind, with some other epoch,
past or future. The passages refer to that timeless age to which
all men belong. Only in a parable, and, even so, only with the
greatest care, can we speak of the 'innocence' of children and of
the guilt of those who have passed beyond the 'age of innocence'!
Only with great circumspection ought we to speak of 'Child-
races' or 'Child-civilizations', &c., or of their 'growing up'. The
life defined as past or future must not be depressed into history,
because the contrast is concerned with the opposition between
eternal life and our present concrete existence. *I was alive* and
sin was dead, because I lived *apart from the law*: *apart from the
law* sin is dead, and men are alive. Only when the creature
stands over against the Creator may it be defined as sinful. The
creation is not questionable, unless it be thought of as mere
Nature, independent of God. The recognition of the opposition
of the world to God, and of its consequent sinfulness, becomes
acute only with the emergence of the titanic possibility of
religion. The creature, in its primal, original, unseen history,
lives and moves without touching the line of death which marks
the separation between God and man ; without touching the tree
of destiny which stands in the midst of the garden. In this
primal life, the union and distinction between the Creator and
the creature is not fraught with the tragic significance which
comes into being with the emergence of religion. In the fresco
of the 'Creation of Adam' Michelangelo depicts God and Adam
looking one another straight in the face, their hands stretched
out towards one another in a delicious freedom of intercourse.
The air is charged with the deep, triumphant, moving peace of
the eternal 'Moment' of creation. And yet, the scene is heavy
with tragedy ; for it portrays the direct relation as not yet lost ;
it portrays the relation in which religion plays no part. And
so it draws attention to the distinction between our present
existence and, not only the 'old' Creation, but also the 'new'
Creation for which men are now waiting. In this direct relationship mankind lives ; not this or that individual man, but
mankind as created by God, in His own image, and as He will
again create them. Out of this relationship, which never has
been, and never will be, an event in history, we issue, and
towards it we move. Nor can sin destroy this primal union, for
it is the act and work of God alone. Marcion described it
admirably as the 'Wholly Other' which is our unforgettable

home; the reality, the proximity, the glory, which we encounter in the last words of the Gospel—Forgiveness, Resurrection, Redemption, Love, God. These are words in which disturbance and promise are joined together; for they direct us towards the realm where there is no law and no religion (iv. 15). Those concrete and historical events which seem to us (as v. 13) relatively pure and innocent are harmless and fraught with hope and meaning only when we behold reflected in them that life from which we come and to which we move.

But·when the commandment came, sin burst into life, and I died. Scattered to the winds is the eternal 'Now' of the Creation. *The commandment came.* It had to come, when men became as God, bearing the burden of the divine secret, knowing good AND evil, election AND damnation, 'Yes' AND 'No'. The time when there was no commandment is beyond our understanding. All we know is that the union between God and man has been changed from divine pre-supposition to human supposition, and that, consequently, every human position has suffered dislocation. On the very brink of human possibility there has, moreover, appeared a final human capacity—the capacity of knowing God to be unknowable and wholly Other; of knowing man to be a creature contrasted with the Creator, and, above all, of offering to the Unknown God gestures of adoration. This possibility of religion sets every other human capacity also under the bright and fatal light of impossibility. Such is human capacity; and we are bound to believe and to make known—for only a weak-chested piety fails to perceive it—that men are compelled to advance along a road which ends in 'Double Predestination'. What then —we are bound to ask the question—are men? *Sin burst into life.* Irrecoverable is the 'Moment' of creation; irretrievable the purity and peace of that existence in which God and men were one and not two. The unity of life has been sundered, and God stands over against men as their counterpart—in power; whereas men stand over against God as His counterpart—in weakness. Men are limited by God, and God is limited by men: both are compromised and rendered questionable. *And I died.* Death is the mark of that passing of eternity into time, which is, of course, not an occurrence in time, but a past happening in primal history. Now everything is concrete and indirect. The whole range of the life we now live is contrasted with our life in God, and consequently stamped with the indelible mark of death. The narrow gate through which our perception widens out from what is finite to what is infinite closes and opens only with critical negation. The recognition that we must die is forced upon us, and such recognition is the point where either we attain wisdom or remain 'fools'—in the most reprehensible sense of the word. In the inexorable 'No' of death, the 'Yes' of God and of life is presented to us: that is to say, it is presented to us in the contrast between what we are able to observe and what is beyond our observation; it is presented to us in recognizable time, which is past and future, but never present; in the concrete form of Nature, which is mere 'world'—COSMOS—but never Creation; in visible history, which is only process, but never completed occurrence. The only world we can know is the world of time, of things, and of men. The final experience to which we have access in this world is summed up in the words—*and I died*, and this is the pre-supposition of all experience. Now, the religious man is bound to encounter this experience, this pre-supposition of all experience, precisely because he is a religious man: *Then said I, Woe is me! for I am undone: . . . for mine eyes have seen the King, the Lord of hosts* (Isa. vi. 5). There is no escape from this vision or from this undoing.

And the commandment, which was unto life, this I found to be unto death : for sin, taking occasion by the commandment, deceived me, and through it slew me. The supreme possibility to which we can attain within the range of our concrete existence under the dominion of sin consists in our capacity to grasp the line of death, to know both good and evil, and in the consequent emergence of the distinction between God as God and men as men. Now, that this supreme and urgent necessity of our existence should be identical with that capacity by which our direct union with God was destroyed, constitutes the final paradox of the Fall.

When we ask what it is that directs us towards that lost, but recoverable life in God, standing as we do within the world of time and things and men, there is but one possible answer: we are directed by the *commandment*, by our capacity for religion, by a vast critical negation—in fact, by the recognition that *we must die*. Is there any other road where the unseen becomes visible, any other road along which those men have passed who have *seen clearly* and to whom the thought of God has been revealed (i. 20), except the narrow way of the 'wisdom of death'? Since we cannot take up our position beyond the line of death, and since we must take our stand somewhere, have we any alternative but to stand on the line 'across which Adam fell' (Luther)? Daring the best and the highest, our place is on the extremest edge of human possibility, where the ' Jesus of History' stands, where Abraham, Job, and all the prophets and apostles stand; the place where men are most evidently men, where they are most completely removed from direct union with God, and where human existence is most heavily burdened with its own questionableness. There is for us no honourable alternative but to be religious men, repenting in dust and ashes, wrestling in fear and trembling, that we may be blessed; and, since we must take up a position, adopting the attitude of adoration. To all this we are urged by the commandment which directs us unto life. Knowing, then, that we have no alternative, knowing also what that alternative involves, ought we to shrink from advancing to take up our position on the very outermost edge of the precipice, on the very brink of the possibility of religion? We may, however, judge the relentlessness of Calvin, the dialectical audacity of Kierkegaard, Overbeck's sense of awe, Dostoevsky's hunger for eternity, Blumhardt's optimism, too risky and too dangerous for us. We may therefore content ourselves with some lesser, more feeble possibility of religion. We may fall back on some form of rationalism or pietism. Yet these more feeble types of religion are also pregnant with implications pointing towards that outermost edge, and some day they may bring this harsh and dangerous reality to birth. If Adam, easily content with lesser possibilities, should ever forget his proper condition and omit to move to his final possibility, Eve soon reminds him of the possibility of religion, for she is more acutely aware of the loss of direct union with God. And yet—for here is the tragic paradox of religion— should we seriously undertake to turn as pilgrims towards that far-off land which is our home, should we undertake the final concrete human action, we do but display the catastrophe of human impotence in the things of God. What is our action, our taking up of a position, but the supreme betrayal of the true pre-supposition? What is our undertaking of a visible relation-ship, our scaling of the summit of human possibility, but our completest separation from the true invisible relationship? Seen from God's standpoint, religion is precisely that which we had better leave undone: *And the commandment—this I found to be unto death*. The necessity of the possibility of religion, the necessity of stretching out towards the tree in our midst, the desire to know good and evil, life and death, God and man— this necessity is no more than a manœuvre, undertaken by men within the concrete reality of this world. By it they are defined as evil and passing to corruption; by it they are defined as—men; by it they are thrown into the contrast between relative and absolute, and there imprisoned. At best they are confronted in religion by the 'No' in which the 'Yes' of God is hidden. Death is the meaning of religion; for when we are pressed to the boundary of religion, death pronounces the inner calm of simple and harmless relativity to be at an end. Religion is not at all to be 'in tune with the infinite' or to be at 'peace with oneself'. It has no place for refined sensibility or mature humanity. Let simple-minded Occidentals (!) retain such opinions as long as they are able. But religion is an abyss: it is terror. There demons appear (Ivan Karamazov and Luther!). There the old enemy of man is strangely near. There sin deceives. There the power of the commandment is deadly—*The serpent beguiled me* (Gen. iii. 13). Sin is the place where our destiny becomes a present, concrete possibility, the place where our knowledge of good and evil becomes an urgent, direct knowledge. The deception of sin is the illusion that such direct knowledge is life, whereas in fact it is death. Deceit runs its full course, because men do not perceive that the necessity of independent human action is what should not be in the presence of God. It is successful, because human determination to retain the possibility of independence before God reveals men to be—merely men. The commandment is therefore the lever or *occasion* of sin: clothing time with the garment of eternity, it presents piety as a human achievement, evokes worship which knows not how to be silent before God, and names such worship 'religion'; concealing from the worshipper, not merely how questionable the world is, but how utterly questionable religion is, it compels him to lift up hands in prayer, then lets them drop back wearily, and in this weariness spurs him unto prayer again. And this is, after all, the situation in which men find themselves under the commandment.

We have now been able to provide a second answer to our question concerning the meaning of religion. Religion is that human necessity in which the power exercised over men by sin is clearly demonstrated. Once again we are compelled to consider what the freedom of God means when it confronts men imprisoned in the closed circle of humanity.

vv. 12, 13. Wherefore the law is holy, and the commandment holy, and righteous, and good. Did then that which is good become death unto me? God forbid! But sin, that it might be shown to be sin, by working death to me through that which is good;—that through the commandment sin might become incomprehensibly **sinful.**

The law is holy, and the commandment holy, and righteous, and good. What, then, are we to do? This is the urgent question which presses upon the man who has come to himself, who has become religious, and is aware of his rebellion against God and of the terrible weight he has to bear as a man of this world. The answer to the question implies a still greater emphasis upon the question. May God never relieve us of this questioning! May He enclose us with questions on every side! May He defend us from any answer which is not itself a question! May He bar every exit and cut us off from all simplifications! May the cavity at the cart-wheel's centre, which Lao-Tse[1] perceived long ago, be delimited by a ring of questions! In that central void the answer to our questioning is hidden; but since the void is defined by questions, they must never for one moment cease. *The law is holy.* We cannot stand on the definition of religion, or indeed of any human possibility, as though it were merely sin. Religion is the place where every human capacity is enlightened by divine light. Placed outside the region of divinity, religion, nevertheless, represents divinity as its delegate or impress or negative. Moving within the sphere of human activity, religion is without doubt *holy*, because it points from humanity to divinity; it is without doubt *righteous*, because it is correlated with the will of God and parallel to it, being indeed the parable of it; and it is without doubt *good*, for it is that concrete, observable, mediated experience which bears witness to the immediacy which has been lost. Should we remove ourselves consciously or unconsciously from the dangerous ambiguity of religion, either we must take refuge in some other less exalted human possibility—in some possibility that is ethical or logical or aesthetic or even lower; or we must side-step into some ancient or modern variety of religion; and, if we are not fully aware of the ambiguity of all religion, to do so will mean inevitably that the alternative variety which we have selected will be a bad one. There is no human advance beyond the possibility of religion, for religion is the last step in human progress. Standing as it does within humanity but outside divinity, it bears witness to that which is within divinity but outside humanity. Let us therefore—within the possibility of religion, and outside the realm of that charity which does *not covet* (1 Cor. xii. 31; xiv. 1; cf. xiii. 4)—*covet earnestly the best gifts.* Let us be convincedly nothing but religious men; let us adore and tarry and hurry with all the energy we possess; let us cultivate, nurse, and stir up religion; and above all, let us reform it; nay more, revolution-

---

[1] *Tao-Teh-King*, ch. xi. 'The thirty spokes of a chariot wheel and the nave to which they are attached would be useless, but for the hollow space in which the axle turns' (G. G. Alexander). [Tr.]

ize it. This labour in the field of the humanities is well worth the vigour of noble and devoted men.

But—the more zealously this labour is undertaken, the deeper we penetrate the valley of the shadow of death. It should cause us no surprise that the majority are reluctant to move to the outer edge of the precipice of religion; for there not only does religion itself become ambiguous, but its ambiguity carries with it the questionableness of all human possibility. We ought not to be surprised at the many attempts which have been made to explore the possibility of some compromise between the spiritual lethargy of the man of this world and the holiness and righteousness and goodness of religion and of the law. The question—**Did then that which is good become death unto me?**—corresponds with the earlier question—*Is the law sin?* (vii. 7). These overlapping questions quite naturally entice men to escape from the twilight of religion. We are fully aware of the tension and disturbance and impossibility of our situation as religious men: we have been led far from the flesh-pots of Egypt deep into the desert. Surely, this eccentric and strange occurrence, this pilgrimage of ours, by which we are cast to the ground and dissolved, cannot be—good? Can God deal with us so harshly? How beguiling and attractive, then, are those many simpler alternatives! How enticing to us is some semi-antinomianism, or indeed, complete antinomianism! Shall we not yield to those who attempt to rid men of the terrifying earnestness of religion by inviting them to something less vexatious; by offering them a joyful, less exacting redemption which takes place outside the danger-zone? Here we are presented with something utterly different from that deadly shadow of the law of God, under which the great men of religion have passed their days bearing witness to the salvation which is by grace only. Can we resist the temptation of easing religion of its heavy burden and uncharging it of its dangerous dynamite? Can we not, at least partially, escape from the accursed relativity of every merely human possibility; from the misery of our present indirect relation to God and of our present segregation on this side the abyss; from the curse which presses so hardly upon the religious man?

God forbid. This is our answer. For, at whatever cost, we must remain at our post and drain the cup to its dregs. Good is not less good because it is not simple or obvious, or because we have no direct access to it. We must submit to the full paradox of our situation. The moment we become aware of ourselves and of our position in the world, through the commandment of God which meets us in the known uncertainty of our present existence we are led onwards to the final possibility of religion. Appealing with tears and longing to the Great Unknown, we stretch out our failing arms towards the 'Yes' which confronts us invisibly in the 'No' by which we are imprisoned. But, nevertheless, we have to learn that we are not justified, not redeemed, not saved, by these appealing cries and tears. Passing, as we are, to corruption, they do but establish and stamp us as—men. I have no alternative but to follow the desire which is above all other desires—the longing for the recovery of the lost immediacy of my life in God. And when I follow it, all my desires are thereby turned to sin, and this last desire supremely so. 'Through the law I become aware of how it is betwixt God and me. Therefore I move about anxious with fears and questionings, unnerved by the slightest trembling leaf, terrified by the thunder's noise. Every moment I expect God to come behind me and crash me over the head with a bludgeon. Wherefore, lest I be forced to hold myself a coward and a weakling, I must dare all, surrender all, sacrifice all, that I may attain the One, and be—like God' (Luther). Thither, then, all the vigour of my energy is directed, that I may attain the eternal 'Moment' of Creation. But, when I have dared, offered, sacrificed everything, I stand with nothing in my hands, mere dust and ashes, separated farther than ever from the One. Do we now at last recognize what sin is, and how impossible it is for us to escape from it? So deeply does it penetrate every human capacity that the attempt to elude it by taking up with religion entangles us more surely in its guilt and plunges us into the destiny of death.—Sin, that it might be shown to be sin, by working death to me through that which is good. Death—through that which is good! through what is necessary and unavoidable! through that which honest and upright men are compelled to snatch at, as a drowning man clutches at a straw! through that possibility which, when first discovered, appears as light shining in the darkness of night! through the purest, noblest, and most hopeful element within the sphere of the competence of men. For what are erotics, alcoholics, intellectualists, mammonites, might-is-right-politicians, what are the armies of the Philistines in comparison with one sinner who believes and prays? He it is, not they, who hears and obeys the destructive command 'Halt'. He it is, not they, who dies the death which is the last word uttered over the man of this world. *Surely he hath borne our sickness, and carried our sorrows* (Isa. liii. 4). He is the sinner; yet he is also the guiltless one, for through him there has entered a divine, not a human possibility. In the mercy of God, he announces salvation and life, for *the chastisement of our peace was upon him* (Isa. liii. 5). Do we now perceive what sin is and what is the significance of religion? Do we understand the words **—That through the commandment sin might become incomprehensibly sinful?** Here we have reached the meaning of religion. In the inexorable reality (vii. 7b–11) of this supreme human possibility sin is shown forth as the power which reigns within the closed circle of humanity. Nevertheless, its power is bounded by the freedom of God, of God Himself, and of God alone. But it has no other boundary. This is the meaning of the law: it sharpens our intelligence that we may perceive (vii. 6) the sheer impossibility of our attaining that freedom from the law, that service *in newness of the spirit*, at which we have gazed— outside the frontiers of religion.

THE REALITY OF RELIGION

VII. 14–25.

Apprehension of the meaning of religion depends upon the clarity with which the dominion of sin over the men of this world is disclosed to our view. When we recognize the peculiar sinfulness of the religious man and see sin *abounding* in him, we are able to understand the meaning of *grace more exceedingly abounding* (v. 20), and the necessity that the divine mercy should act in spite of sin. But, before turning our attention once more to the goal of our investigation, we must make sure whether religion, although incapable of providing a theoretical answer to the problem of sin, may not be perfectly competent to provide a practical answer. We may have established religion to be in theory no more than the last human possibility; but it may turn out to be in actual practice the sure and solid answer to guilt and destiny. The Psychology of Religion, concerned as it is with the reality of religion, with the religious man in the peculiarity of what he is and has, must now be allowed to say what it has to say. Will the religious man agree that sin celebrates its triumph in religion? Has he not something to say to all this? Will he admit that he is branded as a slave and handed over to death (vii. 13)— through the good, by means of the noblest, most necessary, most hopeful of all human possibilities? Yes, he does say this; he does agree with the theorist. The romantic psychologist may make many attempts to hush this up: he may represent religion as that human capacity by which 'all human occurrences are thought of as divine actions'; he may define it as 'the solemn music which accompanies all human experience' (Schleiermacher). Against such representations, however, religion is always on its guard. Religion, when it attacks vigorously, when it is fraught with disturbance, when it is non-aesthetic, non-rhetorical, non-pious, when it is the religion of the 39th Psalm, of Job and of Luther and of Kierkegaard, when it is the religion of Paul, bitterly protests against every attempt to make of its grim earnestness some trivial and harmless thing. Religion is aware that it is in no wise the crown and fulfilment of true humanity; it knows itself rather to be a questionable, disturbing, dangerous thing. It closes the circle of humanity completely; so completely that it completely opens it—covertly! Religion confronts every human competence, every concrete happening in this world, as a thing incomprehensible, which cannot be tolerated or accepted. Religion, so far from being the place where the healthy harmony of human life is lauded, is instead the place where it appears diseased, discordant, and disrupted. Religion is not the sure ground upon which human culture safely rests; it is the place where civilization and its partner, barbarism, are rendered fundamentally questionable. Nor does the frank judgement of honest men of the world disagree with the opinion of religion about itself.

> The curtain is raised; the music must cease.
> The temple is gone: and far in the distance
> Appeareth the terrible form of the—Sphinx.
>
>   Fr. Schlegel on Schleiermacher's speeches.

Religion must beware lest it tone down in any degree the unconverted man's judgement. Conflict and distress, sin and death, the devil and hell, make up the reality of religion. So far from releasing men from guilt and destiny, it brings men under their sway. Religion possesses no solution of the problem of life; rather it makes of the problem a wholly insoluble enigma. Religion neither discovers the problem nor solves it: what it does is to disclose the truth that it cannot be solved. Religion is neither a thing to be enjoyed nor a thing to be celebrated: it must be borne as a yoke which cannot be removed. Religion is not a thing to be desired or extolled: it is a misfortune which takes fatal hold upon some men, and is by them passed on to others; it is the misfortune which assailed John the Baptist in the desert, and drove him out to preach repentance and judgement; which caused the writing of that long-drawn-out, harassed groan, which is the Second Epistle to the Corinthians; which laid upon Calvin's face that look which he bore at the end of his life. Religion is the misfortune which every human being has to endure, though it is, in the majority of cases, a hidden suffering.

The first piece of evidence is: **vv. 14–17. For I know¹ that the law is spiritual: but I am carnal, sold under sin. For that which I do I know not: for not what I would, that do I practise; but what I hate, that I do. But if what I would not, that I do, I consent unto the law that it is good. So now it is no more I that do it, but sin which dwelleth in me.**

I know that the law is spiritual. To know this is the first requirement of a religious man. Whence does he come? And whither does he go? He comes from the realm of the Spirit; he passes relentlessly to death. When, therefore, he stands under the compelling impression of the Spirit, an intolerable tension is introduced into his life. He is engaged inevitably and hopefully in a conflict from which there is no escape, because it is the battle for his very existence. A demand is made upon him which he is bound to accept, because the vast inadequacy of his life in this world means that the demand is not only right but necessary. A question is asked him, to which he must find an answer. A call is given him, which he is bound to obey. The existence of God rises up in the midst of his life, like an immense boundary-wall shutting out some poor neighbour's view; or like a fortress occupied by the enemy; or like a boxer's closed fist, Yet he must stand up to it, come to terms with it, and live with it. Paul knows its meaning, when he calls himself elsewhere *a prisoner in bonds* (Eph. iii. 1, iv. 1; 2 Tim. i. 8; Philem. 9). *O Lord, thou hast persuaded me, and I was persuaded: thou art stronger than I, and hast prevailed* (Jer. xx. 7).

But I am carnal, sold under sin. The tension becomes acute. If God be God, who then am I? If my human relation to Him be bondage and captivity, who then am I? The answer of experience to such questioning is quickly made. I see that the law which proceeds from the Spirit, compelling, necessary, and

¹ Adopting the reading οἶδα μέν, because, in agreement with Hofmann and Zahn, I regard an appeal to a consensus of opinion among the Christian readers (οἴδαμεν) as unsuitable in the context. Nevertheless, the reading οἴδαμεν cannot be ruled out, for the passage is no biographical intermezzo! The contrasted ἐγὼ δέ, which opponents of the reading οἶδα μέν (for example, Kühl) think should in that case have been εἰμὶ δέ, is, however, intelligible, if it be borne in mind that the ἐγώ of the person dedicated to God is contrasted throughout with his knowledge and desire and action and achievement as *the* wholly ambiguous factor. Consequently, σαρκικός εἰμι must not be unduly emphasized (against Beck).

inevitable though it be, is excluded from my existence as a man. What form of human existence is competent to receive THIS impress, to arrange itself according to THIS misery and hope, and to accept THIS demand? Surely no human existence of which I have experience. What answer can I give? How can I obey a call which has emerged from beyond the boundary of my existence? *I am carnal*: never can flesh become spirit, for that would mean the resurrection of the flesh. *I am sold under sin*: a transaction which may not be undone, save by the forgiveness of sin. I am a man: and no emotion or enthusiasm of religion can obscure what this means. Only a new man, only a victory over my humanity, only eternal life, can release me from the enigma of my being. What, then, doth the Spirit profit me? What advantage does the law which proceeds from the Spirit afford me? Of what use is my piety to me? How does the persuasive and prevailing power of God affect me? Is it not only too evident that I have no strength to bring forth? *Depart from me; for I am a sinful man, O Lord* (Luke v. 8). There is no bond of union between me, as I am, and God.

For that which I do I know not : for not what I would, that do I practice ; but what I hate, that I do. Yes, this is clearly the case. If the law of my religious being and having, were itself Spirit ; if sensitive 'apprehension of the absolute'—'feeling and taste for eternity' (Schleiermacher)—could seriously be regarded as lying within the realm of human competence ; if God and such a man as I am could be treated as co-partners ; I should be in a proper position to contemplate and comprehend my words and acts and deeds from the point of view of eternity, or, at least, to think of them as the first stages of a movement in conformity with the movement of the Spirit of God. Then I should be led on to describe and comprehend myself quite properly as the answer to the problem of life, as obedient to the demand of God, and therefore as the new divinely inspired reality in the midst of other realities. I may, of course, be sufficiently humble and simple-minded only to make this claim occasionally. But facts are hard, and it is difficult for me to retain even this confidence for long. The more luminously clear it becomes that the demand requires my actual obedience to the will of God, and that His commandments are not grievous, the more luminously clear it becomes to me that, even in the simplest occurrences of my life, His will has not been done, is not done, and never will be done. For not even at the most exalted moments of my life do I fulfil His commands. Does any single thought of mine express the all-compelling power of the Spirit? Does one single word of

mine formulate the Word after which I am striving and which
I long to utter in my great misery and hope? Does not each
sentence I frame require another to dissolve its meaning? And
are my actions any better? Does my lack of fidelity in little
things make amends for my great infidelity, or vice versa? Take
the case of any reputable and serious-minded philosopher,
poet, statesman, or artist. Does he ever suppose his actual
achievement to be identical with what he wished to achieve?
When my piece of work is done, do I not take leave of it sorrow-
fully? Woe is me, if I have unduly celebrated what I have
accomplished. If, then, my thoughts and words and actions are
of such sort as this, can I seek refuge in the restless sea of my
emotions? Can I find in the witches' cauldron of my unconscious
achievements an adequate substitute for the failure of my
conscious attainments? None but those who are past reclaiming
really believe in the eternal significance of their emotions. No!
there is no achievement of mine which I can recognize as legitimate. All my products are foreign bodies testifying to my inadequacy. I have no affection for them, no comprehension of them.
If I could, I would deny them. They appear before me as hideous,
evil-looking changelings. Fragmentary is our knowledge, and
partial our understanding (1 Cor. xiii. 9). I am unable to apprehend what I have done. What I would, I do not; what I hate,
that I do. Who then am I? for I stand betwixt and between,
dragged hither by my desires and by my hates, and thither by
my inability to do what I desire and by my ability to practise
what I hate.

If what I would not, that I do, I consent unto the law that it is
good. We have just said: *what I hate, that I do.* It would seem,
therefore, that a point of contact has been established between
myself and the incomprehensible, unapproachable, incommunicable, world of the Spirit. Surely, my hatred of my life as it is,
my protesting against it, my dislike of my own behaviour, the
disturbance which accompanies my passage through time, are
points of contact. Is not such negation the means by which
I am brought into harmony with myself? Am I not a doer of
the law, at least in so far as I am aware of my deep-seated sinfulness and am disgusted at it? Can I not console myself with
my own disconsolateness? 'If thou dost discover in thyself the
conflict between the Spirit and the flesh, if thou doest often what
thou willest not, thou dost declare thereby thy heart to be
faithful. So long as a man maintains this conflict, he is not
under the dominion of sin; so long as he struggles against sin
and disapproves of it, sin is not reckoned unto him' (Joh. Arnd).

These are perilous opinions. Who does not know this sunset glow, this quiet and secluded nook of pious dialectic? Who does not recognize here that middle way of compromise and resignation, where conscience is soothed by contemplating a conflict accepted and embraced?

So now it is no more I that do it, but sin which dwelleth in me. What, then, is the meaning of my protesting hatred of myself and my actions? It has clearly no further meaning than that an abyss is disclosed between myself and—myself. Can this really be regarded as a satisfactory starting-point for answering the question: 'If God be God, who then am I?' The EGO which *practises* what I—the other EGO—contemplate with evident horror, cannot be an EGO capable of surviving the question. May not, however, the other EGO, that horrified, dissatisfied, ever-protesting EGO, survive the question? But what is this other EGO? Can this impotent outsider, this poor innocent, who merely shakes his head and disclaims what I am actually doing and practising, saying it is contrary to his will,—can such an EGO, with all his powers usurped, really survive the question? Can my justification rest upon the claim that it is not I who am doing what I am doing, that another rules in my house, that I am no longer master of it, and that this other thinks, speaks, acts, feels, whilst I merely protest? This, surely, is no justification at all; my agreement with the law is simply my own condemnation of myself—the recognition that *sin dwelleth in me.* Faced by so vast a condemnation, I have no ground upon which I can stand; for who is able to entice me to the opinion that my EGO which acts as it wills is to be distinguished from my other EGO, in spite of its expressed disapproval? Is my onslaught upon myself more than a Münchhausen adventure,[1] which never gets beyond the four walls of that house of sin, which is my EGO? Then it is that religion is never competent to speak of that EGO whose existence lies beyond the boundary of the realm of sin. Religion speaks only of dissension: I practise perpetually what I do not will, and I will what I do not practise. Religion merely exposes the disunion of human knowledge and human life; for it speaks of one reality only—the reality of sin.

The second piece of evidence: **vv. 18–20. For I know that in me, that is, in my flesh, dwelleth no good thing: for to will is present with me, but to perform that which is good**

---

[1] *The Original Travels and Surprising Adventures of Baron Münchhausen* appeared first in England under the title of *Gulliver Revived; or, the Vice of Lying Exposed* (London: Printed for C. & G. Kearsley, 46 Fleet Street, 1786). [Tr.]

I find not. For the good that I would I do not: but the evil which I would not, that I practise. But if what I would not, that I do, it is no more I that do it, but sin which dwelleth in me.

I know that in me, that is, in my flesh, dwelleth no good thing. To know that *in me dwelleth no good thing* is the second require-ment of the religious man. This knowledge follows at once from the first requirement. Here again we run up against the 'peculiarity' of all to whom the revelation of God is entrusted (iii. 1–20), namely, that they, as such, can and ought to know this. Into this sinister secret men are initiated also through the revelation which is in Christ Jesus, precisely because it is the revelation of Revelation. 'Paul, good man that he was, longed to be without sin, but to it he was chained. I too, in common with many others, long to stand outside it, but this cannot be. We belch forth the vapours of sin; we fall into it, rise up again, buffet and torment ourselves night and day; but, since we are confined in this flesh, since we have to bear about with us everywhere this stinking sack, we cannot rid ourselves completely of it, or even knock it senseless. We make vigorous attempts to do so, but the old Adam retains his power until he is deposited in the grave. The Kingdom of God is a foreign country, so foreign that even the saints must pray: "Almighty God, I acknowledge my sin unto thee. Reckon not unto me my guiltiness, O Lord." There is no sinless Chris-tian. If thou chancest upon such a man, he is no Christian, but an anti-Christ. Sin stands in the midst of the Kingdom of Christ, and wherever the Kingdom is, there is sin; for Christ has set sin in the House of David' (Luther). *For I know* (vii. 14) is, then, not peculiar to some few men. Every religious man has this knowledge concerning himself. *I am flesh* (iii. 20), this is what he knows. We must, of course, bear in mind the meaning of the word *flesh*: unqualified, and finally unqualifiable, worldliness; a worldliness perceived by men, and especially by religious men; relativity, nothingness, non-sense. That is what I am! The man of property or of fashion may not be required to have this opinion of himself. How, indeed, could he, or ought he, to speak thus of himself? for his knowledge of himself may be a ray from the pity of God, which is more powerful than His wrath. No! it is rather the man dedicated to God who must speak of himself thus; the man of genuine and serious religious experience, the prophet, apostle, reformer; the man to whom the oneness of God's holiness and mercy has become the personal problem of his own existence. *Why callest thou me good? none is good save one, even God* (Mark x. 18). So Jesus spake ; and because He spake thus, we cannot dismiss the recognition that God and man, that is, the man that I am, do not cohere together, as though it proceeded from a purely pessimistic view of life. Indeed, we have already attained this perception from our knowledge of the Spirit (vii. 14). It is clear, then, that what we have established from the consideration of human experience corresponds with the real and logical situation, and that THIS knowledge about men is the proper rider to the knowledge of God.

For to will is present with me, but to perform that which is good I find not. For the good that I would I do not : but the evil which I would not, that I practise. My will merely reminds me of the good which is not in me, and agrees with my knowledge that the law is divine (vii. 14) ; for I cannot know what is divine without willing it. *To will is present with me.* But what is meant by *to will*? It means, presumably, to strive after, desire, demand, question, seek, pray, knock; in other words, it constitutes the theme and purpose of all preaching and of all pastoral work. Appealing to the cloud of witnesses in all ages, preachers and pastors breathlessly repeat this theme with every conceivable variation and with all manner of emphasis. How desperately simple the theme is! and, because of its simplicity, it is the final word of religion. If it does not entice men, what can ? And they are assuredly attracted by it. The exhortation to 'seek God' does not fall on deaf ears; for it is the final exhortation which the human ear is able to receive. It is certain that the number of those who genuinely *will* and who genuinely *seek after God* is far greater than the casual observer would suppose. Who can be deprived of this earnest *will*? Do I not also perhaps *seek after God*? *To will is present with me.* Maybe it is so! but the comfortable nook into which I am tempted to creep, when I have said this, is no more comfortable than that other place over which is inscribed the words: *What I would not, that I do* (vii. 16). As there, so here, everything depends upon action, upon the performance of *that which is good*. I require that the good should exist in me. But it is quite certain that the most sincere, most upright, most deep-seated vigour of *will* remains uncrowned by the performance of *that which is good*. Consider once again that vast cemetery where lies the history of the Church and of Christian piety. Surely there was there no lack of upright *will*! What is it, then, which distinguishes the *doing* of Jeremiah from the *doing* of the false prophets, with whom he is so sharply contrasted? What distinguishes the 'success' of Primitive Christianity which reached its zenith with Constantine —untheologically-minded historians please understand!—from the contemporary 'success' of the worship of Mithras and of Cybele? What distinguishes the 'success' of the Reformers of Wittenberg, Zürich, and Geneva, from the 'success' of the Roman Pontiffs and of the architects of the loftiest towers of Babel? What distinguishes the 'achievement' in delineating the inner piety which shines out of the eyes of the Sistine Madonna from the 'achievement' in delineating the bigotry which peers out of the eyes of the Madonnas of El Greco? May we not conclude that we should be right in setting every human achievement upon one single ladder, although perhaps upon different rungs of that ladder? Are they not, at best, parables of an achievement which lies on a wholly different plane? Yes, no doubt; but nevertheless, must we not also say that the Lord permits to some human achievements a maturity which is lacking in others, even though the distinction which we note and with which we are satisfied cannot be identified with a human will-to-achieve? Are we not bound to own that the path which leads from our will-to-achieve to the 'success' bestowed by the Lord lies wholly beyond our comprehension? We know nothing beyond the frontier which bounds our work and renders it fragmentary and incomplete: *the good that I would I do not: but the evil I would not, that I practise.* The religious man must answer questions concerning human 'success', by saying that, so far as he succeeds, his success lies beyond the competence of his will. I cannot identify my will to do good with the good itself. The characteristic mark of the good is that it persistently demands realization, for action is the end of knowledge and of will. But this end is foreign to me. I do not practise what is good; I perform all manner of evil that I would not. And so the question arises once again: Who then am I? I am he that wills and he that does not perform: I am intolerably both at once. When my will is most steadfast, it does but remind me that the good is—not in me.

But if what I would not, that I do, it is no more I that do it, but sin which dwelleth in me. Seen from the standpoint of my will, there is, then, no performance of *that which is good* (vii. 18b, 19). We return therefore to the decisive question: What is performed? Answer: *I do what I would not.* I am therefore no more justified by the nobility of my desire to do good than I am by my desire not to do evil (vii. 16, 17). For the second time the judgement pronounced by myself upon myself is wholly justified: *it is no more I that do it.* Excluded from responsibility for what is happening in my house, I am thrust up against the wall merely as an observer. An appeal to my goodwill only proves that *sin dwelleth in me.* It is sin that acts, sin that performs, and to sin that the 'success' belongs. And yet, this does not mean that I am, in fact, released from all responsibility: it means, rather, that I stand self-condemned. I have no reason to suppose that the EGO which performs and the EGO which disapproves can escape identification. Reality, even the reality of religion, knows but one man, and I, and not some other, am that man. It is one man that wills and does not perform; one man that does not will, and yet performs: within the four walls of the house of sin dwells but one man. Religious experience, then, simply bears witness to the fact that sin is all-embracing.

Conclusion from the evidence: **vv. 21-3. I find then** the reality of **the law** exposed in that, **to me who would do good, evil is present. For I delight in the law of God after the inward man: but I see a different law in my members, warring against the law of my mind, and bringing me into captivity under the law of sin which is in my members.**

Religion spells disruption, discord, and the absence of peace. A man at one with himself is a man still unacquainted with the great problem of his union with God. Our whole behaviour proves us to be in no way at one with ourselves; and for this reason, our relation to God is a disturbed relation. Happy the man who is able to deny this evident truth! May he long remain innocent of his own questionableness! The reality of religion, however, lies precisely in the utter questionableness of my EGO, confronted, as it is, by my inability to do what I would and by my ability to do what I would not. The subject of these contrasted predicates—my EGO—becomes an *x*, capable neither of life nor of death. By the law, through which I know God, I am enabled *to will to do good*: by the same law, through which I am known by God, my success in *doing evil* is clearly exposed. Thus my noblest capacity becomes my deepest perplexity; my noblest opportunity, my uttermost distress; my noblest gift, my darkest menace. It is almost incredible that, on the day when Schleiermacher finished writing his 'Lectures about Religion', his joy in creation, apparently suddenly, was crossed by the fear of death. 'What a shame it would be', he said, 'were I to die to-night!' One would have supposed

that, whilst writing so many beautiful and moving words
'about religion' (!) he would have been faced continually by
the fact of death. Is it possible to recommend religion to
men who long sincerely and simply for peace? Can religion
be presented, not merely as a tolerable thing, but as a thing
of such absorbing interest that it may be welcomed as an
enrichment of life, a valuable addition to civilization, or even
as a substitute for it? When men are already sufficiently
burdened by the inner uncertainty which attaches both to
civilization and to barbarism, is it credible that religion
should be brought triumphantly into connexion with science,
art, ethics, socialism, the State, Youth Movements and Race,
as though we had not had abundant experience of the waste
land of 'Religion and . . .'? Is it possible to justify these
strange prophets, when we see hosts of men and women flocking
to enlist willingly under their banners, eager to lay hold of religion, in order that their complacent capacities may be sanctioned,
developed, and consecrated; when we behold them zealous to
add to their passions one further emotion, the emotion of
eternity, and to their other capacities yet one more good thing,
the capacity for piety? We may be surprised that all this should
go on before our eyes; but surprise cannot alter the fact that all
of them, teachers and taught alike, are busily engaged in sawing
off the branch upon which they are sitting, in setting fire to the
house in which they dwell, and in scuttling the ship in which they
are sailing into the 'maelstrom'. Those who are genuinely concerned to preserve their own peace of mind, to retain humanism
on an even keel, and to assist the steady progress of culture—or
of barbarism!—will, with Lessing, Lichtenberg, and Kant, so
long as they are able, do their best to prevent the intrusion of
religion into this world. They will lift up their voices to warn
those careless ones, who, for aesthetic or historical or political
or romantic reasons, dig through the dam and open up a channel
through which the flood of religion may burst into the cottages
and palaces of men, after first overwhelming those thoughtless
pioneers! Such warning guardians of humanity will, at any rate,
have displayed more sense for reality than the futile amateurs
in piety—How cruel, in fact, these dilettantes are!—who, without knowing what they are doing, with romantic enthusiasm
conjure up the spirits of religion but are powerless to exorcize
them. But such warning wisdom is unavailing, since the capacity
for religion is deep-seated and cannot be disregarded. Even our
western civilization is powerless to protect men from it. The
watchman at the gate of humanity has only to take care lest,

at the eleventh hour, he too may be compelled to conclude a
short armistice with the adversary of whom he is so terrified.
Religion, though it come disguised as the most intimate friend
of men, be they Greeks or barbarians, is nevertheless the
adversary. Religion is the KRISIS of culture and of barbarism.
Apart from God, it is the most dangerous enemy a man has on
this side of the grave. For religion is the human possibility of
remembering that we must die: it is the place where, in the
world of time and of things and of men, the intolerable question
is clearly formulated—Who, then, art thou? 'The Law of God
brings men under condemnation; for, in so far as they are under
law, they are slaves of sin, and consequently guilty of death'
(Calvin).

**For I delight in the law of God after the inward man: but I
see a different law in my members, warring against the law of
my mind, and bringing me into captivity under the law of sin
which is in my members.** In religion, dualism makes its appearance. The man who conceals this with the fine-sounding phrases
of monism is the 'supreme betrayer of religion' (Overbeck), and
does the greatest possible disservice to those who are satisfied
with them. But the secret he endeavours to conceal cannot be
hidden. The bomb, which he has so carefully decked out with
flowers, will sooner or later explode. Religion breaks men into
two halves. One half is the *spirit* of the inward man, which
delights in the law of God.—Am I to identify myself with this
spirit? Am I merely *inward*? But no one dares to make this
claim. The other half is the *natural* world of my members; a world
swayed by a wholly different law, by a quite different vitality
and possibility. This latter wars against the *law of my mind*,
and denies what it affirms. This corporeality, this essential
second factor, this emergent opposition to my soul, is manifestly the supreme law and the supreme human possibility;
and here undoubtedly is the sin by which I am imprisoned.
Am I to be identified with this sin-laden *nature*?—Who dares
to claim this? The contrast may be defined as inwardness and
outwardness, idealism and materialism, that side and this side.
But to which dost thou belong? Who art thou? Art thou
'Spirit' or 'Nature'? Thou canst not deny 'Spirit', and hold
thee only to 'Nature'; for, as a religious man, thou hast knowledge of God, and thy most particular perception is that
'Nature' desires to be altogether 'Spirit'. Neither canst thou
deny 'Nature', and hold thee only to 'Spirit'; for, as a religious
man, thou hast knowledge of God, and thou knowest only too
well that 'Spirit' desires to be altogether 'Nature'. Am I then

both together?! Well, try: Art thou 'Spirit-Nature' or 'Nature-
Spirit' . . . ?! Once attempt any such arrogant anticipation,
and thou wilt soon perceive that the desired union cannot be
manœuvred merely by ranging the two alongside one another,
or by amalgamating them, or by conglomerating them. The
more thou dost madly endeavour to synthesize things which are
directly opposed to one another, the more surely do they break
apart and become manifestly antithetic. And thou thyself art
harried hither and thither, from one to the other, but never
wholly attaining the one or the other. At one moment one has
excluded the other—and yet not finally or mortally; for, when
the banished one seems weakest, there always remains a way for
it to return in the fullness of its power.

**vv. 24, 25a. O wretched man that I am! who shall
deliver me out of this body of death ? I thank God through
Jesus Christ our Lord.**

And so we retrace our steps to the place from which we set
out at the beginning of the chapter. We know only the religious
man, the man of human possibilities, the man of this world, the
man *as long as he liveth* (vii. 1). Such a one can never be what he
is, and he is not what he ought to be. Indissolubly and undis-
tinguishably one with his mortal body, he bears about with him
always the reminder that he—yes, precisely he—must die. Yet,
once the reality of religion is established, there arises an ultimate
ambiguity concerning the future of the man of the earth. He
can neither live nor die! In his piety he is suspended between
heaven and earth. But what does this ambiguity profit me?
In spite of all the contortions of my soul, of all the gymnastics
of my dialectic, the brutal fact remains that *I am*—a man. And
it is precisely my religion which compels me to recognize this
so clearly. No other possibility is open to me except the possibility of being a man of the earth—**O wretched man that I am!**
We have seen at last the reality of religion; we have recognized
what men are. How vast a gulf separates the nineteenth-
century conquering-hero attitude to religion from that disgust
of men at themselves, which is the characteristic mark of true
religion!—But Jesus Christ is the new man, standing beyond all
piety, beyond all human possibility. He is the dissolution of the
man of this world in his totality. He is the man who has passed
from death to life. He is—what I am not—my existential I—
I—the I which in God, in the freedom of God—I am! Thanks
be to God: through Jesus Christ our Lord I am not the wretched
man that I am.

v. 25b. So then I myself, as a man, **with the mind serve the law of God; but with the flesh the law of sin.**

Wretched man that I am! We must not deprive this *am* of its heavy significance. Paul is not describing the situation before his conversion! If conversion means the dissolution of the man of the earth, what relevance has this preposition 'before'? What Paul is here asserting was well understood by the Reformers; but it is misunderstood by those modern theologians who read him through the spectacles of their own piety. Paul describes his past, present, and future existence. He portrays a situation as real after the episode on the road to Damascus as before it. He is writing about a man, broken in two by the law, but who, according to the law, cannot be thus broken. Paul is thrust into a dualism which contradicts itself. He is shattered on God, without the possibility of forgetting Him. Do we now understand the meaning of the Grace of God and of His Freedom?

The Eighth Chapter

THE SPIRIT

THE DECISION

VIII. 1–10

vv. 1, 2. There is therefore now no sentence of death
against those **that are in Christ Jesus. For the law of the
Spirit of life in Christ Jesus made** thee **free from the law
of sin and of death.**

**There is therefore now no sentence of death against those that
are in Christ Jesus.** Of what, then, have we been speaking? Of
religion as a human possibility—or of that freedom in God which
is ours beyond all human possibility? Of sin—or of righteousness? Of death—or of life? What sort of a man is this man, who
is able to apprehend—as we have apprehended—the frontier,
the meaning, the reality, of religion? Whence has he come?
Whence does he observe? Whence does he know? Who tells
him that he is—man? Once these questions are asked—formulated indeed before we have asked them—we become like the
interlocutors of Socrates: we have touched the torpedo-fish, and
are benumbed.[1] It is evident that no man can of himself utter
the humiliating fact that he is—a man. It must have been said,
the answer must have been given, before he has cried out.
Clearly, he has not sought it out, thought it out, worked it out,
willed it of himself; for it is in itself the pre-supposition of all
searching and thinking and working and willing. The point
from which the circle is seen to be closed cannot be situated
within the circle. The possibility of comprehending human
possibility to be, as such, limited, is manifestly an altogether unheard of, new possibility; especially so, if, in agreement with
Kant, we deny ourselves every prospect beyond that by which
we are limited. The man who not only criticizes, disapproves
of, and deplores himself, but is able finally to set his whole
being in question and to be appalled at himself (vii. 24), is,
at any rate—not I! If we go on to ask: 'Who then?' 'What
then?', we must be quite clear that, the moment we have—even
though carelessly or half in fun—asked such questions, there has

---

[1] In the *Meno* (80 A–C) Socrates, because of his power of bringing his interlocutors to complete helplessness (ἀπορία), is compared to a torpedo-fish
(νάρκη). [Tr.]

already entered within our horizon something radically foreign
to us. We cannot revoke the questions or formulate them
differently. Whoever or whatever we may then be lies, at any
rate, beyond the frontier of human life, for it overturns the significance of our present existence and transfigures it into a reality
which is constituted totaliter aliter. A gaze has been fixed
upon us, strange and yet familiar, familiar and yet strange, to
which our present existence appears upside down, for it beholds
the reality of our life in this world as altogether sinful and passing to corruption. When we ask whence comes this knowledge
of ourselves which is the consequence of the perception of our
utter sinfulness and mortality, we are at once faced by the new
man confronting the man of this world—existentially. The new
man—IS. This turning-point or decision has not, however, taken
place in time, but in that eternity which is the frontier of time.
It is true, of course, that the turning-point is encountered apart
from the particular question with which we have touched the
torpedo-fish, but it is in that question that it is met finally and
quite clearly. And moreover, the question contains in itself
the answer, namely, that the Spirit—IS. The Spirit is the 'Yes'
from which proceeds the negative knowledge which men have
of themselves. As negation, the Spirit is the frontier and meaning and reality of human life: as affirmation, the Spirit is the
new, transfigured reality which lies beyond this frontier. By
this knowledge men are related to their Primal Origin and
placed within its light; by it they apprehend the relativity
of every human possibility, and see themselves entangled
in their own relativity yet nevertheless confronted by the
Absolute; by it I am seen, from above, from outside, to be
the miserable man that I am (vii. 24), and yet I am thus perceived by myself; by it I recognize myself to be confronted
paradoxically by the vast pre-eminence of a wholly different
man—which I am not. Thus related, apprehended, seen, and
recognized, we are not under the sentence of death by which
all men, and especially religious men, are threatened. Thus
related, apprehended, seen, and recognized, we become aware
of the impetuous roaring of heaven, as it were a rushing mighty
wind, which fills all the house (Acts ii. 2) ; we see the Holy City,
the New Jerusalem, coming down from God out of heaven
(Rev. xxi. 2), and know that we—*are in Christ Jesus*. Comprehended in the dissolution of the man of this world, which is
revealed in Jesus as the Christ, we are established as new men
and pass from death to life. This is the meaning of the words
—*in Christ Jesus*.

**For the law of the Spirit of life in Christ Jesus made thee free
from the law of sin and of death.** The negation of sin is not a
possibility among other possibilities, but the possibility beyond
all other possibilities, the lowest common denominator of all
possibility. There exists therefore a once-for-all event, but so
completely once-for-all that it can only appear on the frontier
of all happenings as that which never took place. There is a
supreme law, by the constitution of which every law stands and
falls. This possibility, this event, this law, is the Spirit. The
Spirit is that new, existential, once-for-all, universal life, which
has been revealed in Christ.

WE SPEAK CONCERNING THE SPIRIT. But can men dare to
undertake such conversation? For the description of other possibilities we possess a large vocabulary, but we have no single
word which we can make use of to define the impossible possibility of our lives. Why, then, are we not silent concerning
Him? We must also be silent; but none the less we must bear
in mind that our silence compromises Him no less than our
speech. We do the Spirit no greater service by our silence. The
Spirit remains the Word whether we proclaim Him in silence
or in speech. Whether being speechless we are compelled to
speech, or speaking we are compelled to silence, confronted by
the Spirit we are equally embarrassed and have no means of
escape. Could we but take care that we should speak or be
silent as He willeth, in order that we might at once recognize
that, if we should do right, it is not that WE do so in the speech
or in the silence of religion, but that the Spirit Himself has
spoken with or without words!

WE HAVE THE SPIRIT. He who has encountered the Spirit
existentially has encountered his own existential existence in
God. We can neither conceal, nor deny, nor obscure the fact that
we have heard the sound of the wind of heaven, that we have
seen the New Jerusalem and have encountered the decision of
eternity: we cannot deny that we *are in Christ Jesus*. But what
is the meaning of this hearing and seeing and being? If we
emphasize *we* or *have*, we move at once into the sphere of
religion. We make no mention of the Spirit if we bind Him to
ourselves or to our having. And yet, we must link ourselves to
Him; we cannot, in fact, do otherwise. If we do not say that
we have the Spirit, we think it; and if we do not think it, we
feel it. There is here, however, a quite inevitable inadequacy;
and it is vital that we should recognize it,—recognize, that is to
say, that *we* means 'not we', and *have* means 'not have'. It
may then be that in our recognized inadequacy we encounter

T

the truth. This qualification of ourselves and of our possession bears witness to a reality of our being and having, existing in their ambiguity and in their critical questionableness. Perhaps *we* are not merely men of this world, but—as 'not we'—the representatives and first-begotten of the new world. Perhaps also we *have* not only a psycho-physical experience of this world, but—as 'not having'—are in possession of our eternal human constitution, of our existence *in Christ Jesus*, which is not merely the tangible existence of a community, but the communion of spirits in the unity of the Spirit. Perhaps also—in so far as *we* are 'not we' and 'have not'—those 'others', that is to say, the many who are contrasted with us, cease to be others who do 'not have', but are they who hear us speaking in their tongues the wonderful works of God (Acts ii. 11). In any case, our fear of denying the Spirit is far greater than our fear of betaking ourselves to the ambiguous and questionable realm of religion.

WE RECKON WITH THE SPIRIT. Yes, we reckon Him to be an effective factor and influence in our lives, a theme of our discourse. And yet we know that this is not so. We know Him to be actus purus, pure reality and occurrence, unlimited and unconfined, without beginning or end, place or time. We know Him to be no thing among other things, not even a thing at all, not even the supreme thing. Nevertheless the paradox remains: the Spirit becomes a thing in the midst of other things; what is intangible and impossible, unknown and unobservable, becomes concrete and possible, known and observable. Such is the paradox of the Spirit. Describable only in negatives, He nevertheless exists, and we must preserve the paradox; that is to say, daring to account Him as though He were a thing among other things and the occasion of our behaviour, we must, paradoxically, worship Him as the third Person of the Godhead, await Him, pray for Him, and, confident in His peculiar and particular and quite definite action, be silent in the presence of His power and take care lest we should cause Him tribulation. Though such an attitude involves on our part our own perpetual dissolution, it nevertheless imposes upon us a necessary determination that our behaviour should perpetually correspond with the existential reality of the Spirit. Though we know full well that no behaviour of ours can correspond with the Spirit, yet it is precisely this recognition that may occasion the Spirit to intervene on our behalf, to correspond with us, and to justify those who are not justified. Therefore once again, lest we should sin against the Holy Ghost, we choose for ourselves the behaviour of religion by which we cannot be justified.

The Spirit thinks and acts and works. Thou dost not know what this means. Neither do I. He has already spoken, already acted. But He has spoken and acted in direct contradiction of everything that I can say or thou canst hear—He contradicts even our questioning. He is completely the Other. Confronting Him, we are confronted with perfected speech and with perfected action. We are perplexed, not by the reality of this perfection, but by the extreme difficulty of comprehending it. The Spirit has made thee free from the law of sin and of death—yes, *thee*, that is, thine existential self. In Christ Jesus the transformation, the decision, the conversion is—thine. Thy possibility is given —in Him. Thy life has appeared—in Him. The whole realm of thy speech and action has been comprehended by a dominion wholly indistinct, incomprehensible, and incomparable. The commandment of God, which appeared to thee as the law of thy sin and of thy death, has itself become relative by being related to the law of all laws. Thy sin is sin—in relation to the righteousness of this 'Other'. Thou diest—in relation to the life of this 'Other'. Thy 'No' is 'No'—only in relation to the 'Yes' of this 'Other'. What then becomes of thy sin, of thy death, of thy negation, when, in Christ Jesus, their relativity in relation to this Otherness, this complete Otherness of God, is made known? There remains then no relativity which is not related-ness, no concrete thing which does not point beyond itself, no observable reality which is not itself a parable. Therefore, thou art free— in the knowledge of thy slavery; thou art righteous—in the knowledge of thy sin; and thou dost live—in the knowledge of thy death. The Spirit makes thee free and righteous and alive; and the Spirit is understanding. The Spirit is the eternal discovery, apart from which, encompassed as we are by the law of sin and death, we should not have undertaken the search: 'He writes the Law of God with living fire in our hearts', and, consequently, the law is 'not doctrine but Life, not word but Existence, not a sign but very Fullness' (Luther).

vv. 3, 4. For that took place which was impossible for the **law, in that it was weak through** the opposition of **the flesh: God sent his own Son in the likeness of** sin-controlled **flesh and,** on account of the destructiveness of **sin,** spake the death-sentence over **sin in the** midst of the **flesh:** in order that **the righteousness of the law might be fulfilled in us, who walk not after the flesh, but after the Spirit.**

For that took place which was impossible for the law, in that it was weak through the flesh. What was it that the law could not do ? As we shall hear later, it could not pronounce the death-sentence over sin: as we have just heard, it could not make men free. That is to say, the law could not set human feet upon the rock of Eternity and rid them of the sentence of death which had been pronounced over them. No religion is capable of altering the fact that the behaviour of men is a behaviour apart from God. All that religion can do is to expose the complete godless-ness of human behaviour. As a concrete human being and having and doing, religion is—flesh: it shares, that is to say, in the profligacy and essential worldliness of everything human, and is in fact the crown and perfection of human achievement. Reli-gion neither overcomes human worldliness nor transfigures it; not even the religion of Primitive Christianity or of Isaiah or of the Reformers can rid itself of this limitation. Nor is it merely fortuitous that an odour of death seems, as it were, to hang about the very summits of religion. There proceeds, for example, from Zwingli an insipid bourgeoisdom, from Kierke-gaard the poison of a too intense pietism, from Dostoevsky an hysterical world-fatigue, from the Blumhardts, father and son, a far too easy complacency. Woe be to us, if from the summits of religion there pours forth nothing but—religion! Religion casts us into the deepest of all prisons: it cannot liberate us. Flesh is flesh; and all that takes place within its sphere, every step we undertake towards God, is as such *weak*. Because of the qualitative distinction between God and man, the history of religion, Church History, is *weak*—utterly *weak*. Since religion is human, utterly human history, it is flesh, even though it be draped in the flowing garments of the 'History of Salvation'. *All flesh is grass: the grass withereth, the flower fadeth. But the Word of our God endureth for ever.*

God sent his own Son. This is the Word of God, and *God's own Son* is Jesus Christ. We are here concerned with the particularity—*God sent his own Son* once for all—and with the existentiality of divinity. When it is uttered, it is the Word of freedom which religion is unable to discover. And it is proclaimed by *God's own Son*. In Jesus existentiality is illuminated by par-ticularity. The scandal of the historical revelation of Christ criss-crosses every form of rationalism. God is not 'inevitable reasonableness'. His eternity is not a constant factor which we can affirm safely and directly and non-paradoxically, as though it were a series of universal ideas—such as the idea of God, of Christ, and of Mediation. His omnipotence has not the necessity of a logical mathematical function. God is Personality: He is One, Unique, and Particular—and therefore He is Eternal and

Omnipotent. To Him the human historical Jesus bears witness. But Jesus is the Christ: that is to say, the particularity of God is illuminated by His existentiality. Therefore, in spite of all believing and unbelieving historicism and psychologizing, we encounter in Jesus the scandal of an eternal revelation of that which Abraham and Plato had indeed already seen. The Truth of God is not liable to the 'flux of history'. His action can neither be perceived everywhere nor be dismissed as being nowhere. It can be neither described historically, nor dissolved in a myth, nor treated pragmatically. In Jesus, and precisely in Him, the Love of God breaks through all historical and psychological analysis, and in directness and in mediation transcends both, for it is bound neither to this or that thing nor to this or that place. Because God is eternal and omnipotent, He is unique and once-for-all. To this, Jesus, the Christ, the eternal Christ, bears witness. At these cross-roads, then, God's own Son stands, and He stands nowhere else. GOD SENDS HIM—from the realm of the eternal, unfallen, unknown world of the Beginning and the End. Therefore—but let no orthodox person rejoice—He is 'begotten not made'—that is, He is contrasted with every creature familiar to us. Therefore, He is 'born of the Virgin Mary'—that is, He is our protest against assigning eternity to any Humanity or Nature or History which we can observe. Therefore, He is 'very God and very Man'—that is, He is the document by which the original, lost-but-recoverable union of God and man is guaranteed. GOD SENDS HIM—into this temporal, fallen world with which we are only too familiar; into this order which we can finally interpret only in biological categories, and which we call 'Nature'; into this order which we can finally interpret only from the point of view of economic materialism, and which we call 'History'; in fact, into this humanity and into this flesh. Yes—the Word became flesh, became, as we shall hear later,— *sin-controlled flesh*. GOD SENDS HIM—not to change this world of ours, not for the inauguration of a moral reformation of the flesh, not to transform it by art, or to rationalize it by science, or to transcend it by the Fata Morgana of religion, but to announce the resurrection of the flesh; to proclaim the new man who recognizes himself in God, for he is made in His image, and in whom God recognizes Himself, for He is his pattern; to proclaim the new world where God requires no victory, for there He is already Victor, and where He is not a thing in the midst of other things, for there He is All in All; and to proclaim the new Creation, where Creator and creature are not two, but one.—Do we desire a test as to whether we have spoken rightly

of the mission of the Son? Well, if we have not mightily
offended every possible human method of investigation, and
offended it at its most particularly tender spot, then assuredly
we have spoken about—something else.

God sent His Son—**on account of sin.** For this reason the
Word of God, if it be rightly proclaimed, must always out-
distance other words, and, since the mission of the Son of God
is the divine reaction against sin, it can be described only in
weighty negations, preached only in paradoxes, understood only
as that absurdum which is, as such, incredibile. The offence
which it occasions us is the reflex of the scandal which we are to
God. The Word of God is the transformation of everything that
we know as Humanity, Nature, and History, and must therefore
be apprehended as the negation of the starting-point of every
system which we are capable of conceiving. The mission of the
Son is the divine answer to the last insoluble question which is
forced upon the man of this world as a consequence of the
dominion of sin. It cannot therefore be identified with any
human answer, not even with any of those answers which men
disguise as penultimate and soluble questions. The divine
answer is given only in the veritably final and veritably insoluble human problem. The divine answer is the righteousness
of God, of God alone, which as such pre-eminently and victoriously confronts the last possible definition of men, namely, their
essential sinfulness. And so, as the divine answer, the mission of
the Son is itself no human quality or righteousness or possession,
it fits into no human reckoning and composes no harmonious
human picture—rather we can only conceive of it as beyond our
reckoning, ambiguous, problematical, poised, as it were, upon
the edge and periphery of what is rational: in fact, we can only
conceive of it as inconceivable.

God sent His Son in the likeness of **sin-controlled flesh.** The
innocent and direct life of the garden of Eden is not reproduced
in the mission of the Son. That, indeed, could not, and must not,
be, for His mission took place *on account of sin.* Had it been
a direct and observable manifestation of divinity, it would not
be what it is—the divine transformation and answer and
righteousness: it would not be that 'Otherness' of God by which
the whole realm of humanity is confronted and dissolved; it
would be, rather, some second thing within the human sphere,
another series of notions and illusions tossed up like foam from
the rough and prosaic reality of this world. So utterly distinct
from this world is it, that it can be displayed only where there is
no 'otherness', where, that is to say, it is a thing neither side by

side with, nor pre-eminent over, other phenomena in this world.
Contrasted with the reality of this world and with all its possible
improvements, it is the wholly pre-eminent Truth, which must
not be received as some peculiar intrusion of direct reality.—Such
is the 'divine artifice' (Kierkegaard). If this be so, the mission of
the Son is recognizable only by the revelation of God. We must
therefore be on our guard against that 'fibrous, undialectical,
blatant, clerical appeal that Christ was God, since He was so visibly and directly'! May we be preserved from the blasphemy of
men who 'without being terrified and afraid in the presence of
God, without the agony of death which is the birth-pang of faith,
without the trembling which is the first requirement of adoration,
without the panic of the possibility of scandal, hope to have
direct knowledge of that which cannot be directly known . . .
and do not rather say that He was truly and verily God, because
He was beyond our comprehension' (Kierkegaard). There is
then no mission of the Son except—**in the likeness** *of sin-
controlled flesh*, except in the form of a servant, except in His
impenetrable incognito. Jesus Christ was in no wise a 'very
serious-minded man, almost as earnest as a parson' (Kierkegaard). His true divinity is manifested, as is His true humanity,
in the likeness of the flesh of sin. To such an extent is this the
case, that for the observer many various interpretations of Him
are possible. He may pronounce Him to be human and divine
because of His peculiar awareness of God or because of His
religious-ethical heroism—to this Kierkegaard referred when he
spoke of the 'clerical appeal' to the visible Jesus. Or he may
pronounce the visible figure of Jesus to be something well known
to the student of ancient mythology, or he may dismiss Him as
a madman. Nor is it otherwise with the sinlessness of Jesus.
Judged by the record of what He did and omitted to do, His
sinlessness can be as easily denied as ours can, more easily, in
fact, than can the sinlessness of those good and pure and
pious people who move about in our midst. And, indeed, His
matter-of-fact contemporaries—who did not know what we
think (!) we know—quite openly denied it. The sinlessness of
Jesus is guaranteed only by God; and He speaks secretly both
in what Jesus did and in what He left undone. So is it also
with His power to work miracles. They lend themselves to all
manner of psychological, historical, medical, and theosophical
explanations. So is it also with His call to repentance. It may
be treated as ethical idealism, or as the romanticism of religion,
or as the religion of Socialism; and we may pay the same
attention to it as we pay to other sermons delivered in the open

air, in the forest, or on some well-kept, grassy lawn. So is it also with His sense of mission, with the intimate communing of His soul with God, and with His proclamation of the Kingdom of God. Does not the key to all this lie in Jewish eschatology, or in psycho-analysis, or in a materialistic philosophy of history? So is it also with His death on the Cross. We can say what the Jews on Calvary said; or that after having been an enthusiast He died in despair; or, quite simply, we can remove from His death its sting by reference to other similar occurrences in the history of religion. So it is also with His resurrection. What is to prevent theologians—believers and unbelievers alike—from embarking, with equal success, upon a controversy as to whether it should be interpreted by this analogy or by that, as may the better suit this or that general hypothesis? What is to prevent those who claim to be in touch with other worlds from bringing their grist to the mill of its understanding? And what is to hinder Friederich Strauss from pronouncing it to be 'World-Historical Humbug!'?—Is there any historical occurrence so defenceless against brilliant and stupid notions, against interpretations and misinterpretations, against use and misuse; is there any historical happening so inconspicuous and ambiguous and open to mis-understanding—as the appearance in history of God's own Son? There is no single incident in His life known to us in such a way as to be free from ambiguity and free from the possibility of giving offence. A hundred incidents are manifestly offensive: so much so that modern theologians blurt out awkwardly and with touching simplicity: 'Here we feel otherwise than Jesus felt'— a truth so desperately obvious that one would have thought it hardly worth while mentioning. *Sin-controlled flesh*: human, worldly, historical, natural, scintillating with every variation of ambiguity, a playground where men can exercise their ingenuity in propounding all manner of noble and absurd ideas and notions, but a playground so covered with stones that each man stumbles after his own fashion—such is the life of Jesus, more than any other life. And it must needs be so. Blasphemy is not the stumbling-block that we all—some here, some there—discover in the life of Jesus. We stumble when we suppose that we can treat of Him, speak and hear of Him—WITHOUT BEING SCAN-DALIZED.

In the likeness of sin-controlled flesh God sent His Son, and thereby—**spake the death-sentence over sin in the midst of the flesh.** Jesus Christ is shown forth and accredited as the Son of God, because in His Sonship sin-controlled flesh becomes a parable or *likeness*. What is human and worldly and historical and 'natural' is shown to be what it veritably is in its relation to God the Creator—only a transparent thing, only an image, only a sign, only something relative. But that it IS a sign and a parable is surely in no wise trivial or unimportant. Indeed, men and things may perhaps be vastly more important when seen as signs and parables than when we first separate them from their proper relation to God, and then regard them, in their opaque detachment, as the supreme and ultimate reality. This is the illusion of the flesh which has been *done away* in Christ. In Him the flesh has been deprived of its independence and restored to God who created it. In Him the disorder and corruption under which it groans has been laid bare, and thereby the hope of redemption which it awaits has also been exposed. In Him its independent might and importance and glory have been condemned, and thereby its glory and significance as the creation of God have been restored. God sends His Son in the midst of sin-controlled flesh, in order that there—and if not there, where?—sin and rebellion against God with all its consequences may be condemned and struck down; in order that, where the arrogance of the flesh has willingly taken to itself a false infinity which is its own dissolution, the curse of death may be done away. This condemnation of sin dwelling in the flesh, this exposure of the true nature of the flesh, this parable of the Spirit, takes place, as has been frequently pointed out (v. 6–8, vi. 8), in the ever-increasing deprivation and diminution of the life of Jesus, emphasized first in the Temptation, then in Gethsemane, and finally on Golgotha. In order that the condemnation might be perfected, this KENOSIS of the Son of God, this *form of a servant*, this impenetrable incognito, is not accidental but essential. It is imperative that the incognito of the Son of God should increase and gain the upper hand, that it should move on to final self-surrender and self-abandonment; imperative that we, from the human point of view, should be scandalized; imperative that we should recognize that not flesh and blood but only the Father which is in heaven can reveal that there is more to be found here than flesh and blood. Were it not so, were Christ to be ranged with those directly recognizable sons of god, were it possible for us to assign positive human predicates to His divinity, did there proceed from His mouth and sound in all the world that supreme melody which we name 'piety', were we to discover in Him a road of faith which skirts round the edge of the final scandal of the Cross—then the relativity, the dissolution, the parabolic nature of the flesh would not have been set forth, the assault of sin would not have gone finally home, and neither would sin have been condemned nor men have been saved—existentially. But it is not so. In His unknowableness Christ is the contradiction of all those other brilliant sons of god. He can be glorified with no positive human predicates, for He has stopped up the trumpet of human arrogance: 'With sin He has cursed sin; with death He has hunted out and unearthed death; with law He has overcome law. How, we ask, is this so? As a sinner He hung on the Cross; Himself the chief villain, He undergoes the condemnation and punishment of sinners publicly in the midst of rogues' (Luther).

The purpose of the mission of the Son of God, a purpose veritably attained, is—**that the righteousness of the law might be fulfilled in us, who walk not after the flesh, but after the Spirit.** In so far as we recognize ourselves in the Son of God and see in Him our flesh dissolved and our sin condemned, we behold the existential new man who lives in God. Here then we reach and find the eternal turning-point and decision. At the incredible point where we discover the question-mark which is set against us—set against us manifestly by One that we are not—we encounter eternity; united with Christ, we are apprehended and known by God, and we possess the possibility which is beyond all possibility, the impossible possibility of walking *after the Spirit*. Are we then to deduce from this that we no longer walk *after the flesh*? Yes, we must assuredly make this deduction. But we must rightly understand that not walking after the flesh means that the direct possibility here and now accessible to us is depressed—nay, exalted—to a parable: that is, to relativity. Our whole behaviour, the course of our existence, is lived after the Spirit and is defined by the knowledge of the Son of God. The Son of God, the Lord, in whom we recognize ourselves to be united to Him in the likeness of His death—that is to say, in our death (vi. 5)—is the turning-point, the decision, the divine Victory; He is the wholly Other of God; He is—the Spirit (2 Cor. iii. 17). Since we have participated in the final and inexorable questionableness of His mission, and, consequently, in the answer which He gives to this ambiguity, how can we fail to possess the Spirit of God? How can we fail to be *translated*, beyond the boundary of our human life, *into the kingdom of God's dear Son* (Col. i. 13), into His new transfigured reality, into the transformation of His mind? How can we, who walk after the Spirit and in whom has occurred so incomprehensible, irresistible, and irrevocable a transformation, fail to stand completely above the life we lived in the flesh—before this transformation? Can this flesh—now displayed in Christ as a corruptible thing, the parable of an incorruptible hope—simply continue its course undisturbed? Must it not share in the spiritual life of those who have been liberated? May THIS world pass away and THY Kingdom come! Such is the truth under which we—nay rather, under which humanity and nature and history—stand in the power of the Son's mission. This is the fulfilment in us of the *righteousness of the law*, the solution of the insoluble problem of liberty proposed by the possibility of religion, the doing away of the death-sentence pronounced over men, the annulment of the sentence which the supreme capacity of religion can only rivet the more firmly upon us. Thus the condemnation of sin in Christ is the revelation of the righteousness of God, which religion seeks after but never finds (v. 16, 18).

vv. 5–9. For they that are in the flesh have the mind of the flesh; but they that are in the Spirit have the mind of the Spirit. For the mind of the flesh is death; but the mind of the Spirit is life and peace: for, because the mind of the flesh is enmity against God, it is not subject to the law of God, neither indeed can it be: and they that are in the flesh cannot please God. But ye are not in the flesh, but in the Spirit, if so be that the Spirit of God dwelleth in you. Now if any man hath not the Spirit of Christ, he is none of his.

Spirit means the eternal decision by which God decides for men and men for God. Spirit is the pleasure which God has in men and the goodwill which men have towards God. Spirit means to belong to Christ, to participate in His question and, consequently, in His answer; in His sin and, consequently, in His righteousness; in His 'No' and, consequently, in His 'Yes'; in His death and, consequently, in His life. The Spirit is existential meaning and sense. He makes and creates sense. With Him sense enters into existence and existence into sense. There is no partner or opponent of the Spirit; for He is at once conflict and conquest; He is the victorious dictator who admits no peace, if peace be equilibrium, synthesis, or toleration. Spirit means that 'Either–Or' in which all antithesis is already destroyed by the victory of the 'Either' over the 'Or'. Spirit means that election where no rejection is possible. Spirit admits of no other possibility which is not already excluded, overcome, and non-existent.

The other possibility which exists no longer is the existence of men in the flesh. Flesh is the decision which occurs in time, and by it God decides against men and men against God. The flesh is contrary to the Spirit, and can therefore be defined only as *sin-controlled* (viii. 3). Flesh means to be absent from Christ, to formulate no question, and therefore to hear no answer. We shall understand the meaning of flesh, if we simply reverse all that has just been said about the Spirit. Flesh is non-sense. In flesh non-sense comes into existence and existence becomes non-sense. Flesh is enmity to God, is sin, is the mind which is not and cannot be subject to God, but which, contrariwise, discovers in religion its supreme manifestation as the non-sense of our present existence. As the mind of the Spirit is life and peace, so the mind of the flesh is death. Flesh also means an already decided 'Either–Or', compared with which all other contradictions and notions and judgements and movements are altogether trivial. The world—the world of Christendom and of morality— 'is aghast at the evil in the world; it bemoans it, but knows not whence it comes. It beholds the stream flowing on and on; it watches the tree of life putting forth its shoots and bringing forth its fruits; but it is wholly ignorant of the source of the stream and of the root of the tree. The world sets out to offer advice, to check the evil, to make men good by passing laws and by inflicting punishments. It sets itself against the stream—and still more water pours forth from the spring; it lops off the fresh green twigs—but the vigour of the root is undiminished. The labour of the world is lost labour and ineffectual, so long as the busy improvements affect only the outside, and the stock, root, and source of evil remain untouched. The stream must be dammed at its source, and the tree must be destroyed at its roots; else thy tinkering reforms will only cause them to break out at ten different places. Evil must be cured at its origin; otherwise, however bravely thou dost plaster the cracks and plug up the chinks, it does but continue festering and discharging worse than ever' (Luther).

It is beyond our capacity to decide between flesh and Spirit. We can neither reject the one nor select the other. Nor are some small or large companies of men—**in the Spirit,** whilst others are —**in the flesh.** Should some one claim that he is competent to distinguish between those *in the flesh* and those *in the Spirit*, he thereby proclaims himself to be undoubtedly *in the flesh*. In time, it has already been decided that we are all *in the flesh*: in eternity, it has already been decided that we are all *in the Spirit*. We are rejected *in the flesh*, but elected *in the Spirit*. In the world of time and of men and of things we are condemned, but in the Kingdom of God we are justified. Here we are in death, there we are in life. Both decisions—rejection and election, condemnation and justification, death and life—form the foci of an ellipse, which approximate more and more closely to one another until they unite as the centre of one circle. The unity of both decisions—which is incapable of mathematical representation—is not the unity of an equilibrium, but of the infinite pre-eminence which the one has over the other, whereby time is swallowed up in eternity, and the flesh in the infinite victory of the Spirit. Such is the unity of the road which unites here and there; and it is revealed in the absolute 'Moment' of apprehension, of resurrection, and of God, and lighteneth as lightning out of the one part under heaven and shineth unto the other part under heaven (Luke xvii. 24). So is Jesus Christ, *the Son of man, in his day.*

v. 10. And if Christ be in you, the body is dead because of sin; but the Spirit is life because of righteousness.

Christ in you. This is the condition of that liberty which is ours beyond the law; this is the solution of the riddle which religion sets before us with such intolerable precision. *Christ in you* must never be apprehended as a subjective status which will some day be inaugurated and fulfilled: rather, it is an objective status already fulfilled and already established. Christ is the occasion by which men are enabled to apprehend themselves as existentially free. This apprehension is, however, conditioned by Christ. Men achieve this status neither by a process of logical thought, nor by aesthetic intuition, nor by a moral act of will, nor by means of some religious experience. The status is theirs already by the faithfulness of God (iii. 21) displayed in the mission of His Son (viii. 3). Obedience to the faithfulness of God (i. 5) means that subjection to the conditioning of our liberty which has been given apart from our surrender and apart from our obedience. As the *sin that dwelleth in me* (vii. 17, 20) is the pre-supposition of my rebellion against God, whatever human action or inaction may subsequently take place; so *Christ in us* is the divine pre-supposition of our existence, whatever human action or inaction may subsequently take place. *Christ in us* is the Word of God addressed to us; it is His question and His answer. *Christ in us* is both question and answer: question, because thereby the whole course of human existence is thrust critically upon the road which leads from life to death; answer, because thereby we are set upon the road which leads from death to life. *Christ in us* reveals this road to us, making it *clearly seen* (i. 20) and everywhere accessible. Christ reveals it by setting it clearly and existentially and once for all in the midst of historical phenomena, on their edge, as the point to which all historical phenomena are directed and from which they may be apprehended, as the point where sin is condemned and righteousness enthroned. *Christ in us* is therefore both the place where we are deprived of our liberty and the place where we receive it, both the place where we are judged and the place where we are justified. It follows also that *Christ in us* is never the process by which 'we' apprehend the divine word addressed to us, and therefore that it must never be identified with 'our' perception.

The body is dead because of sin ; but the Spirit is life because of righteousness. Christ is our freedom, our advance beyond the frontier of human life, the transfiguration of life's meaning, and the appearance of its new and veritable reality. In Christ is uttered the eternal decision that flesh is flesh, world is world, man is man—because sin is sin; that the existence of the man of this world, whether upon the lowest or the highest rung of the ladder of human life, must become non-existence, must in fact, when it encounters God, die; that those who stand on the highest pinnacle of religion—prophets, apostles, reformers—cannot advance beyond the tribulation of humanity (vii. 24); that the *body* of man—the totality of his 'I am', whether past, present, or future—*is dead because of sin.* Dust to dust, ashes to ashes, illusion to illusion!—Yes, this is the decision; but, precisely because the decision is eternal and the condemnation eternal, both constitute the already trodden ground of redemption, of righteousness, and of life. In fact, men can apprehend their unredeemed condition only because they stand already within the realm of redemption; they know themselves to be sinners only because they are already righteous; they perceive their death, only because they are alive. Only in God can men be so utterly dismembered. If they had not passed into the land of freedom beyond the frontier of all human possibility, how could they perceive that even the loftiest human possibility is insignificant and unreal, save as the boundary which marks their slavery? How could they bring themselves to sigh for the longed-for redemption, if they were not already redeemed and already blessed? The life of the Spirit shines forth in the light which displays the death of the body: death, because of the sin which has been condemned in Christ; life, because of the righteousness which has been established in Him. Both cohere together, and the one is known and measured by the other. But the second, because of its eternal, qualitative pre-eminence, is the dissolution of the first; and is therefore the freedom of men in Christ Jesus.

Truth exists, and if it is bitter, this very bitterness is not purposeless. Our sighing for redemption from this body of death has an object. Christ is risen. Profoundly significant is it, then, that all that is not existential should have been handed over to death through His death.

THE TRUTH

VIII. 11–27

v. 11. But if the Spirit of him that raised up Jesus from the dead dwelleth in you, he that raised up Christ Jesus from the dead shall also quicken your mortal bodies because of his Spirit that dwelleth in you.[1]

The Spirit dwelleth in you. The Spirit is the Truth. When the Spirit enters into men, it brings them within the sphere of bitterness and sweetness, of misery and hope, of perplexity and promise. There is no objective observation of the Truth; for its objectivity is that by which we are observed before ever we have observed anything at all. Truth is that primal objectivity by which the observing subject is itself constituted. Truth cannot therefore depend upon my observation: that is to say, it cannot be 'subjectivized'. Truth is that redeeming subjectivity which secretly confronts every 'I' and 'Thou' and 'He', critically and immanently dissolving them by the objectivity which everywhere accompanies them. Truth permits no one to use it as a plaything; and it puts an end to all tragedy. Truth is far too merry and noble for us ever to justify our present life and address the present moment: 'Remain with me! thou art so fair!'[2] Truth is far too grim and terrible for us ever to desire to wrest it to ourselves, for example, by despairing and putting an end to our life. The man who, after reading the 'Phaedo', drowned himself in the sea, had as little understanding of the meaning of immortality as those who could bear to read it, and not throw themselves into the sea! We cannot question Truth as to why it is what it is;

---

[1] Adopting the reading διὰ τὸ ἐνοικοῦν αὐτοῦ πνεῦμα. From the evidence of the MSS. Zahn judges this to have been the original reading. Lietzmann, however, draws an opposite conclusion. Without daring an opinion on the complicated history of the transmission of the text, and judging rather from the run of the argument, it seems to me improbable that Paul, in view of the close connexion between the preceding accusatives—διὰ ἁμαρτίαν and διὰ δικαιοσύνην (v. 10)—and the subject of the bodily resurrection which he is now concerned to emphasize, would have suddenly introduced a sensitive—διὰ τοῦ πνεύματος, thereby suggesting a psycho-physical operation of the Spirit, which would be more in harmony with the notions of some later theologian.

[2] Goethe, *Faust*, Part I, scene iv (l. 1700); and Part II, Act V (l. 11582). [Tr.]

for it has already asked us why we are what we are; and in the
question has provided also the rich answer of eternity: 'Thou',
it says, 'art man, man of this world; and thou dost belong to
God, Creator and Redeemer.' All our questions and answers
move upon the background of this previous question and of this
previous answer. We cannot begin with Truth, for it is our
beginning. We must therefore range ourselves under it and make
up our minds to live with it; under its destructive assault and
with its indestructible blessing (Ps. cxxxix. 1–12). *Christ in us*
is the Truth; He is the Spirit that dwelleth in us—both as
judgement and as righteousness (viii. 10).

The Spirit of him that raised up Jesus from the dead is the Spirit
that dwelleth in you. He that hath intercourse with the Spirit
hath intercourse with God, with the hidden, holy, Unknown God,
who dwelleth in light unapproachable. His Life is beyond life
and death. His Goodness is beyond good and evil. His 'Yes is
beyond 'Yes and No'. His Beyond is beyond 'Here and There'
(iv. 17). Truth, therefore, does not stand and fall with us,
does not live and die with us, is not right when we are right and
wrong when we are deceived, does not triumph in our victory and
fail when we are defeated. Truth is death poised above the
cradle; it is life breathing o'er the grave. A Francis of Assisi is
condemned by the Truth by which a Caesar Borgia is set free.
Therefore Truth deposes the mighty from their seats and
exalts them of low degree. Therefore it can turn every human
'Yes' into 'No' and every human 'No' into 'Yes'. Therefore
Truth is where we climb up into heaven and also where we
make our abode in hell. Because Truth is eternally pre-eminent
over all that we have and are, it is our hope, our undying
portion, and our indestructible relation with God.

And yet, as men, we have no calm hope, no immortal position,
no undisturbed relationship with God; but—**He that raised up
Christ Jesus from the dead shall also quicken your mortal bodies
because of his Spirit that dwelleth in you.**—The body is dead because of sin; but the Spirit is life because of righteousness (viii.
10). Only in the light of the Resurrection and of the knowledge of
God does this contrast become apparent. But by the same
illumination the contrast is overcome and dissolved. Whenever
the bright light falls upon this contrasted 'object', there is also
directed against it a charge so well aimed and so destructive
that the second, other, contrasted thing simply perishes. The
same God that raised Jesus from the dead shall also quicken
your mortal bodies. Only in parable can we represent what is
finite as though it were a thing contrasted with what is infinite.

Only in a parable can we contrast the death of our body with the
life of the Spirit of God in us. According to the reality which is
beyond our observation, what is finite is not set over against
what is infinite, but rather by it is wholly dissolved and therefore
wholly established. Its dissolution is that by which it is established. Thus, according to the unobservable reality, our body
is no second, other thing, existing side by side with the Spirit
of God that dwelleth in us: the Spirit is rather the altogether
restless death of the body, and as such also its altogether restless life. But all this is—according to the unobservable reality.
Therefore the Gospel of the Resurrection of our body—which
must be distinguished radically from every form of Pantheism
and Spiritualism and Materialism—cannot refer to any past or
present or future, but only to the all-embracing Futurum
resurrectionis: *He shall quicken.* We must therefore dissociate ourselves from any kind of enthusiastic belief that we are
here in the presence of a claim to some higher perception
(intuition) mediated through a particular condition of soul. The
more coldly we speak of the resurrection of the body the better.
The fact that it is put into words at all involves almost inevitably the emission of sufficient psychic smoke to obscure
the truth. We must beware of all those attempts which have
been made from Oetinger to Beck and from Rothe to Steiner—
and also, though with some reserve, in the first edition of this
book—to utilize the speculations of natural philosophy, in
order to establish the existence of an observable and real Spirit-
Body. All these attempts must be discarded as leading to misunderstanding. They falsify the Gospel, and evacuate it of its
meaning. We can dare to express the Gospel of the Resurrection in words, only if, convinced of the impossibility of any
observable apprehension of divinity, we proclaim it as the absolute miracle. Such a proclamation of the Gospel of the Resurrection is simply a declaration that it is in itself credible. Should
we, however, pressed by secret unbelief, endeavour to make it
credible, we thereby merely discredit it. The body is the totality
of my existence in the flesh, in the world of time and things
and men, the totality of my existence as 'I', as the man of this
world encircled by all manner of concrete and conceivable possibilities. By the knowledge of God this body of mine is defined
as altogether mortal. When, however, a subject is related to
its origin, all its predicates are dissolved, including its identity with itself. No substance, however refined or deep-seated,
can withstand this negation. Physical death, every relative
inner or outer negative occurrence by which physical death is

U

accompanied, all mortifications, all acts of self-denial and self-abnegation, are no more than parables of that final negation. Every practice of devotion, every spiritual discipline of mind or body, does, of course, suggest the 'Mystery',—but is, nevertheless, completely misunderstood the moment it is regarded as effective for the salvation of that 'Body' which is passing to corruption. The process of natural death, with its many related derivatives in crude or refined forms of asceticism, is known to us only in the framework of its relatedness to other processes which are, as such, rendered questionable by the knowledge of God. Therefore even the logical analogy of natural death is a parable, and only a parable. Explosions are the inevitable consequence of our bringing infinity within the range of concepts fitted only for the apprehension of what is finite. For, in so far as we admit infinity as a concept, that is to say, in so far as we make it observable to ourselves as infinity, since we are unable to rid it of its characteristic 'otherness' in relation to what is finite, our concept of eternity emerges as an ALMOST infinitely finite thing! But such an observed notion of infinity is in no way infinity itself; for when our notions are related to the Source of all that is ours, they are shown to be things that have been dissolved. Therefore 'not-I' am the waiting, undying, incorruptible subject, which is apprehended as apprehending, which is not concrete; and this 'not-I' is, in fact, the Spirit of God that dwelleth in me beyond the catastrophe in which 'I', in the totality of my concreteness, am helplessly engulfed. And so, the plain meaning of the 'Beyond' with which we are now concerned lies in the dissolution of every observed 'Here' and also of every observable 'Beyond'. But, precisely because the body—as an observable factor in the past, present, and future—is corruptible and passing to death, it must—unobservably, in the Futurum aeternum—be incorruptible and immortal. Flesh and blood—that is to say, corporeality which is not related to its Primal Origin—cannot inherit the Kingdom of God; no more awaits them than some pseudo-resurrection, some relative 'There-ness', or rather, some elongated 'Here-ness'. But this corruptible and this mortal—that is to say, flesh and blood when they are qualified as corruptible and mortal by their relatedness to God—must put on incorruption and immortality. Disregarding their visible reality, they are born from above; in their temporality, they await their eternity. With the dissolution of their 'Hereness', and with the removal of their relatedness to all that belongs to this world, they participate in a new definition and in a new qualification. This new definition and qualification, of which we know nothing because it does not concern 'us', is the resurrection of the body. The indwelling of the Spirit in us, the self-inaugurated motion of the Spirit towards us, by which men are related to God, and which is their death and their life, is necessary for the establishing of our relation to God. There is no other means of union, and this one is sufficient. Only if the Spirit were not Spirit, and if the Truth were not Truth, and if God were not God; only if they were observable, second things, pseudo-beyonds, would it be impossible for us to claim and formulate in words the Futurum aeternum of the Resurrection of the Body, which is the most outrageous, but most indispensable, interpretation of what the Spirit means for our life.

vv. 12, 13. So then, brethren, we are debtors, not to the flesh, to live after the flesh: for if ye live after the flesh, ye must die; but if by the Spirit ye mortify the deeds of the body, ye shall live.

We are debtors, not to the flesh, to live after the flesh. The Spirit and its equivalent, the Truth—the pre-eminence of which we have so seriously accepted that we have dared to formulate it as the resurrection which, because it lies beyond all corporeality, awaits all corporeality—involve us at once in a quite definitely critical attitude to the body and all its doings. We come from the all-embracing dissolution of every predicate of our known existence, and we advance to meet the equally comprehensive, but totaliter aliter predication of our unknown existence in God, the predication of the new man, which I am not, but which, nevertheless, dwells in me, and which is, undeniably, my existential EGO. We come from the observable possibility of our existence in the flesh, and we advance to meet the unobservable possibility of our existence in the Spirit (viii. 5–9). We come from death and we advance to life. We have orientated ourselves; we have turned our backs to the west and our faces to the east. We cannot now reverse our position. *To live after the flesh*, to live the unbroken life of the world of time and things and men, to take that life seriously and to treat it as the real life, to live naïvely as though we were satisfied with the possibilities of this world, to submerge ourselves in its lowest or to revel in its highest possibilities, to commit ourselves to a conservatism which is unable to quiz itself or to a revolutionary radicalism which recognizes no limitations, is henceforth for us quite impossible. All that stands midway between Beginning and End is for us excluded. Through the

Spirit, through the Truth, we are once for all rid of the debt by
which, without recollecting the necessity that we must die, we
were compelled to live passionately within the possibilities of
the flesh; to live solemnly, without glancing at our very diminu-
tive stature; to behave busily, without being straitened by
eternity; to be zealous, without noticing that our actions pass to
corruption; to be lazy, without the terror of irrevocable time;
to be pious, without remembering our essential godliness; to
be impious, without a thought of the pre-eminent glory of God;
to be distracted and dismembered, in forgetfulness of Him
who is the cause of our misery and who gathers up all our
absent-minded splinters into one united whole. We are not
debtors, bound to *live after the flesh*. The flesh, in which we
are, has, it is true, its own roots, its own earnestness, its own
brilliance and power; but only in the shadow of a wholly different
possibility. Our life in the flesh is observed from a vastly
superior vantage-point, whence it is neither affirmed nor denied
—but whence, if it be regarded as a power to which we are
altogether indebted, it is utterly discredited. Now, the significance of this ambiguity of the whole complex variety of our
observable concrete existence, of all our highways and byways,
of all our earnestness and carelessness, of our righteousness and
sinfulness, of our belief and atheism and incredulity, is that there
is laid, like an axe at the root of a tree, a final 'perhaps and
perhaps not'. This ambiguity is the liberty which we have in
God beyond the frontier of the law: this is the freedom from
which we cannot escape, because it is the Truth, the freedom, of
God Himself. So every human height and depth, strength and
weakness, righteousness and unrighteousness, finds itself confronted by that which frees men and quickly hurries them away;
by that which mourns over them and smiles over them from a
distance, and yet from an infinite proximity comforts them and
demands from them obedience; by that which accuses and excuses them, kills them and makes them alive; by that which
remains ever unobservable, and yet ever speaks and makes itself
known. What then is this known Unknown? It is what Dostoevsky's queer, doubtful characters, deep in their swamp,
remember of the Lord: that He will one day say to those
debauched, weak-willed, shameless creatures—'Come unto Me,
though ye be swine and like unto beasts'. It is also what
enables Luther to die with those unedifying words on his
lips: 'Beggars we are'. And moreover, all this is true, and
we may paraphrase it thus: the man of this world has no
solid ground upon which he can stand; there is accessible to

us no blessed redemption existing in some corner of our
unredeemedness; there is no warm sunset glow which succeeds the storm of our lives—save by the orientation which is
given to men by God Himself and by God alone. This orientation is embarrassment, threatening, promise, the final security
of insecurity, which, as the reflection of light uncreated, encompasses every created thing. This orientation is the End which
announces the Beginning, is the eternal disturbance and the
eternal peace, is the command which banishes us from every
quiet or unquiet nook and compels us to faith, because our
veritable redemption can only be believed in.—Such is the peace
of God which passeth all understanding.

**For if ye live after the flesh, ye must die ; but if by the Spirit ye
mortify the deeds of the body, ye shall live.** The vast display of
noble and ignoble human vitality, all the actual realization of
human positive and negative capacities, in fact, all which we
name 'Life' (BIOS), is—*after the flesh*. As such it stands under
the shadow of death. Its birth is the beginning of death; its
establishment is its dissolution, and its righteousness its condemnation. Existing in time, it has its future and therefore its past.
Nature, in so far as it steps from non-existence into the turmoil
of the course of this world, is dead. History, in so far as what
occurs in it is that which cannot genuinely and properly occur, is
dead. Dead and done with is motion which issues only in commotion. Dead and done with is personality which is self-conscious and recognizable by others. Ought we, must we, can we,
to-day and always, live *after the flesh*? We must, at any rate,
never forget that, since our life moves relentlessly towards
its death, we are riding our horse upon the waves of the sea.
The vitality of our desires, whether manifested in lower or
in higher forms, presses negatively or positively towards full-
grown and healthy maturity, towards a ripe expression of
power. But, though this development be allowed to us,
nay, even be laid upon us as a command, and though its
inherent justification—which may, however, be bounded by
a corresponding absence of justification—generates the steam
and electricity which sets our whole energy in motion, from
the energy of respiration to the energy of prayer:—yet nevertheless, we must never forget the hand uplifted against all
this vitality of ours; lifted up not only against that which is
forbidden, but also against that which is allowed; the hand uplifted in a final, comprehensive gesture of warning. We must
never forget that in the midst of all our activity there is set
a *fruit of the Spirit* (Gal. v. 22), a *fruit of the light* (Eph. v. 9), a

doing which is justified by God. We must not forget the absolute miracle which has occurred. Morality is truly grounded only upon the pure will of God; it can never rest upon the immanent justification of our vitality, even should our power of will have reached its highest development. When, therefore, the will of God is displayed, it must manifest itself in radical criticism of what we possess and do and shall do, both individually and socially. It can never be manifested as sanctioning and justifying us, or even as a thing which contradicts and opposes us: 'The idea of freedom lies beyond our investigation, for it bars the way to every positive representation' (Kant). Therefore we must not fail to observe the hand uplifted against the totality of human capacity. By the Spirit we must *mortify the deeds*, the busy energy, *of the body*. Obviously this does not mean that we must substitute a negative for a positive ethic, and devote ourselves to a morality of flight from the world; of detachment or revolution or asceticism, or to a behaviour which supposes the innocence of Paradise to be recoverable. The practice of such negative morality may, it is true, be permitted, even commanded, here and there, as a parable. The real point, however, is that the whole edifice of human life, including its modern attics and outhouses, is undermined and rendered questionable. The earth quakes quite absolutely: not only the ground upon which Ludendorf and Stinnes and Hölz take their stand, but also the ground upon which the pillar of Simon Stylites rests, the ground upon which all those confident and noble armies of pilgrims are marching—primitive Christians, nature-men, anarchists. All human activity, negative and positive, is radically questionable and insecure. We must, then, recognize the ambiguity of our ambiguity, the death of our wisdom of death; we must make it evident that no man, not even the humble, upright, broken man, has any right-ness; that all the busy *deeds of the body* must be, not checked, nor limited, nor directed into a new channel, but, in their full activity,—mortified. Life emerges at the point of mortification. Set under complete corruption and mortality, words and deeds and movements bear witness to life out of their ambiguity. Only when men take up their position within this insecurity can they perceive the witness which it bears. Perhaps it is to be perceived with a sense of discovery where no one perceives it; perhaps it is seen with quite ordinary eyes where it is perfectly obvious to every one. And yet, it is necessary to emphasize in passing that men are not justified by their perception of so fruitful an insecurity, as though it were a human achievement by which they could be reconciled to God.

Not even this apprehension is sufficient to provide them with the longed for certainty. The flesh is mortified by its relation to the Spirit and by this alone, precisely in order that it may be thrust by this death into the light of hope and of life: 'This pure, soul-exalting, merely negative representation of moral behaviour' (Kant) is the ultimate position—which is no position—to which we are led when we encounter and accept the pre-eminent Truth concerning our *body*.

vv. 14–17. For as many as are led by the Spirit of God, they are sons of God. For ye have not received the Spirit of bondage again unto fear; but ye have received the Spirit of adoption, whereby we cry, Abba, Father. The Spirit himself beareth witness with our spirit, that we are children of God: and if children, then heirs; heirs of God, and joint-heirs with Christ; if so be that we suffer with him, that we may be also glorified together.

'It were good that this text were written in letters of gold; so admirable is it, and full of comfort' (Luther).

As many as are led by the Spirit of God, they are sons of God. What is this vast criticism of our corporeality, by which we are first overwhelmed and then filled with hope, but a making evident that we are gripped by the power and led by the Spirit of God? Clutched by the very Truth, men have no way of escape and can find repose neither in 'Yes' nor in 'No'. The Truth, by germinating death, mortifies our activity and our inactivity, but will also re-orientate them, so that all our acute and complacent questionings, when exposed in unflinching negation, remind us of the positive 'Yes', which men can only seek after and therefore cannot seek after. This positive factor is the Kingdom and Dominion of God. The contrast between subjective and objective, autonomous and heteronomous, 'Here' and 'There', rational and irrational, is obliterated, when we stand at its Origin and Goal. God exists. God leads from death to life. God wills, and a necessity is laid upon us. This is the real situation. We are not debtors to the world of time and things and men (viii. 12). This is our freedom in God, the freedom which is also slavery to Him. In God! There is here no enthusiasm, no mystical experience, no 'feeling of dependence'. By the Resurrection of Jesus from the dead, by the knowledge of God, we are invisibly disposed and orientated from west to east, from death to life; the Holy Spirit exercises His function of judgement and of consolation; the Truth is the Truth—this is the meaning of our being *led by the Spirit of God*, whatever may be the condition of our souls. Thus *led by the Spirit*, under the assault and blessing of the Truth and powerfully controlled by it, we know that we are *sons of God*. In naming myself *son of God*, I mean precisely what is meant when Christ is so named (viii. 3). I do not mean to designate 'myself', the man of this world, thus. I mean always that new, unobservable, other man, who stands before God and lives in Him. I designate thus him that I am—not. I denote thereby Christ in me.—The unparalleled paradox of this statement ought to protect it against that process of humanizing with which practical theologians—far too practical!—are accustomed to gloss the assertions of Christology.—I mean that I can give to the Prime Cause and Power, in whose hands I perceive myself turned from death to life, no name save that of—God. He is the Truth which veritably is, the Truth that wills, the truth that compels. And I—yet veritably not 'I' but Christ in me—am, when I obey the Truth, irresistibly obey it, not the slave of God, not a stranger to Him, but—His Son. How could I be led by the Spirit, how could I experience the infinite bitter-sweet tribulation which the Spirit prepares for me, were it not that the chasm between 'Here' and 'There' was originally no chasm, were it not that originally I shared in the Truth and was originally God's Son? God and His creatures originally one stock and one family! Yes, when we are led by the Spirit, this occurrence is Truth. But the Spirit is: *the Spirit of him that raised up Christ Jesus from the dead* (viii. 11). There is therefore no occasion here for romantic experience, no opportunity for enthusiastic rhapsody, no case for psychological analysis. There is no sign here of 'germ-cells' or of 'emanations' of divinity. There is nothing here of that overflowing, bubbling life in which we think we can discover a continuity of existence between us and God. End and beginning, death and life, judgement and righteousness, is what is meant by the leadership of the Spirit under which our Sonship occurs. Yes, our Sonship is occurrence, and as such it is the answer to that insoluble riddle of our existence which religion finally propounds.

Are we then, nevertheless, left with existence as that which lies outside and not within us? Does our freedom in God still remain slavery? So far as we are men of this world, at best, religious men, the answer is 'Yes'. But in so far as we are— miracle beyond all miracles!—identified with the new man in Christ, 'very man and very God', the answer is 'No': **Ye have not received the Spirit of bondage again unto fear ; but ye have received the Spirit of adoption, whereby we cry, Abba, Father.**

The service *in newness of the Spirit* (vii. 6), in which, led by the
Spirit, we stand unobservably, is no bondage; nor is there in it
any 'otherness' or opposition between God and men, between
Creator and creature. There is here no fear, for perfect love
has cast it out. Here is the hiddenness and clarity and peace
whereby the bondage which men suppose to be their freedom is
measured. What a surging mass of unquiet is that other hiddenness and clarity and satisfaction in which men seek and find their
rest! Here is dissolved the terrible weight which infinity imposes upon what is finite. Dissolved also is that embarrassment
which everything finite imposes upon infinity. Dissolved also is
that untrustworthy complacency which clings to bourgeois affirmations and that precarious vagabondage which is the product
of the poison of human negations. Dissolved is the senseless
multitude of possibilities and the empty vacuity of impossibility.
Dissolved is the impotence of life and the power of death, the
mere humanity of men and the mere divinity of God. Dissolved
is the duality of our life, by which at every moment we are
pressed up against the narrow gate of critical negation. For it is
this duality which gives us to fear, which makes us appalled by
the ambiguity of our being and by the riddle of our existence.
The Spirit, which we have received and by which we have
passed from death to life, brings this duality to an end. Christ in
us, the new man, stands in the singleness of His victory of life
over death. By this One-ness the Gordian knot is severed, and
men stand no longer over against God, as trembling, banished
strangers, subjected, as bond-servants, to an external and
heteronomous law; no longer, with their sense of independence
wounded, revolting against the superstition and fanaticism of
religion and clinging nervously to the autonomy of modern
culture. Now they are Sons, hearing the voice of their Father,
forgetting the 'otherness' of God but first forgetting their own
'otherness'—and from henceforth neither knowing nor willing
aught else but the glory and blessedness of God: God Himself,
and God only! This Spirit of Sonship, this new man who I am
not, is my unobservable, existential EGO. Thence I am known,
directed, enlivened, and beloved. In the light of this unobservable EGO I must now pass my visible and corporeal life. In its
light I must live within the realm of that old duality, pressed
against the narrow gate of critical negation where the fear of the
Lord must be the beginning and end of my wisdom. I must live
in the darkness, but not now without the reflection of light uncreated; God's prisoner, but as such His freedman; His slave,
but as such His Son; mourning and yet blessed. I must still cry

unto Him who confronts me only as unknown and undiscoverable, as the enemy who has vanquished me, and as the judge
who has sentenced me to death—but nevertheless, crying to
Him, *Abba, Father*: 'Such is the description of the Kingdom
of Christ; such is the veritable work and the notable service
of God; such is the operation of the Spirit in the believer'
(Luther). Has there then emerged in all this my final human
possibility? Does this crying ascend to the throne of God?
Does He pronounce it to be righteous? Is this that concrete
behaviour which is not dissolved? Is this religion AND faith?
Who dares make such an assertion, which is contradicted by
all the consequences which follow from it? And yet, who,
arguing from the consequences, can dare to deny it? 'God
is in the flesh, who can apprehend the secret!' If no more is
meant than is expressed in these words, we need not contradict
or criticize what Tersteegen and his disciples say. They are
right, if they really mean no more than this. For assuredly
in such crying the possibility of God is secreted: assuredly
it is possible, when human action has become quite thin and
transparent, for the glory of God to shine through it or,
maybe, to rend it asunder.

The Truth itself has proclaimed to us that Truth is Truth and
that we originally participate in it:—**The Spirit himself beareth
witness with our spirit, that we are children of God.** We are led
beyond all observation to apprehend ourselves as children of God,
not by a spirit, not through some soaring imagination, not in the
midst of some demonic experience or at a moment during some
journey to Damascus. We are led to apprehend our Sonship by
the Spirit, who is neither rational nor irrational, but who is the
LOGOS, the Beginning and the End. We are led by *the Spirit himself*—by Jesus Christ in His full particularity and existentiality
—from life to death and from death to life. He it is who, embracing heaven and earth, bears witness for God to us and to
God for us. He is the dominion of God, established before we
have any experience of it, established also even though we have
never experienced it at all. *The Spirit beareth witness.* Ecstasies
and illuminations, inspirations and intuitions, are not necessary.
Happy are they who are worthy to receive them! But woe be
to us, if we wait anxiously for them! Woe be to us, if we fail to
recognize that they are patchwork by-products! All that occurs
to us and in us can be no more than an answer to what the
Spirit Himself says. Only as this answer can the motions of our
spirits be strong and true and living. The Spirit Himself speaks
beyond our strength and truth and life. That of which God

speaks is immeasurably greater than the greatest of which our
spirits can speak; for He speaks of our non-existent existence;
He speaks of us as—His Children.

If children . . . We—God's Children! Consider and bear in
mind the vast unobservability, impossibility, and paradox of
these words. Remember that, in daring this predication, we are
taking the miraculous, primal, creative step which Abraham
took; we are taking the step of faith, the step over the abyss
from the old to the new creation, which God alone can take.
We—God's children! In uttering these words either we are
talking blasphemy or we are singing the song of the redeemed.
Whether it be on our lips the one or the other, we have dared
to say it, when we have uttered the cry, *Abba, Father*. We
never know or shall know or have known what it means, for we
have done what no mortal man can or ought to do: we have
made use of human words, 'as though' we had seen what no
eye hath seen, 'as though' we had heard what hath entered into
no human ear, 'as though' there had come into our heart what
no heart has contained. And yet, we cannot deny what we have
said; for we have encountered height in the depth, righteousness
in sin, life in death, Christ in us. Hath God prepared this for
them that love him?! Who dares to range himself amongst those
that love God, for whom this hath been prepared? Yes, but who
dares to exclude himself from their number? We have already
included ourselves: we have uttered the word. There is—not,
of course, as an experience—a seeing and hearing which puts
all our questioning to silence, and which remembers only the
decision which has been pronounced. Human sorrow and guilt
and destiny—as they are manifested dark and inexorable
in the countenance and life-story of every single individual, in
the madness of our cities and the dullness of our villages, in the
banal operations of our most primitive necessities and in the ideo-
logical aloofness of our knowledge and conscience, in the horri-
bleness of birth and death, in the riddle of Nature as it cries
out at us from every stone and from the bark of every tree, in
the riddle presented to us by the futile cycle of History, by the
squaring of the circle, and by parallel lines which intersect at no
finite point—have, nevertheless, a voice and a brightness. And
the man who has once heard the voice and seen the brightness—
not psychologically or sociologically or historically or scientifi-
cally; not by some superior and detached academic power of
perception; not by means of some pious illumination of religion;
not by introducing surreptitiously the assumption of a harmony
or providence by which the whole is regulated; but existentially,

earnestly, unavoidably, unescapably, unambiguously, with the ears and eyes of an Ivan Karamazov! himself burnt up, thrown from the saddle—such a man questions no more, but hears and sees—what?—himself as believing and loving and hoping? 'No', a thousand times 'No'; he hears and sees himself confronted by the wholly impossible, by the absolute contradiction, by that which can never be justified and can never be enthroned in any 'concept of God'. Set over against the totality of existence and occurrence, suffering, overwhelmed, asking, and receiving no answer, as impotent in protesting as in rebelling, wholly incapable of doing anything except cry out or be silent, he yet—and here is the point—sees himself as some other, ultimately and primarily distinguished from all this, and yet not altogether detached; free from all this and pre-eminent over it, and yet uneasily woven into its texture. He discovers himself to be in the altogether incomprehensible position of being able to say 'No' to what, in spite of protest and rebellion, he must nevertheless affirm. He sees himself as God's child. What has occurred? In the midst of this seeing and hearing is clearly heard the cry *Abba, Father*. Though men may never have heard the name of God, though, having heard it, they may have blasphemed it; yet, in the midst of the horror they have of themselves, stands clearly the new man, born into a new world. In the midst of it all God has justified Himself in our presence and us in His presence. The theodicy has occurred, beside which all our endeavours to justify God are merely taunting ridicule. Speaking with His own voice, and encircled by the glory of His brightness, God has done once for all the existential deed—He has received men as His children.

And inasmuch as God has once for all acted existentially, we are—**heirs, heirs of God, and joint-heirs with Christ.** Like Abraham (iv. 13), we are heirs of the promise, heirs of the world which God has blessed and made good, heirs of the eternal life and being and having and doing of God Himself, which, because of sin, had become invisible and indescribable, unreal and impossible. Living in the flesh, we await and hope for resurrection, we await our body with its new predicates. Of this hope our present life is the reflection, impress, and witness. Pledged to hope, our life finds there its goal. Quite apart from any conceivable change in us, we are constituted by eternity and qualified by what is to us invisible. With Christ we are sons of God, with Him we are joint-heirs of God, who stands beyond our 'Yes and No', good and evil, life and death. He is the Victor, because

He is God. As His Sons, being what we are not, we stand at His side, participating in His Victory; and our present existence looks forward to this glory, which is already ours.

Have we said too much? Yes, too much—and too little! Too much, when WE contemplate our hope; too little, when WE speak of its fulfilment. Truth is not what we say about God, but what He does and will do and has done. We are *heirs of God*; but we remember that we are so—**if so be that we suffer with him, that we may be also glorified together.** The action of God is the Cross, the Passion: not the quantity of suffering, large or small, which must be borne with greater or with lesser fortitude and courage, as though the quantity of our pains and sufferings would in itself occasion our participation in the glory of God. Participation in suffering means to *suffer with Christ*, to encounter God, as Jeremiah and Job encountered Him; to see Him in the tempest, to apprehend Him as Light in the darkness, to love Him when we are aware only of the roughness of His hand. Those personal sufferings which we are called upon to endure can be no more than harsh reminders of the *sufferings of this present time* (viii. 18) in which heaven and earth are comprehended; and this holds good even should we suffer in a righteous cause—on behalf of Christianity, for example—for there is no 'good cause' which is, in actual fact, God's. Our present human existence—itself not eternity, yet bearing within it eternity unborn—is overshadowed by suffering, as by a dark mantle, by a drawn sword, by an overhanging wall. As such, our life is wholly debatable; there is in it no repose, because, as finite, it is defined and constituted by ambiguity. Our experiences of the temporal limitations of our existence, of the narrow emptiness of our natural powers, of the great and petty tribulations which, as fragments of earth, we must 'endure in pain', are but the shadows of our essential finiteness. That sooner or later we must encounter the final barrier is the Pain in our pains. Nor ought we to remain in ignorance that at this point God directs His question to us, and that here also He prepares His answer. In the Spirit, the secret of God cannot be hidden. In the Spirit, we are enabled to know the meaning of our life, as it is manifested in suffering. In the Spirit, suffering, endured and apprehended, can become our advance to the glory of God. This revelation of the secret, this apprehension of God in suffering, is God's action in us. Such comprehension is the witness of the Spirit by which the Truth is permitted to be the Truth, and is also the guarantee that we are children of God and, as such, heirs of His glory.

vv. 18–25. **For I reckon that the sufferings of this present time are not worthy to be compared with the glory which shall be revealed to us-ward. For the earnest expectation of the creature waiteth for the manifestation of the sons of God. For the creature was made subject to vanity, not willingly, but by reason of him who hath subjected the same in hope, because the creature itself also shall be delivered from the bondage of corruption into the liberty of the glory of the children of God. For we know that the whole creation groaneth and travaileth in pain together until now.** And not only the creation, **but ourselves also, which have the firstfruits of the Spirit, we ourselves** also **groan within ourselves, waiting for our adoption, to wit, the redemption of our body. For by hope we are saved: but hope that is seen is not hope: for what a man seeth, why waiteth he yet ?**[1] **But if we hope for that we see not, then do we with patience wait for it.**

I reckon that the sufferings of this present time are not worthy to be compared with the glory which shall be revealed to us-ward. 'The writer now undertakes to console the Christians who are set in the midst of so great tribulation: he speaks as one who has himself suffered and is confident of what he has to say. He speaks as though he saw that other life with wide-open eyes, but this life blinkered or, as it were, through painted glass. See how he turns his back on this world and confronts the coming revelation, beholding the earth, rid of all misery and disappointment, filled with radiant happiness. See how he contracts the suffering of the world into a single drop and a tiny spark, whilst he expands its glory into a mighty ocean and a blaze of fire' (Luther). This astonishing manner of observing the affairs of men requires explanation. Clearly there is here no exuberant stretching of our normal observation upwards or downwards. There is here no overlooking or toning down of human suffering in order to offer some more solid consolation. The writer does not, for example, redress the tribulation of the world by fixing our attention upon the compensating harmony of another world. No careless attitude to present tribulation can stand even before the aching of a tooth, and still less before the brutal realities of birth, sickness, and death, before the iron reality which governs the broad motions of the lives of men and the stern destiny of nations. Beneath each slight discomfort, and notably beneath

---

[1] Following Lietzmann, and reading (v. 25): ὃ γὰρ βλέπει τις, τί καὶ ὑπομένει; This, at first sight, very uneasy reading is made intelligible by the final words of v. 25.

the greater miseries of human life, there stands clearly visible
the vast ambiguity of its finiteness. How are we able to meet
this? All our answers, all our attempts at consolation, are but
deceitful short-circuits, for from this vast ambiguity we ourselves emerge; we cannot escape from it, not even if we evoke in
our imaginings an infinite divine harmony beyond this world of
ours. The infinity of our imagination is measured by our limitation and achieves no more than infinite-finiteness. The harmony
which we imagine is relative to our discord, the Fata Morgana
of our wandering in the desert; and the God whom we permit to
reward and compensate us in some other world is—if observed,
for example, with the eyes of an Ivan Karamazov—'No-God',
the god of this world, fashioned after our image and, consequently, subject to our criticism—and to our denial. Not for
some relative thing does the ambiguity of our finiteness cry out,
but for the Absolute: it cries for an answer beyond our comprehension, for the true and Unknown God; it cries out for His
consolation, with which the sufferings of this present time are
not *worthy to be compared*, a consolation opposed to this present
time as the immeasurable 'There' is opposed to the measurable
'Here'. If we are even to begin to find consolation, we must
first recognize that we have no consolation, we must acknowledge
that our comfort is in vain: 'Therefore the Holy Spirit must be
our school-master, and send comfort into our hearts' (Luther).
Only by the interpolation of a new and unheard-of manner of
reckoning does comfort enter our lives. We have already met this
unromantic word *reckoning* (iii. 28, iv. 3): we know that by it no
stretching of our human manner of observation is intended; that
all suggestion of a continuity of human thought is foreign to it.
By this manner of *reckoning* the results of human observation are entered on the debit side of the balance-sheet which
God Himself and God alone draws up. The observation which,
according to this *reckoning*, is entered on the credit side, is the
observation sub specie aeternitatis, the observation from
God, which, because it is beyond human capacity but within the
capacity of faith, can be defined only as the action of God. In
so far as 'we' undertake to co-operate in God's reckoning or endeavour to see as God sees, we shall never attain the conclusion
which Paul attained; we shall only conclude as Job did—before
God spoke to him out of the whirlwind. If I say quite simply
'I reckon with God', the final leap into the Absolute is obscured.
Only if these words be inverted is their inexpressible truth displayed—'God reckoned with me'. Here is the occurrence: and
we proclaim it only inasmuch as we—but not 'we'—let the

Truth be the Truth; inasmuch as we—but not 'we'—demonstrate the power of the Spirit and apprehend, in the question
and answer of the Cross (viii. 17b), the action of God. Then
it is that we perceive the time in which we stand to be the
present time, that is to say, the ocean of concrete, observable
reality, in which the submarine island of the 'Now' of divine
revelation is altogether submerged but remains, nevertheless,
intact, in spite of its shallow covering of observable things.
This 'Now' (iii. 21), this 'Moment' beyond all time, when
men stand before God, this 'Point' from which we come, but
which is no point in the midst of other points, Jesus Christ crucified and risen,—is the Truth. All that is before and after
this 'Moment of moments', everything which encircles, like a
plane, this 'Point' which cannot be produced,—is time. At
this 'Point' time, wherein the past is past and the future is
future, emerges as the denial of Eternity; and we name time
this present time, because of that which it obscures and of that
to which it bears witness, and because of that by which it is
measured and apart from which it would not exist. And so, the
time in which we live conceals and yet preserves Eternity within
it, speaks not of Eternity yet proclaims it in its silence. Inasmuch, therefore, as we, by the power of God and by the question
and answer of the Cross, have our primal origin in the absolute
and present 'Now', and inasmuch as God manifestly reckons
with us here and enables us thereby to reckon with Him, we
apprehend Eternity in time. We see our existence lived in the
shadow of the Day of Jesus Christ, the Day which has not as yet
dawned but is inscrutably *at hand*; we see time rolling on in the
shadow of the 'Now'; we see human things running their course
in the shadow of God. *Led by the Spirit* (viii. 14), and crying,
Abba, Father (viii. 15), we declare ourselves to be—no, are declared to be—sons of God (viii. 16) and heirs of His glory (viii.
17). And so once again we must formulate the question: What
place does suffering, that vast and immeasurable factor of human
life, occupy in the context of our Sonship? Evidently, suffering
cannot be compared with the glory of God so as to disturb or
prevent our entering into that 'Now' to which we have free
access, because the conscious recognition of suffering is the gate-
way to knowledge and redemption which is in the 'Now', in the
Spirit, in Jesus Christ. God reckons with us precisely at the
door of suffering. There it is that He justifies Himself in our
presence and teaches us through His Spirit to cry, *Abba, Father*.
It is thus evident that time is the negation of infinity. In that
negation men encounter the barrier which confronts them, and

discover also the place of exit. Where then should the power of
the Spirit be displayed, if not in the action of God by which He
makes us participate in the sufferings of Christ (vi. 5) and thereby brings us within the sphere of the freedom and glory of the
new man? *The sufferings of the present time* cannot, therefore,
be compared with this glory. In Christ Jesus they have indeed
been compared, and have been shown not merely to be simply
characteristic of our life in this world, but actually to mark the
frontier where this life is dissolved by life eternal. The time in
which we live and suffer is the *present time*, the time when glory
is made manifest in suffering. So clearly does God manifest His
glory in the secret of suffering, that, so far from shrinking for
His sake from the contemplation of suffering, it is for His sake
that we are bound to gaze upon it, to see in it the step, the movement, the turning-point from death to life, and to apprehend it as
the place where Christ is to be seen. To overlook suffering is to
overlook Christ. To ask the question why there should be suffering, is to fail to hear that the same question is addressed to us.
To answer that suffering is unintelligible to us, that we cannot
bear it or master it or turn it to any good account, means that
we are deaf to the divine answer which is given precisely in our
inability. Here is both the secret and the revelation of suffering:
God wills to be God, and is God; in His will and in His being He
requires to be known and loved. The child of God does not overlook suffering, does not frame his own questions and answers
concerning it; because God has framed both question and answer,
and he has heard God speak. In suffering he hears the voice of
the Truth, detecting it at the heart of his own questions and
answers: 'He rests not till he finds hopelessness everywhere'
(Nietzsche), until he finds hope in this hopelessness—ave crux
unica spes mea! 'Wilt thou be joint-heir with Jesus Christ?
Wilt thou be like unto Him, His brother?—and not suffer?
Then, at the Last Day, He will certainly know thee not as
brother and joint-heir. Then He will ask thee: "Where is thy
crown of thorns? Where is thy cross? Where are thy nails and
scourge?" And He will ask thee: "Wert thou an abomination
to the whole world, as I and all mine have been since the foundation of the world?" If thou have naught to say to all this,
He will not count thee as His brother' (Luther).—'With great
energy the thinkers of old sought happiness and truth; but with
deep-sounding, evil voice Nature decreed that they should never
know what they perforce must seek. But he who of his own free
will seeks falsehood everywhere and pursues misfortune, to him
Nature perchance draws near and offers her gift—not misfortune,

x

but a miracle; something no words can frame, something of which happiness and truth are forms idolatrous. Maybe the earth lets go its heavy weight; maybe its powers and solid happenings dissolve in dreams, and are transfigured as on some glowing summer eve. And to the man who sees, it is as though his first awakening is girt about with sportive, dreamy, floating clouds, which later disappear, and it is day' (Nietzsche). When we are blind and dumb, then we see and speak; when we are bereft of question and answer, then we ask and find; when they suffer, then the children of God know and love their Father—triumphantly. For his glory *shall be revealed to us-ward.—Shall be!* This future is our misery and our infinitely greater hope. The Futurum resurrectionis reminds us that we have been speaking of God and not of some human possibility.

For the earnest expectation of the creature waiteth for the manifestation of the sons of God. All temporal, created things bear witness to the truth that the time in which we live is the time of the divine 'Now', and that it bears in its womb the eternal, living, unborn Future. Whither can men turn their eyes—men, disconsolate in what they are and longing restlessly to be what they are not—without encountering the eyes of others equally disconsolate and filled with a longing equally restless. Nay more, these other eyes are bent on men, directing to them their earnest questioning. Men suffer—we cannot for one moment be in doubt as to this—in a world which suffers with them. Men suffer, because, bearing within them—at least as a problem—an invisible world, they find this unobservable, inner world met by the tangible, foreign, other, outer world, desperately visible, dislocated, its fragments jostling one another, yet mightily powerful, and strangely menacing and hostile. Not for long can we suppose the peace of our direct union with God to lie in the harmony of the external world. For it is itself a cosmos of things, themselves limited, indirect, and questionable. The more men are aware of their own insecurity and find themselves, under the poignant influence of Christianity, unable to kick against the pricks and to forget that they are men, the more is their attention fixed upon the world by which they are encompassed, the more certainly do they recognize their solidarity with it, and the more passionately do they seek to penetrate its secrets. If this be not so, how can we explain that strange and modern desire to understand the glaciers—on whose brink even Goethe stayed his march—the desert, the North Pole, the bottomless ocean, the trackless air, the abyss of the infinitely great and the infinitely small, Nature's vast millions of years, the many tiny, wretched futilities of the history of men, and the absurdities which congregate and exercise themselves— so competent observers tell us—in the occult, subconscious, marsh-land of our non-existential existence? Were men themselves unbroken and self-sufficient, and did they live in the bright sunlight of directly apprehended truth, they would not long to know and to experience such things as these. Why is it that in its reaction upon our lives, our deeper and more perfect understanding of the COSMOS does nothing to lessen our insecurity or to dissolve our questionableness? Why does the understanding we have reached merely set us on our course more madly energetic than before? And yet, maybe, we do not fail to note a gigantic and expectant eye, observing us from 'over there', strangely investigating us as we investigate, but with a hundredfold more accurate research. Perhaps we do not over-look how interlocked are the two sides of the abyss, how close-related are the inner and the outer world, how, despite the distinction of subject and object, the same question-mark is set against them both. 'In every creature St. Paul, with his sharp, discerning, apostolic eye, perceived the holy and beloved Cross' (Luther). The question, then, which is directly asked of men from 'over there', concerns the meaning of this *earnest expectation*. What is it which men perceive and discover, find and apprehend, in their research and in their experience? They know the COSMOS to be theirs: they seek to find their rest in Nature and in History. But instead, with fatal necessity, they discover everywhere—their own unquiet. The language of creatures and elements, of worlds above and beyond, of times both near and far, turns out to be, when once it is deciphered, a strangely human tongue. It speaks of beauty and disgust, of peace and war, of life and death, of finiteness and infinity, of good and evil. It seems as though the contradictions, so well known to us, were also theirs, the very ground of their existence too; as though our sufferings were theirs, and our diseases also theirs. 'From this pressing forward of Nature to Mankind we must understand that men are necessary to Nature's redemption from the curse of the life of beasts; and that in Mankind a mirror is presented to all existence, in which life is no longer meaningless, but stands forth in its metaphysical significance. But we must pause to ask a question: "Where does the beast end and man begin?"—I mean, of course, the man concerning whom Nature is so seriously anxious ! . . . We have not normally emerged from the beast. We are beasts who seem to suffer meaninglessly. Yet there are moments when we comprehend, and see ourselves in company with Nature pressing forward to Mankind, as to something standing far above us. . . . But we feel ourselves so weak that we cannot for long endure that moment of deep communion. We know that we are not the men to whom all Nature presses for its redemption. It is as though for one brief moment we had raised our heads above the flood, and seen how deep we are submerged. And even so, we have not raised ourselves by our own power' (Nietzsche). That is the truth: *The earnest expectation of the creature waiteth for the manifestation of the sons of God.* The creation waiteth together with us—no, for us.

For the creature was made subject to vanity, not willingly, but by reason of him who hath subjected the same in hope, because the creature itself also shall be delivered from the bondage of corruption into the liberty of the glory of the children of God. 'There is no fragment or particle of the world, which, in the grip of the knowledge of its present misery, does not hope for resurrection' (Calvin). The occasion of the dislocation and longing and *vanity*, presented to us in the whole creation, is not this or that particular pain or abomination or absence of beauty, not even the sum of observable disadvantages attaching to the world as we see it: the occasion is rather createdness itself, the manifest lack of direct life, the unsatisfied hope of resurrection. We cannot, surely, pronounce the created world to be direct, genuine, and eternal life. The perpetual interaction of energy and matter, of coming into being and passing to corruption, of organization and decomposition, of thirst for life and the necessity of death: this *bondage of corruption* which encompasses all living creatures from the microbe to the Ichthyosaurus, and from the Ichthyosaurus to the most distinguished professor of Theology—everything, that is to say, which we know as 'life' or, by the analogy of anything that we comprehend as life, can conceive as such, this surely is not direct, genuine, and eternal life. Whence comes the sad courage with which men, and especially we Europeans, refuse with desperate optimism to see the vanity of the creature, deprived of the direct life of Creation, which cries out at us and will continue to cry out at us in its beauty (as in the human body) as well as in its ugliness, in its grand nobility (as in a chain of mountains) as well as in its paltry insignificance, in its light (as in the moon or in some recently published masterpiece) as well as in its darkness? But we are deaf and do not hear. We must rid ourselves of reverence for pseudo-life, if we are to apprehend; for it is not by such reverence that we are led to the apprehension of the divine secret of the cosmos.

We must recover that clarity of sight (i. 20) by which there is discovered in the COSMOS the invisibility of God; we must recover that sacred terror in the presence of the creature, not terrified by it, but—jolted out of our dreary optimism—terrified at the mere createdness of the things which attract us as well as of the things that frighten us, until we see in their createdness the mirror of our own. Beyond the interminable interplay, which is the mark of createdness, lies—as a problem!—the Creation in the creature, God in the COSMOS. If God be not found in the COSMOS, He is to be found nowhere. When the excitement of 'Life's affirmation' has, no doubt for some quite valid reason, cooled off, men will turn to 'Life's negation', complaining that the world is in itself evil, that it is created in *vanity—willingly*, or the plaything, maybe, of some demiurge. For pessimism is the inevitable counterpart of optimism. But the vanity of the creature is not, however, *willing* vanity. Vanity is not the creature's primal constitution; nor, whether it be overlooked by the optimist or discovered—only to be at once misunderstood—by the pessimist, is vanity its final constitution. But the creature is *subject to vanity by reason of him who hath subjected it*, and therefore—*in hope*. Now, He who has subjected the creature is God: and thence emerges hope. All those things which are so manifestly observed by men are hidden in God: life and death, light and darkness, good and evil, rise and fall, idealism and materialism, inner and outer. In God break forth the contrasts which mark the vanity of the creature. The suffering, by which the whole created world of men and of things is controlled, is His, His action, His question, and His answer. For this reason the creature is placed under hope. Beyond pessimism and optimism, where the origin of the vanity of the COSMOS in the unobservable Fall of the creature from the Creator is apprehended—there emerges hope, hope of the restoration of the unobservable union between the Creator and the creature, through the Cross and Resurrection of Christ. Once the utter bondage is recognized, then freedom is seen. Once perceive the frightfulness of corruption, and there is hope of resurrection. The final check is the first step forward!—in Christ, of course, in the Spirit, and because God is God. The Truth is advance and movement and turning from death to life. The freedom in glory for which the new man, the child of God—he that I am not—waits, with sighs and yet in blessing, is what has been promised; and in this promise even the body, even man—he that I am—even the world, share. For to me, the child of God, it is precisely a blessed world, the world of Creation and of the life that has been

promised. If men are free, the world must be free also. If men
are one with another because they are one with God, there must
be in the world also no inner and outer, no this and that,
no growth and decay. When the sons of God shall appear,
'because of their appearing, Nature, which never leaps, makes
one leap, and that a leap for joy: for then it knows that at last
and for the first time it has attained its goal' (Nietzsche). The
world also is eternal—in God, as the world of the new heaven
and the new earth, as the world which the Father hath subjected
to Himself through the Son (1 Cor. xv. 25–8). He that would
know this, can, by knowing that he knows nothing, know it now
already: 'Truly, the earth shall yet be a place of refreshment;
and indeed, it is already fragrant with a new odour, with a new
hope that bringeth salvation' (Nietzsche).

What, then, do we know? We know that we have cause to be
dumb before God. We know that when we speak of the glory
of God, we speak of a future which never can be in time.—
**We know that the whole creation groaneth and travaileth in
pain together until now.** The whole creation! Yes, even that
which has been hidden and submerged, and so made more
difficult of access by our knowledge! Our knowledge itself! for
we know that what we know and shall know is a thing *groaning*
and *travailing in pain*, a thing loosed from its Primal Origin, a
relative thing, separated from the absolute by an abyss. When,
therefore, something is known by us, we know it as a thing, as
something relative, and what we know is precisely its createdness, and, because it is but a creature, it too *groaneth and travaileth in pain*. But we know that every created, temporal thing—
of uncreated, infinite things we have no knowledge—bears its
eternal existence in itself as unborn, eternal Future, and seeks to
give it that birth which can never take place in time. We know
that everywhere this hope-ful distress and this distress-ful hope
are linked in one all-pervading unity. This knowledge may, it is
true, be further deepened and established, and more precisely
defined, by the exercise of our intelligence. But our intelligence
can never be stretched to a 'higher' knowledge, for we know
by our intelligence that the veritably 'higher' knowledge, the
knowledge of the creature which does not *groan and travail in
pain*, is the knowledge of God. But God is in heaven, and thou
art on earth. Therefore it is precisely our not-knowing what
God knows that is our temporal knowledge about God, our
comfort, light, power, and knowledge of eternity. The creature
sighs *until now*, and in so doing makes reference to the truth
which is revealed in Christ, interpreting our temporal life to

those who have ears to hear both as *this present time* and as the
opportunity of eternity. Have we now heard the groaning of the
creature, which, if we interpret it aright, tells us all we need to
hear? If Christ be in us, we hear what He proclaims. And is this
not the secret of all secrets? 'No human intelligence or human
wisdom can thus think and believe it. . . . The eyes capable of
beholding this glory in the creature must be veritably apostolic
and spiritual' (Luther). *We know* . . . and what further knowledge do we require?

**And not only the creation, but ourselves also, which have
the firstfruits of the Spirit, we ourselves also groan within ourselves, waiting for our adoption, to wit, the redemption of our
body.** From the broad expanse of the created, temporal, corporal
world we turn now to consider once again the narrower sphere of
men who inhabit this world—bodily. We consider the subject
by which the world is observed; but we consider it only in so far
as it is itself an object of observation. For the questioning eyes
which have contemplated us in the mirror of the created world
are our own eyes which, in regarding the universe, see us ourselves as an object. Who, then, are we? And who am I? Well, I
am the man who possesses the firstfruits of the Spirit, who knows
that the law is spiritual (vii. 14), who is invisibly redeemed by
the redemption which is in Christ Jesus (iii. 24), who is seized,
driven, dedicated by the Truth, a free man, a child of God. Were
this not so, how could I really suffer under the weight of the
present order? How could I cry, Abba, Father? How could I hear
the groaning of the travailing creature? I am a citizen of the
coming order. In the light of the 'Now' revealed in Christ Jesus,
I have the requisite knowledge concerning the present temporal
order. I have been saved (viii. 24), and from this salvation I
advance . . . but to what goal, and along what road? And where
does the path begin or end? Once again we have to be reminded,
lest we fall into some romanticism or other, how complex is our
life on this side of the Resurrection. This way and that, our
path is crossed by every kind of human possibility, high and
low, noble and vulgar, significant and trivial. Art, science, and
morality display the passionate longing of men for infinity. Yes,
but, God knows, we also hunger and thirst; we digest our food,
and sleep, and lust. And where is the boundary line between the
two? Can any one rid us of the clear conviction that all our
activities are interlocked? Can any one rid me of the suspicion,
amounting almost to a certainty, that the story of my life and
the history of humanity could be more honestly described if the
stomach rather than the head were adopted as the point of

departure? Even the greatest genius is born, dies, and lives as we do. Nor can his peculiarity be disentangled from our common lot. Can we not, by adopting a purely materialistic philosophy of life, offer a better, or at least a more plausible, interpretation of the general course of the history of humanity or, to select particular aspects of it, of Primitive Christianity, of the Crusades, and of the Reformation? What, for example, is left of Blumhardt in Möttlingen,[1] if he be investigated first by a psychiatrist and then by a psychologist? And what alternative method of investigation have we to offer? No, men—created, temporal, corporal men—are like that; and only as such are they objects of our knowledge. Spirit! What is Spirit? According to our normal understanding, Spirit tends to be no more than a mist hanging above a marshy land. Whence comes the mist? And, when it clears away, what permanent, solid element remains? We need not answer these questions: let it suffice us that, when men emerge from their unobservable, Primal Origin in the Spirit of God, they enter completely into observable and unending ambiguity. In this ambiguity we stand: in most of our activities, manifestly so, but, in fact, ambiguous in all. Well, granting all this and speaking quite frankly: What are we? Clearly, we who *have the firstfruits of the Spirit, we ourselves also groan within ourselves*, just as much as the creation does. We too are subjected to *vanity*, to the contrasts of life and death, light and darkness, beauty and ugliness. We groan, as the creation does; we travail in pain *together* with it. We too bear within us the eternal Future, which we know can never be realized in time. We too are God's prisoners, and therefore we too—hope. *We ourselves also groan—waiting for our adoption.* Waiting! The Spirit bears witness that we are children of God. The new man, the inheritor of the world of the Father, has been born. But I, the temporal and corporal man of this world, am not the new man. My final possibility is to groan—and to await the promise. Now, *adoption* means *the redemption of the body*, that is, the

---

[1] In 1842 at Möttlingen, near Calw in Württemberg, Johannes Christoph Blumhardt (i.e. the elder Blumhardt) healed by prayer a woman suffering from severe hysteria. The case, which was regarded by Blumhardt and by the woman herself as one of demoniacal possession similar to those recorded in the New Testament, formed the starting-point of a widespread movement of conversion and healing, which was marked for Blumhardt by the forgiveness of sins. The confession 'Jesus is Victor', which the demon was supposed to have uttered through the mouth of the woman at the decisive moment, became, as it were, the motto both of the original movement and of the message of the Kingdom of God which was later spread abroad from Bad Boll in Baden, as well as from Möttlingen itself.

The occurrence was, of course, both in 1842 and afterwards, given a purely physiological explanation. [Tr.]

complete identification between Christ and me. The resurrection
of the dead is, in the present order, a matter of faith only. The
whole creation *waiteth for the manifestation of the sons of God.*
From this manifestation of redemption no hair of our head can
be excluded. The vast ocean of reality, which now embraces and
submerges the Island of Truth, subsides and is established so that
only Truth remains: the Truth of veritable Reality! Time, immense and vast, from its first beginning to its furthest future, is
Eternity! There is no without which is not within, and no within
which is not without. It is not some other man that is redeemed,
but I myself; not a fragment of me, but I in my totality. I am
transformed, renewed, purified, made a participator of the divine
nature and of the divine life, with God, by His side, and in Him.
This is adoption. On this side of the resurrection, however, religion is the final word: and we recall its meaning. We remember
the disturbance of desire which gazes at us from our own eyes.
We too stand under the Cross, unable to do more than bear
witness to the 'Now' of eternity which is ours, to the Day of
Jesus Christ, which is no day, but the Day of Days, before and
behind and above the days of our life. 'It is no wonder that we
are moved by great tribulation. For it is not that we have just
one wish: we have rather one long yearning cry. When men
become aware of the tribulation, they can but cry' (Calvin).
And so we ourselves become witnesses: for our ability to know
that we ourselves also must groan within ourselves, and that we
can know no more than this, is the divine justification of the
possibility of religion; and our ability to pronounce and bear
witness to the significance of this precise knowledge which we
have of ourselves means that God is our Father.

Ought we then to regard this knowledge as too scanty for us?
Is it not enough for us to know the groaning of the creation and
our own groaning? Ought we to demand some higher or better
knowledge, which takes no account of the Cross or of the tribulation of time? If so, we must, perforce, take no account of
the Resurrection—of the 'Now' which is time's secret—or of
God:—**For by hope we are saved : but hope that is seen is not
hope : for what a man seeth, why waiteth he yet? But if we
hope for that we see not, then do we with patience wait for it.**
Harsh and holy and powerful is the Truth; so also is our salvation; so also is God Himself on our behalf. The victory and
fulfilment and presence of the Truth is ours only by hope. The
Truth would not be Truth, if we, as we are, could apprehend it
directly. How could the Truth be God, if it were for us but one
possibility among others? How could we be saved by it, if it

did not with compelling power urge us to hazard the leap into eternity, to dare to think what God thinks, to think freely, to think anew, and to think wholly? *By hope we are saved*—inasmuch as in Jesus Christ the wholly Other, unapproachable, unknown, *eternal power and divinity* (i. 20) of God has entered into our world. Could we wish anything else than that this saving hope should always be declared at the Cross, should always set a boundary against everything in our world, and should always manifest itself at that boundary? Were we to know more of God than the groans of the creation and our own groaning; were we to know Jesus Christ otherwise than as crucified; were we to know the Holy Spirit otherwise than as the Spirit of Him that raised Jesus from the dead; were the incognito in which salvation has come to us, does come to us, and will come to us, broken through—then there would be no salvation: *For hope that is seen is not hope.* Direct communication from God is no divine communication. If Christianity be not altogether thoroughgoing eschatology, there remains in it no relationship whatever with Christ. Spirit which does not at every moment point from death to the new life is not the Holy Spirit: *For the things which are seen are temporal* (2 Cor. iv. 18). All that is not hope is wooden, hobbledehoy, blunt-edged, and sharp-pointed, like the word 'Reality'. There there is no freedom, but only imprisonment; no grace, but only condemnation and corruption; no divine guidance, but only fate; no God, but only a mirror of unredeemed humanity. And this is so, be there never so much progress of social reform and never so much trumpeting of the grandeur of Christian redemption! Redemption is invisible, inaccessible, and impossible, for it meets us only in hope. Do we desire something better than hope? Do we wish to be something more than men who hope? But to wait is the most profound truth of our normal, everyday life and work, quite apart from being Christians. Every agricultural labourer, every mother, every truly active or truly suffering man knows the necessity of waiting. And we—we must wait, as though there were something lying beyond good and evil, joy and sorrow, life and death; as though in happiness and disappointment, in growth and decay, in the 'Yes' and in the 'No' of our life in the world, we were expecting something. We must wait, as though there were a God whom, in victory and in defeat, in life and in death, we must serve with love and devotion. 'As though?' Yes, this is the strange element in the situation. In our journey through time, we are still men who wait, as though we saw what we do not see, as though we were gazing upon the unseen. Hope is the solution of the riddle of our 'As though'. We do see. Existen-

tially we see what to us is invisible, and therefore we wait.
Could we see nothing but the visible world, we should not wait:
we should accept our present situation with joy or with grum-
bling. Our refusal to accept it and to regard our present
existence as incapable of harmony, our certainty that there
abides in us a secret waiting for what is not, is, however,
intelligible in the unseen hope which is ours in God, in Christ, in
the Spirit, in the hope by which we are existentially confronted
by the things which are not. We can then, if we understand
ourselves aright, be none other than they who wait. We are
satisfied to know no more than the sorrow of the creation and
our own sorrow. We ask nothing better or higher than the
Cross, where God is manifested as God. We must, in fact, be
servants who wait for the coming of their Lord.

vv. 26, 27. Likewise also the Spirit forestalleth **our infirmities: for we know not what we should pray for as we
ought: but the Spirit** with pre-eminent power **maketh intercession for us with groanings which cannot be uttered.
And he that searcheth the hearts knoweth what is the
mind of the Spirit, that he maketh intercession for the
saints according to the will of God.**

Likewise also the Spirit forestalleth our infirmities. Of what
have we been speaking? Have we been speaking of the Truth
itself or of our search for it? Have we been describing a divine
occurrence to us-ward, or a quantity, or quality, or intensity
of human experience? Have we been speaking of the Spirit,
or of sensitive and enthusiastic spirituality? Verily, our speech
throughout has been of the latter; for how can we speak of
the former except in negations of the latter? But, repeating
what we have said before, it has always been our intention to
speak of the former: *The Spirit himself beareth witness with our
spirit that we are children of God* (viii. 16). The groaning of
the creation and our own groaning is naught but the impress
and seal of the Spirit: our cry, *Abba, Father,* is naught but
the echo of the divine Word. The action of the Spirit is independent: He goeth as He listeth. We do not possess Him:
He possesses us. He anticipates us, and *forestalleth our infirmities.* He is Creator Spiritus. For our groanings are *infirmities*: they are flesh, not Spirit: human, not divine: sinful,
not righteous. If they are heard and accepted by God, it is in
His presence and only there. Our awaiting, however patient and
faithful it be, is also infirmity: for there is an awaiting in Hell—
a purposeless, undefined, ineffective, worthless expectation, a

waiting for nothing, a waiting which is therefore incapable of fulfilment. And no one can assure us that our awaiting is not of such a kind—no one, that is, except God. That the Spirit forestalls us, that the Truth is in itself true, is the power in our infirmity. We must also recognize that we cannot lay hold on this power, even by the strictest abnegation. The mystic's 'Way of Denial' is a blind alley, as are all 'ways'. The only way is the Way, and that Way is Christ.

For we know not what we should pray for as we ought. Do we, now that we have reached the end of this section of the Epistle to the Romans, understand what this means? Did not Paul pray when he wrote these words? And did he not pray aright? Are these words aught else but one quite precise prayer? And where could we find a prayer so penetrating, so courageous, and so selfless? Yet, even whilst writing these words, he knew that he did not know what he should pray for as he ought. But why was he ignorant? Evidently, because prayer is not at all the 'Miracle of miracles, which takes place daily in pious souls': evidently, because the motive of all prayer is not at all the 'Striving after the strengthening and consolidating and enhancing of a man's own life': evidently, because the essential element in prayer is not at all 'Communion with God, thought of as personal and experienced as present' (Friederich Heiler). But because even the most sincere, most heroic, most powerful prayers —and this applies also to the prayers of Prophets, Apostles, and Reformers, not to mention the artistry in prayer of the Ama-Xosa and the 'Kekchi-Indians'[1]—do but serve to make clear how little the man of prayer is able to escape from what he himself has thought and experienced; how utterly he—yes, precisely he—is a man and no more; how completely the bravest leaps and the boldest bridge-building activities of so-called 'piety' occur within the sphere of this world, and have in themselves nothing whatever to do with the incomprehensible and unexperienced but living God. If prayer—and prayer particularly—be thought of as a tangible experience and glorified as such, the objection is justified which Feuerbach brought against all religion: 'We do not know.' Beyond this 'we–not'—in no way related to the technique of 'absorption' practised by eastern and western 'adepts in prayer', but in vehement protest against so great an ocean of misunderstanding—lies the reality of communion with God.

But the Spirit with pre-eminent power maketh intercession for

[1] The allusion here and the quotations which precede it are taken from Friedrich Heiler's book, *Das Gebet: eine Religionsgeschichtliche und Religionspsychologische Untersuchung.* For the 'Kekchi-Indians' see the fifth edition, p. 59 (English Translation, p. 28). [Tr.]

us with groanings which cannot be uttered. We wait: but, because we wait upon God, our waiting is not in vain. We look out: but, because we have first been observed, we do not look out into the void. We speak: but, because there emerges in our speech that which cannot be uttered, we do not idly prattle. And so also we pray: but, because the Spirit maketh intercession for us with groanings which—since His groanings must be songs of praise—are beyond our competence, our prayers and groanings are distinct from that groaning which is weakness—and nothing else. The justification of our prayer is not that we have attained some higher eminence on the ladder of prayer; for all ladders of prayer are erected within the sphere of the 'No-God' of this world. The justification of our prayer and the reality of our communion with God are grounded upon the truth that Another, the Eternal, the Second Man from Heaven (1 Cor. xv. 47), stands before God pre-eminent in power and—in our place.

And he that searcheth the hearts knoweth what is the mind of the Spirit, that he maketh intercession for the saints according to the will of God. Let us set aside our investigation of God. He searcheth us. Our mind is never right. But God knows the mind of the Spirit in us; and this mind, because it is known of God and is the mind of the Spirit, is right-minded. In human fashion no man and no thing can make intercession for us. We stand alone, and are lost. But, according to the will of God, the Spirit intercedeth for us, and we are saved. Apart from the intercession of the Spirit we are sinners. But God names us saints. He makes us saints, using for our fashioning nothing that we are or have been or shall be. He makes us His saints, His separated ones, His instruments, because of that intercession. And He that intercedes for us is the Spirit, the Hope, the Truth, Jesus Christ.

LOVE

VIII. 28–39

vv. 28–30. And we know that all things work together for good to them that love God, to them who are called according to his purpose. For whom he foreknew, he also foreordained to be conformed to the image of his Son, that he might be the firstborn among many brethren: and whom he foreordained, them he also called: and whom he called, them he also justified: and whom he justified, them he also glorified.

We know—not some concrete, visible, corporal divine thing! If that were the object of our knowledge, God would not be God.

Men do not force their way into His Kingdom; nor is it projected
into this world. To us God is the Stranger, the Other, whom
we finally encounter along the whole frontier of our knowledge.
Our world is the world within which God is finally and everywhere—outside. 'The cycle of our existence must be completed by
all of us, according to iron laws, mighty and eternal.' The man
of this world knows only the groaning of creation and his own
groaning (viii. 22, 23), and, moreover, he can have this knowledge
(i. 19, 20) only in so far as he does not turn his back upon the *vanity*
of his existence (viii. 20) and upon the dialectic of its contrasts,
and does not refuse to perceive the relativity and home-sickness
of everything which is merely concrete, observable, and tangible.
The health-bringing function of suffering is to open our eyes; for
joined to suffering and at its extreme limit is that true and
worthy philosophy whose nature and function is to interpret
the sorrow of the world. Ignorant therefore of God and of His
Kingdom, but familiar with the groaning of all creation, we
lend our support to all honest, secular, scientific and historical
research; but we dissociate ourselves from every semi-theological
interpretation of Nature and of History. And we act thus,
because such ignorance and such knowledge together compose the flint and steel from which, when they meet in Spirit
and in Truth, there is kindled, as a new and third thing, the
not-knowing apprehension of God and the apprehending not-
knowing of the vanity of our existence. The fire of the love
of God, because He is God (v. 5), breaks forth. But the pseudo-
theological knowledge of God and the corresponding pseudo-not-
knowing of the vanity of our existence meet neither in Spirit nor
in Truth, and can kindle no fire, certainly not the fire of the love
of God.

To them that love God. The love of God is not a particular
form of behaviour within the sphere of human competence. It
can ring in our ears, only if we detect the groaning of creation;
it can spring to our lips, only if we ourselves cry out. It can be
in our prayers, but also in our inability to pray; it can be in our
religion, but also in our indifference to religion, in our antipathy
to it, and in our assault upon it; it can inhabit the basement of
our most violent passion, but it can also make its home in the
drawing-room of our mature composure. Yet it must not be
identified with any one of these; for it is the power and significance which God can bestow upon this or that form of human
behaviour through its relationship with Him. The love of God,
contrasted with the questionableness of our life, is its deepest
reality. Men love God, whatever their visible behaviour may

be, when, veritably and existentially, quite clearly and once
for all, without possibility of avoidance or escape, they encounter the question: 'Who then am I?' For the contrasted
and inevitable 'Thou' involved in this question is—God. In
being thus compelled to face themselves, men do in fact manifest love towards God. Surely it is not beyond the competence
of men to know the arrows within them, the poison whereof
their spirits drink, and the terrors which set themselves in
array against them (Job vi. 4). Surely they know that they
are engaged upon a constant warfare, and that their days are
like the days of a hireling (Job vii. 1). Surely they can cry:
Am I a sea, or a sea-monster, that thou settest a watch over me?
(Job vii. 12). Surely they can encounter One above whom they
know there is no—Daysman that might lay his hand upon us
both (Job ix. 33). Surely they may be men whose way is hid
and whom God hath hedged in (Job iii. 23). Surely their knowledge of God is sufficiently precise and intimate for them to be
aware that they can neither see, nor know, nor seriously consider, nor recognize the authority of any other, second, thing
beside His veritable reality. Surely, too, they cannot resign or
devote or surrender themselves to Him fatalistically or in the
comfort of religion, but must abandon themselves existentially
with groanings which cannot be uttered (viii. 26)—*I know that
my redeemer liveth* (Job xix. 25). In such knowledge men love
God, not before or after, but in the 'Moment' which is no
moment in a series, and which is the meaning of every moment
in time: Magna et incomprehensibilis res est, amare Deum
nempe hilari pectore et grato complecti per omnia volun-
tatem divinam, etiam tum cum damnat et mortificat
(Melanchthon). Wherever (to paraphrase Melanchthon's words)
the love of God occurs, religious possibility inevitably appears
consciously or unconsciously as a temporal happening. But the
accompaniments of religion, such as gifts of prophecy, of speaking with tongues, of knowledge, are no more essential than
were the admirable speeches of the friends of Job. What is
essential in the occurrence is the answer of God; the presence
of Christ; the outpouring of the Spirit; the *more excellent way*
(1 Cor. xii. 31) of God to men and of men to God which is there
opened up and entered upon; the necessity and freedom by
which men are then touched; the existential constitution of
their personality, which meets them there; and the significance
of every human possibility, which is there manifested to them
as the eternal Meaning. The eternal Meaning occurs, however,
beyond that which is *put away* when the child becomes a man,

when, instead of seeing in a glass darkly, we see face to face, and, instead of knowing *in part*, we know even as we are known (1 Cor. xiii. 8–12). Love towards God—AGAPE—is separated from all religious or other forms of EROS by the flaming sword of death and eternity. Love proclaims that the new man stands before God, and that He cannot be wooed by any love-song as Baal and his like are wooed. This is the Love which *never faileth* (1 Cor. xiii. 8), which abideth—with Faith and Hope, these three: but the greatest of these, because it is the existential occurrence in faith and hope, is Love. *Faith worketh by love* (Gal. v. 6). Love, therefore, is intelligible only as the *more excellent way* (1 Cor. xiii. 13) which is wrought by God: Carni contraria voluptate sponsus sponsam suam afficit Christus, nempe post amplexus, amplexus vero ipsi mors et infernus sunt (Luther).

To them all things work together for good. Love towards God is a humiliation, so well aware of its intention that it excludes confident questionings and no longer claims its rights. Love is a desire so intense that it has already tasted its fulfilment, and therefore cannot be disturbed or extinguished. Love is a peace, so deep that it is at once the highest rest and the highest unrest. Love is an awaiting of redemption, so great that it need wait for no time or event. Not-knowing, it already apprehends God; and apprehending, it knows no longer the vanity of our existence. Love of God is therefore the unobservable place where the consummation of all things has already been completed. Job, in his insistent outcry against the hiddenness of God, had spoken—*of me the thing that is right*: therefore God restored to him—*twice as much as he had before* (Job xlii. 7–10). Unlike his far too religious friends, Job had passed beyond the place of death and had attained the summit of life, where men and their world no longer stand in darkness; and where, in the reflection of the glory of the coming Day, God, the great Unknown, becomes the great Known, and the secret of the COSMOS is manifested as the Creation of God. All things work together for good to them that love God. The Good is the beholding of the Redeemer and of Redemption, the attainment of the living Point beyond the point of death, the beginning of that awaiting which is no awaiting, of that not-knowing which is the supreme apprehending, and of that apprehending of sin and death, devil and hell, which is the supreme not-knowing. The Good is the very love of God towards men who stand before Him rich and well-clothed, because they are still poor and naked. Everything must work together, in order that the man whom God loves may be fitted to participate in that good thing. Everything: the wholly un-edifying visibility of the world, as well as the equally unedifying invisibility of God; the misery of our createdness, as well as the darkness of the divine wrath; the incurable ambiguity of time, as well as the contrasted ambiguity of eternity. For God, as the God of love, stands where two negations are first mani-fested in sharp antagonism and are then seen to meet and dis-solve one another. The Love of God stands where there is disclosed, beyond and above and in the twofold negation, the pre-eminent affirmation—Jesus Christ, the Resurrection and the Life. Blessed discovery! God stands in light inaccessible. Blessed discovery! All flesh is as grass and all the glory of men is as the flower of the field. When, in Spirit and in Truth, one of these discoveries is made, the other is involved in it, for both are in fact operations of the One God, whose universal majesty is the 'Yes' in the 'No'. The Love of God dares to see everywhere on this side and on that side the great riddle, not a 'Here' and a 'There', but wholly and altogether, beyond all tension and duality, the revelation of the one Truth, proclaiming that the free and righteous, blessed and living God, knows us, prisoners and sinners and condemned and dead, to be His own. And so, in our apprehension which is not-knowing and in our not-knowing which is apprehension, there is shown forth the final and primal unity of visibility and invisibility, of earth and heaven, of man and God. In that duality, which now and to the end of our days is alone accessible to our perception, is announced the ultimate unity, which is the glory of the children of God and our hope. Thus God rewards those that love Him.

Who then are those that love God?—They—**who are called according to his purpose.** Not, that is, these men or those men; not indeed men considered as a whole: for we are forbidden to give a quantitative answer to the question. The Love of God cannot be tangibly observed or concretely assessed either in individuals or in the generality of men. The Love of God is not a 'property', which men may achieve or inherit, or which inheres in them. Rightly understood, there are no Christians: there is only the eternal opportunity of becoming Christians—an opportunity at once accessible and inaccessible to all men. As men of the world, we are all at all points and always confronted by God Himself as God. For it is He who has first loved men; He who opens up the gulf on the right hand and on the left, and deprives men of every possibility, except one, of returning His love; He who so sharpens the contrasts that their very duality *works together* until men are unable altogether to escape their

Y

hidden unity; He who, through this unedifying duality, edifies
those that love Him *according to His purpose,* calling them to an
activity which they can neither perform themselves nor require
others to perform. Has any one who has loved God ever thought
otherwise? Has any one boasted that he has turned the key and
opened the door, that he has achieved the negation of negation,
and passed along the narrow way between the abyss on his right
hand and on his left? Has any one vaunted himself that he
has reversed the unedifying signs of the times, and achieved
the consummation of all things? However much 'Christian
assurance'—which exists, fortunately, only in the imagination of
theologians—may treat the absolute paradoxes of the divine
government of the world and the trust of men in God as counters
with which to reckon or rather to juggle; however much it may,
from genuine embarrassment, or in order to secure a deceptive
certainty, or in order to secure an apologetic success, play them
off as 'values' against other values: love towards God knows
that assurance is not a 'thing', not a heroic and glorious achievement of this or that man, not a haven at which men 'put in' after
a long and arduous voyage, not a 'property' into possession of
which the Christian lawfully enters. Love knows itself to be
altogether the gift and operation of God, altogether the calling
which is grounded upon the purpose comprehended in God
before all time and before every moment in time: *When thou
givest them, they gather; when thou openest thine hand, they are filled
with good. When thou hidest thy face, they are troubled; when thou
takest away their breath, they die, and are turned again to their dust*
(Ps. civ. 28, 29). Human duality finds its unity only in God.
God reveals Himself when the duality of human life reveals love
towards God. But His revelation can never be extended onto
the plane of time, so as to be thought of as a concrete possession.
Only in God is 'life' death and 'death' life; only God manifests
the Creation in the cosmos and Himself as the Redeemer; only
God brings into being the existential transformation of unredeemed knowledge from the vanity of the world into the freedom of not-knowing. Such are they that love God, or rather
they that have been called by Him. Is it not, however, within
our competence to provide a less restless and more satisfying
answer to the question—How ought men to be lovers of God?

**Whom he foreknew, he also foreordained to be conformed to
the image of his Son, that he might be the firstborn among many
brethren : and whom he foreordained, them he also called.**
Those who love God are named *called,* in order that they may be
distinguished clearly from those who suppose that they love

Him or pretend to do so but, in fact, do not. It is this 'Call' which distinguishes prophets from false prophets, and Paul from the seven sons of Sceva (Acts xix). Those who love God have no defence against being ranged so completely in the company of those worthless 'thyrsus-bearers' that they become indistinguishable from them. Those who love God will not be surprised if they are confounded with them, and will, in fact, give glory to God, if they be *not* so confounded. Neither will they appeal to their *calling*, for they will remember that it is the 'Call' itself which is their sanction, not their appeal to their *calling*. Nor will they resist the taking from them of all peace and security, for they will remember that they are neither more nor less than men who have been *called*. The love of God which has been shed abroad in their hearts through the Holy Spirit will never be for them a self-evident, settled fact and occurrence. *I will be that I will be* (Exod. iii. 13–15)—the Unknown, the Invisible, the Eternal, is He that hath called you; and as such ye love Him. Whenever God becomes something else; whenever men seek to love Him directly, as though they had an assured possession and enjoyment; God is no longer God, and their *calling* is no longer a 'Call'. For they who are *called* are they who have been *foreordained* by God to be *conformed to the image of his Son*: and the *image* to which they are *conformed* is the death of Jesus (Phil. iii. 10). Under this image, under this incognito, the Son of God came into the world. The transparency of this occurrence was the characteristic and controlling factor in the life of Jesus (v. 6, vi. 5, viii. 3). Those who love God were foreordained to bear witness to the death of Jesus and consequently to His resurrection; and, whatever precise form their lives may take, these must be lived under the final tribulation of men who fully recognize that there exists no third and intermediate thing between the Unknown God and the altogether too well-known world. They proclaim and show forth the tribulation of Jesus in Gethsemane, a tribulation which begins with the Baptism in Jordan and ends with the Crucifixion on Golgotha. To accompany Him along His road and become messengers on His behalf—that is to say, to allow the word of reconciliation to be spoken over them as a genuine condemnation against which they have no defence (1 Cor. v. 19, 20)—this it is to love God. When, like Job or Paul, men proclaim the death of Jesus; when they are able to rejoice in tribulation (v. 3) as their glory and salvation; when in their distress, in spite of it and because of it, they shine forth as lights in the world (2 Cor. i. 3–11); then is fulfilled in them the occurrence of divine foreordination, and God operates in them and through them. This does not mean that some form of self-chosen negation of the world, some ascetic 'wisdom of death', some martyrdom or voluntary 'suicide', creates the divine negation which shines forth in the death of Christ. No experience of death is a substitute for the death which the living God utters in and through His elect; no 'discipleship of Christ' can, as a human undertaking, enrol men in the number of the existential brethren of the firstborn Son of God. It is a divine, unobservable, eternal constitution, a being *led by the Spirit* (viii. 14), that creates the divine sonship of men, that gives to their observable existence such significance, that gives to their thought and will and action such orientation. The fire which kindles this illumination is the fire of God. God is the Creator and Redeemer when tribulation is not merely tribulation, death not merely death, negation not merely negation, and not-knowing not merely absence of apprehension, but when, as in the image of His Son, all things are transfigured by the presence of His Word; when the decision is His, not man's; and when His eye sees and is seen as the brilliance of the sun. Thus, before every moment in time, God foreordains; and the very broken-ness and indirectness of our relationship with Him sanctions and authenticates the calling of those who love Him. Men are there-fore foreordained by God, because they are known of Him: *If any man love God, the same is known of him* (I Cor. viii. 3). Here it is that we encounter the secret of predestination to blessedness, which Augustine and the Reformers represented in mythological form as though it were a scheme of cause and effect, thereby rob-bing it of its significance. No doubt human love of God, the ordination of men to Sonship, and their calling to be witnesses of the Resurrection, are genuine occurrences, consequent upon God's knowledge of men and taking place in the knowledge of the true and only God. But this must not be taken to mean that His love has brought into being a particular temporal human being and having and doing, which is the result of a divine causation which took place concretely as the first of a series of temporal occurrences. Predestination means the recognition that love towards God is an occurrence, a being and having and doing of men, which takes place in no moment of time, which is beyond time, which has its origin at every moment in God Him-self, and which must therefore be sought and found only in Him. The man who loves God can never ask 'Is it I?' or 'Is it Thou?'. Such questions are relevant only in the context at which the Apostles formulated them at the Last Supper. The Lord knoweth His own. He knows the prisoner to be free, the sinner righteous, the damned blessed, and the dead alive. He is the

Judge; and men have sinned and can sin only against Him. The truth of the love of men towards God is His Truth, not man's; in Him it is constituted and realized; He sees it and rewards it; He knows it; and it is existential only in Him. But the knowledge of God is eternal and unobservable: it occurs altogether beyond time. It must therefore be distinguished absolutely from temporal human knowledge, of which it is the KRISIS, the presupposition, and the dissolution: *If any man thinketh that he knoweth anything, he knoweth not yet as he ought to know* (1 Cor. viii. 2).—For the things which are seen—that is, what is known—are temporal; but the things which are not seen are eternal (2 Cor. iv. 18). That is Spirit, that is Truth! Such also is the peace and the assurance of those who love God. The eternal decision in Spirit and in Truth is the ground of their ordination and calling. Embarrassed before God, they have peace; insecure, they have assurance. Fear and trembling is the lever with which they are and have and do. Condemned, they are justified; blind, they see; slain, they live. And yet, these contrasts are never cause and effect. Those who love God are so utterly dependent upon Him that at every moment of time they remain what they are.

Perhaps we are now in a position to understand what is meant when we say:—**Whom he called, them he also justified: and whom he justified, them he also glorified.** Once the calling to love God is assured in Spirit and in Truth, in God Himself, men possess assurance also, by the mercy of God, of pure and un-observable justification and of citizenship in the Kingdom of God; they are, in other words, assured of the fact that God takes sinners to Himself. In those whom He has called and ordained and known, in the secrets of human being and having and doing (ii. 16), God discovers what is well-pleasing to Him. He discovers the new man created for redemption. Called to love God, men are unobservably new and righteous.—We have now discovered the adequate explanation of why it is that all things work together for good to such new men; and we know now why they encounter the one existential truth as their eternal hope. Since love beareth all things, believeth all things, hopeth all things, endureth all things (1 Cor. xiii. 7), human past, present, and future, is, as such, already the eternal Future. Love is the existential recognition of God; for it is God's recognition of men. The Spirit searcheth out the deep things of God (1 Cor. ii. 10). Love, therefore, remains the *more excellent way*; for it is apprehended, not by experience, nor by argument, nor by the assertion of assurance, but only by God Himself.

vv. 31, 32. What then shall we say to these things ? If God is for us, who is against us ? He that spared not his own Son, but delivered him up for us all, how shall he not also with him freely give us all things ?

What then shall we say to these things? How are we to provide any further elucidation, explanation, and interpretation, of the words of God to those who love Him—words which only He can utter at the place where He wills that men should seek and find Him? Is it not inevitable that anything we say must be said 'about' or 'in addition to' or 'contrary to' what God has said? Must not our silence also, quite as much as our speech, obscure the truth concerning the knowledge of love? Do we not do equally wrong, whether, in answer *to these things*, we burst into speech or relapse into silence? If, however, God acknowledge us, we can do right both by speech and by silence.

If God is for us, who is against us?—'Si Deus pro nobis, quis contra nos?—Were we competent to decline the pronoun nos—nobis and to fathom its meaning, we should be bound also to transform the noun Deus into a verb and conjugate it thus: Deus—dixit—dictum est. And when this were done, it would follow that contra would become an altogether scandalous and disgraceful preposition, which must be interpreted as though the words were in fact infra nos, which is what has occurred, and indeed must occur. Amen' (Luther). *God for us*—so is it spoken to those who love God. The words are, however, unprecedented: for they mean that the realm of contrasts lies behind us, and that the duality in which we stand, which conditions everything we see, and which renders the world darkness to God and God darkness to the world, has been overcome. Overcome is the relativity into which men, and pre-eminently religious men, have been thrust, so that in all their knowledge and in all their desire God encounters them as the Wholly Other. Having *imprisoned the truth in unrighteousness* (i. 18), and being opposed by both God and the world, by both death and sin, human thought is able to move only in the tension of contrast and antinomy, and unity lies beyond the comprehension of unredeemed humanity. But if God be with men, if God takes the initiative and men stand at His side, there is no division and no duality, they think no longer in paradoxes, and they are opposed by no man and by no thing. Then is fulfilled the word, *Death is swallowed up in victory* (i Cor. xv. 54): for this corruptible hath put on incorruption and this mortal hath put on immortality. In the words *If God be with us* is summed up all that can be said concerning fulfilment, perfection, and redemption, all that can be said of the unobservable central Point. *That God may be all in all* (1 Cor. xv. 28) is the beginning and the end. We have, of course, no words to express this; for if we had, it would not be what it is. We must therefore be content to have concluded that all roads move in that direction and are impassable.

And so we must break off, not because we now know that we have been dreaming, but because we know that we have seen the final unforgettable truth:—**He that spared not his own Son, but delivered him up for us all, how shall he not also with him freely give us all things?** If we fix our eyes upon the place where the course of the world reaches its lowest point, where its vanity is unmistakable, where its groanings are most bitter and the divine incognito most impenetrable, we shall encounter there—Jesus Christ. On the frontier of what is observable He stands *delivered up* and *not spared*. In place of us all He stands there, delivered up *for us all*, patently submerged in the flood. And if He was delivered up, how much more are we all submerged with Him in the flood, dragged down into the depth, and included in the 'No' which God utters over the men of this world and from which there is no escape! How much more are we led to the place where we stand under the universal judgement of God, where, embarrassed by the conflict between righteousness and sin, life and death, eternity and time, there remains naught but the existentiality of God. But the transformation of all things occurs where the riddle of human life reaches its culminating point. The hope of His glory emerges for us when nothing but the existentiality of God remains, and He becomes to us the veritable and living God. He, whom we can apprehend only as against us, stands there—for us. That Christ, who deprives us of everything but the existentiality of God, has been delivered up, means—we must dare to say it, dare to storm the fortress which is impregnable—and already captured!—that *God is for us* (viii. 31), and we are by His side. Christ who has been *delivered up* is the Spirit, the Truth, the restless arm of God. If so be that we suffer with Him, how can it be that we should not also be glorified with Him (viii. 17)? If we die with Him, how can it be that we shall not also live with Him (vi. 8)? If God has delivered us up with Him to the judgement which threatens all, how should He not also with Him give us all things, and thus secure that all things should work together for our good (viii. 28)? *All things—freely!* Concerning the dawn upon which we have gazed we are able neither to speak nor to be silent.

vv. 33–9. Who shall lay anything to the charge of God's elect ? Shall God—that justifieth us? Who is he that shall condemn ? Shall Christ Jesus—that died, yea rather, that was raised from the dead, who is at the right hand of God, who also maketh intercession for us ? Who shall separate us from the love of Christ ? Shall tribulation, or anguish, or persecution, or famine, or nakedness, or peril, or sword ?—It is with us even as it is written, For thy sake we are killed all the day long; we are accounted as sheep for the slaughter (Ps. xliv. 22)—Nay, in all these things we are more than conquerors through him that loved us. For I am persuaded that neither death, nor life, nor angels, nor principalities, nor things present, nor things to come, nor powers, nor height, nor depth, nor any other creature, shall be able to separate us from the love of God, which is in Christ Jesus our Lord.

Can we not now at last claim that we have stormed and occupied the stronghold—*God for us*? No, we must at once surrender it, for it is God's fortress; and it is ours to occupy neither in the past, present, nor future. The accusation remains against every man, whatever his position may be. Confronted by God, how indeed can men be other than accused? Measured by the standard of Christ Jesus, we are inevitably condemned and *delivered up*. When the door opens and the light of Christ exposes us as we are, who can be justified? How vast is the gulf which separates us from the love of Christ! How incommensurable is the love of God displayed in His death compared with the tiny spark of our love! How immense is the contrast between the tribulation of the life we have to live and the divine, eternal, glorious Future which we behold and believe and encounter in Him!—**In all these things we are more than conquerors.** We! Does this refer to 'us' as men holding this or that belief, occupying this or that position, convinced, busy, and enthusiastic? If we are to answer this question, we must be quite honest with ourselves and keep strictly and modestly to the point. We must speak neither too quickly nor with too great emphasis and assurance, even if we think we have sufficient insight to pronounce an opinion of our own, and have not merely taken over somebody else's opinion. There is, in fact, no very great difference between what we say as a consequence of our own experience and what we borrow from the experience of others: indeed—horribile dictu—the latter is often more nearly true than the former. But—and this conditions our

answer to the question—immeasurable is the distinction between
the eternal 'Moment' when the stronghold 'God-for-us' is
stormed, and every moment in time, whether past or future,
when we stand once again outside the fortress boasting of a
victory which, so far as can be observed, is always our defeat.

And yet, in spite of our observable defeat, we must not abandon the assault, for the love of those who have been called and
ordained and known (viii. 29, 30) by God does reach the heart
of the Judge, however great may be His wrath against the man of
this world. Christ—the new man that I am not—has set His
foot where I cannot stand. What I cannot say of myself is said
of Him. Not only is He the firstborn, but—and here the transformation occurs—He stands risen from the dead at the right
hand of God, and there intercedes on my behalf. He comprehends that I, a sinner, am righteous. He knows my imprisonment to be my freedom and the most grievous anguish of my
death to be my life. And so it is that I know that no man and
no thing can separate me from the wholly incomprehensible love
of God which is in Christ Jesus. Monstrous to us are even those
final inevitable contrasts—knowing and not knowing; death and
life; divine and human nature; past, present, and future on the
one hand, Futurum aeternum on the other; here what can be
observed, there what is invisible; relativity and absoluteness;
earth and heaven—to us they are endless finiteness, endless
concretion, endless createdness—but in God, as negations which
have been negated, as positions which have been dissolved, they
are at peace, reconciled, redeemed, and resolved; in Him they
are one. For the love of God in Christ Jesus is the oneness of the
love of God towards men and the love of men towards God. In
His love our love celebrates its victory. In it the point has been
reached where the unattainable identity has been attained. But
when this is said, we turn ourselves about, knowing that we are
in no sense competent to attain this identity or even to conceive
of its attainment. It sufficeth us to know that thence we came
and thither we go.

The Ninth Chapter

THE TRIBULATION OF THE CHURCH

SOLIDARITY

IX. 1–5

vv. 1–5. I say the truth in Christ, I lie not, my conscience bearing witness with me in the Holy Ghost, that I have great sorrow and unceasing pain in my heart. For I could wish that I myself were accursed from Christ for my brethren's sake, my kinsmen according to the flesh: who are Israelites; whose is the adoption, and the glory, and the covenants, and the giving of the law, and the service of God, and the promises; whose are the fathers; of whom is Christ concerning the flesh; and whose is God that ruleth all things[1]—**blessed for ever, Amen.**

God, the pure and absolute boundary and beginning of all that we are and have and do ; God, who is distinguished qualita-

---

[1] The commentator has to choose between various possible renderings of this passage:

1. The words ὁ ὤν ἐπὶ πάντων, &c., may be taken as a relative clause, of which Χριστός, the subject of the preceding sentence, is the antecedent. This is strongly supported by the analogous grammatical constructions in Rom. i. 25 and 2 Cor. xi. 31. I cannot, however, bring myself to accept 'so unparalleled an attribution of θεός to the exalted Lord' (Zahn) for the following reasons: first, I do not find the attribution either in 2 Thess. i. 12 or in Titus ii. 13: secondly, it does not seem to be required by Rom. x. 11–14: thirdly, such an attribution would, in my judgement, betray a lack of delicacy of which a thinker and writer who differentiates so clearly as Paul does would hardly have been guilty: fourthly, the passage does not, as is clear from the citations of Wetstein, B. Weiss, and Zahn, play as large a part in the early Christological controversies as it must have done, had it been taken in this way: quite apart from the words ἐπὶ πάντων θεός, εὐλογητός occurs frequently in the Psalms where the reference to the God of Israel seems quite obvious.

2. Hofmann and Zahn insert a comma after πάντων—Beck even adding a second comma after θεός—and all three, to whom Kühl must be added as a fourth, emphasize the absence of the definite article before θεός. 'The sentence merely expresses that the dignity of a θεός may be truly ascribed to Christ' (Kühl). In form this explanation is too ingenious, whilst in matter it is open to the gravest objection. To so ambiguous a statement as this I would certainly prefer the previous interpretation.

3. ὁ ὤν ἐπὶ πάντων, &c., may be taken as an independent doxology referring to God. Other Pauline doxologies support this. I cannot, however, agree with Jülicher in finding this to be 'the only satisfactory explanation'. It should be noted that Lietzmann, whilst adopting this interpretation, writes much more guardedly. An independent doxology addressed to God—it is here an asyndeton —is too foreign to Paul's general practice and too unnecessary in the present context for me to feel comfortable with this solution of the problem.

4. I should like to support the conjecture made some 200 years ago (see

tively from men and from everything human, and must never be identified with anything which we name, or experience, or conceive, or worship, as God; God, who confronts all human disturbance with an unconditional command 'Halt', and all human rest with an equally unconditional command 'Advance'; God, the 'Yes' in our 'No' and the 'No' in our 'Yes', the First and the Last, and, consequently, the Unknown, who is never a known thing in the midst of other known things; God, the Lord, the Creator, the Redeemer:—this is the Living God. In the Gospel, in the Message of Salvation of Jesus Christ, this Hidden, Living, God has revealed Himself, as He is. Above and beyond the apparently infinite series of possibilities and visibilities in this world there breaks forth, like a flash of lightning, impossibility and invisibility, not as some separate, second, other thing, but as the Truth of God which is now hidden, as the Primal Origin to which all things are related, as the dissolution of all relativity, and therefore as the reality of all relative realities. Though—nay rather, because—human life is temporal, finite, and passing to corruption, it is revealed in the Gospel that the glorious, triumphant, existential inevitability of the Kingdom of God cannot be hidden. It is made manifest that the knowledge of God—faith working through love—is presented to men as the possibility which, though realized at no particular moment in time, is, nevertheless, open to them at every moment,

Wetstein), and to read: ὤν ὁ ἐπὶ πάντων θεός. The passage would then run parallel to the series of statements in vv. 4, 5, which are introduced by the relatives οἵτινες, ὧν ἡ, ὧν οἱ, ἐξ ὧν, and the doxology would commence with the word εὐλογητός. The present text may be the result of a pure error in transcription, aided perhaps by assimilation to 2 Cor. xi. 31. The emendation is supported by the following considerations. If the received text be adopted, the enumeration of the prerogatives of Israel lacks the decisive and all-embracing prerogative, namely, her possession of the supreme God. The emendation fills up the gap. Against this Jülicher appeals to iii. 29. But Jülicher does not seem to me to perceive that the thesis that God is the God of the Jews and of the Gentiles is in iii. 25, and always for Paul, the consequence of a dialectical attack. For Paul it is no simple, obvious, and generally agreed proposition upon which to base an argument. When he is dealing, as in ix. 5, with the religious, ecclesiastical point of view, God is quite simply the God of Israel. Paul does not, of course, stop here. He admits (ii. 17) the right of the Jew καυχᾶσθαι ἐν θεῷ, since he does not regard the advantage possessed by the Jew in his relation with God as simply dissolved by the ambiguity of his position (iii. 1). Similarly, the recognition of the universality of God does not prevent Paul, or some one influenced by him, from describing those alienated from the πολιτεία τοῦ Ἰσραήλ as—ἄθεοι ἐν τῷ κόσμῳ (Eph. ii. 12). Were the appeal of Jülicher (and of Lietzmann) to iii. 29 correct, Paul, if he were consistent, ought not to have regarded as the peculiar prerogatives of Israel either the υἱοθεσία (cf. viii. 14), or the νομοθεσία (cf. ii. 14, 15), or the δόξα (cf. iii. 32), or the ἐπαγγελίαι and the πατέρες (cf. iv. 16). The relationship is everywhere the same. If the peculiar direction given to all these conceptions and their dialectical movement be overlooked, they are altogether unintelligible.

as the new and realizable possibility of their being what they are in God—His children—cast, as men of this world, under judgement, looking for righteousness and awaiting redemption, but, under grace, already liberated.

And now, in contrast with the Gospel of Jesus Christ, there is thrust upon our attention—Israel, the Church, the world of religion as it appears in history, and, we hasten to add, Israel in its purest, truest, and most powerful aspect. We are not here concerned with some debased form of religion, but with the ideal and perfect Church. Does the Church stand over against the Gospel as one point of view against another? Are we setting one company of men who think rightly over against another company who do not?

Yes, undoubtedly we are. The Church confronts the Gospel as the last human possibility confronts the impossible possibility of God. The abyss which is here disclosed is like to none other. Here breaks out the veritable God-sickness: for the Church, situated on this side of the abyss which separates men from God, is the place where the eternity of revelation is transformed into a temporal, concrete, directly visible thing in this world. In the Church, the lightning from heaven becomes a slow-burning, earth-made oven, loss and discovery harden into a solid enjoyment of possession; divine rest is changed into human discomfort, and divine disquiet into human repose. In the Church, the 'Beyond' is transfigured into a metaphysical 'something', which, because it is contrasted with this world, is no more than an extension of it. In the Church, all manner of divine things are possessed and known, and are therefore not possessed and not known. In the Church, the unknown beginning and end are fashioned into some known middle position, so that men do not require to remember always that, if they are to become wise, they must die. In the Church, faith, hope, and love are directly possessed, and the Kingdom of God directly awaited, with the result that men band themselves together to inaugurate it, as though it were a THING which men could have and await and work for. To a greater or lesser extent, the Church is a vigorous and extensive attempt to humanize the divine, to bring it within the sphere of the world of time and things, and to make it a practical 'something', for the benefit of those who cannot live with the Living God, and yet cannot live without God (the Grand Inquisitor!). To sum up: the Church is the endeavour to make the incomprehensible and unavoidable Way intelligible to men. In all this busy activity the Catholic Church has been granted very considerable success, whereas Protestantism has had to suffer much more

severely from the fact that what is so dear to the heart of a
Churchman is unattainable. From this it is obvious that the
opposition between the Church and the Gospel is final and all-
embracing: the Gospel dissolves the Church, and the Church
dissolves the Gospel.

But what do we mean by this contrast? Assuredly, not a distinction between men and men, but between God and men!
Not between Saul–Paul and—other Pharisees! Not between
Evangelicals and other Churchmen! These would not be eternal but temporal contrasts. However clearly and precisely the
Gospel is preached, the divine incognito still remains. The pure,
non-ecclesiastical Gospel is proclaimed by no human mouth. The
Evangelical, as such, remains always an ecclesiastic, for he
suffers the tribulation and shares in the guilt of the Church. All
human thought and action and possession—however orthodox—
are no more than a parable. Men are not competent, even if they
are gifted with tongues of fire, to speak of God otherwise than in
a parable. We too suffer under this limitation, for the whole
paraphernalia with which we erect, sustain, and order the relation between men and God, is ecclesiastical machinery. We, too,
seek to make the *more excellent way* intelligible. No doubt we
endeavour to preserve its unintelligibility, but has any Churchman ever wished not to do so? Whenever we fail to perceive the
incorruptible in the parable of the corruptible, we have served
the Church and not the Gospel; and who except God can
protect us against this most natural failure of perception? The
fatal prattle of systematic theology, which we are bound to
employ in speaking about God, if we are not to become superficial
and undisciplined, is a parable of the indivisible unity of the
Truth. The appalling fact that no one is able to speak about
God without speaking a great deal about himself is a parable of
the Personality of God by whom all things are eternally upheld.
The paradox of the final, despairing inadequacy of human speech
as a medium for expressing the Truth is a parable of the absolute
miracle of the Spirit. Our almost intolerably one-sided and
narrow-minded presentation of the thought of eternity, which
we can avoid only by talking about—something else, is, nevertheless, a parable of the violent and direct claim eternity imposes
upon us. Can any Evangelist alter the situation by which—
unto them that are without, all things are done in parables? Can he
prevent men from supposing him to be inventing some new and
remarkable and strange orthodoxy, against which, lest they be
themselves thrown from the saddle, they passionately seek to
defend their own familiar orthodoxy and to justify it as skilfully

as they are able, not always, however, without loss of temper?
Can he prevent such men from asserting that what he says
cannot be so very important, since after all he has only spoken
as one man to another, and that too within the sphere of the
Church, where nothing need be taken seriously, since no existential truth can be spoken ecclesiastically!? Who can put
a stop to this scandal, this failure of the Gospel? No one. We
might, for the honour of God, adventure the wildest leap and
land ourselves in the mud (1 Cor. xiii. 1–3); but even so, it
would be interpreted ecclesiastically and not existentially.
Who can teach us to speak existentially and not ecclesiastically?
No one except God. And even should we be taught of God, His
incognito still remains.   There is no opportunity given us
whereby we are in the right and others in the wrong, for God's
point of view is strictly protected against every human point
of view: He is righteous, and we are all unrighteous.

Are we then to deduce that we should forget God, lay down
our tools, and serve men in the Church—as though there were
no Gospel? No, the right conclusion is that, remembering God,
we should use our tools, proclaim the Gospel, and submit to the
Church, because it is conformed to the Kingdom of God. We
must not, because we are fully aware of the eternal opposition
between the Gospel and the Church, hold ourselves aloof from the
Church or break up its solidarity; but rather, participating in
its responsibility and sharing the guilt of its inevitable failure,
we should accept it and cling to it.—**I say the truth in Christ, I lie
not, my conscience bearing witness with me in the Holy Ghost,
that I have great sorrow and unceasing pain in my heart.** This
is the attitude to the Church engendered by the Gospel. He who
hears the Gospel and proclaims it does not observe the Church
from outside. He neither misunderstands it and rejects it, nor
understands it and—sympathizes with it. He belongs personally
within the Church. But He knows also that the Church means
suffering and not triumph. He knows the business of the Church;
and knowing it, he is bitterly in earnest. He does not console
himself by supposing the Church to be a human affair of which
men can rid themselves. He does not think its ministry is a
vocation just like any other. He knows that there must be
beliefs and preachings and interpretations. He knows that men
must call upon God in prayer. He knows that such things must
be, and that the God-sickness of men will always tend to break
out in new forms. He knows that the religious-ecclesiastical
possibility is inevitable. He knows that a non-ecclesiastical
relation between men and God is no more a reality in this world

than is the innocence of paradise. He wears his cassock (gown) without so much as even a glance at those representatives of 'lay' religion, who are widely supposed to be both better and happier men. But he knows also that the venturesome under-takings of ecclesiastical religion are an impossibility. He knows that they must come to grief, because they are as such unattain-able. He sees the inadequacy of the Church growing apace, not because of its weakness and lack of influence, not because it is out of touch with the world; but, on the contrary, because of the pluck and force of its wholly utilitarian and hedonistic illu-sions, because of its very great success, and because of the skill with which it trims its sails to the changing fashions of the world. He recognizes that, precisely when the Church attains the goal of service rendered by men to men, the purpose of God has been obscured, and judgement knocks at the door. The more the Church is the Church, he stands within it, miserable, hesitating, questioning, terrified. But he does stand within the Church, and not outside as a spectator. His possibility is the possibility of the Church, and the Church's impossibility is also his. Its embarrassment is his, and so too is its tribulation. He is one with the solidarity of the Church, because it is the lack of the glory of God which creates fellowship and solidarity among men (iii. 23).

Humanly speaking, there is no limit to this fellowship and solidarity: **I could wish that I myself were accursed from Christ for my brethren's sake, my kinsmen according to the flesh.** Better no grace, no freedom, no Spirit, no expectation of the coming Day, than, possessing freedom and Spirit and expecta-tion, to be an observer, a non-participator, a non-sufferer, an unembarrassed, unmourning, cowardly, separated person. May I not be such an one! How paradoxical it is that Paul quite honestly, without condescension and without any esoteric reser-vation, calls the Pharisees his brethren! Quite seriously he treats them as his *kinsmen according to the flesh*. Fully aware of their lack of knowledge, and because he too shares the same deprivation, he bows himself with them under the pressure of the divine incognito, which is the characteristic mark of the Church. He must occupy this position, though he lose his soul thereby, though he may seem to be untrue to him-self, and though he be exposed to abuse as a dishonest oppor-tunist. And the position is a lost position. Yes, a lost post which must nevertheless remain occupied. All posts which men occupy as men are lost posts. It is this that must be made evident. And, indeed, it is made evident whenever the Gospel

is proclaimed IN the Church, whenever in the solidarity of prophet and priest the impossible becomes possible and the possible
becomes impossible. The prophet proclaims his solidarity with
the priest, because he knows that he too stands face to face with
the question which only God can answer. The solidarity of prophet and priest would be unintelligible were it merely a matter
of finding some new human terminology in which to formulate
the question, if it were merely a matter of propounding new
tasks for the old Church or of founding a new Church to perform
the old tasks. The prophet knows that a 'Settlement' or even
a technical institute is also a 'church'. He knows that human
'sickness' is healed neither by a 'complete change of scenery'
nor by selecting a new medical adviser—but only by God. He
knows that controversy and personal disagreements can never
be wholly avoided, because the reaching of no final conclusions
does in fact expose the ultimate distinction between the Gospel
and the Church. The prophet will indeed undertake from time
to time to warn those who seem to have altogether forgotten
eternity; but he will do this not without a certain grim humour,
for he is aware that his warning is no more than a parable; and
in no case will he imagine that in voicing this warning he is
fashioning some new truth which brings him into personal
opposition to the Church. However much he may be tempted to
dislike the Church and to pour scorn upon it, he will never
entertain the idea of leaving it or of renouncing his orders, for
that would be even less intelligent than if he were to take his own
life. He knows the catastrophe of the Church to be inevitable; and he knows also that there is no friendly lifeboat into
which he can clamber and row clear of the imminent disaster.
He knows that he must remain at his post in the engine-room
or, maybe, on the bridge. The prophet will adopt no particular point of view without the secret intention of abandoning
it as soon as he has gained a merely tactical advantage; for
there is no question but that his point of view will be shown
to be finally inadequate. He will never build up without at
the same time making preparations to demolish what he has
built; and he will always guard against any stability of his
which would militate against the freedom of God. Nothing
will occasion him so great fear as that which threatens to turn
the eternal contrast between the Gospel and the Church into a
contrast between 'us' and 'them', even did 'we' have the right
ever so much on 'our' side. He will make it his business to
open fire on and disperse all such tumultuous assemblies. And
after each violent attack has been launched upon the Church he

will return to the place where the man of the world—especially
the religious-ecclesiastical man is—*accursed from Christ*, in order
that he may hope for salvation by the grace of God only.
Nothing but the honour of God can make any sense whatever
of anti-clerical propaganda. Attacks on the Church which proceed upon the assumption that its enemies possess some superior
knowledge or some superior method of justifying and saving
themselves are—non-sense. Consequently, when the prophet
raises his voice to preserve the memory of eternity in himself
and in the Church, he will always prefer to take up his position
in hell with the Church—and this is applicable to the study
of Theology—rather than to exalt himself with the pietists—
whether they be crude or refined, old-fashioned or modernist, is
irrelevant—into a heaven which does not exist. He that hath
ears to hear, let him hear: Christ is where men are disconsolate,
knowing that they have been banished from His presence.
Christ is not, and can never be, where men think they have
insured themselves against the anguish of this knowledge.

Or are we taking the Church too seriously, paying it too much
honour, and reckoning it to be too important, when we find
manifested in it the eternal opposition of God and man, when
we deny outright any finite distinction between it and 'us', and
when, in pointing to its destiny, we proclaim our solidarity
with it? Why should we not end with the eighth chapter of
the Epistle to the Romans and abandon as trivial all serious
consideration of the Church? Why should we not treat the
Church simply as presenting an interesting historical problem,
a problem, however, which is, in the end, unimportant? This is
impossible, because it is the Church which causes us to be disturbed, because the problem, to which Rom. iii–viii provides
the answer, is precisely the fact of Israel, the fact of the
Church. The Church is that visibility which forces invisibility
upon our notice, that humanity which directs our attention
towards God. To suppose that a direct road leads from art,
or morals, or science, or even from religion, to God is sentimental, liberal self-deception. Such roads lead directly to the
Church, to Churches, and to all kinds of religious communities—of this the experiences of so-called 'religious' socialism
provide an instructive illustration. Only when the end of the
blind alley of ecclesiastical humanity has been reached is it
possible to raise radically and seriously the problem of God.
All that occurs up to this point is harmless illusion. We require
real ammunition when we discover that we can neither walk
round the Church nor make our way through it. And this

discovery is made when he who proclaims the Gospel—and who does not wish to do this?—recognizes Churchmen—and who does not come under this category?—as *brethren* to whom he has nothing 'new' to offer.

Who are Israelites ; whose is the adoption, and the glory, and the covenants, and the giving of the law, and the service of God, and the promises ; whose are the fathers ; of whom is Christ concerning the flesh. This is not said because Paul is 'overwhelmed with grateful awe' (Jülicher). It is, rather, a quite sober statement that Paul is making when he asserts that the other Pharisees know and say and represent and possess all that he knows and says and represents and possesses of the Gospel. Nothing that MEN can say or know of the Gospel is 'new'; for everything which they possess is identical with what Israel possessed of old. Historically, and when it is treated as the negation of divine revelation, the NEW Testament seems to be no more than a clearly drawn, carefully distilled epitome of the OLD Testament. What is there in Primitive Christianity which has not its clear parallel in later Judaism? What does Paul know which the Baptist did not? And what did the Baptist know which Isaiah did not? Those who proclaim the Gospel are compelled to acknowledge again and again that there is nothing new under the sun; that, humanly speaking, everything relevant has been said and heard already; and that at humanity's highest eminence there is always erected a Church of some kind or other, as a living witness in history that men have exhausted every human possibility. Similarly, there is no great truth which the Church has not crystallized into an institution, a doctrine, a 'way', or a symbol, and by so doing rendered it more or less accessible to the generality of men. From simple straightforward morality to the deepest mystical experience, from individual conversion to an extensive cosmic eschatology, from reverent and intensely sympathetic representations of the human personality of Jesus to the most narrow-edged and dynamic concentration upon the thought of God, from a blood-and-thunder theology to a most precise and detailed instruction as to what men ought-to-do-now, from refined and well-intentioned proposals for a reform of the liturgy to the crudest and most Kierkegaardesque preaching of a scandal—all these things have been DONE BEFORE. And we must add that even the patient research of those scholars who are concerned to prove that all these things have been done before—has also been already done! The Gospel can achieve no more than the Church has done and is now doing (Exod. vii. 11). If it is a matter of being Israelites, of possessing the adoption, the glory, the covenants, the fathers, the giving of the law, the service of God, the promises, and the Christ according to the flesh, does not the Church also possess precisely all this? Is anything that we can possess more than the whole fullness of the Old Testament? The banks of the canal are solidly dug and well protected. And if no water flows between its banks, its inhabitants are safe in the assurance that we have no alternative but to construct similar canals. We, no more than they, are competent to control the living water of revelation. We know that, however vigorous our endeavours may be, we can bring forth nothing better than some kind of variation of the age-long work of the Church. However 'new' the undertakings of men may seem to be, they will always be crowned by the spire of a Church. And moreover, the dreadful possibility faces us that men will adopt the same attitude to us as they have always done to the Church. The wise man, therefore, knowing that he cannot progress beyond the Church, humbly recognizing his limitations, and refusing every compromise, embarks upon an ultimate radicalism, as Paul does in Rom. iii–viii. Only so can the axe be laid at the root of the trees.

Whose is God that ruleth all things—blessed for ever, Amen. Israel—the Church—even possesses 'God'. We are bound to lay down this proposition, for it is undeniable. But the very assertion sets a question-mark against ourselves and against the Church. In so far as 'God' is that which we, in the company of all other men, can know and define and worship, the assertion stands. In so far, however, as God is He that *ruleth all things*, there is embedded in the assertion a doubt, nay more, a complaint and an accusation: God does not belong to the Church. The protest of the anti-clerical that the canal is empty is in this context the protest of God Himself. We cannot disregard the objection that our possession of the adoption, the glory, the covenants, the giving of the law, the service of God, the promises, the fathers, the Christ according to the flesh, our possession of 'God', is not an existential possession. When the existential lion roars, who can but fear? The action of God Himself is not a thing which has been DONE BEFORE. The action of God is *new*. In God—as God!—the solidarity between Paul and the Pharisees is broken, and there appear protests and contrasts. Seen from God—as God—the Church is even now already done away. Do ye not hear the *sign*?

THE GOD OF JACOB

IX. 6–13

v. 6a. But I do not sorrow **as though the word of God hath come to nought.**

The Church suffers from many well-known human failings, which are not difficult to discover and expose. Indeed, all through the pages of history they have been shown up again and again, both in the recurrent attacks made upon the Church from outside and in the controversies which have raged within it. And yet, it is unprofitable for us even to speak of these exposures except in the context of the veritable tribulation of the Church —a tribulation lying far deeper than this or that corruption, however corrupt it be, which men suppose they can remove. Were it merely a question of human failings, or of some kind of deterioration, the fiery wrath of Prophets and Apostles and Reformers in setting forth the contrast between the Gospel and the Church would be inexplicable. Why, if that were so, did they not patiently set themselves to introduce reforms? And if that failed, why did they not forthwith erect a new and better Church? Why did both Paul and Luther for so long avoid the construction of a new road? And why did they finally only construct it under compulsion? Why is it only the lesser, over-wrought, hysterical, religious spirits who, when their righteous indignation has run up against clerical opposition, against the worldliness of the Church, against its political and cultural obscurantism, against its religious corruption and lack of progress, and against its feebleness and hypocrisy, have been led, not without a certain complacent self-satisfaction, to lay quick and sudden hands upon this ultima ratio of all true prophecy? Why does all this direct, anti-ecclesiastical behaviour, even when aimed at the Church in the hour of its greatest depravity, turn out to be so vulgar and unconvincing? Why is it also so ineffective and lacking in stability? And why, too, have all those patient movements of reform from the days of Josiah down to our own time failed to achieve any solid success? Why do we meet—standing, as it were, between violent anti-clericalism on the one side and quiet reform on the other—Paul's melancholy acknowledgement of his solidarity with Israel? The answer is obvious: neither Paul nor any one else who is concerned with the proclamation of the radicalism of the Gospel can afford to overlook the truth that, quite apart from the Church's perfections or imperfections, organized religion is at any rate concerned with the relation

between men and God. Now, the veritable anguish of this
human concern with God proceeds from the fact that the Word,
round which all this busy human endeavour revolves, is not a
fortuitous, transient, human word, but the eternal and absolute
Word of God. Should any one think otherwise, should he regard
this unprecedented theme of the Church as a thing among
other things, as a historical-psychological function among other
functions, as a quantity which may be increased or decreased,
as some concrete affair which man or any other creature is
competent to add to or subtract from—then he might, it is true,
join himself to those who complain that—**the word of God hath
come to nought,** and set to work to consider how he may best
repair the breach. He will, in that case, judge some human
deterioration to be responsible for the signs that the Church is
suffering from a chronic disease, and will undertake to restore it
to its former health. Such action is, however, ruled out by the
paradox of the Truth. The Theme of the Church is the Very
Word of God—the Word of Beginning and End, of the Creator
and Redeemer, of Judgement and Righteousness: but the Theme
is proclaimed by human lips and received by human ears. The
Church is the fellowship of MEN who proclaim the Word of God
and hear it. It follows from this situation that, when confronted
by the adequacy of the Word of God, human lips and ears
must display their inadequacy; that, though men are bound to
receive and proclaim the Truth as it is with God, as soon as they
do receive it and do proclaim it it ceases to be the Truth; that,
however true the Theme of the Church may be, as the theme of
the Church it is untrue. This is at once the miracle and the tribulation of the Church, for the Church is condemned by that which
establishes it, and is broken in pieces upon its foundations. Such
is the blessed terribleness of the Theme of the Church; and such is
the Word by which men are related to God: *Let God be found true,
but every man a liar* (iii. 4). And so by its Theme the Church is
divided into the Church of Esau—where no miracle occurs, and
where, consequently, men are exposed as liars, precisely when
they hear and speak about God; and the Church of Jacob—where
miracle is, and where, consequently, the Truth appears above the
deceit of men. The two Churches do not, of course, stand over
against one another as two things. The Church of Esau alone is
observable, knowable and possible. It may be seen at Jerusalem,
or Rome, or Wittenberg, or Geneva. The past and the future
can be comprehended without exception under its name. The
Church of Esau is the realm where failure and corruption may be
found, the place where schisms and reformations occur. But the

Church of Jacob is capable of no less precise definition. It is
the unobservable, unknowable, and impossible Church, capable
neither of expansion nor of contraction; it has neither place nor
name nor history; men neither communicate with it nor are
excommunicated from it. It is simply the free Grace of God, His
Calling and Election; it is Beginning and End. Our speech is of
the Church of Esau, for we can speak of none other. But we
cannot speak of it without recollecting that its theme is the
Church of Jacob. The very life of Esau, questionable as it is,
depends upon Jacob; and he is Esau only because he is not-
Jacob. This being so, all problems concerned with the purification of the Church of Esau from its many corruptions are
altogether secondary; and it is not worth while wasting time in
discussing them, except in relation to the veritable tribulation
of the Church, the tribulation of its virtues, not of its vices. The
disease from which the Church suffers is that God is God, and
that He is the God of Jacob. Only one thing can cause us *great
sorrow and unceasing pain* (ix. 2): and that is the rugged problem
as to whether the theme of the Church does anything more than
disclose the deceitfulness of men. Does it also disclose the Truth
of God? Have we lost the Church of Jacob? Or do we possibly,
in some way or other, actually belong to the impossible, unknown, and invisible Church? Must we merely leave this
problem as a problem and—'await a miracle', as they say who
have no hope? Must we listen for the Gospel, and whisper
stammeringly that the Church of Jacob is established in eternity?
Assuredly not: our duty is to take seriously to heart the known
tribulation of the Church, and to wrestle with God, the God of
Jacob: *I will not let thee go, except thou bless me.*

vv. 6b–9. For not because they are all of the seed of Israel,
are they Israel: **neither, because they are Abraham's seed,
are they all children** of God: **but, In Isaac shall thy seed be
called. That is, it is not the children of the flesh** as such
**that are children of God; but the children of promise are
reckoned** as the **seed** of Abraham and of God. **For this is a
word of promise, According to this season will I come,
and Sarah shall have a son.**

**Not because they are all of the seed of Israel, are they Israel :
neither, because they are Abraham's seed, are they all children.**
The word 'Church' denotes the many-limbed, many-graded
totality of those who, touched by the breath of revelation, call
earnestly upon God, wait for Him, and keep His commandments. All such are *of the seed of Israel.* Now—and this is the

miracle!—if they so hear and speak the Word of God that it veritably is the Word of God, then there is hidden in that historical moment the eternal 'Moment' of revelation, and they are existentially what they are said to be. They are then—and here again is the miracle!—the invisible Church of Jacob, they possess the promise of Abraham (iv. 16), and are the children of God (viii. 16). Is this really possible? Why should it not be so? Why should not all, from the greatest even unto the least, be children of God? Are not the Law and the Prophets signs and witnesses unto them all (iii. 21)? In Christ they are, without exception, all children of God. And, inasmuch as the miracle has taken place; inasmuch as men are what they are by the free grace of God, by His calling and election; inasmuch as they are known by God—they are *in Christ*. But they are not otherwise *in Christ*: for here it is not a question of being *of the seed of Israel*; not at all a question of participating in whatever may be the perfection of the Church of Esau, or of occupying a position on the topmost rung of the ladder of the evolution of religion. The blessed possibility of veritably receiving and pronouncing the Word in which men have trusted proceeds from God and from Him alone. If such, then, be the relation of the Church to its Theme, must we not admit that the situation is one of tribulation, and that this deep-seated sorrow underlies all the merely external tribulations of the Church? All our many endeavours to uphold the present state of affairs, or to undertake their reformation, or to inaugurate a new order altogether, are rendered fruitless by our failure to recognize this simple fact.

In Isaac shall thy seed be called (Gen. xxi. 12). **That is, it is not the children of the flesh as such that are children of God ; but the children of promise are reckoned as the seed.** The totality of those who are of the *seed of Israel*, the type—they are not more than this—of all who lift up hands to God in prayer, stand, then, under the KRISIS of the twofold nature of the Church: or, putting it another way, they are under a 'Double Predestination'. All are confronted by the eternal two-sided possibility, which moves and rests in God alone. As *the seed of Israel*, they are elected or rejected; as *children of the flesh*, they inhabit the House of God or are strangers to it ; with the Word of God ringing in their ears or on their lips, they belong to the Church of Jacob or to the Church of Esau. In Christ the KRISIS breaks forth. In Him is encountered that by which men are finally established, inasmuch as the roots of their being are lit up, as by a flash of lightning, at the eternal 'Moment' of revelation; for, since men are what they are not, the roots of their existence are deeply buried in the unity of God.—But in Christ is encountered also utter desolation, inasmuch as, at that same 'Moment', men recognize that they are and were and will be established only in God, in the One whom they are not. Peculiar, incomprehensible, inexplicable, established neither by history nor by some inner capacity, are they who not only bear the name of 'Abraham's seed', but also are what is designated by that name. They are not of their own establishment, for they are established by God—children of promise, as Isaac was. They are what they are, not by virtue of their excellent gifts, not on account of their achievements as *children of the flesh*, not because of any describable thing—even the most refined and the most spiritual—which is, or shall be, in this world; but, when their whole peculiarity is dissolved and rendered questionable, they are what they are by virtue of the power of God's new *reckoning* with men (iii. 28, iv. 3, vi. 11, viii. 18), and in the light of the Futurum aeternum. There is no other means by which men are what they are not. When the Church is again and again thrown back by its own theme upon what it is not; when it is repeatedly compelled to attack and to surrender, and offer up itself and all that it is; when this is its one and only task—is it not in tribulation? And yet the Church seeks to live: it struggles to preserve its life by turning its back on its veritable tribulation, by engaging in a tenacious defence of its traditions and customs, by attempting to galvanize itself into life or by setting out to erect new religious societies. This unwillingness-to-die is the real tragedy of the Church.

For this is a word of promise, According to this season will I come, and Sarah shall have a son (Gen. xviii. 10). The eruption of the triumphant Truth of God Himself into the reality of this world is the fulfilment of the promise of God to men. The promise of God is comprehended in everything that points to the Truth, that is to say, to miracle, to the Spirit, to impossibility, and to redemption. Men encounter the possibility of election only in the form of a promise. Adventurous belief is required of them. They possess no guarantee or earnest, save the earnest of the Spirit and of faith, which is itself the hazard. Isaac means 'Laughter'. At what, then, do men laugh? And why? Laughter is scepticism with regard to the impossible possibility and enthusiasm for the possible impossibility. Nor is it as difficult to pass from the one to the other as those who are ignorant alike of true scepticism and of true enthusiasm generally suppose. The Church ought not to conceal from men the fact that its theme thrusts them out on to a narrow, rocky edge; for this is the Church's aim and purpose. Direct fulfilment in the Church of the promise of God is the denial and loss of His veritable promise—*Hope that is seen is not hope* (viii. 24). The direct presence of the Truth is therefore its veritable absence. When the Church dares to hear the Word of God with human ears and to utter it with human lips, it lives by promise: and by this promise all that is human must die, in order that it may live unto God. Clearly, therefore, it is precisely the Church which ought not to shun this death, since by its death it veritably lives of the promise, lives in the reflection of the eternal 'Coming' fulfilment, which lies beyond life and death. Whenever the Church sets itself forth as 'alive' and triumphant—it hath a name that it liveth, but lo, it is dead. That the Church, in common with everything human, is compelled towards fulfilment in this world; that it should long to live triumphantly; whereas, in fact, it lives only of promise and must decrease in order that He may increase—this, we repeat, is the tribulation of the Church which cannot be taken too seriously. The ground of the tribulation of the Church is the ground of the hope of the Church. Failing to recognize its tribulation, it is vacant of hope: refusing to believe without sight, without faith, it sees only what men can see.

vv. 10–13. And not only so: but Rebecca also having conceived by one, even by our father Isaac: for when **the** twins were **not yet born,** and had therefore **not done anything good or bad, it was said unto her—that the purpose of God according to election might stand,** and that the issue might be decided, **not by works, but by him that calleth—the elder shall serve the younger. Even as it is written** concerning this decision, **Jacob I loved, but Esau I hated.**

There were, then, within the seed of Abraham two unborn twin sons, the children of one man and of one woman. The rending asunder of the Church by its theme is made even more evident by what had already been said of these two children— **The elder shall serve the younger** (Gen. xxv. 23). Who, but God only, could approve of one and disapprove of the other, whilst they were still hidden and humanly indistinguishable in the womb of their mother—itself a reminder to us of the ultimate invisibility of God. Why Jacob and not Esau? Neither had any pre-eminence over the other: both were legitimate sons of Isaac: both were grandsons of Abraham: neither had done—**anything good or bad.** And yet, though begotten and conceived together, though hitherto inseparable, vertically between them descends the inexorable critical line. Here election, there rejection; here the Church of God, there the Church of men; here the Truth as judgement, there as righteousness. Why! Oh! why? We repeat this question again and again.

The answer:—**that the purpose of God according to election might stand, and that the issue might be decided, not by works, but by him that calleth.** Since God is God, when once the seed of Abraham has entered into relationship with Him, He continually makes Himself known as God, by electing and rejecting, by building up and pulling down, by making alive and putting to death. How otherwise could He, the Lord of life and death, manifest Himself to men whose minds burrow ever deeper and deeper into the concrete things of this world? How otherwise could He reveal to us that He is neither bound to any independent, relative, human peculiarity, nor bounded by any second, other, contrasted thing? How otherwise could we recognize the theme of the Church, if it—yes, the Church primarily—were not brought continually under KRISIS? The seed of Abraham ought to have no other desire, but that, in its oppression, *the purpose of God according to election might stand*, and that His righteousness should be upheld in its vast freedom. The joy of the elect and the remorse of the rejected combine together in raising the hymn of His praise. The inevitable doctrine of eternal 'Double Predestination' is not the quantitative limitation of God's action, but its qualitative definition (Kühl). The doctrine does not mean that a certain human being or having or doing is as such approved and some other human behaviour is as such rejected; nor that, whereas some are able to comfort themselves in the temporal enjoyment of eternal election, others are in possession of a temporal knowledge of their eternal rejection. Indeed the doctrine of predestination expressly rules this out, by concentrating attention upon the eternal foreordination of temporal men, by reminding them of the decision of *him that calleth*, and by insisting that God is veritably God. No doubt, the contrast between election and rejection is paradoxical and therefore open to grave misunderstanding. We must assuredly take great care how we sing the praises of the 'things upon which WE stand'. The seed of Abraham and the Church desire to praise God. But 'He comes to thine aid for His own sake, and not for thine' (Schlatter). Should He aid thee for any other reason, He aids thee not at all, and thy assistance is not from God. In accomplishing His work, He wrests our things—in so far as they are ours—out of our hands. His is miracle or absence of miracle. His is the establishing of Israel as His Israel; His also is the rejection of everything that bears

IX. 11-13 THE GOD OF JACOB 347

only the name of Israel. He it is that lighteneth the people that do Him service; and He it is that covereth with darkness those others who only think they do Him service. He gives the inheritance to His children and disinherits those who are strangers to Him. He blesses with His presence those whom He has called, and He punishes with His absence those whom He has not called. He makes those who are humanly first to be His last and those who are humanly last to be His first—for He is God, the Unknown, and His is the Kingdom, the Power, and the Glory.

Jacob I loved, but Esau I hated. This (Mal. i. 2, 3)—we again repeat it—is descriptive of the behaviour of God and of the quality of His action. Only as free, regal, sovereign, unbounded and incomprehensible, can we comprehend God and do Him honour. Only because He elects and rejects, loves and hates, makes alive and puts to death, can He be apprehended and worshipped by men of this world. The paradox that eternity becomes time, and yet not time, is the tribulation of the Church and the revelation of God. He makes Himself known in the parable and riddle of the beloved Jacob and the hated Esau, that is to say, in the secret of eternal, twofold predestination. Now, this secret concerns not this or that man, but all men. By it men are not divided, but united. In its presence they all stand on one line—for Jacob is always Esau also, and in the eternal 'Moment' of revelation Esau is also Jacob. When the Reformers applied the doctrine of election and rejection (Predestination) to the psychological unity of this or that individual, and when they referred quantitatively to the 'elect' and the 'damned', they were, as we can now see, speaking mythologically. Paul did not think either quantitatively or psychologically, nor could he have done so, since his emphasis is set altogether upon God's concern with the individual, and not upon the individual's concern with God. And how indeed can the temporal, observable, psychologically visible individual be at all capable of eternal election or rejection? The individual is not more than the stage upon which election and rejection take place in the freedom of men, that is to say, in the freedom of the individual who rests in God and is moved by Him—the stage can surely bear no further weight! We know already what this duality in God means. We know that it involves no equilibrium, but that it is the eternal victory of election over rejection, of love over hate, of life over death. But this victory is hidden from us in every moment of time. We cannot escape the duality, since the visible Jacob is for us Esau, and we can only conceive of Jacob as the unobservable Esau. Thus it is that the Church, as we observe it, is confronted only by the possibility of rejection —which is in God eternally overcome. The election of the Church stands only by faith. The truth of the Word of God, which the Church receives and proclaims, has its existence only in the Spirit. The promise, which has been fulfilled already, belongs to the Church only in hope. And Faith, the Spirit, and Hope, belong to God, and are His only. The Church, which desires to be the Church of Jacob, goes therefore on its way in perpetual fear of Esau. Having, with uneasy conscience, done all it can to be reconciled to its angry brother, it must finally and inevitably wrestle with God *until the day breaketh* (Gen. xxxii. 24). Such is the great tribulation of the Church, a tribulation which we cannot prize too highly: and, compared with it, all other troubles are mere child's-play.

THE GOD OF ESAU

IX. 14–29

vv. 14–18. What shall we say then? Is there unrighteousness with God? God forbid. For he saith to Moses, I will have mercy on whom I have mercy, and I will have compassion on whom I have compassion. So then it does **not** depend upon the man **that willeth, nor** upon the man **that runneth, but** upon **God that sheweth mercy. For the scripture saith unto Pharaoh, For this very purpose did I raise thee up, that I might shew in thee my power, and that my name might be declared throughout all the earth. So then he hath mercy on whom he will, and whom he will he hardeneth.**

Is there unrighteousness with God?—*Jacob I loved, but Esau I hated.* This is a terrible truth: and it is no less terrible because it is here set forth without a trace of any psychological explanation. Who is the God that speaketh thus? How dreadful to fall into the hands of One who can prepare such tribulation for His own people! Who is this God, that is so completely God as to do miracles? Who is He, who cannot be known and apprehended as God, except in the miracle of revelation and by the transformation from rejection to election? Who is He, who, whilst always making Himself accessible, yet, for that reason, always demands that men should search Him out; who, though eternally the God of Jacob, is yet, for that reason, always the God of Esau; who is so completely the God of truth that no man can ever be

'assured' of Him? In pondering this, who can but shudder?
Est enim predestinatio Dei labyrinthus, unde hominis
ingenium nullo modo se explicare queat (Calvin). No
Church worthy of its name can refuse to think thus of God; and
yet every Church which does so think is pierced through to the
heart. If this be the true God, our pyramid is set upon its apex;
for thereby all our religious and moral ideas are thrown about
headlong, like trees and houses in a futurist painting. We can
understand only too well the many hasty protests against the
doctrine of predestination which have been made by religion and
by the Church in the interests of threatened humanity. Is it not
inevitable that from the highest pinnacle of human faith there
should ring out the mad, questioning cry (iii. 5):—'Is not such a
God unrighteous?' Yes, is He not indeed a capricious, spiteful
demon, seeking to make fools of us all? Does He not rebel against
the law of righteousness, which He ought to obey? Can anything
be so revolting to us as the majestic secrecy of one who is incomprehensible, unapproachable, inaccessible, self-sufficient, and
completely free? Must we not, all of us, cry out instinctively that
such an one cannot and must not be God? We must, at any
rate, own that, so long as the Church fails to recognize how
menacing is the possibility of these questions and complaints
and accusations, it neither understands its own tribulation nor
apprehends the transformation of its misery. For precisely in
the possibility of such questioning there is exposed the utter
inadequacy of every notion which men have of God and of
everything which they can do for Him. There is no knowledge of
God, no consolation, and no hope, apart from the catastrophe
to which this possibility directs our attention. God would not
be God, were He not liable to such accusations. The characteristic mark of the Gospel of Christ both in the Old Testament
and in the New is that, contrasted with easier and more acceptable gospels, it always evokes contradiction. Wherever men are
serious, the scandal of predestination must be set forth and
received—and then it is that the God of Esau speaks. Nietzsche,
when he wildly and passionately rejected God, seems to have seen
the issue far more clearly than the thoughtless 'direct' believers
who condemned him. The words stand then: *Jacob I loved,
but Esau I hated.* 'This and other passages—as, for example,
where the pillar of cloud came between the camp of the
Egyptians and the camp of Israel, and was darkness to the
former but light to the latter—are two-sided. To the believers
who trust in the love of God, they have a tender and delightful
meaning: to those, however, who prefer to confide in their own

works, they appear as a dark cloud. The more a man finds these texts to be harsh, the more is he wedded to his own righteousness. Inasmuch, however, as he is able to live quietly with them, his heart rests altogether in grace' (Steinhofer).—**God forbid** that we should accept such an antithesis, however plausible it may seem, and however true may be the perception which lies behind it. Such a separation of men can only be allowed to appear, if it be at once broken down, and if by its immediate disappearance God be manifested as He is. For God is the God of Esau, BECAUSE He is the God of Jacob. He is the creator of tribulation, BECAUSE He is the bringer of help. He rejects, IN ORDER THAT He may elect. We must not avoid the KRISIS or vacate the two-sided pillar of cloud of its scandal. And so we come to speak of the endurance which is necessary in this KRISIS.

I will have mercy on whom I have mercy, and I will have compassion on whom I have compassion. So then it does not depend upon the man that willeth, nor upon the man that runneth, but upon God that sheweth mercy. Is God *unrighteous*? No; but He has His own standard! The righteousness of God is eternal! The love of God is infinite, and not finite! What does this mean? According to human conceptions such a God can be described only as a 'Despot', and men are bound to rebel against His tyranny. But He whom men would not naturally wish to name 'God' is, nevertheless, God. Through the knowledge of God which is in Christ, He whom men name 'Despot' (Luke ii. 29, Acts iv. 24, &c.), is known and loved as the eternal, loving Father. The God of Esau is known to be the God of Jacob. There is no road to the knowledge of God which does not run along the precipitous edge of this contradiction. If we conceive of God as conformed to our human ideas, as one cause in a series, as one factor among other factors, He is not the Cause, the Absolute, the Eternal, Personal God—but rather the 'No-God'. And even this 'No-God' is the parable and image whereby we are led inexorably to the point where the contradiction occurs. For the 'No-God' points beyond himself, and is himself dissolved to the honour of the true and only God. The will of God is not some good thing, operating independently, to which God is subject. His will is rather the source and sanction of all good, and it is good only because it is what He wills:—Deo satis superque est sua unius auctoritas, ut nullius patrocinio indigeat. Therefore—Faciam quod facturus sum. And: haec Deo libertas eripitur, ubi externis causis alligatur ejus electio (Calvin). What is it, then, which fashions Moses into Moses, so that he becomes the bearer and the herald of the divine Covenant of grace and of the Gospel of salvation? *Wherein now shall it be known that I have found grace in thy sight, I and thy people, if it be not that thou goest with me?* Answer:—*I will make all my glory to pass before thee, and will proclaim my name, Lord, before thee, and I will have mercy on whom I have mercy, and have compassion on whom I have compassion.* And we must not forget how the passage continues:—*Thou canst not see my face ; for no man shall see me and live* (Exod. xxxiii. 16–20, LXX). Thus it is that Moses becomes Moses. The righteousness of God is His righteousness: in no sense is it the righteousness of the man that *willeth* or *runneth*. To the man of this world nothing is given which belongs to him independently. What God gives, He gives of His mercy and compassion. And His mercy and compassion are genuine and powerful. They must be honoured as the ground of our hope, simply because they are altogether His: that is to say, they are free and unconditioned, resting and moving in themselves. Aware that its hope lies in its tribulation, the Church should know no other God, but Him who is seen, directly and in linear fashion, only as the God of Esau; but who, nevertheless, in the absolute miracle, reveals Himself to be the God of Jacob.

For this very purpose did I raise thee up, that I might shew in thee my power, and that my name might be declared throughout all the earth. So then he hath mercy on whom he will, and whom he will he hardeneth. Again we ask the question, 'Is God unrighteous?' and again we answer, 'No'. Since we cannot measure His action by our behaviour or by our expectations, we must abide humbly by the recognition that His procedure is altogether beyond our powers of observation. But how do we arrive at this perception? We attain it when we apprehend that we should never have formulated that insane and hopeless question, we should never have been in a position to protest against the visibility of the God of Esau, never have been in a position to cry for help and to look for the revelation of the God of Jacob, had the primal light of Creator and Redeemer not shone forth victoriously beyond what we are now able to observe of God. The very fact that we do protest against our direct, but undeniable, rejection, reminds us of the proper, but to us indirect and unobservable, justice, in accordance with which God directs His action. Though the command be laid upon us to worship Him as the visible God of Esau, to honour Him when He brings us into tribulation and when He rejects us, to lay hold on the hand which strikes us—yet we obey, because this harsh God is much more than harsh. He is, in fact, the wholly different God

of Jacob, who helps us and elects us. How could we apprehend
the God of Jacob, save when we bow before the God of Esau?
How can we comprehend election, save as the transformation of
our rejection? Even Moses could see God only when he took
up his position—in the cleft of the rock: and then he only saw
Him from behind, as He passed by (Exod. xxxiii. 21-3). To see
Him otherwise would involve our death. What the triumphing
Church names 'God' has never been veritably God. The Church is
related to the living God only when it is in tribulation, when it
recognizes that it is in tribulation, when it knows that, in the
whole expanse of its historical manifestation, it is rejected by
God, and when it, nevertheless, holds on firmly, pronouncing
this terrible God to be God, but to be also much more and vastly
different from this—to be, in fact, the God who can and will elect.
Moses, it is true, was *raised up* in his invisible office to be the
man of God; but so also was Pharaoh, when he acted as the visible
opponent of Moses. In predestinating Pharaoh to hardening,
God pays no attention to his human qualifications. Moses has
no human pre-eminence over Pharaoh. Both stand humanly
under the harshness of God; and from this point of view Moses
and Pharaoh are interchangeable. We can far more easily understand the figure Esau-Pharaoh than we can that of Jacob-Moses,
for when we speak of Moses, the elect, we do not refer to the
observable Moses whom the observable Pharaoh opposed, whose
human failings, lack of success, and melancholy end lack something of the tragic dignity of Pharaoh's hard and steady opposition. When we contrast Moses and Pharaoh, we are not concerned
with some nice differentiation of soul, or with the distinction between two 'personalities' but with the unobservable paradox
of election and rejection. Strictly speaking: ineffabile est
individuum. The widespread notion that there dwell in the
human breast two—why not three or more?—souls, leads us
nowhere. We are concerned with that quality which lies beyond
psychological description, and which cannot therefore be treated
as a quality belonging to this or to that psychological subject.
Our definition of the man Moses as elected and of the man
Pharaoh as rejected is repellent, meaningless, and utterly incapable of proof. The election of the one and the rejection of
the other have meaning only in the freedom of God and by the
miracle of revelation, and the very purpose of the occurrence
is—to show in thee My power, and that My Name may be declared throughout all the earth (Exod. ix. 16). The purpose of
the rejection of Pharaoh could be, and in fact is, identical with
that of the election of Moses. Both are servants, not masters:

servants of the will of God. The one manifests the 'Yes' of God,
the other His 'No'; the one His mercy, the other His hardening;
both, the good and the bad, are made use of to maintain and
expose the invisible glory of God. The man that is *hardened* is the
visible man, who, because of his ultimate separation from God,
neither knows nor practises repentance. But who among us either
knows or practises repentance? This is our hardening. The man
to whom God shows mercy is the invisible man, the man who is
miraculously united with God, the new-born man whose repentance is God's work. And who is excluded from the sphere
of this divine operation? Such is the mercy under which we
stand. In our present condition, how could God speak to us,
save in the ruthless disclosure of this contrast? And in what
could this vast contrast be grounded, except in the one God in
whom is hidden also its dissolution? It is God that willeth, God
that showeth mercy, God that hardeneth; and this God is the
tribulation of the Church. The work of the Church is the work
of men. It can never be God's work. Even the Church's adoration is in the end a human work. If the Church desires to be
altogether Moses—and what Church or conventicle does not so
desire?—then it must recognize and ponder the fact that it is
Pharaoh, the Church of Esau. By this recognition and by this
pondering room is made for the absolute miracle; and when the
Church bows before this miracle, it can be Moses, the Church
of Jacob.

An Episode.

**vv. 19–21. Thou wilt say then unto me, Why doth he
still find fault ? For who hath resisted his will? Nay
but, O man, who art thou that repliest against God ? Shall
the thing formed say to him that formed it, Why didst
thou make me thus ? Or hath not the potter a right over
the clay, from the same lump to make one part a vessel
unto honour, and another unto dishonour ?**

Why doth he still find fault? For who hath resisted his will?
This is no new objection (iii. 8; vi. 1, 15). Human action neither
assists the victory of God nor hinders it. It must follow, then,
from His freedom and sole-dominion, that men are irresponsible,
and, from His overcoming of sin by grace, that men are free to do
both good and evil. Yes, when men undertake seriously to consider the thought of God, this deduction does follow inevitably.
But, the deduction once made, we must tremble with fear, for
we are close to the Burning Bush, we are nigh unto God. The

Church ought not to be prevented by its responsibility for human
conduct from pondering seriously over this conclusion; it ought
not to be dissuaded by fear lest those who dare to reckon with it
may find themselves within the domain of crime and immorality,
of insanity and suicide, or by the dread lest the Church's responsibility for the moral stability of society may thereby be jeo-
pardized. The appalling disturbances which can occur on the
frontier where the Gospel is proclaimed, and which indeed have
actually occurred on the loftiest summits which run along that
frontier, do not constitute an argument against the Truth, but
against men who are unable to bear the Truth—not, of course,
merely against particular individuals, but against all men. It is
by no means irrelevant that certain particular men—as, for
example, Nietzsche—should, just because of their strength or
their weakness, demonstrate in their body and in their general
view of life, that the Truth is intolerable. For such disturbances
show that, when mankind and the world approach the ordering
of God too nearly, they are thrown out of gear. The conclusion of Dostoevsky's 'Idiot', the end of men like Hölderlin
and Nietzsche, the inevitable catastrophes in the history of the
'Baptists'—Muck-Lamberty![1]—make it only too clear that, in
spite of its supposed richness and healthiness and righteousness,
humanity has no alternative but death when confronted by the
Truth. These catastrophes serve as significant parables to those
who, perhaps not to their credit, are spared so great temptations,
and therefore escape so great a fall. The sufferings of such men
do, at any rate, make clear how grievous is the sickness which
men suffer at God's hands. It is not fitting that we should refuse
to think the thought of God because of the objections which may
be brought against it, or because the symptoms of the sickness
terrify us. We do all suffer from the sickness, and the most
terrible aberrations and disasters which befall the few or the
many are after all no more than symptoms. We engage with
safety in active love of men only when it is the love of God; and
love of God will not permit us for fear of men, or because of our
anxiety on their behalf, to silence the fear which we owe to Him.
And so we think we understand the danger which threatens us
at the point where the objection arises: *Why doth he still find
fault?* The danger lies in the possibility of our speaking of the
freedom and power and grace of God in such a way that, instead

[1] The allusion is to a scandal which took place on the frontier of religion
and the Youth Movement in the immediately post-war period in Germany.
The episode is now forgotten, and the allusion is therefore best left in its
obscurity. [Tr.]

of leading men to apprehend His will, we encourage them to
discard all sense of responsibility. For this reason it is impossible
for us comfortably to repose in the thought of the sacrifice demanded of us by the indirect road of the Truth. Rather, we are
compelled to abandon directness and unbrokenness at all points,
and precisely when we most earnestly undertake to think the
thought of God. We must maintain quite firmly that the objection against God is untruth and must be rejected. Once again,
therefore, we proceed to reject it (iii. 5, 6, vi. 1, 2, 15, 16).

Nay but, O man, who art thou that repliest against God? All
that must be said about the objection is comprehended in the
words—*O man*. The objector overlooks the infinite qualitative
distinction between God and man. He proceeds as though God
and man were two things. He speaks of men as though they
were God's partners, junior partners perhaps, but nevertheless
competent to conduct an argument with Him.   Regarding
human conduct as an operation of which the will of God is the
efficient cause, he sets both within a single chain of causality
in such a manner that human conduct confronts the will of God
as a second thing. But this is preposterous. Human conduct is
related to the will of God neither as cause nor as effect. Between
human responsibility and the freedom of God there is no direct
observable relation, but only the indirect, underivable, un-
executable relation between time and eternity, between the
creature and the Creator. The freedom of God confronts men
neither as a mechanism imposed upon them from outside nor as
their own active and creative life (see the 1st edition of this
book!). The freedom of God is the pure and primal Origin of
men: the Light, the presence or absence of which renders
their eyes brightness or darkness—the Infinite, by the twofold
measurement of which they are great or little—the Decision, by
which they stand or fall. Men are competent by their action
neither to increase nor to decrease, neither to assist nor to
obstruct, God's freedom. In fact, so little is their action relevant
that it is precisely the indirectness of the relation between their
freedom and God's freedom that establishes and sanctions the
relative necessity, the relative seriousness, the relative ordering,
of their freedom. And so it is precisely the knowledge of God's
freedom and power and grace which does NOT throw men wholly
out of gear, because such knowledge is indissolubly one with the
knowledge that they are men and not God. It is precisely the
man who respects God as God who will have no occasion to
object, for he will neither fear nor desire the dissolution of his
responsibility: such a man will become NOT insane, NOT immoral,

NOT a criminal, NOT a suicide. And should he, in spite of this, become one of these, he certainly will not make of it a 'sacrament' (Blüher),[1] but rather, like the murderer Raskolnikoff in Dostoevsky's novel,[2] will take it as a warning monument to the possibility of a final misunderstanding of the command that men should fear and love God above all things. The catastrophes of religion warn us how strange to men is the honouring of God, how incapable we are of watching but one hour with Christ, how difficult we find it to support the paradox of life without attempting to satisfy our need for an equilibrium by falling into some kind of Titanism! But when it is recognized that God is the tribulation of His people, it will at once become evident that, whether moral or immoral, men are blameworthy and opposed to the will of God (ix. 19); that they can achieve no equilibrium; and that neither moral uprightness nor immoral depravity provides them with an opportunity of arguing with God, of justifying themselves before Him, and so of escaping the tribulation. If, on the other hand, the tribulation be accepted, men will discover that their relative sense of responsibility is thereby guaranteed —'These things have not been said in order that we might by our lethargy checkmate the Holy Spirit, who hath given us a spark of His brightness, but in order that we might perceive that what we have comes from Him, and in order that we may learn to hope in Him, to surrender ourselves to Him, and to pursue our salvation with fear and trembling' (Calvin).

Shall the thing formed say to him that formed it, Why didst thou make me thus? Or hath not the potter a right over the clay, from the same lump to make one part a vessel unto honour, and another unto dishonour? Such is the relation between God and man. We introduce at this point the familiar prophetic parable (Isa. xxix. 16, xlv. 9, lxiv. 7; Wisd. of Sol. xv. 7), for it is relevant to the problem we are considering. Men are related to God as the thing formed is related to him that formed it, as clay to the potter. Who now dares to speak of partners or of links in a chain of causality? On the one side stands the purpose-full master, on the other side the material which serves his purpose and becomes his work. No bridge, no continuity, links the potter and the clay, the master and his work. They are incommensurable. The distinction between them is infinite and qualitative; the link which connects them is altogether indirect and unob-

---

[1] Hans Blüher was formerly a leading exponent of the ideals of the German Youth Movement. In his book—*Die Rolle der Erotik in der männlichen Gesellschaft* (1921)—he maintained that suicide is a sacrament. Blüher is now a supporter of the German Nationalist Party. [Tr.]
[2] *Crime and Punishment.* [Tr.]

servable—or so, at least, it is in the parable. 'Here' is confronted
by 'There'. And this situation remains, when we have said all
that can be said about the state of the material or about the
requirements, skill, temper, and success of the master. The
freedom of the master to propose this or that remains intact,
even when we have investigated the complicated process which
is involved in any kind of creative work, even when we have
explained how it is possible for the same hand to fashion flower-
vases and chamber-pots out of the same material, and how the
master can change from this work to that, and from this purpose
to that. In spite of all observations, which may so easily be
stretched to appear as a chain of causation, there remains the
freedom of the master. And so it is with God and men. God
confronts men as their Primal Origin, not as their immediate
cause. Are men righteous?—It is before Him that they are so.
Are men sinners?—It is against Him that they sin. Are men
alive?—It is in His life that they participate. Do men die?—It
is at His hands. Men are not merely conditioned in the course
of their lives: they are, like everything which does, or can,
condition them—even though it bear the name of 'god'—
created. The parable of the master and his work, the potter and
his clay, is not, of course, adequate to explain what 'creation'
means. But it does point the way to the proper understanding
of it. Men are related to God as a visible and concrete thing
is related to what is invisible and immaterial, as existence is
related to non-existence. Whenever it is possible for us to point to
the existence of human independence or freedom, we are, in fact,
simply deferring the problem of primal origin, of the right and
freedom of God, the problem of beginning and end, creation and
redemption. The thought of predestination is, however, the
final abandonment of this deferring of the problem. Its abandonment is bound to occur when God is known to be God in His
relation to the being and having and doing of men. God must be
apprehended as the God of Jacob and of Esau; otherwise we
shall not understand that, whilst He is, in every moment of
time, the God of Esau, He is in eternity the God of Jacob. How
could the conception of human responsibility—the undermining
of which the objectors either feared or desired (ix. 19)—be more
securely protected, than by the complete relativity (relatedness!)
of men when they are confronted by God?

We now return to the main theme.

**vv. 22, 23. What if God, willing to shew his wrath,
and to make his power known, endured with much**

long-suffering the vessels of wrath fitted to destruction, that he might make known the riches of his glory upon vessels of mercy, which he afore prepared unto glory?

Why is God the God of Esau and of Jacob? Why is He the God of anger and of mercy? We know the question to be childish and formulated in mythological terms. For in God is no 'and', nor any duality. In Him the first is dissolved by the second. He is One. In eternity He is the God of Jacob manifesting Himself to men. But our thought cannot escape from dualism. We know that we are unable to comprehend otherwise than by means of a dialectical dualism, in which one must become two in order that it may be veritably one. So it is that when He manifests Himself to the men of this world as God, He must do so as the angry God who is bound to make His power known. Inexorably He declares that He is not to be confronted with the gods—even with the highest god—whom men are accustomed to worship. And conversely, when men receive His revelation, they cannot do so otherwise than as vessels of wrath, incapable of conceiving of Him or of obeying Him. When men undertake to receive His revelation they either produce a compromise or are forced to the experience that they must die at His hands. Have true men of God, in their human creatureliness, ever acted otherwise or encountered any other experience? Were they not men of God, precisely because they recognized that they were vessels fitted unto destruction; precisely because they saw that no man is as such righteous, that the lives of men are forfeit (Exod. iv. 24–6!), and that the form of this world is passing away? Have we any other ground of hope but the knowledge of our tribulation: the knowledge, that is, that we can hope and be only the obverse of revelation, and that as men we can have intercourse only with the God of Esau?—But, when we have said this, inasmuch as it is God who does reveal Himself to men, He confronts creatureliness with the 'And Yet' of the Creator, the immensity of human sin with the 'And Yet'—remember the *Kapporeth* (iii. 25)!—of His covering forgiveness. As the God that showeth mercy, He stands over against them, making known the riches of His glory, His pre-eminent, infinite, and victorious Truth. He reveals Himself as the Redeemer of men. In so far as men receive the revelation of God they are vessels of mercy. Then it is that the absolute miracle occurs, and that the eyes of men are opened to behold themselves repentant and already new creatures. Then they see the love of God in His harshness, and, loving Him in

return, receive the Gospel of Salvation as the message of joy, in
spite of, nay, because of, the altogether unlimited scandal with
which it confronts them. Men have wrestled with the God of
Esau, and have shown themselves thereby to be Jacob-Israel.
God—who prepared for Jacob, Moses, and Elijah such tribulations that we are unable to deny that, humanly speaking, their
opponents, Esau, Pharaoh, and Ahab, had chosen the better
part—is in eternity the shield of His people and their exceeding
great reward.—But what if the process of the revelation of this
one God moves always from time to eternity, from rejection to
election, from Esau to Jacob, and from Pharaoh to Moses?
What if the existence of—**vessels of wrath**—which we all are
in time!—should declare the divine endurance and forbearance (iii. 26), should be the veil of the long-suffering of God
(ii. 4), behind which the *vessels of mercy*—which we all are in
Eternity!—are not lost, but merely hidden? What if the man
Esau, who is—**fitted to destruction**—to whom also the man
Jacob belongs—endures the wrath of God only in a representative capacity, in order that the road may be prepared for the
man Jacob, who is fitted for glory—to whom also the man
Esau belongs—to enter the righteousness of God, which is
hidden in His wrath and which emerges from it? Crossing and
dissolving the continuous process of history is the terrible and
incomprehensible process of revelation! Terrible and incomprehensible is the true and hidden significance of all existence!
Incomprehensible and beyond all thinking is the emergence
of the righteousness of God, as it passes vertically through all
human righteousness and unrighteousness. What then remains
of our childish question, 'Why should God desire this dualism?',
the question which we have inevitably formulated mythologically, if all this be really true, and if this 'process' of revelation be the will of God for us?

**vv. 24–9. Even us, whom he also called, not from the
Jews only, but also of the Gentiles. As he saith also in
Hosea, I will call them my people, which were not my
people; and her beloved, which was not beloved. And it
shall come to pass, that in the place where it was said
unto them, Ye are not my people; there shall they be
called the sons of the living God. And Isaiah crieth concerning Israel, Though the number of the children of
Israel be as the sand of the sea,** only a remnant shall be
saved. For the Lord will bring upon the earth a curtailing
and a cutting short of his word of promise! **And, as Isaiah**

hath said before, Except the Lord of Sabaoth had left us a seed, we had become as Sodom, and had been made like unto Gomorrah.

We said 'if'. But we do not mean that, for there is no doubt about it. The process of revelation in Christ is decisive. In Time, we are *vessels of wrath*: in Eternity, we are not merely something more, but something utterly different; we are— *vessels of mercy*. Wonderfully saved beyond our whole visible existence, we are they who have been called of God. We are— and here occurs the absolute miracle—the Church of Jacob, the community of the elect. But who are 'we'? Not, of course, this or that collection of people who can be quantitatively defined. Not, of course, a numerus clausus. Indeed, not a numerus at all. Not the historical and describable Israel. It is God who here loves and elects and shows mercy. This means that all the visible distinctions which emerge, and must emerge, among men, are subjected to an invisible dissolution. Only for the Church of Esau are fences necessary to mark off Israel from Edom, Jews from Gentiles, believers from unbelievers. When in the eternal 'Moment' the Church of Jacob dawns in Christ, the fences are broken down, and the Gentile Esau enters the service of God and participates in the divine promise. And with Esau enter the hosts of those who stand outside. Then what is without becomes within, what is afar off becomes nigh at hand, what is not-beloved becomes beloved, and the place of rejection becomes the place of acceptation (Hos. ii. 23, ii. 1). And then it is, when Israel rejoices in its assured security, that Isaiah—**crieth**. He cries out the secret of the 'Double Predestination' with that 'love-lessness' which befits the announcement of the love of God as the Word of judgement and the Word of promise—the two are inseparable in Isa. x. 22, 23. He cries that the Jew is not as such the servant of God. When it is God that loves and elects and shows mercy, who that is within can be certain that he is not without? What promise is not in peril of being automatically curtailed and cut short, in order that it may conform to the truth of Him that made it? What visible body of righteous men is not crumpled up and dissolved into the invisible and incomprehensible—**remnant** and—**seed** of those who are righteous before God? What Jerusalem can escape the possibility that, to-morrow or even to-day, it will become a **Sodom** and a **Gomorrah**—unless it has already been protected by the grace of the God of judgement (Is. i. 9)?

Our familiar Church, the Church of Esau, is therefore set up on the brink, the razor-edge, of the abyss. And this is so, precisely because its goal, its promise, its Sion, is the Church of Jacob; precisely because it is concerned with the living God, and is His people. There is no security, except the security which is in God. All knowledge is uncertain, except our ignorance and God's knowledge. And God is unknown, apart from the knowledge which He Himself—as the Unknown—gives to us in Christ. This is the tribulation of the Church.

The Tenth Chapter

THE GUILT OF THE CHURCH

THE *KRISIS* OF KNOWLEDGE

IX. 30—X. 3

vv. 30–2a. What shall we say then? That the Gentiles, which followed not after righteousness, have attained to righteousness, even the righteousness which comes from the faithfulness of God. **But Israel, which followed after a law of righteousness, did not arrive at that law.** Why not? **Because** their pursuit comes **not** from **faith, but** from **works.**

What shall we say then? Unlike those who are accustomed to make hasty and direct attacks upon the Church, we have been compelled hitherto to speak simply of its tribulation, of that tribulation imposed upon it by the knowledge of God, which is its proper theme, and gift, and task. We have, moreover, spoken of this misery as something from which no man is exempt, whatever his attitude to the Church may be. For it is not a misery from which some men can hold themselves aloof, and then proceed to pity or to blame those who suffer from it; but a misery which all men, as religious men in their relationship to God, are compelled to endure. In the Church humanity becomes conscious of itself and is manifested as religious. And then it suffers, because God is God. Humanity does not suffer from this pain and from that pain, not here and there, not more and less. It suffers, because every concrete and temporal thing is confronted, not, it must be remembered, by some second thing, but by non-existence, by Primal Origin, by the Creator of all things visible and invisible. But how could God prepare such tribulation for men—unless they were guilty? In this connexion we must remember (vii. 7–13) that our creatureliness is a curse only in virtue of our sin. It is not otherwise a curse. When once we comprehend the immensity of the Church's failure, past, present, and future, then we not only ought and can, but must speak of the wrong done by the Church. We should not as yet have penetrated to the heart of its tribulation, were we to omit to denounce it, and to define and name its guilt, its sin, and its wrongness. For a tribulation imposed merely by fate, and therefore admitting of no indictment, would not be a recognizable, burning tribulation. And if, contrariwise, we were to transfer our accusation and direct it against God, we should do no more

than expose once again the failure of our analysis of the situation. We should have failed to perceive that the deep-seated
cause of the tribulation is, in fact, our recognition that we
are the accused party. The fact that we are under accusation
occasions our apprehension of the tribulation. Men cannot comprehend the nature of their tribulation apart from their knowledge of God; and this knowledge is precisely the knowledge that
God is the standard by which they are, and know themselves
to be, judged. This is the real anguish of humanity.—To
put the matter another way. The misery of men is occasioned
by the fact that their knowledge of God is itself embarrassed,
troubled, and under KRISIS, and by their inability to escape from
a sense of guilt and responsibility for this whole situation. For
however true it may be that the tribulation of men is grounded
in the freedom of God, yet it takes place within a context of
human freedom and responsibility. So the knowledge of God
involves not merely that men are suffering from a disease, but
also that they are guilty sinners.

**Gentiles, which followed not after righteousness, have attained
to righteousness, even the righteousness which comes from the
faithfulness of God.** The KRISIS appears here first. We have to
recognize that, side by side with those who have knowledge and
who are saints and children of God, there exist ignorant and
unholy men of the world. However the Church be defined, it is
encompassed by Gentiles and strangers, who do not comprehend,
do not communicate with it, and do not follow after righteousness. This creates—at least for those of delicate sensibility—a
disturbing and, in its quiet eloquence, perhaps an intolerable
situation. How can it be that the Gentiles, when confronted
with the Church, are, and remain, Gentiles? How is that their
response is continued apathy to the Holy Place over which the
Church mounts guard? Is not the Sanctuary seriously affected,
if it remains permanently just the peculiar property of a peculiar
people, and fails to command universal respect? What are we
to say concerning a *Word of God*, when we are compelled to
acknowledge that, uttered by us, it evokes very little opposition
and very little approval among those 'outside'? What are we
to say about the Church, when, threatened, in these tolerant
days, by no external persecution, it continues to live its peculiar
life undisturbed, but without any very great prospects; and
when it finds itself finally in a situation in which it has to search
out for itself within its own borders opportunities of exercising
its spirit of pugnacity; and when it almost begins to long for a
little persecution, in order that this oppressive live-and-let-live

may be brought to an end? Sharper eyes, looking out from the windows of the Church, have, however, seen farther than this. They have seen that the Church cannot defend the peculiarity of its being by accusing the world of sinful hardness of heart, and by launching an offensive against it. The Church can neither prick the world with needles nor assail it with bludgeons. With horror they have perceived what is fully set out in ii. 14–29: *Gentiles, which have not the law, do by nature the things of the law.* The Gentiles do not hunt after righteousness, for they have already laid their hands upon it. They refuse to be taught, because they have already learnt. They have no interest in religion, because long ago God interested Himself in them. They do not give attention to our *Word of God,* because they have heard it long ago apart from us, and have long ago proclaimed it. The unholy and unbelieving children of the world are—in spite of their quite naked misery and in spite, maybe, of their merry freedom—not 'objects' of our preaching and pastoral care, of our evangelistic, missionary, and apologetic activities, of our busy efforts for their salvation; they are not objects of our 'love'—for, long before we appeared upon the scene to have mercy on them, they had been sought and found by the mercy of God, they had entered into His righteousness, shared in His forgiveness, participated in the power of resurrection and obedience; long ago Eternity had struck them with terror and they had set their hope upon it— long ago, in fact, they had been thrown existentially upon God! From the standpoint of human righteousness this possibility can be controverted with much plausible argumentation. Who, for example, would wish to overlook the observable *poverty* of the heathen? But we are concerned here with what is open only to the indirect perception of the eyes of the Saviour. We are concerned here only with the impossible, unheard of, unobservable possibility of God. We are concerned here with the righteousness of God, unconditioned by any corresponding righteousness of men, and with the faithfulness which is His alone. We are concerned with the new creation, and not with the sequence of cause and effect. In short, we are concerned with the Truth of God in Christ Jesus. Though the arguments against the existential salvation of the heathen were never so many and never so unanswerable, how can we wholly repudiate it or make our recognition of it depend upon the emergence of this or that possible and observable human righteousness? How can the Church indeed, which claims God for its God, fail to recognize that God is God? How can it deny that He is the God of the Jews and of the Gentiles (iii. 30)? Does it not sing the praises of

Abraham, Israel's own ancestor, when he was in—uncircumcision (iv. 9)? And yet, suppose it be allowed and granted that
there is also salus extra ecclesiam, that both Esau and Jacob
can be elect, what becomes of the backbone of the Church, what
confidence can it have in its own mission? Does the Roman
Church, in advancing its own well-known claims, do more than
protect the proper interests of every Church? What becomes of
Israel's following after righteousness, of its zeal for God, if it be
granted that the goal has been reached by those 'others' who
take no part in this zealous pursuit? Can the Church fail to
recognize the reproach which is implicit in God's undertaking
to do, alongside of, and apart from, the Church, the work with
which it has been entrusted, and which is the justification of its
very existence? What attitude does the Church adopt to this
reproach?

Were we to see still further, we should say—**Israel, which
followed after a law of righteousness, did not arrive at that law.**
What if the elect Jacob could be also Esau? What if God's
warrior could be just one of the many unsuccessful human
warriors, runners, taskmasters, and orators, unable to succeed,
because men are men? This is a possibility which the Church—
the Church especially—cannot refuse to consider. No doubt
much can be said against this possibility from the standpoint of
human righteousness, particularly if the earnestness and pro-
fundity and success of the Church's activity be taken seriously
into account. But the life of the Church depends upon its
recollection of the qualitative distinction between God and men,
and this is preserved in the law of the Church. The Church must
therefore know that men do not *follow after* the righteousness of
God; that they have no means whereby they can condition or
compel or claim or display or guarantee the presence and reality
of God; that the divine 'Why?' of forgiveness can be answered by
no human, but only by a divine 'Therefore'. Fundamentally the
Church does, in fact, know this. But it must know yet more. It
must know that even it itself cannot *follow after* faith. For faith
is that invisible relation of men—who are not of this world—to
God—whom we do not know: a relationship which exists only
through the faithfulness of God. The Church must therefore
know that nothing is gained by replacing an objective by a
subjective religion, by transforming the service of God into
'pious practices' and righteousness into *a law of righteousness*,
because even so it does not find what it is seeking. The Church
can, of course, pursue religion and busy itself in the human work
of the law. It can cultivate religious experience aesthetically,

ethically, and logically. But it cannot do more than this: for religious experience is not the same thing as faith or righteousness; it is not the presence and reality of God, nor is it the divine 'Answer'. Religious experience is our human and, consequently, our very questionable, relation to God. The law is not itself revelation, but a worldly, limited, negative impress of revelation. The Church can, and presumably should, mount guard over the course down which the sacred stream may flow when the Hour of God be come. But it has no power of compulsion; and it is important that it should not forget its incompetence. This unforgetfulness—this open wound—is the supreme advantage of the Church. Religion is not the Kingdom of God, even if it be the Kingdom-of-God-Religion of Blumhardt's decadent successors. Religion is a human work. Maybe the Church is ignorant that there exists no such *law of—righteousness*, and that it is following after a phantom. In any case, it continually forgets it. In any case, we all, without exception, have the greatest difficulty in remembering it even for a moment. The *law of righteousness* which is the reality of the phantom, which is pursued by every Church and by every conventicle, is the *law of faith* by which all boasting is excluded (iii. 27). When the Church speaks of faith, however, it means notoriously a profitable 'something', which men of the world can 'have', and which this or that man can strive after, attain, and boast about. But how can such a human work be the faith by which men are justified by God? Is not rather such work simply religion decked out with faith as a predicate? And, presenting such a claim, is not the supreme religion a phantom? Can there be a 'supreme' religion, a highest pinnacle of all human work, in the relation between God and men? If such a religion were to be found anywhere, it would be in the 'religion' of the prophets and psalmists of Israel, which is nowhere excelled, certainly not in the history of Christianity, and not even in the so-called 'Religion of Jesus'. But, in fact, a religion adequate to revelation and congruent to the righteousness of God, a law of righteousness, is unattainable by men, except in the miracle of the absolute 'Moment'. And Faith is miracle. Otherwise it is not faith. The word, which enters human ears and is uttered by human lips, is the Word of God—only when the miracle takes place. Otherwise it is just a human word like any other. The Church is the Church of Jacob— only when the miracle occurs. Otherwise it is nothing more than the Church of Esau. But the miracle cannot be striven after, or attained, or boasted about. It is the unexpected, new, divine occurrence among men.

We are tempted to ask—**Why not?** Why should not the miracle of faith, about which the Church speaks, be *followed after*? Why does the object of the Church's pursuit remain always a phantom? **Because their pursuit comes not from faith, but from works.** Men come to faith, only from and through faith. Faith is to fear and love God above all things; to fear and love Him as He is, and not as we think Him to be. Faith is to bow ourselves under the judgement by which the whole relationship of God and man is governed. And to be under judgement means that we cannot comprehend God or follow after Him, for He is and remains for us the altogether Other, the Unknown and the Unapproachable. That *pursuit*, of which we have been speaking, cannot come *from faith*, and therefore cannot attain the faith which is its goal. The *pursuit* of the Church comes *from works*. But *works* bring men into relationship with a god whom they can comprehend, and such a god is not the God who of necessity doeth miracles. *Works* are the behaviour of men, when they do not apprehend the judgement regulating the whole relationship of God and man; or—which amounts to the same thing—when they suppose that there are gaps in the judgement of God. We imagine that we are able to hunt the righteousness of God and faith and miracle through supposed gaps in His judgement. But there are no gaps. And yet the Church can lay hold on faith—but only if it begins with faith in the unknown, living God. It can attain righteousness—but only if, itself under judgement, it bows before the gap-less judgement of God. It need not die—if only it would not so grimly struggle to live. It can hear and proclaim the Word of God—if, without any pretensions of becoming great through the Word, and without any anxiety for the morrow, it would care only for the Truth of the Word. It could be the place of understanding—if only it sought pre-eminently to be a place where the incomprehensible God, before whom no flesh is righteous, is worshipped. If the Church were sufficiently humble to recapture its understanding of the communion of saints as the fellowship of sinners dependent upon forgiveness, and so be rid of that nervous, devastating, vigorous founding of new societies; if it were sufficiently humble to endure patiently the sneers of the rationalists, to fear and love God, and so to outstrip even Kant in the careful preservation of the boundaries of humanity; if it were courageous enough to keep its eyes fixed upon its own theme, to abandon all striving after, attaining, and boasting about, visible goals and successes; if only it would cultivate experience of God by a robust criticism of all mere experience, and religion by a fearless 'relativizing' of all

religion; if only it would bring forth good and pious people—
that most obstinate species of the human genus!—by persistently
and tirelessly confronting them with the hosts of men who have
been justified by God, such as Gentiles, Publicans, Spartacists,
Imperialists, Capitalists, and other unsympathetic persons, as
for example, those who are not devoted to Social Reform; if only
the Church were directed wholly and altogether towards the unknown, living, free God, and would concentrate its preaching
upon the Cross of Christ—then the Church could be, unobservably and in a manner unheard of, the Church of Jacob, the
Church of faith, and the Church of the righteousness of God.
And such indeed the Church has, in fact, always been. But in
order that the Church may be what it is, it must dare to begin
in faith, in the 'darkness' of faith (Luther). And this the Church
has never dared. Its activity proceeds *from works*. It is
orientated to what can be seen of men. Its faith is not at all
what is described in Hebrews xi. The Church does not love the
solitariness of the desert. Even when it speaks expressly of
solitude, it is speaking about something else. Even when it
enters the desert, it rids its solitude of all real terror and its
desertedness of all real danger. The Church does not fast as
those who have not the Bridegroom, but endeavours and is able
to console itself for the vacuity of its history by all manner of
romantic sentimentalities. The Church does not wish to be a
stranger in the world. It does not wait for the City which is
built upon a foundation. It cannot stay itself in the position of
Christianity before the Resurrection, in the Passion of the
rejected Christ. The Church is in great haste; it is hungry and
thirsty for the concrete joys of the marriage-feast. It refuses,
in spite of many defeats, to retire from the lost outposts upon
the main position. It wishes to advance—but whither? At
any rate, in the direction of those who desire to avoid being
bowed down under judgement; at any rate, in the direction of
the things which are definite, observable, comprehensible, direct,
and tangible. Faith, as it appears in Hebrews xi, seems to the
Church too unsympathetic, too loveless, too dangerous, too
unpsychological, too unpractical. The Good News ought to be
altogether direct, 'positive', and, as far as may be, enjoyable.
It ought to be something which would survive as Good News
apart from faith and without God. But if, when the Church is
confronted by the impossible possibility of remaining true—a
loyalty which involves the risk of ruin—to its proper Theme, it
selects rather the possible possibility of making humanity—
religious humanity, of course—its theme, it enters within the

danger-zone and perishes. For men, even religious men, even
those who have reached the highest summit of religion, cannot
avoid the curse that is laid upon their mere createdness. How
should Israel, in so far as he is engaged upon the finite goal of
religion, not be put to shame when confronted with God? How
should he, when once everything comes to depend upon existentiality, not be caught up and surpassed by the first, best
Gentiles, not himself stand with empty hands? How can men
be grateful to the Church, so long as it continues to make con-
cessions to a world which expects from it something quite
different? The Church follows after a phantom, and, engaged
in its pursuit, misses the reality which it could have grasped.
And so the Church suffers, not merely because it is Esau and not
Jacob, but because of its own guilt. And who does not bear this
guilt? Who can rid himself of it? Who has ever set himself
seriously to undertake the task of the Church, knowing it to be
a duty that has been laid upon him, without at the same time
knowing that, in undertaking it, he displays his own guiltiness?
For does not guilt emerge precisely when what is possible with
God is discovered to be impossible with men? Indeed, this is
the one, the only guiltiness of men: a guiltiness which breaks
out as a disease when men dare to hear about God and to
speak of Him, but do NOT dare to give Him the honour that
is His due.

vv. 32b, 33. They stumbled at the stone of stumbling; even as it is written, Behold, I lay in Sion a stone of stumbling and a rock of offence: and only he that believeth on it shall not be put to shame.

This admirable Biblical citation is composed by bringing
together Isa. viii. 14 and xxviii. 16. The stone of stumbling, the
rock of offence, which is, however, at the same time the precious
corner-stone laid in Sion, is—Jesus Christ. In Him God reveals
Himself inexorably as the hidden God who can be apprehended
only indirectly. In Him He conceals Himself utterly, in order
that He may manifest Himself to faith only. In Him He makes
known His infinite love by allowing the miracle of His freedom and of His Kingdom to be proclaimed with penetrating
absence of all ambiguity. He that is of the truth heareth His
voice. And yet, who is *of the truth*? Who sees God as He is?
Who does not advance a thousand excuses for keeping out of
His way? We do not endure the truth. Indeed, were we to
endure it, our endurance would be itself the miracle, and through
it the truth would save us from the misery of our createdness.

If this cannot take place, because we are not open to the miracle of the truth or ready for it, the truth will bring us under judgement without any miracle, simply by its own inner logic, and so, in the full course of their pursuit after the finite goal, which they define as faith, righteousness, love, and God, men must be put to shame. In the midst of Sion, in the midst of this earthly heaven, God has set the fact of His Eternity, and has uttered the truth that He is found by grace and must be sought in Eternity. When this offence and scandal is encountered, only the believer will not be put to shame. He that *follows after* (ix. 31) but does not believe will inevitably gather nothing but empty nuts; he will run like a man who charges up a blind alley. And so there breaks forth the KRISIS of knowledge and the catastrophe of religion. There is no avoiding the shame and nakedness which accompany an impracticable undertaking. The Church of Esau is, and remains, what it is. It must nail Christ, its only hope, to the Cross. There is no alternative: when men do not joyfully accept the divine order, whereby God chooses us and not we Him, they must inevitably overthrow it. However apparent the failings of the Church may be—its superficiality and dullness, its worldliness and its asceticism, its useless humility and its equally useless pride, its misplaced zeal in trivial matters and its equally misplaced and helpless unconcern with the things of existence and non-existence,—these, and many other accusations which may be brought against the Church, would not be sufficient to secure its condemnation, were it not that it stood already condemned by its failure to accept the judgement pronounced over men as men, before ever they have committed this or that offence or failed in this or that particular. Were the Church to appear before men as a Church under judgement; did it know of no other justification save that which is in judgement; did it believe in the stone of stumbling and rock of offence, instead of being offended and scandalized at it; then, with all its failings and offences—and certainly one day purified of some of them—it would be the Church of God. The Church, however, which sings its triumphs and trims and popularizes and modernizes itself, in order to minister to and satisfy every need except the one!; the Church which, in spite of many exposures, is still satisfied with itself, and, like quicksilver, still seeks and finds its own level; such a Church can never succeed, be it never so zealous, never so active in ridding itself of its failings and blemishes. With or without offences, it can never be the Church of God, because it is ignorant of the meaning of repentance.

x. vv. 1–3. Brethren, my heart's desire and my prayer is, that they may be saved. For I bear them witness that they have a zeal for God, but not according to knowledge. For being ignorant of God's righteousness, and seeking to establish their own, they did not subject themselves to the righteousness of God.

My heart's desire and my prayer is, that they may be saved. The description of the Church which we have just given is often blamed as being typical of those who oppose the Church or who, at least, hold themselves aloof from it. But blame such as this does not affect us. When, however, our critics go on to propose that we ought to leave the Church if we think of it thus, we are bound to state that we could not contemplate such a proposal, and would do our best to dissuade others from even considering it. It would never enter our heads to think of leaving the Church. For in describing the Church we are describing ourselves. Before ever we have spoken to others, we have conversed with ourselves, and continue to do so. In fact, we are perhaps more ecclesiastically minded than many who are known as 'good Churchmen':—indeed, Vere verbum Dei, si venit, venit contra sensum et votum nostrum. Non sinit stare sensum nostrum etiam in iis, quae sunt sanctissima, sed destruit ac cradicat ac dissipat omnia (Luther). This it is—and here the Church is handled most severely— which frees from guilt the man who proclaims the Word of God in the Church against the Church. For in acting thus, he is himself most hardly hit of all. In the affairs of God it is impossible for one individual to range itself against another, or one person against another. We cannot examine men, and then proceed to justify some and to condemn others. In the affairs of God, prosecutor and defendant alike appear on behalf of one another; for all who are seriously concerned with the problem which confronts the Church are alike prosecutors and defendants.

I bear them witness that they have a zeal for God. We can also defend ourselves against the accusation that we have been unfair to the intelligence and to the achievements of the Church. The point is, however, that our position enables us to be entirely just to the attainments of the Church both in the sphere of history and in the inner world of the mind. Indeed, we are ready to undertake the role of an eloquent advocate of the Church, and to plead her cause in the forum of men. Let us say, once and for all, that we fully recognize her zeal for God. But when it comes to matters which concern the relation between God and man, an exchange of compliments between men and men is totally irrelevant. However well mounted we may be—however deep our piety, and deeper still our religious experience—however great our confidence in God and our love of our brother men—we have not entered ourselves for a number of events on the racecourse of the *law of righteousness* (ix. 31). We cannot engage ourselves in the stupid controversy as to which of us has greater ' gifts ', which is the most pre-eminent in inward intensity, and in enthusiasm for love and hope and peace. Our business is to break off all such futile rivalry; for we know that, though human piety may in quality attain a most exquisite refinement of delicacy and in quantity pile up a veritable Tower of Babel, in the presence of God it possesses no final and decisive validity. We know also that the meeting-place of God and man is not an arena where men crown each other with laurels or refuse to confer that distinction, but a point where God and man meet in order to separate and separate in order to meet. In other words, we know that we—all of us—can only fear and love and worship God.

But not according to knowledge are they zealous for God. The lack of this knowledge is the guilt of the Church—a lack which is world-wide and age-long. For who possesses true knowledge? Whom does it not always elude? Who does not enter his name as a competitor in those races? What otherwise is the meaning of the whole series of religious explosions— each louder than the last—of which we have had such terrible experience since 1918? What about this book, in so far as it enters nolens volens into the midst of competing rivalries? What is the significance of the whole history of Theology up to the present day? Yes, Theology!—that eloquent section which may be carved out in order to illustrate the universal struggle for existence; a struggle in which animals furnished with younger teeth and horns do to death those older and weaker than themselves, until their own time comes. What do these changing scenes import? Does any one really suppose them to be meaningless? Again and again we all forget to consider how it is with us. This forgetfulness is the Church's peculiar guilt. And we are bound to acknowledge that, however much we may protest against it, we ourselves are implicated in it.

Being ignorant of God's righteousness, and seeking to establish their own, they did not subject themselves to the righteousness of God. Zeal for God according to knowledge exists when men are in subjection to the righteousness of God, of God Himself, and of God only; when they bow before the secret of divine predestination; and when they love God, because He is God, enthroned in that secret. For the righteousness of God is His freedom: the freedom in virtue of which He is the standard, by which He alone can call, and on account of which it is fitting (ix. 12) that he should love Jacob and hate Esau (ix. 13). By His freedom He hath mercy upon whom He will, and whom He will He hardeneth (ix. 18); by it, in fact, He is God alone, ruling yesterday, to-day, and to-morrow, with the same unrestricted sovereignty. To know God is the continuous, never-completed acknowledgement of this divine sovereignty, an acknowledgement which in no sense lies behind us, an acknowledgement which carries with it an unceasing critical distinguishing between the righteousness of God and every—yes every—human righteousness. To know God means a relentless honouring of Him in His pre-eminence over all human eminence—even over the eminence of our noteworthy thoughts about Him. It means that we consciously and of our own will endure the absolute assault which is launched upon men by His righteousness. Out of such knowledge zeal for God can arise—a zeal which does not need to participate in those races, and which sits in judgement upon itself. But who 'possesses' this knowledge and who can exercise it? For whom is it not too wonderful and excellent? Who can abide its brilliance or breathe its air? Who does not fear lest *all things should come to an end*? Who does not perhaps—nay, probably—nay, certainly—substitute for the righteousness of this unapproachable God some very refined, very excellent, very significant, righteousness of his own, to which is added, of course, some such phrase as *with the help of God* or *trusting in God*? Who does not substitute some plan or programme or method, some new thing, some new 'interpretation of the truth', some movement or task, which gives us less to create but more to do, less to ponder but more to talk about, less to endure but more to undertake, than does the righteousness of God? And so we introduce a 'thing' by which men—and especially religious men—secure an advantage for themselves. Immersed in the happiness of doing and speaking and inaugurating, busy with reforms and revolutions, they are able to forget the judgement hanging over their heads, and so the 'thing' on which they are engaged turns out more to their credit than if they were to seek naught else but to fear and to love God above all things. Was there ever a period when the Church was free of the temptation to substitute a human righteousness of its own for the righteousness of God? Was there ever a time when the temptation was resisted? The Church of Rome may excel in the skill with which it organizes itself to protect the proper interests of humanity against God, and to conceal and suppress the truth of divine predestination, but it excels only in the success with which it does what every Church tries to do. Has the Church ever been courageous enough to cut the ropes which bind it to the desires and needs and strivings of the men of this world, and to subject itself wholly to God? Can the Church do this? Can it even conceive of so doing? If, then, the Church cannot do what it exists to do, its knowledge of God breaks down under His KRISIS. For if men, as men, avoid recognizing God as God, can the Church be surprised, if it stands under no mere human indictment? And if this be so, how can it escape the necessity of conducting the case against itself?

THE LIGHT IN THE DARKNESS

X. 4–21

If, then, the tribulation of the Church be its guilt; if the guilt of the Church be its steady refusal to acknowledge the tribulation imposed upon it by its own peculiar task and its own peculiar Theme; and if the refusal of the Church to acknowledge its theme be nothing less than the Church's avoidance of God—then the very fact of the possibility of this refusal and avoidance points to another opposite possibility. The Church, on its own showing, cannot fall back on the excuse that it is being driven simply by blind fate and necessity. The Church is itself responsible precisely because it fails to lay hold of this opposite possibility. Therefore in the darkness the light shines. This is of great importance, not merely in order that we may not doubt that the tribulation of the Church lies in its burning guilt, but in order that we may perceive the hope of the Church to be manifest precisely where its guilt is proven. In the midst of the possibility of the Church lies the impossible possibility of God. The Church is therefore enlightened by the light of eternity, by light from light uncreated. The question is whether the Church is able to recognize this light.

vv. 4, 5. For Christ is the end of the law unto righteousness to every one that believeth. For Moses describeth the righteousness which is of the law, when he saith **that the man which doeth those things shall live thereby.**[1]

Christ is the end of the law unto righteousness to every one that believeth. There is but ONE truth, ONE freedom of God, whether

---

[1] Reading with Zahn and Kühl: γράφει τὴν δικαιοσύνην τὴν ἐκ νόμου ὅτι ὁ ποιήσας αὐτὰ ἄνθρωπος ζήσεται ἐν αὐτῇ.

it be exercised in election or in rejection. There is but ONE
righteousness of God. This one righteousness of God is encountered by us whether we meet it in the *righteousness which
proceeds from the faithfulness of God*, and which we lay hold of
and affirm and appropriate by faith (i. 17); or whether we
meet it in the *righteousness which proceeds from the law*, that is,
in the authoritative standard of human behaviour, in the goal
towards which human conduct is directed and by which it is
governed. In the first case the righteousness of God is invisible,
in the second it is visible. But it is nevertheless the same
righteousness. The righteousness which proceeds from the law
is the same righteousness that proceeds from the faithfulness
of God. For *the end of the law*—its sense and meaning—is
the righteousness of God. The Church is therefore concerned
with the law. This does not mean, however, that it is engaged
in chasing the phantom of some *law of righteousness* or of
some Kingdom-of-God religion (ix. 31). All human religion is
directed towards an *end* beyond itself (iii. 21); and that *end* is
Christ. For Christ is the goal of all the needs and longings and
endeavours of men. Ostensibly, of course, the Church exerts its
care and affection in fostering human endeavour and in satisfying it. Would that it were in fact so! If only the Church understood what it really means to be active in the law of righteousness! If only it knew how to evoke religion, and to defend it—as
a sign and as a witness! If only it could awaken that last and
most deep-seated human desire, by which every penultimate
longing is dissolved! If the Church were seriously engaged in
carrying out its proper programme, it would veritably encounter
the truth and the freedom and the righteousness of God. For it
is with the Church as it is with Israel. When once religion and
worship and a relationship between time and eternity have been
taken into account as serious human possible possibilities, then
there appears on the fringe of all this and beyond all visible
things, as their pre-supposition and as the point from which they
can be observed—the impossible possibility of the man of faith.
No serious human piety or righteousness, no earnest-minded
Church, can—as is seen quite clearly on every page of the
Psalter—remain satisfied with itself. And in fact all human
piety does point beyond itself, for it knows that it can be no
more than an imprint, a signpost and an intermediate station, a
reminder and a negation. The Church—if it be aware of itself
and is serious—sets fire to a charge which blows up every sacred
edifice which men have ever erected or can ever erect in its
vicinity. When men are in earnest with the law, every kind of

peace and quiet and security is at an end, save the peace and the quiet and the security of the eternal 'Moment' of the revelation of God. Every *following after righteousness* is done with, save that pursuit which is conducted within the context of the problem of apprehension (x. 2). There can be on the part of men no going about to *establish their own righteousness* (x. 3). All that must stop; for we have been brought to the point where we must recognize that a miracle takes place, but that the miracle of the existential relationship between God and man is an occurrence comprehended in no moment of time. Faith believes and God speaks. Now this means that wherever the Church is—wherever, that is to say, religion is taken account of as a penultimate human possibility—there occurs within the realm of human competence the impossible possibility of God. And so it is that the Church of Esau, of which alone we have knowledge, lives of the Church of Jacob.

The man which doeth those things shall live thereby. Thus Moses describes the *righteousness which is of the law* (Lev. xviii. 5). Now, Moses is not ignorant of the meaning of his words. He does not merely represent a law, which is no more than a human work, and which of itself has no further significance. Moses is not merely a typical, well-informed ecclesiastic, not merely an undiscerning man, aware that he represents religion at its highest point. He may, of course, be all this, as all prophets and apostles and reformers are. But as Prophet or Apostle or Reformer, in fact, as Moses, he is more than this. He insists that the law must be done, in order that men may live by the righteousness which is of the law—*not the hearers of the law are just before God, but the doers of the law shall be justified* (ii. 13). This is how Moses understands the righteousness which is of the law. Who, then, is a *doer of the law*? We recollect that to do the law means to bow before Him by whom the law was given and from whom we have received it. To do the law means to comprehend that human righteousness comes into being only through the majesty of the nearness of God and of His election. Human righteousness exists only in order to bear witness to that nearness and to that election. Accordingly all—yes! all—human righteousness is surrendered to Him to whom it belongs, and thus pays honour to Him. Only when the law is actually done, only when the impossible possibility of miracle, of existentiality, of faith, in fact, of God, becomes itself possible, can men live thereby. This means, of course, that this possibility is capable of fulfilment neither within the realm of time, nor on the plane of history or experience. There is here no occasion of boasting (iii. 27, 28!). This

is what Moses means. By using the Futurum aeternum, he
cannot fail to make us understand that neither the promise nor
the condition which is linked to it is direct and observable.
Both are used to denote the possibility which is messianic and
eschatological. So likewise the Church must apprehend the
righteousness which is of the law as affording it a task to
perform and a gift to bestow. The Church must lay hold
firmly upon the dialectical truth that Christ is the end of
the law. Dialectical, because from the law no righteousness
emerges, yet nevertheless, from the requirement of the law—
that is, from Christ—righteousness proceeds. In Christ men,
busily 'pursuing', are dissolved, and exalted to be with God.
And all this takes place through the faithfulness of God. When
the Church understands its programme thus, it cannot but
contemplate with horror the depth of its humiliation. It is
indeed a terrible thing to fall into the hands of the living
God. And yet, the guilt of the Church is thereby removed; it
understands its task, and, in that moment,—the light shineth
in the darkness.

vv. 6–8. But the righteousness which cometh of the
faithfulness of God **saith thus, Say not in thine heart, Who
shall ascend into heaven ? (that is, to bring Christ down:)
or, Who shall descend into the abyss ? (that is, to bring
Christ up from the dead.) But what saith it ? The word
is nigh thee, in thy mouth, and in thy heart** (Deut. xxx.
12–14): **that is, the word of** the faithfulness of God, **which
we preach.**

As we have seen already—**The righteousness which cometh
of the faithfulness of God** is declared by Moses to be *the end of
the law.* The Church may hesitate to give honour to God; but it
cannot defend its hesitation by supposing that men are merely
men, endowed only with human possibilities. The Gospel of the
Unknown God, who is Creator and Sole Ruler, is foreign neither
to the Church nor to humanity. As the boundary of humanity
the Gospel is no doubt strange. But what is really strange is
that this is not unfamiliar. When men pursue their own way to
the bitter end, they stand before God. And the Church too, in
the same way, is, with humanity, finally confronted by that Other
Possibility. At the point where the Church advances into the
presence of God and is thereby enabled to take itself seriously,
all chasing after the righteousness of the law (ix. 31), all ignorant
zeal for God (x. 2), all striving to set up a righteousness which
can be observed (x. 3), comes to an end. The Church is then

what men look for in it and expect from it. The Church is the
place of fruitful and hopeful repentance; and it is nothing else.
When the Church crashes up against this point, it is overwhelmed with disgust at its convulsive attempts, at one moment
to—**ascend into heaven,** at another to—**descend into the abyss ;**
it is appalled that it should have tried to be both 'height' and
'depth', to occupy them, speak of them, point them out, and
apportion them. There is a certain horror at all attempts to
bring about the work of God, to effect the incarnation of divinity
or the resurrection of humanity, by employing the dynamic,
demonic power of the Church's own word. The Church may
refine its liturgy; popularize its technical language; broaden the
basis of the education of its clergy; see that its administration is
made more efficient; yield hurriedly to the demands of the laity,
however doubtful they may be; encourage theological jour-
nalism; approximate more closely to the uncertainties of the
'spirit of the age', to romanticism, liberalism, nationalism, and
socialism; may, in fact,—'bring Christ into the picture'! But
when He is brought into the picture, it is discovered that we
cannot introduce Him thus, either by *bringing* Him *down*, or by
bringing Him *up*. For Christ is not the exalted and transformed
ideal man. He is the *new man*. Christmas is not the festival of
mother-and-child, with which we are so familiar, and which we
find so attractive. Good Friday is not an occasion for us to ponder
upon our sufferings, for that requires no encouragement. Easter
is not a representation in concrete form of the triumph of our
lives or of our aspirations—of socialism, for example, or of the
'resurrection' of Germany. The Ascension is not a symbol of
the lifting up into heaven of our idealism. The Pentecostal fire
has nothing to do with our manipulated extravagances or with
our enthusiasms, however genuine they may be. Once this were
perceived, the Church—and in the term is included every conceivable little conventicle which passionately denies that it is a
Church—would be the place where, contrasted with all other
places, the proper, inexhaustible distance of 'height' and 'depth'
would be apprehended, set forth, and maintained. Then the
Church would be able to express itself. The Church is not bound
to be silent—with or without incense! For silence before God
gives meaning both to our silence and to our most eloquent
speech. Then the Church would be the place where men receive
the message of joy and the positive Word of God. For it would
be the place where—distinct from all moralizings and sentimentalities—the supreme negation of the Word of the Cross
could be heard without the disturbance of other words. But we

must guard ourselves at this point against misunderstanding. We must not clothe the final and abiding Word of the Cross with a positive human negation. For that would be precisely to *descend into the abyss.* We must not substitute for normal Christian idealism a mere command to stand still, and then proceed to use our full-blooded artistry to persuade men to embark upon a gospel of 'demolition'. This would merely be to make out of the radical negation of all things human, and out of the abyss which is here disclosed, a new, very peculiar, very high-minded, theological point of view. We must not preach 'demolition' as a means of 'winning souls'; for that would be merely a new manner of 'moralizing' the Gospel, and making of it a human position and a possible human behaviour. We must not substitute for the vigour of the Church a highly artificial passivity; and for its extensive, wide-flung propaganda a waiting, vaunted as very intense and significant, but in reality most questionable, because so carefully manipulated. We are not permitted to seek salvation by doing nothing or by remaining unmoved.

The word is nigh thee, in thy mouth and in thy heart, that is, the word of the faithfulness of God, which we preach. That is to say, no skill in manipulation, no positive or negative dislocation, is required. It is necessary only to look into what is nigh at hand and to perceive the tribulation and promise of life, as it is set before us in every word we speak and in every motion of our heart. Being a man, thou dost assuredly behold the question-mark standing at the boundary of humanity, to which the *word of the faithfulness of God, which we preach,* is the answer. The only pre-supposition required of us, then, in order that we may come nigh unto the Word, is that we should make ourselves aware of the actual course of the world and of our own lives, simply and soberly, critically, and stripping ourselves of every illusion. A Church capable of retiring from all its sacred heights and depths, from all its extensive and intensive ecclesiastical possibilities; a Church determined to retrace its steps from every distant country, in order that it may move in the 'nearness' of the lives of men and in the ambiguity of their existence, would thereby embrace its true task, and in its own misery and responsibility would encounter Him, who has ordered human affairs that in them He may be nigh at hand. In thus describing the resignation of the Church and its severe concentration upon the matter in hand, we are not demanding some new 'reformation' Rather, we are thinking once again of the Church of Jacob, of the Church in the desert; we are thinking of miracle and of faith, of the impossible possibility, which is beyond our observation, and which, therefore, we cannot think of in terms of some new movement of reform or of some new school of thought. We mean that which is everywhere and always present in every possible Church as soon as it in any way takes itself seriously. The retirement of the Church upon its inner lines is not a manœuvre which we can plan, set in motion, and accomplish. The retirement of the Church is the strategic significance of its already existing manœuvres—a significance which already exists and which occurs without any preparatory circulation of orders, without any practical consideration whatever, and without any increase of establishment. What we mean is the new orientation of all possible human activity, the step from hope to tribulation and from tribulation to hope, the eternal advance, which accompanies or does not accompany, which assists or hinders, all human progress. Set. over against all human possibilities, it is the 'Wholly Other'; and because it is this, it is the possibility that is always and everywhere open— the possibility for the living, Unknown God to be what He is. Now, this open possibility means that behind and above and in the Church of Esau—however degenerate and priest-ridden it may be—is the Church of Jacob. When we say that the *word is nigh thee*, we are simply speaking once again of the righteousness of God (Deut. xxx. 14), ever awaiting our serious consideration, ever waiting for us to hear it and proclaim it, ever ready to display its efficacy in causing us oppression and in setting us free. Yet, because it is the Word of Christ, it is beyond our hearing and beyond our speaking; for, to hear it and to proclaim it—we must wait. Weighed down by the ambiguity of our existence, we must await the trumpeting forth of the last question and the last answer. The sound of the last trumpet lies beyond—but because veritably beyond, therefore within—the noise of all penultimate questions and answers. Far too transcendent, far too important, far too full of significance, is the Word of God by which the Church is constituted! We cannot endure it—even though it be heard by human ears and proclaimed by human lips!—save when it is trumpeted forth in the final question and in the final answer. The Word is nigh unto us. Wherever we cast our eye, the dynamite is prepared and ready to explode. But if there is no explosion, or if something less final takes place, can we not take just the smallest risk which is, in fact, the greatest? Are we always to prefer a thousand other days to one day in the outer courts of the Lord? Shall we never permit our hands to be empty, that we may grasp what only empty hands can grasp? Must our hands be on the tiller and the wind be in the sails, before we know the direction of our journey? Do we start to build a tower or do we make a declaration of war, before we have reckoned the cost or numbered our troops? So in like manner is it with the Word of God. But here we must not forget to reckon with impossibility. For impossibility is, as such, nigh at hand, ready at our elbow, possible. Impossibility presses upon us, breaks over us, is indeed already present. Impossibility is more possible than everything which we hold to be possible. The light shineth in the darkness.

vv. 9–11. Because if thou shalt confess with thy mouth Jesus as Lord, and shalt believe in thine heart that God raised him from the dead, thou shalt be saved: for with the heart man believeth unto righteousness; and with the mouth confession is made unto salvation. For the scripture saith, Whosoever believeth on him shall not be put to shame (Isa. xxviii. 16).

Speaking of righteousness, Moses saith—*The man that doeth it shall live thereby* (x. 5). It is now possible to define more clearly the meaning of the word *doeth*. The promise emerges once more as the Futurum aeternum—**shalt be saved—shall not be put to shame**. We might paraphrase thus—shall be the Church of Jacob. What, then, is the condition which the Church must fulfil? What is the *doing* of the law with which the promise corresponds? Now we have the answer—**if thou shalt confess Jesus as Lord, and shalt believe that God raised him from the dead—thou shalt be saved**. And again—**whosoever believeth on him—shall not be put to shame**. Jesus the Lord, Resurrection, Faith, are, then, the condition. It is as Moses proclaims it: nothing less is required than that subjection to the righteousness of God (x. 3), which we know to be demanded of us always, but which we persistently reject; nothing less than the Word which Israel discovers in its heart and on its lips; nothing less than that Word which is eternally ready, eternally nigh, when Israel recognizes the meaning of the name Israel, and when the Church takes itself seriously (x. 6–8). Set unobservably over against the place where the Church stands with all its possibilities, we encounter—as the impossible possibility of all possibilities, as the abyss into which no man can leap, and yet into which we do all leap—these three: the Lord, Resurrection, and Faith. LORD denotes the unconditional imperative; RESURRECTION the utterly strange; and FAITH the free initiative of the absolute 'Moment' of the righteousness of God. But it is Jesus, in His historical particularity and contingency and finiteness (viii. 4), who is to be acknowledged as 'Lord' and believed in as 'risen'. This means the existentiality of this 'Moment'; and existentiality must not be confounded with 'idealism'. So it is that—**with the heart man believeth unto righteousness, and with the mouth confession is made unto salvation.** The sequence *heart–mouth* is of no particular importance, nor is the selection of these two organs of any peculiar significance; it might just as well have been feet or hands or eyes or ears. What is important is that the mention of human organs in this context secures the correct emphasis. It emphasizes the ambiguity and contingency of the course of human existence, in order to make it clear that this contingency is answered by the corresponding existentiality of the turning-point and decision. Since this occurs in Jesus, it occurs in the domain of human possibility, though at its outer limit. The man who DOES this—that is to say, who confesses and believes—shall live by righteousness. In speaking of the existentiality of this action, we have not, of course, forgotten that it is unobservable and unheard of. It is true that in laying emphasis upon the existentiality of Jesus, of the mouth which confesses, and of the heart which believes, we have spoken quite freely of law, of religion, of history, and of the human soul. But nevertheless we have only spoken of the existentiality of Jesus, as 'Lord', as 'risen', and as 'believed in'. We have spoken of righteousness only as COMING, as the impossible which becomes possible. Righteousness does not, however, come of the law, but of the faithfulness of God. The condition, therefore, which corresponds with the promise, itself corresponds with the Futurum aeternum of that promise. We now propose to show that the condition which corresponds with the promise is neither unknown to the Church nor impossible for it to fulfil.

vv. 12–15. For there is no distinction between Jew and Greek: for the same Lord over all is rich unto all that call upon him: for, Whosoever shall call upon the name of the Lord shall be saved. How then shall they call on him in whom they have not believed? and how shall they believe in him whom they have not heard? and how shall they hear without a preacher? and how shall they preach, except they be sent? even as it is written, How seasonable **are the feet of them that bring glad tidings!**

Seen to be beyond human observation, known to be the Unknown who proclaims the final question and the final answer—such is the risen Lord to all who call upon Him. He is no founder

of a new religion. He erects no new Church which may be compared or contrasted with other Churches. He is the imperative
of the righteousness of God—in its strangeness and in its freedom. He is the master-key which opens every door. He is the
wave which overtops even the highest building. He is the point
from which the vast horizon of life is seen in true perspective.
By the Resurrection of Jesus the whole length and depth and
height of human existence is directed towards that other length
and depth and height; it is directed towards fulfilment and
salvation. Jesus is the goal to which all law and all religion
move. Wherever, in the rough and tumble of human life, men
become even dimly conscious of this movement, wherever they
do but feel its rhythm, and ask that it may be explained, law
and religion make their inevitable appearance. And is human
life ever vacant of law and of religion? Is there any longing
and anticipation which is not potentially a *calling upon God*,
a calling upon the name of Him who reveals God to be God?
Is there any consciousness of the sentence of death hanging
over human life which is not an—incomprehensible!—awareness of the—impossible!—possibility of resurrection? Can men
recognize and name the universal tribulation without bearing witness also to the universality of salvation of which it
is the shadow? The questioning concerning the secret meaning
of life which is manifested in every law and in every religion, is
assuredly a calling upon the Lord who is the deep and hidden
answer to this questioning. Men call upon God, because, and
only because, He has answered before they call. Men suffer at
His hands, because they require to be healed at His hands. Such
is the case between God and man, as it is manifested in Jesus.
And He is master of the situation in virtue of His Resurrection.
For in the tribulation of our existence, in our sighing and
questioning, in our seeking and crying, He reveals the riches of
divine salvation and divine healing, which are the hidden roots
of our tribulation. If this be our situation—**There is no distinction between Jew and Greek: for the same Lord over all is rich
unto all that call upon him : for, Whosoever shall call upon the
name of the Lord shall be saved** (Joel ii. 32); or as we have
already said (x. 11): *Whosoever believeth on him shall not be put
to shame.* What is the relevance of all this for the Church, for
every Church? Does it not mean that every serious-minded
Church will become the Church of Jacob? And yet there is a
difficulty here. Are we to understand *whosoever . . .* and *there is
no distinction between Jew and Greek*, when addressed to Israel,
as involving judgement or promise? Whatever answer be given

to these questions, we are bound to recognize that to Paul the words *whosoever* and *no distinction* constitute the most vitally significant comment upon the conceptions of faith and righteousness; for, whether the Church approve of them or not, in the light of the decisive death of Christ upon the Cross these words mark the unlimited freedom of God. It is this free *Lord over all* whom we call upon, who is *rich unto all that call upon him, whether they be Jew or Greek*. In justifying the Jew, He justifies Himself. But He is not bound to the Jew; for in His ability to justify the Greek, He also justifies Himself. Manifesting Himself as Lord in Jesus, He confronts all men as God. The Church, if it be wise, will recognize this sovereignty of God, since it will not then be excluded, for it calls upon Him who is Lord over all. If, however, the Church be foolish, if it be pained that God should reveal Himself in Jesus, it will be excluded, even though it call upon the Lord. Indeed, fearing His harshness, the Church in its folly will cease to call upon Him. Be that as it may, the Lord seeks those who call upon Him—as He is. And to *call upon the Lord* means existential knowledge and faith and fear and love. There are men who, in subjection to the righteousness of God, await eternal life (x. 5), eternal salvation (x. 9, 13), eternal not-being-put-to-shame (x. 11). But are these men within the Church, or outside it, or are they members of some Church of their own founding? The question is trivial. And because it is trivial, it is the disturbance of the Church. We are not speaking of a small company of 'converted' men in Rome or Ephesus or Corinth. These companies of men bear witness to a wholly different conversion. Nor are we speaking of certain noble pagans, such as Seneca and other pious men of the world. We are not speaking of atheists who are unconsciously Christians or of any other such men. They too are no more than signs of the light in which all men stand in Christ—apart from any human righteousness. The faithful heathen, of whom we say that they call upon the Lord, do not compose a definite and analysable number of men. They are an eschatological quantity, embracing potentially the totality of psychologically analysable individuals, whether they belong to the Church or not. The Lord knoweth His own. There are men who, recognizing the reality of this divine order, bow before the Lord who knoweth His own and perceive the possibility of fulfilling the divine condition. We set such men over against the Church. But who is of the number of these men, and who is excluded from it? The Church can also bow before the divine order and the divine condition, without adding to it or substituting anything for it.

The Church need not dissolve the secret of Predestination by imposing upon it some human 'way of salvation'. The Church can stand upright and be recognized among the successors of the uncircumcised Abraham (iv. 9-12), for it can be strong enough to recognize its weakness in the presence of God.

And so we say—**How then shall they call on him in whom they have not believed? and how shall they believe in him whom they have not heard? and how shall they hear without a preacher? and how shall they preach, except they be sent?** Men do invoke Jesus the Lord. But this crying of men from the depth of their tribulation—a crying disclosed in all law and in all religion —would not take place were it not that behind all that can be analysed there lies a knowledge of God which, although unobservable, is none the less real. This knowledge of God, which is the God-given pre-supposition of all observation and definition, is faith in all its hiddenness. Faith, however, presupposes hearing and preaching and mission, which are likewise hidden. In other words, knowledge of God presumes the possibility—nay, the reality—of the hidden Church of Jacob, whose ear hears and whose mouth speaks the Word of God.

We are not ignorant of the possibility of which we are now speaking. We speak of the—**seasonable** time, of the time of the End, of Judgement, and of Grace. We speak of the Time and Hour of God, when—**the feet** draw nigh—**of them that bring glad tidings** of the Kingdom, the Power, and the Glory of God; when the new and true system of co-ordinates is laid down and God and man are drawn apart in order that men may be drawn together in His presence and may be confronted by the new Israel to which all belong, not by right, but by the mercy of God. If God be veritably God, why should the *seasonable* time not be already present? And if it be already present, why should God not send forth His emissaries, and why should His name not be proclaimed and heard and believed in and called upon? We cannot doubt but that there is no time when it is not seasonable for men to reckon with the righteousness of God, with His all-humiliating wrath, and with His all-embracing pity. It is, however, open to question whether we are the *seasonable* ones, whether we are men who can thus reckon. That the light shineth in the darkness is not open to question. There is, however, grave doubt as to whether it has been seen even by the Church, even by the children of Abraham.

vv. 16, 17. But they did not all hearken to the glad tidings. For Isaiah saith, Lord, who hath believed our

report ? (For **belief** must come **of hearing, and hearing by the word of Christ**).

They did not all hearken to the glad tidings. The word which is the end of the law demands obedience—*The doers of the law shall be justified* (ii. 13). Here is the separation of spirits. Here the tribulation of the Church becomes its guilt, and its guilt the cause of its tribulation. We must be careful here. The universal pre-supposition set forth above (x. 12, 13) must not be confused with some rationalistic general religious a priori, which, in fact, blunts the edge of a genuinely critical rationalism. We must not erect behind or in front of all so-called positive religions a universal 'religion of reason'. When we say, *Whosoever shall call upon the name of the Lord shall be saved* (x. 13), we mean the universalism of grace, and we speak of revelation. This universalism and this pre-supposition, contrasted with every religious a priori, carry with them, not the con-stitution of all human religions, but their de-stitution. Accordingly, at the supreme point we are bound to proclaim the entire absence of every human presupposition. We proclaim that God is free. The Gospel is the glad tidings, precisely because all human conjunctions and adjustments and presuppositions—however transcendentally conceived of—are there confronted by the sovereignty of God. For very good reason and with admirable acuteness Kant did not set out upon a critique—that is to say, an establishing—of the pure reasoning of piety. From the human side we are able to take account only of the freedom of God: that is to say, we are concerned only with obedience. And here Kant was possessed of far greater insight than his—religious!— opponents. But obedience means repentance; and repentance means preparedness to enter upon the divine, seasonable, eschatological possibility, to bow before the wrath and before the mercy of God, to be accessible to the one-sided, passionate, and exclusive claim which God makes upon men. Repentance means being open to the strangeness of resurrection and to the free and boundless initiative of faith. Obedience means that there is encountered in the known man of this world a vacuum, a place of irruption, where the new man is able to breathe and move. Obedience is the sense for the specific peculiarity of the Divine and for the Wholly-Other-ness of God, the King, the Monarch, the Despot. It follows from this that obedience means being committed to a particular course of action, a readiness to surrender individual freedom of movement to the free movement of God, a readiness to offer up everything that the known man of the world supposes to be important and necessary and right, a readiness to retreat from every concrete position which we have occupied, from every undertaking, alliance, compromise, or daring venture upon which we have embarked; in fact, from every method of thought or manner of behaviour. Obedience means that the pendulum is allowed to swing to and fro, freely and without interruption, from its point of suspension; and that we are free to walk—free, that is to say, to move along the same road backwards and forwards again and again without ever standing still, free to understand and to withstand human life with the same energy upon whatever part of the road we may happen to be, free to permit our position to be subjected to the full frontal attack of God, and free never to lose sight of the check which all things encounter in God. This is the obedience which is congruous to the Gospel of Salvation. But who is competent for such obedience? Speaking soberly and very obscurely, we answer—*not all*. In any case, not this or that man, not this or that assessable number of men. No doubt the Church of Jacob and those who *walk in the steps of that faith of our father Abraham which he had in circumcision* (iv. 12) are competent. But who are they? And where can they be found? What are we to say of our Church, of the known Church of Esau? Is it obedient? Surely it must be. For the Word of God is nigh it, and the —**report** which its preachers proclaim must surely proceed from the Word of God. Surely men do discover from the *report* of the preacher the faithfulness of God, and surely faith and obedience are thereby generated. But ARE they generated thus? Do not these preachers appear strangely deserted, isolated, helpless, and embarrassed, not only when confronted by their hearers, but also when confronted—by themselves? **Lord, who hath believed our report** (Isa. liii. 1)? Can we honestly say that the Church everywhere provokes men to repentance in fear and trembling and to veritable respect for God? Can we say that it creates and guards the abyss which separates God from man, that it assaults—religious!—men and bombards the very structure of human life? Can we say that it sets in motion that *walking* which does not halt when some happy nook has been discovered in which men suppose they can rest? Can we say that the Church presents us with a veritable embarrassment, permanent, fundamental, bitter-sweet, relentless, and piercing to the very marrow of human existence, which must be endured and from which there is no escape, an embarrassment, in other words, which is prepared for us by God? How is it that the Church—and now we must call attention to certain symptoms

↓ of its disease—how is it that the Church continually shuns the
rupture, the leap, the sacrifice which God demands? Why does
the Church perpetually keep half an eye on its contemporaries,
the nobility, the crowd, the educated classes, the proletariat,
youth, the bourgeoisie, asking what they will say, what they
will make of the Church, asking whether they will understand
or whether they can fail to understand? Why is the Church so
incredibly skilled in discovering in Divinity a thing capable of
historical description or of psychological analysis? How easy
the Church finds it to bring in 'interesting parallels', to draw
up pedigrees of spiritual experience, to note differences and to
illustrate the dependence of one religion upon another, to disclose or invent 'types', and then to puff them about like so
many peas out of a pea-shooter! What a strange, elastic power
the Church has, when twanged in the face by its own elastic,
of speaking complacently of the religious value of such a rebuff!
How distressingly correct and friendly the Church manages to
make itself! Were an Amos or an Elijah to appear as a modern
preacher, he would be rendered perfectly harmless. With what
uncanny facility the slightest trace of the impossible possibility
is transformed into the possible possibility of a movement, a
school of thought, a point of view, or of a fellowship, each claiming that some shibboleth or other represents the most peculiarly
modern enthusiasm for God, each having its own 'Press' which
does business under a title indicating some form of accommodation of the Gospel, and indicating also a quite certain failure!
Why is the Church so quick to muzzle any one who displays
conspicuous intelligence by at once making him a leader? And
finally, whence comes its ability to discover some refuge where
men need no longer fear dissolution, where, rid of the necessity
to defend themselves, they can enjoy the security of their
own righteousness? And all this is compatible with the quite
devastating illusion shared by almost every one, that, of course,
as far as they are personally concerned, the Church is not itself
the supreme thing, not an end in itself. We are speaking here
of the only Church we know or can ever know, of the Church
which has never been materially different, and never will be,—of
the Church (and all these symptoms make it abundantly plain)
which is inevitably and always the Church of Esau,—of the
Church—we have said it and we do not retract it (ix. 1-5,
✗ x. 1)—to which we belong. That the tribulation of the Church
is its guilt, and that its guilt consists in a perpetual avoiding of
the tribulation which it suffers from the secret of God, must
not be in any way minimized, but rather must be vigorously

asserted. The Church needs to be continually reminded of the most serious of all symptoms. It was the Church, not the world, which crucified Christ.>

v. 18. But I say, Did they not hear ? Yea, verily, Their sound went out into all the earth, and their words unto the ends of the world (Ps. xix. 4).

Is it possible to remove the guilt of the Church by saying that it did not hear, that it has not yet heard? The *word of Christ* would then be a new thing which some men have heard and some have not. It would then be a gift bestowed upon those who dwell in some particular corner of the world, in some other street. There would then be some further knowledge which we do not as yet possess. There would then be something more which we could know, if an angel descended from heaven to-day, and smote upon the table, and uttered the new thing with a voice of thunder. But no, this is not so. Whoever we are, we have heard the *word of Christ* and we are within the picture. It is an objective impossibility for us to discover that we have not heard.

vv. 19, 20. But I say, Did Israel not know ? First Moses saith, I will provoke you to jealousy with that which is no nation, with a nation void of understanding will I anger you. And Isaiah is very bold, and saith, I was found of them that sought me not; I became manifest unto them that asked not of me (Deut. xxxii. 21; Isa. lxv. 1).

Is it not, perhaps, possible to remove the guilt by pleading that we heard indeed, but could not understand. But what is meant by understanding? Does it require leisure or great maturity of judgement? Does it need special moral stamina or power of intellect, or a particularly strong faith? Where, we ask, is such understanding to be found? Shall we discover it in some unknown Gentile Church of Jacob? Is there any one anywhere who thus understands? Who is possessed of sufficient leisure, maturity, poise, and ability, to understand the things pertaining to God? Can we not understand that what is required of us in the things of God is to understand that we do not understand? Those who understand are—**no nation : a nation void of understanding.** But which of us dare say what Isaiah said? God permitted Himself to be discovered in His boundless mercy—by those who did not seek Him. He revealed Himself to those who asked not of Him. There is no lofty pinnacle of religious insight, up which we are able to drag ourselves. Here is no final rhythm of faith. What is demanded of us here is that we should know that we are understood by God—in our lack of understanding.

v. 21. But to Israel he saith, All day long did I spread out my hands unto a disobedient and gainsaying people (Is. lxv. 2).

Here we must stop. Guilt is not innocence. Guilt means that we can, but we will not. We will not sacrifice ourselves. We will not cast ourselves down from that pinnacle of ours. We will not recognize the validity of that other system of co-ordinates. We remain in our own tents and in our own dug-outs, and we will not go forth to meet God (Exod. xix. 17). Characteristic of men is a tenacious, profitless opposition to God. And this is also characteristic of the Church. The light shineth; but it shineth in real darkness.

The Eleventh Chapter

THE HOPE OF THE CHURCH

THE ONENESS OF GOD

XI. 1–10

vv. 1, 2a. I say then, Did God cast off his people ? God forbid. For I also am an Israelite, of the seed of Abraham, of the tribe of Benjamin. God did not cast off his people which he foreknew.

Did God cast off his people ?—*The light shineth in the darkness* (John i. 5). How are we to translate what follows? *The darkness apprehended it not*, or, according to more recent and better interpretation, *The darkness overcame it not*. And yet, the first seems to represent more closely the actual situation. Must we not retain that bald 'No'! which is the final observable human word? Can we escape from that essential atheism of the Church, which is set forth whenever it is compelled to make a decision for or against its own Theme? Are we free of the Satanism of the 'Grand Inquisitor', who, though he knows God, yet for the love of men refuses to know Him, and would rather put Christ to death than allow the Word of the freedom of God to run its course? Has God then spread out His hands in vain (x. 21)? Has the terrible thing occurred? Has God been betrayed by the Church, by every Church? Has He been betrayed by men who, in serving Him, refuse to serve Him, and who, with all their skill and might, deny that He is God? Can there be any hope? Can hope emerge from this death? Can there be hope for those who with their own hands have murdered hope and buried it? Is there hope for Judas Iscariot? However uncomfortable this question is, we are bound to formulate it. We dare not pass it by, however difficult it may be. If hope be hope, it must continue to burn after it has put out every false hope.

Did God cast off his people? Hope is not hope unless it rises from the background of this question. But how can there be such hope? Whence have we the courage to answer this pressing, but destructive, question with a straight—**God forbid?** It is impossible for us to secure courage from some argumentation by which human behaviour is placed in a more favourable light. We cannot set our confidence upon some other observable possibility attained outside the Church or in some

new, reformed Church. The only possibility open to the Church
and to men is the unobservable, divine possibility which men
in their guiltiness have neglected. We can only say *God forbid*,
if we really mean that God does forbid it. For the hope which
looks forward to the attainment of visible human possibilities,
to the reformation of old things and the erection of new things,
does but increase our guilt: it cannot dissolve it.

And so we must establish hope after we have considered the
paradox—**For I also am an Israelite, of the seed of Abraham, of
the tribe of Benjamin** (cf. ix. 1–5, x. 1). How can the hope of the
Church be apprehended by one who does not himself hope in
God? And how can any one hope in God who has not bowed
himself altogether before God? And how can any one bow before
God who does not recognize that *I also am—an Israelite, of the
seed of Abraham, of the tribe of Benjamin.* I also am—the 'Grand
Inquisitor', the betrayer, the disobedient opponent of God. I also,
under the pretext of serving God and man, set out to protect
men from the presence of God. I also am that mature person
who, being perfectly aware of the true issue, makes use of what he
has heard and apprehended (x. 18, 19), simply in order to conceal
from himself and from others the truth that honour must be paid
unto God. Whoever we are, we must lay down our arms. For we
are the Church with all its appurtenances. We are most question-
ably engaged. We are marked men. We have embarked upon
this or that religious enterprise, even if it be upon a religion
which we have ourselves invented. We are Jews or Catholics or
Lutherans or Reformed. We have already been warned against
side-stepping from one to the other. We mount all kinds of
pulpits, or sit under them. And we have failed as laymen and as
theologians, as parish priests and as professors. We trundle
along the broad track of some venerable Christian tradition, or
along the narrow way of some new Christian fellowship. We
think we understand the tragedy—or is it the comedy?—of this
busy, cumbersome existence, of this standing or sitting or
trundling along. We have heard what Kierkegaard said about
it all, and we agree with him. Every day we sigh over this *I also
am*, over its power and glory even more than over its pain and
weakness. We hope that we are not unmindful of its ambiguity,
and that we bear witness to its questionableness in all we say
and do. But we know that this *I also am* is not merely a human
judgement, but a far less avoidable judgement of God. For
the divine possibility cannot be apprehended save in the catastrophe of that human possibility which is the Church. There is,
then, no justification save through the utter radicalism of the

XI. I, 2   THE ONENESS OF GOD   393

divine 'And yet'. This is the supreme witness of the Church. It follows therefore that we cannot be rid of Judaism except as Jews, of Pharisaism except as Pharisees, of theology except as theologians. The Church hopes, in its tribulation and guilt; and the Church hopes in God, precisely because, humanly speaking, it has no hope.

God did not cast off his people which he foreknew. These words are not spoken from the security of the shore, or from the safe refuge of a lifeboat as it approaches, or pulls away from, a wreck. These words are spoken from the deck of a ship—as it sinks. Only one who is himself a Churchman knows what it is to sin against God, to betray Him and to deny Him. The man who does not know this, but thinks he is able to discover something better than the Church and its anguish, some private by-path which skirts the embarrassment of the Church and avoids that *I also am*, knows neither the tribulation which God has prepared for men, nor the guilt in which they are imprisoned in His presence, nor, consequently, the hope which arises in the evident misery of the Church. Hope is made known to us when we recognize that our tribulation comes from God, that it is in His presence that we are guilty, and that it is He who spreads out His hands unto a disobedient and gainsaying people (x. 21). This being so—existentially so—we do not need first to join ourselves to this people. In any case we are His, for it is on Him that we are broken in pieces, and for this reason we also participate in His people's victorious and unconquerable hope. If God really does spread forth His hands to us, what are we to make of our disobedient gainsaying, even though it be utterly satanic? What of the death, which is our end? What of that murder and burial, which is the prelude to our hope? What of our betrayal of Christ? Well, He kissed the Grand Inquisitor 'upon his old and bloodless lips—and this was His complete and only answer'. But it is just this 'complete and only answer' which is the hope of the Church; for, established in God only, mercy is eternal, unconditional, unfathomable, it passeth all understanding. We are not saved by our knowledge of God. Our knowledge brings us under judgement. God is Alpha, and therefore Omega; He rejects, and therefore elects; He condemns, and therefore is merciful. God conducts men down into Hell, and there releases them; He formulates the Question—which breaks forth in the Church as a disease and in human society as an open wound— and therefore He is also the Answer. God is One. One in the identity of the God of wrath with the God of mercy. One as the Deus absconditus and as He who raised up Jesus from the dead.

One as the God of Esau and as the God of Jacob. This Oneness—and it is summed up and manifested in all its invisibility and inaudibility in the Cross of Christ—is our hope. And so, deprived of every other hope, without support or bridge, when nothing intervenes for us or co-operates with us—*the light shineth in the darkness; and the darkness overcame it not*—For the Lord will not cast off his people for his great name's sake: because it hath pleased the Lord to make you a people unto himself (1 Sam. xii. 22, LXX).

vv. 2b–6. Or wot ye not what the scripture saith in the story **of Elijah ? how he pleadeth with God against Israel, Lord, they have killed thy prophets, they have digged down thine altars: and I am left alone, and they seek my life. But what saith the answer of God unto him ? I have left for myself seven thousand men, who have not bowed the knee to** the shame of **Baal. Even so then at this present time also there is a remnant according to the election of grace. But if it is by grace, it is no more of works: otherwise grace is no more grace.**

Lord, they have killed thy prophets, they have digged down thine altars : and I am left alone, and they seek my life. If then the Oneness of God is the hope of the Church, the Church must believe in it, however paradoxical and inadequate its own position may be. It were better that hope should be altogether hidden and the Church altogether hopeless than that men should endeavour to see, or claim that they have seen, what can be only a matter for faith. Since the hope of the Church is the final and only hope, it must be pure, genuine, and real. We must recognize that, inasmuch as the question has been formulated by God, He alone can provide the answer. The desperate situation of the Church cannot be exaggerated. Put quite bluntly, the Church is the Church of Ahab and Jezebel. Looked at from the standpoint of the Gospel, the complaint of Elijah (1 Kings xix. 10, 14) may be applied also to the Church. If it were not applicable yesterday, it is certainly so to-day; and if not to-day, it will certainly be so to-morrow; if not in one respect, certainly in another. One failure is sufficient to justify the complaint. There can be no wobbling from one side to the other: there can be no relative relationship between Jehovah and Baal. If Baal be detected peering out from any one of our windows—if he appear at all in our theology, or in our preaching, or in the relation between the Church and politics—he is the Lord of the House, for Jehovah does not share with him the sovereignty. When a

Kierkegaard or a Kutter, measuring the Church by an absolute
standard, proceeds to utter his complaint against it, we are
bound to uphold his criticism, indeed we must underline it and
endorse it.   In matters pertaining to God—and they are after all
the concern of the Church—a single failure involves complete
failure. Nor is it possible to 'exaggerate' a single failure, for it
does but remind us of the vast ambiguity of our whole situation.
The circumstantial evidence against us is overwhelming. We
cannot defend the Church by claiming that, though no doubt
there is in it something of Baal, yet it possesses also something
of Jehovah. We have no protection against the necessity of
repentance. We stand in need, not of patience, but of the impatience of the prophets, not of well-mannered pleasantry, but
of a grim assault, not of the historian's balanced judgement—
neither the priests of Baal nor the Swiss or Danish clergy are
after all quite so bad as they are painted!—but of a love of truth
which hacks its way through the very backbone of the matter,
and then dares to bring an accusation of unrighteousness against
every upright man.

I have left for myself seven thousand men, who have not
bowed the knee to the shame of Baal (1 Kings xix. 18). That is
the reverse side, which Elijah does not see. But who can see
these 7,000, however delicate may be his insight into the hidden
piety of the Church? Surely the Word of God reveals here, not
some hidden undercurrent, but the 'wholly other' side of the
history of the Church. These 7,000 are not—paradoxical though
it may seem, and contrary to the plain meaning of the text—a
numerical quantity, a 'tiny fraction of the nation' (Jülicher), a
minority of the 'quiet in the land'. The 7,000 are not men whom
Elijah might have met and known and pointed out. He was
right when he said, *I am left alone*. A prophet as such is always
isolated and alone. The Quantum of his lonely soul cannot be
increased or decreased. The 7,000 are not so many individuals.
As one whole, they represent the vast, mighty, invisible host,
encompassing the lonely Elijah: as only 7,000, as a diminished
number, they represent invisibly the whole people of God in
their quality as objects of election in the midst of rejection; they
represent the invisible Church of Jacob in the midst of the
Church of Esau. The 7,000, then, are the people of God whom
He has not cast off. They stand upright—but only in the
presence of God. The answer of God to Elijah does not mean
that there are a number of men who know God, but that there is
no limit to the number of those who are known by Him. It does
not mean that there are just 7,000 men upon whom God has

mercy: it means that His mercy is infinite. It does not mean that there exist a calculable number of men who are at peace within themselves: it means that the Oneness of God triumphs over the whole questionableness of the history of the Church. The Word speaks of miracle, of election, of God: it does not speak of some oasis in the desert, of Assisi or of Bad Boll[1]—indeed, neither Assisi nor Bad Boll were havens of rest for St. Francis or for Blumhardt, even at the height of their success! It is of course true that the invisible quality of election is here and there displayed; but even so, it is displayed in its unobservability, that is to say, it is displayed as miracle and as revelation. The Island of Truth is, as we have explained earlier (viii. 18), a submarine island. *I* have left *for myself* 7,000 men. God alone justifies. God alone saves. But He DOES justify: He DOES save. Elijah is not alone: all Israel is not cast off. Where human hope comes to an end, God enters upon the scene. ·He has waited in His wrath for the cry of the lonely man in Israel, only in order that He may declare His mercy to him and to all Israel.

Even so then at this present time also there is a remnant according to the election of grace. But if it is by grace, it is no more of works : otherwise grace is no more grace. The relation of the Church to its Theme is the relation between time and eternity, between men and God. The Church, every Church, is thereby dethroned—but perhaps also justified. Yes, justified, if the dethronement and judgement inherent in this relationship be veritably the Word of God, if the utter humiliation and powerlessness and brokenness of men be guaranteed by the power of God, if the veil of time be rent asunder in the eternal 'Moment' of revelation, if Christ the Lord incline towards men. The Gospel which we proclaim is that this does occur, has occurred, and will occur; and that this occurrence is Truth. When the Truth occurs, Elijah is not alone, and the Church—the whole Church and every Church—has not been cast off. The Church of Jacob is already *at this present time* in the midst of the Church of Esau. Already it is there, for eyes which see and for ears which hear, in the love which is poured forth into the heart by the Holy Spirit, in words which are more than words, in the readiness of many to obey the will of God. But who are the many? Once again, they are no numerical 7,000. Mention a number, and it diminishes to an invisible *remnant*. Attempt to disembark upon the Island of Truth as it emerges from the sea, and the water rushes in to submerge it—and we are drowned. The number here disclosed is the number of the elect. Election

[1] See note on p. 312. [Tr.]

is not an affair of this or that man; no man can claim it as his
own; and yet it concerns all men. Those peculiar men, in whom
the thoughts of God—which are beyond all thinking!—are, as
it were, revealed, are what they are by grace alone; only by
grace can their divine quality be made known; and moreover,
it is only grace—universal grace—that is visible in them by
grace. It follows then that the remnant must not be looked for
by direct observation; it must not be located in particular cases
of piety, in particular epochs of faith, in revivals, or in reformations, where it is supposed that the grace of God breaks through;
for then *grace is no more grace*. This does not mean that grace
may not also be where these things are, but that it is there only
inasmuch as God can also permit Himself to be found at such
high-water marks of human religious development, inasmuch as
there also 'obedience' (x. 16) does occur. But, in order that all
direct observation may be put to shame, Grace is not there
alone—indeed, if it be SOUGHT there, it is assuredly precisely
not there—but rather just as much, and perhaps much more
properly, at the quite different low-water mark, where there are
no *works* such as ecclesiastical historians delight to describe.
Grace is where all time and every period of time is an 'interim',
where God alone can open men's eyes to God, and where God
alone can discover and recognize Himself in poor, forlorn
humanity. Thus, whether the curve of history be moving upwards or downwards, whether uncouth Teutons or cultivated
nineteenth-century religious men be the objects which are
perceived, it is the knowledge of God which itself makes the
decision. God has not cast off His people—because He foreknew
them (xi. 2). The election of men is by grace: this is the humiliation of the Gospel. But it justifies and saves, because it humi-
liates. This is the Gospel of the remnant which verily exists,
whose light shines *at this present time* in the misery and guilt of
the Church. The one hope of the Church is that God should
now justify Himself and bear witness to His own Oneness. And
this is in fact the hope of the Church, because in Christ God is
now revealing Himself as the cause of our tribulation and of our
guilt.

**vv. 7–10. What then? That which Israel seeketh for,
that he obtained not; but the election obtained it, and the
rest were hardened: according as it is written, God gave
them a spirit of stupor, eyes that they should not see,
and ears that they should not hear, unto this very day.
And David saith, Let their table be made a snare, and a**

**trap, and a stumbling block, and a recompense unto them:
Let their eyes be darkened, that they may not see, and
bow down their back alway.**

Once again we pause at the 'No!' spoken by God against the
Church, in order that it may be quite plain that, when we speak
of the hope of the Church, we mean God. If hope is to be pure
and genuine and real, if the Church of Jacob is to appear, it can
be only as men wrestle with this negation. As has been pointed
out (ix. 31), the negation occurs in the fact that Israel hath not
obtained that which he—**seeketh for.** Not only does Israel
not obtain, but he never will obtain. We know what he is seeking for—his own righteousness, camouflaged as the righteousness of God (x. 3). He endeavours to justify and save men by
enthroning piety. Has there ever been a Church which has not
—no doubt after some hesitation—done this? Is there any
one, sharing in the inner life of the Church, who is free from
this guilty endeavour? The real significance of the Church lies,
however, elsewhere. Is not the Church aware that men cannot
undertake this search, because they are men, and because, if they
do undertake it, their whole questionableness becomes apparent.
The search itself is not guilty—*Seek ye him, and your soul shall
live.* We are guilty, because we forget that the search is beyond
human competence. We are guilty, because of the pride which
makes us suppose that we can seek without having already
found, and because of the thoughtlessness with which we throw
away what has already been found, in order that we may continue to seek—in vain.

On the frontier of human possibility, that is to say, upon the
frontier of the Church, stands the man who does not forget, is
not proud or thoughtless, the man who, bowed under the judgement of God, has obtained righteousness, even the righteousness
of God. **The election obtained** what is really meant by the quest
of the Church. It has been pressed home to us that the elect are
not this or that group of men who can be named and pointed out.
The elect cannot be included in any programme of ours. We
cannot start our investigation with them as lights of the Church
with whom we must first reckon. They are not a particularly
inspiring 'school of thought'. They are not an 'inspiration' to
us, save in so far as they incite us to eternal life; and they do
this only in the form of a scandal. They are here and they are
there, but they certainly are not where we cry, 'Lo, there'.
They have this and that name, but they have assuredly no name
by which we can address them. They are known in order that

they may be unknown. They emerge only in order that they may be submerged. Their election and the success with which they *obtain* is not a thing capable of description in books of devotion; nor can their 'influence' be set out in the pages of Church history. The historian can describe only what is not their election, not their success, what they have not *obtained*. In these bearers of hope the Church can see only the unfathomable freedom of God, for the hope of the elect is centred upon His grace. In them we can learn only the lesson—*Israel hath not obtained that which he seeketh for*.

The rest were hardened. The light shineth in the darkness— and was not overcome! The light does shine in the darkness. Hopelessness is hopelessness, and death is death. There is no continuity between the bearers of hope and those to whom hope is brought. There is no infection of the one by the other, no influence of the one upon the other. Nothing is transferred. They meet only in God. Only from God do they obtain that which, if they do not obtain it from Him, they seek in vain. The elect can be for others no more than signposts to God. They cannot be the divine beginning or seed or kernel. According to the synoptic narrative, Jesus sent out His disciples to proclaim the Kingdom (Matt. x. 7), not to establish it. Moreover, the disciples, as is expressly mentioned in Matt. x. 28, are in grave and mortal danger of being unmindful of God, of being themselves 'outside', of being *hardened* and hermetically sealed against the divine possibility. It is clear, therefore, that the Church needs to apprehend its hope, to understand that there is no hope, save when God works the miracle. And the miracle of God is the message of the elect. In fact, the only observable truth which the Church can proclaim—and it ought to be inscribed on every church door, to be written on the first page of every sermon, and to form the title of every religious book—is the truth that *The rest were hardened*. *The rest* are, however, no more a definable quantity than are the elect. In so far as God is not recognized, all are the *rest*; and they are so through Him. God must be known by Himself. Thence comes the inclusion of the elect and the exclusion of the *rest*; and to the latter the elect belong, in so far as their existence is not their election.

Thus it is that we cannot escape the tribulation of the Church of Esau. God has smitten it with a—**spirit of stupor,** with eyes that —**should not see,** and with ears that—**should not hear.** He has made their table—that is to say, their whole behaviour—**a snare and a trap, and a stumbling block, and a recompense.** He has —**bowed down their back** under an inexorable judgement, which they do not perceive to be justification and salvation. This God—who, in revealing His mercy, so mercilessly utters His 'No'; who, in turning His face towards all, so sternly excludes all; who, in making Himself known, remains hidden and is first known as the Hidden God—is the hope of the Church. His is the Oneness, the Identity, the Grace, and the Truth. And through Jesus crucified and risen, and by no other means, He is our Father. Whence then, we ask, comes so great a hope to the Church, that it should set its hope upon THIS God?

A WORD TO THOSE WITHOUT

XI. 11-24

v. 11. I say then, Did they stumble that they might fall? God forbid: but by their fall salvation is come unto the Gentiles—for to provoke them to jealousy.

Did they stumble that they might fall? We now see, contrasted with the Church, with every Church, the 'Others'—the **Gentiles.** No doubt even they constitute some kind of Church; but we will, for the time being, regard them, in comparison with what we are wont to call a Church, as, at least relatively, unecclesiastical persons, as men who do not hear what we hear or see what we see, as men who observe the work of the Church from outside and bear witness to its failure. The *world* sees—and this is the case even when the *world* is itself a Church observing another Church, perhaps silently—that there is in the Church a lack of success. The Church is seen tripping up, *stumbling* over an unseen obstacle. In so far as we ourselves are to some extent healthy, romantic, undamaged *Gentiles*, we shall, for example, find it exceedingly difficult to 'assist' at a Mass without a strong, deep feeling that the whole action is simply impossible: our feeling may even vent itself in the very strong language of the Heidelberg Confession. If, on the other hand, we are ourselves somewhere or other *within*—and we do, all of us, belong to some *within* or other!—we must be under no illusions; for, without doubt, those whom we call 'outsiders' feel precisely the same thing about us. *Gentiles* are always in the fortunate position of being able to say that the Church fails to impress them, that its work is trivial, or that, though perhaps it may be worthy of some respect, at any rate it cannot be BELIEVED IN. Gentiles see the Church concerned with the Word of God, but they see no sign of the Word. Outsiders as such have a most delicate insight into the tribulation and guilt of the Church. They perceive the divine

'No' which is set against it. They see the pricks against which
those inside are unable to kick. The indictment which God
brings against the Church is also drawn up against it by the *world*,
sometimes with rare intelligence, sometimes unintelligently.
And yet, the indictment of the world is meaningless except in
the context of God's indictment. That is to say, the impotence
and embarrassment and incredibility which are displayed to the
world by the Church are not a final, metaphysical reality. Even
were the Gentiles to see ten times more clearly what they do see,
the Church would not therefore be defeated, done with, and
finished. As God does not permit the world in its tribulation and
guilt to fall to the ground, so He does not permit the Church—
which is the world's loftiest peak—to be destroyed. The World
and the Church are what they are only because they are related
to one another. Neither can say that the other is excluded
absolutely. What is absolute is simply the fact that both are
opposed to God. Seen from God's point of view, the Church is
done with—but then, so is the World. Israel AND the World are
both done away. It is, therefore, impossible that they should
have stumbled—against the rock of offence and the stone of
stumbling (ix. 33)—merely in order that they might fall.

But by their fall salvation is come unto the Gentiles. The
tribulation and guilt of the Church is a 'Moment' in the invisible, divine scheme of advance from rejection to election,
from 'No' to 'Yes', from Esau to Jacob, from Pharaoh to Moses.
By this scheme the sovereign freedom of God is set in motion.
By it He makes Himself known, and reconciles the world to
Himself (ix. 22, 23). The tribulation of the Church is no final
occurrence; it is no second metaphysical reality side by side
with the glory and righteousness of God. The tribulation of the
Church is simply the expression in time of His glory, of His
righteousness, of His will to help all men. It is the cloud of the
wrath of God covering the hope of the Church. *His anger
endureth but for a moment; in his favour is life. Weeping may
endure for a night, but joy cometh in the morning* (Ps. xxx. 5).
Rejection is no more than the shadow of election. The 'No' of
God is no more than the inevitable turning to the man of this
world of the reverse side of His 'Yes'. Esau is Esau only in so
far as he is not Jacob. The invisible hardening of Pharaoh bears
witness to the same divine power as the invisible calling of
Moses. He who receives the revelation of God must submit to
the tribulation and guilt involved in his position, in order that
he may be himself the guarantor of the revelation of the hope
which is his. Israel and the Church stand in the first position.

The second is born in the catastrophe of their disruption—*By their fall salvation is come unto the Gentiles—where sin abounded, grace did abound more exceedingly* (v. 20). Election is the real and possible, though utterly incomprehensible, salvation of men from the inevitable destiny of rejection. The 'Yes' of God consists only in the transformation of His 'No'. Jacob is Jacob because he is not Esau. There is no vocation of Moses which is not also the vocation of Pharaoh—in his incurable hardening. Thus it is that the salvation of the Gentiles comes into being through the fall of the Church. But in what fashion does it come into being? Through the guarantee that the divine grace is above all human unrighteousness. For the unrighteousness of the Gentiles, which cries loudly to heaven, is less of an obstacle to the righteousness of God than the human righteousness of the Church. The fruitful 'moment' of heathenism is its relative and negative opposition to the Church. The Gentiles are justified only because of their opposition to the Church; they are not otherwise justified. Salvation is theirs, inasmuch as God willeth to display His almighty power over against the Church, inasmuch as the human work of the Church must again and again be broken in pieces on God. Salvation comes to the Gentiles, inasmuch as the Church crucifies the Christ.

To provoke them to jealousy (cf. ix. 19). The context which we have outlined above shows that the moment we formulate a metaphysical distinction between two concrete classes of individuals—those without and those within—the distinction falls to the ground. Both are, in fact, objects, instruments, bearers of one divine operation. As a divine possibility, election involves the possibility of rejection. The 'Yes' of God illuminates the place where His 'No' is complete and radical as the divine negation. Esau is provoked by the recollection that God prefers Jacob. In his hardening, Pharaoh participates in the divine origin of the call of Moses. By *jealousy* he shares in the vast disturbance which of necessity the existence of the elect —in whom the freedom and grace of God are demonstrated— prepares for the rejected. This *jealousy* or disturbance is, humanly speaking, the hope of the Church. Disturbance is the final description in human categories of that which men are, have been, and will be, when they are not the elect. The stumbling of the Church, its failure, its inability to impress and convince, the inevitable irony of its whole situation, in short, the deep-seated disease from which Jacob suffers, do but serve to reawaken in it the recognition of the freedom of God. The Church is thereby forced back upon that health-bringing jealousy and fruitful disturbance which are pregnant with the promise of God. The Church is thereby opened to God. This reawakened recollection, this disquiet, this openness, mean that the tribulation and guilt of the Church have attained their end and their goal. The Church has reached its fulfilment—in God.

vv. 12–15. Now if their fall is the riches of the world, and their loss the riches of the Gentiles; how much more their fulness ? But I speak to you that are Gentiles. Inasmuch then as I am an apostle of the Gentiles, I glorify my ministry: if by any means I may provoke to jealousy them that are my flesh, and may save some of them. For if the casting away of them is the reconciling of the world, what shall the receiving of them be, but life from the dead ?

Now if their fall is the riches of the world, and their loss the riches of the Gentiles; how much more their fulness? To stumble upon the reality of God, to be put to shame by Him, to have to die at His hands is, then, an occurrence pregnant with hope. When it occurs, a man may fall, it is true, but he falls only to rise to his feet precisely with the aid of that obstacle which brought him to the ground. Such a man has not fallen finally. His *fall* is not metaphysical, utter, absolute, and infinite. Because God is God, and because He is free, to stumble over Him involves the possibility of rising again. And those who observe the *loss* of the Church from outside, and are convinced of its failure, are bound to reckon with this further possibility. The fall of the Church is not the end. The tribulation and guilt of the Church, the *fall* and *loss* of Israel, as they are manifested in the crucifixion of Christ, are the *riches of the world* and the *riches of the Gentiles*. But only in the light of the Cross of Christ is this wealth revealed to the world; for it is in the perception of this catastrophe that God makes known that He has not renounced His freedom and invisibility, His *eternal power and divinity* (i. 20). In this catastrophe He makes the assertion that He Himself and He alone is God—above all human works. Election occurs at the point where this is displayed and seen— whether by those outside or by those inside. There the risen Lord —who is *rich unto all that call upon him* (x. 12)—is proclaimed. There He gives grace unto the humble. Beyond the Cross stands the Resurrection, unobservably shown forth by God, and seen by eyes which God has made to see! There God authenticates Himself, and asserts His validity. There He sets Himself forth as the

Origin of all things, Creator and Redeemer. Where human
possession in all its fullness falls to the ground, and appears as
void and loss and failure, as a minus quantity which cannot be
perceived, there is exposed the fullness of the possession of God.
His Fullness! yes! His plus quantity, His riches, His mercy, His
observability. This is the goal of the emptying of all human
possession. Yes! and human emptiness ends also. Only the
Fullness of God, the divine PLUS which takes the place of the
human MINUS, has no end. The end of the Church is the beginning of the Fullness of God. His Fullness is both unlimited and
eternal. Not only does it erect a barrier; it also dissolves that
finiteness with which it is contrasted. There is in the Fullness of
God no election AND rejection, no Gentile AND Jew, no outer AND
inner. All are one—in Christ Jesus. Negatively, therefore, the
end of the Church—the Crucifixion of Jesus—is the action of
God, by which He frees Himself from every limitation which
men impose upon Him. It is the possibility and reality of
the divine election by grace, of man's reconciliation with God.
It is the bursting forth in time of the eternal 'Moment'.
Positively, however, the end of the Church—the Resurrection
of Christ—is the eternal light itself. It is eternity—beside
which there is no time—the risen life, the effective, final
redemption, the election which makes rejection impossible.
Those who observe the failure of the Church from without
must understand that the end of the Church concerns the
Last Things—the destruction of death (xi. 15, 1 Cor. xv. 26).
Where the *loss*—the sacred loss—of the Church is, there stands
before the door that 'Wholly Other' Fullness. To say that the
Church is done with, is a statement which should be made only
in fear and trembling; indeed, it had better not be made at all.
For who is able to the bear the knowledge of that doing away?

**I speak to you that are Gentiles. Inasmuch then as I am an
apostle of the Gentiles, I glorify my ministry : if by any means I
may provoke to jealousy them that are my flesh, and may save
some of them.** It is necessary for those outside to hear this and
to ponder it. By the tribulation and guilt of the Church they
are justified. The moment of the rejection of those who are
within is the moment of the salvation of those who are without.
Israel is judged by the sole dominion of God. By it the Gentiles
are saved. Void of any ground of justification, and almost
devoid of any extenuating circumstances, they are saved in the
utter nakedness of their almost total worldliness. They have
no claim on God that can for one moment be taken seriously.
For it is to be hoped that they will not erect their weakness into

a claim. Paul is their apostle, and to them he directs the Gospel.
In their weakness and nakedness he sees a parable of the poverty
of all who stand before God and are justified by Him. He sees
them contrasted with those others who, robust in their own
righteousness, do not stand before God, and are not justified.
It is this parabolic insight that rivets Paul so firmly to Israel
and brings him back to them. He always begins his preaching
with Israel, as Luke so clearly records. And this is because
the nakedness of the Gentiles which, contrasted with the fullness of Israel, occasions their openness towards God, is simply
the condition in which all men—Israel included—stand in His
presence. Human nakedness is the point where, beyond human
righteousness, the divine 'And Yet' of the forgiveness of sins is
made evident. This concerns Israel also. And conversely: How
can forgiveness be apprehended as that which lies beyond the
human nakedness of the children of the world, if the whole
meaning of human life be not perceived in the final, supreme,
religious, human possibility? Forgiveness cannot be proclaimed
to the world save through the capitulation of the Church. On
the one hand, therefore, the world is the mirror in which the
Church recognizes its own humiliation and its own promise. On
the other hand, the Church is the mirror required by the world,
if it is to perceive its own relation to God. It must be borne in
mind, however, that 'Church' and 'World' are to be understood,
not as historical, but as dialectical, factors. Mankind cannot be
rent asunder into two distinct groups. For as it is inevitable that
the Church should be provoked to jealousy when it is disturbed
by the World, so also it is inevitable that the Gentiles should be
compelled to recognize that this justification involves also the
justification of the Church. And so an immediate pressure is
exerted *to save some of them*, and to break them loose from their
hardening. For this activity is the sign that salvation and not
destruction is the eternal future of all. Were the *apostle of the
Gentiles* concerned only with the Gentile in the Gentiles, and not
also with the Gentile in the Jew, he would not be an emissary of
Jesus Christ. Nor would the Gentile be the elect of God, if he
rested simply in the opinion that the Jew as such was reprobate
and that the Church had simply come to an end.

**For if the casting away of them is the reconciling of the world,
what shall the receiving of them be, but life from the dead?** The
casting away of the Church is the fact that its undertaking of the
last, supreme, human possibility, its attempt to hear and speak
the Word of God, has been pronounced a titanic action, and
therefore impossible. Having undertaken this impossibility, the

Church is weighed down as it can be weighed down by no other activity; and the proof of this is that it has—crucified Christ. The Church seeketh after God; and when it meets Him, being unable to comprehend Him, it rejects Him. But when this catastrophe is recognized, the *reconciling of the world* with God occurs. When the old man, at the highest peak of his possibility in the Church, encounters God and becomes a sinner, he must die. But this moment of death is the 'Moment' when the new man is born, who is at *peace with God* (v. 1): *While we were enemies, we were reconciled to God through the death of his Son* (v. 10). How, save in the collapse of the Church, can we perceive that we are enemies and that we are *reconciled*? Did not Paul stand on the threshold of the new world, precisely because the collapse of Pharisaism ran longitudinally through his life in this world? The final justification of the Church consists in its perpetual collapse, just as Pharisaism is justified by its power of self-destruction. And both are justified, because it is the self-destroyed Jew and the collapse of the Church which are of supreme interest to the Gentiles and to the World. Humanity is thereby made aware that there is always in its midst a place where the consequences of its inherent possibilities are fully worked out, and where its proved impossibility makes room for the appearance of the possibility of God. And so we know that rejection is not the final word either for humanity as a whole or for the Church. And we know also that neither the word *reconciliation* nor the phrase *peace with God* is final, for they are altogether beyond our hearing. Beyond our *rejection* there awaits us our *receiving*—the receiving, that is to say, of human impossibility into the possibility of God, the oneness of concrete existence and Primal Origin, the clothing of corruption with incorruption, the passing of time into eternity,—in fact, the new Heaven and the new Earth. This is what the impossibility of the Church awaits. Nowhere is the meaning of rejection so unmistakable as it is in the Church—and nowhere else is the reception of the man of this world into union with God so unmistakable. When mankind realiter and in truth hears and utters the Word of God; when the Gospel—really the Gospel and not Christianity!—is preached to the whole world; when the programme of the Church is carried out as the programme of God; then—but dare we say 'then', for we speak of no time, but of all time? Ought we not, in order to counteract the misunderstanding of a temporal eschatological possibility, to say rather 'there'—there, where the human possibility embodied in the Church is identical with its true meaning and significance, appears the possibility of God Himself and of God only. And this is more than reconciliation, it is—*life from the dead*. Let us put this in another way. The non-rejection, or rather the receiving of the Church, the realization of the Church of Jacob, is identical with the dawning of the Day of Jesus Christ, with the manifestation of the glory of God—for which we now hope (v. 2), and can only hope—and with the world redeemed by God. Where hope is, there is also hope for the Church. And this hope must be announced *to you that are Gentiles*, to you spectators from without, to you who are justified as outsiders. All true hope is hope for the Church; for hope for all is included in hope for the Church. If there is to be health anywhere, it must appear where the sickness of the world breaks out in manifest disease What is it, then, for which we are waiting? We await our existential hearing of the Word of God and its existential utterance. If mankind as a whole are to have their attention drawn to this existential occurrence, it can be only within those walls where the attempt to hear and to speak the Word of God is continually undertaken, and where it as continually fails.

vv. 16–18. And if the firstfruit is holy, so is the lump: and if the root is holy, so are the branches. But if some of the branches were broken off, and thou, being a wild olive, wast grafted in among them, and didst become partaker with them of the root of the fatness of the olive tree; glory not over the branches: but if thou gloriest, it is not thou that bearest the root, but the root thee.

If the firstfruit is holy, so is the lump : and if the root is holy, so are the branches. The holy *firstfruit* and the holy *lump* embrace the final eschatological possibility, which is the Theme, and consequently the judgement and the promise, of the Church. This Theme is the permanent soil and life of the Church; and it is also that by which it is perpetually put to shame. Nevertheless, hoping where there is no hope (iv. 18), and bound to its Theme, the Church is not put to shame (v. 5, ix. 33, x. 11). The parables of firstfruit and lump, of root and branch, must not be taken as referring to some immanent or 'organic' continuity between the Church and its Primal Origin and Final End. Paul may, it is true, when he speaks of *firstfruit* and *root*, have in mind the patriarchs or the elect in Israel (xi. 9); but even so, he thinks of these historical personages only as hearers of the eschatological possibility. Not for one moment is he thinking of some supernatural tradition in history or in the context of this world. The holiness of the Primal Origin and of the Final End breaks through every human analogy. There is no human language adequate

to express the participation in this holiness by that which lies
in the middle—betwixt Beginning and End—or to express the
connexion between the known Church of Esau and the unknown
Church of Jacob. The hope of the Church is directed towards
the holiness of God, who dwelleth in light unapproachable,
towards a holiness which is utterly transcendent and miraculous.
And the holiness of God is, as we have seen (xi. 13-15), the hope
of the Church, because in the Church suffering and guilty
humanity is able to comprehend the question to which the
holiness of God is the answer. In its vast and permanent un-
holiness the Church is sanctified by hope.

But if some of the branches were broken off, and thou, being a
wild olive, wast grafted in among them, and didst become
partaker with them of the root of the fatness of the olive tree;
glory not over the branches. The parable, as Paul employs it is,
of course, an agricultural impossibility—'Paul is a child of the
city; but Jesus is a countryman' (Jülicher). But that is not the
reason why Paul has uttered an impossibility. Rather, the incomprehensible occurrence with which Paul is concerned defies
every correct and natural analogy. The breaking off of the
branches of the true olive tree is—the rejection of the Church.
The grafting in of the wild olive is—the election of those without.
The one is as monstrous as the other—and indeed, this is the
point. God is not found of them that seek Him, but of those who
do not seek Him (x. 20). And this simply because He is God and
willeth to make Himself known to both—as God. He is the holy
root of the tree. Broken off, the branch withers up and dies.
Grafted into it, the wild olive lives and grows. This does not
mean that the wild cutting is preferred to the root's own proper
branch, the Gentile to the Jew, the outer to the inner. Indeed,
the pride with which the outsider, luxuriating in his supposedly
wild freedom, looks down upon those within the Church, is less
defensible than the opposite sense of superiority. The outsider
may not be more completely naked before God than those within;
but his nakedness is certainly not a better nakedness than the
respectable human righteousness of the Church. The point is
that it is nakedness pure and simple before God which is acceptable to Him; it is the status of childlikeness and misery which
renders men accessible to His justification and salvation. Men
simply stand before God and His grace; they do not stand by
virtue of their being Gentiles, or men of the world, or men outside the Church. The nakedness of the Gentiles is not more than
a parable of that nakedness which is acceptable to God! If self-
conscious adherence to the Church does not justify men before

God, neither does natural simplicity, nor the unpretentious honesty of the proletariat, nor the nowadays much-vaunted superiority of the religious-minded 'layman' who has discarded theological thought and language, nor any other selfconscious or unselfconscious carelessness and weakness. All human activity, from the devotional exercises of a Benedictine monastery to the vigorous and comprehensive programme of the Social-Democrats, is enacted on the rungs of one single ladder. No man can boast of the possession of that poverty in spirit, of that absolute removal from the Church, which Jesus blessed, and which makes the Gentiles righteous before God—because that poverty has no concrete existence. If those within the Church are clearly unable to claim as a right the divine possibility of forgiveness which meets absolute poverty, neither can it be claimed as a right by those outside, as though they were in possession of some peculiar advantage. Divine forgiveness must be reverenced as a miracle.

But if thou gloriest, it is not thou that bearest the root, but the root thee. If then, friend of Nature, thou must boast; if thou, beloved Gentile, outsider, unecclesiastical person, must vaunt thy superiority over the Church; if thou, O highbrow intellectual socialist, must praise thy independent and autonomous relation to God or to something thou hast put in His place—and apparently thou must boast, because thou hast long since formed thyself and thy friends into a little Church!—nevertheless, the fact remains that in thy greatest prosperity thou art living of the possibility which the Church shows to be impossible; that thy right is at best precisely that for which the Church is condemned; that—we say it again—in thy greatest happiness thou art moving in the 'Yes' which for the Church is moving relentlessly to 'No'. Thy life is depending upon that which lies beyond thy possibility and the Church's impossibility, beyond thy right and its wrong, beyond thy 'Yes' and its 'No'—*The root beareth thee*. It is mere illusion to suppose that this can be reversed. It is illusion to suppose that thy pure sincerity, thy nobility and religious amateurishness, could be the root, the source of divinity. For a time, perchance, thou mayest be untouched by the tribulation and guilt of the Church, but thou canst not rid thyself of that by which it is oppressed and condemned. What thou art, thou art only inasmuch as thou art released from thy superiority by that same Unknown. Whosoever exalts himself beyond the necessity of release shares the tribulation and guilt of the Church. He is no longer 'outside', but altogether and far more desperately 'within', and therefore—a lopped-off branch. And so we are brought to the point where we are forced to recognize the possibility that the branches of the wild olive, should they vaunt superiority over the Church, may also be cut off. Of this possibility we must now speak.

vv. 19–22. Thou wilt say then, Branches were broken off, that I might be grafted in. Well; by their unbelief they were broken off, and thou standest by thy faith. Be not highminded, but fear: for if God spared not the natural branches, neither will he spare thee. Behold then the goodness and severity of God: toward them that fell, severity; but toward thee, God's goodness, if thou continue in his goodness: otherwise thou also shalt be cut off.

Branches were broken off, that I might be grafted in. Such is the triumphant claim which 'outsiders' are accustomed to advance against the Church. But is the claim true? May not the opposite be the truth? We suppose that to-day we—yes, we!—have seen God and His Kingdom, that we have understood 'Life' and 'Decision'; that we apprehend, experience, are convinced; that we are vigorous in propagating—the truth. We have left the old ways, broken the old 'tables of stone', overcome the 'men of yesterday', and thrown down the idols which men worshipped aforetime. And now our day has come. Do not our claims run in some sort after this fashion?

Well!—is the comment on all this. No one would wish to contradict it flatly. The claim is nothing new or unfamiliar. For it is ever so. The icy wind of God opens one door and bangs another. His freedom releases some and oppresses others, creates one vessel for honour and another for dishonour, lightens one place and plunges another in deep shadow. All this talk and all this freedom are, therefore, in some manner a parable of truth—so long as they do not proceed from complete misunderstanding. Why should the elect who are outside be forbidden to lift up their voices and praise God? Why should they not sing the song of the time when it is a good and a delightful thing to be alive?

But—by their unbelief they were broken off, and thou standest by thy faith. This is the criterion of election: a criterion which should at least put men on their guard. For a man to assess his own position in the Kingdom of God is a risky proceeding. To discover oneself in the picture of the history of salvation and to compare oneself with others is exceedingly dangerous. Hazardous it is to know too certainly who and what we are. Better that we should leave it to God to know us. For it lies within His competence to decide whether what we are is true or whether it is not at the same time a lie and a delusion. The ground of election is faith, and the ground of rejection is unbelief. But who is a believer? and who an unbeliever? Belief and unbelief are established only in God. For us they are unobservable, incomprehensible, and uncertain. Only the root is effective. And in regard to the root, what pre-eminence have the wild branches over the natural branches which have been cut off?

Be not high-minded, but fear. 'The note of absolute certainty, present in viii. 28, 29, is absent here' (Jülicher). Of course it is. The reference in viii. 28, 29, was to *those that love God*; and love of God emerges always on the background of fear, which, as we are once again reminded, is the beginning of wisdom. Faith, unlike piety, is not a thing which can be vaunted and paraded before God and man, or played off against them. Faith is not a visible ladder, up which we can climb. Faith is born in fear and trembling from the knowledge that God is God. All that is not thus born is not faith, but that unbelief which is the cause of rejection. 'Assurance of salvation'—the phrase is of doubtful legitimacy—is not a possession which can be claimed either against or on behalf of the Church. Only complete misunderstanding of the Reformers could lead to such an opinion. The decision is God's. His goodness and His severity are—because they are His—new every morning. Election stands by grace: we must never forget this. An 'assurance of salvation' apart from the most exclusive 'Double Predestination', that is to say, as assurance has been understood in recent Protestantism, is—worse than heathenism.

'The servile spirit of Hagar grew proud the moment she had been given something. And that is the way to be turned out of the house' (Steinhofer). So it is that the shouts of triumph which have so often been raised against the Church by those outside it are no more than the sound of bells ringing in a new church. Not for long does this new church escape the tribulation and guilt of the old Church. Soon it must take its place amongst the branches which have been cut off—**For if God spared not the natural branches, neither will he spare thee. Behold then the goodness and severity of God : toward them that fell, severity ; but toward thee, God's goodness, if thou continue in his goodness : otherwise thou also shalt be cut off.** Laymen who make a parade of the fact that they are laymen, and men of the world who affect to be satisfied with their worldliness, constitute, if that were possible, a greater menace than the claims of an arrogant priesthood. The genuine elect who stand outside the Church avoid the language of victory.

vv. 23, 24. And they also, if they continue not in their unbelief, shall be grafted in: for God is able to graft them in again. For if thou wast cut out of that which is by nature a wild olive tree, and wast grafted contrary to nature into a good olive tree: how much more shall these, which are the natural branches, be grafted into their own olive tree?

The hope of the Church is inextinguishable and unassailable. *He that scattered Israel will gather him* (Jer. xxxi. 10). Rejection and election are of God. Both are wonderful, inscrutable, and incomprehensible. More wonderful, more inscrutable, and more incomprehensible than the election of those who ever seek God is the election of those who never seek Him. They indeed have good reason to set their hope on grace alone, to hope with the Church and for it.

THE GOAL

XI. 25-36

vv. 25-7. For I would not, brethren, have you ignorant of this mystery, lest ye be wise in your own conceits, that a hardening in part hath befallen Israel, until the fulness of the Gentiles be come in; and so all Israel shall be saved: as it is written, There shall come out of Zion[1] the Deliverer, and shall turn away ungodliness from Jacob: For this shall be my covenant unto them, when I shall take away their sins.

I would not, brethren, have you ignorant of this mystery, lest ye be wise in your own conceits. To gaze steadily at hope-less reality, to apprehend its relativity, to perceive the goal to which it presses and by which alone it is provided with significance—this is Hope. Hope-less reality broken through by an indirect apprehension of hope and penetrated by a hidden meaning—this is the 'Secret' or mysterium. By *mystery* Paul means what we call 'paradox'.—The existence of the *man of sin* who restrains the dawning of the Day of Jesus Christ is a *mystery* (2 Thess. ii. 7).

---

[1] Paul quotes here the LXX Version of Isa. lix. 20; with, however, the remarkable alteration of ἕνεκεν Σιών into ἐκ Σιών. In spite of its authentication in the MSS., and in spite of the ease with which commentators have passed over the difficulty, I am unhappy about the reading. Beza suspected ἐκ to have been an abbreviation of ἕνεκεν, or the mistake of a scribe. Calvin rightly comments: *Aptius ad propositum quadrabat loquutio, qua utitur propheta.* If ἐκ is Pauline—and I dare not for the present accept the suggestion proposed by Beza—some attempt must be made to do it justice. This I have tried to do in the exposition which follows.

The disturbing distinction at the resurrection between the living and those who have already died is a *mystery* (1 Cor. xv. 51). The union of husband and wife which at first sight appears extremely questionable is a *mystery* (Eph. v. 32). Above all, the Gospel itself, regarded as a human word from which the divine Word may break forth, is a *mystery*. Calvin writes—Quoties desperationem nobis iniicit longior mora, occurrit mysterii nomen. It follows, therefore, that the whole relationship between God and man, as set forth in the Church, is a *mystery*. The fact that we are able to observe only the Church of Esau, in its tribulation and guilt, presents a riddle which we cannot endure. In the place of the revelation proper to the existence of the Church, we find always and everywhere nothing but concealment. Revelation and election pass bluntly by the Church, by every Church. This whole situation constitutes a mystery from which there is no escape. It is of paramount importance that we should not be *ignorant of this mystery*, for it is the God-given riddle, in which we verily encounter God. The divine mystery of consolation in despair, of exhortation to hope, stands in direct opposition to all those final human words, to all that wisdom of our *own conceits*, to all those riddles which we propose. Faced by the actual course of observable human life, our words are altogether irrelevant. Confronted by the tribulation and guilt of the Church, our restless, subjective explanations, our excited, irritated dogmatism, our disappointment and distress, our heroism and assurance, do but compose our *own conceits*, for they proceed from a failure to apprehend the final ambiguity of the real situation. The contrast between the Church and the Kingdom of God is infinite (ix. 6). And no man can escape the condemnation involved in this contrast, for we all stand within its context. The righteousness of God means that men must think of Him in fear and trembling. No one is competent to despair of human righteousness without doubting his despair. No one is permitted to disbelieve in the Church, unless at the same time he refuses to justify himself by his disbelief. No one is outside the necessity of hope. Faced by the mystery of the Church, we are in fact faced by the mystery of God. And for this reason we are directed towards hope, and towards hope only.

A hardening in part hath befallen Israel, until the fulness of the Gentiles be come in. The catastrophe of the Church means that there is no point from which God can be excluded—*For of him and through him and unto him are all things* (xi. 36). Through Him the task of the Church becomes inevitable. But He is the

impossibility which deprives the Church of the possibility of
fulfilling its task. He renders men guilty in their attempt to
fulfil it, and holds them bound and helpless, as with fetters of
iron. By thus binding them, He makes Himself known as the
One God, beyond human misery and guilt, and as the goal of
human hope. The same God who selects Saul also rejects him,
in·order that He may select David. Why should this be? Simply
because He is God—*My soul truly waiteth still upon God, for of
him cometh my salvation.* This intolerable behaviour is divine.
God's action requires that men should be still; and in this still-
ness hope is possible and necessary. Were the action of God less
intolerable, it would not be divine, and men would have to do
otherwise than be still and hope. Before Israel, God covered and
hid Himself, made Himself unknown and impossible. Men, as
men, cannot apprehend God. They can neither see with their
eyes nor hear with their ears. Vain is their will, and vain their
searching and their reflection. Their energy breaks down at the
supreme moment, and indeed must break down. For none of
these things do, or can, or should, attain unto repentance. If
they did attain, repentance would not be what it is. 'Men snap
at repentance, as a dog snaps at a fly; but it escapes them'
(Luther). Such is *hardening*; and such is the Church of Esau.
And yet, the tribulation of Israel at God's hands, being so great
because it is the tribulation of eternity, has a veritable 'Beyond',
a veritable 'End'—in God. He is the Beyond. He is the End,
even of that which seems unending. Because the *hardening* is of
God, we must, in the first place, recognize it to be essentially
relative and *in part*. The totality of the reprobate is always
confronted by the invisible 7,000 (xi. 4), in whom are comprehended those elect ones who are already comforted in their
tribulation and saved from their misery. When the miracle
occurs, the massive wall, which separates God and man, becomes
transparent. But the miracle takes place at no time and in no
place. The Lord knoweth His own. We must, however, recognize secondly that this *hardening* is no more than a temporal
condition of mankind. Eternity, as the boundary of time, is the
end of time; as the primal origin of time, it is its goal. The
eschatological possibility of the advent of the *fulness of the
Gentiles* is therefore the end and the goal of *hardening* (xi. 12,
13). The exhaustion of human possibility clearly pre-supposes
the possibility of God. The death of the old man pre-supposes
the birth of the new. The catastrophe of the Church pre-
supposes the breaking forth of redemption. The nations shall
walk in the light of the glory of God and of the Lamb. Their

salvation is in that Jerusalem where there is no Temple (Rev. xxi. 22–4). Aware of this end and of this goal, and fixing our gaze upon the present, hopeless reality of the hardening of Israel, we must be still, and hope.

And so all Israel shall be saved. The salvation of the lost, the justification of those who are not justified, the resurrection of the dead, comes whence the catastrophe came. The Church is concrete mankind, receiving the revelation of God. As mankind, men are lost, unrighteous, and dead. In the Church the misery of Joseph breaks out as a disease. Salvation, justification, resurrection can be expected only in so far as, through the revelation of God to men, the new man is created: the new man who unobservably takes the place of the old man and is his meaning, goal, and fulfilment. The reverse, however, is also true. In the course of this world, the old man takes the place of the new man. He bears witness to him, opens the road to him, exposes him; but suffers and waits for him. The old man is the *figure of him that was to come* (v. 14). The coming new man, saved, justified, and made alive by the revelation of God, is made up of the elect of Israel, together with the Gentiles who have been elected in Christ. Once again, we must bear in mind that this does not mean a particular number of historical men or of psychologically recognizable individuals, of conscious or unconscious 'Gentile-Christians'. The actual existence of Gentiles who have become Christians has, in this context, no more than a demonstrative significance. The poverty and nakedness and blindness and hopelessness of the Gentiles, contrasted with the fullness and healthiness and repletion and assurance of Israel, points to the man who has been elected in Christ by grace. This is Paul's meaning. The new man, the elect Jacob, the man created by God, cannot be better defined than by contrasting him with his elder brother, Esau, who hears and speaks the word of God—as a man. This does at least make clear that the man who selects God must make way for the man who is selected by Him. This is the meaning of 'Double Predestination', the revelation of the *mystery* of God, and the goal of His carefully preserved freedom. The revelation of God to man occurs when this is said and heard. For we are here made aware of the impossible, eschatological, possibility—the possibility that he who receives the revelation, and as such must yield and decrease and pass to corruption, is he who has been saved and justified and raised from the dead: saved, as one that has been lost, justified as beyond justification—this is the resurrection of the dead, which in Christ enters within the realm of possibility. Thus God manifests Himself. He authenticates Himself as God both in His wrath and, in totally different fashion, in His mercy. All other methods of helping the man who, having raised himself to the highest peak of human possibility, imagines that there he can hear and speak the word of God, are barred. All other roads involve some direct, historical, psychological salvation, justification, and resurrection. But men are saved only in the Futurum resurrectionis, when they perceive the unobservable existentiality of God. Now, this salvation concerns *all Israel*, the whole Church, every Church. And so, the Church is the figure of the Coming One, the fulfilment of prophecy, the canal through which flows the living water of salvation. 'Only where graves are, is there resurrection' (Nietzsche); rather, wherever graves are, there is resurrection. Where the Church ends—not, of course, by a human act of will, but by a divine decree—there is its beginning. Where its unrighteousness is altogether exposed, their its righteousness dawns. The divine demolition of any Church means that every Church arises as signpost, threshold, and door of hope. It is then that the Church appears, as it were, as an arrow shot from the other bank; it appears as the messenger of Christ and as the tabernacle of God with men. When the Gentiles advance as missionaries to the Church, when it has been humbled by the promise which is its own message, then perhaps the time has come for the Church to undertake its mission to the Gentiles. The mission of the Church, as we learn from Paul himself, requires great speed and zeal, and should, moreover, be carried out with overflowing joy. Broken, the Church can bear its message with head erect, for the Gospel of salvation belongs to the Church which is lost. Shattered, the Church can, and indeed must, speak of God, by whose help men leap over the wall. Confronted by an impassable barrier, the Church can confidently and vigorously dare its terrible, boundless task. Here is the veritable fulfilment of the prophecy of the second Isaiah concerning the Servant of God, whom the nations are to see and hear. The reality of Christ risen, the possibility of God in spirit and in truth, is apprehended, when once the Word of the Cross is understood, and the impossibility of God is seen barring the way of all flesh.

There shall come out of Zion the Deliverer, and shall turn away ungodliness from Jacob : For this shall be my covenant unto them, when I shall take away their sins (Isa. lix. 20, xxvii. 9). These reminiscences of Old Testament eschatology gather round the divine possibility which, once it is apprehended, provides the key to the *mystery*, and is the end or goal of those obscure

movements of the Church in which we play our part. We have
spoken to unredeemed humanity of the Last Things, of the
miracle of the divine 'Yes', of the PAROUSIA of Jesus Christ, who
is the *Fulness of the Gentiles*. Jesus Christ is the Redeemer, the
individual standing existentially before God. In Him duality
has become unity, for in Him rejection has been overcome
and swallowed up in election. He comes *out of Zion*, that is,
from above, from the unobservable Origin of the Church. He
comes from the glory of the throne of God, whence came the
rejection of the Church; and with Him come regal dignity
and regal power. His appearing is the Creation which takes
place at no time, for it is the mystery in which all time is dissolved and established. His Coming is eternity, and His work is
ineffable—*He shall turn away ungodliness from Jacob*. He tears
away the veil which now hides the unobservable Church of
Jacob. What is this veil but the inevitable contingency and
perversion of the Church of Esau? He inaugurates the new
covenant of God Himself, of God alone. He *turns away*, clears
out, quenches, demolishes, annihilates, both sins and Sin. He
restores to men the union with God which they have now lost.
Once again we must break off; for we stand once more at the
point where what we have to say is unutterable. Yet this
boundary is the end of *hardening*, the incomprehensible goal of
the road of God.

**vv. 28–32. As touching the gospel, they are enemies for
your sake: but as touching the election, they are beloved
for the fathers' sake. For the gifts and the calling of God
are irrevocable. For as ye in time past were disobedient to
God, but now have obtained mercy by their disobedience,
even so have these also now been disobedient, that by the
mercy shewn to you they also may now[1] obtain mercy.
For God hath shut up all unto disobedience, that he might
have mercy upon all.**

As touching the gospel, they are enemies for your sake : but
as touching the election, they are beloved for the fathers' sake.
We must now attempt to formulate as precisely as possible the
main theme of chaps. ix–xi. We have seen the ambiguity of the
Church; and we have seen embodied in it the vast ambiguity of
human nature and of human civilization. Regarded purely from
a human point of view, the Gospel of Christ and the human work

---

[1] I find myself no longer able to defend the deletion of the second νῦν in *v.* 31.
The whole passage is controlled by an almost intolerable eschatological tension.
The νῦν is therefore entirely congruous. Moreover, the word is equally sur-
prising in *v.* 30, where a τότε might have been expected to follow the πότε.

of the Church operate in diametrically opposite fashions. In the Church the hostility of men against God is brought to a head; for there human indifference, misunderstanding, and opposition attain their most sublime and also their most naïve form. In the Church, the dead no-man's-land between two opposing forces becomes visible; for there the advance of human achievement, even though it imagine itself to be invested with divine power, is finally checked. All the piety which the Church encourages and to which it attains, all the knowledge, work, and prayer, by which it claims to be justified, are piled up so as to form one mighty obstacle on this side of the barrier which separates God and man. The Churchman, standing armed to the teeth, gathers together and focuses in himself everything which men have built up as a defence of themselves against God. Hence the Cleansing of the Temple! And hence the abandoning as useless of the whole conception of a direct road between God and man. Thus precisely in the Churchman is opened up the possibility of an indirect road, the road of forgiveness and of the mercy of God. It is at this point that there appears upon the horizon the 'other' man, the man of the world, the outsider, the Gentile, who, unlike the Churchman, announces to us this indirect road. He appears before us in visible poverty, evidently abandoned and without protection. He is no obstacle. In him the situation as it is between God and man is made known; for in him the forensic righteousness of God is revealed in all its glory. Since God has determined to reveal His glory and His mercy in this 'other man', it follows that those who embody in themselves the purpose and achievement of the Church on this side of the barrier must stand as the *enemies of the gospel— for your sake*. Sin must abound, in order that grace may abound more exceedingly (v. 20). But in fact there are no such Gentiles; for all Gentiles are in fact solidly one with Israel. They too are *enemies*, they too abound in sin, they too are lost. Regarded from the invisible standpoint of God, the operation of the Gospel of Christ cannot be distinguished from the operation of the Church. As the unworthy bearer of the divine Word, the Church is the revelation of election by grace. And that is what the *enmity* of the Church (v. 10) means. In so far as the man who is unable to justify himself possesses the divine promise, and in so far as he stands in his vast disobedience under the mercy of God, he serves the honour of God—*for the fathers' sake*, for the sake, that is to say, of the faith of Abraham the Gentile. He too, then, is the *beloved of God*, and it is precisely he who is 'within'. The pious man, with all his dangerous, godless, human arrogance, is sacrificed and abandoned—in the Church. And so, room is made in the Church for the forensic justification of the Gentiles. For the Church is the communion of saints seeking forgiveness, of the lost who are saved, of the dead who are alive. In the tribulation and guilt of the knowledge and work and prayer of the Churchman there appears, gathered together and focused, hope for all men, the justification and salvation of all those things which men in their ignorance undertake and accomplish. The man of piety is himself—a Gentile. Arriving at the end of the direct road to God, he announces the indirect road. Bearing witness to the catastrophe of human righteousness, he witnesses to the resurrection. A vessel of the wrath of God, he becomes the vessel of His mercy. Where can there be found an Israel which does not participate in the blessedness of the Gentiles? If Israel would venture to take its stand upon the election of the Fathers, if the Church would dare to be moved and sustained by the faith of Abraham, if it would descend into veritable humility, how great the Church might be! Great, because it is no longer great: great, only in the mercy of God!

For the gifts and the calling of God are irrevocable.—*Shall their want of faith make of none effect the faithfulness of God* (iii. 3)?— *It is not as though the word of God hath come to nought* (ix. 6).— *God did not cast off his people* (xi. 2). The Theme of the Church has in it more truth than the righteousness of those outside, more truth than the unrighteousness of those within, more truth even than the visible opposition of the Church and the world. The Theme of the Church is the freedom of God, His divine and unobservable working, whereby He Himself and He alone provides and removes both righteousness and unrighteousness. The freedom of God involves both the judgement and the establishing of the Church; it involves its terrible purgation and also its fulfilment. The Truth in all these truths is none other than God Himself. The rejection of the elect does not destroy His *gifts* and His *calling*. They are as much established by it as they are by the election of the reprobate. Both operations are in God invisibly one and the same. In every Church the in-alienable longing of mankind is concentrated, and in every Church this longing is doomed to remain unsatisfied. In-separable from the conscious recognition of this longing is the irrevocable sense of mission, even though it sweeps men into the catastrophe of all mankind. But whenever men apprehend their misery as having been prepared for them by God and their guilt as wrong done to Him, and when in consequence there is for them no other hope but God—then there is opened up the possibility which can never be locked against them.

As ye in time past were disobedient to God, but now have obtained mercy by their disobedience, even so have these also now been disobedient, that by the mercy shewn to you they also may now obtain mercy. 'Paul is speaking here of the wondrous sovereignty of God in His Church, by which those who bear the glorious name of the "People of God", and who, as the people of Israel, constitute the Church, are rejected for their unbelief; whereas others, hitherto outside God's people and under disobedience, but now receiving the Gospel and believing in Christ, become in God's sight the true Church, and are blessed' (Luther). Yes, the manner of the operation of the rule of God in His Church is indeed a wondrous and unspeakable paradox. Over the Church, as over all humanity as such, there are written the words 'Darkness—Rejection—Disobedience—Esau'. With this *time past* is, however, contrasted the altogether invisible *now* of revelation, when what is becomes what was. *But now*—in the light of the eternal Moment, in the light of the Day of Jesus Christ—ye Gentiles, outsiders, incurable, ye hopeless ones, *have obtained mercy*. Now the reprobate are the elect, and in them is manifested the Church of Jacob. Now the hour has struck for them—and it is the clock of God which strikes. How can we apprehend this? The power—the divinity—of the mercy which is theirs displays itself in the sharp contrast of itself with human disobedience, in the removal of the elect from the ranks of the reprobate, in the opposition between light and darkness. This mercy is the mercy of God, directed towards human disobedience, that is to say, towards all men, whilst at the same time disclosing disobedience and punishing it relentlessly. Mercy which did not manifest the holiness of God would not be the mercy of God. We are speaking of the mercy manifested in the death and resurrection of Christ. The elect encounter God turning towards them: this is the resurrection of Christ. The reprobate encounter exposure and punishment: this is His crucifixion. That which befell Christ is the mercy of God. He alone, because of what befell Him, stands surety for the elect. Their cause is veritably His. And so it is said to the elect—*ye obtained mercy by their disobedience.* But, once again, the mercy of God is real and powerful, because, in order that He may turn His face towards the disobedient, that is to say, to all men, He discloses and punishes the disobedience of the reprobate. It is quite true that darkness does cover the reprobate; but it is a darkness apprehended only in the light of the mercy of God—

These have now been disobedient by the mercy shewn to you. What can this mean, but that *now*—the eternal 'Now' which dethrones 'Here' but exalts 'There', and displays both 'Here' and 'There' the freedom and the majesty of God—*now* the elect are sureties for the reprobate, that they, bearing the burden of the elect, may participate also in the mercy which belongs to the elect. And so the new invisible title of all humanity is made manifest in the 'Now' of revelation.

For God hath shut up all unto disobedience, that he might have mercy upon all. 'With this joyful and comforting summary the investigation which had been begun in chap. ix reaches its conclusion' (Jülicher). Amazing comment! when we recognize that it is precisely this conclusion which brings into prominence the grim disturbance underlying the whole Epistle, and not this Epistle only. Our understanding or our misunderstanding of what Paul means—and not only Paul—by the key words, God, Righteousness, Man, Sin, Grace, Death, Resurrection, Law, Judgement, Salvation, Election, Rejection, Faith, Hope, Love, the Day of the Lord, is tested by whether we do or do not understand this summary. How are we to spell out the meaning of those great words? In what context are we to interpret them? Well! it is this passage which provides the standard by which they can be measured, the balance in which they can all be weighed. In its own way, it is the criterion by which every one who reads or hears the Epistle is himself judged; for by it the final meaning of 'Double Predestination' seeks to make itself known. Pregnant with meaning is the divine *shutting up*; pregnant also is the divine *mercy*. Most significant is the first *all*; most significant also is the second *all*—for even these last run the risk of being reckoned among those who, as Calvin says, nimis crasse delirant. Here it is that we encounter the hidden, unknown, incomprehensible God, to whom nothing is impossible, the Lord, who is as such our Father in Jesus Christ. Here is the possibility of God pressing upon us, vastly nigh at hand, vastly rich, but also vastly beyond our understanding. Here is Beginning and End, the road and the goal of the thought of God. Here is the object of faith, which may never be depressed to an 'object'. Here is the inner meaning of Christianity, which defies analysis. The Church hopes. Well, this is the hope of the Church. There is no other hope. Would that the Church might comprehend it! 'Take to heart this great text. By it the whole righteousness of the world and of men is damned: by it the righteousness of God is alone exalted, the righteousness of God which is by faith' (Luther).

vv. 33–6. O the depth of the riches and the wisdom and the knowledge of God! how unsearchable are his judgements, and his ways past tracing out! For who hath known the mind of the Lord? or who hath been his counsellor? or who hath first given to him, and it shall be recompensed unto him again? For of him, and through him, and unto him, are all things. To him be the glory for ever. Amen.

The depth of the riches and the wisdom and the knowledge of God is—correcting here what was written in the first edition of this book—unfathomable. The Epistle moves round the theme (i. 16, 17) that in Christ Jesus the Deus absconditus is as such the Deus revelatus. This means that the theme of the Epistle to the Romans—Theology, the Word of God—can be uttered by human lips only when it is apprehended that the predicate, Deus revelatus, has as its subject Deus absconditus. The theme can, and indeed must, be uttered. The work of re-formulating the theme is both possible and full of promise. But it is a work which must be undertaken with wise reserve and with full recognition that 'nothing' is in fact thereby accomplished. For it must be remembered that the subject—Deus absconditus—of the predicate—Deus revelatus—which is the Spirit Himself, the Fullness of divine Truth, the existentiality of the divine 'Yes', is not set forth in the Epistle to the Romans, for it can neither be written nor uttered, and it certainly cannot be 'done', because it cannot be in any way an object of human endeavour. The Moment when God, not man, speaks and acts, is the Moment of Miracle. And men have attained the utmost limit of their vigorous action when, possessing the status of John the Baptist, and filled with awe, they bear witness to God and to His Miracle. Luther presumably did not write without due consideration, when he said: 'He who hath this Epistle in his heart, hath in him the light and power of the Old Testament.' For no man hath the light and power of the New Testament 'in his heart', that is to say, in the sense that they are concrete things in the midst of other things. No man, then, can rightly deplore the absence of 'positive' revelation in the Pauline Epistles or in the whole realm of Theology. The word of Paul and the word of Theology has done its work when men are driven by it to ask of God why it is that His Word stands written in no book—not even in a 'table of contents'—and has been attained by no man. What is *clearly seen* in the works of God is His invisibility (i. 20). What is searched out in the deep things of

God is His unsearchability (1 Cor. ii. 10). To know God means to
stand in awe of Him and to be still in the presence of Him that
dwelleth in light unapproachable. And so we are brought back
again and again to stand before the HIDDEN depth of His Riches,
His Possibility, His Life, and His Glory! before the HIDDEN
depth of His Wisdom, His Thoughts, His Judgements, His Way!
before His movement from 'Here' to 'There'! before the HIDDEN
depth of the Knowledge by which He knows us before we know
Him and with which He holds us to Himself although we are
always separated from Him!

**How unsearchable are his judgements, and his ways past
tracing out !** How then is it possible for us to speak of election
and rejection? There is but one answer to our perpetual and
inevitable questioning. God would not be God, were His election
not unsearchable and His rejection not past tracing out, were
the writing of His hand not altogether hidden, and did He not
proclaim Himself in this hiddenness to be the God of victory,
who has mercy, and will have mercy, upon all.

**Who hath known the mind of the Lord? or who hath been his
counsellor** (Isa. xl. 13)? **or who hath first given to him, and it shall
be recompensed unto him again** (Job xli. 11)?—This is presumably an echo of the description of Leviathan–Crocodile in Job
xli.—There is no direct knowledge of God. He decides without
the assistance of counsellors. It is impossible to lay hold of Him.
Men cannot bind Him, or put Him under an obligation, or enter
into some reciprocal relationship with Him. There can be no
'Federal Theology'. He is God, and God only. This is the
affirmation of the Epistle to the Romans.

**For of him, and through him, and unto him, are all things.
To him be the glory for ever. Amen.** Marcus Aurelius said much
the same in his 'Meditations'. The formula is found in a hymn
to Selene and is inscribed as a charm upon a gem. It was not unknown to Philo and to others. But why were its implications
not drawn out more clearly in the mysticism of the Hellenistic
world? Why were its terror and its promise not emphasized?
If Paul simply borrowed the formula, why is it that the theory
of borrowing provides no more than an utterly superficial
explanation of what he has actually done? Why is Paul's use
of the formula so much more original than in the source from
which he borrowed it? Whatever the truth may be about the
method of his borrowing, Paul could not have provided the
chapter with a more appropriate conclusion. For by it he renders
audible the threat and the hope implied in what those outside—
already know.

The Twelfth to the Fifteenth Chapters

THE GREAT DISTURBANCE

THE PROBLEM OF ETHICS

XII. 1, 2

**vv. 1, 2. I beseech you therefore, brethren, by the
mercies of God, to present your bodies a living sacrifice,
holy, acceptable to God—which is your** veritable worship
of God!—and not to fashion yourselves[1] according to the present
form **of this world,** but according to its coming transformation,[1] **by the renewing of your mind, that ye may prove
what is the will of God, even what is good and acceptable
and perfect.**

I beseech you therefore, brethren. The problem of ethics is
presented once again (vi. 12–23, viii. 12, 13) as a great disturbance. How, indeed, can it be otherwise? for human behaviour
must inevitably be disturbed by the thought of God. Every
conversation about Him ends in disharmony, since it is undertaken by men lacking sufficient perception to enable them to
keep a firm hold upon the subject about which they are talking.
The fact that ethics constitutes a problem reminds us that the
object about which we are conversing has no objectivity, that
is to say, it is not a concrete world existing above or behind our
world; it is not a treasury of our spiritual experiences; it is
not even some transcendental vastness: for we are not meta-
physicians. Our conversation is about men living in the world
of nature and of civilization; and, moreover, we ourselves are
also men living of necessity from minute to minute a quite concrete life. The fact that ethics are presented to us as a problem
means that the concepts which we make use of in our conversation are, as we have so often pointed out, existential concepts;
and it provides us with a guarantee that, when we repeat—somewhat tediously perhaps—the formula 'God Himself, God alone',
we do not mean by it some divine thing, or some ideal world

---

[1] Adopting the variant reading, which has infinitives and not imperatives.
I consider it unlikely that Paul would have introduced an imperative at this
point: partly because, in view of the actual meaning of the verbs, the peculiarly
Pauline nuance of the word *exhortation* would be disturbed, were *I exhort
you* to be followed by an imperative; and partly because, since the syntax of
the passage would be easier if the verbs were in the imperative mood, their
presence here is most probably due to later smoothing out of the text.

contrasted with the visible world. We mean by the formula that
unsearchable, divine relationship in which we stand as men. It is
in the actual tension and movement of human life, in the actual
being and having and doing of men, that our existential concepts
and formulations emerge. And it is precisely here that they
emerge in their abstract contrast with everything human and
everything of this world. There can, moreover, be no more
complete misunderstanding of the abstraction of these concepts
than to abstract them from the context which has given them
birth and to attempt to understand them otherwise than in their
relation to the concrete world in which we live. A wide reading
of contemporary secular literature—especially of newspapers!—
is therefore recommended to any one desirous of understanding
the Epistle to the Romans. If our thinking is not to be pseudo-
thinking, we must think about life; for such a thinking is a
thinking about God. And if we are to think about life, we must
penetrate its hidden corners, and steadily refuse to treat anything—however trivial or disgusting it may seem to be—as
irrelevant. To be sincere, our thought must share in the tension
of human life, in its criss-cross lines, and in its kaleidoscopic
movements. And life is neither simple, nor straightforward, nor
obvious. Things are simple and straightforward and obvious
only when they are detached from their context and then
treated superficially. The reality to which life bears witness
must be disclosed in the deep things of all observable phenomena,
in their whole context—and in their KRISIS. Only dialectical
human thinking can fulfil its purpose and search out the depth
and context and reality of life: only dialectical thought can lead
to genuine reflection upon its meaning and make sense of it.
For when our thought moves onwards direct and unbroken,
when it is comprehensive, it is quite certain that we are not
thinking about life; we are not thinking, that is to say, about the
KRISIS in which human life is in fact being lived. It is not 'complicated' thinking which is doctrinaire, but that much-praised
'simplicity'. Men think 'simply' when they pretend to know
what they do not know. The straight-moving thought which we
so earnestly desire is not genuine thought at all. Genuine thinking
is always strange to the world and unsympathetic. For thinking
is not a biological function. To think is to formulate the question,
the answer to which is itself the possibility of the very existence
of any biological function. Thought, therefore, as the search for
this answer, is not action, but pre-supposition. Since, however,
no presupposition exists in its own right, but always presupposes
action, it follows that genuine thought must always be broken

thought, and cannot escape the criticism of being merely intellectual. To this criticism we must now do justice. The preceding apology for intellectual thought is, strictly speaking, applicable only to pure thought, that is, to the thought of God Himself. We are unable to apprehend thought otherwise than as action, as a biological function, and the 'complexity' of our thinking would be really superior to other 'simpler' forms of thought only if it had so passed beyond the chance and whim of this world as actually to participate in the purity of the pre-supposition. We cannot, however, be so uncritical as to suppose that, when Paul in the Epistle to the Romans performs an action of thought, and when we in following him do likewise, his dialectic or our own can be represented as a reflection of divine thought, or that his thought or ours is really the actual thinking of the thought of life. We should like to think that the requirement that the Pauline 'Dogmatic' should be followed by a peculiar 'ethic' is altogether superfluous and meaningless. But this is not so. For it is the ethical problem which forces upon our attention the great disturbance. The problem of ethics reminds us that our act of thinking cannot be justified. What is justified is its unobservable origin, its pure pre-supposition. And this is justified because it makes sense of the whole fullness of concrete things—in its complete separation from them. The problem of ethics reminds us of the Truth of God, which is never actually present or actually apprehended in our act of thinking, however sublime. And so, paradoxically, the fact that our act of thinking is encompassed by the busy world of daily occurrence proves to us that our conversation about God is not undertaken for its own sake, but for the sake of His will. As the thought about God disturbs all human being and having and doing, so the problem of ethics disturbs our conversation about God, in order to remind us of its proper theme; dissolves it, in order to give it its proper direction; kills it, in order to make it alive. This is the meaning of the words:—*I beseech you therefore, brethren.* Break off—all ye who follow my thoughts, worship with me, and are pilgrims with me—break off your thinking that it may be a thinking of God; break off your dialectic, that it may be indeed dialectic; break off your knowledge of God, that it may be what, in fact, it is, the wholesome disturbance and interruption which God in Christ prepares, in order that He may call men home to the peace of His Kingdom.

I beseech you—**by the mercies of God.** We are not now starting a new book or even a new chapter of the same book. Paul is not here turning his attention to practical religion, as though it were

a second thing side by side with the theory of religion. On the
contrary, the theory, with which we have hitherto been concerned, is the theory of the practice of religion. We have spoken
of the *mercies of God*, of grace and resurrection, of forgiveness
and Spirit, of election and faith, of the varied refractions of the
uncreated light. But the ethical problem has nowhere been left
out of account. The questions 'What shall we do?'—'How are
we to live?' have nowhere been excluded. We have not been
searching out hidden things for the mere joy of so doing. It has
not been abstract thought which has led us again and again to
the point which is beyond our observation, to the light to which
no man can attain. Rome in the first century, all places at all
times, in fact, the whole concrete situation—this has always been
our starting-point (i. 18, 19). In following the road of thought,
this it is which has caused us to enter dark recesses. The need of
making decisions of will, the need for action, the world as it is—
this it is which has compelled us to consider what the world is,
how we are to live in it, and what we are to do in it. We have
found the world one great, unsolved enigma; an enigma to
which Christ, the mercy of God, provides the answer. And
because the *mercies of God* are the answer to the great enigma,
we have perforce to return to the point whence we set out, and
to formulate even more pointedly, even more thoroughly, its
essential insolubility. Only so can the mercies of God be its
solution; for they finally define the world as this world without
being themselves in any way depressed into things of this world.
Once again, then, we are confronted by the problem of the
'This-sidedness' of the whole course of our concrete existence.
Once again—and now quite unavoidably—our life and will and
acts are brought in question. For the freedom of God, the 'Other-
sidedness' of His mercies, means that there is a relationship
between God and man, that there is a dissolution of human
'This-sidedness', and that a radical assault is made upon every
contrasted, second, other, thing. When, however, the mercies of
God form a subject of exhortation, they advance to this side,
whilst belonging wholly to the other. It follows, therefore, that
the point from which the exhortation is made cannot be that
eminence from which well-meaning pedagogues are wont to
moralize, from which the true or false prophetic eye is accustomed to roam over the world, or from which arrogant or
genuine martyrs chant their woes over mankind. If, therefore, the Church is to be a place of exhortation, it must be a
Church altogether aware of its final and indissoluble solidarity
with this world of 'dry bones'; it must be a Church which has

set its hope upon God only. When such a Church embarks upon
moral exhortation, its exhortation can be naught else but a
criticism of all human behaviour, a criticism which moves
through every one of the 360 degrees of the circle of our ambiguous life. This means that very great reserve is necessary
when judgements concerning human capacity of will and action,
whether they be positive or negative, have to be made—not for
fear lest the criticism should be too sweeping, but lest it should
not be sweeping enough. The criticism which proceeds from the
high-places of which we have just spoken—the criticism which
peals forth from all those triumphant Church towers—is never
the great disturbance by which mankind is damaged. Such
criticism, however transcendent it may be, is human, all too
human; for it is a 'beyond' which still remains of this world.
(The man who, in attacking others, does not also destroy himself
had better keep silence in the congregation. The whole problem
of ethics is so delicate, so dubious, that the addition of one word
too much is far more disastrous than the omission of one word
which might have been said. The decisive word about ethics
must disclose their full ambiguity, an ambiguity covering every
aspect of human behaviour.) The decisive word must be the
word which cuts down to the roots. And the only sufficiently
radical word—apparently pure 'theory'; but alone, in fact,
eminently practical—is the word which, leaping over all so-
called intermediate stages, points directly to the mercy of God
as the only adequate cause and purpose of the ambiguity of life.
Utterly radical, this decisive word is, then, the word of pity and
of understanding; for it perceives that all particularity, all
concreteness, belongs to the course of this world; and all the
while it itself remains universal, existential, and beyond all
concreteness. EXHORTATION can therefore never be merely a
demand, since it is the demand that grace should come into its
own. EXHORTATION lets what is be as it is, because of what it is
not. Grace means not judging, because the judgement has already
taken place. Grace means the recognition that a bad conscience
must be assumed in the daily routine of an evil world. But
precisely for this reason grace means also the possibility, not of
a 'good' (!) conscience, but of a consoled conscience. If then—
in agreement with Luther and Dostoevsky against Tolstoy and
the Franciscans—exhortation be the exposition of the validity
of grace, it involves a perception of the pre-supposition of grace
in all concrete phenomena. This pre-supposition, moreover, must
be so set forth that it is asserted as a general pre-supposition, and
not as some separate concrete thing existing independently, in

its own right or side by side with other concrete things. In medio inimicorum regnum Christi est (Luther). Exhortation can therefore be undertaken only where the Pharisee and the Publican have been thrust together onto one step; only where no separation of sheep and goats has been even contemplated; where there is no superiority of those who claim to be 'impelled by Christ'; and where moral indignation against—shall we say? —a Tirpitz, or a Bethmann-Hollweg, or even a Lenin, has entirely ceased to exist. EXHORTATION is evoked when all these dubious characters are seen to be no more than exaggerations of what we all are; and to be pointing to a wholly different ambiguity before whose secret all men are dumb. Exhortation occasioned by the putting forward of some clear-cut scheme of reform, and which therefore issues in a long string of ready-made complaints, is no—EXHORTATION. Preached from the pinnacles of humanity, all such moral exhortations bear the marks of their inevitable weakness. For the voice of the preacher, even though it be pitched in the key of absolute truth, wobbles from note to note, is raucous, croaking, and utterly unimpressive. It is, in fact, the cry of a Titan. And, whether the preacher himself be good or bad, he simply bears witness to the judgement which hangs over all Titanism. Human exhortation, therefore, is justified only when it is seen to be void of human justification; that is to say, when it is grounded upon the *mercies of God.*

I beseech you—**to present your bodies.** We remember (vi. 13, 19) how important was our apprehension that grace, being the power of the resurrection, demands nothing less than that we should present our *members* unto obedience, and *yield* them as *servants* to the divine contradiction which is set against us. The demand concerns our *body* and its *members.* Now, the body is the observable, historical man, of whom alone we have knowledge. When this man encounters the new man in Christ, he is impounded and rendered altogether dubious—*by the mercies of God.* The task of ethics, thus defined and directed, becomes both serious and impressive, for it lies wholly beyond this world. It admits of no retreat. It rules out an obedience affecting only the 'inner' life of the soul or of the mind. In the light of 'critical' ethics, 'inwardness', 'soul-fulness', 'thought-fulness', are seen to be either—when regarded from below—merely higher functions of the body, in which case no distinction can be drawn between higher and lower functions that is sufficiently clear to admit of the latter being simply left behind in disobedience; or—when regarded from above—the new man in

Christ whence comes precisely that disturbance from which the old man of the *body* has no means of escape. When, therefore, our attention is directed towards grace, towards the mercies of God which no man has merited or can merit, when we apprehend the KRISIS which is involved in that movement from death to life which is the only hope of men, the relation of man to God carries with it the compelling demand of an absolute ethic. That is to say, the ethical problem possesses an eschatological tension; otherwise it is not ethical. Grace means divine impatience, discontent, dissatisfaction: it means that the whole is required. Grace is the enemy of every thing, even of the most indispensable 'Interim-Ethic'. Grace is the axe laid at the root of the good conscience which the politician and the civil servant always wish to enjoy, and which modern Lutheranism, with its weak humanitarianism, knows so well how to provide. What a ghastly misunderstanding it is when men hope that grace may be a place of repose for 'Theorists' and mystics, or fear lest it may be so (vi. 15, 16)! What method of defence could be more underhand than when upright, moral(!) men, genuinely and rightly concerned about their own existence, and wishing to avoid the Lutheran misunderstanding, suppose that ethical behaviour rests upon a number of moral ideals realizable in this world, rather than upon a critical negation of all such ends and purposes and possessions, rather than upon the forgiveness of sins! What behaviour could be more foolish than the behaviour of those newly-converted men who, after their conversion, leap to embark with confidence upon an adequate moral life? This is, however, to lay grace wholly under suspicion by making it, and human ethical conduct, two separate functions, as though it were possible first to pass under grace and then to proceed to build up a positive ethic. The result of such procedure is not open to doubt: the *body* is then left securely in possession of the field. In point of fact, it is grace alone that is competent to provide men with a truly (ethical disturbance;) and if grace is to perform this function, it must be treated as covering the whole field of human life, and must be permitted to make that absolute assault upon men without which ethics are completely meaningless.

A living sacrifice, holy, acceptable unto God—which is your veritable worship of God. The general situation between God and man being what it is, how can the primary ethical action be defined as a *veritable worship of God*? What can this mean? Previously (vi. 19, 22) it was defined as *sanctification*. Clearly this now requires further consideration. To *sanctify* something means to separate and prepare it that it may be presented and offered to God. This is more precisely defined in the conception of *sacrifice*. The exhortation which is grounded upon the mercies of God and is directed towards men is summed up in the demand that men should present their bodies—that is, their concrete, observable, historical existence—as a *sacrifice*. Now, sacrifice means surrender; it means an unconditional gift; it means the renunciation of men in favour of God. If men are themselves the object to be surrendered, renounced, and given up, their sacrifice can mean nothing less than the relentless acknow-ledgement of that questionableness and confiscation which occurs when they are confronted by the unfathomable God; the sacrifice which they have to offer by means of an ever-renewed, but never completed, return to His mercy and freedom; the sacrifice, of which the harshness and greatness can best be understood by recollecting the meaning which 'Double Pre-destination' has in chaps. ix–xi. By such an *exhortation* to primary behaviour we are recalled to Him apart from whom there is no exhortation. The problem of 'ethics' is, therefore, identical with the problem of 'dogmatics': Soli Deo gloria! It follows, then, that all secondary ethical behaviour—about which we shall have to speak later—must be both related to the primary behaviour and conditioned by it. Our secondary moral be-haviour can be defined as *living, holy*, and *acceptable to God*, only in so far as this connexion is maintained. Goodness is that be-haviour which stands under the TELOS of life (vi. 23). From this certain consequences follow. Sacrifice is not a human action whereby the will of God is fulfilled, if 'fulfilment' means that he who makes the sacrifice becomes thereby an instrument of God. Sacrifice is, rather, a 'demonstration' demanded by God—for His glory. The act of sacrifice is in itself simply a human act as good or bad as any other human act. God remains God even when confronted by the greatest sacrifice; and after the sacrifice His will goes its own way as it did before. It is, surely, childish to suppose a May Day Procession to be itself the Labour Move-ment. It is a Demonstration. Nevertheless, any class-conscious 'worker' would feel bound to take part in it. Similarly, all ethical behaviour, even the primary ethic of the broken line, even the worshipper bowed before the merciful God, is no more than a demonstration: the demonstration is, however, necessary and obligatory. There is no such thing as the 'building up' by men of an adequate ethical life, not even if the quality of their moral behaviour were so sublime that it might be claimed that the will of God had been united with the human will, or that the

human will had been absorbed into the divine, or that the
divine will had been fulfilled in the human will. All human doing
or not-doing is simply an occasion or opportunity of pointing to
that which alone is worthy of being called 'action', namely, the
action of God. In the sphere of ethics this rule is adamant.
There is no overlapping of act and pre-supposition! Whenever
men claim to be able to see the Kingdom of God as a growing
organism, or—to describe it more suitably—as a growing building, what they see is not the Kingdom of God, but the Tower
of Babel. There is, no doubt, a great and universal human
'building' at which we all in our various ways labour in fear and
trembling; but it is a work in which the will of God at no single
point touches or overlaps with the will of man. Pure ethics
require—and here we are in complete agreement with Kant—
that there should be no mixing of heaven and earth in the sphere
of morals. Pure ethical behaviour depends upon its primal
origin, an origin which needs to be protected by a determination
on our part to call God God and man man, however much we
may be tempted to stray into romanticism. If this means that
men are thereby slowed down, disappointed, and discouraged—
well, this slowing down is only from the Good. Would that the
man of this world could comprehend what is really meant by his
'discouragement', and how it serves to confront him with the
problem of ethics, if this is still unknown to him! Within the
limits of that great and general 'building' upon which we are engaged, we can do no more than arrange demonstrations; we can
act only so as to provide significant signposts and witnesses to
the glory of God. Whether our actions do in fact serve His glory
must be left entirely to His decision, precisely because their
purpose is the service of His honour. He accepts and rejects: He
will *render to every man according to his works* (ii. 6). Yes, it is He
who selects; it is He who will assign to them their value. And
moreover, it is not only the primary ethical action which
demonstrates to His honour, but all those secondary actions also
which flow from the primary action and are linked to it: for they
are legitimately bound to it, and are properly 'good', only when
they constitute a veritable abandonment by men of their power
and their right, and thereby proclaim the mercy and freedom of
God; only when they are, all of them, appeals to Him to accept
them or to reject them, claiming thereby to be no more than
parables and tokens; only when it is left entirely to Him to
pronounce upon their meaning and their value. There is, then, no
sacrifice which is *living, holy, acceptable unto God*, except that
sacrifice which—seen from below, merely one in an unending

series: seen from above *once for all*—claims to be nothing but
sacrifice and demonstration; and which does not also, in claiming
this 'nothing but', impinge upon the freedom of God. Thus
it is that all human duties and virtues and good deeds are set
upon the edge of a knife. They hang on a single thread. Is the
man who practises them and cherishes them really prepared to
sacrifice them; really prepared to see in them no more than
demonstrations, and thus to give glory to God? What is more
than this is of the evil one—even if it be the holiness and purity
of a martyred virgin. Does a man suppose that thereby God
shows Himself to be too harsh a master? Is He unwilling to
offer Him this *veritable service*? Then let him turn back, for he
has too many possessions!

We have now reached the point where it has become clear for
what reason and to what extent the ethical demand which is
based upon the mercies of God must issue in the great disturbing
of all men. I beseech you—**not to fashion yourselves according
to the present form of this world, but according to its coming
transformation.** The exhortation refers clearly to 'secondary'
ethical behaviour, that is to say, to that conduct in which
the broken line is evident. What is it, then, against which
our actions are demonstrating? And what is their purpose?
The answer is obvious. Our actions, even our quite fundamental actions, are the actions of men who have been sacrificed. They are the unjustified actions of men who have been
defeated; and this is the case even though they may assume
a triumphant, victorious form of righteousness! The world of
which Paul is speaking is this aeon; the world of time, and
of men, and of things; the world of which alone we have knowledge, and which alone lies within our comprehension. In this
world in which we live we are indissolubly and indivisibly one
with our *body*—and the term includes any form of supposed
'astral' body! In this world men are and remain men, even
though they may be stretched into some conceivably possible
middle world betwixt 'Here' and 'There'. This world has,
moreover, *form* and shape; and it possesses a law, a general
pressure towards concreteness, to light-created light!—to life
and fullness, to begetting and being begotten. This pressure
towards enjoyment, possession, success, knowledge, power,
rightness; this vigorous movement towards an attainable,
comprehensible perfection; this pressure, in fact, towards—
works, forms the mysterious pivot round which the whole world
of human genius revolves. But we must remember that the
word genialis means etymologically that which is 'fitted for

marriage', and so genius is—well!—our beloved EGO! We should perhaps catch the meaning of the *form of this world* if we glossed it by the 'figure of EROS'. Our whole behaviour, always and to the world's end, bears stamped upon it the *form* of this world. We must not delude ourselves. There are no moral actions, such as love, or honesty, or purity, or courage, which ᵧhave rid themselves of the *form of this world*, which are not 'erotic'. As there is no pure act of thought, so there is no pure act of will. The significance of this whole situation cannot be over-emphasized. If there is no man who fails to bear the mark of the form of this world, there is also, nevertheless, no man who does not bear it in the context of the 'primary' ethical act of sacrifice: for—the *fashion* (form)—*of this world passeth away* (1 Cor. vii. 31). The purpose of the 'pressure towards life' is that it comes to an end. Generation is directly confronted by death. All that has been produced, concreted, worked, has been formed in and for the temporal order. When a human work or production sings to us a theme of supreme beauty—Mozart!—then, precisely then, it strikes chords of deep distress. Are we really ignorant of this? Do we not know that our *body* is the *body of death* (vii. 24), and that our busy activity cannot but cease (viii. 13)? There is for us no alternative. Is there any man of us who has not been offered up existentially as a sacrifice? Thus oppressed existentially we are bound to affirm the profound existential truth which presses upon us in our profound ambiguity— and who does not affirm this truth? for the Lord knoweth His own. Our whole 'secondary' ethical conduct, then, presupposes this 'primary' ethic. It follows, therefore, that we do not *fashion ourselves according to the present form of this world, but according to its transformation.* Where human particularity and arbitrary self-will and arrogance break down; where men have been offered up as a sacrifice—it may be at the highest eminence of human development; there is the end of the world and the resurrection of the dead. ⎣The ethical factor in human conduct depends upon the light which shines in it: it depends, that is to say, since we ✓ can here speak only negatively, upon men being overcome.⎤This 'being overcome' is, moreover, congruous, not with the present form of this world, but with its coming transformation. To sum up: there is no human action which is not in itself fashioned according to the form of this world.; and yet there are actions which seem almost to bear in themselves the mark of the divine protest against the great error. There is no human action which is in itself fashioned according to the transformation of this world; but there are actions which seem so transparent that the light of the coming Day is almost visible in them. Human conduct is therefore in itself only—but why should we say 'only'? —a parable, a token, of the action of God; and the action of God cannot occur in time; it can occur only—and again, why should we say 'only'?—in eternity. Is 'only' a relevant description of a cloud of dust, if that cloud of dust betrays the whereabouts of a column on the march? Is a shell-hole 'only' a shell-hole, if it marks the spot where an explosion has taken place? Is the shaft of a mine sunk in the side of a mountain 'only' a shaft, if it enables us to conceive of a part of the mountain where no mountain is? So it is that every human position, every far-reaching, deeply penetrating human achievement, is to be sought out and recommended, for it is an urgent testimony to the power of the Spirit. This means that we must be prepared for men to take up new positions, new points of view; we must expect new dogmas; we must not be surprised if new motor power is attached to the old carriage of this world, for surely these new things appear every day! But all these novelties—in spite of, or rather because of, their gravitation towards concreteness—are necessarily fashioned according to the *form* of this world and not according to its *transformation*. In all this 'real business' it is still men who triumph or suffer; it is still their success or their failure; it is still they who gain or lose, live or die; it is still they, and they only, who are engaged. In the midst of such great possibility of genius, men are able to dress themselves up in the festal wedding-garments of their own beloved EGO and to feel that they are unassailable, unbroken, and secure. The grave objections that can also from this point of view be brought against Nietzsche's defence of suicide as an act of freedom need only to be indicated here. All these great possibilities of genius may, however, be just promethean possibilities—and indeed, the higher they reach and the more final they are, the more Prometheus-like they become. How then can the gravity and power of ethics, the gravity and power of the great disturbance, lie in such acts and deeds? Nevertheless there are actions from which the light of sacrifice shines, actions where men are offered up, not in order that a new human achievement, positive or negative, may be brought to view, but that the peculiarity of God, His particular will and power and might, may be disclosed, and that He may be known as—Lord. It is this enlightenment which disturbs men, whether they be formed according to the idealism of a Ludendorf and a Lenin or of a Foerster and a Ragaz. This enlightenment is an assault upon all men. It is an assault upon the man of this world with all his giftedness—and who among us is not gifted in some way or other? We are all frightened of this attack, because we all desire it and expect it, because, presumably, we are all aware that there could be for us no better thing than that we should at last be rid of our—genius. The assault upon our genius constitutes the KRISIS that announces our passage from death to life. There is no department of human life outside the realm of this KRISIS; no person who does not yield a willing ear to this *exhortation*; no one who opposes it. All engage in the assault, for all are subjected to the attack. Here all are in the right, since all are in the wrong. No more damaging offensive against the fortress of the Devil can be imagined than that which is here undertaken. It may even be that in this assault some supposed outposts of God collapse and are destroyed! This whole destructive occurrence is clearly not—*fashioned according to the present form of this world, but according to its transformation*.

But what is it possible for us to do in order that the sacrifice, by which men are overcome and God is glorified, may shine forth in our actions? How can we ensure that our deeds are fully ripened fruit and not mere empty husks? What are we to demand of men? and to what are we to invite and exhort them? Since the truth lies in the ambiguity of human existence, we must exhort them to affirm that ambiguity. It is possible for us to encourage them to the 'primary' ethical action. We can exhort them—and above all we can exhort ourselves—to repentance. Repentance is the 'primary' ethical action upon which all 'secondary' ethical conduct depends and by which it is illuminated. Repentance is—**the renewing of your mind, that ye may prove what is the will of God, even what is good and acceptable and perfect.** And so we are brought back to thought. Yes, repentance, as the 'primary' ethical action, is the act of re-thinking. (This transformation of thought is the key to the problem of ethics, for it is the place where the turning about takes place by which men are directed to a new behaviour.) But —and we must repeat what has been said before—even our thinking is conducted within the sphere of relativity; even our thinking can never be in itself the righteousness which is valid before God; even our thinking of the thought that God thinks in us is a majestic illusion of romantic philosophy, which can do no more than form the advance guard in the demonstration to the honour of God. In our thought dwells no creative power; for the esse which lies in the nosse is the word and work of God alone. It follows, therefore, that we cannot exhort men to participate in pure thought. Nevertheless, there is an act of human thinking to which a promise is attached. There is an act of thinking which, because it dissolves both itself and every act, is identical with the *veritable worship of God*, with utter, bowed adoration of Him. There is an act of thinking which, because it is perfected, and therefore, as an act, dissolved, constitutes a *proving what is the will of God*; there is an act of thinking by which sufficient wisdom is given men to choose the road which is for the moment the right road. There is—and this is what we mean—a thinking of the thought of grace, of resurrection, of forgiveness, and of eternity. Such thinking is congruous with our affirmation of the full ambiguity of our temporal existence. When once we recognize that the final meaning of our temporal existence lies in our questioning as to its meaning, then it is that we think the thought of eternity—in our most utter collapse. For the vast ambiguity of our life is at once its deepest truth. And moreover, when we think this thought, our thinking is *renewed*; for such rethinking is repentance. We know too that our thinking of the thought of eternity is never a thing completed in time, for it is full of promise. As an act of thinking it dissolves itself; it participates in the pure thought of God, and is therefore an accepted sacrifice, living, holy, acceptable to God. And yet we know that this thought does actually take place, because it is the KRISIS of all our other thoughts. And so, as men focus their attention upon the creative work of God, to which *their thoughts one with another accusing or else excusing them bear witness* (ii. 15), it is possible for them to exhort others to think eternity; to summon them to a renewal of mind; and to demand repentance. It is possible to beseech them not to allow this familiar KRISIS of *x* all thought to fade away into the background, but to remember it; to pay attention to the word of God; and to make room for His work. And this is enough: for grace is sufficient, even for ethics! Like the turning of a key in a lock, it is the prelude to a new action, to that conduct which is marked by the divine protest against the great illusion, and through which the light of the coming Day shines clear and transparent. Grace is sufficient to destroy the noxious assurance of men and to give them the status of the new man in Christ. Grace is sufficient to awaken them from the sleep of righteousness, and to make of them men who have been sacrificed. Grace is sufficient to prevent men being removed altogether from that which is *good and acceptable and perfect*; from the behaviour which is well-pleasing to God and in which His glory and the downfall of men shine forth. Neither the superficial nor the legitimate protests of the anti-intellectuals are applicable to the thinking of the thought of grace. For it is precisely the THINKING of the thought of eternity which dissolves the possibility of any adequate human thought. It is wholly meaningless for us to busy ourselves with pointing out how futile the intellectualists are; because, in so doing, we also are sinners. As LOGOS—reason—is reminded of its primal origin by our actual behaviour, so our conduct is reminded by LOGOS—reason—of the problem of that action which is existential. Thus, it is our actual observation of life as it is that thrusts us back upon the necessity of hearing and speaking the Word of God. So also, it is our pondering over the question, 'What shall we do?' which compels us to undertake so much seemingly idle conversation about God. And it is precisely because our world is filled with pressing, practical duties; because there is *wickedness in the streets*; because of the existence of the daily papers; that we are bound to encounter 'Paulinism' and the Epistle to the Romans. If all that ought to be done had in fact been *done*, our easy-going counsellors would be right, and we should not need to be bothering our heads about Paul. But since nothing has been *done*, the exhortation to *renewal* of mind, to re-thinking, to repentance—an exhortation which can be obeyed and which, being obeyed, can lead to action—is inevitable. But, when this has been said, we need to be reminded again of the limitation under which all exhortation lies—the final word of our instruction is spoken by God Himself and by Him alone; for it is He who mightily disturbs both the dogmatist and the moralist.

THE PRE-SUPPOSITION

XII. 3–8

v. 3a. For I say, through the grace that was given me, to every man that is among you, not to think of himself more highly than he ought to think; but so to think as to think soberly.

This is the great disturbance—that 'God should first be the love that loves men, and should then display Himself as the God who willeth to be loved. God is, of course, no egoist. Yet, nevertheless, He is the eternal EGO. God cannot be refashioned according to thy good pleasure: thou it is that must be re-fashioned according to His good pleasure. . . . As the arrow, loosed from the bow by the hand of the practised archer, does not rest till it has reached the mark; so men pass from God to God. He is the mark for which they have been created; and they do not rest till they find their rest in Him. . . . The moment I make of my words an existential thing—that is to say, when I

make of Christianity a thing in this world—at that moment I explode existence and have perpetrated the scandal' (Kierkegaard).
Only he who has been exposed to this terrible disturbance can
dare to exhort others (xii. 1) or can, indeed, be himself exhorted.
Such a man is Paul (i. 1). *The grace that was given him* (cf. v. 2)
constitutes the peculiarity of his position and the paradox of his
apostolate. He has been 'commissioned and seconded to be a
scout in the highest service' (Kierkegaard). Yet he assumes that
his hearers are similarly placed; and the whole conversation
between them forms one long reminder of the vast disturbance
which has taken place. For this reason the Epistle to the Romans
is nothing but *exhortation*. God is God: this is the pre-supposition ✓
of ethics. Ethical propositions are therefore ethical only as
expositions of this pre-supposition which may never be regarded
as a thing already known, or treated as a basis of further routine
operations, or as something from which it is possible to hurry on
to a new position. Rather, it is precisely the pre-supposition
which seeks to make itself known, which seeks to condition and
carry out the daily routine, which itself hurries on. What manner
of man, then, is summoned to speak about ethics and to hear the
speech of others? Surely, the man who knows that it behoves
him from first to last—**not to think of himself more highly than
he ought.** We know already these dangerous eminences, but we
can never be sufficiently aware of them (xii. 1); for hardly have
we been thrown from one horse than we have our foot in the
stirrup of another; hardly have we found ourselves to be out of
our depth in one 'subject' than we immerse ourselves in another;
hardly have we left school before we begin to teach others.
Disillusioned with psychology and history, we betake ourselves
to the Bible, and undertake to fashion one more idol out of the
wisdom of death and out of the *living God*. Unaware of our
frequent failure, it would seem that we must always be mounting
some eminence, always be entering some Church. To our shame
we must own that a Church appears on the scene (ix. 6) whenever
men hear from human lips what can be spoken about human
life only by God. But what Church is it that then appears?
The probability of our erecting a Church in which men will seek
to ascend some *high place* seems infinite: and, in that case, what
God has to say is notoriously absent. The more men seem to
speak deeply and really about God, the more unreal is what they
say. The unobservable and impossible Church of Jacob brings
this Church to an end, as it brings to an end all *high places* with
their *Baals* and their *Asherahs*. The exhortation *so to think as to
think soberly* is therefore manifestly not an encouragement of

some particular form of human righteousness, of some special condition of soul. The words point, rather, towards the eternal √'Moment' when before God we are unrighteous and humiliated, in order that by Him we may be justified and exalted. This does not render exhortation superfluous; for, as a secondary ethical action, it may prove of supreme importance by pressing upon us the knowledge of our folly in resorting to those eminences. In so far as our thought and will and action are titanic—and when is our engaging of ourselves in thought and will and action not titanic?—in so far as they bear upon them the unmistakable marks of Cain's struggle for existence, even though it be a struggle on 'God's' behalf; in so far as they mean that—unavoidably, no doubt—we plant our standards, establish our business houses, build our towers—our vast energy must break in pieces upon the disturbance which threatens the whole *form of this world* (xii. 2), must be shattered upon the law of death which can be avoided by no thing that thinks itself to be some thing. There may be a real value in exhortation, if by it we are led to know all this; if it hammers into our heads the fact that we should —so think as to think soberly. We must, however, at this point remember that it is not to the pagan virtue of sobriety that we are here exhorted—that also is titanic, even when it is dressed up in Christian clothes. Nevertheless, even there the miracle may take place; for the light of a sobriety which is not of this world, which is not of men, the light of the demand which God makes upon us, may shine forth through a secondary act of human ethics. It can happen that, if we are obedient to exhortation, the mist of arrogance and pride and dogmatism with which men envelop themselves may be *rent asunder*; it may be that the doors of the circus where men vie with one another in displaying their agility on the high trapeze may suddenly be closed to us; it may be that we shall hear the parable of the thoughts and wills and actions of men; and that then God will be glorified in the full humanity of the man of this world. This is the Miracle; but its achievement lies beyond our competence. We are competent, however, so to conduct ourselves and so to recollect ourselves as to live mindful of how utterly empty our existence is, even upon some *high place*, if the Miracle does not occur. So to recollect ourselves is full of promise, since thereby the claim of God, upon which all else depends, is recognized and made room for. So then we are led back to the mainspring of ethics.

vv. 3b–6a. Strangely enough, the protection against Titanism and the return to the Primal Origin—that is to say, to the presupposition of ethics—are guaranteed by a conception of the INDIVIDUAL, but by a conception of the individual in which he is rid of his ambiguity.

I beseech you . . . to think soberly—according as God hath dealt to each man a measure of faith. For even as we have many members in one body, and all the members have not the same office: so we, who are many, are one body in Christ, and severally members one of another. And having gifts differing according to the grace that was given to us.

When the Parable of the Body and its Members is examined carefully, it will be found that it does not support that romantic, conservative attitude towards individual human personality which underlies the Catholic doctrine of the Church and other similar doctrines which are derived from it. Paul does not set forth individual human personalities as 'partial' things comprehended in a larger whole, as so many cells are united into one living organism. If the parable were to be thus interpreted, it would then refer—in very crude form, no doubt—to a series of phenomena which belong properly within the spheres of sociology and biology. In that case, the parable would not refer—as in Paul's writings we should expect it to do—to the Kingdom of God, nor would the exhortation to think soberly follow as an ethical necessity. For why should the conception of human life as an organism—adequate though it appears at first sight—impose so severe a limitation upon men as to remind them of God? Have we really any reason to suppose that the Christian 'corporation' is competent to represent to the individual the claim of God, or that the totality of the community—the mass of the faithful—is competent to judge between God and man? Such an interpretation of the parable may seem transparently obvious, and the relation between God and man which is involved in it may seem self-evident—so self-evident that even Protestants seldom rid themselves of it!—but for these very reasons—please note that we are here contradicting what was said in the first edition of this book—it cannot be the right interpretation; for the parable would then fall altogether outside Paul's horizon. God does not delegate His claim upon men to any directly observable human formation, however spiritual. They encounter Him in their own particular, individual, tribulation and hope, and not through some notion of the 'whole'. In fact, the individual is not a 'part', but is himself the 'whole'. A limit must, it is true, be set to his arrogance and lack of sobriety. This, however, is not secured by means of some Entelechy or

perfecting of the whole natural organism, but by his being confronted by that which is common to all men, namely, by the
eternal distinction of God. Natural Philosophy, then, provides
no adequate interpretation of the Parable of the Body and its
Members.

But the parable does, of course, remind the individual of the
fact of the community. That is to say, it reminds him of the
existence of other individuals. And, indeed, the ethical problem—
what shall we do?—appears at the point where the existence of
these 'others' itself emerges as a problem. The subject and object of the exhortation are not, however, the empirical 'other'
individuals as such, but those OTHER believers who, oppressed by
the tribulation and hope of the problem of God, have been established as individuals in Christ. In other words, their OTHERNESS
is unobservable and impenetrable. What is here meant is the pure,
transcendental 'I' which is the unobservable subject of every
observable, concrete 'Thou'. The concept of time within which
this 'Thou', this empirical, concrete, particular, individual, is
apprehended by us, shows clearly that the observable 'Thou'
can, as such, be no more than a parable of the eternal Individual,
can be no more than an 'opportunity' for making known his
existential reality. We must not take this to mean that the
parable or 'opportunity' is not itself real, or assume that,
because this 'I' is eternal, it is therefore not present in every
moment of time. No, the Good Samaritan was quite right, the
neighbour is obviously meant (xiii. 9, 10, cf. Mark xii. 28–31, Luke
x. 25–37). But the *neighbour* is—'every man. A man is not thy
neighbour because he differs from others, or because in his
difference he in some way resembles thee. A neighbour is that
man who is like unto thee before God. And this likeness belongs
to all men unconditionally' (Kierkegaard). We are now in a
position to understand the meaning of the ethical demand that,
when one individual is confronted by another, he should *so think
as to think soberly*. What we can actually see in the 'other' is
here totally irrelevant. Irrelevant here is that impressive complexity of the varied observable distinctions which we might be
able to discover in the 'other' when he appears on the scene and
stands before us. Irrelevant also here is the impressiveness of
the directly visible community as it confronts us with the
external authority of its numbers, of its cohesion, and of its
weighty demands, or with the so-called 'inner' authority of its
formulated or unformulated creeds, of its 'view of life', and of
its past tradition. With all such direct governance of individual
human ethics we are not now concerned; and we are unable to

subscribe to the Catholic doctrine of the Church, since exhortation cannot be undertaken by any 'other' individual or group of individuals. It must be Fellowship which is encountered in the community: but this means an encountering of the OTHER in the full existentiality of his utter OTHERNESS. In the *neighbour* it must be the ONE who is disclosed. Thus understood, Fellowship is not an aggregate of individuals, nor is it an organism. In fact, Fellowship is no concrete thing at all. It is, rather, that Primal synthesis and relationship and apprehension of all distinct concrete things which is their final unobservable ONENESS. Fellowship is communion. It is, however, not a communion in which the 'otherness' of each particular individual is blurred or limited or dissolved, but that ONENESS which both requires the 'otherness' of each individual and makes sense of it. Fellowship is the ONE which lies beyond every 'other'. The ONE, the INDIVIDUAL, is therefore not one among others, not a cell in a larger organism, but simply the HOLY ONE—sanctus. In him is focused and summed up that OTHERNESS of the ONE which is contrasted with every other kind of 'otherness'. He is free; and by his freedom the Fellowship is established and rid of every form of hierarchy and of all possibility of disintegration. Similarly, it is the Fellowship by which the individual is established and rid of all caprice. Fellowship is communio—sanctorum! There is no other communio; and there are no other sancti. The Body in the parable is therefore neither the sum of its particular members, nor the consequence of their interaction. The Body confronts the members, establishes them, and makes them ONE: is, in fact, the INDIVIDUAL, and, as such, is an altogether unobservable, transcendental, factor, which is contrasted with every single member, with the aggregate of them all, and with their organic unity. What the members are and do in their observable, varied peculiarity, they owe to their relation to the unobservable ONENESS of the Body which transcends every particular individual whether isolated or gathered into one whole. The meaning of the parable—in which Body and Individual correspond as picture and reality—lies, then, in the contrast between the unobservable, transcendental ONENESS of the INDIVIDUAL and every particular individual, whether isolated or grouped together. The *believers*—men in relation to God—are therefore, in their full-grown and in no way attenuated individuality, ONE BODY, ONE INDIVIDUAL in Christ. They are not a mass of individuals, not even a corporation, a personified society, or a 'totality', but The Individual, The One, The New Man (1 Cor. xii. 12, 13). This ONE, this Body of Christ, it is which confronts us in the problem of the 'other' in the fellowship of the believers. The *Body of Christ* is, however, as we remember (vii. 4), the crucified Christ. Thus we perceive at once how critical, how directly critical, for the pre-supposition of ethics, is this conception of the Individual. If the crucified Christ is *the measure* of faith which God hath dealt to each man—to each man in his particularity; if we have—**gifts differing according to the grace** which kills men in order to make them alive; if each single one of us must, in his particularity, *put on the Lord Jesus Christ* (xiii. 14), that is to say, put on the New Man; if the 'other'—the neighbour—who stands at the side of each one of us is the uplifted finger which by its 'otherness' reminds us of the WHOLLY OTHER; if the community is that fellowship which reminds us of the Fellowship which is the ONENESS of every man and of all mankind in the unsearchableness of God—then, for each one of us who is thus reminded of his INDIVIDUALITY, all Titanism, all mounting of *high places*, is excluded; and to *think soberly*—that is to say, to recollect that God alone occupies the High Place—is set forth as √ THE ETHICAL ACTION. In order to correspond with their veritable situation men must therefore—bow. This proper humiliation cannot really be brought about by any pressure of numbers, by any weighty human requirements, by any exercise of observable authority, by any mystical middle world of ecclesiastical organism; for the humiliation of men before God is a compelling and →inevitable demand. With this reminder, the secondary ethical action of self-recollection is bent backwards to its origin, to the primary ethical action; and there it participates in the power and dignity of its origin. Thus it is that the secondary action in demonstrating its own transcendental purpose, is itself fulfilled; and the individual stands before God. But he stands with his 'individuality' shattered and disturbed, as only God can disturb it; and yet, in his disturbance, nevertheless under the sign of victory and the sign of hope.

vv. 6b–8. We have, then, different gifts—Perhaps, one bears the word of **prophecy**—let him **prophesy** in accordance with **faith! Or,** perhaps, one is capable of **ministry**—let him understand his **ministry! Or,** perhaps there is one **that teacheth**—let him do it for instruction! Perhaps there is one that preacheth—let him preach! **He that giveth—let him do it with simplicity! He that ruleth**—let him do so earnestly! **He that sheweth mercy**—let it be **with cheerfulness.**

As Fellowship, the community is constituted by Christ, the ONE, the INDIVIDUAL. This means that only by submission to

God, and by the complete correspondence of what is particular
with its ultimate purpose, can unity be established in diversity.
Tolerance is, no doubt, a virtue without which none of us can
live; but we must, nevertheless, at least understand that it is,
strictly speaking, destructive of fellowship, for it is a gesture by
which the divine disturbance is rejected. The ONE in whom we
are veritably united is Himself the great intolerance. He willeth
to rule, to be victorious, to be—everything. He it is who disturbs
every family gathering, every scheme for the reunion of Christendom, every human co-operation. And He disturbs, because He
is the Peace that is above every estrangement and cleavage and
faction. The maxim, 'To every one his own', can never lead to
ethical action. 'To every one the ONE', is the true maxim. For
what can preserve the community from disruption? What can
protect the problem presented by 'others' from the misunderstandings of the struggle for existence, if, so long as we are men,
grace meets us only as a number of various kinds of *gifts*; if the
WHOLLY OTHER meets us only in the 'otherness' of the concrete
man who confronts us here or there; if we find in 'others' only
what is, in fact, their 'own'? A careful psychological analysis
will no doubt prove that things are precisely so. But are we
thereby protected from disruption? The psychologist may press
us to the conclusion that men are always in conflict with one
another, and that between individuals there is possibly no—yes,
no!—reconciliation. But psychology is not ethics; and the more
honest a man the psychologist is, the more certainly he will own
it. The situation being what it is, nothing can help us save the
recollection that as an individual, and precisely in the appalling
particularity of his individuality, every man is a parable of the
ONENESS of men—in God. This means that it is not in spite of a
man's particular gifts that he is a particular person and can think
and do only what is particular, but precisely because of HIS
particular gifts. There is, however, a particularity which all
men share alike; and it consists in the knowledge of the KRISIS
from death to life. And this particularity is theirs in Christ—in
the ONE. It consists not in a man's strength, but in his weakness;
not in his possession, but in his deprivation; not in his rightness,
but in his wrongness; not when he ascends his *high place* with all
that is his, but when, in order that God alone may be exalted, he
descends from his height, and every secondary ethical action—
even this negative action—is bent back to its Primal Origin. If
this descent be quite radically understood—but where can such
understanding be found?—; if everything which is a man's 'own'
be completely surrendered to the One—but where has such

surrender ever been found?—; if each one of us, perceiving that his *gift* is grace, has placed HIS power, HIS possession, HIS rightness at God's disposal—; then, because of grace, each one may regard his own particular possession as his *gift*. And so it is that—recollecting, of course, the great cautionary *perhaps* by which we are reminded of grace, that is to say, of the ONE—each man's 'own' comes to its own honour. Yes, it does in very truth COME to honour! For it is not only that the ONE is honoured thereby, but that the plurality of the members, of the individuals, is established—by their relation to the ONE. And moreover, the community is established thereby as Fellowship. But what a community it is! Only with hesitating steps dare we follow the text at this point. For once again there comes into the picture the vanishing-point of the Resurrection. It is in this context that secondary ethical actions begin to assume full and weighty significance. The purposeful 'demonstration' now moves over from *thinking* (xii. 3a) to the words of the witnesses. Their actual speech is a real witness. In the description of the community which follows none are mentioned save these active, combatant, sharp-shooting witnesses. Every one of them seems to be—a parson! But what parsons they are! Not a word about human requirements! Everything revolves round the demand of God to which all must submit. Each man moves like a shell shot from the mouth of a gun. Indeed, they must and can so move, because each one has a purpose, the Purpose. None of them are engaged on 'piece-work'; nothing is neatly arranged by a disciplined administration. In performing his own work, each one does the One thing, which is the Whole.

Perhaps one is a bearer of the—**word of prophecy.** We are not likely to be taken in by the many allurements of prophecy which appear before us, claiming to represent the Wholly Other. For we are, alas, only too familiar with alluring prophets. We have seen them crumble into fragments. We have seen them bring the Wholly Other once more into disrepute, by being themselves no more than 'very strange'. Yet, in spite of their frequent collapse, the longing that one should arise who will truly set before us the complete strangeness of the Wholly Other still remains. If there is *perhaps* some particular one who has so completely submitted his own particularity to the 'Perhaps' of the grace of God, who speaks so much—**in accordance with faith,** who so genuinely renders unto God what is His that God is able to speak through him, as though he were not; if such a one be the ONE, then would his prophecy be the only ethical possibility. There could be no other; for it would need nothing to supplement or counterbalance it. Since the meaning of such particularity is ONE-NESS, it is itself sufficient and the arrogance of particularity has been thereby excluded.

Perhaps one is—**capable of ministry,** that is of rendering practical assistance. The exercise of this capacity can also be, paradoxically, the only ethical possibility; and the particular one who possesses it, without arrogance, can also be the ONE. We have every reason to be disgusted with those who cry out at us the word 'Service' and demand that we should be 'practical' Martha still declares her intention of *serving* without any intention whatever of hearing. Yet, in spite of all these busy Marthas, the longing for help still remains. Service means so to bind up our temporal wounds that our eternal wounds, which no human operation can heal, are left gaping. Service means so to care for the body that the souls of men are not destroyed thereby. Service means not passing by the man who has fallen among thieves, as did that Priest and that Levite. Busied with the knowledge of God, and persuaded that on it everything depends, it is for the Priest that the question *And who is my neighbour?* has no longer any meaning. SERVICE is the active sight of that which Priests and Levites refuse to see. 'Practical' is that which thrusts men back upon 'theory' and makes them 'see' their great tribulation and their great hope. *Perhaps* there is some particular one who does nothing but minister to men, who ministers to them in their veritable tribulation and ministry, in the KRISIS of their existence. Perhaps such a one, having heard that men are not justified by being practical, IS the servant of God, the Good Samaritan, IS in other words Mary who has chosen the good part. Then his very action is sufficient and without danger.

Perhaps there is one that teacheth. Can the Gospel of Christ, the Word of God be—teaching?(!) Can theology be a science?(!) We think that we understand these questions; and we add the exclamation marks without difficulty. We have heard what Kierkegaard has to say—'To be a Professor of Theology is to have crucified Christ'. We know that Overbeck pronounced Theologians to be the 'Blockheads of human society'. No, the Word of God cannot be—taught! But once again we say: *Perhaps.* In spite of all this abuse, the longing for Theology still remains, precisely because of the mark of exclamation, which is the exclamation mark of resurrection. Omit the exclamation mark, and Christianity is betrayed not only by our speech, but also—which Overbeck forgets—by our silence. Nevertheless, the longing remains: first—because men desire to be instructed from the Bible concerning the meaning of the Word of God at the

moment when, having left its source, it has become the word of
man: secondly—because they desire an 'historical' exposition
of the irreconcilable conflict between 'Christendom', the representative of this word of man, and all human culture and lack of
culture; they want, that is to say, a quite honest record of the
defeat of 'Christendom' during its 1,900 years' history: thirdly—
because they desire the frontier of human capacity as such to
be surveyed and mapped out as accurately and dispassionately
and 'systematically' as possible, in order that thereby the true
meaning of the problem of God may be formulated by reference
to the complete inadequacy and limitation of the contrasted
word of man: and fourthly—they require theology because all
who dare to become clergymen need to be forewarned seriously
against illusions and securities, and against the various ministries
of men; because, in fact, they need 'Practical' Theology to direct
them to their real ministry. Strange it is, then, that Theology
too can be not merely an ethical possibility, but the only ethical
possibility, and the particular one who *teacheth* so as to—do it
for instruction can also be—the ONE.

Perhaps there is one that preacheth—exhorteth, consoleth,
calleth. We are here bound to think very particularly of the
parson. Can his work be the only ethical possibility? This is,
indeed, surprising. But why! We might well be surprised if the
themes which drove men to the necessity of seeking ordination
were psychology, morals, a smattering of Biblical history, a few
platitudes, the tradition of the Church, and personal experience.
But these are not the clerical themes. The theme of the clergy
is the disturbance which has been prepared by God for men, and
the promise which He has given them. *Perhaps* there is some
particular one to whom, stumbling upon it in fear and trembling,
this theme has become so existential, so full of significance, that
there is no other theme, that the subject of his preaching, if he
is to preach at all, must be—Cross, Resurrection, Repentance.
In such a case as this preaching is the only ethical possibility.
Then verily he preacheth, exhorteth, consoleth, calleth. Then
verily this particular one is in his peculiarity—the ONE. Then,
precisely as clergyman, he is called, and justified, and elected,
and is well-pleasing to God.

**He that giveth—with simplicity : he that ruleth—earnestly :
he that sheweth mercy—with cheerfulness.** The demonstration
now moves from the description of the various witnesses to
describe conduct in the narrower sense of the word. Why, however, this particular selection? Why distribution, authority,
and mercy? The meaning of grace is that it is clearly more

blessed to give than to receive; that an impressive authority
which demands respect, and an open heart which is not niggardly
and unsympathetic, are obviously relevant. In the community
where fellowship is constituted by the ONE, each man is thereby directed precisely to this particular conduct and to these
particular gifts, which are, moreover, actually operative in the
community. Now, these particular 'offices' come into being
because men are disturbed by God. Apart from that, men would
not, as they are, behave precisely in this manner. The undisturbed man is neither generous, nor impressive, nor merciful; or,
if he is, his conduct in such matters lacks the peculiar brilliance
of that behaviour which, because it is exercised in the midst of
complete human ambiguity, points to the disaster by which men
are overcome. Whenever men are offered up as a sacrifice (xii. 1)
the witness of speech tends to be reinforced by the witness of this
particular conduct, this particular disposition, by these particular 'offices'. We must not, however, forget that these 'offices'
are, in fact, one: varied and particular though they are, they do
but express one and the same reality. They do not exhaust
themselves in a display of natural human good-heartedness, but
are all for the glory of God, and they all stand under the Cross—
we do not say that they ought to be BROUGHT under the Cross,
but that they DO veritably stand there. Mindful of this, *he that
giveth* will do so *with simplicity*, with that inner freedom which
does not make of giving so solemn an affair that to receive becomes a bitter thing, but so gives that both giving and receiving
bear witness together to the unfathomable simplicity of God.
Similarly, authority will be exercised naturally, as something
which actually exists, not as something which must be brought
into being. Thus constituted, authority is exercised *earnestly*.
Mercy, however, will be shown *with cheerfulness*, because the
mercy which God has vouchsafed to men makes it impossible
for them to be merciful without a certain sorrowful humour;
for the merciful man is aware that he himself is desperately in
need of mercy. Thus it is that all these human possibilities
become ethical only in the shadow of the final eschatological
possibility. When, however, they do stand there, they become
at once the only possibility, for they are an urgent, compelling
necessity.

Is the foundation of Ethics to be found, then, in the constitution of the Community as Fellowship? Yes; for this is what these
verses mean. The Community is fashioned out of particular
men in their relation to God. In the One-ness of the particular
individual this relation is realized. Now, Christ is the One-ness

of each particular one, and He is therefore the Fellowship of them all. There is no other protection of conduct against the subtle, ever-present danger of Titanism. There is no other relating of human behaviour to God. When we speak thus we are speaking in notoriously ecclesiastical fashion. But we are speaking really of the Coming Church of Jacob; and it ought not to surprise us if this is nowhere and at no time visible. For us it is sufficient if, in spite of its ambiguity, the visible Church of Esau is capable of reflecting the coming light. This light need not be altogether hidden, and indeed is not altogether hidden; for wherever men are gathered together—*perhaps* their particular community is constituted by reference to the One— there men are found to be wrestling with the ethical presupposition, hoping for it, suffering for it—and this cannot be all to no purpose.

POSITIVE POSSIBILITIES

XII. 9–15

vv. 9–15. Let love be without dissimulation. Abhor that which is evil; cleave to that which is good. Be kindly affectioned one to another with brotherliness! **In honour preferring one another !** Be **not slothful in** seriousness! Be **fervent in spirit !** Serve the time![1] Rejoice **in hope!** Be **patient in tribulation!** Continue **instant in prayer !** Participate in all that is done for the good **of the saints!**[2] Be **given to**

---

[1] I feel bound, in spite of Jülicher's protest, to retain the opinion that the reading κυρίῳ δουλεύοντες (*v.* 11c) is insipid. The demand that men should *serve the Lord* seems to me to be, in the context, a quite intolerable generalization. The words occur, it is true, in Col. iii. 24; but there they are wholly relevant, whereas here they are not. The suggestion that they refer to δοῦλος Χριστοῦ Ἰησοῦ (Rom. i. 1) seems to me to make them, at this point, still more irrelevant. Jülicher attempts to support the reading by interpreting it to mean 'serve the Lord—only'. But in the series of exhortations it is the verbs which are emphatic; the nouns merely indicate the different occasions. Are we to suppose that *v.* 11c is an exception?—which it must be, if we are to accept Jülicher's 'only'. The reading καιρῷ δουλεύοντες, which I prefer, presents an entirely suitable paradox. Lietzmann dislikes it because it has a sinister ring about it. But this, surely, may mark its authenticity. It is intelligible that some copyist, lacking a sense of humour, should have been guided by Athanasius: ὅτι οὐ πρέπει τῷ καιρῷ δουλεύειν ἀλλὰ τῷ κυρίῳ; but it is surely unintelligible that a later copyist should have made the opposite correction. I understand from Lietzmann's critical note that an unintentional alteration is unlikely.

[2] μνείαις (*v.* 13) seems to have been sacrificed by the same corrector who got rid of καιρῷ (*v.* 11). Here he substituted the easier χρείαις. μνεία, of course, has nothing to do with the cult of the saints. It denotes—as in i. 9—a 'rendering of assistance to some one'; or, as Zahn has it, a 'recollection expressed in concrete and friendly support'.

hospitality! Bless them that persecute you; bless, and curse not! Rejoice with them that rejoice, and weep with them that weep!

The phrase 'Positive Ethics' means that volition and action which constitute a negation of the *form of this world* (xii. 2), a behaviour which contradicts its erotic course, and which protests against its great error. Properly speaking, 'Positive Ethics' belong only to the volition and action of God. Absolute, positive, ethical, human volition and action which are genuinely detached from the course of EROS, and which genuinely protest against it, lie beyond our knowledge. We do, however, know a relative positive human behaviour which, although it belongs to the human possibilities of this world, and although it is marked—as, indeed, all human possibilities are marked—by the *form of this world*, nevertheless possesses, even in its *present* form, by virtue of the imperishable and primary constitution of the universe, a parabolic capacity, a tendency towards protest, an inclination to enmity against EROS. We must, however, be careful how we express this. We may find it easier to regard some kinds of human behaviour as being more pregnant with parabolic significance than others. We may, for example, choose love rather than hatred. Certain particular human possibilities may appear to be more closely related to the divine disturbance and transformation than others are. It may seem to us more probable that we should attain to that 'sacrifice', that demonstration to the honour of God, within the framework of a particular series of concrete actions: more probable, that is to say, that we should be able to fulfil the four commandments written on the first 'Table', if we do so having first fulfilled the commandments written on the second 'Table'. But when we say 'easier', 'more closely', 'more probable', we mean that the ethical necessity even of these particular kinds of human conduct does not lie in their 'matter'—for materially they belong to *this world*—but in their 'form', that is to say, in their Primal Origin, in the Oneness of the subject of the action. The possibility that from time to time God may be honoured in concrete human behaviour which contradicts the commandments of the second Table must therefore be left open.

Let love be without dissimulation! Side by side with EROS stands AGAPE, Love, the love of one man for another. AGAPE is the supreme, positive, ethical possibility. AGAPE includes in itself all the commandments of the second 'Table'. In it is summed up the whole behaviour of men which, though relative, and though remaining within the *form of this world*, yet runs counter to it. As the love of men towards God, AGAPE is, however, the supreme, unobservable work demanded in the first 'Table'. As such it is the existential action of the man who is under grace (v. 5, viii. 28, 29); and it is represented in the primary ethical action of worship. We know that grace is the grace of the hidden God by which the vitality of the known man of this world is fundamentally disturbed. We know also that in grace the supposed unity of mankind meets and is disturbed by a Wholly Other majestic and unobservable unity, which is the true One-ness. Now, it is the existence of others which constitutes a riddle by which we are reminded of that true and wholly other One-ness. It follows therefore—and here we pass over into the realm of what is observable and concrete—that the primary act of worship must be extended, or rather translated, into the secondary action of love towards our brother men. Indeed, it is precisely by this extension or translation of worship that the honour of God is demonstrated. Worship, it is true, represents love towards God; it represents the existential action of men which is directed towards the unsearchable majesty of God. But worship can represent existential love only in so far as it is significantly engaged in the corresponding love of men which is the parable of love towards God. Love of men is in itself trivial and temporal: as the parable of the Wholly Other, it is, however, of supreme significance; for it is both the emissary of the Other and the occasion by which it is apprehended. In the visible and concrete existence of our contemporaries the problem of God is therefore formulated concretely and in such a manner as to demand a concrete answer. As the love of men towards men, AGAPE is the answer of the man who under grace is directed towards the unsearchable God. AGAPE is the concrete analogue of election. Thus understood, AGAPE borders on infinity. And further, as the love of men towards men, AGAPE demonstrates the existential existence of my neighbour who is unobservable. The man fallen among thieves provides the opportunity by which we are enabled to apprehend the neighbour who cannot be observed. For this reason, and only for this reason, is he really our neighbour. But we must be careful not to say too much. Suffice it that Love in this passage does not in the end refer to some general and directly visible neighbourly or brotherly love, not even to the love of foreigners or of negroes. Much has been said about the significance of the love of men towards men; but we are bound to recall what has been said already about 'Double Predestination', and about the freedom of God as God. It remains there-

fore to bring this into relation with even the greatest love of
which we are capable. In fear and trembling we must mention
the possibility of a 'remnant' which cannot be comprehended,
even in the most absolute extension of the ethics of love. There remains a worship the significance of which is expressed otherwise
than in terms of brotherly love. With penetrating insight Luther
refers to this when, in commenting on xii. 14, he declares that
cursing is an 'operation of the Holy Spirit'. If we follow Luther
here we need not suppose that we are contradicting the First
Epistle of John: 'As the first commandment is the standard to
which all the other commandments must be referred; so God's
word against the neighbour is the measure by which love itself
must be judged' (Luther). There can be therefore no absolute
exhortation to love, any more than there had been (xii. 3–8) to
fellowship, or to prophecy, or to theology, &c. Wherever the
disturbance by God is, these relative possibilities exist, and also,
of course, love which is the greatest relative possibility. But we
must not forget that love is peculiarly and characteristically
under KRISIS, precisely because it is within the sphere of grace
that love is the supreme, positive, relative possibility. Love,
therefore, must conduct itself according to its real significance.
Love must be worthy of its—borrowed!—name AGAPE. It must
display its positive ethical quality by protesting against the
force which is impelling men as men. This protest can never be an
inherent quality in human love; for how can human love appear
otherwise than in the form of EROS—a form to which it should
not, strictly speaking, be adapted? Where is there a human
worship of the Unknown God which is not moved by the rhythm
of a worship of the god whom men know? Is our human love
ever veritably pure and veritably free from the lust which is
fashioned according to this world—the desire to see and to
create, to shape and to possess? EROS is not—*without dissimulation*. EROS deceives. As a biological function it is now hot,
now cold. But AGAPE is—*without dissimulation*. AGAPE is our
recollection that the existence of our fellow men presents us
with the problem of the hidden God. AGAPE reminds us that
in our whole conduct towards them it is God who must be
honoured; that the purity of our relation to them can never
consist in our observable intercourse with them, but only in that
renewing of the mind by which human intercourse is perpetually
transformed and reconstituted. AGAPE reminds us that the
purity of human intercourse cannot be measured by positive
'success', for the endeavour to bring about positive 'results' is
a motion of EROS. AGAPE consists, rather, in the offering of a

pure sacrifice—in human intercourse. It consists in the purity
of obedience and in respect towards Him who is able to accept
or to reject our sacrifice. Love is without dissimulation when
our ethical behaviour bends backwards from the commandments
of the second 'Table' to those of the first, from secondary
ethical actions to the primary ethical action. The true intercourse is to be related to the Primal Origin! This means to seek
and to serve the One in the others, which is the meaning of the
much-misunderstood 'Song of Love' (1 Cor. xiii). 'Let every
man set his face steadfastly towards Jerusalem' (Tersteegen)—
with the certain risk that then he will 'approach too nearly'
both himself and others.

Abhor that which is evil; cleave to that which is good. This
refers still to our fellow men. The distinction does not agree at
all with the pattern of EROS. EROS does not merely deceive: it is
also uncritical. EROS knows nothing of that 'Other' in the
others. In others EROS sees only what they are, and loves them
only in their non-existential existence. EROS does not perceive
that it is precisely this which is their *evil*. AGAPE, on the other
hand, consistently accepts and rejects. It selects what the
others are not—that is, their *good*—and rejects what in their
totality they are—that is their *evil*. Blüher points out that the
word πονηρόν means literally 'burdensome'. The *earthy*, which
must be borne painfully, is the ambiguity and impurity attaching to everything which in the observable world is real and
analysable. This is as such—the Evil. AGAPE is the question
which is addressed to the others—What is good? What is evil?
AGAPE is the KRISIS in which the others stand. AGAPE can never
be the simple, direct, unmistakable thing which sentimentalists
yearn after—because it is indissolubly linked with the AGAPE
which is directed towards God. Love is therefore both sweet
and bitter. It can yield; but it can also be harsh. It can preserve
peace; but it can also engage in conflict. 'All the good works
that I might perform on behalf of my neighbour and all the love
that I might display towards him ought to be governed by the
will of God. Should I be able to make the whole world happy
for one day, nevertheless I must not do so—if it be not God's
will' (Luther). Only the love which is strong enough to abhor
that which is evil can cleave to that which is good. Love forgets—and knows; forgives—and punishes; freely receives—
and utterly rejects. Love beholds the concrete neighbour, sees
his positive 'Yes', and knows it to be veritably 'No'; and
yet, nevertheless, apprehends him as he has been already
apprehended by God. Such is love. And men, in spite of the

contradiction in which they stand, await it, claim it, knowing that EROS can never answer their problem, can never justify them and redeem them.

Be kindly affectioned one to another—with brotherliness! When we all stand before God, brotherhood is not a difficult notion. But inasmuch as that which is 'before God' is not *conformed to this world*—of which alone we have knowledge—so assuredly brotherliness before God can never be a concrete present thing. Horrible in His sight is brotherliness which is unaccompanied by fear and trembling, and which forgets that men can be brothers only in God. Grossly immoral (i. 27!) is all direct and particular brotherhood unless it be strictly a matter of service. In the Epistle to the Romans, to be *kindly affectionate* means—means, that is, when it is understood existentially—to be serviceable, veritable, directed towards the goal, critical. Only when it is thus defined and conditioned is brotherliness a demonstration against the form of this world. Only so can it withstand the rebound of failure and disappointment, which is inevitable in all brotherliness with which we are familiar.

In honour preferring one another! That we should respect personality is also not unnatural, if it be true that in the Community—that is, in the person of the other—we encounter in visible form the secret of God. This simple requirement is, however, complicated by the suspicious fact that the demand is normally made by those who think themselves not sufficiently respected. This serves to remind us of the KRISIS which attaches also to this ethical possibility. We are familiar with the honour paid by one man to another according to the form of this world. But in all this removing of hats and paying of compliments men do but honour themselves. If, on the other hand, the honour we pay to another is to be an ethical action, it must be an unconditional, genuine preference, which expects nothing in return. Only so can it represent the honour which we owe to God; for it is ethical only as a type. When, however, it is thus understood, the honour we pay to others is a genuine respect for the holiness of men; and without it society is naught but a collection of imbeciles.

Not slothful in seriousness! Paul does not, as Jülicher maintains, regard every moment as fraught with seriousness. *Seriousness* (xii. 8) represents, rather, that true and commanding impressiveness which belongs to a man when he is invested with real authority. And real authority belongs to the accredited representative of the 'One' to the others. The requirement that men should love one another is, of course, involved in this authority; and, as men greatly disturbed, we ought to stand up and demonstrate on behalf of this disturbance and against all brazen-faced human security. We ought seriously to strangle and exclude all opposition of men against men, and drive them to preferential respect for others; we ought to raise the standard of the dictatorship of genuine self-lessness. But can we maintain that the 'moment' of our authority, of our *seriousness*, is like that? Certainly not, for our authority is fashioned according to this world, and partakes of its supremacy. And this is true of every known authority. All our impressiveness is weighed in the balance. *Be not slothful*: do not rest lazily upon your authority. Stand up for that which ye are not, and know not, and do not. Busy thyself in asking questions, not in answering them. Renounce all impressiveness, and be impressive. Nothing is solemn, save the solemnity of the 'Matter', which is not your matter at all. The 'Moment' when your serious speech embraces the true 'Matter'; the 'Moment' when therefore you are able to enjoy true and ethical respect—is no moment in time!

Fervent in spirit! Is spirit, then, an ethical possibility? Yes! in the same sense as love is. For all the visible and derived conceptions mentioned in this passage refer back to an invisible reality lying behind them, which thrusts its way with promising disturbance into the life of men. Here *spirit* clearly means subjective, inner, impelling power governing human life; and it is contrasted with the Spirit, which is objective and external. The psychologically analysable force which is the motive power of human action we may, perhaps, call 'conscience' or 'conviction', for it lies very close to the relation between man and God. In any case, however, Paul does not mean, as Jülicher supposes, that we could be led at all times by the Spirit. What is the Spirit? Is it that by which we are led always? Is it that cool, warm, hot, burning spirit which we call 'conscience' or 'conviction'? If so, it remains inevitably within the sphere of EROS; and, moreover, by it 'others' also are certainly moved. Be *fervent* in the Spirit. If for one moment—at all times, forsooth!—the final, direct, unquestionable, motive power should burn within us intuitively and with inner necessity, then, conforming to the majesty of the 'Matter', so powerful would be the blow that we should be dissolved, so relentless would be the decision that we should be judged and consumed; and it would be wholly unnecessary for us to pause and argue that it was neither A spirit nor OUR spirit, but THE Spirit. 'Come rack, come rope—don't flinch!' (Zwingli). No, the 'Moment' of this occurrence also is no moment in time.

Serve the time! This is complementary to what has just been said. Is not the particular occasion or time when we set about our urgent tasks conditioned by the 'Moment' of the great divine disturbance? Is time—history!—anything else but the objective Spirit that speaks to us from without? The question is not whether our spirits are altogether governed by time; of course they are—and every Tom, Dick, and Harry in this sense *serves the time*. The real question is whether our time is conditioned by the Spirit, whether our time is the 'present' time (viii. 18, xiii. 11), whether our time is time filled with meaning, whether our time is a time by which we ought to, and can, be regulated. This is always the question. If this be so, then —*serve the time*: plunge into the KRISIS of the present moment, for the decision is there. Why should it not be that the vast ambiguity of the ebb and flow of time constitutes its vast significance? If for this reason ye serve time, then obey it wholly, press onwards through its ebb and flow, onwards, till ye perceive that time itself is also under KRISIS. Then is your service an ethical service; and then serving the time ye are not time-servers.

Rejoice in hope! Hope, an ethical behaviour? Yes, of course. The great hope which God sets before men compels them to demonstrate against the course of this world. But is there any one who does not hope? What is it that makes of our hope an ethical action? Surely, it is our rejoicing! Not to see, to be deprived and empty-handed, to be confronted by negation (viii. 24, 25)—this is what hope means. The sense of present possession, to have and not to need to wait—this is the opposite of hope. To *rejoice in hope* means to know God in hope without seeing Him, and to be satisfied that it should be so. This is what makes of hope an ethical action; for to hope in God turns hope into a joyful act which cannot be brought to naught.

Patient in tribulation! Tribulation, an ethical action? Assuredly it is. For how can we do homage unless we be oppressed? *We glory in tribulation* (v. 3). To be oppressed is a positive human action. When men are pressed down, God presses on. His pressure, however, is neither direct nor obvious. *Upon every soul of man that doeth evil* (ii. 9) tribulation falleth. Tribulation is the negative correlation of the course of human life. Only when it is borne patiently, however, is it a protest against the course of the world. Patience means to love those who oppress us. It means to know God in tribulation without seeing Him, and to be satisfied that it should be so. This patience it is which makes of tribulation an ethical action, and gives it its significance of an advance from 'Here' to 'There'. Patience means faith in God—here and now.

Continue instant in prayer! Prayer, an ethical action? Certainly. For prayer—the reference here is not, of course, to the primary act of worship which, as we have seen, is the presupposition of all action, but to a secondary action, to prayer as a concrete occurrence—is a quite precise action. Placed as we are and grievously oppressed, how can we avoid calling upon God? How can we avoid being of the company of those who, like the Psalmists, saw things as they really are, and in their misery cried out unto God? Can we do otherwise than submit ourselves to Him, because He is God; than thank Him—never, however, without evident dread; than beg Him to be our God and to continue to be our God? Uncomfortably this energy of prayer presses into the world of men. It is almost as though the normally parabolic action of men were in prayer disturbed by the intrusion of an absolute human act. And yet, what a paradox it is! For is there any human activity so utterly questionable as the busy praying of men? How profane a world this world of prayer is, how it verges upon the ridiculous, Heiler has made abundantly clear:—*we know not how to pray as we ought* (viii. 26). Only when it is persisted in does prayer become an ethical action. To *continue instant in prayer* does not mean to pile up a greater quantity of prayers or to refine their quality, but to hold fast their direction and to retain their proper continuity. To *continue instant* means that God is sought and intended in prayer, that it is God's will that we should pray. Thus directed, prayer is the groaning within us of the Spirit which is not our spirit (viii. 27).

Participate in all that is done for the good of the saints! Be given to hospitality! These two particular and immediate requirements show that all the ethical demands with which we are now concerned are quite direct and concrete. The reference here is first to the collection for the poor saints in Jerusalem— the demand is made in 2 Cor. viii, ix, with mysterious emphasis —and then to the necessity of providing hospitality to the faithful who settle in Rome or who are passing through the city on their way to some other place. Both requirements deal with conduct which, humanly speaking, expresses the unity of the community in Christ. In both requirements there is also, however, something remarkable and strange, the meaning of which is not at first sight obvious. It is this last which needs to be comprehended. In all modern acts of charity its material purpose and content exhaust the meaning of what is done. To

Paul—here as in 2 Cor.—this is in the end trivial. For him the
significance of charity lies in its 'form', not in its 'matter'. By
charity the tension between self and others is overcome; and, for
this reason, charity is a demonstration of the recognition of the
'One' in the others. It is this recognition which makes of charity
an ethical action. Consequently, the range of what is strange
and foreign is capable of unlimited expansion.

Bless them that curse you ; bless and curse not ! Since the
disturbance by God affects also the 'others', it cannot be but
that persecution should break out against the man who is first
hurt by it. The more unobservable and indirect the attack
which Christianity makes upon society, the more liable must
it be to persecution. Persecution belongs inevitably within
the context of grace. What, however, does not belong within the
context of grace is the behaviour which persecution normally
evokes. To *curse* belongs to the *form* of this world. Cursing—
and this is why it is expressly mentioned here—is also recognized in the Bible as the final, solemn possibility of protest.
Cursing in the Bible is the 'Curse of God against the curse of the
devil. Wherever the devil makes use of his followers to resist,
and to hinder, and to destroy, the Word of God . . . it is time
for faith also to break out in curses, and to desire that the
obstacle be put out of the way, in order that room may be
made for the blessing of God' (Luther). Here, however, the
case is different; for, inasmuch as the persecutor threatens
personal suffering to those who are under grace, he is not the
enemy of God but His messenger; and as such he must be
welcomed. The persecutor is the dark, mysterious stranger,
who provides an unparalleled opportunity for doing something
which is relatively unambiguous—in this case, not to have
recourse to arms, to bless and not to curse,—in order that, by
quite unexpected and unyielding conduct, the disturbance, of
which the persecutor is so afraid, may be thrust urgently back
upon him. This blessing means that in the midst of the human
struggle for existence honour is paid to God, and in the most
impressive manner we recognize the 'One' in the 'other'.

Rejoice with them that rejoice, and weep with them that weep !
A fresh vista is opened up at the end of this series of ethical
demands. If the 'other' is the emissary of God as persecutor,
why should he not also be his messenger—in his joy and in his
sorrow? Are joy and sorrow to be regarded only as extremes
of biological-erotic emotion? Are we to meet these emotions—
and they are the questions which the 'other' puts to us—by
confronting joy with the deliberate calm of a stoic, and pain

with the stoic's aloofness? Surely not. Laughter and weeping
remind us that the extremes of human emotion are so ambiguous
that they point beyond themselves to their parabolic significance.
There is a laughter which represents life; and there is a weeping which signifies death. Both are pointing to the 'One'. All
stoicism and moralism, all instruction, every attempt to inter-
fere with human emotion or to set one emotion against another,
may dangerously upset their parabolic witness. Such inter-
ference may turn out to be enmity against God; as, for example,
when Michal tried to stop David dancing before the Ark, or
when the friends of Job tried to check his cry of pain. The true
protest against the world is, strangely enough, here brought
about by affirming even the ecstasies of human joy and sorrow.
The affirmation is, however, ethical only if the paradox of the
unknowableness of the Son of God be apprehended, and if we
recognize that *sin-controlled flesh* is a parable (viii. 3). If, then,
we are to move freely in the depths of human emotion, we must
do so as being not free. If we know what we are doing, we must
know that we do not know. We demonstrate against the form of
this world, in this case, by allowing the 'other' to forget his
'otherness'. He must be enabled to see for himself that we
discover in his supreme and most passionate emotions the witness which he bears to the 'One'. There is, then, a rejoicing and
a weeping with men, as they are wrenched hither and thither by
the deceptive passion of EROS, which itself proclaims the truth
and bears witness to the mercy of God. And so it is that precisely
in this demand the KRISIS in which all positive ethical possibilities are involved is quite clearly displayed. At this point, no
attempt is made to draw out the implications of this KRISIS;
and consequently, the demand seems almost frivolous. We
might, indeed, be led by it to include Jesus Christ among the
sinners. This is, however, a possibility so questionable that we
are now pressed onwards from all secondary conduct to the
primary ethical action, and beyond it again to its Primal
Origin.

NEGATIVE POSSIBILITIES

XII. 16–20

vv. 16–20. **Be of the same mind one toward another.
Set not your mind on high things, but condescend to the
things that are lowly! Be not wise in your own** haphazard
**conceits! Render to no man evil for evil! Take thought
for the things honourable in the sight of all men! If it be**

possible, as much as in you lieth, be at peace with all men! Avenge not yourselves, beloved, but give place unto the wrath of God! For it is written, Vengeance belongeth unto me, I will recompense! saith the Lord. But if thine enemy hunger, feed him! If he thirst, give him to drink! For in so doing thou shalt heap coals of fire upon his head.

By 'negative ethics' we mean things that are willed and done, which, being congruous to the *transformation of this world* (xii. 2), stand in a positive relation to the Coming World. Properly speaking, this is applicable only to the will and action of God; for we know no human possibility, not even a negative possibility, a not-doing, that is in itself a possibility of the Kingdom of God. As, however, there are things willed and done by men which, in spite of their relativity, are pregnant with parabolic significance, powerful in bearing witness, capable of concentrating attention upon the 'Beyond'; so there may be things not willed and not done which are endowed with a like gravity. Human action may be interrupted; and this interruption may speak so earnestly of the invisible action of God that it drives human action, as it were, out of the field (xii. 18). The direct line of human behaviour may be so strangely bent out of the straight as to suggest and proclaim the presence of some invisible, disturbing force. We must, however, be on our guard lest we should at this point introduce a series of negative actions, of things forbidden, and then go on to claim that these secondary actions constitute an accurate and absolute ethic. All possibilities, negative or positive, which are capable of precise definition, are human possibilities, and are, as such, open to question; for they are subject to the right which must be reserved for God alone; they are liable to the judgement of the first 'Table' and to the KRISIS of the passage from death to life. Indeed, they are ethical possibilities only because they are thus strictly related to their Primal Origin. Destroy this relationship, seek their essential nature in what they are in themselves or in what they contain in themselves, and their ethical character is done away.

Be of the same mind one toward another. Set not your mind on high things, but condescend to things that are lowly! These words do not seem to refer, at least in the first instance, to the universal rule that governs all human doing and not-doing. They do not refer to the 'sobriety of thought' with which all meaningless 'high thinking' is contrasted (xii. 3). The reference is here rather to the casual and quite concrete happenings of life, to the observable behaviour of men in relation to what is plainly exalted or plainly lowly, to their straightforward affirmations or negations. The disturbance of men by God renders everything which in this world is 'set on high' open to grave suspicion, whilst at the same time investing with definite attractiveness everything which in this world is lowly and depressed. The Resurrection is, it is true, as we have often heard, the negation not only of human position but also of human absence of position. Nevertheless, in spite of this, it is on the brink of a negation of the order of this world that we are confronted by the Resurrection; and its observable parable is disclosed, not in the fullness of life's development, but in the bodily death of the Christ according to the flesh. In the haphazard happenings of this life the things that are *lowly* have, at least relatively, a greater parabolic capacity than have those things that are set on *high*. Our negations submerge us more deeply than do our affirmations. We might indeed say that a clear apprehension of the disturbance of the equilibrium of human life is a sine qua non for any real understanding of the Epistle to the Romans and of its message. Seen in the light of the Resurrection, every con-crete thing that we appreciate as life and fullness, as great and *high*, becomes primarily a parable of death; death, however, and everything that is related to death—weakness and littleness, de-crease, deprivation, and *lowliness*—become a parable of life. *He must increase, but I must decrease.* This is the great disturbance of men. This is the undeniable shadow of insignificance, of doubt and suspicion, that falls on every human eminence. Since each daily occurrence in our lives is weighed down by this shadow, we must not dismiss it with some vague generalization. Since the problem which it presents is a permanent problem of our existence, it cannot be legitimate for us to treat it as an 'interim' situation or as an 'interim' problem. Christianity does not set its mind on *high things*. It is uneasy when it hears men speaking loudly and with confidence about 'creative evolution'; when it marks their plans for perfecting the development of pure and applied science, of art, of morals and of religion, of physical and spiritual health, of welfare and of well-being. Christianity is unhappy when men boast of the glories of marriage and of family life, of Church and State, and of Society. Christianity does not busy itself to support and underpin those many 'ideals' by which men are deeply moved—individualism, collectivism, nationalism, internationalism, humanitarianism, ecclesiasticism. Christianity is unmoved by Nordic enthusiasm or by devotion to Western Culture, by the visions of Youth or by the solid

and mature wisdom of middle-age. Christianity sees no clear
distinction between concrete and abstract idealism. It observes
with a certain coldness the cult of both 'Nature' and 'Civilization', of both Romanticism and Realism. It watches with some
discomfort the building of these eminent towers, and its comments always tend to slow down this busy activity, for it
detects therein the menace of idolatry. Christianity's suspicion
may appear unsympathetic; but can we seriously pronounce it
unjustified? In all these growing towers Christianity beholds at
least a parable of death. It sees the rich man, not of course
actually dead, but still in the torment of Hades. Finding truth
more in 'No' than in 'Yes', Christianity recommends men to
condescend to things that are lowly. Seeing men balanced midway
between earth and heaven, and perceiving the insecurity of their
position, it finds itself unable to place serious confidence in the
permanence of any of these human *high places*, in the importance
of any of these 'important' things, or in the value of any of these
'values'. Christianity perceives men moving, it is true, but
moving to deprivation. It beholds a hand shaking the foundations of all that is and will be. It hears the joists creaking
mysteriously. Christianity cannot simply disregard what it has
seen and heard. We can now understand why Christianity loves
the poor and the oppressed, the sorrowful, the hungry, and the
thirsty. We can understand why it can seriously recommend
celibacy, and why it does not fear lest, by checking the reproduc-
tion of the human race, it may dissolve the 'prime assumption
of all positive thought—the assumption that human life is in
some way in itself of value' (Harnack). Christianity knows
itself at least more akin to ascetics and pietists, strange though
their behaviour may be, than to 'healthy evangelical national
piety'; more closely related to the 'Russian Man' than to his
western brothers. To Christianity no problem of life, be it
great or small, is trivial or irrelevant. But this is because its
interest is centred upon the Problem in the problem. Christianity is nigh at hand when human problems are discovered
to be insoluble; it is far distant when men regain their balance.
Christianity displays a certain inclination to side with those who
are immature, sullen, and depressed, with those who 'come off
badly' and are, in consequence, ready for revolution. There is,
for this reason, much in the cause of socialism which evokes
Christian approval. Christianity beholds Lazarus—that is, the
poor man as such—not, of course, *with God*, but, nevertheless,
in Abraham's bosom. It sees in the *lowly* at least a parable of
life. This is because it cannot forget the meaning of resurrection.

In all probability, then, the man 'down there' is blessed, whereas the man 'up there' is not blessed Christianity dare not say more than 'in all probability'; for it cannot be unmindful that the objects of its suspicion and of its approval, of its threatenings and promises, are after all concrete things whether they be *high* or *lowly*; and because they are concrete things, they can be no more than parables. Christianity is therefore at a loss to know what, in the concrete happenings of life, is at any given moment really *high* and what is really *lowly*, to what it ought at any given moment to extend its favour and from what it ought to turn away. This, however, is at any rate clear: Christianity is concerned with human exaltation on the one hand and with lowliness before God on the other. If this be applied to the particular situation—we must not here forget what was said concerning 'Double Predestination'—the last may be first and the first last. It may therefore be that those whom we think to be *lowly* have long ago become in fact exalted. It may be that their humility has been turned long ago to horrid pride. It may be that their ambiguity has been formed into an idol, and their 'brokenness' into some new popular theology. The Proletariat may have become blunderingly and coarsely dogmatic. The revolt against culture may have become naught but an irrational fancy. The busy activity of tower-building may long ago have passed from those who affirm to those who negate. The 'No' may long ago have become 'Yes', and men may now, for the time being, be finding security in positive negation. If so, the time has come for Christianity to turn sadly away from all such negation. If so, the time has come when we are bound to ask whether the solid western agricultural labourer—the Bavarian peasant, for example—is not nearer the Kingdom of God than the 'Russian Man'; whether the skilled mechanic and the industrious man of business are not nearer to the truth than the parson brooding over the deep things of God. If so, the time has come for us to consider seriously whether it would not be good for us to condescend to the things that are lowly, to arise, that is, and plunge into the world—to marry and care for wife and children, to enter politics—not merely on the side of the socialists!—to hold art in high esteem, to be cultured, and perhaps, with the last grim comedy of life, to become—a Churchman. The theses of Christianity here become its antitheses; for it is possible for the parable of death, though it be but a parable, to overstep itself. We must never forget the freedom with which Christianity allots its 'Yes' and its 'No'. It sets up and it tears down; it recalls the emissary it has dispatched; it gives and it takes away. Its purpose, however, remains always the same. It acts always in accordance with the same rule. Opposing what is *high*, it befriends what is lowly; loaning men certitudo, it permits them, for the honour of God, no securitas; measuring our time by the eternity of God, it allows us no established rights, gives us no rest, and preserves no strict continuity in its own action. Does it frighten us to discover how completely all that we are and do moves within the sphere of relativity? Perhaps it does, but this is precisely what we must discover. What, however, is this relativity? Relativity is our relationship to our Primal Origin, our being related to it. This relativity or related-ness affects every concrete human action or position; conse-quently it affects all human ethical behaviour. The function of Christianity, its achievement, is to bring this to our notice. The absolute character of Christian ethics lies in the fact that they are altogether problematical. Their evolution consists simply in the fecundity with which it puts forth more and more questions to which God Himself alone can be the answer. Once apprehend this, and it becomes obvious, terribly obvious, that human ethical behaviour can only demonstrate, only signify, only offer a sacrifice. Nor are we able to extract peace and comfort even from this 'only'; for by it we are reminded that it is God who confronts us with that earnest, inexorable question, What shall we do? The 'No' of Christianity is all-embracing; by it we are thrust deep down to the level of what is *lowly*; by it there is brought upon us a shattering disturbance; by it we are enveloped and overshadowed; by it we are forced to encounter the One in the other—*Be of the same mind one toward another*. But ye will be *of the same mind* only in so far as ye *set not your mind upon high things, but condescend to the things that are lowly*. From the dialectic of this rule, that is to say, from the Rule in the rule—Soli Deo gloria!—the great contradictions emerge, world-denial and world-acceptance, enthusiasm and realism, the wisdom of death and the wisdom of life. But sub specie aeterni they are resolved into one comprehensive and unified view of life. This comprehensive view of life has never, however, had any concrete existence in itself, no man possesses it, for it is not what men comprehend, but that by which they are compre-hended. For this reason it is without doubt both comprehensive and unified. Are we not all patients in one hospital? Do we not all stand under one accusation? Are we not all fallen under one condemnation? What, then, can we do, but be of the same mind one toward another?

Be not wise in your own haphazard conceits! (Prov. iii. 7).

H h

This is the negative rule consequent upon our condescension. Up aloft, on whatever high place they may stand, men have *their own haphazard conceits* (xi. 25). Up there their opinions are conditioned by the necessity of self-preservation, self-expression, self-defence; and this 'self' is haphazard. Up aloft men are bound to adopt the uncritical standard of the struggle for existence; they are bound confidently and naïvely to make use of the categories I—Thou, We—Others. Having taken up one position or—how ridiculous they are!—one point of view, they regard the pre-eminence or victory of their opponents as though it were a tragic disaster; but their own pre-eminence or their own victory is, in fact, equally tragic, equally disastrous. They 'win their way through' or they do not; they 'rise in the world' and are deposed again from their position; they are fortunate or unfortunate; they may perhaps be successful, but even so, they are wounded and buffeted and disappointed and humiliated. Therefore, being the product of the moment, their conceits are haphazard, unqualified, and occasional notions; varying with each heart-throb, they depend upon the condition of the 'enemy', but even more upon the state of a man's self. Let us not deceive ourselves. Our conceits are haphazard. To this rule there are no exceptions. And yet, though the straight line of our haphazard behaviour is never broken through, it can, nevertheless, be strained to breaking-point. There are upon it traces of the fundamental assault that is made upon men by grace. We have seen already that the power and earnestness of Christian ethics lie in its persistent asking of questions and in its steady refusal to provide answers to these questions. Christian ethics only demonstrate, only bear witness that there is an answer. This relativity of the ethics of grace is the axe laid at the root of *our own haphazard conceits*. The root from which our conceits spring, the secret which lies behind all human exaltation, is disclosed in the persistent regularity with which men crown themselves with the security of some absolute answer. By putting an end to all absolute ethics, Christianity finally puts an end to all the triumph and sorrow that accompanies the occupation of any human eminence. To Christianity every human *high place*, every human position, every battle and controversy between men of this world, however sacred and inevitable the conflict may be, is no more than a parable. We are deprived by THE Truth of the energy with which we immerse ourselves in A truth. We are deprived by THE Wrong of the courage with which we put up with A wrong, supposing it to be something peculiar to ourselves. We are deprived by THE

Victory of the vast excitement with which we await A victory
here or there. Is this deprivation 'demoralizing'? Does it involve the breaking of every bone in our body? Assuredly it
does; for that, indeed, is its purpose. Death is the inevitable lot
of everything which lies on this side of the discouragement of
our courage. Human behaviour that has not passed through pur-
gatory can never be ethical, it is simply BIOS, PATHOS, EROS; it is
not governed by necessity, but simply haphazard and fortuitous;
it is not freedom, but simply slavery; it is not of God, but is
capable of some explanation that is merely psychological, if not
psychiatric. Christian ethical behaviour—in so far, of course,
as it is not dramatized into a concrete, observable thing—is THE
Courage compared with which all OUR courage is just cowardice.
By breaking down all 'individualism', Christianity establishes
the Individual. Though its purity is nowhere to be found, Christianity is human behaviour purified of all biological, emotional,
erotic factors. Christianity is the final protest against every high
place that men can occupy. For this reason it is the absolute
ethic, and for this reason it proclaims the Coming World.

Render to no man evil for evil! *Evil* means, in Christian
language, the necessary condition of all visible human action.
Evil is the inert mass of human activity as such. *Good* is not a
second possibility contrasted with *evil*. *Good* is the dissolution
of *evil*, its judgement. *Good* is the impossible possibility of
redemption from *evil*. *Good* is the justification of men by God.
*Why askest thou me concerning that which is good? One there is
who is good* (Matt. xix. 17). Our relation to others, even when
we name it a relationship of *love*, is governed by the law that
we should *render evil for evil*. We do not perceive (xii. 9) in the
other the One—that is, the *good* which he is not. Rather, we
hold him liable for being what he is. Abiding by our neighbour's
visible aspect, and content with observing him directly, we
judge him to be utterly lost to the *good*, even though we see in
him all manner of good. This making men liable for what they
are is to render to them *evil for evil*. Long before we have begun
a conflict with the other, long before we have adopted his *evil*
tactics and have attacked him and counter-attacked him, we
have rendered to him evil for evil, simply because we have made
him liable, simply because we have not apprehended what he is
not. It is this failure of apprehension which makes of our whole
behaviour an inert mass of evil. Along this line of evil we all,
without exception, move. And yet, this line also can be, if not
broken through, at least strained to breaking-point, if we bear
in mind that in affirming, quite rightly affirming, the evil of

others, we are also affirming our own evil; if we also remember that it is only by affirming the One in the other—that is, the good which is in him—that we can even imagine the possibility of our own justification. It may be that, for serious ethical reasons, we find ourselves unable to acquiesce in any interruption of rendering evil for evil. To this we must reply: *to no man* should we render evil for evil. For even the worst that others can do serves only to make our own judgement more obvious and our own justification more grave. In so far as this critical attitude results, to a greater or lesser degree, in concrete non-retaliation and non-resistance, in treating the other as irresponsible, and, in spite of seeming weakness, in overlooking his evil, there is demonstrated in this world what is in fact invisible, namely the One in the other and the overlooking of sin by God. It is to this demonstration that we referred when we said that the line of inevitable human behaviour is strangely deflected. But we must nevertheless remember that it is not, and must not be, broken. This memory it is which prevents us from turning non-resistance into an absolute ethical action and so damaging the hope of the Coming World.

Take thought for the things honourable in the sight of all men! (Prov. iii. 4). Once again we have affinities with the ethics of Kant. If an action be approved by the unobservable One which is in all, it is an ethical action. That is to say, an action is ethical if it is contrasted with the visible behaviour of the 'Many'. All ethical action is of the nature of a protest. This must not be obscured. The One which is in all protests against the behaviour of the 'Many', and indeed provides the standard of the protest. What is good is that which is good in the sight—the perceiving eyes!—of all men. An action which represents really and genuinely the disturbance of men by God, and is not merely a casual and unauthorized disturbance of men by their fellow men, must possess a universal validity, must come out into the open. This means that the paradox of genuine protest must not be thought of as a private matter, valid merely for this or that particular individual. This would be to overlook the One in the particular. The ethical paradox consists precisely in the recollection of this invisible One. There must be no subsidiary, second, paradox side by side with the primary ethical paradox. Here Kierkegaard needs to be corrected from time to time by reference to Kant. The action which is properly ethical must not be directed towards some hidden or secret happiness or unhappiness. Though the behaviour of a given individual—for example, the work of an apostle (i. 1)—may fail to be co-ordinated with the concrete behaviour of human society, it must, nevertheless, be co-ordinated with the truth by which human society is in fact constituted. That is to say, behind the apparent disharmony of the prophet and his environment there must exist a real and final harmony. We are justified in our refusal to submit ourselves to the judgement of the 'Many', but not for one moment dare we refuse to accept the judgement of 'All'. This is the criterion by which every apparently irregular human action must be judged. To this criterion every outstanding character— the hero, the leader of men, the ascetic, the pietist, the preacher of a new moral code—must submit. And, indeed, it is by an appeal to this criterion that all manner of supermen, 'personalities', artists, and geniuses, feel themselves to be justified. There is, then, no especial morality for peculiar people; and there is also no ordinary morality for the average man. So it comes about that a course of moral action which we admire or of which we merely express approval—the action of a prophet, for example—becomes for that very reason a duty for us. We cannot rid ourselves of our responsibility by saying simply—'Well, that was Luther'. Human action becomes abnormal only when it is related to God. But then it becomes normal for all men. When, however, we say for *all men*, we must remember the unobservability of this 'All'; otherwise we shall fall into misunderstanding. The exhortation, *Set not your mind on high things—Be not wise in your own haphazard conceits* (xii. 16), points, therefore, to the truth of the Coming World, to the truth of the One in the 'All'.

If it be possible, as much as in you lieth, be at peace with all men ! The preservation of peace can be an admirable demonstration. It can mean that men are so restrained by God that they have no energy left to deal out blows to others, however justified and well directed those blows might have been. The situation as it is between men and men is so confused and unpeaceable that it requires a distribution of blows to right and to left. Our fellow men have no right to peace. Everything they do irritates us. Unattractive, crotchety, impenitent, they are the incarnation to us of the unteachableness of the known man of this world, who presents us with ever recurring new varieties of provocation. So hardly does this man of the world press upon our own EGO that we can hardly be expected to welcome him as a friend when we meet him in others. Why, then, should we not engage in conflict, particularly if our own struggle with ourselves is, to some extent at least, eased by being transferred to a contest with our fellow men? What is more natural than war? War is, moreover, a parable of what lies beyond it, for in the end war is always directed against the known man of this world. War is the concrete expression of our recognition of what men are, of their impossibility, and of our determination to be rid of them. But war is, nevertheless, a mistaken demonstration; for our conflict with our fellow men never does in fact bring about the denial of the known man of this world. He does not die, even though we continue to fight until we have exterminated our enemies. The denial of the known man of this world is evidently—Jesus Christ, the One in the 'All'. The moment this is apprehended conflict must cease both with ourselves and with others, for it is clearly fruitless. In Christ war seems impossible. He is our peace! It is not for us to impose as it were an additional burden upon this or that man. It is not for us to make known to him that he too is—a man! It is not for us to add to God's right against every man the right of one man against another! We must not fail to apprehend that all that is visibly provocative in men is precisely that which points to their invisible justification. War is a natural human activity. Yes, but it is the activity of men engaged in making themselves God by making of their attitude to their fellow men an absolute moral attitude. It is the apprehension of this which bids us at all costs preserve peace with all men. Whence comes the energy and passion of war, if we know that we are not God? Does it then follow that we must preserve peace in order that we may demonstrate on behalf of the freedom and of the mercy of God? Be at peace—*as much as in you lieth*. We are fully aware why it is that we dare not say more than this. God is the boundary of human possibility. Nothing that we call 'peace'—here we are unable to follow Kant —is even a preparation for eternal peace, for the 'kingdom of practical reason'. When we assert that we behold Christ Jesus in our fellow men—when, that is, we behold peace in war— when we think that we can or ought to express this insight by the preservation of peace, we must remember that we are talking about God's perception and about His peace. But God is not known; He will be known. God therefore remains free. So the possibility that we must engage in conflict with ourselves remains; and the possibility that we must engage in conflict with our fellow men also remains, though it is somewhat more distant. The reservation that God can forbid us to see Jesus Christ in this or that particular fellow man remains. We must not, however, misunderstand this. The reservation is God's reservation. We must not, therefore, confuse His reservation with the reservation which Lutherans made when in their distress they proclaimed a 'moratorium for the Sermon on the Mount'. We must not identify with God's reservation a reservation made by men under the pressure of peculiarly difficult circumstances, however great or even noble the pressure may be. We must not make God's reservation a pretext for the preaching of war-sermons in which men are encouraged to engage in war with a 'good conscience'. There is no such thing as a 'good conscience' either in war or in peace. Even the most sturdy defender of peace knows that we are always in the position of being unable to see the One in the other. He knows, too, that we must always abhor the evil which is in the other (xii. 9). The One in the other has no concrete, visible existence. In relation to the problem of war the knowledge of God means that we must descend from every warlike *high place*; but this does not mean that we must then proceed to ascend at once some *high place* of peace. The knowledge of God directs us to God; it does not direct us to some human position or to some human course of action either in time of war or in time of peace. A Church which knows its business well will, it is true, with a strong hand keep itself free from militarism; but it will also with a friendly gesture rebuff the attentions of pacifism. The earnestness of the command that we should *be at peace* lies in its capacity to illustrate the first commandment; it directs us, that is, to God. We must, therefore, recognize that the command that we should be at peace is no absolute command; it has no final accuracy. And so, because it is a broken command, it bears witness to the peace of the Coming World.

Avenge not yourselves, beloved, but give place unto the wrath of God! For it is written, Vengeance belongeth unto me, I will recompense! (Deut. xxxii. 35) saith the Lord. But if thine enemy hunger, feed him! If he thirst, give him to drink! For in so doing thou shalt heap coals of fire upon his head (Prov. xxv. 21, 22). We must carefully bear in mind what is meant by an *enemy*. The *enemy* displays clearly what we ought not to do. As we have heard already (xii. 14), he is the other in his extreme unknowableness. There seems no doubt that we are bound not to be at peace with him. The moment I am confronted by my fellow man as an *enemy*—the enmity may be personal or national, it may be the product of class antagonism or of a general difference of temper—the whole obscure riddle of the existence of others seems to be focused into one point. When confronted by the *enemy*, all the surly misgivings and pessimistic judgements which we harbour concerning our fellow men seem to be justified. It then appears impossible for us to escape from that biological relation to our fellow men which is the relation of conflict. But who is the *enemy*? The Psalmists knew, at any rate. They saw in the *enemy* not merely a rival or an unpleasant person, an opponent or an oppressor, but the man who to my horror is engaged before my very eyes in the performance of objective unrighteousness, the man through whom I am enabled to have actual experience of the known man of this world and to perceive him to be evil (xii. 17). The *enemy* is the man who incites me to render evil for evil. It is not surprising, therefore, that Luther found in his enemy—the Papacy—not merely an enemy, but the ancient Enemy of men vigorously at work. We can now also understand why it is that in the passionate language of the Psalmists the enemy attains BEFORE GOD a stature which is almost absolute, and why it is that they cry unto God that they may be avenged of him. The *enemy* opens my eyes to what it really is that I find so strangely irritating in my fellow men. I see that it is the *evil*. The *enemy* shows me the known man as finally and characteristically evil. He shows me, moreover, the evil freely running its course without let or hindrance, without obstacle or contradiction from within or from without. He lets loose in me a tempestuous, yearning cry for a higher—non-existent—compensating, avenging righteousness, and for a higher—non-existent—judge between me and him. Naught but an enemy can bring me into so critical a position. What, then, shall I do, when I pass through the elemental, overpowering experience of discovering that no avenging righteousness is available? What am I to do, when I realize that everything that can be done against the enemy is itself evil?—But can it be evil to bring into operation against the enemy that higher righteousness for which I so earnestly yearn? Then it is that the last, supreme temptation to Titanism lies so strangely near at hand. Shall I take the matter into my own hands? Shall I undertake to battle for the right? Shall I become myself the invisible God? Shall I, as an enemy, set myself against the enemy? Shall I, as a Titan, war against the Titan? Who will pronounce judgement upon me, if I do this? I may perhaps be uncertain as to my authority for acting thus, but I shall, at any rate, have answered the more pressing question, What shall I do? I shall, at any rate, have acted. And if action be necessary, what else could I do in the presence of the enemy but, as the representative of the absent God, advance against him with word and deed, with the force of law and of arms, with the whole offensive and defensive might of the world? What else could I do but arise in my anger and punish him, execute judgement upon him? Once it is granted that men can and ought to perform objective righteousness, this whole forceful procedure on behalf of right is clearly inevitable. Once grant this presupposition, and the whole 'Tirpitz morality' stands secure, and no moral refutation of it is possible.—But it is precisely this presupposition, the presupposition that men can and ought to do what is objectively right, which the disturbance of men by God renders altogether questionable. Men can always, of course, attempt to advance against the enemy, claiming that what they are doing is objectively right. But they cannot do this without Titanism, without seizing the sceptre of God. There can be no misunderstanding here, especially if men angrily propose to occupy the field which is already occupied by the wrath of God. But this is precisely the secret of the enemy. He too has laid hands upon the sceptre of God. He too has in some way recognized the absence of a higher righteousness. He too has been confronted by the question, What shall I do? He too has been pressed on till he has decided to erect this righteousness with his own hand. Have even our most bitter enemies ever failed to suppose subjectively that they were doing objectively the thing that is right? It is this claim to objectivity that has so deeply wounded our sense of what is right, that makes their behaviour seem to us objective unrighteousness, and that makes them criminals before God and man. The enemy is, however, delivered over by the burning wrath of God to his own heart's desire (i. 24), and in him I encounter the wrath of God. Am I then also to be engulfed by the wrath of God? Am I also to take into my own hands the preservation of right? I can do so, of course. I may, indeed, have to do so, for is there any alternative to withstanding the Titan titanically? If, however, I do this, I must not be surprised if I have to learn from my titanic, tragic, terrible, pitiable fate that I too, in intending to do what is objectively right, have in fact done objective unrighteousness. Our determination to introduce the higher righteousness is precisely that which renders it altogether lost: *For the wrath of God is revealed against all ungodliness and unrighteousness of men* (i. 18). The wrath of God is revealed against human ungodliness in doing evil and in doing good; it is revealed against the enemy and against me, if I purpose to be the enemy of my enemy. This is the criticism of militarism, but it is, in passing, a criticism of pacifism also.—But who among us does in fact leave room, not for the wrath of men, but for the wrath of God? Who among us does seriously reckon with the fact that human action will, not only here but everywhere, be driven off the field by the preeminent action of God? Who among us recognizes that in the dialectic of life objective right remains merely a question? That it is no more than a question is what is clearly revealed to us by the enemy. It is he who tears away from us our last illusion, for in him we perceive that the righteousness of God can be 'done' only by doing evil. Thus it is in the enemy that the righteousness of God is represented as something altogether distant from us, as something strange and undo-able. In the enemy the righteousness of God appears only as His wrath, and God Himself is revealed to us as—Deus absconditus. Guided by this critical perception, what, then, can I do to the enemy save withdraw from doing to an original not-doing? What can I do but turn away from every answer to an ever-persistent questioning? What can I do but turn from every action to the pre-supposition of all action? If the gesture of conflict is forbidden, what attitude am I to take up towards the enemy? I must surely do the irrational, impossible, and altogether unpractical thing: *If thine enemy hunger, feed him! If he thirst, give him to drink!* What does this mean but that through the enemy, through the One disguised completely in the other, I have received, in most strange fashion, the clear call to give glory to God: *Vengeance is mine, I will recompense! saith the Lord.* Me—I. In order to demonstrate this—*if thine enemy hunger, feed him! If he thirst, give him to drink!* These actions demonstrate that precisely in the enemy the coming Kingdom of God Himself and of God only has been recognized. They draw attention to the fact that the enemy has presented us with a problem that presses upon us too hardly for us to regard him as some one who can be attacked whilst we ourselves remain unbroken. And yet, we have to be careful here. Suppose that we do feed the enemy. Suppose that we do give him to drink. There arises at once the temptation to make of these actions a new human possibility, a new, plausible, human behaviour, a new practical goal to which we can direct our energy. We know, however, how fruitless it is to yield to such temptation. We must not, therefore, make of the 'love of the enemy' that is here required of us a visible human action which is in itself ethical. We are here in the presence of the ethical paradox of the One in the other. On the head of the enemy we must heap *coals of fire.* That is to say, the other must be driven by our action out of his position as an enemy. The other, being secretly the One though he is the enemy, must be compelled to come out of his concealment and stand forth as the One. If this is to be so, I must see him as one of those who *hunger and thirst*, I must perceive that, though, when viewed from outside, he goes on still in his triumph, yet in fact he is naught but a sacrifice to his own tragic fate, naught but a man smitten by the anger of God. I must be led to apprehend that the objective righteousness, which I sought to establish by opposing him, has been established already. In the enemy smitten by God the other no longer remains unknown. In the parable of death he is One. This apprehension is, however, genuine only if it has passed into action. Therefore, feed him! give him to drink! Thou and the enemy smitten by God are one. Between thee and him there is complete solidarity. His evil is thy evil; his suffering thy suffering; his justification thy justification. Thy redemption can only be that by which he is redeemed. Every 'action' which effectively makes known the correlation between thee and him is good. Measured by the standard of what Titans are wont to do to one another, such doing can only be described as not-doing. When, therefore, thou dost ascend the high place of 'love of the enemy', remember that thou art in fact descending to what is lowly, and that thy action is no more than a significant action. The question, What shall I do? is capable of no material answer. It simply raises the question of the ground and purpose of all human action, and then the question, What shall I do? is transformed into a question to which the action of God Himself provides the only answer. The peculiar interest which in Christian ethics attaches to the love of an enemy is that it is a significant action which announces the Coming World.

THE GREAT NEGATIVE POSSIBILITY

XII. 21—XIII. 7

Be not overcome of evil, but overcome evil with good. Let every man be in subjection to the existing ruling **powers: for there is no power but of God; and the powers that be are ordained of God. Therefore he that resisteth the power, withstandeth the ordinance of God: and they that withstand** draw **to themselves judgment. For rulers are not a terror to the good work, but to the evil. Wouldest thou then not be afraid of the power? do that which is good, and thou shalt have praise of the same. For he is a minister of God to thee for good. But if thou do that which is evil, be afraid; for he beareth not the sword in vain: for he is a minister of God, an avenger for wrath to him that doeth evil. Wherefore ye must needs be in subjection, not only because of the wrath, but also for conscience sake. For for this cause ye pay tribute also; for they**—the rulers—**are God's** priests, **attending continually upon this very thing. Render to all their dues:**

tribute to whom tribute is due; custom to whom custom; fear to whom fear; honour to whom honour.

It is now time for us to speak of the various ordinances by which human society is regulated and governed. Moreover, our theme is that, since they provide the great demonstration to the order of the Coming World, they must not, as such, be broken through. It is clear that here both we and our readers are entering upon a very controversial subject. Accordingly a warning will not be out of place, a warning to those who are at the moment deeply involved in the controversy and also, very particularly, to those who may expect something sensational to be said about it. Should this book come into the hands of such persons, they ought not to begin with the Thirteenth Chapter. Those who do not understand the book as a whole will understand least of all what we now have to say. They will be puzzled as to why we say what we do say, why we do not say more, and why we do not say less.

The whole problem of the One in the other, which we encountered last in an acute form in the conception of the *enemy*, is now concentrated in the fact of the existence of the ordinances by which human affairs are regulated. The 'Moment' of the recollection of God is eternal only as the qualification of a moment in time, as that which qualifies the temporal past and the temporal future. The ethical KRISIS of our conduct is absolute only in relation to an action which has not yet been *done away with*, or which has ceased to be *done away with*. The discovery of the One in the other can occur only as each single individual is confronted by particular concrete others; only as he is confronted by the concrete 'Many', itself composed of a number of particular individuals; and only when, in this whole concrete situation, the great ethical riddle is propounded to him and requires solution. The critical revision—*the renewing of the mind* (xii. 2)—to which our conduct is subjected by being related to its Primal Origin in God, by the thinking of the thought of eternity, encounters, however, the remarkable fact that there already exist qualifications of time, that human conduct has already been related to the absolute, that there are in existence combinations of particular individuals which claim to have already solved the riddle of the One. Our critical revision encounters, therefore, a number of ethical factors that are not merely the more or less tempestuous experiments of single individuals, but which, far from being capricious and haphazard, have, so it seems, reached the level of high objectivity. To speak plainly, our critical revision encounters the great positions of Church and State, of Law and Society. And these positions claim to possess the answer to the question, What shall we do? because in all of them the plurality of individuals has been limited by the Whole. These concrete, visible powers claim—and their claims are supported by very convincing arguments—to be, not merely things in human life, but that order and direction which constitute the solution of the problem for which we have been seeking with such unnecessary pain. These powers demand recognition and obedience, and we have to decide whether we shall or shall not yield to their demand. If we admit their authority, we concede quite clearly the principle of Legitimism; if, on the other hand, we reject it, we are bound to accept the principle of Revolution. Being, however, concerned to demonstrate the honour of God, we do not—as the impatient reader desires, or rather, since every one is as a matter of course a party man, as the opponent of revolution quite naturally desires—concede the principle of Legitimism. But, on the other hand, neither do we—as so many readers of the Epistle secretly hope—concede the principle of Revolution. On the contrary, for reasons which will appear later, we find in the Epistle a direct denial of Revolution. We have, however, already suggested that we find in it also a denial of Legitimism. Why we did not say this explicitly will also become clear later.

The Great Negative Possibility! Great, because we are now concerned, not with the demonstration to the honour of God effected by the behaviour of particular individuals towards their neighbours, but with the demonstration made by a collective attitude and behaviour in relation to the plurality of neighbours, a plurality which itself borders on totality. Negative, not because 'the State is to be reckoned without question among the moral forces' (Jülicher), not because 'all State authority and every office has its origin in God' (Wernle), but because here again we find an assault being made upon men, upon their *setting their minds on high things* (xii. 16), upon their Promethean arrogance. It is not upon secular authority itself, not upon the conduct of those who accept and keep its ordinances, not upon the 'duties of citizenship' (Jülicher), that our attention is concentrated, but upon the requirement that men should NOT break through these regulations. In other words, we are interested in a negative behaviour, in a human not-doing. We are therefore most anxious about the man who embarks upon revolution. And even here we do not wish to prejudice his action in any way, for we have no material interest in legitimism. We are

concerned to wrest from his hands the principle of revolution
—simply for purposes of instruction. Why is it that we have
to watch so carefully the forces of revolution? Why are we not
equally anxious about the manifest dangers of conservatism?
This question must be answered. In the dialectical scales revolution and reaction are not equally balanced. But in pointing out
against which side the balance is weighted we must be on our
guard lest we give a totally false impression of the situation as a
whole. We are anxious about the forces of revolution and not
about the forces of conservatism, because it is most improbable
that any one will be won over to the cause of reaction—as a
result of reading the Epistle to the Romans! On the other hand,
it is not unlikely that its reading may foster a contempt for the
present order and an attitude of negation towards it. The disquiet, the questioning, the negation, the emphatic insistence upon
the parable of death, to which Christianity. is definitely committed (xii. 16), may be so misunderstood as to be transformed
into a positive method of human behaviour, into a means of
justification, indeed, into the Titanism of revolt and upheaval
and renovation. The revolutionary Titan is far more godless, far
more dangerous, than his reactionary counterpart—because he
is so much nearer to the truth. To us, at least, the reactionary
presents little danger; with his Red brother it is far otherwise.
With this danger we are vitally concerned. For the honour of
God we have to bring the revolutionary within the orbit of
sacrifice; and his sacrifice is a sacrifice of quite peculiar dignity!

Be not overcome of evil, but overcome evil with good. The
problem of the victory of right over wrong is presented to us in
a far more essential form in the existence of human ordinances
than in the existence of the *enemy* (xii. 19, 20). Must not the
existing order, the order that has already been FOUND, seem the
very incarnation of triumphant unrighteousness to the man who
is SEEKING after God and His Order? Is not the existing order
a reinforcement of men against God, a safeguard of the normal
course of this world against its disturbance by the great ambiguity and its defence against the pre-supposition by which it is
threatened on all sides? Are not the ordinances of men simply a
conspiracy of the Many—far too many—against the One who
manifests Himself, and can only manifest Himself, when the
mature wisdom and authority of the Many crumbles in pieces?
Rulers! What are rulers but men? What are they but men
hypocritically engaged in setting things in order, in order that
they may—cowards that they are—ensure themselves securely
against the riddle of their own existence? Are we not once again

confronted by fools begging a few moments' delay before the sentence of death is pronounced upon them? The invectives that have been hurled against 'Governments' from the days of the Revelation of John to the fulminations of Nietzsche, from the Anabaptists to the Anarchists, have not been directed against defects in government but against the right of governments to *exist* at all. That men should, as a matter of course, claim to possess a higher right over their fellow men, that they should, as a matter of course, dare to regulate and predetermine almost all their conduct, that those who put forward such a manifestly fraudulent claim should be crowned with a halo of real power and should be capable of requiring obedience and sacrifice as though they had been invested with the authority of God, that the Many should conspire to speak as though they were the One, that a minority or a majority—even the supreme democratic majority of all against one—should assume that they are the community, that a quite fortuitous contract or arrangement should be regarded as superior to the solid organization of the struggle for existence and should proclaim itself to be the peace which all men yearn after and which all should respect; this whole pseudo-transcendence of an altogether immanent order is the wound that is inflicted by every existing government—even by the best—upon those who are most delicately conscious of what is good and right. The more successfully the good and the right assume concrete form, the more they become evil and wrong— summum jus, summa injuria. Supposing the right were to take the form of theocracy, supposing, that is to say, superior spiritual attainment were concreted into an ideal Church and all the peoples of the earth were to put their trust in it; if, for example, the Church of Calvin were to be reformed and broadened out to be the Church of the League of Nations;—this doing of the supreme right would then become the supreme wrong-doing. This theocratic dream comes abruptly to an end, of course, when we discover that it is the Devil who approaches Jesus and offers Him all the kingdoms of this world. It ends also with Dostoevsky's picture of the Grand Inquisitor. Men have no right to possess objective right against other men. And so, the more they surround themselves with objectivity, the greater is the wrong they inflict upon others. Others are, it is true, awaiting the right of the One. But when and where has the right of the Many really become the right of the One? Has it not been always and everywhere acquired fraudulently? Is there anywhere legality which is not fundamentally illegal? Is there anywhere authority which is not ultimately based upon

tyranny? There is a certain imperfection in the existing ordinances by which we are enabled to detect that their existence is,
as such, evil. There is a certain uncontrollable tendency to freedom which causes both good and bad men to resent the chain
which the Many—no doubt with the best intentions—put upon
them. There is a certain strange and penetrating perception
which sees through the fiction that lies behind our bondage.
From this perception of the evil that lies in the very existence of
the existing government, Revolution is born. The revolutionary
seeks to be rid of the evil by bestirring himself to battle with
it and to overthrow it. He determines to remove the existing
ordinances, in order that he may erect in their place the new
right. This is, of course, a wholly intelligible course of action,
and one in which we might very well take part; it is, in fact, as
intelligible as is hostility against the *enemy* (xii. 19) and conflict
against our fellow men. (The revolutionary does not begin by
betaking himself to the generally decried shedding of blood. He
begins by simply harbouring a certain secret poisonous resentment against the existing order—many indeed go no further
than this; they detest the *Power*, and become wholly enslaved
to feelings of resentment!) The revolutionary must, however,
own that in adopting his plan he allows himself to be *overcome
of evil*. He forgets that he is not the One, that he is not the subject of the freedom which he so earnestly desires, that, for all
the strange brightness of his eyes, he is not the Christ who stands
before the Grand Inquisitor, but is, contrariwise, the Grand
Inquisitor encountered by the Christ. He too is claiming what
no man can claim. He too is making of the right a thing. He
too confronts other men with his supposed right. He too usurps
a position which is not due to him, a legality which is fundamentally illegal, an authority which—as we have grimly
experienced in Bolshevism, but also in the behaviour of far
more delicate-minded innovators!—soon displays its essential
tyranny. What man has the right to propound and represent
the 'New', whether it be a new age, or a new world, or even a
new—spirit? Is not every new thing, in so far as it can be
schemed by men, born of what already *exists*? The moment it
becomes a human proposition, must it not be numbered among
the things that are? What man is there who, having proposed
a novelty, has not proposed an evil thing? Far more than the
conservative, the revolutionary is *overcome of evil*, because with
his 'No' he stands so strangely near to God. This is the tragedy
of revolution. Evil is not the true answer to evil. The sense of
right which has been wounded by the existing order is not

restored to health when that order is broken. *Overcome evil with good*. What can this mean but the end of the triumph of men, whether their triumph is celebrated in the existing order or by revolution? And how can this end be represented, if it be not by some strange 'not-doing' precisely at the point where men feel themselves most powerfully called to action? The revolutionary has erred. He really means that Revolution which is the impossible possibility. He means forgiveness of sins and the resurrection of the dead. He means Jesus Christ—He that hath *overcome*—who is the true answer to the injury wrought by the existing order as such. But the revolutionary has chosen another revolution: he has adopted the possible possibility of discontent and hatred and insubordination, of rebellion and demolition. And this choice is not better, but much worse than choosing the possible possibility of contentment and satisfaction, of security and usurpation; for by it God is far better understood, but far more deeply outraged. The revolutionary aims at the Revolution by which the true Order is to be inaugurated; but he launches another revolution which is, in fact, reaction. The legitimist, on the other hand, himself also overcome of evil, aims at the Legitimism by which the true Revolution is inaugurated; but he maintains another legitimism which is, in fact, revolt! And so, as always, what men do is the judgement upon what they will to do (vii. 15, 19). When, however, the revolutionary becomes aware of the judgement, he is dispossessed of his well founded, concrete, justifiable action, and is turned towards the action of God. But how can he demonstrate the action of God save by dying where he was born? by dying, that is to say, where he first perceived the evil of the present order. What more radical action can he perform than the action of turning back to the original root of 'not-doing'—and NOT be angry, NOT engage in an assault, NOT demolish? This turning back is the ethical factor in the command, *Overcome evil with good*. There is here no word of approval of the existing order; but there is endless disapproval of every enemy of it. It is God who wishes to be recognized as He that *overcometh* the unrighteousness of the existing order. This is the meaning of the commandment; and it is also the meaning of the Thirteenth Chapter of the Epistle to the Romans.

Let every man be in subjection to the existing ruling powers. Though subjection may assume from time to time many various concrete forms, as an ethical conception it is here purely negative. It means to withdraw and make way; it means to have no resentment, and not to overthrow. Why, then, does not the rebel turn back and become no more a rebel? Simply because the conflict in which he is immersed cannot be represented as a conflict between him and the *existing ruling powers*; it is, rather a conflict of evil with evil. Even the most radical revolution can do no more than set what *exists* against what *exists*. Even the most radical revolution—and this is so even when it is called a 'spiritual' or 'peaceful' revolution—can be no more than a revolt; that is to say, it is in itself simply a justification and confirmation of what already exists. For the whole relative right of what exists is established only by the relative wrong of revolution in its victory; whereas the relative right of revolution in its victory is in no way established by the relative wrong of the existing order. Similarly also, the power of resistance in the existing order is in no way broken by the victorious attack of revolution; it is merely driven backwards, embarrassed, and compelled to adopt different forms, and thus rendered the more dangerous; whereas the energy of revolution is dissipated and rendered innocuous—simply by its victory. And so the whole conduct of the rebel in no way constitutes a judgement upon the existing order, however much his act of revolution may do so. The rebel has thoughtlessly undertaken the conflict between God's Order and the existing order. Should he allow himself to appeal directly to the ordinance of God, 'should he boldly and confidently storm the heavens and bring down thence his own eternal rights which hang aloft inalienable, unbroken as the stars themselves' (Schiller), he betrays thereby perception of the true 'limit to the tyrant's power', but his bold storming of the heavens in no way brings about this limitation. He may be justified at the bar of history; but he is not justified before the judgement-seat of God. The sequel shows 'the return of the old natural order where men oppose their fellow men'. When men undertake to substitute themselves for God, the problem of God, His mind and His judgement, still remain, but they are rendered ineffective. And so, in his rebellion, the rebel stands on the side of the existing order.

Let the existing order—State, Church, Law, Society, &c., &c. —in their totality be:

$$(a\ b\ c\ d)$$

Let their dissolution by the Primal Order of God, by which their totality is contradicted, be expressed by a minus sign outside the bracket:

$$-(+a+b+c+d).$$

It is then clear that no revolution, however radical, which takes place within the realm of history, can ever be identical with the divine minus sign outside the bracket, by which the totality of human ordinances is dissolved. Revolution can do no more than change the plus sign within the bracket—the plus, that is to say, which existing ordinances possess within the bracket because they exist—into a minus sign. The result of a successful revolution is therefore:

$$-(-a-b-c-d)$$

And now we see that for the first time the great divine minus sign outside the bracket has transformed the anticipatory, revolutionary minus sign into a genuine plus sign. Revolution has, therefore, the effect of restoring the old after its downfall in a new and more powerful form. [Equally false, however, is the reckoning of the legitimists: false, because they consciously and as a matter of principle—in their consciousness and in their appeal to principle lies the arrogant and titanic element in Legitim-ISM—add a positive sign to the terms within the bracket. But the divine minus sign outside the bracket means that all human consciousness, all human principles and axioms and orthodoxies and -isms, all *principality and power and dominion*, are AS SUCH subjected to the destructive judgement of God. *Let every man be in subjection* means, therefore, that every man should consider the falsity of all human reckoning as such. We are not competent to place the decisive minus sign before the bracket; we are only competent to perceive how completely it damages our plus and our minus. Accordingly, the subjection here recommended must not be allowed to develop into a new and subtle manner of reckoning, whereby we reintroduce once more an absolute right. It is evident that there can be no more devastating undermining of the existing order than the recognition of it which is here recommended, a recognition rid of all illusion and devoid of all the joy of triumph. State, Church, Society, Positive Right, Family, Organized Research, &c., &c., live of the credulity of those who have been nurtured upon vigorous sermons-delivered-on-the-field-of-battle and upon other suchlike solemn humbug. Deprive them of their PATHOS, and they will be starved out; but stir up revolution against them, and their PATHOS is provided with fresh fodder. No-revolution is the best preparation for the true Revolution; but even no-revolution is no safe recipe. To *be in subjection* is, when it is rightly understood, an action void of purpose, an action, that is to say, which can spring only from obedience to God. Its meaning is that men have encountered God, and are thereby compelled to leave the judgement to Him. The actual occurrence of this judgement cannot be identified with the purpose or with the secret reckoning of the man of this world.]

Upon this background we are able to understand what follows —**For there is no power but of God ; and the powers that be are ordained of God.** Here a positive, affirmative authority seems to be assigned to the existing government. This would, however, directly contradict the basis of *subjection* which has been set forth above. It is therefore evident that the emphatic word 'God' must not be so interpreted as to contradict the whole theme of the Epistle to the Romans. We must not give to the word 'God' the value of a clearly defined, metaphysical entity. What will it profit us if a formal fidelity to the meaning of a word is purchased at the cost of complete infidelity to the Word? He of whom the *power* is and by whom every existing authority is ordained is God the Lord, the Unknown, Hidden God, Creator and Redeemer, the God who elects and rejects. This means that the mighty *powers that be* are measured by reference to God, as are all human, temporal, concrete things. God is their beginning and their end, their justification and their condemnation, their 'Yes' and their 'No'. If we adopt an attitude of revolution towards them—and this is the attitude adopted in the Epistle to the Romans, as is shown by the unmistakable fact that the passage dealing with human *rulers* follows immediately after the passage dealing with the *enemy* and is prefaced by the quite clear statement that men are to overcome *evil*—, the attitude of revolution is, nevertheless, crossed by the reflection that it is only in relation to God that the evil of the existing order is really evil. God alone is the minus sign outside the bracket that is able to demolish the false plus signs within the bracket—and, moreover, the romanticists of the present order have also to learn as surely that genuine plus signs can exist only because of the minus sign of God. We, therefore, have to remember that it is not for us to arm ourselves for action with the standard of the measurement of God—as though He acted through us! The revolutionary must also renounce the blue flower of romanticism. If then evil be evil in its relation to God, it is not a thing of which we can complain, any more than good is a thing about which we can boast. Therefore, even the observer who has been directly hurt and wounded by the evil of the existing order must bow before Him who is so strong and wondrous a God, high above all gods. If God be the Judge, who can share in His judgement? And if God be the Judge, where is there then not—righteousness? Where is there then evil which is not pregnant with witness to the good? Where is there then any concrete thing which is not pregnant with that which is Primal and invisible? Is not, therefore, the existing order a pregnant parable of the Order that does not *exist—For the creature was subjected to vanity, not of its own will, but by reason of him who subjected it in hope* (viii. 20)? The existing order falls and passes to corruption because it *exists*. The apprehension of this, however, has been, as we have seen, the source of revolution. But the existing order is justified against revolution precisely at this source; for here the demand is made that the revolutionary should not take the assault and judgement into his own hands, but rather should recognize that the evil of the existing order bears witness to the good, since it stands of necessity as an order contrasted with THE Order. Precisely in this contrast the existing order bears involuntary witness to THE Order and is the reflection of it. The *powers that be* are, therefore, in the general course of their existence—*of God*; and, in the particular form in which they constitute a present urgent problem, especially for the revolutionary, they are—*ordained of God*. The KRISIS to which the powers that be are subjected by God renders the possibility of our revolting against them far less advantageous to us than the possibility of our not revolting. In any case revolution is thereby deprived of its PATHOS, of its enthusiasm, of its claim to be a *high place*; it is, in fact, deprived of all those factors which are indispensable if the revolutionary is boldly and confidently and properly to 'storm the heavens'. *Vengeance belongeth unto me* (xii. 19). Our subjection means, therefore, no more than that vengeance is not our affair. It means that the divine minus before the bracket must not be deprived of its potency by a series of anticipatory negations on our part. [The supporters of the present order, who may perhaps feel encouraged by what has been said, must, however, be reminded that revolution has been *ordained* as evil, in order that they may bear witness to the good; and this means, in order that they may themselves be without justification and utterly unromantic, in order, in fact, that they too may turn and become from henceforth dis-ordered.]

Therefore he that resisteth the power, withstandeth the ordinance of God : and they that withstand draw to themselves judgement. There is a precedent judgement, not for the existing order, but against revolution. This judgement is based upon the fact that the real revolution comes from God and not from human revolt. To the revolutionary, the *power* represents the sovereign right of the divine Revolution. But through the *power*

they have to learn that order and not disorder is the meaning of
the divine Revolt. Through the *power* it is made clear that the
disclosure of the One in the other can be effected by no human
action. Through the *power* they have to learn to practise that
humility apart from which their apprehension of the evil in
the existing order is merely contempt. Their action is the
action of men who, supposing that they have already found
the One in the other, set out to bring in the New Creation.
But this is to fail to recognize a human authority as established and ordered by God, and also to overlook the fact that
the *power* is amply justified precisely at the moment when
they allow themselves to rise in revolt against it. Their laying
hands upon the sword of judgement cannot be excused on
the ground that the *power* has already employed the same
sword against them. That is its judgement, not their right. They
are objectively wrong, however much they may be in the right.
The moment when they rise up in protest is the moment when
a protest must be directed against them—*Wherein thou judgest
the other, thou condemnest thyself; for thou that judgest dost
practise the same things* (ii. 1). With men, no doubt, their action
is possible—as possible as the action say, of the 'White Guard'[1]
—but with God their action—and its!—is impossible. Behind
the existing order—which may itself be new!—stands God.
He is the Judge, and He is the Right. Insubordination—and
there is also a conservative insubordination!—is insubordination against Him. Overcome of evil, men find themselves
in the realm where evil must be under the judgement of evil;
and they ought not to be in the least surprised that this is
their fate.

For rulers are not a terror to the good work, but to the evil.
Wouldest thou then not be afraid of the power? do that which is
good, and thou shalt have praise of the same. For he is a minister
of God to thee for good. We have seen already that it is the sense
of injury done to the consciousness of right, the feeling that
the pressure exercised by the 'Many' in State and Church and
Society is an evil thing, that drives men to revolution. This
sense of injury, this oppressive feeling of evil, is, we must now
say, the *terror* of the superior *power* exercised by the existing
rulers. But to what extent is this terror really justified? It is

---

[1] The allusion is to the 'White' Russian counter-revolution (1920; Denikin,
Koltchak). In socialist and communist circles in Switzerland and Germany
the phrase 'White Guard' became a term of abuse applied to any attempt of the
'Bourgeois' parties to organize themselves against revolution. The phrase
'the action of the White Guard' means, therefore, the conduct of those who
support the existing order and oppose all revolutionary movements. [Tr.]

justified obviously only so far as our action moves upon the
same plane as theirs, only in so far as we oppose evil with evil
thoughts and words and actions, and set what we call freedom
against what we call authority, illegality against legality,
relative disorder against relative order, the 'new' against the
'old'—only, in other words, when we rough-handle the rough
customer. On the known plane of visible human action it is
inevitable that, if we assault and batter, we should ourselves be
assailable and vulnerable. The pressure and counter-pressure of
the Archimedean screw is, of course, endless. To revolutionaries
rulers must be a *terror*, a continual source of irritation and resentment, anxiety and misgiving, bitterness and self-defence—just
as they themselves are to rulers. And this *terror* is wholly justified, for it is nothing but the terror men have of their own evil;
and, since human action is altogether encompassed with evil, it
is nothing but the terror men have of their own existence.
Rightly understood, then, it is the terror of the judgement of
God. The *divine* factor in the existing order—and also in the
revolution that bursts forth against it—is its capacity to bring
the evil conduct of men—and what human conduct is not evil?
—under the judgement of God. For this purpose it is *ordained*.
The existing order has, however, no terror for the *good work*.
How indeed could it? for where good is done rulers have no
power. Our thoughts are, no doubt, free; but how much more
truly free is the invisible behaviour of the One in us all! He does
not revolt: against what, indeed, should he revolt? He is not
assailable, for he makes no assault. He is not vulnerable, for he
does no injury. He does not take up a position where evil is
delivered up to the judgement of evil, and therefore no 'fate'
threatens him. He has already been judged by God, and is
therefore justified. And what is his *good work* but his standing
upon the eternal ground of judgement and of righteousness?
To him, the *good work* is the dissolution of the man of this world
and the establishing of the individual in God. The good work
is the 'not-doing' by which all action is related to its Primal
Origin. To such good work, since it has no temporal existence,
rulers—or anarchy!—have no *terror*. In so far as men are good
they are altogether rid of the convulsion that accompanies the
Promethean conflict against—or for!—the existing order. The
good man beholds the End that lies beyond all his penultimate
activity within the realm of evil. In this realm he becomes ever
more and more invisible, inaudible, and undimensional. He is
no longer an angry god warring against other gods. He becomes
what he really is; and as such he—has *praise* of the rulers. All

unsuspecting, rulers rejoice over a citizen so remarkably well-behaved; but they are, in fact, rejoicing over one whose behaviour means 'only' the judgement of God, who has so much to say against them that he no longer complains of them. And, in spite of the irony of his position, he really does make a 'good citizen', since he has turned back to reality and is rid of all romanticism. Having freed himself of all idolatry, he does not need to engage himself in endless protestations against idols. Nor is he continually busying himself with pointing out the manifest inadequacy of each solution of the problem of life as it is propounded, of each form of government as it is erected, of each human road along which men propose to journey. And this is because he knows that the shadow of the judgement of God which spreads itself over them all is the shadow of righteousness. He knows also that the endeavours which men make to purify themselves have real importance as parables and as witnesses; for, inasmuch as *the powers that be* do, to some extent at least, put a check upon human caprice, they do something to remind men of the sacrifice of their *bodies* (xii. 1) that is demanded of them. Requiring obedience, they have a certain similarity to the obedience required by the grace of God; in some fashion, they represent to the EROS of each single individual the sovereignty of the One, to the splintered fragments of the Many and to the Many collected into a lump the One-ness of fellowship, and to the universal struggle for existence the dominion of peace. The 'good citizen' has, however, no illusions. He knows that all these endeavours are questionable, even when they seem to be almost successful. And, moreover, he never supposes them to form a series of rungs on a ladder, of which the highest rung is—the successful and good human endeavour. He pauses; and beholds *good* contrasted with all human endeavours—however successful they may be—only in the incommensurable pre-eminence of God. He therefore sees, not merely the imperfection of those endeavours, but their pure and complete negativity, compared with the 'endeavour' of God. And yet, in spite of what he sees, he is possessed of sufficient patience and sagacity and humour—it is his critical sense that permits, and indeed demands, this 'interim'!—to recognize that these relative possibilities are, in the midst of their evil, good, and to accept them as shadows preserving the lineaments of that which is contrasted with them. Therefore he takes them seriously; he examines them and participates in them. As routine exercises and representations, they must not be neglected. And so, the existing order is the *minister of God*—and revolution is also the minister of God to those who

are not disturbed and punished, but, encouraged by what has
been said, imagine that they are in the right—in the sense
that, when the negative character of all concrete things has
been perceived, then it is that they begin to shine with the
positive power of what is not concrete; they begin to shine
with the power of God. Calm reflection has thus been substituted for the convulsions of revolution—calm, because final
assertions and final complaints have been ruled out, because
a prudent reckoning with reality has outrun the insolence of
warfare between good and evil, and because an honest humanitarianism and a clear knowledge of the world recognize that
the strange chess-board upon which men dare to experiment
with men and against them in State and Church and in Society
cannot be the scene of the conflict between the Kingdom of
God and Anti-Christ. A political career, for example, becomes
possible only when it is seen to be essentially a game; that is
to say, when we are unable to speak of absolute political right,
when the note of 'absoluteness' has vanished from both thesis
and antithesis, and when room has perhaps been made for
that relative moderateness or for that relative radicalism in
which human possibilities have been renounced. But in saying
this we must remember that 'moderation' is not a compensation
for the good. For us good must always involve questioning.
Subjection, therefore, serves the good only in so far as it rids
human social life of all romanticism and separates God from the
routine of life; only in so far as it does not merely leave the good
as an 'open question' but with supreme urgency unrolls the
great negation and makes the critical recollection unavoidable.
[It follows from all this that the conservative, no less than the
revolutionary, must consider what is here involved in his case;
for neither has he been established.]

   **But if thou do that which is evil, be afraid ; for he beareth not
the sword in vain: for he is a minister of God, an avenger for wrath
to him that doeth evil.** We are wont also to overlook far too
easily that other warning—the warning against the doing of *that
which is evil*. We must indeed be led to see that we continually
overlook it. Every step we take in this world we take in the
shadow of evil. Even the earnestness with which in the midst of
evil we do good, even our patient, busy reforms which for many
of us take the place of revolution, do not bring us out of the
shadow of evil. Our whole visible behaviour is either an acceptance of the present order or a denial of it; and in both cases
we do wrong. We can do right only in the 'not-doing' of
our relationship to God. The warning with which we are now

concerned merely emphasizes that our whole experience does thus move within the shadow of evil, and bids us not be wholly engulfed by it. In the shadow of the kingdom of death we must *be afraid*; for there we are encompassed by enemies and rivals, by jealous and dangerous friends, by men whose success is insecure and by those who gloat over the failure of others. There set-backs and periods of stagnation await us, obstacles and disappointments, failures and defeats, which come upon us unexpectedly one after another. There legal proceedings and quarrellings take place, confusions and all manner of tragic complications. On this board we make no move that is not met by some dangerous counter-move; no step that does not in some way have back at us; no possibility that does not contain its own impossibility. Whether we support or oppose the existing order, we stand on the same level with it, and are subjected to one condemnation. Occupying some position, positive or negative, on the plane of the existing order, we are bound to have to pay for the fact that all are relative. We attack or defend, we build or tear down, fight or are at peace, affirm or deny; but sooner or later we are compelled to halt before a last threatening danger and a last heavy punishment—the danger that, after all, we are men, and the punishment for being so. God does not yield before our encroachments—and when do we not encroach upon His rights? The encroachments of revolution He meets with the *sword* of government; the encroachments of government with the *sword* of revolution. And in the fate of both we behold our own destiny—in fear and in pity. The wrath of God falls upon all of us. Upon each one in some way or other the *sword* is drawn; and it is not drawn *in vain*. Whether we attempt to build up some positive human thing or to demolish what others have erected, all our endeavours to justify ourselves are in one way or another shattered in pieces. We must now assert that all these endeavours of ours not merely cannot be successful, but ought not to be so.

Wherefore ye must needs be in subjection, not only because of the wrath, but also for conscience sake. To experience the wrath of God as wrath only would be eternal death. It is, however, our *conscience* that understands the 'Halt'! of the drawn sword, and recognizes God in His wrath. Our *conscience* prevents us from supposing that the evil we encounter is merely obstruction and fate. It reminds us that we are evil; but it also recognizes in the sword that is drawn upon us the righteousness of the hand of God. Conscience sees in the evil that is done against us the *minister* of good. It interprets our judgement, not to our advantage, but to our salvation. It makes of the injury done to us, not our justification, but our hope. Conscience, therefore, does not allow us to rise up from the severity of our lives— embittered and ready to revolt; rather, it pronounces the end of the grim cycle of evil unto evil. Conscience leads us out of the turmoil of human suffering back to our Primal Origin, back to God—*Wherefore ye must needs be in subjection.* Revolution provides the great opportunity of willing to do what God does. And yet, such an intention is impossible; for we have to understand that our 'new' is not THE 'New'. We have therefore to return to the source of our rebellion, to the apprehension of the evil in the existing order before there had issued from it revolutionary thought and action, before ever revolution was born. Our terror then was a guiltless terror, for we were then terrified with God at the misery of the creature. Then we knew also— and this knowledge was our deepest, most assured knowledge— the hope of the creation. Then was the 'Moment' when our most simple perception of the relation between God and man was identical with the doing *that which is good*. But this pure 'Moment' was no moment in time; and therefore being *in subjection* is also no temporal human action. And yet, to know that we have no Right, even when we are in the right, is a knowledge in time. It is this knowledge which reveals that we have a hope—the hope of the Coming World where Revolution and Order are one.

For this cause ye pay tribute also. A strange conclusion! Ye are actually acting more or less willingly.—Ye are paying taxes to the State. It is important, however, for you to know what ye are doing. Your action is, in fact, pregnant with 'notdoing', with knowledge, with hope. **They are God's priests, attending continually upon this very thing.** Are then the people in power, the Government Officials who represent the existing order—God's priests? Yes, assuredly! precisely they! For their whole existence and authority, their whole strange being-justified-before-you, loudly proclaims the One—the unrighteousness of men and the Goal which is God's World. Would ye, then, destroy this order which speaks so loudly of another wholly different order? Surely not—**Render to all their dues; tribute to whom tribute is due; custom to whom custom; fear to whom fear; honour to whom honour.** How trivial and uninteresting seems the command that men should—do what they are already doing! To our question concerning the right of the existing order and the right of revolution this may indeed seem an 'unsatisfactory' conclusion. Perhaps this is inevitable. Beyond all those

interesting and important problems concerning what we ought
to do lies the great negative possibility of God. Perhaps we
are, in fact, unable to demonstrate on its behalf better than
by doing—as men who know!—what we are already doing.

THE GREAT POSITIVE POSSIBILITY

XIII. 8–14

**Owe no man anything, save to love one another! for he
that loveth the other hath fulfilled the law. For this, Thou
shalt not commit adultery! Thou shalt not kill! Thou
shalt not steal! Thou shalt not covet! and if there be any
other commandment, it is summed up in this word,
namely, Thou shalt love thy neighbour as thyself! Love
worketh no ill to his neighbour: therefore love is the
fulfilling of the law. And this** do, **knowing the time, that
now it is high time to awake out of sleep: for now is our
salvation nearer than when we believed. The night is
far spent, the day is at hand: let us therefore cast off the
works of darkness, and let us put on the armour of light.
Let us walk decently as** though it were already day: no
revelling and drunkenness! no **chambering and wantonness!** no **strife and jealousy! But put ye on the Lord Jesus
Christ, and make not provision for the flesh, to fulfil the
lusts thereof!**

Owe no man anything—save to love one another. No debts!
Paraphrased, this means non-resistance! It means not to enter
the field of evil and seek a decision by negation and demolition!
—This is the significance of all those strange possibilities of 'not-
doing' which we have described first as 'Negative Possibilities'
(xii. 16–20) and then, comprehensively, as the 'Great Negative
Possibility' (xii. 21–xiii. 7). *Save*—and here, making a breach
in our own wall, we turn from the demonstration of 'not-doing'
to demonstrative action, to 'Positive Possibilities' (xii. 9–15)
—*to love one another!* To every man we should owe love. It is not
permitted us to excuse ourselves for the absence of love by saying
that, since we live in the shadowy region of evil, we can only bear
witness to the Coming World by 'not-doing'. Even in the world
of shadows love must come into active prominence, for it does
not stand under the law of evil. Love of *one another* ought to be
undertaken as the protest against the course of this world, and
it ought to continue without interruption. We remember that
human conduct is positively ethical when it is not *conformed to*

this world (xii. 2), when, within the framework of this world and in complete secrecy, it bears witness to the strangeness of God. We define *love* as the 'GREAT Positive Possibility' for the same reason as we had previously defined *subjection* as the 'GREAT Negative Possibility'. We are not now thinking of a single act, but of the combination of all positive—that is to say, protesting —possibilities; we are thinking of a general ethical manner of behaving. We define *love* as the 'Great POSITIVE Possibility,' because in it there is brought to light the revolutionary aspect of all ethical behaviour, and because it is veritably concerned with the denial and breaking up of the existing order. It is love that places the reactionary also finally in the wrong, despite the wrongness of the revolutionary. Inasmuch as we love one another we cannot wish to uphold the present order as such, for by love we do the 'new' by which the 'old' is overthrown. And so, in speaking of the breach in the wall of the incomprehensible 'not-doing', we have to speak now of the much more incomprehensible action of love.

He that loveth the other hath fulfilled the law. In considering the relation between man and God, we have, at crucial moments (v. 5, viii. 28, &c.; cf. xii. 9), encountered the extremely enigmatic conception of love. It has been noteworthy that we have always encountered it lying beyond the possibility, the conceivable possibility, of any concrete or analysable experience of the relation between man and God, beyond, that is to say, Law and Religion, beyond all the demands which they are wont to make upon men's minds and wills; we have encountered it, moreover, as the unobservable point where men's highest endeavours are related to God, and therefore where they are immediately reversed. We have described the conception of love as that reality which, since it is contrasted with the ambiguity of our existence, cannot be defined in terms of an act of human will or thought, but only as the pre-supposition of all that is analysable and observable. We have described it, in fact, as the *outpouring of the Spirit* (v. 5), that is to say, as that reality by which men know God, lay hold of Him, and cling to Him, as the Unknown, Hidden God, as the final 'Yes' in the final 'No' of all concrete, observable life. Love is the existential standing-before-God of men, their being touched by His freedom, whereby their personalities are established, whereby, we might perhaps say, they are 'individuated'. Love is the *still more excellent* (incomprehensible) *way* (I Cor. xii. 31), the eternal meaning of our comprehensible ways, and the realization of their 'highest places'. Love is therefore human religious impossibility—when it is apprehended as the possibility of God: in other words, love is the *fulfilling of the law*. But what can all this mean, when we remember that all these reflections of ours, as our reflections, are disturbed by their relation to the concrete world in which we live? Our conversations about God are always interrupted conversations; for He withdraws Himself from us and opposes Himself to us when we are confronted by the question, What shall we do (xii. 1)? To this question we now answer—**Thou shalt love thy neighbour as thyself** (Lev. xix. 18), inasmuch as *He that loveth the other hath fulfilled the law*, does the truth, and is therefore proceeding along the *more excellent way*.

Thou shalt love thy NEIGHBOUR. In the concrete fact of the *neighbour* we encounter, finally and supremely, the ambiguity of our existence, since in the particularity of others we are reminded of our own particularity, of our own createdness, our own lost state, our own sin, and our own death. That men should be thus confronted by men is the riddle presented to us in the primitive constitution of nature. The solution to this riddle must also be the solution of those perpetually recurring interruptions of our conversations about God. Here a decision must be sought as to whether the impossible possibility of God—which lies beyond all human possibility—is or is not a mere phantom of metaphysics; whether, when we speak of the pre-supposition behind all things that are capable of analysis and description, when we speak of the outpouring of the Spirit in our hearts, we are or are not merely dreaming; whether our apprehension of the final 'Yes' in the final 'No' is or is not merely a wild guess; whether our knowledge of God is or is not simply the 'renunciation of knowledge' (Kierkegaard); whether the Unknown God has spoken to us in Jesus Christ; whether our being touched by the freedom of God, the establishing of our personalities, our proceeding along the still more excellent way, are existential events. The decision lies in our answer to the question—Do we, in the unknowable *neighbour*, apprehend and love the Unknown God? Do we, in the complete Otherness of *the other*—in whom the whole riddle of existence is summed up in such a manner as to require its solution in an action on our part—hear the voice of the One? We must, at this point, remember that our love of God takes place as an event when, in the ambiguity of our existence, a contrasted, unobservable 'Thou' presses upon us so insistently that we are confronted inevitably by the question, Who then am 'I'? Nor do we forget that the answer to the problem of the opposing 'Thou' lies in the question concerning this 'I', since we cannot but recognize that our most questionable 'I' is one with the 'Thou' by which we are confronted. And moreover, as we have already seen, it is in the ambiguity of the neighbour who *fell among thieves* that we encounter primarily and supremely the 'Thou' which is both question and answer. If I hear in the *neighbour* only the voice of *the other* and not also the voice of the One—that is to say, if I do not detect in him both question AND answer,—then, quite certainly, the voice of the One is nowhere to be heard.

Therefore—*Thou shalt love thy neighbour* AS THYSELF. Hidden and invisible is the *neighbour*, the *other*, whom, if I am really to love God, I must love *as myself*, to whom, that is to say, I am not and cannot remain another. In Christ—the turning point from question to answer, from death to life—I am not only one with God, but, because 'with God', one also with the neighbour. Love, then, is the 'spiritual relationship' (Kierkegaard) with the neighbour: that is to say, it is that unity—*fellowship*, communio —with him which is brought into being by means of the question and answer presented to me in the 'Thou' by which I am confronted, in so far as I am really one (*fellowship*, communio) with God. *Who then*, asks the scribe, *is my neighbour?* There is no escaping the answer—*He that shewed mercy unto him that fell among thieves. Go and do thou likewise.* Be thyself the neighbour; and there is no need for any further question (Luke x. 29, 30–7). And so the neighbour is found to provide the answer to the question, Who, then, am I? and in this apprehension of him as the One who is 'Thou' and 'I' and 'He' lie the authorization and confirmation of our love towards God—whom we do not see.

Therefore—*Thou shalt* LOVE *thy neighbour*. Love is the relation between men and their fellow men which is grounded— and therefore broken!—in the knowledge of God. In this relationship of love it is not men who confront men, but God who confronts God. Whether in this relationship we experience peace or conflict, whether, that is to say, love is what we are wont to call 'love', or whether it is not something far more austere, far more bitter, is another question (xii. 9). However that may be, love is always the disclosing of the One in the other, in this and that and every other. Love, being altogether independent of its object—the concrete 'neighbour'!—is, for that very reason, altogether bound to it. Love beholds in every concrete neighbour only the parable of him who is to be loved; but nevertheless it does really see, it really does see in every temporal 'Thou' the eternal, contrasted 'Thou' apart from whom there is no 'I' (xii. 3b–6a). Love, therefore, is love of men, of concrete, particular men; and it is this precisely because it has no pre-ference for any

particular man. Love of the neighbour is love for him in his
strange, irritating, distinct createdness and constitution, because and inasmuch as it undoes and loosens this constitution
of createdness, as though it were a garment which must fall from
his shoulders (Kierkegaard). Love is 'eternal, levelling righteousness' (Kierkegaard), because it justifies no man according to his
desire. Love edifies the fellowship, because it seeks fellowship
only. Love expects nothing, because it has reached the goal
already. Love does not intend, because it has already done.
Love asks no questions, it already knows. Love does not fight,
it is already the victor. Love is not the EROS that lusteth
ever, it is the AGAPE that never faileth.

For this reason, then—*Thou* SHALT *love thy neighbour.* Understood strictly as the action of the NEW man, love is duty; and as
such, it is protected against caprice and disappointment and
misuse. In this *Thou shalt* every divine *Thou shalt not—not
commit adultery; not kill; not steal; not covet* (Exod. xx. 13–17,
Deut. v. 17)—is summed up! In it the man who has been compelled to that 'not-doing' which is his turning back to God is
once again impelled by God to action; cast down, he now again
stands upright; a sinner, he now becomes righteous; dead, he
is once more alive. In this *Thou shalt!* there is manifested the
flaming sword of death and of eternity. Therefore love is in
itself perfect: it is the NEW doing, THE new doing, which is the
meaning and fulfilment of all 'not-doing'. Love is the breath
we breathe when, in the realm of evil, we have no breath left.

Therefore—**Love worketh no ill to his neighbour.** Love is the
good work by which the evil is *overcome* (xii. 21). Love is that
denial and demolition of the existing order which no revolt can
bring about. In this lies the strange novelty of love. In the
cycle of evil unto evil, of reaction unto revolution, it plays no
part. Love is the inversion of all concrete happening, because it
is the recognition of the pre-supposition that lies in every concrete event. Love, because it sets up no idol, is the demolition of
every idol. Love is the destruction of everything that is—*like
God*: the end of all hierarchies and authorities and intermediaries,
because, in every particular man and also in the 'Many', it
addresses itself, without fear of contradiction—to the One. Love
does not contradict; and therefore it cannot be refuted. Love
does not enter into competition; and therefore it cannot be
defeated. Capable of being defined only in negative terms in the
sphere of evil (1 Cor. xiii!), it is, therefore, the action which is
altogether pre-eminent over all evil. No impossibility of my not
doing good in the realm of evil—the only realm we know!—can

rid me of the duty of love. If, therefore, as a protest against the course of this world, I cease to love, I thereby simply—do not love God, offer no sacrifice, and do not *renew my mind* (xii. 2). This is the relentless, impelling, earnestness of the command of love; and—**Therefore love is the fulfilling of the law.**

And this do, knowing the time. When and where can men do the incomprehensible work of love—the work whereby, when they are impelled to God by the riddle of the neighbour, they are turned back again from God in order that they may find themselves in the neighbour? When and where are we to discover the impossible possibility of fulfilling the law? If we are to see clearly what the real problem is which meets us in the command of love, we must not foreshorten the perspective. An unparalleled occasion must correspond with the unparalleled significance of the action of love. And so, our answer to the question must be that the possibility occurs when we perceive that time shall be as eternity and eternity as time. This is what is meant by—*knowing the time.* Between the past and the future—between the times—there is a ' Moment' that is no moment in time. This 'Moment' is the eternal Moment—the *Now*—when the past and the future stand still, when the former ceases its going and the latter its coming. Then it is that time reveals its secret: it is not time which goes and comes; man it is who has been and will be in God, who dies and lives, falls and stands; it is man who is what he is and is also what he is not; men it is who have been created as this or that particular man and who have been also created anew as the One; men it is who are individuals both in their particular once-for-allness and in their universality. Men are always the first AND the second; but they are the second in the overcoming of the first, in Christ; that is to say, in the invisible New Age. *We spend our years as a tale that is told*—this is the secret of time which is made known in the 'Moment' of revelation, in that eternal ' Moment' which always is, and yet is not. Time is, then, irreversible; and of this the irrevocable hurrying away of the past and the relentless approach of the future are a parable. But a parable of it also is the completely hidden, unobservable, intangible present which lies 'between' the times. Facing, as it does, both ways, each moment in time is a parable of the eternal 'Moment'. Every moment in time bears within it the unborn secret of revelation, and every moment can be thus qualified.—*This do, knowing the time.* And so, the known time—apprehended and comprehended in its transcendental significance—provides the occasion for the incomprehensible action of love. Wherever a moment in the past or in the

future has been qualified by the *Now* of revelation that lies in
the midst between the two, there is the opportunity for the
occurrence of love—for its 'living regiment' (Kierkegaard). And
faith which sees the revelation is the fulfilling of the law. The
human action of love is, then, an action that springs from
supreme knowledge; for he who loves is he who has been touched
by the freedom of God. When, therefore, we say that love, as the
great positive possibility, has become a command, we presume
this last and central relating of time to eternity—in fact, we
presume that love is a miracle. We can, then, only *do* what we
are doing, inasmuch as we are—*knowing the time*; and with this
knowledge no action of ours can be 'already done'. And so,
paradoxically, what we are doing can be no more than that
which points to the victory which has occurred, does occur, and
will occur in Christ; it can only direct us to the individual who
is born out of 'individuality', it can only await the End—the
end of the world of time and things and men—which is the
Beginning. By thus keeping severely distant from everything
that has been done already, by thus pointing away from itself
to the End which is the Beginning, love *worketh no ill to his
neighbour* and is the *fulfilling of the law*, the fulfilling of every
Thou shalt not. Love enters the realm of evil, in order to leave it
again at once. Love builds no tabernacles, for it seeks to create
nothing that abides, nothing that 'exists' in time. Love does
what it does only in the knowledge of the eternal 'Moment'.
Love is therefore the essentially revolutionary action.

**Now it is high time to awake out of sleep : for now is our
salvation nearer than when we believed. The night is far spent,
the day is at hand.** Being the transcendent meaning of all
moments, the eternal 'Moment' can be compared with no
moment in time. *Salvation—the day*, the Kingdom of God—
being the fulfilment of all time, is incomparable. We, however,
live in the flux of time; and if we do not love within a succession
of moments, we love not at all. Jesus was the Christ, not somewhere outside this flux but within it, not outside this succession
of moments but within it. For us, too, knowledge of the eternal
'Moment' must occur within the same flux. For us, too, there
must be within this knowledge a place, a time, an occasion for
love. The knowledge of the 'Moment' must occur in a moment:
the turning back to eternity must occur in a time. This present
moment, this present time, is the *high time* for us *to awake out of
sleep*. But what is this moment or this time save a past and a
future that have been qualified by the *Now !* that is set unobservably in the midst between them. This *high time* is, then, not that

moment or that time. No moment in time can be in itself the *high time*. Every moment in time—including the time *when we believed* (iii. 28)—is in itself a stranger to the *Now* that lies invisibly in the midst, incommensurable with it and unable to approach it. Faith cannot be a concrete thing, that once began, and then continued its course. Faith is the Beginning, the Miracle, the Creation in every moment of time; and as such it confronts even the moment when we believed. All concrete things—even the thing which men are wont to name 'faith'—belong within the unqualified time of *sleep*. There is no belief that does not need to be reminded of revelation, no action that does not need to be recalled to a necessary knowledge, no man who does not need to be recalled to the freedom of God. In so far as this recollection has *not yet* taken place—and when indeed has it ever 'already' taken place?—men are asleep, even the apostle, even the saint, even the lover. Men are sold under time, its property. They lie like pebbles in the 'stream of time', and backwards and forwards the ripples hurry over them. They do what they ought not; what they ought they do not. The qualified time, the time of withdrawal and of advance, the time of negative and of positive ethical possibility, has yet to be. And yet, there are distinctions of time within this final separation between time and that strange 'Moment' of eternity. There are times that are *near*, and there are times that are far; there is night-time and there is the time when the day begins to dawn; there are times of sleeping and there are times of awakening. There is therefore not only an eternal but also a chronological qualification of time—*To day if ye will hear his voice, harden not your hearts* (Heb. iii. 7, 8; Ps. xcv. 7, 8): and by contrast—*The word of the Lord was rare ; and there was no frequent vision* (1 Sam. iii. 1).—*Now is our salvation nearer than when we believed.* There is always a tension between the 'Then' of our unruffled existence and the 'Now' of our disturbed recollection of non-existence. There is always a tension between the times of the revelation that have 'already' occurred, between the deeds that have been 'already' done, between the God who has been 'already' known, and our waiting for the existential occurrence of what has only apparently 'already' taken place, our expecting and looking for the eternal 'Moment' of the Appearance, the Parousia, the Presence of Jesus Christ. This tension of the times has as much or as little to do with the well-known nineteen hundred years of the history of the Church—which quite obviously have 'not yet' ushered in the Parousia—as it had with those weeks or months during which the Epistle to the Romans lay in Phoebe's trunk

(xvi. 1), or with the moments which elapsed between Paul's
dictation and Tertius' writing (xvi. 22). For the *hour* of awakening, the striking of the last hour, the time of fulfilment, which
is here announced, certainly does not mean some succeeding
chronological hour, as though the life which proceeds from death,
the non-existence by which all 'existence' is dissolved, the *Now*
which is between all past and all future, could be a period of time
succeeding another period in time. What is time but the *times
of ignorance*, the times of recollection, when men are bidden to
repent? It is not time but Eternity that lies 'beyond'. Standing
on the boundary of time, men are confronted by the overhanging,
precipitous wall of God, by which all time and everything that is
in time are dissolved. There it is that they await the Last Hour,
the Parousia of Jesus Christ. But that Day and that Hour no
man knoweth—*not even the angels in heaven, neither the Son, but
the Father* (Mark xiii. 32). Do not our ears burn when we hear
this? Will there never be an end of all our ceaseless talk about
the *delay* of the Parousia? How can the coming of that which
doth not *enter in* ever be *delayed*? The End of which the New
Testament speaks is no temporal event, no legendary 'destruction' of the world; it has nothing to do with any historical, or
'telluric', or cosmic catastrophe. The end of which the New
Testament speaks is really the End; so utterly the End, that in
the measuring of nearness or distance our nineteen hundred years
are not merely of little, but of no importance; so utterly the End
that Abraham already saw the Day—and was glad. Who shall
persuade us to depress into a temporal reality what can be
spoken of only in a parable? Or who, knowing that here every
word can be ONLY a parable, shall be able to set us to rest with
this 'only'? Who shall persuade us to make of God an idol, and
then, on the basis of so grave a misunderstanding, bid us shame-
lessly make light of Him? Who shall persuade us to transform
our expectation of the End—the 'Moment' when the living shall
be changed and the dead shall be raised, and both shall stand
together before God (1 Cor. xv. 51, 52)—into the expectation of a
coarse and brutal spectacle? Who, when this spectacle is quite
rightly delayed, shall be able to lull us comfortably to sleep by
adding at the conclusion of Christian Dogmatics a short and
perfectly harmless chapter entitled—'Eschatology'? Is this to be
our only reminder of that of which we must be reminded and of
which, indeed, we wish to be reminded? What *delays* its coming
is not the Parousia, but our awakening. Did we but awake; did
we but remember; did we but step forth from unqualified time
into the time that has been qualified; were we only terrified by

the fact that, whether we wish it or not, we do stand at every
moment on the frontier of time; did we, standing on the frontier,
dare to love the Unknown, to apprehend and lay hold of the
Beginning in the End—then, neither should we join the sentimentalists in expecting some magnificent or terrible FINALE, nor
should we comfort ourselves for its failure to appear by embracing the confident frivolity of modern protestant cultured piety.
We should, then, refuse both methods of escaping so shamefully
from the bitter earnestness of the Day that is *at hand*. But rather,
knowing that the eternal 'Moment' does not, has not, and will
not, *enter in*, we should then become aware of the dignity and
importance of each single concrete temporal moment, and apprehend its qualification and its ethical demand. Then we should
await the Parousia: we should, that is to say, accept our present
condition in its full seriousness; we should apprehend Jesus
Christ as the Author and Finisher; and then we should not
hesitate to repent, to be converted, to think the thought of
eternity, and therefore to—love. Apart from *knowing the time*,
all this is, however, impossible; for without knowledge there is
no love.

As though it were already day. To act knowing the 'Moment'
in the moment, looking towards that which lies midway between
the times of our life as it is; to love, because we have been loved
in Christ—this is the establishing of the great positive possibility
in its totality; and in this all other ethical possibilities are comprehended. Far too *nigh at hand* is the Kingdom of God, far too *near*
is the overhanging wall of eternity—in every stone and flower, in
every human face!—far too oppressive is the boundary of time—
memento mori!—far too insistent and compelling is the presence of Jesus Christ as the turning-point of time. The direct
and concrete movement of life, governed as it is by BIOS and
EROS and PATHOS, cannot remain undisturbed. Indeed, it has
already been disturbed. The form of this world passeth away,
and the Kingdom of God cometh. Love, and all that proceeds
from love, demonstrates this passing away and this coming.

**Let us therefore cast off the works of darkness . . . no revelling
and drunkenness ! no chambering and wantonness ! no strife and
jealousy . . . make not provision for the flesh.** And these words
were spoken—*to all that are in Rome, beloved of God, called to be
saints* (i. 7). Do we not also stand in the realm of the 'Brothers
Karamazov' where all these evil things are possible? This realm
of evil and what we are wont to call the Kingdom of God seem
therefore to be two circles which overlap at many points. If the
separation between these two worlds is to be complete, if *the*

works of darkness are to be utterly *cast off*, the separation must be
a final separation, a separation of *knowing the time*. But what can
we say to this, save that the direct, concrete line of human life
remains always unbroken? The *provision for the flesh* remains
in the pious and in the men of the world. The threads of time
are not severed, no, not for a second. Clear, direct, observable
human righteousness has not appeared. The world is the world
and men are men. Questionable at all times is human conduct
whether it be delicate or coarse. Even the saints have not rid
themselves of the possibilities of a Karamazov. But—*knowing
the time!*—it is in God's sight that men are so questionable, so
impossible, and so foolish. Can they be surprised, then, to find
themselves so near the edge of the abyss, so deeply entangled in
ambiguity? *What is man that thou art mindful of him?* If, however, men can no longer be sustained upon the high places of
human morality, can they not, perhaps, breathe more easily in
the region of the beasts? May not the riddle of life be more
easily solved down below than up aloft? But suppose we fly
from the One, what will our flight profit us, if it is love from
which we are escaping? The assault of God embraces the whole
man. The Kingdom of God robs him of breath, oppresses him,
whatever position he occupies, whatever may be his lusts. We
cannot repair our damage. The disturbance affects the saints
and the swine. We have in the end no choice; we cannot withdraw out of range. We must yield to God all along the line. And
love is the fulfilling of the law.

Therefore—Let us put on the armour of light. Let us walk
decently. . . . Put ye on the Lord Jesus Christ. What an antithesis it is! These words are spoken to the same men. Nevertheless, we are then the beloved of God. Yes, this is true also.
These eternal, heavenly possibilities are also ours. Ours is the
great possibility of *being clothed upon* with the offensive and
defensive armoury which God alone can provide. We can be
armed with the Lord Jesus Christ Himself. And who will dare
to exclude any single one of us? Who will dare to exclude even
himself?

THE *KRISIS* OF HUMAN FREEDOM AND DETACHMENT

XIV. 1—XV. 13

The Pauline 'exhortation' ends—and its ending concludes the
whole Pauline 'conversation'—with a warning to all who find
themselves in entire agreement with what has been said and are
persuaded that their own opinions have been fully confirmed.

Once again these busy hands are held back; once again the energy of partisans is damped down, and their oratory interrupted. What shall we now say? We think, no doubt, that we have caught a glimpse, even though from a distance, of a place, beyond all the words and thoughts and questions and apprehensions that have from time to time appeared and disappeared, where men may stand and live out their lives. This place, at once both near and far, we have frequently described and defined as the freedom of God. There can be no doubt that, according to the Epistle to the Romans, there is demanded of us a quite precise manner of life. Shall we formulate it as the life of 'free detachment'? Detached, because it seems to be a direct and practical manner of life proceeding from the great divine disturbance and from nothing else: free, because it seems to be the consequence of a shattering discovery of the freedom of God. Where is the man—this is the question asked of us in the Epistle to the Romans—who will venture not merely to think the thought of freedom but actually to live under its guidance? If, then, we are to live in Pauline fashion we must dare to live freely. Oppressed on all sides by God and wholly dissolved by Him; reminded constantly of death and as constantly directed towards life; scared out of the petty trivialities of human relationships in which men are normally imprisoned and therefore free to apprehend what is certain and living and eternal; depending only upon the forgiveness of sins and therefore able to direct our conduct with real clarity of insight; our reverence for all relative values and factors so completely shattered that we are enabled to make genuine and proper use of them; so securely bound and chained to God that we can preserve a calm independence with regard to those many problems and requirements and duties of life which are not imposed upon us directly by God Himself and by Him only; loosed—or shall we say, 'relativized', in the negative and positive sense of the word?—from the whole compulsion of authority and regimentation, from the whole multiplicity of godlike powers and authorities which make up our world—is not this the Pauline freedom and detachment? Is it not wholly intelligible that those who dare to embrace this manner of life should—and we are speaking here of the essence of Protestantism—call themselves *strong* (xv. 1)? And indeed, they are strong and free and pre-eminent; they know; they bear the terrible divine burden; and therefore they—yes, precisely they—are the instruments of the unheard-of divine undertaking. Putting from them all those positive and negative ethical possibilities of which we have spoken, do they not dare the impossible possibility?

do they not dare to believe? Do they not, that is to say, dare to live under the one restriction of God, free from all other restrictions of good and evil, because by that one restriction the good is manifestly assured and the evil manifestly condemned? Is not the man who dares thus to believe undoubtedly *strong*?— And now, at the moment when the friendly lights of the harbour seem so invitingly near, at the moment when, having passed per varios casus, per tot discrimina rerum, we are at last able to formulate the question which can only have 'Yes' for its answer, there comes a final command—'Halt!'. Once again, as so often before, we are warned; once again the door is barred against us; once again our position is rendered critical and un-certain; once again our brokenness is broken. Paul against 'Paulinism'! The Epistle to the Romans against the point of view adopted in the Epistle! The Freedom of God against the manner of life which proceeds inevitably from our apprehension of it! Such is the amazing facing-about which takes place in the Fourteenth Chapter of the Epistle to the Romans. And yet, surely, to any one who has really apprehended, this facing-about ought not to be in the least surprising.

AGAINST? Yes, because—FOR! The free and the strong are what they are because the great question-mark must be set also against their freedom and their strength. It is not against faith that we are warned, but against OUR faith; not against the place that has become visible where men can stand and live, but against OUR taking up a position there and proceeding to live out our lives there; not against freedom and detachment, but against their ambiguous appearance in OUR lives, against the certainty with which WE advance in freedom and in detachment. The warning is uttered against any position or manner of life or endeavour that WE think to be satisfactory and justifiable, as though WE were able in some way or other to escape the KRISIS of God. The KRISIS, the knowledge of which makes the strong man strong, is turned round upon his knowledge and upon his strength. There can be no doubt, from the First Chapter of the Epistle on-wards, that the free, Pauline, sacrificed 'Christian' is not in him-self justified (xii. 1). It is, of course, true that a quite definite manner of life is demanded in the Epistle. Those who, overlooking the clarion call of its demand 'Thou art the man! Thou shalt!', treat it merely as a diatribe of theological philosophy—which assuredly it is—have wofully misunderstood it. It is true, also, that freedom is the essential meaning of the manner of life which is here required: the freedom which was brought by Christ and which the Grand Inquisitors of all ages have found so awkward and so

dangerous—the freedom of the prisoner of God. But the freedom in this freedom is the Freedom of God; and the life in this
manner of life is the unjustifiability of everything that men name
life. The man therefore who, armed with the knowledge of the
Epistle to the Romans, himself advances to the attack, has
thereby failed to perceive the attack which the Epistle to the
Romans makes upon him. And so, when at its ending the Epistle
dissolves itself, when it quite deliberately gives to its sympathetic,
understanding, naturally Pauline readers the sharp command,
'Halt!', it does but corroborate itself. It is now that the reader
is really tested. Can he, at this last point, bear to see everything that he thinks he has apprehended and comprehended
wrenched from his hands? For must not the great disturbance
be carried through to the KRISIS of all conscious knowledge, and
especially to the KRISIS of the conscious perception that we are
under KRISIS, if God is to be the Unknown, Hidden God, if He is
to remain alone in His eternal power and divinity, the only
Strength of the strong? If the KRISIS be not pressed home to the
end, all would be but sounding brass and a tinkling cymbal.
Once again, therefore, at the end of the Epistle to the Romans—
just as at the end of the novels of Dostoevsky—there is presented
to us the impenetrable ambiguity of human life—even of the life
of the Christian and of the Christian Community. Once again,
it is the fact of the existence of our fellow men—the ethical
problem—by which we are brought face to face with the great
disturbance.

vv. 1–4. Maintain fellowship with **him that is weak in
faith.** Do not provoke him to doubt his own convictions!
**One man hath faith to eat all things: but he that is weak
eateth** only vegetables. **Let not him that eateth set at
nought him that eateth not; and let not him that eateth
not judge him that eateth: for God** maintaineth fellowship
**with him. Who art thou that judgest the servant of
another? to his own lord he standeth or falleth. Yea,
he shall be made to stand; for the Lord hath power to
make him stand.**

Maintain fellowship with him that is weak. The free and detached manner of life is no more than one variation of the many
endeavours that men propose for themselves. Of all human
endeavours it is, however, the most subtle; for, lacking pronounced characteristics, it is apt to pass unnoticed. Were this
not so, it would not be properly detached. Its whole significance
lies, not in directing attention to the action of the particular

person as such, but in pointing to the action of the One in the particular. Its meaning, therefore, is fellowship; and any pronounced, particular characteristic would clearly damage its importance. Its peculiarity, then, lies in its absence of peculiarity. Aware, consciously aware, that in the midst of other possibilities it is the only possibility, it thereby, however, acknowledges the existence of other possibilities. It is *strong*, but there is nothing it fears so much as any explosive exhibition of strength: it is, in fact, strong—as though it were weak. Being THE movement, it does not put itself forward as A movement; at most it represents itself as the motive-power behind all other movements, and even then at once applies a brake to their energies. Others may be concerned to show how peculiar their manner of life is, but the proper 'Pauline' Christian takes no interest in such differentiations and has no real capacity for making himself conspicuous—Paul, it is true, did not always reach this standard himself, and we certainly do not. The 'Pauline' Christian does not complain of those who hold opinions differing from his own, nor does he abuse them; rather he stands behind them sympathetically asking them questions. He has discovered that he is his own worst enemy long before he has experienced the hostility of others. He admits without arrogance that there are many non-Pauline possibilities, but he pays them so little attention that they never become, so far as he is concerned, so clearly defined that he has to reckon with them as opposing possibilities: were this to take place, he would be lost, for his position is no position, and woe betide him, if he were to allow himself to be enticed onto ground where one point of view stands solidly and honestly in opposition to others. He is, if possible, more reserved than even the Socratic philosophers; for he does not assume an attitude of reserve, in order to provoke another to—**doubt his own convictions.** No, so fundamentally does he presume the One in the other, that the other must be permitted to follow his own road to the end. He who is free and detached does not win his victory in the midst of clashing convictions; he wins by recognizing the common END of all convictions. This attitude is very far removed from 'toleration', for he certainly does not intend to LET the convictions of others BE; but it is equally far removed from 'intolerance', for he certainly does not wish to TAKE AWAY their convictions from them. He treats the convictions of others seriously, merely because he is aware of the KRISIS which lies before them and behind them. His own way is peculiar only in the sense that whereas others forget this KRISIS, he is mindful of it. He is right, only because he does not desire to be right. His work is, there-fore, always exercising itself in criticism; it is destructive and Socratic; it dissolves the endeavours of others. But how does he exert his influence? Not by leaving the community, nor by disturbing it actively from within. He is not schismatic. Remaining within the community, he upholds the fellowship by taking it for granted. He leads by refusing all initiative. He breaks up the community by leaving everything as it is. He is a shining light by remaining altogether invisible. He wins his victory by always *conforming*. He inaugurates the great divine disturbance by disturbing nothing at all. But it is necessary, if this programme is to be carried out, that the descent from every high place of the Epistle to the Romans be an inconspicuous descent.

One man hath faith to eat all things. Who is not aware of the grim humour in these words? As soon as the faith of the Third and Fourth Chapters of the Epistle becomes OUR faith, the faith of this or of that intelligent, awakened, well-instructed person, this is the kind of faith that emerges. It becomes the faith *to eat all things*: the belief that the enjoyment of wine and flesh is not sinful; that the Kingdom of God cannot be inaugurated by busy movements of reform; that men are not justified by the practice of asceticism; that the Christian is not concerned with rules and regulations, with programmes and policies, with absolute com-mands and prohibitions; that neither the conduct of Jesus as set out in the Synoptic Gospels nor the words of the Sermon on the Mount are adequate to provide direct guidance for Christian behaviour; that, to take an example, even the non-employment of military force must not be exalted to a principle of conduct which must never be broken (xii. 18). Is this faith? If so, in what does this 'believer' believe? Jülicher answers: 'He believes magnificently in the conception of the unfettered con-science of the believer.' Truly, a grand point of view, but one that has long ago been adopted by all liberals and caught up from them by their clerical disciples. Is there any particular advantage in BELIEVING that men can *eat all things*? Is it as easy as that to become a *strong* man? And suppose we do take unto ourselves such strength; suppose we do free ourselves from all authority and tradition, from all ecclesiastical discipline, &c., &c.; suppose we do know ourselves to be prodigiously free; will the relationship between heaven and earth, will the condition of men, be in the least altered thereby? Surely, a very humble Paradise, a Paradise which, as we look at it, makes us unconsciously yearn after—yes, a monastery! But when

questions are asked as to the way in which this free detachment
is to be put into actual practice—as to what human doing or
not-doing it involves—or when, perhaps, as in modern Protestantism, we are told that we ought to be satisfied with a mere
asking of questions,—what more can we, in fact, do than simply
call attention to our 'freedom of conscience' and to our *faith to
eat all things*? Ought we not to be humiliated by this lack of
resource, so humiliated that we become clear about one thing;
namely, that the standpoint of the *strong* is no standpoint at
all, or, rather, that it is the worst of all illusions?

Contrasted with the strong man is the **weak** man who—**eateth
only vegetables.** This, at any rate, is a clear, concrete standpoint.
The uninstructed, non-Pauline man has this advantage at least.
His ambiguity is not at once obvious; he does, at any rate, do
something. Party-men, Sectarians, Churchmen, are vigorous
and full of life. They occupy a position. They have pronounced
characteristics. Their lives form a proper subject for the bio-
grapher. They are concerned with 'deeds and facts'. Ranged
behind the vegetable eaters at Rome we see the devotees of
Orpheus and of Dionysus, the Neo-Pythagoreans, the Thera-
peutes, and the Essenes, of the Ancient World; the Monks of
the Middle Ages; the Baptists of the Age of the Reformation;
the Total Abstainers, the Open-Air Enthusiasts and the Vege-
tarians of the Present Day. But now we can understand also
both the grandeur of the Catholic system and the dignity
of the rigorous Reformation ethic; we can sympathize with
Tolstoy as well as with some of the more religiously minded
Socialists and Pacifists. We cannot be blind to the deep earnestness which has brought and still brings into being such human
endeavours. We are not ignorant of the great personal perplexity
and disintegration, of the great courage and sacrifice, which lie
behind them. We remember with genuine reverence the long
succession of heroes and saints, martyrs and prophets. Without
doubt, the noblest figures in history are marshalled behind the
Roman eaters of vegetables. We need not now, at the conclusion of the Epistle to the Romans, waste words in pointing out
the tragedy which is bound up with it all. Our present concern
is only to contrast these *weak* ones—historically and psychologically they are, of course, in no way weak—with the *strong*,
so as to be reminded of the tragedy of the strong by putting to
them certain questions. Are they so superior in faith to the weak
vegetable eaters that they can dare to separate themselves and
refuse to maintain fellowship with them? Indeed, if it were
a question of making a comparison between different stand-

points, would not the point of view of the Catholic, or of the
Particular Baptist, or of some one of their derivatives, at least
be preferable to that of modern Protestantism? If the paradox
of the *strong* is that the strength of their character lies in an
absence of pronounced characteristics, ought they to continue to
cultivate this character-less character? Or, at any rate, seeing
how bad their case is when they are compared with the *weak*,
ought they not to cease seeking their strength in THEIR strength?
    We say both—**Let not him set at nought** and—**Let not him
judge.** That is to say, we do not think it profitable to play off
'rigorism' and 'freedom of conscience' one against the other. In
any case, we have no ground for judging the *strong* to be in the
right. These spiritually minded men are wont, it is true, to *set
at nought* those who are busied in 'good works'—the 'enthusiasts' and the 'Pharisees'; but they are themselves liable to the
still more vigorous rejoinder of those reformers who pronounce
them to be 'soft-living, fleshy men of Wittenberg'.[1] What a
circulus vitiosus it is! And both accusations are justified,
though the vegetable eaters have the advantage—but only in
making accusations. We need proceed no further in this direction.
The strong who are really strong know how fruitless the whole
controversy is. Here the parties are not equally balanced, for the
weak cannot have this knowledge. All reformers are Pharisees.
They have no sense of humour. Deprive a Total Abstainer, a
really religious Socialist, a Churchman, or a Pacifist, of the
PATHOS of moral indignation, and you have broken his backbone.
The vegetable eater, in spite of his peaceable diet, lives upon
secret and open protestation; he sighs and shakes his head over
the folly of the world; he differentiates himself from others—
because he is unaware of the real tragedy of human life, before
which every mouth must be dumb. But we are not now concerned
with him. We are concerned with the 'Pauline' man, who makes
of his freedom a concrete thing, and in so doing makes himself
weaker than the weak. He ought to know what his opponent—
whom he ought not to regard as an opponent—does not know,
namely that—**God maintains fellowship with him,** that is to say,
with the OTHER—**Who art thou that judgest the servant of another?**
If thou knowest what justitia forensis is, thou canst not play
off thy knowledge against another's ignorance. It speaks on

[1] The phrase occurs in the title of a pamphlet published by Thomas Münzer,
the Anabaptist, in 1524. The title runs: *Hoch verursachte Schutzrede, und
Antwort wider das geistlose, sanftlebende Fleisch zu Wittenberg welches mit
verkehrter Weise durch den Diebstahl der h. Schrift die erbärmliche Christenheit
also ganz jämmerlich besudelt hat* (see *Die Religion in Geschichte und Gegenwart*,
2nd ed., vol. iv, p. 280). [Tr.]

behalf of that other—**To his own lord he standeth or falleth.**
Shall not the hidden, unsubstantiated righteousness of God
benefit also, and indeed precisely, the weak in faith, the uninstructed, non-Pauline man? Can any one with any understanding of the unparalleled mercy of God set at nought the
OTHER, simply because he has not understood the mercy of God,
simply because he continues his busy, optimistic work on the
very edge of the precipice of his unbroken morality? Does
the behaviour of the OTHER lie so far outside the freedom of God
that the strong man should suppose that, though he may continue in fellowship with publicans and whores, Pharisees must
be excluded? But—**He shall be made to stand; for the Lord hath
power to make him stand.** Is it not, then, as it should be that, at
the moment when the 'Pauline' Christian *sets at nought* the
moralists and becomes an anti-pharisaic Pharisee, he himself is
also found to be unrighteous? He, too, sits in judgement when
he sets at nought the weak man who sits on high and condemns
others. Weak is the man who allows himself to be pushed into
a position from which he judges others. Who is the Lord? Who
hath authority to judge? Who hath power to exalt and to cast
down? Man or God? The strong man knows which of the two.
He who knows what 'we' know has no superiority or advantage.
He hath, God knows, no pre-eminence. Whosoever thinketh
that he excelleth in aught, knoweth not what 'we' know. There
is but one advantage—divine election; and in it a simple
vegetable eater can share even now in his complete unbrokenness, rather than the man who knows the Epistle to the Romans
by heart backwards and forwards. God can even now take more
pleasure in the life of a monk than in thy confident Protestantism. Thou fool!—*God maintaineth fellowship with him, and hath
power to make him stand.* If this be really possible, surely we ought
also to maintain fellowship with him. If not, we shall be the
strong, and then we shall be most assuredly *weak*. If we are not
sufficiently intelligent to descend from the high place of our
knowledge almost as soon as we have clambered up to it, we are
certainly ignorant men. If we seek once more to be men of
character, we shall certainly have thereby abandoned the
character indelebilis.

vv. 5, 6.—a remark in passing—For[1] **one man esteemeth
one day above another: another esteemeth every day
alike. Let each man** be happy **in his own** conviction. **He**

[1] γάρ should not be deleted. These verses contain an 'additional parallel
and instructive illustration of lack of uniformity in Christian practice being
held to be admissable'.—I am here following Zahn against Kühl.

that regardeth the day, regardeth it unto the Lord: and he that eateth, eateth unto the Lord, for he giveth God thanks; and he that eateth not, unto the Lord he eateth not, and giveth God thanks.

There are points where disagreement is admissible. In such cases the strong are wont to recognize the rigorism of the *weak*, even though they make no practice of it themselves. The strong man is silent: he observes and waits and knows. 'He does not press his opinions upon others or enter into controversy with them; but is, nevertheless, quite certain that his opinion is right before God and that further experience will prove this to be so. Such an attitude often admits of greater flexibility of behaviour than is possible for a scrupulous conscience' (Steinhofer). That is to say, the strong man, in this case, recognizes that the rigorist is in some way acting—**unto the Lord,** and that the divine disturbance, though misunderstood, does in fact underlie his behaviour. His point of view may be thus expressed: 'The ship undoubtedly sails better in the open sea; but it can if necessary, make some progress in a narrow canal' (Bengel). The strong man has the responsibility of understanding the rigorist better than he understands himself and of interpreting rigoristic practises by the generalization—**He giveth God thanks.** Whether an action is valid or invalid depends upon its relation to God. By this standard the precision of the rigorist is judged— but by the same standard the freedom of the strong man also: 'The basic principle of human life consists in the complete dependence of men upon a gesture of God. So vacillating and questionable is their spiritual condition that they cannot be trusted to move even a finger' (Calvin). To the onlooker, however, the application of this basic principle always remains wholly invisible. We have, therefore, no alternative but to accept the claim of the *weak* that they do mean God when they obey their precise monastic rules, however much we may imagine that an idol has intervened between them and God. God can be meant; meaning and significance can reside in their practices; their action can be a necessary demonstration offered to the glory of God. On the other hand, it cannot for one moment be admitted that in itself eating is more pleasing to God than not eating. It is, then, the thought of predestination— which the weak are unable to accept—that causes the strong man to range himself wholly on one step with them.

vv. **7–12.**—returning to the main theme—**For none of us liveth to himself, and none dieth to himself. For whether**

we live, we live unto the Lord; or whether we die, we die
unto the Lord: whether we live therefore, or die, we are
the Lord's. For to this end Christ died, and lived again,
that he might be Lord of both the dead and the living.
But thou, why dost thou judge thy brother? or thou
again, why dost thou set at nought thy brother? for we
shall all stand before the judgement-seat of God. For it
is written, As I live, saith the Lord, to me every knee
shall bow, and every tongue shall confess to God. So
then each one of us shall give account of himself to God.

To be strong means that as men we find ourselves involved
in a final, unavoidable KRISIS—None of us liveth to himself—
Whether we live, we live unto the Lord. There is no such thing
as life in itself: there is only life in relation to God. That is to say,
there is only life under His judgement and under His promise;
there is only life characterized by death but qualified, through
the death of Christ, as the hope of life eternal. Rigorism and
free detachment are therefore both under KRISIS. But both are
also directed towards life. The life that is in 'life' is, however,
the freedom of God which for us is death. We live only—*unto
the Lord.* Can this qualification be less drastically critical for the
man who is free and detached than for the rigorist, simply
because, whereas the former has consciously paid attention to
eternal life, the latter's conception of the life at which he is
aiming is still suspect as being bounded by biological ideas?
But is not the former's consciousness also biological? Is all that
we know or hold to be valid more than an act of our thinking?
If so, can even the supreme act of our thought have residing in it
the assurance and righteousness which would render it pre-
eminent above all other acts of human thinking? The Lord
alone is the assurance of promise—*Except the Lord build the
house, their labour is but lost that build it.* But the Lord is in all
circumstances also the Judge; and only through the death of
Christ is our hope a living hope.—And now we must formulate
the same truth in an opposite manner—None dieth to himself—
Whether we die, we die unto the Lord. There is no such thing as
death in itself; there is only death in relation to God. That is
to say, there is only death as both barrier and place of exit; the
death of that which we call life, but which, through the resurrection of Christ, is qualified as the sign of reconciliation. Rigorism
and free detachment are, therefore, both under KRISIS. Both
are in different ways directed towards death. But the death
that is in 'death' is the freedom of God which is, for us, life.

We die only—*unto the Lord*. Once again, the *weak* need to be rid of the suspicion that the relative negations and dissolutions and controversies with which their manner of life is so vitally concerned have reference to biological death. The *strong*, being possessed of far more mature discretion, are, it is true, aware that the death which we seek after must be a death that is qualified by resurrection and no other. This does not mean, however, that, death being thus qualified, the strong are less drastically under criticism than the weak. For what have the strong established? No more, surely, than that their awareness is a perception which is itself involved in biological death, and is, therefore, no more than a parable. How can we be justified by OUR thinking the thought of eternity? How can we be reconciled by OUR apprehension of death as a reconciliation? The Lord alone guarantees resurrection—*Except the Lord keep the city, the watchman waketh but in vain*. Once again, the Lord is in all circumstances also the Judge; and only through the Resurrection of Christ is meaning assigned to the cross under which we all stand.—Therefore—**Whether we live or die, we are the Lord's. For to this end Christ died, and lived again, that he might be Lord of both the dead and the living.** So, then, to be strong means to recognize God in Christ. And this is to recognize Him in the final and unavoidable KRISIS both of our life and of our death. To be strong means to fear and to love God above all things. To fear and to love Him as He encounters us in the dialectic of the supreme categories of our thought; to fear and to love Him as the Lord. If we know that we *live unto the Lord* and *die unto the Lord*, we acknowledge thereby that both our life and our death, our 'Yes' and our 'No', can claim no other justification—no justification existing in its own right!—side by side with the justification that God alone can bestow upon us. Neither our life nor our death, neither our 'Yes' nor our 'No', is in itself justified. And therefore, when regarded from these two boundary points, neither rigorism nor the life of free detachment is in itself justified. This is, of course, what the *weak* do not know—indeed, their ignorance is the cause of their weakness. But the *strong*, having a perception rendered more acute by reason of the manifest ignorance of the *weak*, instead of waiting for them to move, ought themselves to bow before the secret of God, to cease all opposition, and to take the first step in the humility that knows that we know nothing, because it knows that—God knows.

But thou, why dost thou judge? The question is repeated with still greater urgency—**Or thou again, why dost thou set at nought**

thy brother? He that is set at nought is thy brother. There is no reason to disrupt the community: on the contrary, there is every reason to maintain fellowship. The great critical truth of that *unto the Lord* under which we stand as MEN—not as strong or as weak, but as men; and, because mankind is in Christ summed up in the One who stands before God, therefore also as BROTHERS! —means that—**We shall all stand before the judgement-seat of God.** The Lord, as we have just heard, is the Judge over life and over death. The implications of this must be thoroughly examined and applied. Because we SHALL all stand before the judgement-seat, because this Futurum aeternum is the critical truth of our being and existence, it must follow that we all, being what we ARE, ARE standing before the judgement-seat, some of us in our strength, some of us in our weakness. Terrified before the final, unheard-of fact that *we are the Lord's*, we all in some fashion or other—what does it signify whether intelligently or unintelligently?—venture upon some attempt to be righteous in the presence of God. The two roads of rigorism and of detachment diverge from the same point; they both start from the same embarrassment and from the same hope. Because we shall stand before the *judgement-seat* of God, because the judgement of God, the 'Double Predestination', is the critical truth of our life and of our death, it must follow that some are *strong* and others *weak*; it must follow that the conduct of the former implies election, whereas the conduct of the latter implies rejection. For the real meaning of 'freedom of conscience' is quite clearly the recognition of the freedom of God and of His action; whereas the real meaning of 'rigorism' is equally clearly the recognition that men and their whole conduct are in chains. But because we shall all stand before the judgement-seat *of God*, because the critical truth under which we stand is that it is God who elects and rejects, it follows that the strong—the elect— have not the slightest right against the weak—the rejected. As the faithfulness OF GOD, faith justifieth; as the knowledge OF GOD, human knowledge is true; as the hope OF GOD, hope is our salvation; as the love OF GOD, love is the still more excellent way. But all this is true only in so far as there emerges from the action of the man who believes, knows, hopes, loves, no merit or right or claim—**To me every knee shall bow, and every tongue shall confess to God** (Isa. xlv. 23). In so far as men and their 'piety' are substituted for God and His freedom, human conduct, whatever form it may take, means simply rejection. Human conduct means election only in so far as it is the renunciation of merit, right, or claim, that is to say, in so far as the idol of this or that form of piety is renounced. **So then each one of us shall give account of himself to God.** What do we know of another's renunciation? We observe only his action; we see his 'piety'; but we do not know whether his election may not lie precisely where we see his rejection; we do not know whether he may not be strong in his weakness. In the OTHER we can see only the man who has been condemned and will be condemned; but this means, however, that beyond everything which, as human conduct, can be no more than 'significant' conduct, beyond also the contrast between election and rejection —we see the One who stands before God. We can see only Christ, only the brother; we see Him as the strong in the weak. As the *strong* we can, however, propound the Socratic problem concerning Christ and concerning the brother in him that is weak, only if we have ourselves renounced even the right which we think we have established for ourselves by the quite fundamental renunciation upon which our 'strength' depends. WE have established nothing. All our supposed superiority over others is altogether questionable. Therefore every judgement which we make in accordance with psychological or biological standards is frail and uncertain (Matt. vii. 1). Frail also is our scepticism concerning these standards—for it is not only the position of anxious Churchmen, of strict Sectarians, and of active Socialists, that is shaky, but also the superior attitude of the Pharisees of freedom. Uncertain are all our questions concerning the salvation of others, whatever form our questions take; feeble are all attempts to assess the value of another's relation to God, whether the assessment be conservative or radical. All is subject to the judgement of God. **Judge not** is therefore the only possibility. And yet, even this possibility is no possibility, no recipe; it provides no standard of conduct. We have no alternative but to range ourselves under the judgement that awaits us, hoping—without any ground for our hope—for the impossible possibility of the mercy of God.

vv. 13–15. We have now examined the warning which is directed against the attitude which the free, detached man is wont to adopt 'in theory' towards the rigorist. We have now to consider the warning which is directed against its application 'in practice'—**Let us not therefore judge one another any more: but** prove your capacity of judging in that **no man put a stumblingblock or occasion of falling in his brother's way. I know, and am persuaded in the Lord Jesus, that nothing is unclean of itself: save that to him**

516 THE GREAT DISTURBANCE XIV. 13

who accounteth anything to be unclean, to him it is unclean. For if because of thy meat thy brother is grieved, thou walkest no longer in love. Destroy not with thy meat him for whom Christ died.

Regarded as a 'point of view', the point of view of the Epistle to the Romans is God's point of view! To judge a man from that standpoint would mean, therefore, his authoritative rejection by God. It would mean that he was made to feel the wrath of God; and this would be to place in his path the—stumbling-block and the—occasion of falling with which God confronts him. In fact, however, we are exhorted in the Epistle to the Romans to a particular line of conduct, not in order that we may adopt the point of view of God, but that we might bear it in mind, consider it from all sides, and then live within its gravity. To judge involves the capacity to assign guilt and to envelop an action in wrath. God has this capacity and exercises it continuously. But, as the capacity of God, it is invisibly one with His forgiveness and with the manifestation of His righteousness. Our action in judging possesses, however, nothing of this double-sidedness. We do not possess the divine freedom of rejecting AND electing. When we permit ourselves to judge others, we are caught up in condemnation: the result is that we merely succeed in erecting the wrath of God as an idol. In their monkish vehemence, this is the kind of judgement that the *weak* exercise without interruption. But so also are the judgements of the *strong*. Irritated by the abuse hurled at them by the vegetable eaters, and even more irritated by their habit of 'deploring' what others are doing, the strong *set them at nought*, and thus judge them; and in so doing themselves become, as Pharisees of freedom, the *weak*. The—capacity of judging, which the strong undoubtedly possess, must therefore find some other outlet. It must be turned against themselves, it must be *proved*. And the capacity of judging is proved when a man does not meet his *brother* as though he were the bearer of the wrath of God against him—such behaviour is, as the strong ought to know, improper for men. And so, the capacity of judging prevents him not only from judging his brother but also from setting in his path a *stumblingblock or occasion of falling*. For that also is divine only as a divine action. As a human action, being once again fatally one-sided, it is impossible. To *put a stumblingblock or occasion of falling* means to lead astray, to blind, to be lacking in compassion, to harden, to separate from God, to deprive of the possibility of repentance. This undoubtedly God does (ix. 33)!

But, as the invisible action of God, it is one with its opposite.
By executing His judgement, by preparing stumblingblocks
and occasions of falling, God takes men to Himself. When God
rejects and hardens (xi) there is hope and promise. It is written
—*He that believeth on it shall not be put to shame* (ix. 32, 33). How
different it is when men, putting themselves in God's place, put
stumblingblocks in the way of other men. They seek only to
harden, and not to liberate; only to bind, and not to loose; only
to kill, and not to make alive. Have the well-meaning exertions
of the vegetable eaters ever achieved anything save to blind
the eyes of many, to embitter them and to deprive them of the
possibility of repentance? The finest flower of pharisaism has
always had a negative, hardening effect. But negative also is
the operation of the Pharisee of the freedom of conscience, of the
man who *hath faith to eat all things*, if there be there no capacity of judging, no freedom in the freedom, no possibility—in
spite of his faith—of not eating all things. Here once again the
supreme right is the supreme wrong, if we suppose that right is
our right.

I know, and am persuaded in the Lord Jesus, that nothing is
unclean of itself. The assumption with which the 'brother' starts
is false: in Christ it has been done away. Asceticism and movements of reform have their place as parables and as representations, but in themselves they are of no value. In no sense can
they ever be even a first step towards the Kingdom of Heaven.
There is but one good and one evil, one pure and one impure.
Before God everything is impure; and therefore nothing is
especially impure. All notions of particular impurities arise
from secret or open illusion; for they arise from hidden or open
refusal to repent. The ascetic and the reformer need to advance
in seriousness, if they are to be genuinely earnest men, if, that is
to say, they are to deal honestly with the problem of evil.—To
him who accounteth anything to be unclean, to him it is unclean.
Granted that a man does hold that false and superseded notion;
granted that, on a fundamentally false manner of reckoning, he
is disgusted by particular impurities; then, within the limits of
his reckoning, his conclusions are inevitable and irreproachable,
unless he change his manner of reckoning. His multiplication
tables are not inaccurate; his mistake lies in the restricted field
on which he is operating. His earnest, definite disgust is much
to be applauded: what is deadly is his capricious selection of the
objects of his disgust. He needs to be brought back to his
Primal Origin. How has he come to be what he is? Humanly
speaking, he has come manifestly from thé same health-giving

disturbance of life, from the same final urgent question, from the
same longing that men should be loyal to God, from which the
strong man with his freedom of conscience has also come. If,
therefore, he is to be turned back, this disturbance and questioning and longing must at all costs be retained. The freedom in
which, in his distress, every man stands before God must not be
disturbed. If, therefore, he is persuaded to overthrow the results
of his reckoning without being first persuaded of the wrongness of his manner of reckoning; if his earnest determination be
deprived of its objects without first being provided with its
proper object; if he is made superficial and careless and muddle-
headed where he had previously been strict and precise; then
he is simply disturbed and led astray and hardened, and
stumblingblocks and occasions of falling are piled up in his path.
What he needs, however, is to be persuaded to break through,
with the same earnestness and with the same determination, to
the place where—*to the pure all things are pure* (Titus i. 15).
The possibility of repentance depends upon every man following
his own path to the end. For, as the goal of men and as their
new beginning in God, repentance is an action of which no man
should deprive another, since it is entirely particular, individual,
and takes place once for all.

**If because of thy meat thy brother is grieved, thou walkest no
longer in love.** I *grieve* my neighbour, when I prevent him from
continuing along his own road—to the end; when I cause him to
do what he ought not; when I block up those springs of unrest
which are concealed behind his defiant self-will; when I help
him to be at peace with himself, and so deprive him of the
opportunity of repentance; when I tyrannize over him by leading
him astray; when, failing to perceive the deep purpose which
underlies it, I challenge his titanic moral behaviour, with the
result that, as a consequence of my action, he becomes engulfed
in the far more precarious Titanism of freedom by which I myself
—in my strength—am overwhelmed; when I dangle before his
eyes a freedom which for him is complete imprisonment; when I
present him with a knowledge of God which might be more
appropriately named a knowledge of the Devil—when I have
prepared for him, it may be, the stumblingblock that God will
assuredly prepare for him. *It must needs be that offences come.*
Perhaps in acting thus I do no more than acquaint him with
what is, in fact, the end of his journey—namely, the possibility
of repentance. Perhaps, by leading him into temptation, I am
really leading him away from himself, beyond his unrest, am
really setting him before God. But—*Woe unto him through whom*

offences come!—what do I know of all this? How can I dare to
presume upon this 'perhaps'? By forgetting the brother in my
fellow men, the One in the other, Christ in the neighbour, in the
WEAKNESS of the neighbour—*I walk no longer in love.* I am
justified neither by the possibility that I may be right nor by
the fact that God is right. Therefore—**Destroy not with thy meat
him for whom Christ died.** Christ died for him, and I—eat against
him! This is the ridiculous impossibility of my most possible
possibility: this is the wrong of my supreme right. No triumphant freedom of conscience, no triumphant *faith to eat all things*
justifies me, if, at the moment of my triumph, I have seated
myself upon the throne of God and am myself preparing
stumblingblocks and occasions of falling instead of making room
for God's action. Gone then are my faith and my freedom; and
all my knowledge is as though I knew nothing.

vv. 16–18. **Let not then your good be evil spoken of: for
the kingdom of God is not eating and drinking, but
righteousness and peace and joy in the Holy Ghost. For
he that herein serveth Christ is well-pleasing to God, and
approved of men.**

The strength of the strong is confronted by an iron barrier.
We now stand before the KRISIS of what we think to be our freedom, of the freedom in which we rejoice as our good. But it is
good only when it is the freedom of the Kingdom of God. Do we
understand this? Is our freedom nothing but the freedom
which God takes to Himself in our doing or in our not doing?
Or is it a freedom which we take to ourselves in His name? Or
do we perceive that our freedom is important only when in it
God demonstrates His freedom? Or do we suppose our freedom
to be in itself important? In displaying our strength, are we
anxious that—**righteousness and peace and joy** should be made
known unto men? Or are we, in fact, in the end concerned
with—**eating and drinking?** Ought we to do what we MUST,
or must we do what we OUGHT? Are we mindful of the autonomy
of truth, or are we not far more mindful of our own autonomy?
If the latter be our chief concern, our good will have been already
—**evil spoken of**: for, since we shall have spoken evil of it, it will
quite rightly be subject to the abuse of others. How questionable, how ludicrously accommodating, nay rather, how precarious and hypocritical is Paulinism, if its main theme be—what
is undoubtedly the main theme of modern Protestantism!—the
hideous, mistaken idea that men are justified by their secret knowledge of God. In order to arrive at this mistaken notion there

was surely no need to digress into a study of the Epistle to the Romans. If this were the main theme of Paulinism—and where is the 'Pauline' Christian who is not daily in danger of thinking that it is?—how right has been the chorus of the *weak* in persistently complaining of the Epistle to the Romans! How right also was the Grand Inquisitor when he declared that the freedom which Christ brought was open to the very gravest objection! How right are the vast armies of moralists, educationalists, psychologists, sociologists, and 'historically-minded' persons! How right are all those convinced and upright friends of practical, sane, common sense! How excusably inadequate, nay rather, how well-founded and justifiable, should we then find their lack of perception to be! How urgent would then be the necessity of subjecting ourselves to the nearest best law we can find! In that case we ought to acknowledge that, having advanced far too precariously, there is much to be said in favour of our returning to Catholicism and throwing ourselves into the arms of Mother Church. But we are led into this KRISIS by the righteousness of God. If this be not recognized as the Kingdom OF GOD, we remain inevitably under judgement. We are the servants of Christ *in the Holy Ghost*, never in OUR spirit. If we choose to serve Christ in OUR spirit, then even our free detachment will mean that OUR spirit—and when are we ever rid of this danger? —is taking unto itself glory; and we ought not to be surprised if we are found to be neither—**well-pleasing to God** nor—**approved of men.** It would be a sign of real perception on our part were we to cease CELEBRATING the Reformation and were we to learn seriously to regret it as a venture of Titanism. The time might then come when, measuring the greatness of the promise involved in the Reformation by the greatness of its danger, we might go on to the further truth that we do stand 'on the basis of the Reformation'. For the time being, however, it is our business to discover to what depths men can descend and how grievously they may be damaged on the 'basis of the Reformation'.

vv. 19–23. So then let us follow after things which make for peace, and things whereby we may edify one another. Overthrow not for meat's sake the work of God. All things indeed are clean; howbeit it is evil for that man who eateth with offence. It is good not to eat flesh, nor to drink wine, nor to do anything whereby thy brother is offended. Hast thou faith ?[1] have it to thyself

---

[1] A copyist, not noticing that the sentence (*v.* 22a) is a question, may have inserted ἦν before ἔχεις in order to ease the construction.

before God. Happy is he that judgeth not himself in that which he alloweth to himself. **But he that doubteth is condemned if he eat, because he eateth not of faith; and whatsoever is not of faith is sin.**

Have those readers who have followed our conversation throughout now perceived the twice-broken line of the narrow and never clearly distinguishable track of the Pauline manner of life? Well, once again we summarize its course:

We ought to follow after the—**things which make for peace.** This does not mean that we should follow the first peaceable thing we meet; that would be to obey men rather than God. What is meant is the peace in the freedom of God which may involve us in war with the whole world. Are we to conclude from this that freedom of conscience is the bright sun of our own moral endeavour? Yes assuredly; but it must at once remind us of the freedom of conscience that is in God, of the Peace of God that is beyond the caprice of our intelligence, of the peace in THE Freedom, which is also the freedom of the neighbour. There is no peace apart from the—**things whereby we may edify one another.** Now, proceed on thy way in the midst of human life!

Overthrow not for meat's sake the work of God. We behold the good and the divine in danger. We see men suffering. We recognize that an obligation has been laid upon us to play our part, to offer a sacrifice, to do deeds. Verily, however, this obligation, by which the work of God is overthrown, must not be undertaken *for meat's sake,* that is to say, in order that men may assert and possess their freedom. And more than this—**All things indeed are clean.** *All things !* This is the end of all precipitate moral intervention, the complete stoppage of all direct action. Here is proclaimed freedom of conscience for all men. Protestantism, then, is altogether justified. Yes, no doubt; but there is a second consideration—**Howbeit it is evil for that man who eateth with offence.** The fact, however, remains that my neighbour is in distress, and by my freedom his distress is increased. He is tempted, and I thrust him deeper into temptation. He ought to follow his own road, and I put an obstacle in his way. Ought this to be so? Must I will what I ought? Ought I to set at nought direct action? Ought I to interrupt it? Ought I, in order to preserve my detachment, to pass by the man who has fallen among thieves? And so—**It is good not to eat flesh, nor to drink wine, nor to do anything whereby thy brother is offended.** The Holy Spirit, not the right that *I* have, is the objective right. Dost thou see the stone rising in the midst of

the stream? Well, put just one foot on it, and that only for a
second, and then—jump. That is the only way to reach the
other side!

Hast thou faith? Yes, have it! but—**Have it to thyself and—
before God.** Thou art alone with God in thy faith. To Him only
thou art bound; upon Him only thou art cast. He alone is thy
Judge and thy Saviour—**Happy is he that judgeth not himself in
that which he alloweth to himself.** Yes; but there is a second
consideration.—It is a terrible thing to be thus alone with God
and to know that He who alloweth not Himself to be mocked,
He who, in demanding of us all, deprives us of all, He only is
the Good. Then it is that the possibility of doubt arises, it may
be for the rigorist, it may be for the free, detached man: the
possibility, infinitely nigh at hand, that perhaps much, perhaps
everything, that we do does not spring out of faith!—**But he that
doubteth is condemned if he eat, because he eateth not of faith ;
and whatsoever is not of faith is sin.** Who then is justified? Who
dares to say, 'I have faith'? Who dares to take upon himself
responsibility for others, or even for himself? Who dares to
harp upon the theme of his own autonomy? There is but one
thread in all this grim uncertainty. Hold thee to God! But who
can maintain his hold, if he be not himself held?

vv. 1–6.[1] **Now we that are the strong ought to bear the
infirmities of the weak, and not to please ourselves.** Let

---

[1] An attempt was made in the first edition of this book to justify, on the basis
of the work of Tholuck, Hofmann, and Zahn, the inclusion at this point of the
passage xvi. 25–7, and therefore to undertake its interpretation in the context
provided by the concluding verses of Ch. xiv. As a result, however, of the more
recent textual critical studies of Corssen, Lietzmann, and Harnack, and also of
further exegetical reflection—which, as Zahn rightly points out, must here be,
in the end, decisive—I find myself unable to maintain my former opinion.

The passage in question runs as follows: *Now to him that is able to stablish*
(Zahn: *fortify*) *you according to* (Lietzmann: *in*) *my gospel and the preaching of
Jesus Christ, according to* (Lietzmann: *in*) *the revelation of the mystery which
hath been kept in silence through times eternal, but now is manifested, and through
the scriptures of the prophets* (Zahn adds: *and through the appearance of our
Lord Jesus Christ*), *according to the commandment of the eternal God, is made
known unto all nations unto obedience of faith: to the only wise God, through
Jesus Christ, to whom* (Zahn omits *to whom*) *be the glory unto the ages!* (Zahn:
for ever).

It seems very probable that at the turn of the 2nd–3rd centuries, perhaps
even earlier, the Church in the West was in possession of a certain number of
MSS. of the Pauline Epistles which did not contain Chs. xv and xvi of the
Epistle to the Romans. Since the theme of Ch. xiv is continued, and developed
without any break in Ch. xv, it is extremely difficult to suggest any adequate
grounds, external or internal, for this omission. Completely obscure also is the
relation of this omission to the text of Marcion who, as Origen tells us—*Ab eo
loco ubi scriptus est 'omne autem quod non est ex fide, peccatum est' usque ad
finem dissecuit*. The probability that these chapters were omitted, not only
in the text of Marcion but also, apparently independently, in certain MSS.

each one of us please his neighbour for good, unto edifying. For Christ also pleased not himself; but, as it is written, The reproaches of them that reproached thee fell upon

possessed by the Church, is so great that we have to reckon with the omission as a fact, in spite of the difficulty of explaining how it ever came about. Assuming the omission to have been made, the Epistle would require the introduction of some 'solemn conclusion', and, since it was read during the Liturgy, the Epistle required a 'liturgical conclusion' (Lietzmann). It is, therefore, wholly intelligible—previously I had questioned this—that the Doxology should have been added to satisfy this requirement. Ch. xvi. 25–7 is a Doxology. I ought not to have allowed myself to be led astray by Hofmann's bold proposal—rightly rejected by Zahn—to take τῷ δὲ δυναμένῳ (xvi. 25) as the dative object of ὀφείλομεν δέ (xv. i). Hofmann's proposal involves a grammatical construction of the sentence which is quite horrible. It is, moreover, quite clear from the parallel passages in Eph. iii. 20, Jude 24, 25, and to a lesser extent in Mart. Polyc. 20, that we have here a solemn Invocation independent of the sentence which follows. If this be so—and Hofmann agrees to this—the insertion of xvi. 25–7 between xiv. 23 and xv. 1 results in an intolerable interruption. What is the hymn doing there at all? Even could I accept Hofmann's proposal, I should now find it impossible to regard the hymn as an 'important link' in the development of Paul's argument. If the passage be interpreted as providing a reason for the demand that the weak should be cared for, the reason is very strange and far-fetched. It should be noted that every attempt to interpret the passage thus depends upon the emphasis falling on the word στηρίξαι! Further, the reason given would be in flagrant contradiction to that given in xv. 3–12, which follows quite naturally from the context. Ch. xvi. 25–7 is therefore a superfluous, and, indeed, disturbing, excrescence, intelligible only if it be a liturgical conclusion, unrelated to the context. And so, if the argument of the Epistle did not end at xiv. 23—and, in spite of the existence of some evidence in the MSS., it is difficult to suppose that it did—the Doxology certainly cannot originally have followed xiv. 23. But neither can it have stood originally at the end of Ch. xvi. This conclusion formed the starting-point of what I wrote in the first edition. What was it doing there? It would be 'psychologically entirely intelligible' (Kühl) as the conclusion of a sermon delivered on a Festival of the Church. The Epistle to the Romans is, however, no such sermon. Rather, it is an important communication which ends very appropriately with a short polemic (xvi. 17–20), followed by greetings from Corinth (xvi. 21–3), followed by—and this cannot be deleted—an expression of goodwill (xvi. 24). I find it impossible to conceive that after this Paul again set to work to produce—a solemn liturgical conclusion. Moreover, when I came to examine the passage in detail, especially when I compared it with the parallel passage in Eph. iii. 20, 21, I found its style unpleasingly turgid, its grammatical construction awkward, and its succession of ideas undeniably strange. When to this is added the Marcionite character of these eight lines, to which Harnack has drawn attention, and which, he says, were only rendered tolerable to the Church by the addition of a number of corrections, which have the effect of making the whole passage intolerably formal—the conclusion was forced upon me that the Doxology is not Pauline. It was added—whether in its present form or in a shorter Marcionite form we do not know—as a liturgical conclusion to a copy of the Epistle to the Romans which ended at xiv. 23. (As a matter of fact, an ancient table of headings points to the existence of a Latin Version of the Epistle consisting of Chs. i–xiv plus the Doxology.) The passage was then transferred to MSS. which contained Chs. xv and xvi. Sometimes it retained its position at the end of Ch. xiv, and therefore before Ch. xv; sometimes it was removed to the end of Ch. xvi, thereby displacing xvi. 24; sometimes it occupied both positions. There survived, however, MSS., otherwise complete, which did not contain the Doxology at all, but which did contain xvi. 24. These, I hold, represent the original form of the Epistle to the Romans.

me! (For whatsoever things were written aforetime were
written for our learning, that through patience and
through comfort of the scriptures we might have hope.)
Now the God of patience and of comfort grant you to be
like-minded one with another according to Christ Jesus:
that with one accord ye may with one mouth glorify the
God and Father of our Lord Jesus Christ.

We are the strong. That which makes us strong proceeds from
the KRISIS which breaks forth with ever undiminished power
upon our strength. Therefore we seek no other road between the
two abysses save the narrow way; we seek no other bridge save a
bridge of stepping-stones on which we can place but one foot and
that but for a second. The KRISIS passes through all the self-
assertiveness, all the sense of freedom, all the attainments,
claims, and orthodoxies, in our faith. Our strength, then, does
not lie in OUR faith. If, therefore, our free detachment has this
goal, however secretly, we belong quite properly within the
camp of the rigorists and in the company of the *weak*. What,
then, does survive? Nothing that we can observe! All that we
can make evident to ourselves is that as the men who know, as
the pre-eminent people, as free men, we also are weak. We stand
on the same step as the weak. Consequently, the more we cease
from all setting at nought, from all differentiating of ourselves,
from all desire for superiority, the better!—**We ought to bear the
infirmities of the weak.** But should we do so only seemingly and
with patronizing dissimulation? Should we, whilst appearing to
bear their infirmities, secretly rejoice in our strength and freedom?
But that is not to *bear* infirmity. After all, the New Testament
is not a theatre. The bearing of infirmity is a wholly existential
occurrence; it is a genuine being weak with the weak. The *weak*
do not seriously think they are weak. Their weakness lies in
their supposedly developing strength. We, however, ought to bear
what they cannot or are unwilling to bear—the whole burden of
the unrest which God prepares for men. We ought to be men
who know that we cannot escape from bondage, either by rigorism or by freedom of conscience, either in Catholicism or in
Protestantism, either by asceticism and reforms or by *faith to eat
all things*. We ought to know that to men in their final distress
every road is blocked save at the one gate—and this is opened
by God. Even the weak are not ignorant that there are such
bearers of infirmity, such priests, such men who know. This,
then, is our 'free detachment'. A detachment which is not in
order that we may—**please ourselves.** And yet, the moment we,

by an act of will, attempt to achieve such detachment, we have lost the battle! For God's sake let there be no 'Passionate Protestantism'! no 'Struggle with Rome'! Our strength is so to bear that we ourselves appear not at all, or at least only as men who remember and are rendered questionable. The best element in Paulinism is what is unmanageable and use-less in it The same applies to Protestantism. What is best in it is that it is un-practical and un-popular. When Protestantism becomes a 'factor to be reckoned with', when it attempts 'to play a part', it has lost itself. The KRISIS of Protestantism comes from its refusal to dare to stand on the outermost edge of civilization and society, of world-culture and world-religion, and be the humble —but, nevertheless, decisive—question-mark and mark of exclamation. Protestantism is judged because it determines at all costs to be something, to stand out as the rival of the Roman vegetable eaters.—**Let each one of us please his neighbour for good, unto edifying.** This is the sacrifice, the renunciation, the journey into the wilderness, which is demanded of the strong. The strong man always has his neighbour in mind—and we remember that the neighbour is the One in every man. Here is the end of rivalry, the end of all particularity and superiority of behaviour. The strong man, because he is strong, is in opposition to no one; rather, he lies behind all men. He does not hurry ahead, he waits; he does not criticize—for that he is far too critical—he hopes; he does not educate, he prays, or rather he educates through prayer. He does not stand out, he withdraws; he is nowhere, because he is everywhere.

For Christ also pleased not himself. We are here reminded of all that we heard (especially in Chs. iii and viii) concerning the hiddenness of the revelation of God in Christ. This hiddenness must be retained in ethical conduct:—*He shall not cry, nor lift up, nor cause his voice to be heard in the street.* Therefore, the inevitable destiny of every 'point of view' is in His case irrelevant:—*A bruised reed shall he not break, and the dimly burning wick shall he not quench* (Isa. xlii. 2, 3)—*He counted it not a thing to be grasped to be on an equality with God* (Phil. ii. 6). He proclaimed the Kingdom of God which is, in fact, the freedom of God. His life was altogether a sacrifice, a renunciation, a withdrawal:—**The reproaches of him that reproached thee fell upon me** (Ps. lxix. 9). He passes through the Old Testament as the great Sufferer. It is, therefore, congruous that He should appear before us as the Crucified One. These things were—**written for our learning.** The whole picture is full of—**patience,** full of—**comfort.** And yet it is far more than a picture; for behind it stands—**The God of patience and of comfort.** God does not merely instruct us: He GIVES us the incomprehensible, in order that in all our differences and in all our brokenness we may be— **like minded ;** in order that we may, in all the play of our thoughts, look up to the One, and in order that we may, in the disharmony of the community, hear the voice of fellowship:— **That with one accord ye may with one mouth glorify the God and Father of our Lord Jesus Christ.**

vv. 7–13. Wherefore receive ye one another, even as Christ also received you,[1] to the glory of God. Now I mean **that Christ hath been made a minister of the circumcision for the truth of God, that he might confirm the promises given unto the fathers, and that the Gentiles might glorify God for his mercy; as it is written, Therefore will I confess thee among the Gentiles, and sing unto thy name. And again he saith, Rejoice, ye Gentiles, with his people! And again, Praise the Lord all ye Gentiles; and let all the peoples praise him! And again, Isaiah saith, There shall be the root of Jesse, And he that ariseth to rule over the Gentiles; on him shall the Gentiles hope** (Ps. xviii. 50, Deut. xxxii. 43, Ps. cxvii. 1, Isa. xi. 10). **Now the God of hope fill you with all joy and peace in believing, that ye may abound in hope in the power of the Holy Ghost.**

Christ is the KRISIS of our freedom and detachment. He makes the strong to be strong to the glory of God. But He also leads them again to the weak to the glory of God. He is the Christ of Israel, of the Church. For every witness—however tenuous— which is borne to Him by the weak has as its object, the corresponding truth of God. But He is also the Christ of the Gentiles, the Christ of the World. The mercy of God has found the strong, for they were veritably weak (v. 6). Truth and Mercy hold together Jew and Gentile, Church and World. Who is here strong? Who is here weak? Above, before, behind every human endeavour stands—The God of Hope. To Him the voices of all who have been found by His Truth and by His Mercy are lifted up in a chorus of jubilation. He beholds weakness in the strong and strength in the weak. With His eyes He sees all, whether they stand on the highest or on the lowest step, sharing in the blessed secret of His Freedom and of His Kingdom.

---

[1] ἡμᾶς is a later generalization. Paul is turning once more to address the *strong*.

THE APOSTLE AND THE COMMUNITY

XV. 14–33, XVI. 1–24

v. 14. And I am altogether **persuaded, my brethren, that ye yourselves are full of goodness, filled with all knowledge, able also to admonish one another.**

The Epistle to the Romans offers no new, strange, personal truth, but rather, the Truth which is old, familiar, and universal. It lays no claims to originality, nor does it pretend to be deeply spiritual. It cannot, however, be for this reason overlooked, for it possesses a real claim to serious consideration. It is not a system of dogmatics: for this reason the launching against it of anti-dogmatic tirades fails to confute it. It does not proclaim the authority of Paul; yet neither can it be dismissed when it is discovered that at best the whole is just—Paul. For, that Paul is not Christ, is a quite trivial, obvious truth; Christ, moreover, stands in no book, and to BELIEVE in the man who wrote the Epistle or in what he wrote is out of the question: it is possible to believe only in GOD! This is precisely the thesis of the Epistle, the thesis of 'Paulinism'. And by this thesis Paulinism is itself dissolved, long before its opponents have found sufficient breath to utter their anxious warnings against it. The man who busily engages himself in launching attacks against Paulinism as a 'system' is simply tilting at windmills; he betrays himself as one who has learnt nothing and forgotten nothing. The Epistle to the Romans makes its appeal neither to belief in authority, nor to a capacity for constructive thinking, nor to a sense for a higher world, nor to abnormal experiences, nor to an instructed conscience, nor to religious emotion. The Epistle appeals to the sensus communis—to the 'universal feeling for truth' (Oetinger), to the childlike simplicity—yes, of course!—of those who have seen through and are nauseated by the confusion of that supposed 'simplicity' of which our generation is so proud. The Epistle appeals to the honesty of the Gentiles, to their preparedness not to allow a serious and relevant examination of the condition in which men actually find themselves to pass entirely unnoticed. The Epistle speaks to the—brethren in those whom it addresses, to the existential One in all. It counts upon the sympathy, understanding, and co-operation which no one can seriously withhold who—to the fury of all visionary ideologists—endeavours to take things—'simply' as he finds them. It puts into words what everybody has heard already. It says what everybody can say without any assistance. It discloses what is always and everywhere true. It instructs the instructed. It is a communication to those who know. It exhorts men of good will. It takes the field, unfurls its standards, goes through its manœuvres, overthrows its enemies, occupies the position—but only in a parable. The thing done, it withdraws as though nothing had happened. When any one seeks to prove himself right and it wrong, he finds it wholly without defence and wholly unable to vindicate itself:—**I am altogether persuaded that ye yourselves are full of goodness, filled with all knowledge.** And so, good man, thou needst not be disturbed. Continue to enjoy thy position—if thou canst! Close thine ears to the questions that have been raised—if thou art able! We are —yes, we really mean it—in far closer agreement with thee than thou art willing to allow. And yet we are bound to say that we shall not for very much longer be able to concede more than a purely humorous importance to explosions of resentment against orthodoxy.

vv. 15, 16. But I have written the more boldly unto you in some sort, as putting you again in remembrance, because of the grace that is given me by God, that I should be a priest **of Christ Jesus unto the Gentiles, ministering the gospel of God, that the offering up of the Gentiles might be acceptable, being sanctified by the Holy Ghost.**

The standpoint of the Epistle to the Romans is, however, a standpoint which is—**in some sort the more bold.** It is true that a more peaceable life can be passed in other folds which are not situated under the shadow of THIS possibility. Terribly thin are the threads of the knowing not-knowing which is here presented to us. Perilously nigh unto the abyss is the path along which we are being led. Precariously sharp is the 'Either–Or' by which we are here at every step confronted. Is this necessary? Is it really required of us that we should take up this very exposed position—which is no position? Must every answer be ruled out which is not itself a question? Must every straightforward, peaceable, practical, historical, psychological, friendly via media really be abandoned? Must we always choose the most precipitous knife-edge? We answer: 'No, certainly not!' Not for one moment do we wish to suggest that the kind of behaviour described, and inevitably described, in the Epistle to the Romans as a possible kind of behaviour for men, should be regarded as normal. Indeed, we are bound to utter the gravest warning against all 'normal routes' as such. We are not in the least anxious to speak in radical fashion or to present a radical silhouette. We repeat once more that in the end Paulinism condemns itself. The most precipitous route, being merely one among a number of others, cannot be the meaning of Paulinism; it can only be a parable of its meaning. We can, moreover, fully appreciate the importance and the fruitfulness of other and less harmful possibilities of life. We are able to stand amicably side by side with Catholics and Protestants, with the representatives of Protestant Culture and with the theologians of the League of Nations, and indeed, by whose side can we not stand amicably? We can speak comfortably to them all; we can say what they long to hear—'Thou art right!'. But only upon one condition can we speak these comfortable words: we are bound to add— 'Also, thou art wrong!'. It is when we make this addition that we begin to be—*in some sort the more bold*. For if we are concerned to speak of God, and are not concerned how we may comfort and help ourselves, how we may 'advance in religion' (Wernle), how we may 'set to work', how we may propound a metaphysical x which will satisfy all our postulates; if we are concerned to set forth how God, authentically interpreted in Christ Jesus, encounters us—whether we like it or not—in the reality of our life as the Unknown, Holy God, the Lord of life and of death; if, in the midst of our concern with those more relative and less harmful possibilities of human life, we ought to be concerned also to propound honestly the problem of human existence; if the purpose of all speaking and hearing about God is to put us—again in remembrance, because we have all forgotten the Unknown God, forgotten the One, forgotten the Truth that makes us free—then, that wherein the Epistle to the Romans is *in some sort the more bold* must be propounded from every possible standpoint. There must be sharp-shooting; and, on the assumption that no one of our neighbours will be absent, the problem of all problems must be laid out inexorably and with no trace of 'piety'. The paradox of the crucified and risen Saviour must be set forth so that everything is seen to depend upon the one thread of faith. Every seemingly relevant illustration and every pseudo-reality—Potemkin's Villages!—must be condemned and demolished; and men must advance straight along the road between the two abysses. All Pseudo-Artistry must be opposed with merciless severity. There must be no

yielding, no nervous anxiety about dangerous consequences!
Men must be—*fervent in spirit* (xii. 11). And yet, though to
speak about God is *bold*, we know very well that it is only *in
some sort* bold. We know that the existential *putting again in
remembrance* is not an action which can be compared with other
actions. We know that human language can never break through
to the absolute; for that would be the end of all things, and to
that we can never be so bold as to set our hands. Side by side
with those normal, well-regulated, bourgeois possibilities of life
—no, not side by side with them, but in serio-comical fashion,
hopefully in them ALL!—there exists the abnormal, irregular,
revolutionary—in the most significant sense of the word
'revolutionary'!—possibility of venturing, half seriously, half
jocularly, upon an advance into the absolute. The Epistle to
the Romans is such an advance. It is theology, a conversation
about God, undertaken with penetrating understanding of the
One in all. Abnormal, irregular, revolutionary, the Epistle to
the Romans is the catastrophe of all catastrophes, the predica-
ment in all other predicaments:—**Because of the grace that is
given me by God, that I should be a priest of Christ Jesus unto the
Gentiles, ministering the gospel of God, that the offering up of the
Gentiles might be acceptable, being sanctified by the Holy Ghost.**
Once again, this is only a parable; but a parable it is. The theme
of theology is grace, the absolute 'Moment', the greedy dialectic
of time and eternity. Other sciences have attempted, more or
less successfully, to arrange an understanding with it in order
that they may remain secure; but theology menaces them all.
According to its reckoning the impossible possibility of God
appears as the position which cannot be a position. By this
position all other reckonings are threatened with destruction at
every moment. Theology is a *priest*hood *unto the Gentiles*. That
is to say, it addresses itself to the concrete, visible, historical,
particular man, in order to instruct him about himself, to teach
him that he is the One invisible, unclothed man, standing before
God. Theology interests itself only in the Gentiles—the Gentiles
in the Gentiles and in those who are not Gentiles. It is concerned with men only in so far as they can and must be surrendered to God as an *offering*. It is concerned only with their
being sanctified by the Holy Ghost, with the loosening of their
chains, with their redemption, with their freedom in God.
Theology is a totally unpractical and non-religious undertaking;
and it is so, because it is concerned with the most practical of all
human desires, because it is concerned with the meaning—the
'further' meaning—of all religion. Filled with inexhaustible

purpose and certain of final success, theology must appear on the
scene without any purpose and acknowledging no success as such.
Itself the final venture of men, it is bound to perceive that every
human adventure can be no more than a demonstration and a
parable. Nevertheless, as this final hazard, *as ministering the
gospel of God*, theology is what it is. If it be not this, if it dares
not to be what it is, it were better that it should file a petition in
bankruptcy at once without any further delay. Theology owes its
existence in history and its place in the universitas litterarum
only to this essential, final, necessary, venture, and to its
abnormal, irregular, revolutionary attack. Only by means of
this venture and of this attack can it retain its status. It cannot
retain its status if its primary purpose be the service of the
Church. Still less can it live on what it has borrowed from the
laboratory of historical research! To be scientific means to be
thrown up against reality. The reality of theology is its unconditional respect for the peculiarity of its own chosen theme.
Now, the theme of theology is men—men in their final distress
and hope, men as they stand in the presence of God. Scientific
theology is repentance, the revolution of thought, the *renewing
of the mind* (notice, however, the safeguards with which, in xii. 2,
this conception is surrounded). And so, as the Church sets a
question-mark and a mark of exclamation at the outermost edge
of civilization, so theology performs the same necessary role at
the outermost edge of a university. But we must not forget that
there is no intelligent man who does not somehow or other set
the same question-mark and the same mark of exclamation.
Since, however, neither the Church nor theology has the courage
to be what it is, the pertinent question arises as to whether
it would not be better if both were to be declared bankrupt. If,
however, they have sufficient courage not to go into liquidation,
in the midst of so much modern muffled, half-understood
remembrance of the triviality of all human action, let there not
be in the Church and in theology a too great, too self-conscious,
too triumphant triviality. Let there be at any rate some
recollection of the Epistle to the Romans; let the theologians be
at any rate—*in some sort more bold*. Happy the man who is not
required to stand in this precarious position; but woe to those
who stand there, and know not what they do!

**vv. 17–21. I have therefore whereof I may glory in
Christ Jesus,** that is to say, before **God. For I will not
dare to speak of those things which Christ wrought not
through me, to make the Gentiles obedient, by word and**

deed, through the power of signs and wonders, by the power of the Spirit of God; so that from Jerusalem, and round about even unto Illyricum, I have fulfilled the preaching of the gospel of Christ; yea, being ambitious not to preach the gospel where the name of Christ was already known, lest I should build upon another man's foundation; but, as it is written, They shall see, to whom no tidings of him came, and they who have not heard shall understand (Isa. lii. 15).

Or are we to say that the Pauline glory which is here set out with such evident self-consciousness throws a shadow upon everything that is said in the Epistle, and therefore enables us to escape from it? There is, of course, a self-consciousness radiating out from these pages. The question is, whose self-consciousness is it? Is it Paul's? Yes, it is Paul's also. How indeed could it be otherwise? For, when a man speaks of God, when he speaks of Him as expressly as Paul does, how could he throw too great, too disturbing an emphasis upon his own self-consciousness? Through the forgiveness of sins, it can, however, come about that there is reflected in this human self-consciousness a consciousness of a wholly different self. It may be that the criticisms which humble men feel bound to make at this point run up against a granite wall. For Paul is not, in fact, standing where they suppose him to be standing. He has his glory—in Christ Jesus, before God. Who is this Paul? Paul has been sacrificed. Of what he has experienced, of what he knows, says, and has achieved; he—will not dare to speak. Paul is nothing. Having withdrawn himself behind this *not*, he is perhaps, however, far more dangerous. It may be that the so grievously misunderstood Pauline *glory* is naught but the witness which is borne to a glory existing *in Christ before God* and which cannot altogether be hidden under a bushel. Perhaps it is this glory which is so irritating to those who are proud of their humility and which makes the figure of Paul so intolerable to them. But perhaps it is this glory that must be considered in assessing the importance of the mission of Paul and of Paulinism in history. Clearly, the apostle Paul was not an attractive or congenial person. But this was precisely because of his self-consciousness. When he was convincing, he must have been so in spite of himself. So also with Paul's gospel. In the spiritual history of mankind, it is a disturbing factor; indeed, it could easily and properly be excluded from the story of human evolution, of which it has never really formed a part. It has remained always a grain of sand, or sometimes a pebble, which has got in between the smoothly-moving, interlocking wheels of the machinery of human progress. That his gospel has been effective must be traced back to his strange awareness of the presence of a wholly different and incommensurable factor—Jesus Christ. Its effectiveness is presumably due also to the most characteristic and least attractive feature of Paulinism—to the apostle's proud refusal to—**build upon another man's foundation.** Paul's thought is altogether unhistorical, for, surely, no one would wish to contradict this by appealing to his use of the Old Testament! His relation to existing Christian practices is extremely uneasy. Even the most venerable traditions have for him no essential stability. He does not directly affirm the most important factors in history, not even the greatest of them all—*Christ according to the flesh.* He is strangely suspicious, even sarcastic, with reference to all already existing *pillars* (Gal. ii. 9). He did not consult with flesh and blood, neither—and this was quite fundamental—did he go up to Jerusalem: he went away into Arabia (Gal. i. 16, 17). He allows himself to say expressly that he neither learnt nor received his gospel from any man (Gal. i. 11, 12). Every blow that 'sane' theological and ecclesiastical mediocrity has ever directed against 'enthusiasts devoid of all historical sense' also falls, intentionally or unintentionally, upon Paul. The strangeness of Paul's behaviour is in itself of no importance, for clearly it too is a phenomenon in history; but it may be a significant strangeness, that is to say, it may bear witness to a strangeness which is wholly different. If this be so, it is obviously superfluous and dangerous for us to be content with a mere description of Paul's behaviour. It would be better for theologians to follow the hint which has just been given.

vv. 22–9. Wherefore also I was hindered these many times from coming to you: but now, having no more any place in these regions, and having these many[1] years a longing to come unto you, whensoever I go unto Spain (for I hope to see you in my journey, and to be brought on my way thitherward by you, if first in some measure I shall be satisfied with your company)—but now, I say, I go unto Jerusalem, ministering unto the saints. For it hath been the good pleasure of the communities **of Macedonia and Achaia to make a certain contribution for the poor among the saints that are at Jerusalem. Yea,**

---

[1] πολλῶν may have seemed to a copyist to be an exaggeration. He may therefore have replaced it by ἱκανῶν.

it hath been their good pleasure; and their debtors they are. For if the Gentiles have been made partakers of their spiritual things, they owe it to them also to minister unto them in carnal things. When therefore I have accomplished this, and have sealed to them this fruit, I will go on by you unto Spain. And I know that, when I come unto you, I shall come in the fulness of the blessing of Christ.

Where there is real fellowship, personal contact and personal appreciation are beautiful things (i. 9–13). They are looked forward to and readily enjoyed as stations on the road of service. We should, however, notice the very circuitous route—Corinth–Jerusalem–Rome—, for it is somewhat strange. The contribution, mentioned already in xii. 13, must first be delivered to the Christians in Jerusalem, for it forms a peculiar manifestation of the unity of Gentiles and Jews, of near and far, of known and unknown, which is the theme of the Epistle. The second project of the man who perceives that he has—**no more any place** this side of Italy, is a sortie into Spain, a demonstration to the end of the world. In the course of carrying out this project, which is really more apocalyptic than rational, the author hopes to meet his readers personally, both on his outward and on his return journey.

vv. 30–3. Now I beseech you, brethren, by our Lord Jesus Christ, and by the love of the Spirit, that ye strive together with me in your prayers to God for me; that I may be delivered from them that are disobedient in Judaea, and that my ministration which I have for Jerusalem may be acceptable to the saints; that I may come unto you in joy by the will of God and together with you find rest. Now the God of peace be with you all. Amen.

The proposed circuitous route seems to be neither easy nor lacking in danger. What does Paul foresee? At any rate, he expects STRIFE. Judaea, Jerusalem, is in every way the stronghold of—the Church. And there he is threatened, threatened by the machinations of the Jews. But not only this. In spite of the contribution he is bringing, so uncertain is he of the manner in which he will be received by the saints that he asks that this also should be made a subject of prayer among his readers. The man who here speaks is a stranger wherever he goes; and for this reason he appeals to all his well-wishers to remember him sympathetically before God in his terrible loneliness.

vv. 1–16. I commend unto you Phoebe our sister, who is indeed[1] a servant of the Church that is at Cenchreae: that ye receive her in the Lord, worthily of the saints, and that ye assist her in whatsoever matter she may have need of you: for she herself also hath been a succourer of many, and of mine own self. Salute Prisca and Aquila my fellow-workers in Christ Jesus, who for my life laid down their own necks; unto whom not only I give thanks, but also all the churches of the Gentiles: and salute the church that is in their house. Salute Epaenetus my beloved, who is the first-fruits of Asia unto Christ. Salute Miriam,[2] who bestowed much labour on us.[3] Salute Andronicus and Junias, my kinsmen, and my fellow-prisoners, who are of note among the apostles, who also were in Christ before me. Salute Ampliatus my beloved in the Lord. Salute Urbanus our fellow-worker in Christ, and Stachys my beloved. Salute Apelles the approved in Christ. Salute them which are of the household of Aristobulus. Salute Herodion my kinsman. Salute them which are of the household of Narcissus, which are in the Lord. Salute Tryphaena and Tryphosa, who labour in the Lord. Salute Persis the beloved, which laboured much in the Lord. Salute Rufus the chosen in the Lord, and his mother and mine. Salute Asyncritus, Phlegon, Hermes, Patrobas, Hermas, and the brethren that are with them. Salute Philologus and Julia, Nereus and his sister, and Olympas, and all the saints that are with them. Salute one another with a holy kiss. All the churches of Christ salute you.

Here we have opened out before us a little world of suffering and courage and endurance—in the Lord; a world full of mutual respect and help—in the Lord. This, then, is the proper place for us to ask about the 'facts and deeds' which correspond with the 'words' of the Epistle to the Romans. Here is the simple 'life' which we have so often missed. The answer to our question is provided by the readers of the Epistle, each in his own way, to this very day. Lietzmann and Zahn will give us all the information we want about the antiquarian problems

---

[1] The καὶ following οὖσαν should not be deleted. Lietzmann points out that Paul frequently uses καὶ in order to throw an emphasis upon the word which follows it. A similar καὶ has been removed also in viii. 24.

[2] Μαριάμ might be altered to Μαρίαν, but hardly the reverse.

[3] Read ἡμᾶς not ὑμᾶς. To praise the woman because of her labours among the readers of the Epistle would be altogether foreign to the context, and would, moreover, also be in itself quite exceptional.

which this list of names presents. The suggestion that it originally formed the major part of a letter addressed to the community in Ephesus, and that it has been tacked on to the Epistle to the Romans, is unattractive, if only because the Epistle would be altogether incomplete if it did not itself make clear that it was addressed to particular men possessed of human names and bearing a human countenance. In any case, to such men it was addressed. In the middle of the first century a community-sister took the letter from Corinth to Rome. It was addressed to men and women, to Greeks, Romans, and Jews, to masters and slaves. The possibility that Tryphaena and Tryphosa and the other 'laymen'—not to speak of the 'theologians' included in this long list!—would not have been able to understand the Epistle, does not seem to have been considered. In other words, there was once—and this would hold good even if the 'Ephesian' theory were right—a body of men and women to whom the Epistle to the Romans could be sent in the confident expectation that it provided an answer to their questions; that somehow or other it would be understood and valued. For this body of men and women it seems that theology—this theology!—was THE living theme. Their problems, it seems, began where those of so many others—including those of many theologians!—are wont to end. It seems that these spirits were moving over a wide field. In fact, these men and women are more surprising than are the other historical problems raised by the Epistle to the Romans. We are, however, not surprised that they were able to—**salute one another with a holy kiss.**

vv. 17–20. Now I beseech you, brethren, mark them which are causing divisions and occasions of stumbling, contrary to the teaching which ye learned: and turn away from them! For they that are such serve not our Lord Christ, but their own belly; and by their smooth and fair speech they beguile the hearts of the innocent. For your obedience is come abroad unto all men. I rejoice therefore over you: but I would have you wise unto that which is good, and simple unto that which is evil. And the God of peace shall bruise Satan under your feet shortly. The grace of our Lord Jesus be with you.

A last urgent appeal, which is, however, no foreign element in the Epistle. The whole polemic of the Epistle—and where is it not polemical?—is concentrated in one blow. Take care lest ye be deceived, especially by those who are nearest to you and most plausible! Beware of the annual market of religious goods with its many, busy, glittering stalls! Be especially careful, because ye are yourselves in the midst of it all, and because ye have no criterion by which ye are able to distinguish and segregate yourselves from those who—serve. not our Lord Christ, but their own belly, save the *putting again in remembrance* (xv. 15). Beware—of yourselves! In this *putting again in remembrance* is the power of that wise frankness and simple reserve which is able to prevent men from being altogether submerged in the teeming multitude of conflicting opinions. Etiam cultores saepe veritatis ea, quibus haud assuevere, tardius admittunt. Cum pridem audierunt: HOC EST! quaerunt denique: QUID EST? cumque demonstratio defluxit, postulata sibi proponi queruntur. Nonnulli obitu demum suo veritati, in parte non agnita, officere desinunt. Veruntamen non frustra laboratur: dum alii praeter opinionem desunt, alii praeter opinionem se dedunt vel dedent. Lux crescit in dies: per adversa ad victoriam enititur veritas (Bengel). 'The God of truth, not of slumbering peace, MUST do THE best. What He does, He often does promptly! If men could only be patient, and not too soon intervene with their applause' (Steinhofer). *He that hath ears to hear, let him hear.*

vv. 21–4. Timothy my fellow-worker saluteth you; and Lucius and Jason and Sosipater, my kinsmen. I Tertius, who wrote the epistle, salute you in the Lord. Gaius my host, and of the whole church, saluteth you. Erastus the treasurer of the city saluteth you, and Quartus the brother. The grace of our Lord Jesus Christ be with you all. Amen.[1]

[1] The Doxology (xvi. 25–7) should be deleted, but not *v.* 24. See the note on pp. 522 f.

INDEX TO PASSAGES FROM SCRIPTURE

[**Bold** type is used in certain references to the Epistle to the Romans to show where an extended commentary upon the passage in question is to be found.]

INDEX TO SUBJECTS AND NAMES

REPRINTED LITHOGRAPHICALLY IN GREAT BRITAIN
AT THE UNIVERSITY PRESS, OXFORD
. BY VIVIAN RIDLER
PRINTER TO THE UNIVERSITY